The leading Singaporean series adapted for the N

DISCOVERING MATHEMATICS 3A

Victor Chow
Katie Wood

UK Consultant: Robert Wilne
Singapore Consultant: Berinderjeet Kaur

OXFORD
UNIVERSITY PRESS

OXFORD
UNIVERSITY PRESS

Great Clarendon Street, Oxford, OX2 6DP, United Kingdom

Oxford University Press is a department of the University of Oxford. It furthers the University's objective of excellence in research, scholarship, and education by publishing worldwide. Oxford is a registered trade mark of Oxford University Press in the UK and in certain other countries.

First published in 2021

British Library Cataloguing in Publication Data
Data available

978-0-19-842208-2

1 3 5 7 9 10 8 6 4 2

Paper used in the production of this book is a natural, recyclable product made from wood grown in sustainable forests.
The manufacturing process conforms to the environmental regulations of the country of origin.

Printed in the UK by Bell and Bain Ltd, Glasgow

MIX
Paper from responsible sources
FSC® C007785

Acknowledgements
The authors and publishers would like to thank the reviewer team of **consultants** – Robert Wilne, Laurie Luscombe, Mark Moody, Naomi Norman – and **teachers** – Pippa Baker, Jill Borcherds, Adam Burton, Jemma Sherwood, Jo Walker – who have advised on the content of this book. Their contributions have been invaluable.

Editorial team: Dom Holdsworth, Felicity Acton, Cameron Briggs, Sarah Dutton and Isobel Fray

With thanks also to Rachel Phillipson for her contribution.

The publishers would like to thank the following for permission to use copyright material:

Cover: Kjeld Friis/Shutterstock

Photos: p1: Christos Georghiou/Shutterstock; p6: Elisanth/Shutterstock; p9: Brynjar Gunnarsson/Shutterstock; p11: Yurchanka Siarhei/Shutterstock; p19: okili77/Shutterstock; p24: irin-k/Shutterstock; p25: topseller/Shutterstock; p27(t): Artsiom Petrushenka/Shutterstock; p27(b): diy13/Shutterstock; p30: ChristianZscheile/Shutterstock; p31: Africa Studio/Shutterstock; p36(t): johnfoto18/Shutterstock; p36(b): Olga Pink/Shutterstock; p37: Shaynepplstockphoto/Shutterstock; p58: Inhabitant/Shutterstock; p61: Drozhzhina Elena/Shutterstock; p62: Alexapicso/Shutterstock; p63: Akhenaton Images/Shutterstock; p70: Aleksandra Pikalova/Shutterstock; p74: MPFphotography/Shutterstock; p83: Eric Isselee/Shutterstock; p85: Africa Studio/Shutterstock; p87(t): grebeshkovmaxim/Shutterstock; p87(m): Wellcome Collection. Attribution 4.0 International (CC BY 4.0); p100: anna-nt/Shutterstock; p107: Levent Konuk/Shutterstock; p108: Ian Francis/Shutterstock; p118: Ian 2010/Shutterstock; p119: Can Yesil/Shutterstock; p140(t): Roman Samokhin/Shutterstock; p140(b): Duda Vasilii/Shutterstock; p149: JStaley401/Shutterstock; p151: Alex Staroseltsev/Shutterstock; p153: Triff/Shutterstock; p157: hlphoto/Shutterstock; p158: timquo/Shutterstock; p159: BlueRingMedia/Shutterstock; p160: Karve/Shutterstock; p162(t): Pixel-Shot/Shutterstock; p162(bl): Andrii Yalanskyi/Shutterstock; p162(br): Zerbor/Shutterstock; p176(l): Luis Carlos Torres/Shutterstock; p176(r): Levent Konuk/Shutterstock; p177: Catsense/Shutterstock; p181: pixbox77/Shutterstock; p184: DarwelShots/Shutterstock; p185(t): Szasz-Fabian Ilka Erika/Shutterstock; p185(m): Rawpixel.com/Shutterstock; p185(b): Lubo Ivanko/Shutterstock; p191: JETACOM AUTOFOCUS/Shutterstock; p196: Hans Christiansson/Shutterstock; p197: Jevanto Productions/Shutterstock; p198: brave rabbit/Shutterstock; p211: Anton_Ivanov/Shutterstock; p213(l): MeeRok/Shutterstock; p213(r): Ukki Studio/Shutterstock; p213(m): Richard P Long/Shutterstock; p220(t): ShadeDesign/Shutterstock; p220(b): Yuriy Boyko/Shutterstock; p221(l): Natsutapon/Shutterstock; p221(r): Creative Photo Corner/Shutterstock; p229: Photo Melon/Shutterstock; p230(l): gokturk_06/Shutterstock; p230(r): BigBlueStudio/Shutterstock; p236: Tony Baggett/Shutterstock; p239: Scrudje/Shutterstock; p240: GEORGII MIRONOV/Shutterstock; p252: Marian Salabai/Shutterstock; p260: supergenijalac/Shutterstock; p262(t): vladsilver/Shutterstock; p262(b): serg_dibrova/Shutterstock; p272(l): yuri4u80/Shutterstock; p272(r): PGMart/Shutterstock; p277: Ukki Studio/Shutterstock; p279: Igor Kovalenko/Shutterstock; p290: barbaliss/Shutterstock; p313: StoneMonkeyswk/Shutterstock; p232(l): AMLbox/Shutterstock; p323(r): Dokmaihaeng/Shutterstock; p331(t): CasarsaGuru/iStockphoto; p331(b): Lunatictm/Shutterstock; p332: Dmitry Kalinovsky/Shutterstock; p352(tl): pcruciatti/Shutterstock; p352(tr): M Barratt/Shutterstock; p352(bl): Alena Veasey/Shutterstock; p352(br): Mark William Richardson/Shutterstock; p359: wong sze yuen/Shutterstock; p360: sirtravelalot/Shutterstock; p361: ball2be/Shutterstock; p363: StockphotoVideo/Shutterstock; p365: Alexander Baluev/Shutterstock; p370: Kenishirotie/Shutterstock; p371: Maria Colfer/Shutterstock; p377: Paolo Paradiso/Shutterstock; p378: Raura7/Shutterstock; p380: Linda Bestwick/Shutterstock; p382(l): Dan Kosmayer/Shutterstock; p382(r): Oleksandr Lytvynenko/Shutterstock; p385: STILLFX/Shutterstock; p393(tl): symbiot/Shutterstock; p393(tr): Vladislav Belchenko/Shutterstock; p393(bl): Mike H/Shutterstock; p393(br): EastVillage Images/Shutterstock; p412: August_0802/Shutterstock.

Artworks: Q2A Media Services Pvt. Ltd.

CONTENTS

ABOUT THIS BOOK

This book has been written by an experienced author and reviewed by a team of maths consultants and practising teachers. It is based on the top-selling Singaporean maths series and has been carefully adapted to make it suitable for the English National Curriculum, Year 9. The features and exercises have been designed to help you discover the underlying principles of mathematics and to set you on the road to mastery.

Every chapter starts with an example of how the maths you will learn can be related to real life.

Flashback is a reminder of what you should already know. Revise this content to prepare to build your knowledge.

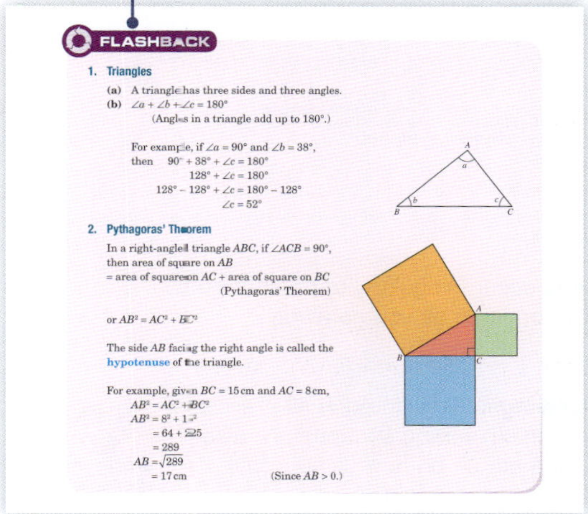

Learning objectives at the beginning of the chapter tell you what you will learn.

At the end of every chapter, **Review** summarises the key learning points that have been covered. This can be used for revision.

You will be told when you should or shouldn't use a calculator. If there is no instruction, you can decide yourself or ask your teacher.

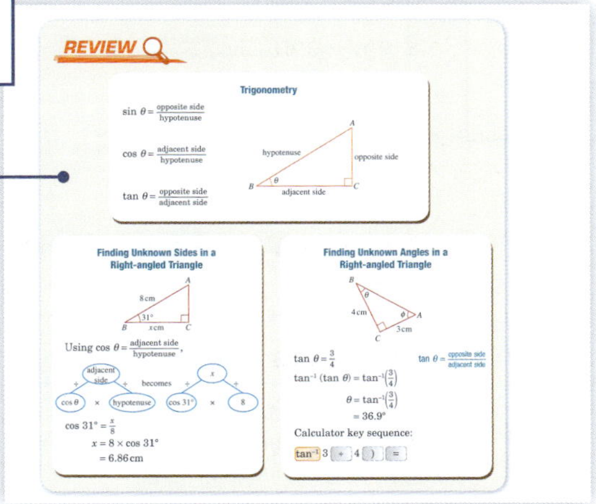

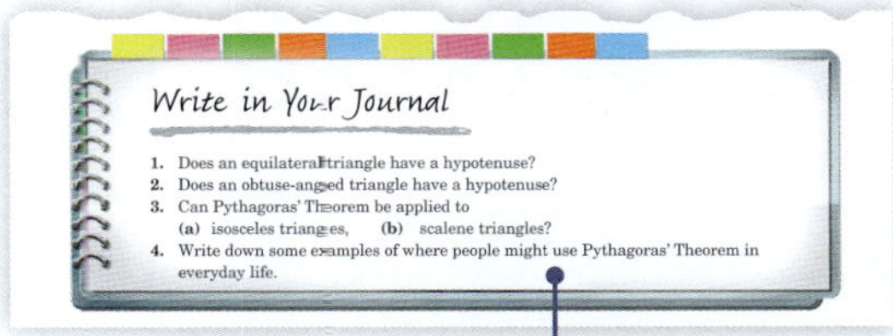

At the end of every chapter, **Write in Your Journal** sections encourage you to reflect on your learning.

Class activities are led by the teacher and allow the whole class to learn through discovery and exploration.

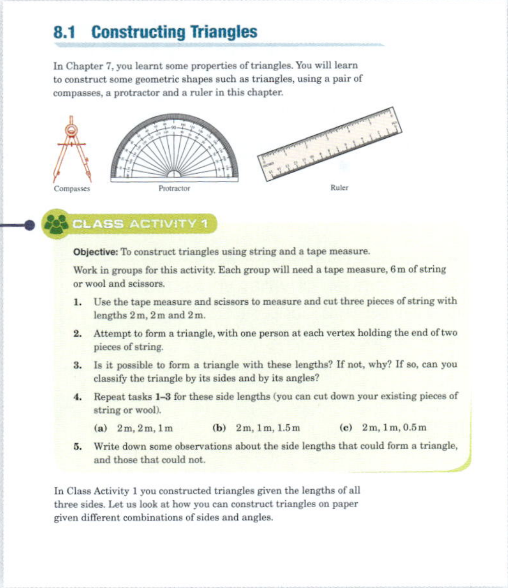

8.1 Constructing Triangles

In Chapter 7, you learnt some properties of triangles. You will learn to construct some geometric shapes such as triangles, using a pair of compasses, a protractor and a ruler in this chapter.

CLASS ACTIVITY 1

Objective: To construct triangles using string and a tape measure.

Work in groups for this activity. Each group will need a tape measure, 6 m of string or wool and scissors.

1. Use the tape measure and scissors to measure and cut three pieces of string with lengths 2 m, 2 m and 2 m.
2. Attempt to form a triangle, with one person at each vertex holding the end of two pieces of string.
3. Is it possible to form a triangle with these lengths? If not, why? If so, can you classify the triangle by its sides and by its angles?
4. Repeat tasks 1–3 for these side lengths (you can cut down your existing pieces of string or wool).
   (a) 2 m, 2 m, 1 m (b) 2 m, 1 m, 1.5 m (c) 2 m, 1 m, 0.5 m
5. Write down some observations about the side lengths that could form a triangle, and those that could not.

In Class Activity 1 you constructed triangles given the lengths of all three sides. Let us look at how you can construct triangles on paper given different combinations of sides and angles.

Worked examples show how ideas and reasoning can be expressed using precise mathematical language. Every worked example is followed by a **Try It!** to practise what you have learnt.

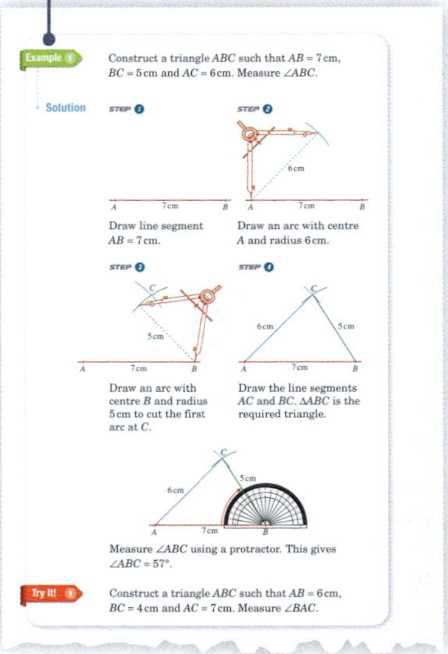

Example 1 Construct a triangle ABC such that $AB = 7$ cm, $BC = 5$ cm and $AC = 6$ cm. Measure $\angle ABC$.

Solution

STEP 1 Draw line segment $AB = 7$ cm.

STEP 2 Draw an arc with centre A and radius 6 cm.

STEP 3 Draw an arc with centre B and radius 5 cm to cut the first arc at C.

STEP 4 Draw the line segments AC and BC. $\triangle ABC$ is the required triangle.

Measure $\angle ABC$ using a protractor. This gives $\angle ABC = 57°$.

Try It! 1 Construct a triangle ABC such that $AB = 6$ cm, $BC = 4$ cm and $AC = 7$ cm. Measure $\angle BAC$.

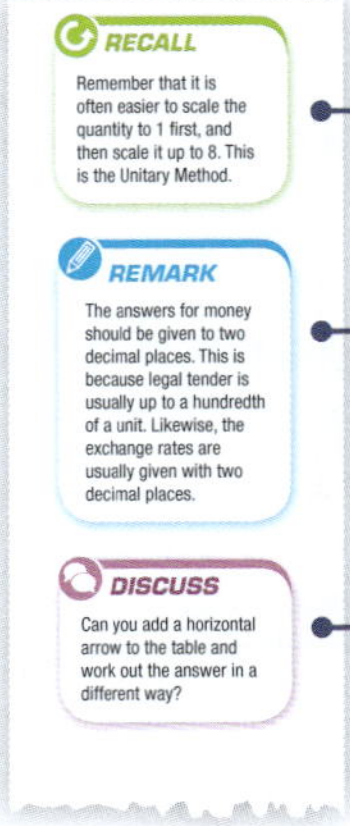

RECALL

Remember that it is often easier to scale the quantity to 1 first, and then scale it up to 8. This is the Unitary Method.

REMARK

The answers for money should be given to two decimal places. This is because legal tender is usually up to a hundredth of a unit. Likewise, the exchange rates are usually given with two decimal places.

DISCUSS

Can you add a horizontal arrow to the table and work out the answer in a different way?

Recall boxes remind you of what you already know.

Remark boxes explain common misconceptions and provide extra hints.

Discuss boxes encourage paired and group working.

A **Challenge** activity in every chapter allows you to develop a deeper understanding of topics. It is also a chance to practise your problem-solving skills.

Assessment occurs regularly to make sure you understand concepts as you go along.

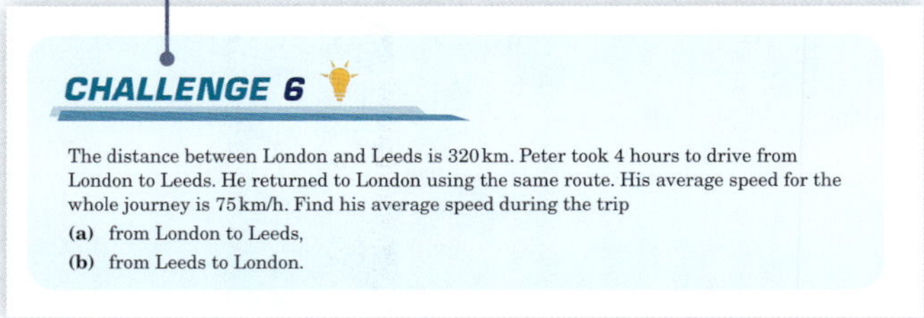

CHALLENGE 6

The distance between London and Leeds is 320 km. Peter took 4 hours to drive from London to Leeds. He returned to London using the same route. His average speed for the whole journey is 75 km/h. Find his average speed during the trip

(a) from London to Leeds,

(b) from Leeds to London.

Problem solving is highlighted in all exercises. Two extra problem-solving sections are also included giving advice on how to approach problem solving, and providing practice of problems in real-life situations.

PROBLEM SOLVING

A **Revision Exercise at the end of every chapter** allows revision of concepts:

Every chapter section ends with a Practice exercise to practise understanding:

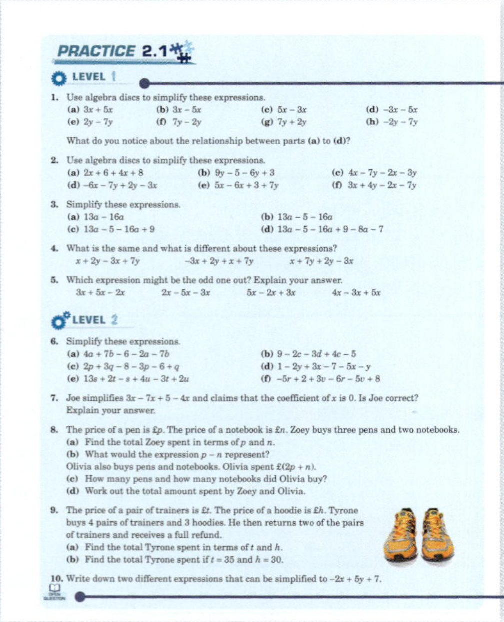

PRACTICE 2.1

LEVEL 1

1. Use algebra discs to simplify these expressions.
   (a) $3x + 5x$ (b) $3x - 5x$ (c) $5x - 3x$ (d) $-3x - 5x$
   (e) $2y - 7y$ (f) $7y - 2y$ (g) $7y + 2y$ (h) $-2y - 7y$
   What do you notice about the relationship between parts (a) to (d)?
2. Use algebra discs to simplify these expressions.
   (a) $2x + 6 + 4x + 8$ (b) $9y - 5 - 6y + 3$ (c) $4x - 7y - 2x - 3y$
   (d) $-6x - 7y + 2y - 3x$ (e) $5x - 6x + 3 + 7y$ (f) $3x + 4y - 2x - 7y$
3. Simplify these expressions.
   (a) $13a - 16a$ (b) $13a - 5 - 16a$
   (c) $13a - 5 - 16a + 9$ (d) $13a - 5 - 16a + 9 - 8a - 7$
4. What is the same and what is different about these expressions?
   $x + 2y - 3x + 7y$ $-3x + 2y + x + 7y$ $x + 7y + 2y - 3x$
5. Which expression might be the odd one out? Explain your answer.
   $3x + 5x - 2x$ $2x - 5x - 3x$ $5x - 2x + 3x$ $4x - 3x + 5x$

LEVEL 2

6. Simplify these expressions.
   (a) $4a + 7b - 6 - 2a - 7b$ (b) $9 - 2c - 3d + 4c - 5$
   (c) $2p + 3q - 8 - 3p - 6 + q$ (d) $1 - 2y + 3x - 7 - 5x - y$
   (e) $13s + 2t - s + 4u - 3t + 2u$ (f) $-5r + 2 + 3v - 6r - 5v + 8$
7. Joe simplifies $3x - 7x + 5 - 4x$ and claims that the coefficient of x is 0. Is Joe correct? Explain your answer.
8. The price of a pen is £p. The price of a notebook is £n. Zoey buys three pens and two notebooks.
   (a) Find the total Zoey spent in terms of p and n.
   (b) What would the expression $p - n$ represent?
   Olivia also buys pens and notebooks. Olivia spent £$(2p + n)$.
   (c) How many pens and how many notebooks did Olivia buy?
   (d) Work out the total amount spent by Zoey and Olivia.
9. The price of a pair of trainers is £t. The price of a hoodie is £h. Tyrone buys 4 pairs of trainers and 3 hoodies. He then returns two of the pairs of trainers and receives a full refund.
   (a) Find the total Tyrone spent in terms of t and h.
   (b) Find the total Tyrone spent if $t = 35$ and $h = 30$.
10. Write down two different expressions that can be simplified to $-2x + 5y + 7$.

Questions step up in difficulty from **Level 1 to 2**.

Science and **Finance** contexts are marked.

Open Questions show that more than one answer is possible.

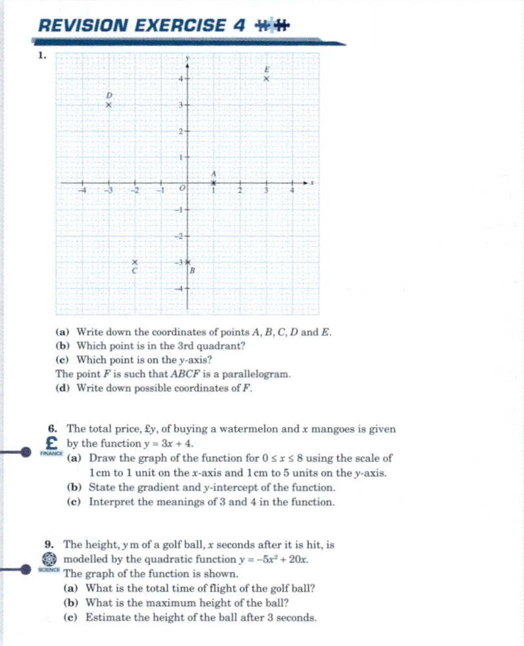

REVISION EXERCISE 4

1\.

(a) Write down the coordinates of points A, B, C, D and E.
(b) Which point is in the 3rd quadrant?
(c) Which point is on the y-axis?
The point F is such that $ABCF$ is a parallelogram.
(d) Write down possible coordinates of F.

6\. The total price, £y, of buying a watermelon and x mangoes is given by the function $y = 3x + 4$.
(a) Draw the graph of the function for $0 \le x \le 8$ using the scale of 1 cm to 1 unit on the x-axis and 1 cm to 5 units on the y-axis.
(b) State the gradient and y-intercept of the function.
(c) Interpret the meanings of 3 and 4 in the function.

9\. The height, y m of a golf ball, x seconds after it is hit, is modelled by the quadratic function $y = -5x^2 + 20x$.
The graph of the function is shown.
(a) What is the total time of flight of the golf ball?
(b) What is the maximum height of the ball?
(c) Estimate the height of the ball after 3 seconds.

Integrated Examples appear after several chapters to help make connections between different topics. These are each followed by a **Review Exercise** to check on your mastery of concepts.

For additional practice and support on any topic, ask your teacher for the **MyMaths links**, which are provided in the accompanying Scheme of Work.

MyMaths.co.uk

1 PRIME FACTORISATION, INDICES AND STANDARD FORM

WHAT IS IN THIS CHAPTER:

There are eight planets in the solar system. What are the distances of these planets from the Sun? The average distance from the Earth to the Sun is about 149 600 000 km. How can you represent this large distance in a concise way? In contrast, the diameter of a DNA molecule is 0.000 000 002 m. How can you represent this very small value in a simpler way?

LET'S LEARN TO

- express a composite number as a product of prime factors
- represent prime factorisation of a number in index notation
- find the HCF and LCM of two numbers using prime factorisation
- use the terms base, index and power
- interpret numbers written in index notation
- understand and use the definitions of zero and negative indices
- express numbers using index notation
- interpret numbers written in standard form
- express numbers using standard form
- solve problems involving indices and standard form

FLASHBACK

1. Large Numbers and Small Numbers

	Millions	Hundred thousands	Ten thousands	Thousands	Hundreds	Tens	Ones
3845 607	3	8	4	5	6	0	7

You can see in the place value table that the number 3845 607 represents three million, eight hundred and forty-five thousand, six hundred and seven.

	Ones	Tenths	Hundredths	Thousandths	Ten thousandths	Hundred thousandths
4.008 32	4 •	0	0	8	3	2

In the place value table, you can see that the number 4.008 32 represents four and 8 thousandths, 3 ten thousandths and 2 hundred thousandths.

2. Square Numbers and Cube Numbers

(a) The value given when an integer is multiplied by itself is called a **square number**.

For example, area of the square $= 4 \times 4$

$= 4^2$

$= 16\,\text{cm}^2$

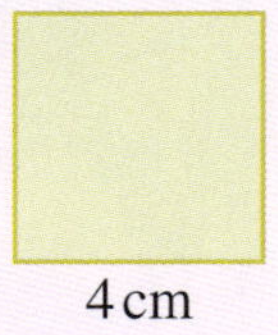

4^2 is read as '4 squared'.

$4^2 = 16$, so 16 is a square number.

The first five square numbers are 1, 4, 9, 16 and 25.

(b) The value given when an integer is multiplied by itself, then by itself again, is called a **cube number**.

For example, volume of the cube $= 4 \times 4 \times 4$

$= 4^3$

$= 64\,\text{cm}^3$

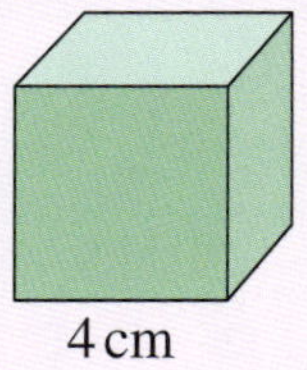

4^3 is read as '4 cubed'.

$4^3 = 64$, so 64 is a cube number.

The first five cube numbers are 1, 8, 27, 64 and 125.

REMARK
An integer is a whole number, for example, 4, 29, −3, −25, 6204.

3. Factors, Multiples, Prime Numbers and Composite Numbers

(a) If a number can be written as a product of two integers, the integers are called the **factors** of that number.

The product of an integer and another integer is called a **multiple** of the original integer.

For example, $18 = 1 \times 18$

$= 2 \times 9$

$= 3 \times 6$

1, 2, 3, 6, 9 and 18 are factors of 18.

18 is a multiple of each of the numbers 1, 2, 3, 6, 9 and 18.

REMARK
You can create a factor wall for the number 18.

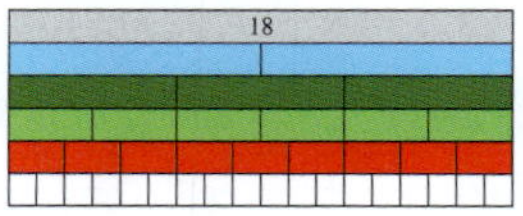

(b) An integer greater than 1 (but not 1) which has only two factors, 1 and itself, is called a **prime number**. The first ten prime numbers are 2, 3, 5, 7, 11, 13, 17, 19, 23 and 29.

(c) A **composite number** is an integer greater than 1 which has more than two distinct factors. The first ten composite numbers are 4, 6, 8, 9, 10, 12, 14, 15, 16 and 18.

The numbers 0 and 1 are neither prime numbers nor composite numbers because they do not have two or more distinct integer factors.

1.1 Prime Factorisation, HCF and LCM

A Prime Factorisation

You have learnt how to find the factors of a number. For instance,

$$\begin{aligned} 42 &= 1 \times 42 \\ &= 2 \times 21 \\ &= 3 \times 14 \\ &= 6 \times 7 \end{aligned}$$

Hence, 1, 2, 3, 6, 7, 14, 21 and 42 are factors of 42.

Of these factors, 2, 3 and 7 are prime numbers, so they are called the **prime factors** of 42.

42 is a composite number, so it can be expressed as a product of its prime factors.

$$42 = 2 \times 3 \times 7$$

prime factors

Expressing a composite number as a product of its prime factors is called **prime factorisation**. This can be done using a **factor tree** as illustrated in Example 1.

REMARK
A factor which is a prime number is called a prime factor.

REMARK
Always write the prime factors in ascending order in your final answer.

Example 1 Express 350 as a product of its prime factors.

Solution

Step 1 Express 350 as a product of 2 factors other than 1, for example, 5 and 70.

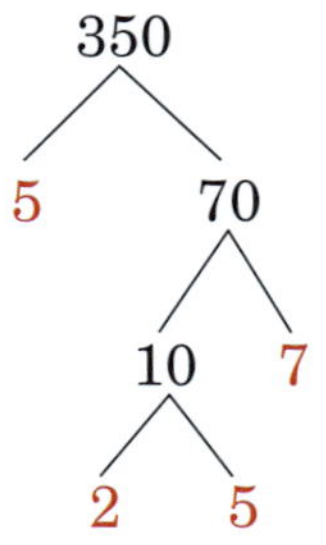

Step 2 Express each number in the factor tree as a product of two factors, if possible.

Step 3 Continue the process until the numbers at the end of each branch are prime numbers.

The prime numbers at the ends of the branches give the prime factorisation of the given number.

Thus, $350 = 2 \times 5 \times 5 \times 7$.

Try It! 1 Express 300 as a product of its prime factors.

DISCUSS

Can you draw up a factor tree for 350 in a different way? For example, try completing this factor tree.

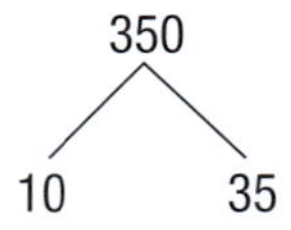

What is the same and what is different about the two factor trees?

B Highest Common Factor (HCF)

A number which is a factor of two numbers is called a **common factor** of the two numbers. The largest common factor of two numbers is called the **highest common factor (HCF)** of the two numbers.

CLASS ACTIVITY 1

Objective: To understand the idea of the highest common factor (HCF).

Number rods of different lengths have been used to make a factor wall for the number 16.

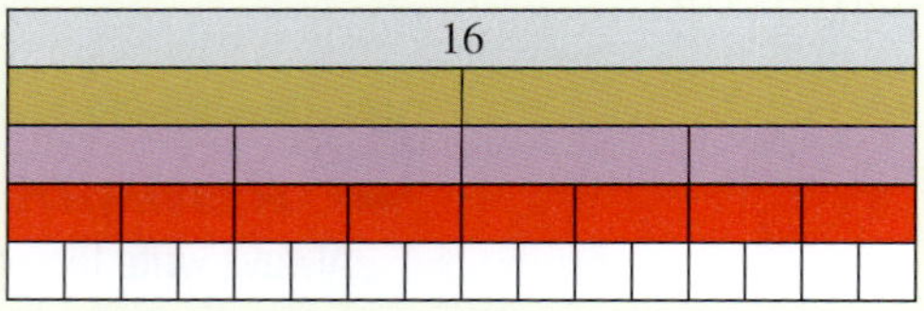

1. Use number rods to make a factor wall for 12.

2. **(a)** Which number rods can be used to make the factor walls of both numbers?

(b) Which is the longest number rod that can be used in the factor wall of both numbers?

(c) What does this longest number rod tell you about the two numbers?

3. Use, or draw, number rods to make factor walls for other pairs of numbers, such as 20 and 30, and repeat **Question 2** for these pairs of numbers.

DISCUSS

What do you call the rods that can be used for both numbers?

DISCUSS

Could a factor wall help you find the HCF of three integers?

In Class Activity 1, the number rods in the factor wall are factors of the given number. The answers in Question 2(a) are the common factors of the two numbers. The answer in Question 2(b) is the highest common factor, HCF.

Another way to find the HCF of two numbers is by writing the two numbers as products of their prime factors, and then picking their common prime factors.

For example, to find the HCF of 28 and 70, first write each number as a product of its prime factors:

$$28 = 2 \times 2 \qquad \times 7$$
$$70 = 2 \qquad \times 5 \times 7$$

Common prime factors are 2 and 7.
Therefore, the HCF of 28 and 70 is $2 \times 7 = 14$.

> The HCF of two numbers is the product of their common prime factors.

The method used in Example 2 is useful for large numbers.

Example 2 Find the highest common factor (HCF) of the numbers 160 and 220.

Solution First find the prime factorisation of 160 and 220.

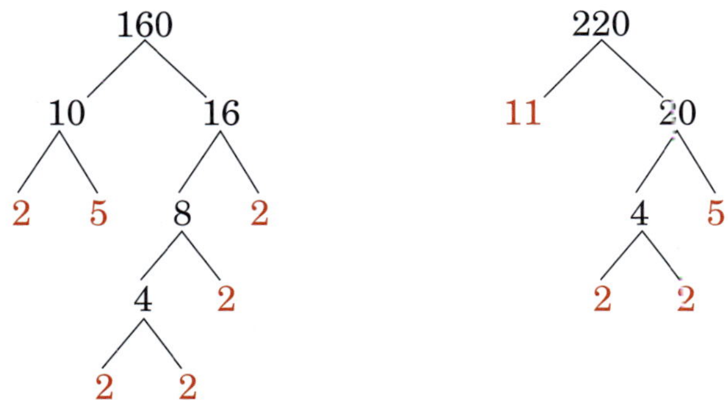

From the factor trees,

$$160 = 2 \times 2 \times 2 \times 2 \times 2 \times 5$$
$$220 = 2 \times 2 \qquad\qquad \times 5 \times 11$$

Pick out the common prime factors.

DISCUSS

Draw the factor trees for 28 and 70 to find these prime factorisations.

DISCUSS

Determine whether each statement is true. Explain your answer.

(a) Two prime numbers always have an HCF of 1.

(b) Two numbers with an HCF of 1 are always both prime.

The common prime factors are 2, 2 and 5.

HCF of 160 and 220 = product of their common prime factors

$= 2 \times 2 \times 5$

$= 20$

Try It! 2

Find the highest common factor (HCF) of the numbers 240 and 360.

DISCUSS

Why is the HCF equal to the product of the common prime factors?

Why is the number 2 listed twice as a common prime factor?

Example 3

A stall sells pizzas. One weekend, the income from pizza sales was £210 on Saturday and £66 on Sunday. What is the highest possible price of a pizza?

Solution

The cost of a pizza must be a common factor of £210 and £66. Therefore, the highest possible price of a pizza will be the highest common factor of £140 and £66.

First find the prime factorisation of 210 and 66 using factor trees.

$210 = 2 \times 3 \times 5 \times 7$

$66 = 2 \times 3 \times 11$

Pick out the common prime factors.

HCF of 210 and 66 $= 2 \times 3$

$= 6$

HCF is the product of the common prime factors.

The highest possible price of a pizza is £6.

DISCUSS

At the highest possible price, how many pizzas are sold on Saturday and how many on Sunday?

DISCUSS

What other prices could the pizzas have been sold at?

Try It! 3

Bar A is 180 cm long. Bar B is 84 cm. Each bar is cut into pieces such that all the pieces from both bars are of equal length. What is the longest possible length of each piece?

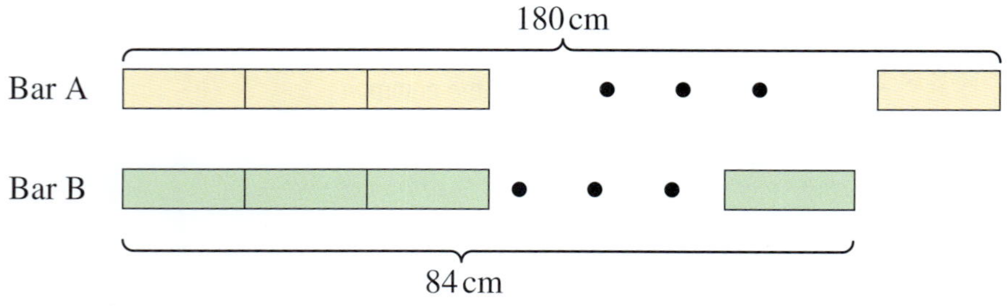

C Lowest Common Multiple (LCM)

A number that is a multiple of two integers is called a **common multiple** of the two integers. The smallest common multiple of two integers is called the **lowest common multiple (LCM)** of the two integers.

CLASS ACTIVITY 2

Objective: To understand the idea of lowest common multiple (LCM).

1	2	3	4	5	6	7	8	9	10
11	12	13	14	15	16	17	18	19	20
21	22	23	24	25	26	27	28	29	30
31	32	33	34	35	36	37	38	39	40
41	42	43	44	45	46	47	48	49	50
51	52	53	54	55	56	57	58	59	60
61	62	63	64	65	66	67	68	69	70
71	72	73	74	75	76	77	78	79	80
81	82	83	84	85	86	87	88	89	90
91	92	93	94	95	96	97	98	99	100

1. Copy the hundred-square.
2. Use one colour to shade all the multiples of 5 such as 5, 10, 15, … on your square.
3. Use a different colour to shade all the multiples of 6 such as 6, 12, 18, … on the same square.
4. List the numbers which are shaded in both colours.
5. What do the numbers you listed in **Question 4** represent?
6. What is the smallest number on your list? What can you say about this number?
7. Repeat **Questions 1** to **6** with another pair of numbers, such as 4 and 14.

DISCUSS

Could you use this method to find the LCM of three integers?

In Class Activity 2, the numbers on the list are the common multiples of the two given numbers. The smallest one on the list is the lowest common multiple, LCM. You can also represent the lowest common multiple with number rods, for example the LCM of 5 and 6 is 30:

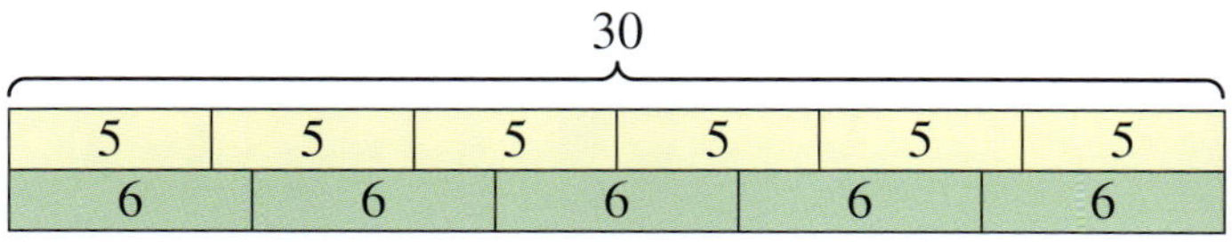

You learnt how to find the LCM of small numbers in Student Book 1A. You can also find the LCM by first writing the two numbers using prime factorisation. The LCM is the product of all their prime factors. You should only count common prime factors once.

For instance, to find the LCM of 28 and 70, first write each number as a product of its prime factors:

$$28 = 2 \times 2 \qquad \times 7$$
$$70 = 2 \qquad \times 5 \times 7$$

LCM of 28 and 70 $= 2 \times 2 \times 5 \times 7$

$= 140$

> **REMARK**
> Line up the factors which are the same in both numbers.

> The LCM of two integers is the product of all their prime factors, counting every common prime factor just once.

Example 4 shows a good way of finding the LCM of larger numbers.

Example 4 Find the lowest common multiple (LCM) of 360 and 390.

Solution First find the prime factorisation of 360 and 390.

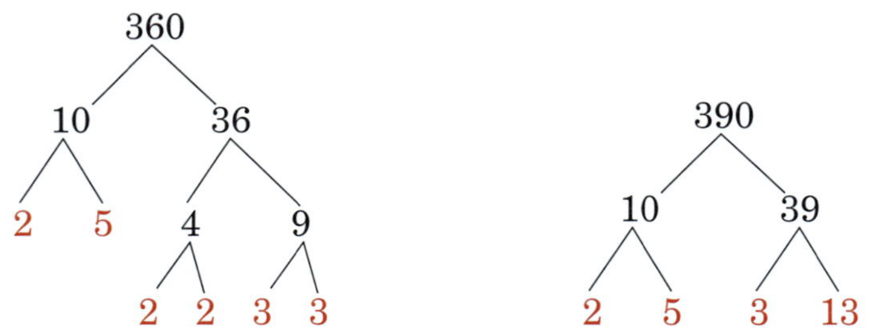

$$360 = 2 \times 2 \times 2 \times 3 \times 3 \times 5$$
$$390 = 2 \times \qquad \times 3 \qquad \times 5 \times 13$$

LCM of 360 and 390 $= 2 \times 2 \times 2 \times 3 \times 3 \times 5 \times 13$

$= 4680$ Include all the prime factors from each number. Count common factors once only.

Try It! 4 Find the lowest common multiple (LCM) of 330 and 132.

Example 5

James wants to make fruit bags that contain one apple and one orange for a school trip. Apples are sold in boxes of 60. Oranges are sold in boxes of 45.

He does not want any apples or oranges to be left over. What is the minimum number of fruit bags he should make?

Analysis James needs to buy the same number of apples as oranges.
The number of apples he buys will be a multiple of 60.
The number of oranges he buys will be a multiple of 45.
In order to have an equal number of apples and oranges, the number bought must be a common multiple of 60 and 45.

Solution First find the prime factorisation of 60 and 45.

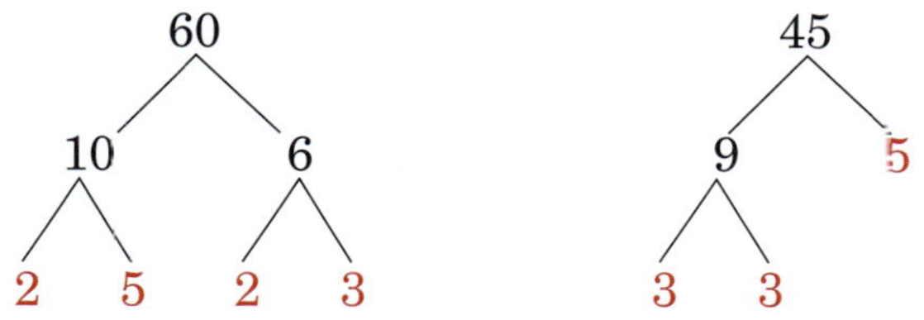

$$60 = 2 \times 2 \times 3 \qquad \times 5$$
$$45 = \qquad\qquad 3 \times 3 \times 5$$

$$\text{LCM of 60 and 45} = 2 \times 2 \times 3 \times 3 \times 5$$
$$= 180$$

James should make 180 fruit bags.

DISCUSS

How many boxes of apples and boxes of oranges will James need to buy?

Try It! 5

A teacher needs to buy the same quantity of pink paper as green paper for a school project. Pink paper is sold in packs of 36 sheets. Green paper is sold in packs of 60 sheets. What is the minimum number of sheets of each colour that they should buy?

PRACTICE 1.1

LEVEL 1

1. Express each number as a product of its prime factors using a factor tree.
   (a) 63 (b) 72 (c) 135
   (d) 154 (e) 380 (f) 440

2. Find the HCF of each pair of numbers.
   (a) 72 and 135 (b) 72 and 24
   (c) 380 and 440 (d) 380 and 228

   Hint: Use your answers to **Question 1** as a starting point.

3. Find the LCM of each pair of numbers.
   (a) 63 and 135 (b) 63 and 252
   (c) 154 and 440 (d) 154 and 231

   Hint: Use your answers to **Question 1** as a starting point.

4. Determine whether each statement is true. Explain your answer.
   (a) 5 is a factor of 40.
   (b) 8 is a factor of 100.
   (c) 88 is a multiple of 4.
   (d) 6 is a multiple of 30.
   (e) The same number can be both factor and a multiple.

5. Determine whether each statement is true. Explain your answer.
   (a) 4 is the HCF of 16 and 24.
   (b) 9 is the HCF of 90 and 50.
   (c) 1000 is the LCM of 10 and 25.
   (d) 16 is the LCM of 8 and 16.
   (e) A multiple of a number can be a prime number.

6. The HCF of 18 and 24 is 6. What is
   (a) the HCF of 180 and 240,
   (b) the HCF of 54 and 72?

LEVEL 2

7. The prime factorisation of two numbers is worked out as Number 1 $= 2 \times 3 \times 3 \times 3 \times 5 \times 11 \times 11$, and Number 2 $= 2 \times 2 \times 3 \times 11 \times 11$.
   Determine whether each statement is true. Explain your answer.
   (a) The HCF of the two numbers is equal to $2 \times 3 \times 11 \times 11$.
   (b) The LCM of the two numbers is equal to $2 \times 2 \times 2 \times 3 \times 3 \times 3 \times 5 \times 11 \times 11$.

8. There are two packs of identical balls. The total mass of balls in the first pack is 136 grams. The total mass of balls in the second pack is 102 grams. What is the maximum possible mass of each ball?

9. Ava earns £180 per day and Dan earns £150 per day for a job. They get the same total wages for the job. What is the smallest number of days each could have worked?

   FINANCE

10. Find two possible numbers with HCF 6 and LCM 168.

   OPEN QUESTION

1.2 Index Notation

A Positive Index Notation

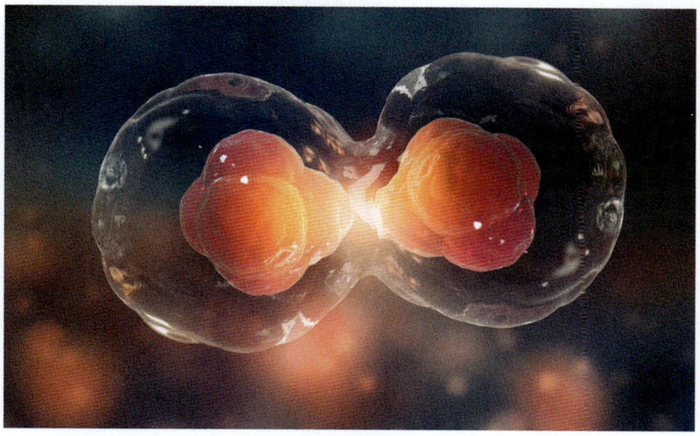

Suppose there are two cells and each cell divides into two cells every hour.

At the beginning of the first hour,
number of cells = 2 $= 2^1$

At the beginning of the second hour,
number of cells = $2 \times 2 = 4$ $= 2^2$

At the beginning of the third hour,
number of cells = $2 \times 2 \times 2 = 8$ $= 2^3$

At the beginning of the fourth hour,
number of cells = $2 \times 2 \times 2 \times 2 = 16$ $= 2^4$

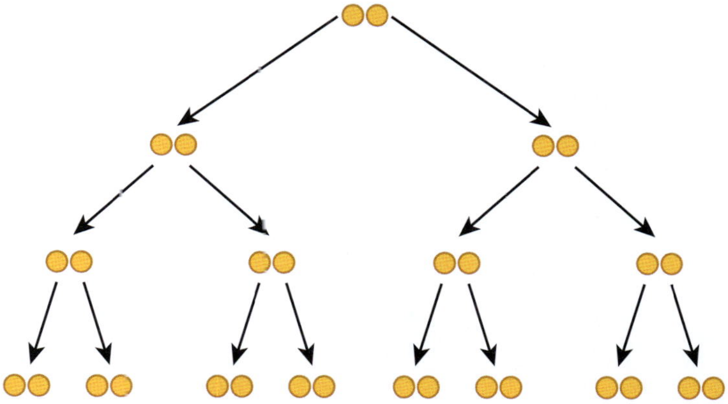

The numbers 2^1, 2^2, 2^3 and 2^4 are written in **index notation**. Each of the numbers consists of two parts: the **index** (or **power**) and the **base**.

2^5 ← index or power; 2 ← base

DISCUSS

What is 2^5 equal to?

For example, $2 \times 2 \times 2 \times 2 \times 2 = 2^5$ is read as '2 to the power of 5'. Here, the base is 2 and the index is 5.

Here are some further examples.

$5^4 = 5 \times 5 \times 5 \times 5 = 625$ and is read as '5 to the power of 4'.

$3^5 = 3 \times 3 \times 3 \times 3 \times 3 = 243$ and is read as '3 to the power of 5'.

$$a^n = \underbrace{a \times a \times \ldots \times a}_{n \text{ factors}}, \text{ where } n \text{ is a positive integer.}$$

DISCUSS

What are the base and the index in each of the numbers 5^4, 6^5 and 7^3?

CLASS ACTIVITY 3

Objective: To write numbers in index notation and explore some properties of index notation.

1. **(a)** Copy the table and write the numbers as a multiplication of the base and in index notation.

Base	Number	Index notation
3	3	3
	? $= 3 \times 3$	3^2
	27 =	
	81 =	
4	4	
	16 =	
	64 =	
	? =	4^4
5	5	
	? =	5^2
	125 =	
	625 =	
10	10	
	100 =	
	? =	10^3
	10 000 =	

(b) What is the same and what is different about 3^4 and 4^3? Are they equal in value?

(c) What is the same and what is different about a^b and b^a? Can they ever be equal in value?

2. **(a)** Copy and complete this table.

Base	Number	Index notation
(−3)	−3	−3
	? $= (-3) \times (-3)$	$(-3)^2$
	−27 =	
	81 =	
(−4)	−4	
	16 =	
	−64 =	
	? =	$(-4)^4$

DISCUSS

Ian says that $3^2 = 6$. Do you agree or disagree?

DISCUSS

Can you show 10 to the power of 2 and 3 using base-ten apparatus? Explain how you could do this.

RECALL

The product of a negative number and a positive number is negative. The product of two negative numbers is positive.

(b) Describe what you notice when the base is a negative integer and the index is an odd integer.

(c) Describe what you notice when the base is a negative integer and the index is an even integer.

DISCUSS

Lauren says that $3^n = (-3)^n$. Do you agree or disagree?

From Class Activity 3, you see that a negative base with an odd index will be a negative number, but a negative base with an even index will be a positive number.

Example 6

Write these expressions in index notation.

(a) $7 \times 7 \times 7$

(b) $8 \times 8 \times 8 \times 8 \times 8 \times 8 \times 8$

(c) $(-9) \times (-9) \times (-9) \times (-9)$

(d) $b \times b \times b \times b \times b$

Solution

(a) $7 \times 7 \times 7 = 7^3$

(b) $8 \times 8 \times 8 \times 8 \times 8 \times 8 \times 8 = 8^7$ — 7 factors.

(c) $(-9) \times (-9) \times (-9) \times (-9) = (-9)^4$ — 4 factors.

(d) $b \times b \times b \times b \times b = b^5$ — 5 factors.

DISCUSS

Is $10 + 10 + 10$ equal to 10^3? Explain your answer.

DISCUSS

Is $(-9)^4$ positive or negative?

Try It! 6

Write these expressions in index notation.

(a) $4 \times 4 \times 4 \times 4 \times 4$

(b) $6 \times 6 \times 6 \times 6 \times 6 \times 6 \times 6 \times 6$

(c) $(-5) \times (-5) \times (-5) \times (-5) \times (-5) \times (-5)$

(d) $p \times p \times p \times p \times p \times p \times p$

DISCUSS

Can you write the prime factorisation $2 \times 2 \times 2 \times 2 \times 3 \times 5 \times 5$ using index notation?

Example 7

Write these expressions with the variables in index notation.

(a) $3 \times 3 \times a \times a \times a$

(b) $d \times d \times 2 \times 2 \times 2$

(c) $(-5) \times (-5) \times (-5) \times y \times y$

(d) $p \times p \times p \times p \times 2 \times 2 \times 2 \times 2$

Solution

(a) $3 \times 3 \times a \times a \times a$
$= 3^2 \times a^3$
$= 9a^3$

(b) $d \times d \times 2 \times 2 \times 2$
$= 2^3 \times d^2$
$= 8d^2$

REMARK

When simplifying expressions like these, it is usual practice to write the numerical part as an integer and the variable parts in index notation.

(c) $(-5) \times (-5) \times (-5) \times y \times y$
$= (-5)^3 \times y^2$
$= -125y^2$

(d) $p \times p \times p \times p \times 2 \times 2 \times 2 \times 2$
$= 2^4 \times p^4$
$= 16p^4$

DISCUSS

How do you know that $(-5)^3$ is negative?

Try It! 7

Write these expressions with the variables in index notation.

(a) $5 \times 5 \times c \times c \times c \times c \times c$
(b) $s \times s \times s \times 2 \times 2 \times 2 \times 2$
(c) $(-1) \times (-1) \times (-1) \times z \times z$
(d) $3 \times 3 \times 3 \times v \times v \times v$

Example 8

Find the values of these expressions using a calculator.

(a) $(-5)^2$ **(b)** $2^5 + 7^2$ **(c)** $(-2)^3 \times 3^2$

Solution

(a) Key sequence: [( ] [−] 5 [ )] [$x^{\blacksquare}$] 2 [=]

$\therefore \quad (-5)^2 = 25$

(b) Key sequence: 2 [$x^{\blacksquare}$] 5 [▶] [+] 7 [$x^{\blacksquare}$] 2 [=]

$\therefore \quad 2^5 + 7^2 = 81$

(c) Key sequence: [( ] [−] 2 [ )] [$x^{\blacksquare}$] 3 [▶] [×] 3 [$x^{\blacksquare}$] 2 [=]

$\therefore \quad (-2)^3 \times 3^2 = -72$

REMARK

When working out by hand, index expressions should be calculated before any multiplication, division, addition or subtraction.
So $(-2)^3 \times 3^2$
$= (-8) \times 9$
$= -72$

REMARK

For x^2 and x^3 you can also use the [x^2] and [x^3] keys on your calculator.

Try It! 8

Find the values of these expressions using a calculator.

(a) $(-4)^3$ **(b)** $2^6 - 3^4$ **(c)** $(-9)^2 \div 3^4$

You can use index notation to express a number as a product of its prime factors.

So, $72 = 2 \times 2 \times 2 \times 3 \times 3$
$= 2^3 \times 3^2$

If you are given numbers in this form, then write the product out in full to find the HCF or LCM.

Example 9

Find the HCF and LCM of $3^2 \times 5^2 \times 11^2$ and $2 \times 3^2 \times 5^3 \times 11$.
Express the answers in index notation.

Solution

First, consider the HCF:

$$3^2 \times 5^2 \times 11^2 \quad = \quad 3 \times 3 \times 5 \times 5 \quad \times 11 \times 11$$
$$2 \times 3^2 \times 5^3 \times 11 = 2 \times 3 \times 3 \times 5 \times 5 \times 5 \times 11$$

Pick out the common prime factors.

Common prime factors are 3, 3, 5, 5 and 11.

HCF of the two numbers = product of their common prime factors

$= 3 \times 3 \times 5 \times 5 \times 11$

$= 3^2 \times 5^2 \times 11$

Write answer using index notation.

Then consider the LCM:

$$3^2 \times 5^2 \times 11^2 \quad = \quad 3 \times 3 \times 5 \times 5 \quad \times 11 \times 11$$
$$2 \times 3^2 \times 5^3 \times 11 = 2 \times 3 \times 3 \times 5 \times 5 \times 5 \times 11$$
$$2 \times 3 \times 3 \times 5 \times 5 \times 5 \times 11 \times 11$$

Include all the prime factors from each number. Count common factors once only.

LCM of the two numbers $= 2 \times 3 \times 3 \times 5 \times 5 \times 5 \times 11 \times 11$

$= 2 \times 3^2 \times 5^3 \times 11^2$

Try It! 9

Find the HCF and LCM of $2^3 \times 5^2 \times 7$ and $2 \times 5^4 \times 7^3$.
Express the answers in index notation.

B Zero Index

You know that $a^1 = a$, $a^2 = a \times a$ and that $a^3 = a \times a \times a$. What is a^0 equal to?

CLASS ACTIVITY 4

Objective: To explore patterns of changing indices.

1. For each of the tables
   (a) copy and describe the number pattern for each row,
   (b) complete the tables based on the number patterns.
   Use fractions where appropriate.

−1 −1 −1 −1 −1 −1

n	3	2	1	0	−1	−2	−3
2^n	8	4	2	1	$\frac{1}{2}$	$\frac{1}{4}$	$\frac{1}{8}$

÷ 2 ÷ 2 ÷ 2 ÷ 2 ÷ 2 ÷ 2

Number pattern
Subtract 1

DISCUSS

Can you use the pattern for 2^n to predict the pattern for 3^n or 5^n?

REMARK

You can use bar models to help you to divide fractions.

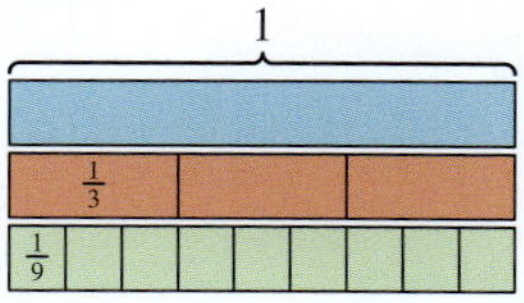

n	3	2	1	0	−1	−2	−3
3^n	27	9					

Number pattern

n	3	2	1	0	−1	−2	−3
5^n	125	25					

Number pattern

n	3	2	1	0	−1	−2	−3
10^n		100	10				

Number pattern

In this table, choose your own base.

n	3	2	1	0	−1	−2	−3

Number pattern

2. What can you say about a^0 when $a \neq 0$?

3. What is the same and what is different about 3^2 and 3^{-2}?

4. What is the same and what is different about 10^3 and 10^{-3}?

5. Can you write two rules for indices based on your tables in **Question 1**?

DISCUSS

Can you predict the pattern for a^n for any value of a?

DISCUSS

What is 0^n when $n \neq 0$? What is 1^n for any value of n? Explain your answers to a classmate.

From Class Activity 4, you can see that each of the bases to the power of zero equals 1.
This is true for all bases except 0.

When $a \neq 0$ $\quad a^0 = 1$.

REMARK

0^0 is undefined.

Example 10

Find the values of these expressions.

(a) 4^0 **(b)** $(-2.5)^0$

Solution

(a) $4^0 = 1$ $\quad a^0 = 1$

(b) $(-2.5)^0 = 1$

Try It! 10

Find the values of these expressions.

(a) 6^0 **(b)** $\left(-\frac{3}{4}\right)^0$

RECALL

$\neq$ means 'is not equal to'.

DISCUSS

Can you get these results using a calculator? If so, what would be the key sequences?

C Negative Integer Index

From Class Activity 4, you can see that a base with a negative power represents a **reciprocal**.

When $a \neq 0$ and n is a positive integer, $a^{-n} = \frac{1}{a^n}$.

Example 11

Find the values of these expressions.

(a) 5^{-3} **(b)** 3^{-4}

Solution

(a) $5^{-3} = \frac{1}{5^3}$ — $a^{-n} = \frac{1}{a^n}$

$= \frac{1}{125}$ — $5^3 = 5 \times 5 \times 5$

(b) $3^{-4} = \frac{1}{3^4}$

$= \frac{1}{81}$ — $3^4 = 3 \times 3 \times 3 \times 3$

Try It! 11

Find the values of these expressions.

(a) 2^{-4} **(b)** 7^{-2}

Example 12

Find the values of these expressions.

(a) $2^0 - 3^{-2}$ **(b)** $9^0 \times 6^{-2}$

Solution

(a) $2^0 - 3^{-2} = 1 - \frac{1}{3^2}$ — $a^0 = 1$, $a^{-n} = \frac{1}{a^n}$

$= 1 - \frac{1}{9}$

$= \frac{8}{9}$

(b) $9^0 \times 6^{-2} = 1 \times \frac{1}{6^2}$ — $6^{-2} = \frac{1}{6^2}$

$= 1 \times \frac{1}{36}$ — $6^2 = 6 \times 6$

$= \frac{1}{36}$

Try It! 12

Find the values of these expressions.

(a) $3^0 - 2^{-3}$ **(b)** $8^{-2} \div 8^0$

RECALL

When the product of two numbers is 1, the two numbers are said to be the reciprocal of each other. For example, $3 \times \frac{1}{3} = 1$ so $\frac{1}{3}$ is the reciprocal of 3.

REMARK

0^{-n} is undefined.

RECALL

Index expressions should be calculated before any multiplication, division, addition or subtraction.

PRACTICE 1.2

LEVEL 1

1. Write these expressions in index notation.
   (a) $6 \times 6 \times 6 \times 6$
   (b) $(-5) \times (-5) \times (-5)$
   (c) $7 \times 7 \times 7 \times 7 \times 7 \times 7$
   (d) $(-9) \times (-9) \times (-9) \times (-9) \times (-9)$

2. Find the values of these expressions.
   (a) 5^3
   (b) $(-5)^3$
   (c) 2^6
   (d) $(-2)^6$
   (e) 8^0
   (f) $(-8)^0$
   (g) 0.5^0
   (h) $(-2.5)^0$

3. Find the values of these expressions using a calculator.
   (a) 3^8
   (b) $(-3)^8$
   (c) 7^5
   (d) $(-7)^5$
   (e) 9^0
   (f) $-(-9)^0$
   (g) 4^3
   (h) 4^{-3}

4. Which of these statements are true? Explain your answers.
   (a) $2^3 = (-2)^3$
   (b) $(-3)^2 = -3^2$
   (c) $5^0 = (-5)^0$
   (d) $(-4)^0 = -4^0$
   (e) $10^{-1} + 10^{-1} + 10^{-1} = 10^{-3}$
   (f) $10^{-1} \times 10^{-2} = 10^{-3}$

5. What is the same and what is different about these numbers in index form?
   $2^3 \qquad -2^3 \qquad (-2)^3 \qquad 2^{-3}$

LEVEL 2

6. Write these expressions in index notation.
   (a) $7 \times r \times r \times r$
   (b) $5 \times 5 \times t \times t \times t \times t$
   (c) $x \times x \times x \times x \times x \times (-3) \times (-3)$
   (d) $(-2) \times (-2) \times (-2) \times z \times z \times z$

7. Find the HCF and LCM of each pair of numbers. Express the answers in index notation.
   (a) $2^3 \times 3 \times 11^2$ and $2^2 \times 3^3 \times 11$
   (b) $2^4 \times 5^3 \times 7$ and $2^3 \times 5^2 \times 7^2$

8. Tina works out the expression $68 + (-3)^4 + (-2)^5$. Her working is shown. Find her mistake and work out the correct answer.
   $$68 + (-3)^4 + (-2)^5 = 68 + (-81) + (-32)$$
   $$= 68 - 81 - 32$$
   $$= -45$$

9. Work out the values of these expressions.
   (a) $13 + 2^0$
   (b) $3^2 - 4$
   (c) 4×5^2
   (d) $2^4 \div 2$
   (e) $17^0 + 2^3$
   (f) 2×5^{-1}
   (g) 3×2^{-3}
   (h) $3^{-2} \div 5^0$

10. Which of these expressions has a value different from the others?
    $2^{-4} \qquad (-4)^{-2} \qquad 8^{-2} \qquad \left(\frac{1}{16}\right)^1$

1.3 Standard Form

In daily life, you often come across very large numbers and very small numbers with many zeros. For instance, the approximate area of the UK is 243 000 km^2, and air pollution particles called PM2.5 are particles with a diameter of 0.000 0025 m or less. **Standard form** is a simpler way of representing these numbers.

Area of the UK = 243 000 km^2

CLASS ACTIVITY 5

Objective: To compare very large and very small numbers.

1. Here are some approximate measurements in metres.

Measurements	Descriptions
0.000 004 m	height of a bear
40 000 m	circumference of the Earth
0.0004 m	height of a skyscraper
4000 000 m	distance from Leeds to Brighton
400 m	length of a bacteria
40 000 000 m	distance from UK to North Pole
4 m	length of a marathon
0.04 m	length of a grain of sand
400 000 m	width of a book

(a) Write down each measurement and each description on separate sticky notes or pieces of paper.

(b) In pairs, match each measurement with a possible description.

(c) Put the measurements in order from smallest to largest.

2. Choose pairs of measurements and write a sentence to compare them. For example, 'The distance from Leeds to Brighton is 10 times longer than the distance of a marathon'. Write sentences for at least three different pairs.

3. **(a)** What is the value at each arrow?

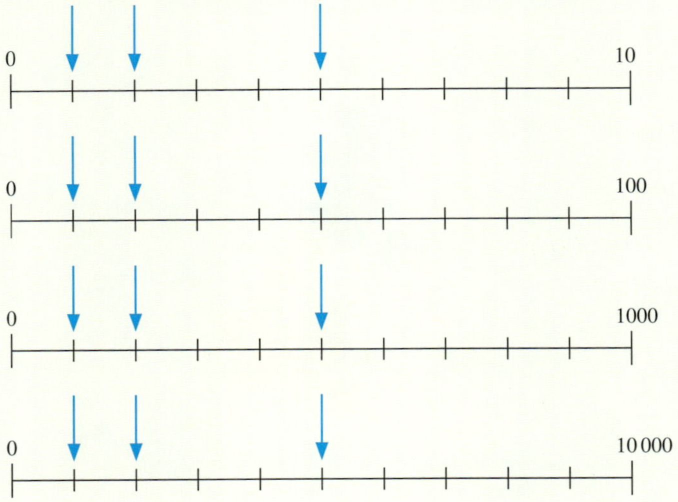

(b) Compare the values at the first arrow on each number line. What do you notice about the relationship between them?

(c) Compare the values at the third arrow on each number line. What do you notice about the relationship between them?

Standard form uses powers of 10 to show the magnitude of a number.

For instance,

$$2 \times 10^6 = 2 \times 1000\,000 \qquad 10^6 = 1000\,000$$
$$= 2000\,000$$

$$3.7 \times 10^3 = 3.7 \times 1000 \qquad 10^3 = 1000$$
$$= 3700$$

The power of 10 can also be negative.

For example,

$$5 \times 10^{-2} = 5 \times \frac{1}{10^2} \qquad a^{-n} = \frac{1}{a^n}$$
$$= 5 \div 10^2$$
$$= 5 \div 100 \qquad 10^2 = 100$$
$$= 0.05$$

As you can see, multiplying by 10^{-2} is the same as dividing by 100.

$$8.1 \times 10^{-3} = 8.1 \times \frac{1}{10^3} \qquad a^{-n} = \frac{1}{a^n}$$
$$= 8.1 \div 10^3$$
$$= 8.1 \div 1000 \qquad 10^3 = 1000$$
$$= 0.0081$$

RECALL

To multiply by 10, you move all the digits one place to the left in the place value table.

Thus, to multiply by 10^3, move all the digits three places to the left in the place value table.

Thousands	Hundreds	Tens	Ones	Tenths
			3	7
3	7	0	0	

RECALL

To divide by 10, you move all the digits one place to the right in the place value table.

Thus, to divide by 10^3, move all the digits three places to the right in the place value table.

Ones	Tenths	Hundredths	Thousandths	Ten thousandths
8	1			
0	0	0	8	1

Example 13

Write each number as an integer.

(a) 6×10^4 (b) 5.34×10^7

Solution

(a) $6 \times 10^4 = 6 \times 10\,000$
$= 60\,000$

$10^4 = 10\,000$

(b) $5.34 \times 10^7 = 5.34 \times 10\,000\,000$
$= 53\,400\,000$

$10^7 = 10\,000\,000$

Try It! 13

Write each number as an integer.

(a) 5×10^3 (b) 9.21×10^6

Example 14

Write each number as a decimal.

(a) 8×10^{-4} (b) 6.17×10^{-5}

Solution

(a) $8 \times 10^{-4} = 8 \times \frac{1}{10^4}$

$a^{-n} = \frac{1}{a^n}$

$= 8 \div 10^4$
$= 8 \div 10\,000$
$= 0.0008$

$10^4 = 10\,000$

(b) $6.17 \times 10^{-5} = 6.17 \times \frac{1}{10^5}$

$a^{-n} = \frac{1}{a^n}$

$= 6.17 \div 10^5$
$= 6.17 \div 100\,000$
$= 0.000\,0617$

$10^5 = 100\,000$

Try It! 14

Write each number as a decimal.

(a) 9×10^{-4} (b) 2.45×10^{-6}

DISCUSS

Glen says that 4×10^{-5} is a negative number. Is he correct?

A number expressed in the form

$A \times 10^n$,

where $1 \leq A < 10$ and n is an integer, is called the standard form of the number.

DISCUSS

Edward says that 4×10^{12} is a very large number and 4×10^{-12} is a very small number. Is he correct?

Consider:

$710 \times 10 = 7100$	Move all digits 1 place to the left in the place value table.
$71 \times 10^2 = 71 \times 100$	$10^2 = 100$
$= 7100$	Move all digits 2 places to the left in the place value table.
$7.1 \times 10^3 = 7.1 \times 1000$	$10^3 = 1000$
$= 7100$	Move all digits 3 places to the left in the place value table.
$0.71 \times 10^4 = 0.71 \times 10\,000$	$10^4 = 10\,000$
$= 7100$	Move all digits 4 places to the left in the place value table.

DISCUSS

Which of these numbers is in standard form? Explain your answer.

0.694×10^{-2}
6.94×10^{-3}
69.4×10^{-4}
694×10^{-5}

These all use powers of 10 to express the number 7100. However, only 7.1×10^6 is in standard form, because 710, 71 and 0.71 are not numbers greater than or equal to 1 and less than 10.

CLASS ACTIVITY 6

Objective: To compare numbers given in standard form or as integers.

(a) Copy and complete the table to show the approximate average distance of planets from the Sun.

Planet	Average distance from Sun (km)	
	Standard form	Integer
Earth	1.5×10^8	
Jupiter	$7.8 \times$	780 000 000
Mercury	5.7×10^7	
Mars	$\times 10^8$	230 000 000
Neptune	4.5×10^9	
Saturn		1 400 000 000
Uranus	2.9×10^9	
Venus	1.1×10^8	

(b) Write the planets in ascending order of distance from the Sun.

Example 15

Write each number in standard form.

(a) 625 **(b)** 13 700 **(c)** 4523 000

Solution

(a) $625 = 6.25 \times 100$

$= 6.25 \times 10^2$

Express the number as a product of a number A such that $1 \leq A < 10$ and a power of 10.

(b) $13\,700 = 1.37 \times 10\,000$

$= 1.37 \times 10^4$

(c) $4523\,000 = 4.523 \times 1000\,000$

$= 4.523 \times 10^6$

Try It! 15

Write each number in standard form.

(a) 7300 **(b)** 325 000 **(c)** 46 520 000

DISCUSS

How can you use place value tables to check your answers?

Example 16

Write each number in standard form.

(a) 0.068 **(b)** 0.0003 **(c)** 0.000 0195

Solution

(a) $0.068 = 6.8 \div 100$

$= 6.8 \times \frac{1}{100}$ Dividing by 100 is the same as multiplying by $\frac{1}{100}$.

$= 6.8 \times \frac{1}{10^2}$

$= 6.8 \times 10^{-2}$ Express the number as a product of a number A such that $1 \leq A < 10$ and a power of 10.

(b) $0.0003 = 3 \div 10\,000$

$= 3 \times \frac{1}{10\,000}$

$= 3 \times \frac{1}{10^4}$ $\frac{1}{a^n} = a^{-n}$

$= 3 \times 10^{-4}$

(c) $0.000\,0195 = 1.95 \div 100\,000$

$= 1.95 \times \frac{1}{100\,000}$

$= 1.95 \times \frac{1}{10^5}$

$= 1.95 \times 10^{-5}$

Try It! 16

Write each number in standard form.

(a) 0.04 **(b)** 0.000 47 **(c)** 0.000 004 78

PRACTICE 1.3

LEVEL 1

1. Which of these numbers are in standard form?

38×10^7 $\quad 1 \times 10^5$ $\quad 0.29 \times 10^3$

2.9×10^{-4} $\quad 290 \times 10^{-6}$ $\quad 3.08 \times 10^{-2}$

2. Write each number as an integer.

(a) 4×10^3 **(b)** 4.2×10^6 **(c)** 6.3×10^5 **(d)** 6.07×10^8

3. Write each number as a decimal.

(a) 9.1×10^{-4} **(b)** 9×10^{-3} **(c)** 8.3×10^{-6} **(d)** 8.03×10^{-5}

4. Express each number in standard form.

(a) 6300 **(b)** 630 000
(c) 0.63 **(d)** 0.000 063
(e) 28 900 **(f)** 289 000 000
(g) 0.000 289 **(h)** 0.000 000 289

5. The diameter of Earth is about 12 700 km. Write the diameter in standard form.

SCIENCE

6. The length of a bee is 0.014 m. Write the length in standard form.

7. What is the same and what is different about these numbers?

4×10^3 $\quad 3 \times 10^4$ $\quad 4 \times 10^{-3}$ $\quad 3 \times 10^{-4}$

LEVEL 2

8. Write each number in standard form.

(a) 48×10^5 **(b)** 0.3×10^6
(c) 360×10^{-4} **(d)** 0.36×10^{-3}

9. Which number in each pair is bigger?

(a) 2×10^{-3} or 2×10^{-5}
(b) 3.45×10^{-3} or 2.67×10^3
(c) 92 000 or 9.3×10^3

10. The diameter of a red blood cell is 0.000 0078 m. The diameter of a white blood cell is 12×10^{-6} m.

SCIENCE

(a) Express these two diameters in standard form.
(b) Which cell has a larger diameter?

1.4 Solving Problems Involving Standard Form

Indices and standard form can be applied in daily life. Let us see some examples.

Example 17

The volume of water in tank A is $76000\,\text{cm}^3$. The volume of water in tank B is $125000\,\text{cm}^3$. Find the total volume of water in the two tanks. Give your answer in standard form.

Solution

$$\begin{aligned}\text{Total volume of water} &= 76\,000 + 125\,000\\ &= 201\,000\\ &= 2.01 \times 100\,000\\ &= 2.01 \times 10^5\,\text{cm}^3\end{aligned}$$

> **REMARK**
>
> Set out in columns:
> 76000
> +125000
> Ignoring the three trailing zeros gives
> 76 + 125 = 201
> Thus, 76 000 + 125 000 = 201 000

Try It! 17

The volume of hot air balloon A is 2100 000 litres. The volume of hot air balloon B is 2850 000 litres. Find the total volume of these two balloons. Give your answer in standard form.

Example 18

The mass of a housefly is 0.000 02 kg. The mass of a mosquito is 0.000 0025 kg. Calculate the difference in mass of the two insects. Give your answer in standard form.

Solution

$$\begin{aligned}\text{Difference in mass} &= 0.000\,02 - 0.000\,0025\\ &= 0.000\,0175\\ &= 1.75 \div 100\,000\\ &= 1.75 \times \frac{1}{100\,000}\\ &= 1.75 \times \frac{1}{10^5}\\ &= 1.75 \times 10^{-5}\,\text{kg}\end{aligned}$$

> **REMARK**
>
> Set out in columns:
> 0.0000200
> – 0.0000025
> Ignoring the four leading zeros gives
> 200 – 25 = 175
> Thus, 0.000 02 – 0.000 0025 = 0.000 175

Try It! 18

The thickness of a hair is 0.000 068 m. The thickness of a piece of paper is 0.000 12 m. Calculate the difference in thickness of the hair and the piece of paper. Give your answer in standard form.

Example 19

The table shows some units in digital data size.

1 megabyte (MB) = 1×10^6 bytes	
1 gigabyte (GB) = 1×10^9 bytes	

(a) Write 1×10^6 and 1×10^9 as integers.

(b) How many megabytes are equal to 1 gigabyte? Express your answer in standard form.

Solution

(a) $1 \times 10^6 = 1 \times 1000\,000$
$= 1000\,000$

$1 \times 10^9 = 1 \times 1000\,000\,000$
$= 1000\,000\,000$

(b) 1 gigabyte = $1000\,000\,000$ bytes
$= (1000\,000\,000 \div 1000\,000)$ megabytes
$= 1000$ megabytes
$= 1 \times 10^3$ megabytes

Try It! 19

The table shows some units in digital data size.

1 kilobyte = 1×10^3 bytes	
1 terabyte = 1×10^{12} bytes	

(a) Write 1×10^3 and 1×10^{12} as integers.

(b) How many kilobytes are equal to 1 terabyte? Express your answer in standard form.

Example 20

A block of clay has a mass of 7500 g. The clay is used to make six identical vases. Use a calculator to work out the mass of each vase. Give your answer as an integer and in standard form.

Solution

Mass of one vase $= 7500 \div 6$
$= 1250$ g
$= (1.25 \times 10^3)$ g

Try It! 20

A pack of 50 sheets of card is 0.015 m thick. How thick is one sheet of card? Give your answer as a decimal and in standard form.

REMARK

This calculation can be represented by a bar model.

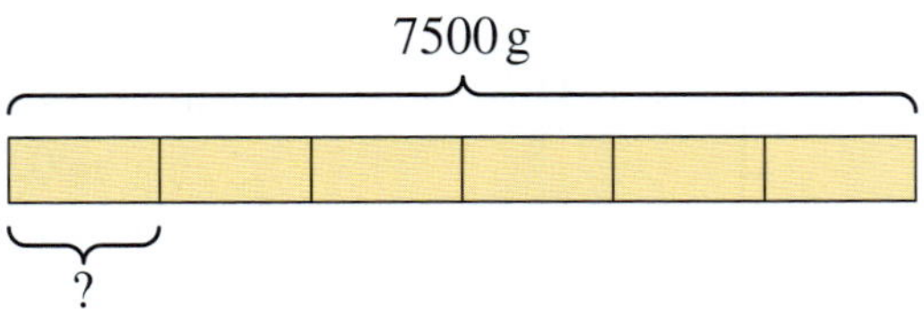

REMARK

Scientific calculators will sometimes give answers in standard form, so you need to understand how to interpret the display.

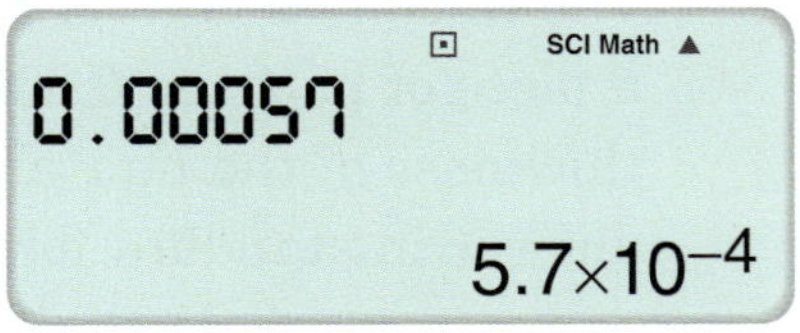

This means 5.7×10^{-4}.

PRACTICE 1.4

LEVEL 1

1. The volume of a piece of copper is 36 000 cm^3. The volume of a piece of zinc is 7800 cm^3. Find the total volume of these two pieces of metal and express the answer in standard form.

2. The area covered by St James's Park is 230 000 m^2. The area covered by Hyde Park is 1420 000 m^2. Find the difference in the area of St James's Park and Hyde Park. Give your answer in standard form.

3. In an Olympic triathlon, competitors swim 1500 m, cycle 40 000 m and run 10 000 m. Find the total length of the triathlon and express the answer in standard form.

4. SCIENCE The diameter of Venus is approximately 12 000 000 m. The diameter of Saturn is approximately 120 000 000 m.
   (a) How many times larger than the diameter of Venus is the diameter of Saturn?
   (b) Find the difference in the diameters of Venus and Saturn. Give your answer in standard form.

LEVEL 2

5. A rectangular block of land is 380 m long and 200 m wide. Find the area of the land. Give your answer in standard form.

6. SCIENCE Each tablet contains 0.000 04 kg of a medicine. A patient takes 60 tablets in one month. Use a calculator to find the total mass of the medicine taken in a month. Give your answer as a decimal and in standard form.

7. A recipe for cupcakes contains 16 g of sugar per cupcake. A factory buys large tubs containing 20 000 g of sugar. Use a calculator to work out how many cupcakes can be made with the sugar in one tub. Express your answer in standard form.

8. The mass of a baby elephant is (9×10^4) g. The mass of an adult elephant is (9×10^6) g. How many times larger than the baby elephant is the adult elephant?

9. PROBLEM SOLVING The file size of a digital photo is 4300 000 bytes. The file size of a video is 22 000 000 bytes.
   (a) Find the total file size of the photo and the video in bytes in standard form.
   Nigel can send an email with attachments up to 25 MB in total.
   (b) Can Nigel send the photo and the video in one email?
   Hint: 1 megabyte (MB) = 1×10^6 bytes.

10. Make up a real-life problem that involves addition or subtraction of two very large or very small numbers. Write your answer in standard form.

REVIEW

Prime Factorisation, HCF and LCM

Writing a composite number as a product of prime factors is called prime factorisation. It can be done using a factor tree.

For example,

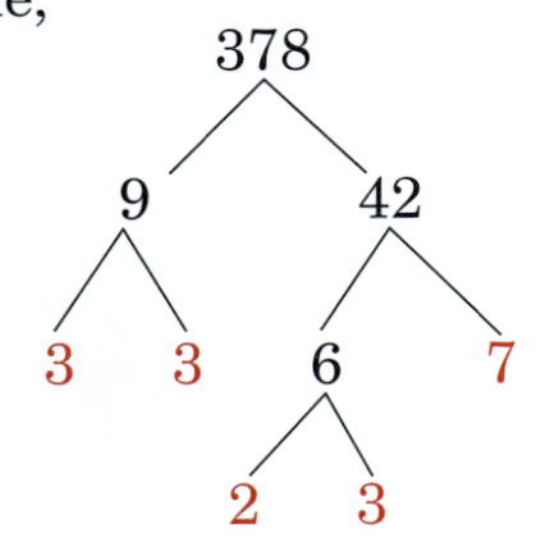

$$378 = 2 \times 3 \times 3 \times 3 \times 7$$

The HCF and LCM of two numbers can be found using prime factorisation.

(a) The HCF of two numbers is the product of their common prime factors

$$378 = 2 \qquad\qquad \times 3 \times 3 \times 3 \qquad \times 7$$
$$360 = 2 \times 2 \times 2 \times 3 \times 3 \qquad \times 5$$

HCF of 378 and 360 $= 2 \times 3 \times 3$
$= 18$

(b) The LCM of two integers is the product of all their prime factors, counting every common prime factor just once.

$$378 = 2 \qquad\qquad \times 3 \times 3 \times 3 \qquad \times 7$$
$$360 = 2 \times 2 \times 2 \times 3 \times 3 \qquad \times 5$$
$$2 \times 2 \times 2 \times 3 \times 3 \times 3 \times 5 \times 7$$

LCM of 378 and 360
$= 2 \times 2 \times 2 \times 3 \times 3 \times 3 \times 5 \times 7$
$= 7560$

Index Notation

(a) If n is a positive integer,

$$a^n = \underbrace{a \times a \times a \times \ldots \times a}_{n \text{ factors}}$$

This is read as a to the power of n. a is called the base, and n is called the power or index.

For example, $5^4 = 5 \times 5 \times 5 \times 5$
$= 625$
$(-4)^3 = (-4) \times (-4) \times (-4) = -64$

(b) $a^0 = 1$ for any $a \neq 0$.
For example, $7^0 = 1$, $(-8)^0 = 1$.

(c) If n is a positive integer and $a \neq 0$,

$$a^{-n} = \frac{1}{a^n}.$$

For example, $a^{-3} = \frac{1}{a^3}$,

$$(-5)^{-2} = \frac{1}{(-5)^2} = \frac{1}{25}.$$

Standard Form

A number expressed in the form

$$A \times 10^n,$$

where $1 \leq A < 10$ and n is an integer, is called the standard form of the number.

For example, the standard form of 4700000 is 4.7×10^6,

the standard form of 0.0000965 is 9.65×10^{-5}.

CHALLENGE 1

The mass of an ant is 0.000 003 kg. It can carry an object of 25 times its mass. Can the ant carry a crumb of bread of mass 6×10^{-4} kg? Explain your answer.

REVISION EXERCISE 1

1. Express these numbers in index notation.
(a) $5 \times 5 \times 5$
(b) $8 \times 8 \times 8 \times 8$
(c) $(-1) \times (-1) \times (-1) \times (-1) \times (-1)$
(d) $(-10) \times (-10) \times (-10) \times (-10)$

2. Find the values of these expressions.
(a) $2^5 + 4^0$
(b) $2^5 + (-4)^0$
(c) 2×4^3
(d) $2 \times (-4)^3$

3. **(a)** Express the numbers 450 and 270 as the products of prime factors using index notation.
(b) Find the HCF of 450 and 270.
(c) Find the LCM of 450 and 270.

4. Two pieces of wire are 150 cm long and 105 cm long. They are cut into small pieces of equal length.

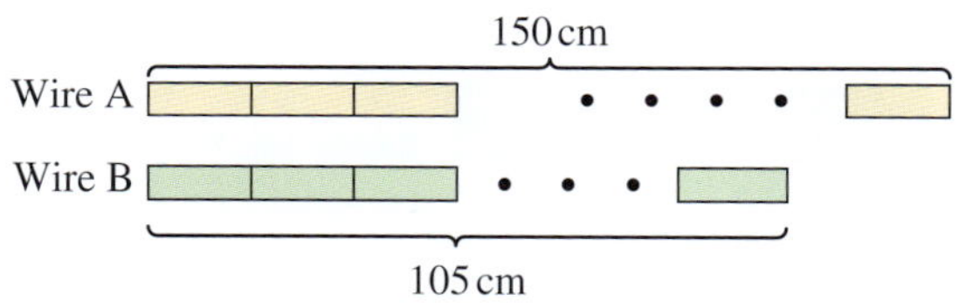

(a) Express 150 and 105 as products of prime factors using index notation.
(b) What is the maximum possible length of each piece?

5. OPEN QUESTION Sajid writes down two numbers. The smaller of the numbers is $2^3 \times 3^4 \times 5^2 \times 7$. The HCF of the two numbers is $2 \times 3^3 \times 5^2 \times 7$. Write down two possibilities for the larger number in index notation.

6. Write down the LCM of $2^3 \times 3 \times 7 \times 11$ and $2 \times 3^2 \times 11^2$ in index notation.

7. Find the values of these expressions using a calculator.
(a) $7^0 + 6^{-2}$
(b) $(-3)^{-4} - (-9)^0$
(c) $5^4 \times (-5)^{-3}$
(d) $4^{-1} \div 7^{-1}$

8. Which of these statements are true? Explain your answers.
(a) $(-5)^2 = 5^{-2}$
(b) $(-3)^4 = -3^4$
(c) $8^{-1} + 8^{-1} + 8^{-1} = 8^{-3}$
(d) $(-2)^5 = -2^5$

9. Arrange these numbers in ascending order.

(a) $5^0, 5^{-1}, 5^3, 5^{-2}$

(b) $(-2)^5, (-2)^2, (-2)^0, -2^3$

10. The area of Blenheim Palace is 8500 000 m². Express the area in standard form.

11. The mass of a butterfly is 0.000 27 kg. The mass of a bee is 0.000 12 kg. Find

(a) the total mass of the butterfly and the bee,

(b) the difference in mass of the butterfly and the bee.

Give your answers in standard form.

12. The distance from London to Sydney is approximately (1.7×10^7) m. The distance from London to Dubrovnik is approximately (1.7×10^6) m. How many times further away from London is Sydney compared to Dubrovnik?

Write in Your Journal

Which of these numbers are expressed in standard form? Explain your answer.

3.5×10^5 $\quad$ 35×10^{-2} $\quad$ 0.35×10^7 $\quad$ 3.5 $\quad$ 3.5×10^{-3}

2 ALGEBRAIC EXPRESSIONS AND MANIPULATION

WHAT IS IN THIS CHAPTER:

Variables in algebra represent unknown values. For example, the total cost of this crockery is 4 × cost of a plate + 4 × cost of a bowl + 4 × cost of a mug, which you might write as $4x + 4y + 4z$. What do x, y and z represent?

LET'S LEARN TO

- identify linear algebraic expressions
- add and subtract linear algebraic expressions
- expand and simplify linear algebraic expressions
- expand the product of two linear algebraic expressions
- factorise expressions by finding common factors

FLASHBACK

1. Algebraic Expressions

(a) An expression that contains numbers, variables and operation symbols is called an **algebraic expression**.

For example, $4x - 2$, $1 - 2x + 3y$ are algebraic expressions.

(b) An algebraic expression can be represented using algebra discs.

For example, $4x - 2$ or $4x + (-2)$: 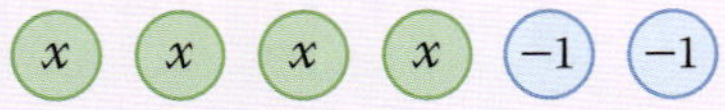

$1 - 2x + 3y$ or $1 + (-2x) + 3y$: 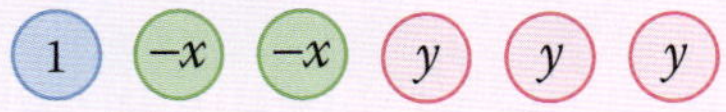

(c) The algebra discs 1 and −1, x and $-x$, y and $-y$ form zero pairs.

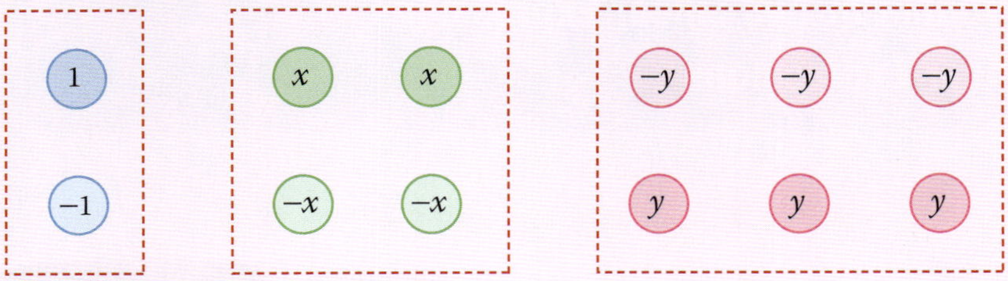

$1 + (-1) = 0$ $\quad$ $2x + (-2x) = 0$ $\quad$ $(-3y) + 3y = 0$

(d) When the values of the variables are known, the value of an algebraic expression can be found by **substitution**.

For example, when $x = 5$ and $y = 3$,

$$\begin{aligned} 1 + 2x + 4y &= 1 + 2(5) + 4(3) \\ &= 1 + 10 + 12 \\ &= 23 \end{aligned}$$

2(5) means 2×5 and 4(3) means 4×3.

2. Like Terms and Unlike Terms

In an algebraic expression, parts separated by addition or subtraction symbols are called **terms**. The number which is multiplying a variable in a term is called the **coefficient** of the variable. Terms which differ only in their numerical coefficients are called **like terms**. Terms which are not like terms are called **unlike terms**.

For example, $3x$ and $-4x$ are like terms because the variable, x, is the same, but the numerical coefficients, 3 and −4, are different. $5y$ and $3y$ are like terms. $3x$ and $3y$ are unlike terms. 7 and $2y$ are unlike terms.

DISCUSS

Are $4x$ and $4y$ like terms?

3. Expanding Algebraic Expressions

The **distributive laws** of multiplication over addition and subtraction are:

$a(x + y) = ax + ay$ — Distributive law of multiplication over addition.

$a(x - y) = ax - ay$ — Distributive law of multiplication over subtraction.

For example, $3(2x + 5) = 3(2x) + 3(5) = 6x + 15$ $3(2x - 2) = 3(2x) - 3(2) = 6x - 6$

DISCUSS

Jonah says 'x and x^2 are like terms because they both only contain x terms.' What would you say in response?

2.1 Linear Algebraic Expressions

Strips of different lengths can be used to make shapes. The length of each longer blue strip is b cm and the length of each shorter red strip is r cm.

Some of these strips are used to make a shape with perimeter $(2b + 6r)$ cm.

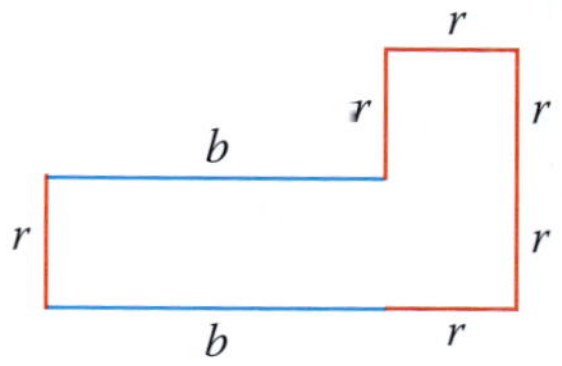

The expression $2b + 6r$ is an example of a **linear algebraic expression**.

DISCUSS

Can you make some more shapes using the strips and write down their perimeters as algebraic expressions?

Remember that the number which is multiplying a variable in a term is the coefficient of the variable. For example, in $2p$, the coefficient of p is 2 and in $-5y$, the coefficient of y is -5. A number which is not multiplying any variable is called a **constant term**. For example, in $2p + 3q - 4$, the constant term is -4.

Expressions can be represented by algebra discs and then simplified by grouping discs that are the same together. This process of grouping is called **collecting like terms**. Let us recap this work from Student Book 2A.

The expression $5x + 2 - 3x - 3$ can be represented using algebra discs.

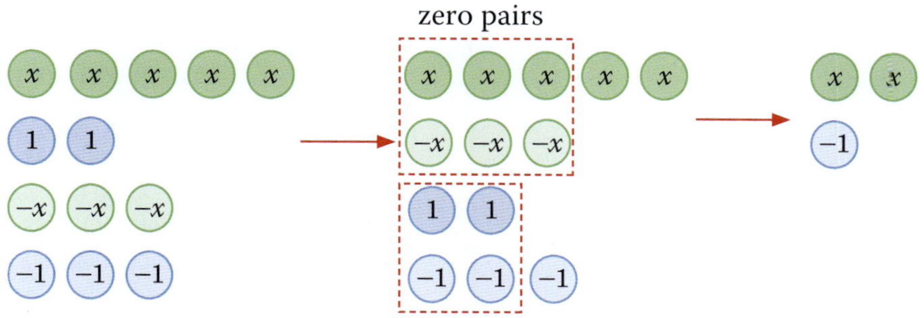

Collect the like terms

$5x + 2 - 3x - 3$ $\underbrace{5x - 3x}_{2x} + \underbrace{2 - 3}_{-1}$ $2x - 1$

$$\begin{aligned} 5x + 2 - 3x - 3 &= 5x - 3x + 2 - 3 \\ &= 2x - 1 \end{aligned}$$

Arrange like terms together.

CLASS ACTIVITY 1

Objective: To use algebra discs to investigate the technique of collecting like terms.

1. **(a)** Use algebra discs to represent $6x + 3 - 2x + 2$.
   (b) Rearrange the discs so like terms are together.
   (c) Use zero pairs to remove as many discs as possible. What expression do the remaining discs represent?
2. **(a)** Use algebra discs to find three other expressions that simplify to the same expression as **Question 1(c)**.
   (b) Compare your answers with a classmate's. Can you find two more expressions that are different from those you already have between you?
3. **(a)** Fill in the blanks with integers to make the expression equal to $2x + 3$.

   $\square\, x - \square - \square\, x + \square$

   (b) Compare your answer with a classmate's. What is different and what is the same about your answers?
   (c) Repeat parts **(a)** and **(b)**, but this time make the expression equal to $-5x + 1$.
4. Find two expressions that simplify to each of these expressions.
   (a) $3x - 7$ **(b)** $3x + 5y$ **(c)** $3x - 5y + 7$

From Class Activity 1, you see that an expression can be simplified by collecting like terms. Two unlike terms in an expression cannot be collected.

Example 1

Simplify these expressions.

(a) $4x + 7x$ **(b)** $4y - 7y$ **(c)** $-3z - 2z + 7z$

Solution

(a) $4x + 7x = 11x$ — $4 + 7 = 11$

(b) $4y - 7y = -3y$ — $4 - 7 = -3$
You can see this on a number line.

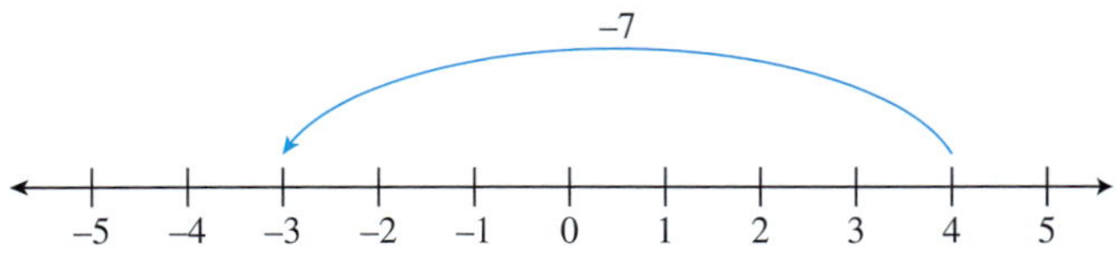

REMARK

You can use algebra discs to work these out. If the variables are not x or y you can draw algebra discs or replace other variables with x or y.

For example, $-3z - 2z + 7z$ can be rewritten as $-3x - 2x + 7x$ so that you can use x algebra discs. Just remember that your final answer needs to be in terms of z.

(c) $-3z - 2z + 7z = -5z + 7z$ $\quad -3 - 2 = -5$

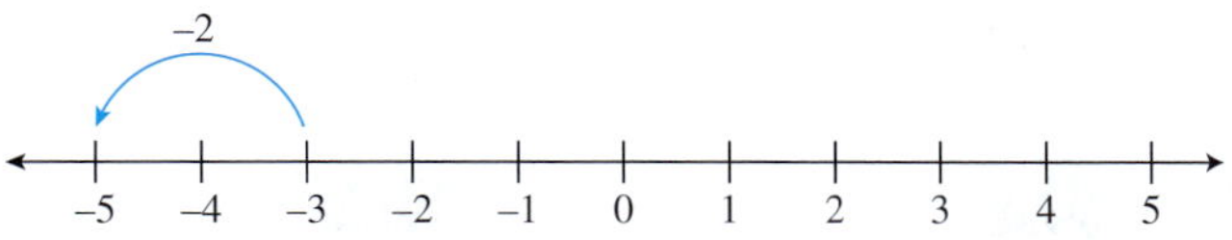

$= 2z$ $\quad -5 + 7 = 2$

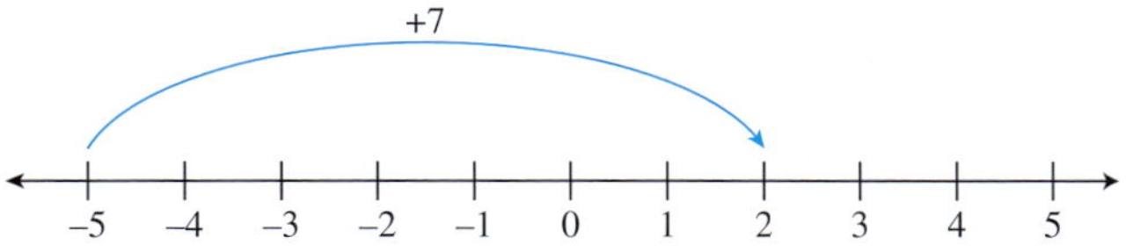

Try It! 1

Simplify these expressions.

(a) $3a + 5a$ **(b)** $-6b + 9b$ **(c)** $2c - 7c - 4c$

Example 2

Simplify these expressions.

(a) $2p + 3q - 5p + 4q$ **(b)** $8 - 7m + 6n - 1 - n - 2m$

Solution

(a) $2p + 3q - 5p + 4q = 2p - 5p + 3q + 4q$ Arrange like terms together.

$= -3p + 7q$ Simplify like terms.

(b) $8 - 7m + 6n - 1 - n - 2m = 8 - 1 - 7m - 2m + 6n - n$

$= 7 - 9m + 5n$

Try It! 2

Simplify these expressions.

(a) $4r + 5s - 3r + 2s$ **(b)** $3u + 2v - 6 - 5u - v - 4$

REMARK

You can use or draw algebra discs for these questions if you need to.

Example 3

The price of a portion of curry is £x and the price of a portion of rice is £y.

Jenny and Luke both buy food for their families.

(a) Luke bought 3 portions of curry and 2 portions of rice.
Work out the amount Luke spent in terms of x and y.

(b) Jenny spent £$(4x + 3y)$. Work out the amount Jenny and Luke spent in total in terms of x and y.

(c) What would the expression $x - y$ represent in this context?

REMARK

'in terms of x and y' means an expression involving x and y.

Solution

(a) The price of a portion of curry is £x, so 3 portions of curry will cost £$3x$.
The price of a portion of rice is £y, so 2 portions of rice will cost £$2y$.
Therefore, total spent by Luke = £$(3x + 2y)$

DISCUSS

Is it possible to simplify the expression $3x + 2y$?

(b) Total spent $= 3x + 2y + 4x + 3y$
$= 3x + 4x + 2y + 3y$
$= £(7x + 5y)$

(c) $x - y$ represents the difference between the cost of a portion of curry and a portion of rice.

Try It! 3

The price of a burger £a and the price of a portion of chips is £b.

Hannah and Abe both buy burgers and chips for their families.

(a) Hannah bought 2 burgers and 3 portions of chips. Work out the amount Hannah spent in terms of a and b.

(b) Abe spent £$(5a + 4b)$. How many burgers and how many portions of chips did he buy?

(c) Work out the amount Abe and Hannah spent in total in terms of a and b.

Example 4

The price of a cushion is £c and the price of a blanket is £b. Lei buys five cushions and two blankets. She then returns one of the cushions and receives a full refund.

(a) Work out the total amount Lei spent in terms of c and b.

(b) Work out the total amount Lei spent if $c = 10$ and $b = 25$.

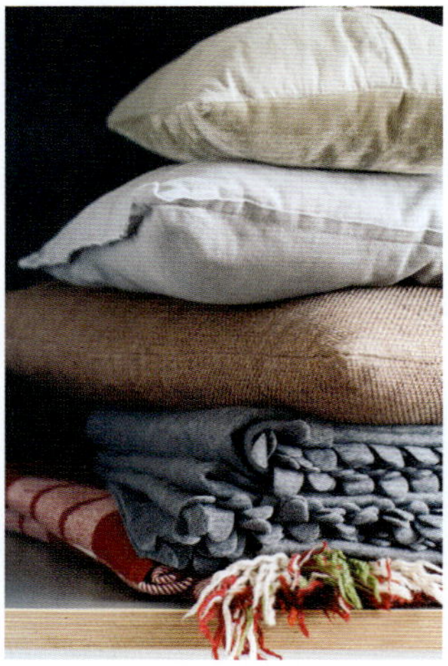

Solution

(a) Total spent $= £(5c + 2b - c)$
$= £(5c - c + 2b)$
$= £(4c + 2b)$

(b) If $c = 10$ and $b = 25$, then
total spent $= £(4 \times 10 + 2 \times 25)$
$= £(40 + 50)$
$= £90$

RECALL

When you know the values of all the variables, you can use substitution to find the value of the expression.

Try It! 4

The price of a T-shirt is £t and the price of a shirt is £s. Greg buys four T-shirts and three shirts. He then returns two of the shirts and receives a full refund.

(a) Calculate the total amount Greg spent in terms of t and s.

(b) Work out the total amount Greg spent if $t = 15$ and $s = 30$.

PRACTICE 2.1

LEVEL 1

1. Use algebra discs to simplify these expressions.
   (a) $3x + 5x$ (b) $3x - 5x$ (c) $5x - 3x$ (d) $-3x - 5x$
   (e) $2y - 7y$ (f) $7y - 2y$ (g) $7y + 2y$ (h) $-2y - 7y$

   What do you notice about the relationship between parts **(a)** to **(d)**?

2. Use algebra discs to simplify these expressions.
   (a) $2x + 6 + 4x + 8$ (b) $9y - 5 - 6y + 3$ (c) $4x - 7y - 2x - 3y$
   (d) $-6x - 7y + 2y - 3x$ (e) $5x - 6x + 3 + 7y$ (f) $3x + 4y - 2x - 7y$

3. Simplify these expressions.
   (a) $13a - 16a$ (b) $13a - 5 - 16a$
   (c) $13a - 5 - 16a + 9$ (d) $13a - 5 - 16a + 9 - 8a - 7$

4. What is the same and what is different about these expressions?
   $x + 2y - 3x + 7y$ $-3x + 2y + x + 7y$ $x + 7y + 2y - 3x$

5. Which expression might be the odd one out? Explain your answer.
   $3x + 5x - 2x$ $2x - 5x - 3x$ $5x - 2x + 3x$ $4x - 3x + 5x$

LEVEL 2

6. Simplify these expressions.
   (a) $4a + 7b - 6 - 2a - 7b$ (b) $9 - 2c - 3d + 4c - 5$
   (c) $2p + 3q - 8 - 3p - 6 + q$ (d) $1 - 2y + 3x - 7 - 5x - y$
   (e) $13s + 2t - s + 4u - 3t + 2u$ (f) $-5r + 2 + 3v - 6r - 5v + 8$

7. Joe simplifies $3x - 7x + 5 - 4x$ and claims that the coefficient of x is 0. Is Joe correct? Explain your answer.

8. The price of a pen is £p. The price of a notebook is £n. Zoey buys three pens and two notebooks.
   (a) Find the total Zoey spent in terms of p and n.
   (b) What would the expression $p - n$ represent?
   Olivia also buys pens and notebooks. Olivia spent £$(2p + n)$.
   (c) How many pens and how many notebooks did Olivia buy?
   (d) Work out the total amount spent by Zoey and Olivia.

9. The price of a pair of trainers is £t. The price of a hoodie is £h. Tyrone buys 4 pairs of trainers and 3 hoodies. He then returns two of the pairs of trainers and receives a full refund.
   (a) Find the total Tyrone spent in terms of t and h.
   (b) Find the total Tyrone spent if $t = 35$ and $h = 30$.

10. Write down two different expressions that can be simplified to $-2x + 5y + 7$.

OPEN QUESTION

2.2 Adding and Subtracting Linear Algebraic Expressions

In Section 2.1 you saw a shape made from long blue and shorter red strips.

The length of the longer strips is b cm and the length of the shorter strips is r cm.

Let us investigate what happens when we use these strips to make shapes of different sizes.

CLASS ACTIVITY 2

Objective: To use strips to explore adding algebraic expressions.

1. **(a)** Choose paper in two colours. Create thin strips of one length with one colour, and create strips of a different length in the other colour. Make two different shapes using several of the strips.

   (b) Write down the perimeter of each of your shapes in terms of b and r.

2. **(a)** Combine the strips from both shapes to make a bigger shape.

   (b) Write down an expression for the perimeter of your bigger shape.

3. Repeat for different pairs of shapes.

REMARK

If you are working with another person then you could make one shape each.

RECALL

The perimeter of a shape is the total length of its boundary.

You can add two expressions using algebra discs. For example, to work out $(2x - 1) + (3x + 4)$, first represent each expression using algebra discs.

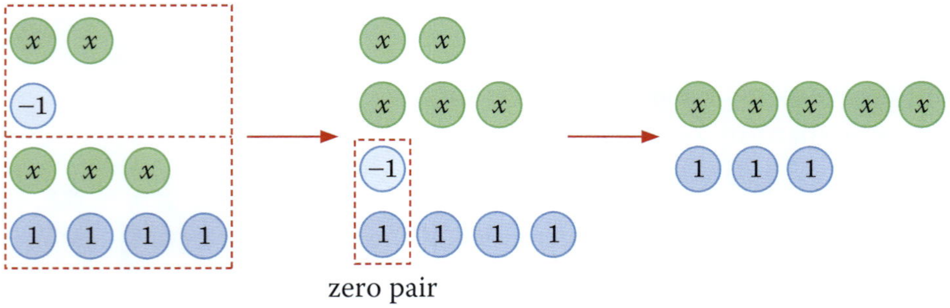

$(2x - 1) + (3x + 4)$ Rearrange and collect like terms. $5x + 3$

$$
\begin{aligned}
(2x - 1) + (3x + 4) &= 2x - 1 + 3x + 4 \\
&= 2x + 3x - 1 + 4 \\
&= 5x + 3
\end{aligned}
$$

Remember that to obtain the negative of an expression, you flip the discs that represent the expression. For example, work out $-(x - 3y)$.

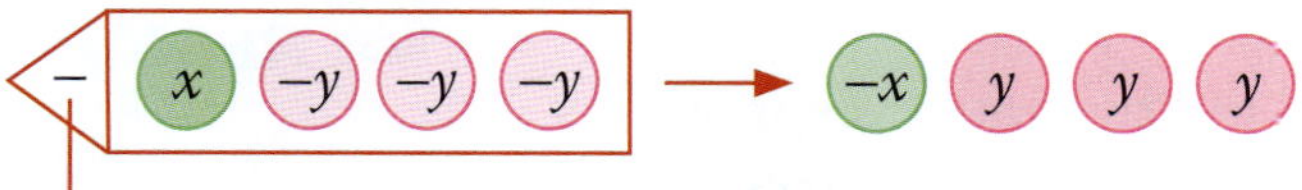

This has the effect of multiplying each disc in the box by −1.

You can show this expansion using algebra.

$\therefore \quad -(x - 3y) = (-1)(x) - (-1)(3y)$ Distributive law of multiplication over subtraction.

$= -x + 3y$ $-(-3y) = 3y$

Recall that subtracting a number is the equivalent of adding the negative of that number.

For example, $8 - 3 = 8 + (-3)$

It is the same with algebraic expressions. Subtracting an expression is equivalent to adding the negative of that expression.

For instance: $8x - 3x = 8x + (-3x)$

$(8x + 2) - (3x + 1) = (8x + 2) + -(3x + 1)$

You can then use algebra discs to add the two expressions.

For example, simplifying $(2y - 1) - (y - 3)$ is the same as simplifying $(2y - 1) + -(y - 3)$.

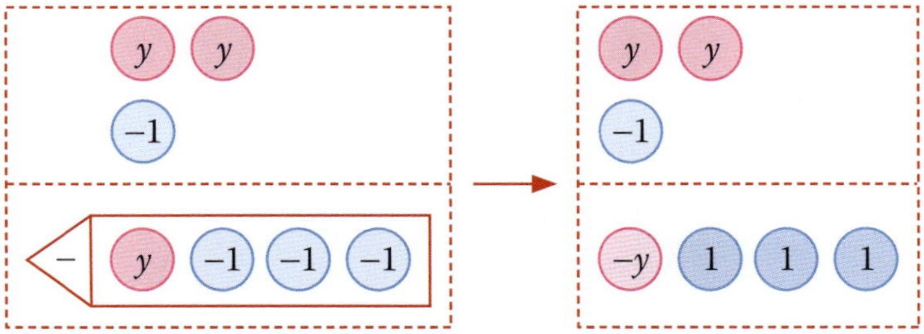

$(2y - 1) + -(y - 3)$

Flip the discs inside the solid box to show they have been multiplied by −1.

zero pairs

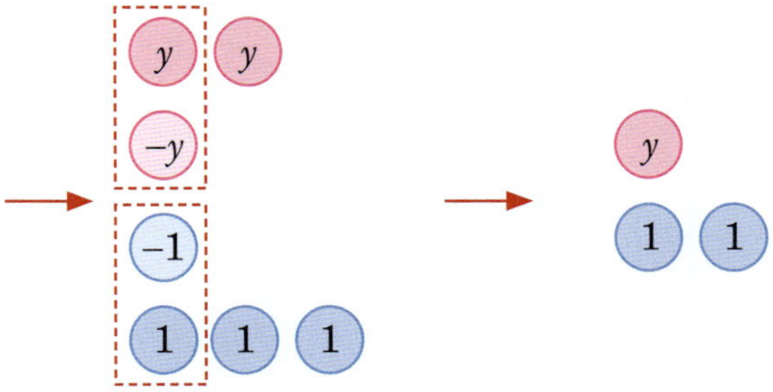

Collect like terms. $y + 2$

$(2y - 1) + -(y - 3)$

$= 2y - 1 - y - (-1)(3)$ Expand $-(y - 3)$ using the distributive law, taking care of signs.

$= 2y - 1 - y + 3$

$= 2y - y - 1 + 3$ Arrange like terms together.

$= y + 2$

CLASS ACTIVITY 3

Objective: Find the sum and difference of linear expressions.

1. Work out the sum and difference of the two linear expressions $3x + 7$ and $4x - y + 1$.

2. Make each of these statements true.
   (a) $(5x + 7y) - (\_\_ x + \_\_ y) = 3x + 2y$
   (b) $(5x + 7y) + (\_\_ x - \_\_ y) = 3x + 2y$
   (c) $(\_\_ x - \_\_ y) - (5x + 7y) = 3x + 2y$

3. **(a)** Write a sum of two linear expressions that is equal to $9x + 12$. Your two expressions should both have a constant term and an x term.
   (b) Write a sum of two linear expressions that is equal to $8x - 5y + 7$. Your two expressions should both have a constant term, an x term and a y term.

4. **(a)** Write a difference of two linear expressions that is equal to $3x + 7$. Your two expressions should contain at least a constant term and an x term.
   (b) Write a difference of two linear expressions that is equal to $5x - 7y$. Your two expressions should contain at least an x term and a y term.

REMARK

You can use algebra discs to help you answer these questions.

DISCUSS

Compare your solutions with a classmate. How many different solutions do you think there are?

RECALL

To find the difference you need to subtract, for example, the difference between $(2x + 7)$ and $(3x - 4)$ is given by $(2x + 7) - (3x - 4)$.

Example 5

Simplify these expressions.

(a) $(2a + 3) + (a - 5)$

(b) $(2m + 3n - 5) + (-8m - 3n + 4)$

Solution

(a) Using algebra discs:

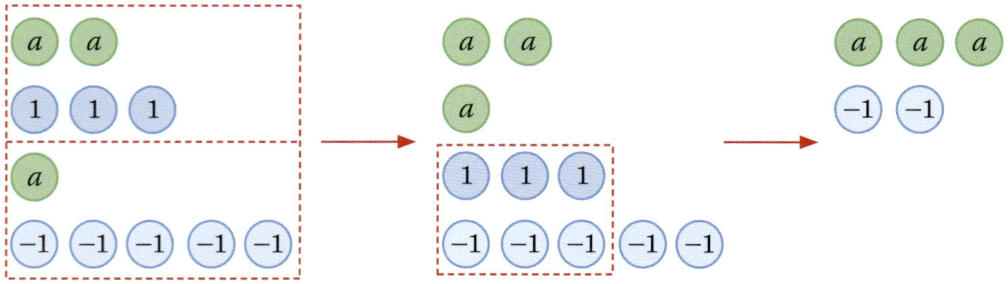

$(2a + 3) + (a - 5)$ zero pairs $3a - 2$

Rearrange and collect like terms.

The simplification can also be done using algebra:

$$\begin{aligned}(2a + 3) + (a - 5) &= 2a + 3 + a - 5 && \text{Remove the brackets.}\\ &= 2a + a + 3 - 5 && \text{Rearrange and collect}\\ &= 3a - 2 && \text{like terms.}\end{aligned}$$

(b) $(2m + 3n - 5) + (-8m - 3n + 4)$
$= 2m + 3n - 5 - 8m - 3n + 4$ Remove the brackets.
$= 2m - 8m + 3n - 3n - 5 + 4$ Rearrange and collect like terms.
$= -6m - 1$ $3n - 3n = 0$

Try It! 5

Simplify these expressions.

(a) $(3b + 4) + (6b - 8)$

(b) $(7p + 4q - 1) + (-7p - 5q - 2)$

DISCUSS

Anish says the answer is $10m + 6n - 9$. What mistake do you think he has made?

REMARK

You can draw algebra discs for these questions if you find it useful.

Example 6

Simplify these expressions.

(a) $(2r - 3s) - (5r - s)$

(b) $(-4u + 3v - 8) - (-2u - 7v + 5)$

Solution

(a) $(2r - 3s) - (5r - s) = 2r - 3s - 5r - (-1)(s)$
Expand brackets using the distributive law.
$= 2r - 3s - 5r + s$
$= 2r - 5r - 3s + s$ Rearrange and collect like terms.
$= -3r - 2s$

(b) $(-4u + 3v - 8) - (-2u - 7v + 5)$
$= -4u + 3v - 8 + 2u + 7v - 5$ Be careful with the signs.
$= -4u + 2u + 3v + 7v - 8 - 5$ Rearrange and collect like terms.
$= -2u + 10v - 13$

DISCUSS

Jane says the answer is $-3r + 4s$. What mistake do you think she has made?

Try It! 6

Simplify these expressions.

(a) $(2x + 5y) - (6x - 3y)$

(b) $(-3a + 4z - 7) - (-4a + 5z + 8)$

Example 7

Two families go swimming. The price for an adult is £x and the price for a child is £y. Family A spent £$(2x + 3y)$. Family B spent £$(x + 2y)$.
Find, in terms of x and y,

(a) the total amount spent by the two families,

(b) the difference in the amounts spent by the families.

Solution

(a) Total amount spent
$= (2x + 3y) + (x + 2y)$
$= 2x + 3y + x + 2y$
$= 2x + x + 3y + 2y$
$= £(3x + 5y)$ Include the units.

(b) Difference in spending

$= (2x + 3y) - (x + 2y)$
$= 2x + 3y - x - 2y$
$= 2x - x + 3y - 2y$
$= £(x + y)$

REMARK

You may use a bar model to show the situation.

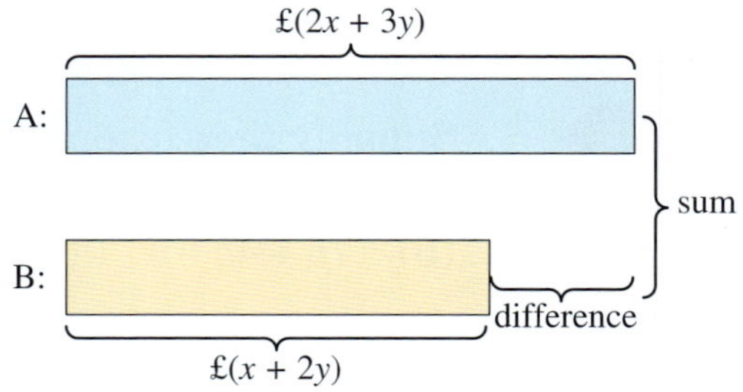

Try It! 7

Two groups of friends go to the cinema. The price of a ticket for a person under 12 is £x. The price of a ticket for a person aged 12 or older is £y.
The amount spent by group A is £$(3x + y)$.
The amount spent by group B is £$(2x + 4y)$.
Find, in terms of x and y,

(a) the total amount spent by the two groups,

(b) the difference in the amounts spent by the groups.

PRACTICE 2.2

LEVEL 1

1. Use algebra discs to simplify these expressions.

(a) $3a + (2a + 5)$ **(b)** $3a + (2a - 5)$ **(c)** $(2b + 1) + (4b + 3)$

(d) $(2b - 1) + (-4b + 3)$ **(e)** $(-3c + d) + (3c - d)$ **(f)** $(-4c + d) + (3c - 2d)$

2. Match the equivalent expressions in the two columns.

(a)

$-(2x + 4)$	$-2x + 4$
$-(2x - 4)$	$-2x - 4$
$-(-2x + 4)$	$2x + 4$
$-(-2x - 4)$	$2x - 4$

(b)

$-(3y + 2x - 5)$	$3y + 2x - 5$
$-(3y - 2x - 5)$	$3y - 2x + 5$
$-(3y + 2x + 5)$	$-3y - 2x + 5$
$-(-3y - 2x - 5)$	$-3y - 2x - 5$
$-(-3y - 2x + 5)$	$3y + 2x + 5$
$-(-3y + 2x - 5)$	$-3y + 2x + 5$

3. Use algebra discs to simplify these expressions.

(a) $5t - (2t + 3)$ **(b)** $5t - (2t - 3)$ **(c)** $(4u + 8) - (3u + 1)$

(d) $(4u - 8) - (-3u - 1)$ **(e)** $(-6v + 4w) - (v - 3w)$ **(f)** $(-6v + 4w) - (-v + 4w)$

4. Which expression might be the odd one out? Explain your answer.

$(2x + 3y) + (-6x + 4y)$ $(2x + 4y) + (-6x + 3y)$

$(6x - 4y) - (2x + 3y)$ $(2x + 3y) - (6x - 4y)$

LEVEL 2

5. Simplify these expressions.

(a) $(2a + 3b - 4) + (3a - 5b + 6)$

(b) $(2a + 3b - 4) - (3a - 5b + 6)$

(c) $(4g - 3h - 6) - (5g + 7h - 2)$

(d) $(-6k + 7m + 3) - (-2k + 7m - 9)$

6. Which expression might be the odd one out? Explain your answer.

$(2a + 4b) + (2a - 4b)$

$(3a - 8b) + (3a + 8b)$

$(7a + 2b) - (7a - 2b)$

$(9a + b) - (-9a + b)$

7. Point out the mistakes in this simplification and work out the correct simplified expression.

$$\begin{aligned}(2x + 3y - 5) - (-4x + 7y - 6) &= 2x + 3y - 5 - 4x - 7y + 6 \\ &= 2x - 4x + 3y - 7y - 5 + 6 \\ &= -2x - 4y - 1\end{aligned}$$

8. Two shapes are formed with coloured strips of length r cm and b cm as shown.

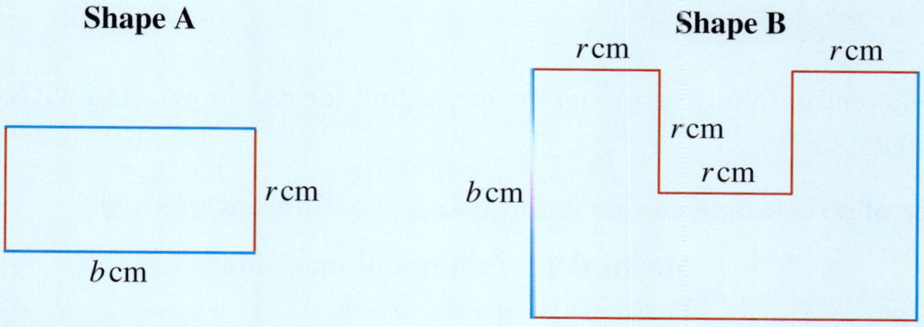

Find, in terms of r and b,

(a) the perimeter of shape A,

(b) the perimeter of shape B,

(c) the difference between the perimeter of the two shapes.

9. Alex gets £m pocket money per week and gets £n extra for doing chores.

£ FINANCE

One week he gets £$(m + 3n)$ pocket money and the next week he gets £$(m + 5n)$ pocket money.

Find, in terms of m and n,

(a) the amount of pocket money Alex got in total over the two weeks,

(b) the difference between the amount of pocket money he got in the two weeks.

10. The width of a rectangle is x cm. The length of the rectangle is y cm more than its width.

(a) Work out the perimeter of the rectangle in terms of x and y.

Hint: Draw a diagram to help you.

A square has a perimeter of $(4x + 12)$ cm.

(b) How much longer is the perimeter of the rectangle than the square?

2.3 Expanding and Simplifying Linear Algebraic Expressions

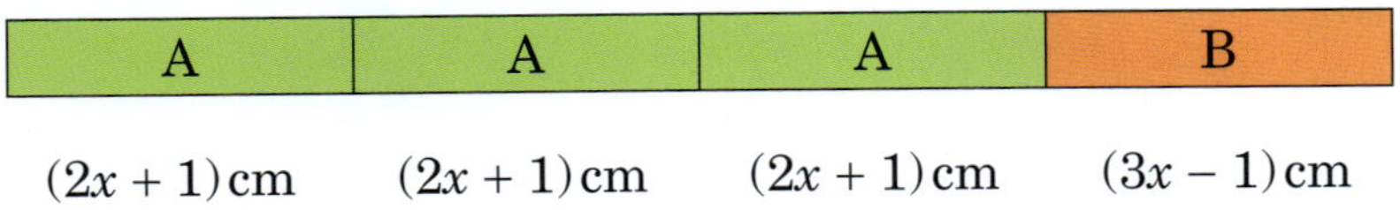

Bar A is $(2x + 1)$ cm long. Bar B is $(3x - 1)$ cm long. The total length of three of bar A and one of bar B in cm is given by the expression

$$3(2x + 1) + (3x - 1).$$

You can simplify this expression by expanding the brackets then adding the like terms.

You have looked at some simple expansion of brackets in Section 2.2, but let us revise some more examples of expansion first.

CLASS ACTIVITY 4

Objective: To investigate how expressions for perimeter can be written with or without brackets.

The perimeter of a rectangle can be found using two different methods:

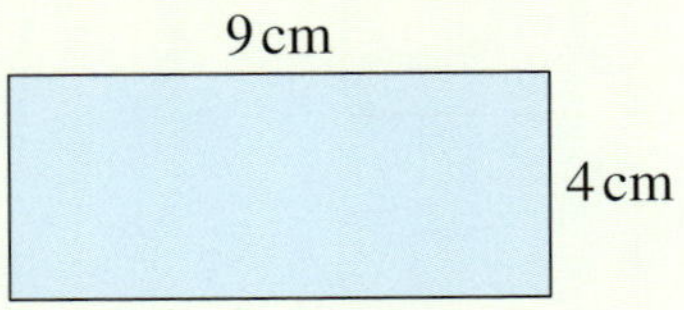

Method 1 – Add up all four sides.

Perimeter $= 9 + 4 + 9 + 4$

$= 26$ cm

Method 2 – Add the width and height then multiply by 2.

Perimeter $= 2(9 + 4)$

$= 2 \times 13$

$= 26$ cm

1. Write the perimeter of these shapes in two different ways, one with brackets and one without.

(a)

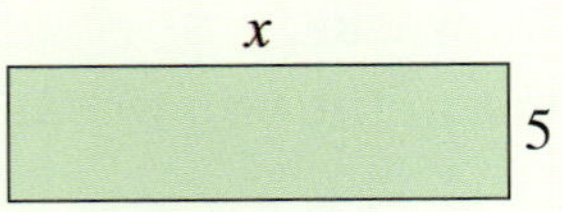

(b)

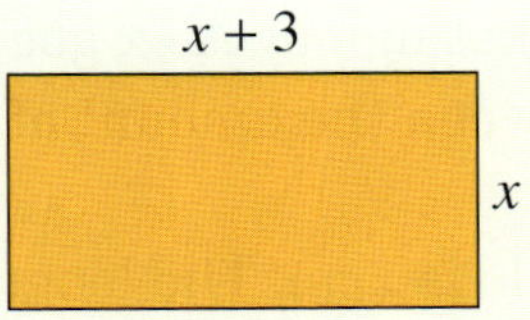

(c)

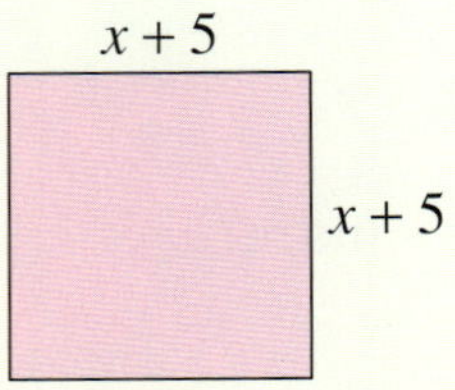

(d)

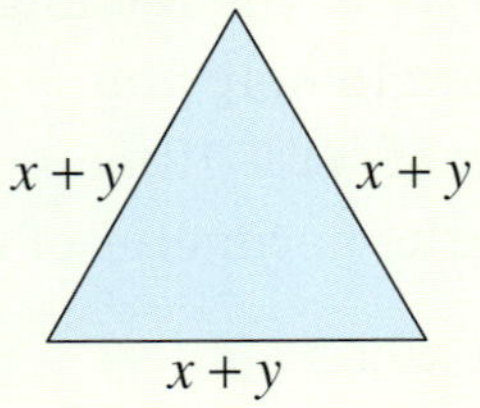

RECALL

Two expressions are **equivalent** if they can be simplified to the same expression.

2. Using your answers in **Question 1**, write down some rules for expanding brackets.

3. Match the equivalent expressions for the perimeter. One of the expressions is missing – can you work out what it should be?

$2(2x + y)$	$2x + 4y$
$2(x + 2y)$	$4x + 2$
$4(x + y)$	$4x + 2y$
$2(x + y)$	$4x + 4$
$4(x + 1)$	$2x + 2y$
$2(2x + 1)$	

4. (a) Draw rectangles with these perimeters.

   (i) $2(2x + 7)$ (ii) $2(2x + 7y)$

   (b) Write the perimeter of each rectangle without brackets.

REMARK

You could draw rectangles to help with **Question 3**.

DISCUSS

Compare your answers to **Question 4** to a classmate's. How many possible answers are there for each part?

In Student Book 2A, you learnt about using algebra discs to expand brackets.

For example, $3(2x + 1)$ can be represented as three groups of two x discs and one 1 disc.
By combining the groups, this gives one group of six x discs and three 1 discs.

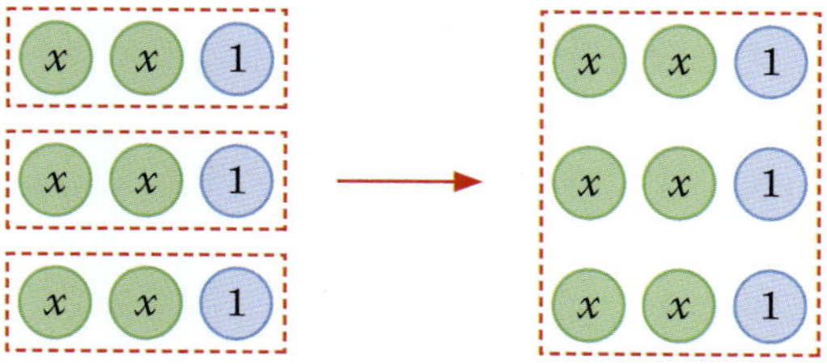

$3(2x + 1)$ $6x + 3$

Thus, $3(2x + 1) = 3(2x) + 3(1)$
$= 6x + 3$

You can see that to multiply a single term by a linear expression, you must multiply the single term by each of the terms within the expression.

You can use a multiplication frame to show the expansion.
For example, write $3(2x + 1)$ in a multiplication frame:

×	$2x$	1
3		

Then complete the multiplication frame by multiplying both $2x$ and 1 by 3.

×	$2x$	1
3	$6x$	3

Thus, $3(2x + 1) = 6x + 3$.

Example 8 Expand these expressions.

(a) $3(4p + 1)$ **(b)** $-3(4p - q)$

Solution

(a) Using a multiplication frame:

×	$4p$	1
3	$12p$	3

$\therefore \ 3(4p + 1) = 12p + 3$

Alternatively,

$3(4p + 1) = 3(4p) + 3(1)$
$= 12p + 3$

Multiply each term inside the brackets by 3.

(b) Using a multiplication frame:

×	$4p$	$-q$
-3	$-12p$	$3q$

Look carefully at the sign of each term.
Recall that the product of two negative numbers is positive.

$\therefore \ -3(4p - q) = -12p + 3q$

Alternatively,

$-3(4p - q) = (-3)(4p) - (-3)(q)$
$= -12p + 3q$

Multiply each term inside the brackets by -3.

Try It! 8 Expand these expressions.

(a) $6(4x + 5)$ **(b)** $-6(4x - 5y)$

REMARK
This uses the **distributive law** of multiplication over addition:
$a(x + y) = ax + ay$.

REMARK
This uses the **distributive law** of multiplication over subtraction:
$a(x - y) = ax - ay$.

DISCUSS
Draw a multiplication frame and show how you would work out $2(3x + 2y)$ using it.

Example 9 Simplify $2(3x + 2y) + (2x - y)$.

Solution

$2(3x + 2y) + (2x - y) = 6x + 4y + (2x - y)$ Expand $2(3x + 2y)$.
$= 6x + 4y + 2x - y$
$= 6x + 2x + 4y - y$ Rearrange and collect like terms.
$= 8x + 3y$

Try It! 9 Simplify $3(2x - 3y) + (4x + y)$.

REMARK
Represent and work out Example 9 using algebra discs.

Example 10 Simplify $(2y - 5) - 3(y - 2)$.

Solution Use a multiplication frame to help expand $-3(y - 2)$.

$\times$	y	-2
-3	$-3y$	6

Thus, $-3(y - 2) = -3y + 6$

Hence, the simplification can be written

$$\begin{aligned}(2y - 5) - 3(y - 2) &= (2y - 5) - 3y + 6 \\ &= 2y - 3y - 5 + 6 \\ &= -y + 1\end{aligned}$$

Expand $-3(y - 2)$.

Rearrange and collect like terms.

Try It! 10 Simplify $(5x - 3) - 4(x - 2)$.

REMARK

Take care when multiplying negative numbers, for example $(-3) \times (-2) = 6$.

Example 11 Simplify $3(2x - 1) + 4(-2x + 3)$.

Solution Use multiplication frames to help expand $3(2x - 1)$ and $4(-2x + 3)$.

$\times$	$2x$	-1
3	$6x$	-3

$\times$	$-2x$	3
4	$-8x$	12

$3(2x - 1) = 6x - 3$ $\quad$ $4(-2x + 3) = -8x + 12$

$3(2x - 1) + 4(-2x + 3) = 6x - 3 - 8x + 12$

The simplification can also be written as:

$$\begin{aligned}3(2x - 1) + 4(-2x + 3) &= 3(2x) - 3(1) + 4(-2x) + 4(3) \\ &= 6x - 3 - 8x + 12 \\ &= 6x - 8x - 3 + 12 \\ &= -2x + 9\end{aligned}$$

Expand.

Rearrange and collect like terms.

Try It! 11 Simplify $2(3y - 4) + 3(-2y + 5)$.

DISCUSS

Is it possible to simplify $-2x + 9$?
How do you know?

Example 12

The cost of hiring a tennis court for x hours in pounds is given by $5x + 3$, where 3 is the booking fee for a court. The organisers of a tennis tournament need to hire four courts. Work out the total cost of hiring four courts for x hours. Give your answer in expanded form.

Solution

Price to hire four courts $= 4(5x + 3)$
$= 4(5x) + 4(3)$
$= £(20x + 12)$

Multiply the expression by the number of courts needed.

Try It! 12

The price of hiring a canoe for y hours is given by £$(10y + 6)$. A family wants to hire five canoes. Work out the total price of hiring five canoes for y hours. Give your answer in expanded form.

DISCUSS

In Try It! 12 Marley says, 'Substitute $y = 5$ into the expression to find the total price.' Explain why she is incorrect.

PRACTICE 2.3

You can draw algebra discs or multiplication frames for these questions.

LEVEL 1

1. Use algebra discs to expand these expressions.

(a) $3(5x + 8)$ **(b)** $-3(5x + 8)$ **(c)** $2(3y - 1)$
(d) $-2(3y - 1)$ **(e)** $4(-2x + 6)$ **(f)** $-4(2x - 6)$

2. Simplify these expressions.

(a) $2 + 4(5a + 3)$ **(b)** $2b + 4(5b - 3)$ **(c)** $4(c - 3) + (2c + 7)$
(d) $3(c - 3) + 4(2c + 7)$ **(e)** $5(2h - k) + 6(3h - k)$ **(f)** $7(-m + 2n) + 2(m - 2n)$

3. Simplify these expressions.

(a) $5 - 3(4p + 1)$ **(b)** $6p - 3(4p - 1)$ **(c)** $4(3q - 1) - (5q - 4)$
(d) $4(3q + 1) - 2(4 - 5q)$ **(e)** $-3(2r + 7s) + 6(5r - s)$ **(f)** $-3(2r + 7s) - 6(5r - s)$

4. Which expression might be the odd one out? Explain your answer.

$3(4x - 5) - 2(6x + 1)$ $2(6x + 1) - 3(4x - 5)$
$-3(4x - 5) + 2(6x + 1)$ $3(5 - 4x) - 2(-1 - 6x)$

5. What is the same and what is different about these expressions?

$2(a + b) + 3(a - b)$ $2(a + b) - 3(a + b)$ $-2(a - b) - 3(a + b)$

LEVEL 2

6. A rectangle is $(5x - 1)$ cm in length and $(3x + 4)$ cm wide. Find the perimeter of the rectangle in terms of x.

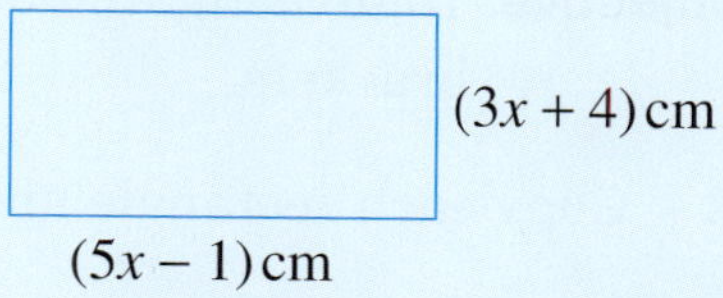

7. The cost of hiring a car for x days is given by £$(30x + 40)$. The cost of hiring a van for x days is given by £$(40x + 50)$. Work out the total cost of

(a) hiring three cars for x days,

(b) hiring two vans for x days,

(c) hiring three cars and two vans for x days.

Give your answers in expanded form.

8. The ones digit of a two-digit number is n. The tens digit is 3 more than the ones digit. Express, in terms of n,

PROBLEM SOLVING

(a) the tens digit,

(b) the value of the two-digit number.

Hint: If the two-digit number is 74, how can you express this number using the digits 7 and 4?

9. Write down two expressions involving the expansion of brackets that sum to

OPEN QUESTION

(a) $18x + 12$, **(b)** $8x - 20y$.

10. Write down two expressions involving the expansion of brackets that have a difference of

OPEN QUESTION

(a) $3x + 6$, **(b)** $4x - 7y$.

2.4 Expansion of the Product of Two Linear Expressions

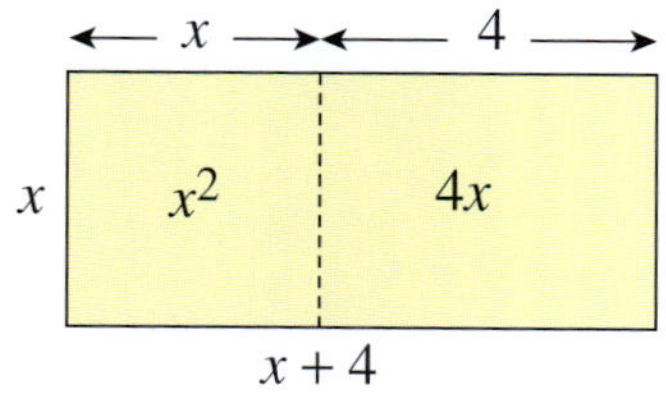

A rectangle is $(x + 4)$ cm long and x cm wide. Its area in cm^2 is given by $x(x + 4)$.

As shown in the diagram, the rectangle can be divided into a square of sides x cm and a rectangle of x cm by 4 cm. Hence, its area can be expressed as $x^2 + 4x$.

As these two expressions represent the same area, this gives

$$x(x + 4) = x^2 + 4x.$$

It shows that the product of two expressions can be obtained by multiplying the single term by both terms inside the brackets.

RECALL

$3 \times 3 = 3^2$
$4 \times 4 = 4^2$
$5 \times 5 = 5^2$
$x \times x = x^2$

CLASS ACTIVITY 5

Objective: To investigate how expressions for area can be written with or without brackets.

1. Copy each rectangle and calculate the total area. The first is done for you.

(a)

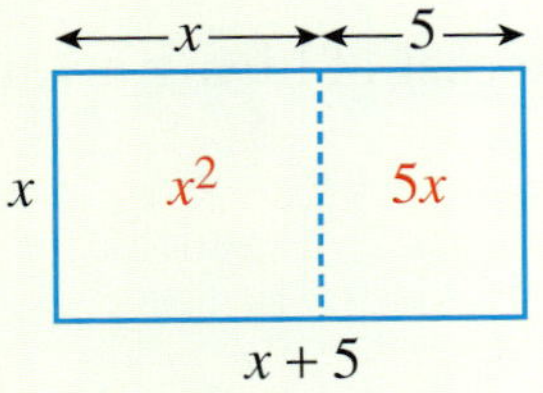

Total area = $x(x + 5)$
$= x^2 + 5x$

(b)

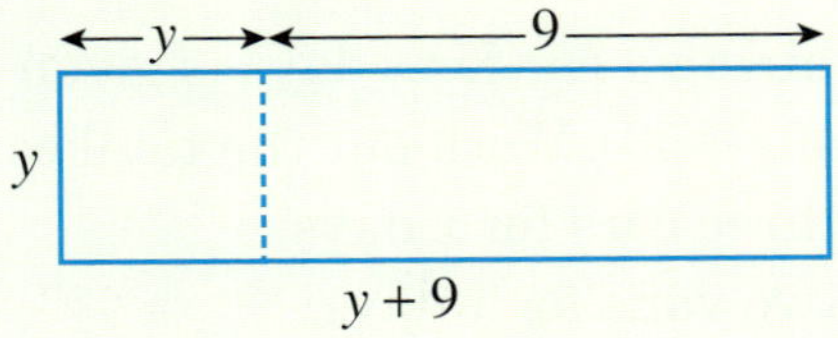

Total area =

(c)

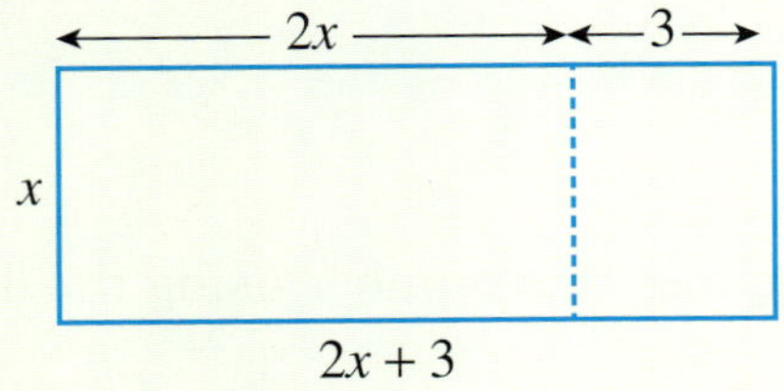

(d)

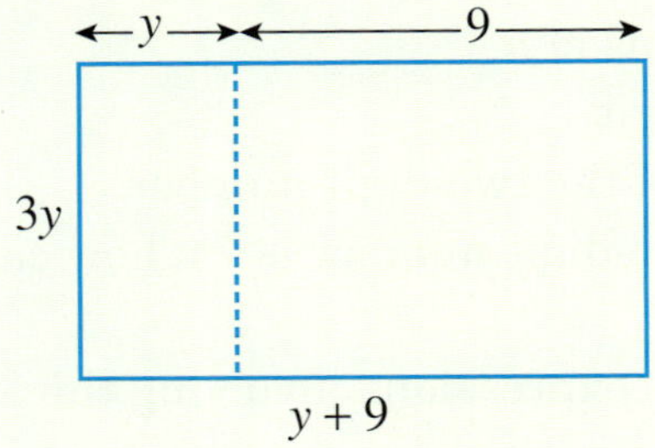

2. Draw some rectangles like those in **Question 1**, then swap with another person and write the area of each rectangle both with and without brackets.

3. Work in pairs to match the equivalent expressions for area. One of the expressions is missing – can you work out what it should be?

$x(x + 3)$	$2x^2 + 3x$
$2x(x + 3)$	$x^2 + 3x$
$x(x + 6)$	$3x^2 + 6x$
$x(x + 3)$	$x^2 + 3x$
$3x(x + 2)$	$2x^2 + 6x$
$x(2x + 3)$	

4. **(a)** Draw a rectangle with area
(i) $x(x + 1)$, **(ii)** $x(2x + 1)$.

(b) Write the area of each rectangle without brackets.

RECALL

$x \times 2x = 2 \times x \times x$
$= 2x^2$

REMARK

You could draw rectangles to help with **Question 3**.

From Class Activity 5, you can also use a multiplication frame to help expand the product of two linear expressions.

For example, write $x(x + 6)$ in a multiplication frame.

×	x	6
x		

Then complete the multiplication frame by multiplying both x and 6 by x.

$\times$	x	6
x	x^2	$6x$

Thus, $x(x + 6) = x^2 + 6x$.

The expression $x^2 + 6x$ is a **quadratic expression** (in x), since the highest power of x is 2. Other examples of quadratic expressions in a single variable are x^2, $y^2 + 3$, $a^2 - 5a$ and $3b^2 + 2b - 1$.

DISCUSS

Which of these expressions are quadratic and which are linear?

$x^2 + 2$ $\quad x^2 + 2x$

$x - 2$ $\quad x^2 + 2x - 1$

Example 13

Using multiplication frames, expand these expressions.

(a) $x(3x + 5)$ **(b)** $6y(4y - 7)$

Solution

(a) Use a multiplication frame:

$\times$	$3x$	5
x	$3x^2$	$5x$

Thus, $x(3x + 5) = 3x^2 + 5x$

(b) Use a multiplication frame:

$\times$	$4y$	-7
$6y$	$24y^2$	$-42y$

Make sure you include any negative signs.

Thus, $6y(4y - 7) = 24y^2 - 42y$

DISCUSS

Jay says that $3x^2 + 5x$ can be simplified to $8x^2$. Susan says that $3x^2 + 5x$ can be simplified to $8x^3$. Are they correct? Explain your answer.

REMARK

The answers to parts **(a)** and **(b)** are both quadratic expressions.

Try It! 13

Using multiplication frames, expand these expressions.

(a) $n(2n + 1)$ **(b)** $5p(3p - 8)$

Example 14

Using multiplication frames, expand these expressions.

(a) $a(2 + b)$ **(b)** $3c(5c - d)$

Solution

(a) Use a multiplication frame:

$\times$	2	b
a	$2a$	ab

Thus, $a(2 + b) = 2a + ab$

RECALL

$a \times b$ is written as ab.

(b) Use a multiplication frame:

$\times$	$5c$	$-d$
$3c$	$15c^2$	$-3cd$

Thus, $3c(5c - d) = 15c^2 - 3cd$

Try It! 14

Using multiplication frames, expand these expressions.

(a) $x(y + 5)$ **(b)** $2t(t - 7u)$

Example 15

Expand and simplify these expressions.

(a) $2x + x(5x - 4)$ **(b)** $2x - x(5x - 4)$

Solution

(a) Use a multiplication frame:

$\times$	$5x$	-4
x	$5x^2$	$-4x$

Hence, the simplification can be written as

$$\begin{aligned} 2x + x(5x - 4) &= 2x + 5x^2 - 4x \\ &= 5x^2 + 2x - 4x \\ &= 5x^2 - 2x \end{aligned}$$

(b) Use a multiplication frame:

$\times$	$5x$	-4
$-x$	$-5x^2$	$4x$

Hence, the simplification can be written as

$$\begin{aligned} 2x - x(5x - 4) &= 2x - 5x^2 + 4x \\ &= -5x^2 + 2x + 4x \\ &= -5x^2 + 6x \end{aligned}$$

Try It! 15

Expand and simplify these expressions.

(a) $5y + y(3y + 7)$ **(b)** $5y - y(3y - 7)$

DISCUSS

Why might it be difficult to use or draw algebra discs for the examples and in this section?

DISCUSS

Lucy says that $5x^2 - 2x$ can be simplified to $3x$. Is she correct? Explain your answer.

DISCUSS

How do you know when an expression is fully simplified?

DISCUSS

Emil says the answer to part **(b)** is $6x - 5x^2$. Is he correct?

PRACTICE 2.4

LEVEL 1

1. Using multiplication frames, expand these expressions.

(a) $a(2a + 7)$ **(b)** $a(2a - 7)$ **(c)** $3a(2a + 7)$ **(d)** $3a(2a - 7)$

(e) $4b(b + 5)$ **(f)** $4b(b - 5)$ **(g)** $4b(5 + 6b)$ **(h)** $4b(5 - 6b)$

2. Using multiplication frames, expand these expressions.

(a) $x(y + 2)$ **(b)** $x(y - 2)$ **(c)** $3x(y + 2)$ **(d)** $3x(y - 2)$

(e) $3x(y + x)$ **(f)** $3x(y - x)$ **(g)** $x(y + 3x)$ **(h)** $x(2y - 3x)$

3. Which of these statements are correct? Explain your answers.

(a) $3t(2t - 1) = 6t^2 - t$ **(b)** $x(5x + 6) = 5x^2 + 6$

(c) $5y(3y - 7) = 15y^2 - 35y$ **(d)** $6a(-2b + 3) = -12ab - 18a$

4. Tristan said, 'The coefficient of x^2 in the expression $2x(3x + 1)$ is 5'.
Is Tristan correct? Explain your answer.

5. Which expression might be the odd one out? Explain your answer.

$3a(3a - 2b)$ $a(6b - 9a)$ $3a(-2b + 3a)$ $a(9a - 6b)$

LEVEL 2

6. Expand and simplify these expressions.

(a) $3a + 2a(a + 1)$ **(b)** $3a(2a + 1) + 3$

(c) $4b(5b + 1) + 5b - 1$ **(d)** $4b(5b + 1) + 6(5b - 1)$

7. Which expression might be the odd one out? Explain your answer.

$4x(3 - 5x)$ $4x(-5x + 3)$ $2x(10x - 6)$ $2x(6 - 10x)$

8. A rectangle is $(3x + 5)$ cm long and $2x$ cm wide.
Find the area of the rectangle in terms of x.
Write your answer in expanded form.

9. A right-angled triangle has a base of $4x$ cm and a height of $(x + 2)$ cm.
Find the area of the triangle in terms of x.
Write your answer in expanded form.

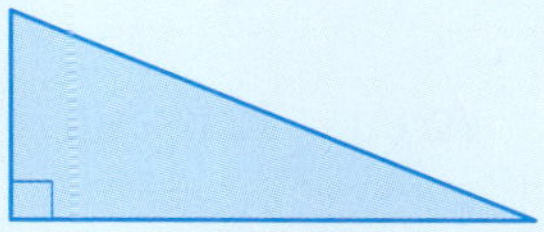

Hint: Remember the area of a triangle is given by area $= \frac{1}{2} \times$ base $\times$ perpendicular height.

10. Write down two different pairs of linear algebraic expressions with a product of $8x^2 + 6x$.

OPEN QUESTION

2.5 Factorisation of Linear Expressions

The process of writing an algebraic expression as a product of two or more of its factors is called **factorisation**. This is the reverse process of expansion.

For example, as $3(x + 5) = 3x + 15$,
$3x + 15$ can be written as the product of the two factors 3 and $x + 5$.
Hence, the factorisation of $3x + 15$ is $3(x + 5)$.
This is written as $3x + 15 = 3(x + 5)$.

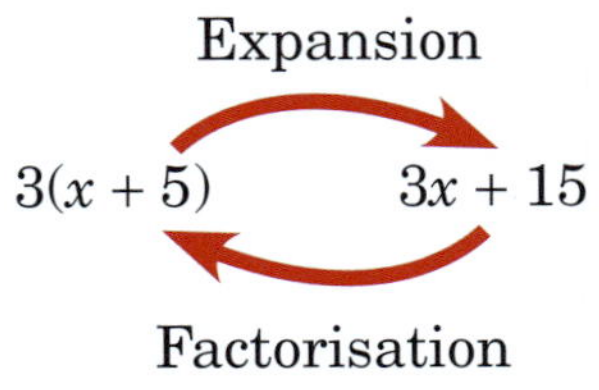

CLASS ACTIVITY 6

Objective: To investigate factorisation of linear algebraic expressions.

1. $6x + 15$ $\quad$ $12x + 6$ $\quad$ $16x - 4$ $\quad$ $8 - 10x$

For each of these expressions

(a) represent the expression using algebra discs,

(b) share the discs into equal groups,

(c) rewrite the expression using brackets,

(d) compare your answers with a partner. Which expressions can be written using brackets in more than one way?

For example

(a) Represent $5x + 10$ with algebra discs.

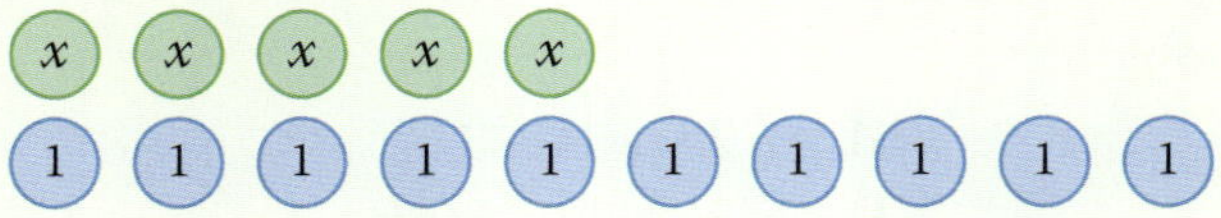

(b) The discs can be shared into five equal groups.

DISCUSS

In this example, the discs can be shared into five equal parts. How does the number of parts relate to the coefficients in the expression $5x + 10$?

(c) Each part represents the expression $x + 2$. There are five lots of $(x + 2)$.
Thus, $5x + 10$ can be written as $5(x + 2)$.

2. **(a)** Suggest possible expressions for the length and width of these rectangles.

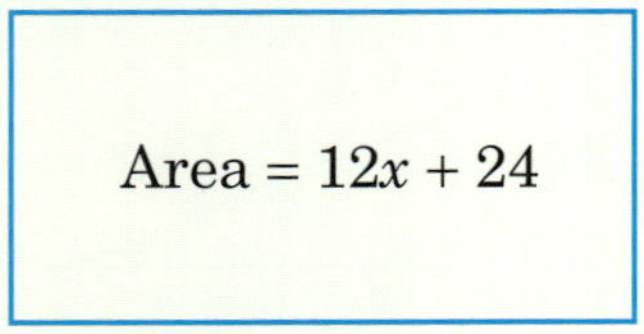

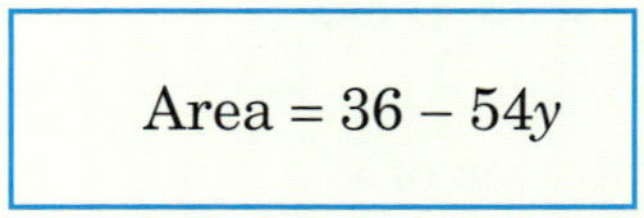

(b) Check your answers by expanding brackets.

(c) Compare your answers with a partner.

(i) What is the same and what is different about your answers?

(ii) How many possible answers can you find for each rectangle?

You can also use multiplication frames to help you factorise an expression.

For example, for the expression $3x + 15$, write $3x$ and 15 in the the multiplication frame as shown.

Find terms for these parts.

×		
	$3x$	15

Then you need to work out what the terms on the top row and the left column are.

×	x	5
3	$3x$	15

Thus, $3x + 15 = 3(x + 5)$

Example 16

Factorise these expressions.

(a) $4p + 6$ **(b)** $24q - 36$ **(c)** $-2x - 4$

Solution

(a) Use a multiplication frame.

×		
	$4p$	6

What could the missing terms be?

×	$2p$	3
2	$4p$	6

$\therefore 4p + 6 = 2(2p + 3)$

Check by expanding: $2(2p + 3) = 4p + 6$

(b) Use a multiplication frame.

×		
	$24q$	-36

What could the missing terms be?

×	$2q$	-3
12	$24q$	-36

$\therefore 24q - 36 = 12(2q - 3)$

Check by expanding: $12(2q - 3) = 24q - 36$

(c) Use a multiplication frame.

×		
	$-2x$	-4

DISCUSS

Which of these expressions cannot be factorised? Explain how you know.

$2x + 3$ $2x - 5$ $2x + 6$

REMARK

You can make a sensible guess then check by expanding.

REMARK

You could also have filled in the multiplication frame like this:

×	$8q$	-12
3	$24q$	-36

Thus, $24q - 36 = 3(8q - 12)$.
This is also a correct factorisation.

DISCUSS

Ana says that $15t - 30$ is factorised as $15(t - 2)$ and Bill says that $15t - 30$ is factorised as $5(3t - 6)$. Who is correct? Explain your answer.

What could the missing terms be?

$\times$	x	2
-2	$-2x$	-4

$\therefore -2x - 4 = -2(x + 2)$

Check by expanding: $-2(x + 2) = -2x - 4$

DISCUSS

Hugh says that $-2x - 4$ can also be factorised as $2(-x - 2)$. Is he correct? Explain your answer.

Try It! 16

Factorise these expressions.

(a) $5r + 20$ **(b)** $16s - 12$ **(c)** $-8s - 12$

In Example 16, you saw that there is sometimes more than one correct factorisation of an expression. An expression is *fully* factorised if the HCF (highest common factor) of the terms inside the brackets is 1. For example, $3(8q - 12)$ is not *fully* factorised since the HCF of $8q$ and 12 is 4, but $12(2q - 3)$ is fully factorised since the HCF of $2q$ and 3 is 1.

Remember that the HCF of two positive whole numbers is the largest number which is a factor of both.

For example,

factors of 12 are 1, 2, 3, 4, 6, 12:

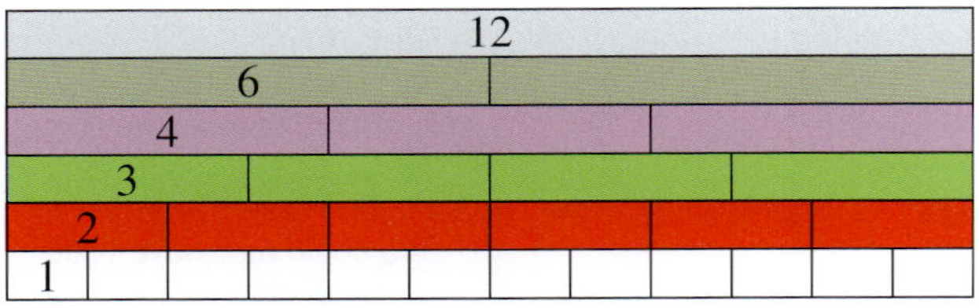

factors of 18 are 1, 2, 3, 6, 9, 18.

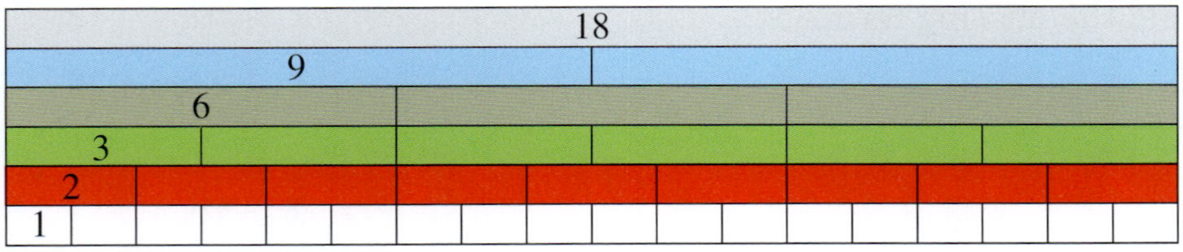

You can see from the factor walls that common factors of 12 and 18 are 1, 2, 3, 6.

Thus, the HCF is 6. You should use your knowledge of HCF when you are factorising expressions.

DISCUSS

Which of these expressions are fully factorised? Explain your answer.

$8(2x + 4)$
$5(2x - 7)$
$12(x + 3)$
$2(3x - 9)$

Example 17

Factorise these expressions fully.

(a) $6t + 12$ **(b)** $15v - 20w$

Solution

(a) Using a multiplication frame, write in $6t$ and 12 as the products, then work out the terms on the top row and the left column.

$\times$	t	2
6	$6t$	12

The factor in the left column of the frame should be the HCF of the given terms.

$\therefore 6t + 12 = 6(t + 2)$.

Check by expanding: $6(t + 2) = 6(t) + 6(2)$
$= 6t + 12$

(b) Using a multiplication frame, write in $15v$ and $-20w$ as the products, then work out the terms on the top row and in the left column.

$\times$	$3v$	$-4w$
5	$15v$	$-20w$

$\therefore 15v - 20w = 5(3v - 4w)$

Check by expanding: $5(3v - 4w) = 5(3v) - 5(4w)$
$= 15v - 20w$

DISCUSS

Sian writes the answer to part **(a)** as $2(3t + 6)$
Is this correct? Explain your answer.

REMARK

To *fully* factorise, find the HCF of both terms. The HCF of $15v$ and $20w$ is 5. This will help you to fill in the multiplication frame, but you should still check your answer by expanding.

Try It! 17

Factorise these expressions fully.

(a) $9x + 3y$ **(b)** $14z - 21a$

PRACTICE 2.5

LEVEL 1

1. Copy and complete the missing terms in the multiplication frames then write a factorisation statement for each. Part **(a)** is done for you.

(a)

$\times$	$2x$	3
2	$4x$	6

Thus, $4x + 6 = 2(2x + 3)$

(b)

$\times$	x	-2
	$6x$	-12

(c)

$\times$		
3	$9x$	3

(d)

$\times$	$5x$	
	$20x$	-8

(e)

×		
	$5x$	10

(f)

×		
	$5x$	-10

(g)

×		
	$-5x$	10

(h)

×		
	$-5x$	-10

2. Factorise these expressions fully.

(a) $4a + 6$ **(b)** $4a - 6$ **(c)** $4a + 8$
(d) $21f - 28$ **(e)** $-21f - 28$ **(f)** $28 - 21f$
(g) $25x + 15$ **(h)** $25 + 15x$ **(i)** $25 - 15x$

3. Factorise these expressions fully.

(a) $6h + 4k$ **(b)** $6h - 4k$ **(c)** $16h - 4k$
(d) $18t + 30u$ **(e)** $-18t + 30u$ **(f)** $18t - 36u$
(g) $14a - 28b$ **(h)** $14b - 28a$ **(i)** $-14b - 28a$

4. Here are the workings of Amy and Ben on the factorisation of $10x + 30$.
Amy: $10x + 30 = 2(5x + 15)$ Ben: $10x + 30 = 5(2x + 6)$.
What is the same and what is different about their answers? Are their answers correct?

5. Which of these expressions are fully factorised? Explain your answer.
$30a + 45b = 5(6a + 9b)$ $30a + 45b = 15(2a + 3b)$ $30a + 45b = 3(10a + 15b)$

LEVEL 2

6. **(a)** Write down three different ways to factorise the expression $8b - 24$.
(b) Which of your answers in part **(a)** is fully factorised?
Explain how you know.

7. Simplify and then factorise the expression $3a + 7 - 8a + 3$.

8. The cost for five people to go ice skating, including hiring skates, is £$(5x + 20)$.
Work out the cost for one person in terms of x.
PROBLEM SOLVING
Hint: Try factorising the expression of the total cost.

9. The area of a rectangle in cm^2 is given by the expression $4x + 12y$.
Write down possible expressions for the length and the width of the rectangle.
PROBLEM SOLVING

Area = $(4x + 12y)$ cm^2

10. Write down two expressions which each have $(4x - 7)$ as one of their factors.
OPEN QUESTION

REVIEW

Linear Algebraic Expressions

Algebraic expressions can be simplified by collecting like terms.

For example

$4x - 6y - 5x + 9y$

$= 4x - 5x - 6y + 9y$ Rearrange and

$= -x + 3y$ collect like terms.

$2a - 7 + 12 - 5a$

$= 2a - 5a - 7 + 12$ Rearrange and

$= -3a + 5$ collect like terms.

Adding and Subtracting Linear Algebraic Expressions

For example

$(2x + 1) + (3x - 8)$

$= 2x + 1 + 3x - 8$ Remove brackets.

$= 2x + 3x + 1 - 8$ Rearrange and

$= 5x - 7$ collect like terms.

$(4x - 7y) - (2x - y)$

$= 4x - 7y - 2x + y$ Distributive law of

$= 4x - 2x - 7y + y$ multiplication over

$= 2x - 6y$ subtraction.

Expanding and Simplifying Linear Algebraic Expressions

Use multiplication frames to help expand expressions.

For example

×	$2x$	-5
4	$8x$	-20

$4(2x - 5) = 8x - 20$

To simplify, for example, $2(x + 3) - 3(x + 2)$, first expand each expression then simplify:

$$2(x + 3) - 3(x + 2) = 2x + 6 - 3x - 6$$
$$= 2x - 3x + 6 - 6$$
$$= -x$$

Expansion of the Product of Two Linear Expressions

An expression in a single variable where the highest power of the variable is 2 is a quadratic expression in that variable. For example, $x^2 + 3$, $2y^2 + y$ and $3a^2 - 5a + 2$ are all quadratic expressions.

Use multiplication frames to help expand.

For example

×	$3x$	5
$2x$	$6x^2$	$10x$

Thus, $2x(3x + 5) = 6x^2 + 10x$

×	$2x$	$-y$
x	$2x^2$	$-xy$

Thus, $x(2x - y) = 2x^2 - xy$

Factorisation of Linear Expressions

Writing an expression as a product of its factors is called factorisation. It is the reverse process of expansion.

You can use a multiplication frame, for example

$\times$	y	$3z$
4	$4y$	$12z$

Thus, $4y + 12z = 4(y + 3z)$

$\times$	$2a$	$-b$
3	$6a$	$-3b$

Thus, $6a - 3b = 3(2a - b)$

An expression is fully factorised if the HCF of the terms inside the brackets is 1.

So, $6(2x + 3)$ is fully factorised since the HCF of 2 and 3 is 1.

$3(4x + 6)$ is **not** fully factorised since the HCF of 4 and 6 is 2, not 1.

CHALLENGE 2

A rectangle is $(4x - 1)$ cm long and $3x$ cm wide. A small rectangle that is $(2x + 5)$ cm long and x cm wide is cut from it.

(a) Express the remaining area in terms of x.

(b) Factorise the answer in part **(a)**.

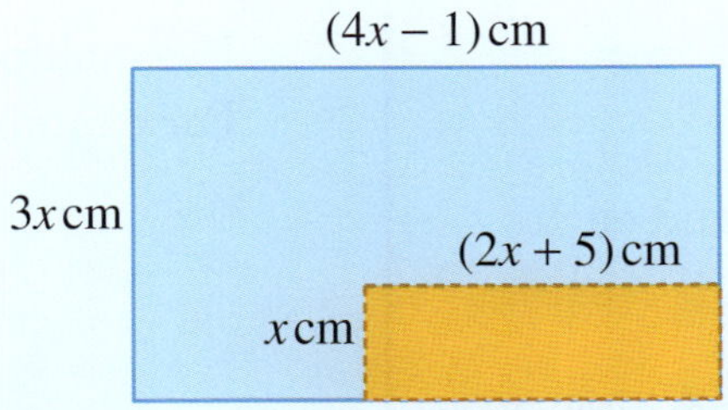

REVISION EXERCISE 2

1. Simplify these expressions.

(a) $4a - 3 + 3a + 7$ **(b)** $2b + 5c - 3b - c$

(c) $4p + 3q - 6 - 6p + q$ **(d)** $-5x - 8y + 2 - 3x + 3y - 9$

2. Simplify these expressions.

(a) $3m + (4m - 7)$ **(b)** $(-4n + 3) - (2n - 8)$

(c) $-(5p - 6)$ **(d)** $7q + (2q - 8)$

(e) $(7r + 3s) + (2r - 6s)$ **(f)** $(2x - 5) - (4x + 9)$

3. Expand and simplify these expressions.

(a) $4(2x + 7)$ **(b)** $3(2x - 5y)$

(c) $9(p - 3) + 2(p + 1)$ **(d)** $5(2q + 3) + 4(6 - 5q)$

(e) $7(2u + 3v) - 5(u - 2v)$ **(f)** $4(y - x) - 5(x - 5y)$

4. Which of these expressions are equal to $3x - 4y$?

$(2x + y) + (x - 5y)$ $3(x + 2y) - 2y$ $2(2x + y) - x - 6y$ $3(x - y) - 2y$

5. Roisin attempts to simplify the expression $4(5x - 3y) - 3(6x + y)$. Her attempt is shown. Point out her mistakes and write out the correct simplification.

$$4(5x - 3y) - 3(6x + y) = 20x - 12y - 18x + 3y$$
$$= 20x - 18x - 12y + 3y$$
$$= 2x + 9y$$

6. Expand and simplify these expressions.

(a) $a(3a + 5)$ **(b)** $b(9 - 4b)$

(c) $3c(c + d)$ **(d)** $d(2e - d)$

(e) $8x + 3x(2x + 1)$ **(f)** $-6y(y - 3) + 2y(4y - 7)$

7. The dimensions of two rectangles are given in terms of x.

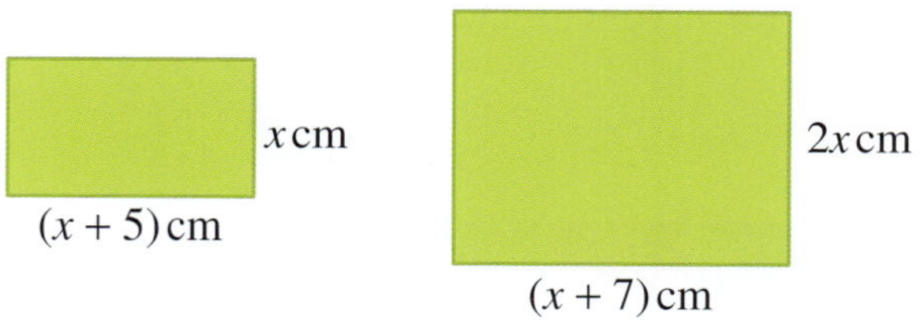

(a) Find the difference between the perimeters of the two rectangles in terms of x.

(b) Find the total area of both rectangles in terms of x.

8. Factorise these expressions fully.

(a) $15a + 25$ **(b)** $8b - 6$

(c) $20 + 28n$ **(d)** $30p - 45$

(e) $24s + 18t$ **(f)** $14x - 21y$

9. Daniel attempts to fully factorise $20x - 16$.

Daniel: $20x - 16 = (2)(10x) - (2)(8)$

$= 2(10x - 8)$

Explain why he is wrong. Work out the correct answer.

10. The price of a sandwich is £s. The price of a can of drink is £d. Nathan and Max bought sandwiches and drinks for their friends. Nathan spent £$(2s + 4d)$ and Max spent £$(5s + d)$.

(a) How many sandwiches and how many cans of drink does each of them buy?

(b) Work out the total spent by Nathan and Max in terms of s and d.

(c) Work out how much more Max spent than Nathan in terms of s and d.

11. The cost of playing x games of bowling including shoe hire is £$(5x + 2)$ for an adult and £$(3x + 1)$ for a child.

(a) Work out the cost for 2 adults and 3 children to go bowling in terms of x. Write your answer in expanded form.

(b) Work out how much more expensive it is for an adult to play x games of bowling than a child.

12. The area of a parallelogram in cm^2 is given by the expression $24x + 12$. Write down possible expressions for the length and the perpendicular height of the parallelogram.

PROBLEM SOLVING

OPEN QUESTION

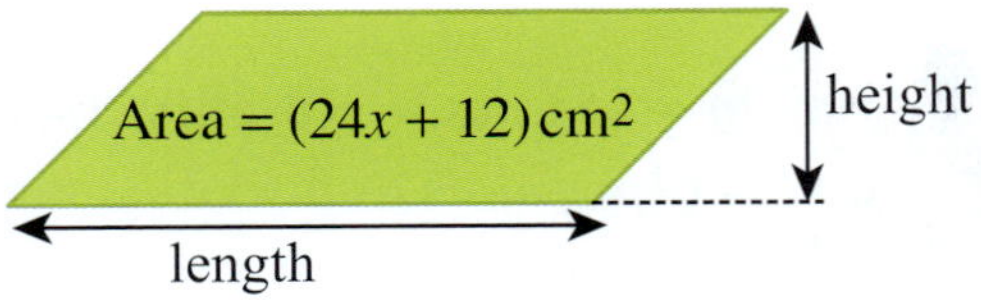

13. The width of a rectangle is x cm. The length of the rectangle is 3 cm more than its width. Work out, in terms of x

PROBLEM SOLVING

(a) the perimeter of the rectangle,

(b) the area of the rectangle.

A square has a perimeter of $(8x + 20)$ cm.

(c) What is the difference between the length of the rectangle and the length of the square?

14. A mobile phone costs £240, but you pay in equal instalments each month of the year. The total cost for the mobile phone and unlimited use for a year is £$(240 + 12x)$. Work out the cost each month of the year in terms of x.

PROBLEM SOLVING

Write in Your Journal

Write two examples to illustrate that factorisation is the reverse process of expansion.

3 LINEAR EQUATIONS

WHAT IS IN THIS CHAPTER:

The total cost, £c, of a mobile phone contract is worked out using the formula $c = 5 + 2d$, where £5 is a fixed charge, £2 is the cost per 1GB (gigabyte) of data and d is the amount of data in GB. The cost of a contract with 4GB of data is given by $c = 5 + 2 \times 4 = 13$, i.e. £13. How much data would be included in a contract which costs £25?

LET'S LEARN TO

- solve linear equations in one variable, including where the variable is on both sides of the equation
- solve linear equations with brackets in one variable
- solve problems involving linear equations in one variable
- change the subject of a formula
- find the value of an unknown variable in a formula

FLASHBACK

1. Linear Equations in One Variable

(a) Equations such as $3x - 5 = 7$ and $2x + 8 = 23 - 3x$, where the variable x is to the power of 1, are called **linear equations in one variable**, x.

Any value of x that, when substituted into the equation, makes both sides of the equation equal, is called a **solution** of the equation. This value of x is said to **satisfy** the equation. Finding a value of x that satisfies an equation is called **solving** the equation.

(b) An equation can be solved by the **balance method** where you carry out the same operations on both sides. For example

$$x - 5 = 7$$
$$x - 5 + 5 = 7 + 5 \quad \text{Add 5 to both sides.}$$
$$x = 12$$

$$3x = -18$$
$$\frac{3x}{3} = \frac{-18}{3} \quad \text{Divide both sides by 3.}$$
$$x = -6$$

$$\frac{x}{7} = 3$$
$$\frac{x}{7} \times 7 = 3 \times 7 \quad \text{Multiply both sides by 7.}$$
$$x = 21$$

You can substitute your value of x back into the equation to check it is correct.

DISCUSS

Why do you choose to add 5 to both sides?

DISCUSS

Why do you choose to divide both sides by 3?

DISCUSS

Why do you choose to multiply both sides by 7?

2. Expansion of Expressions

The distributive law tells you that
$$a(x + y) = ax + ay$$
$$a(x - y) = ax - ay$$

You can use multiplication frames to help expand expressions. For example

$4(3x + 5) = 12x + 20$

×	$3x$	5
4	$12x$	20

$-7(3y - 5z) = -21y + 35z$

×	$3y$	$-5z$
-7	$-21y$	$35z$

$x(3x - 5y) = 3x^2 - 5xy$

×	$3x$	$-5y$
x	$3x^2$	$-5xy$

3.1 Solving Linear Equations

A Simple Linear Equations

If you want to find the value of d that gives $9 + 4d$ as equal to 25, you must solve the equation

$$9 + 4d = 25.$$

Let us recall the balance method of solving basic linear equations first seen in Student Book 2A.

The two sides of an equation can be represented by algebra discs on two sides of a balance. The balance represents 'equal'. For example, to solve the equation $3x + 2 = 8$, place the corresponding algebra discs on the LHS and RHS of the balance.

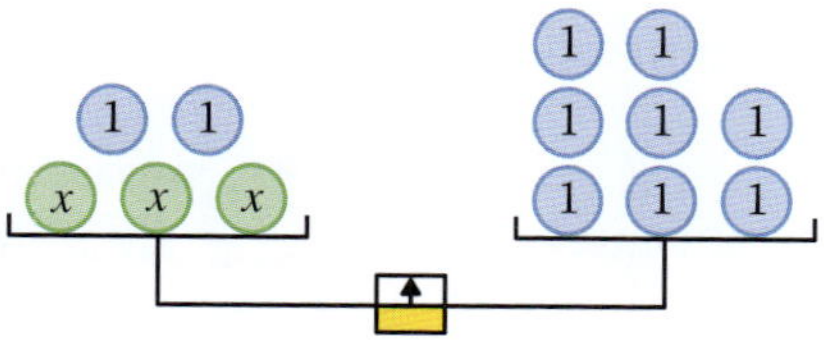

$3x + 2 = 8$

Add two (−1) discs on both sides to make two zero pairs on each side.

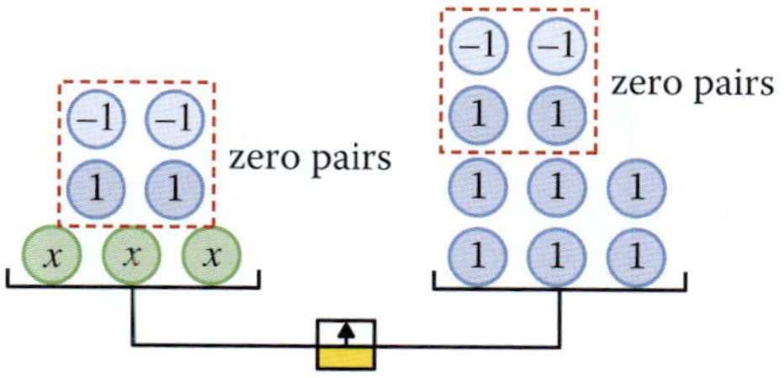

$3x + 2 + (-2) = 8 + (-2)$

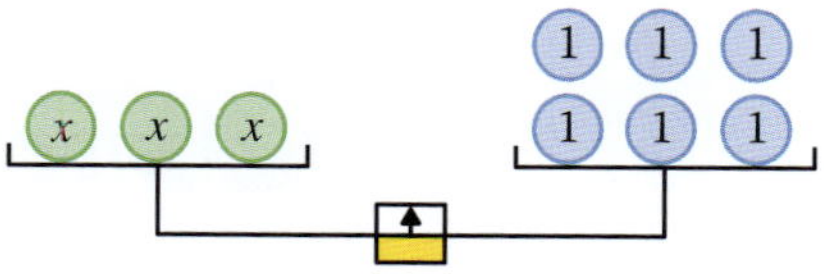

$3x = 6$

Divide both sides into three equal parts so that the LHS just has one x disc.

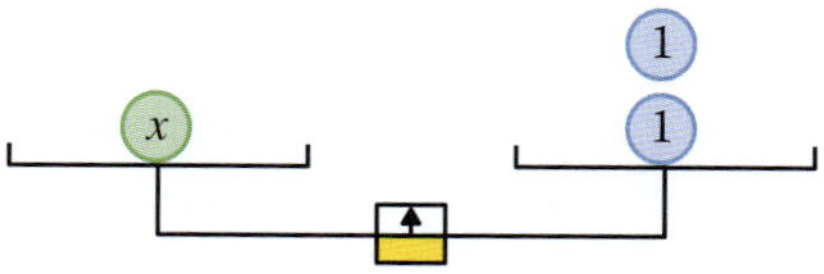

$x = 2$

REMARK

You can check this value of x satisfies the equation by using substitution.
If $x = 2$,
$3x + 2 = 3(2) + 2$
$= 6 + 2$
$= 8$
So, $x = 2$ is the solution to the equation $3x + 2 = 8$.

CLASS ACTIVITY 1

Objective: To investigate methods of solving linear equations.

1. For each of these equations, use a 'guess and check' method to find the value of the variable that satisfies it.

(a) $2x + 4 = 10$ **(b)** $2x - 4 = 10$

(c) $4y + 2 = 10$ **(d)** $4y - 2 = 10$

(e) $4y + 2 = y + 8$ **(f)** $4y - 2 = 2y + 8$

Do you notice any patterns in your answers?

2.

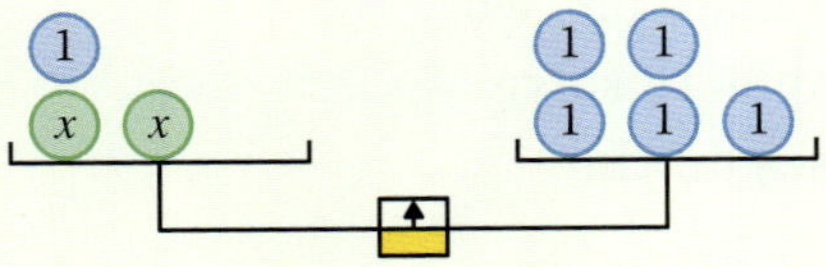

(a) Write down the equation represented by the algebra discs.

(b) Use the algebra discs to solve the equation in part **(a)**.

3. Use algebra discs to solve these equations.

(a) $3x - 5 = 7$ **(b)** $10 = 3x + 4$

(c) $4x - 6 = 2$ **(d)** $2 = 4x + 6$

4. Write down some different equations that have the solution

(a) $x = 5$, **(b)** $x = -2$.

REMARK

Work each of these out by guessing a solution and using substitution to check if it satisfies the equation.
For example, in part **(a)**:
When $x = 2$,
$2x + 4 = 2(2) + 4$
$= 8$
Therefore, $x = 2$ does not satisfy the equation. You need to try a different value for x.

DISCUSS

How many different solutions do you think there are?

Example 1

Solve these equations.

(a) $4x + 3 = 23$ **(b)** $3y - 5 = 16$

Solution

(a) You can represent the equation $4x + 3 = 23$ using a bar model:

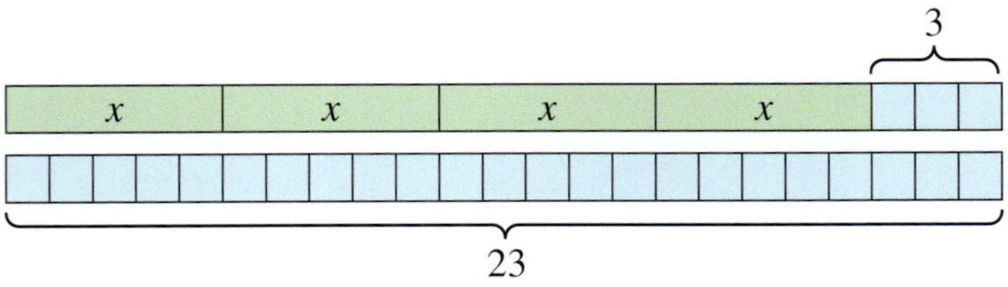

From the bar model you can see that $4x + 3 = 23$

$$4x = 23 - 3$$
$$4x = 20$$
$$x = 5$$

DISCUSS

Use algebra discs to solve the equations in Example 1. What is the same and what is different between using algebra discs, a bar model and using algebra to solve the equation?

You can also solve this using algebra:

$$4x + 3 = 23$$

$$4x + 3 - 3 = 23 - 3$$ Subtract 3 from both sides.

$$4x = 20$$

$$\frac{4x}{4} = \frac{20}{4}$$ Divide both sides by 4.

$$x = 5$$

Check: LHS $= 4(5) + 3$

$= 20 + 3$

$= 23$

$=$ RHS

The solution is correct.

(b) You can represent the equation $3y - 5 = 16$ using a bar model:

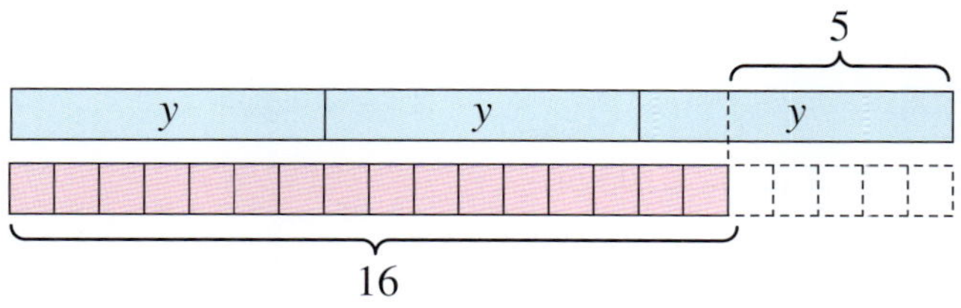

From the bar model you can see that $3y - 5 = 16$

$$3y = 16 + 5$$

$$3y = 21$$

$$y = 7$$

You can also solve this using algebra:

$$3y - 5 = 16$$

$$3y - 5 + 5 = 16 + 5$$ Add 5 to both sides.

$$3y = 21$$

$$\frac{3y}{3} = \frac{21}{3}$$ Divide both sides by 3.

$$y = 7$$

Check: LHS $= 3(7) - 5$

$= 16$

$=$ RHS

The solution is correct.

Try It! 1 Solve these equations.

(a) $3x - 8 = 16$ **(b)** $10y + 9 = 39$

REMARK
Subtracting 3 is the inverse of adding 3. Dividing by 4 is the inverse of multiplying by 4.

DISCUSS
Why do you add 5 to both sides? Why do you divide both sides by 3?

DISCUSS
Use two different methods (algebra discs, bar models or algebra) to solve Try It! 1. Which method do you find easiest?

REMARK
Use substitution to check your answers to Try It! 1.

Example 2

Solve these equations.

(a) $3x - 7 = x + 5$ **(b)** $5y + 1 = 15 - 2y$

Solution

(a) You can solve this using algebra discs:

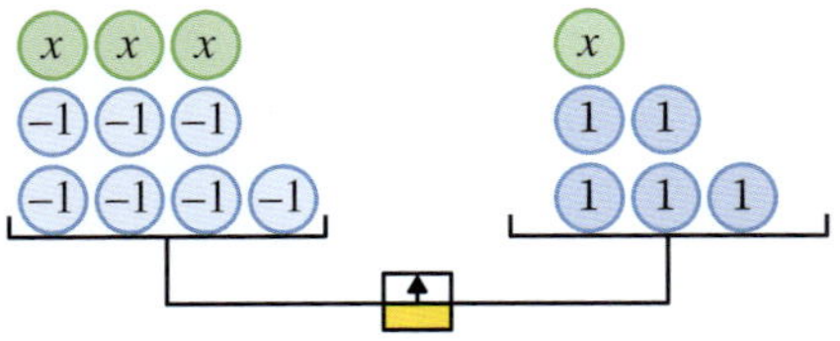

$3x - 7 = x + 5$

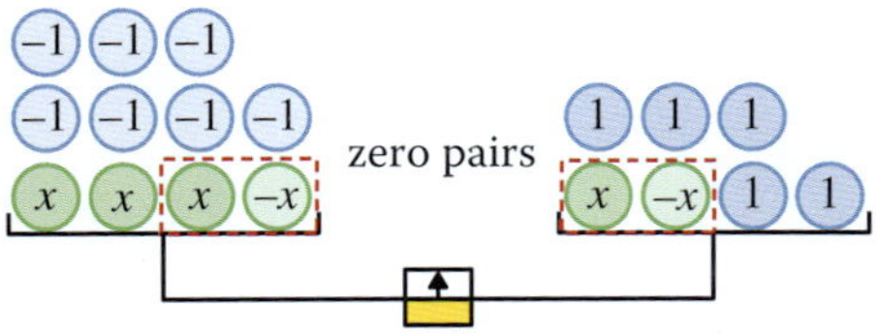

$3x + (-x) - 7$
$= x + (-x) + 5$

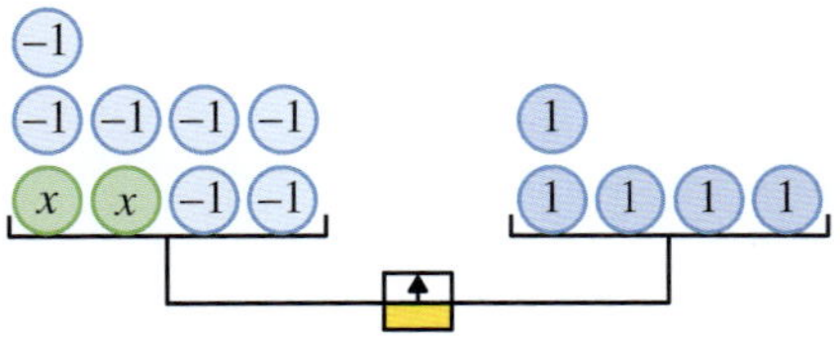

$2x - 7 = 5$

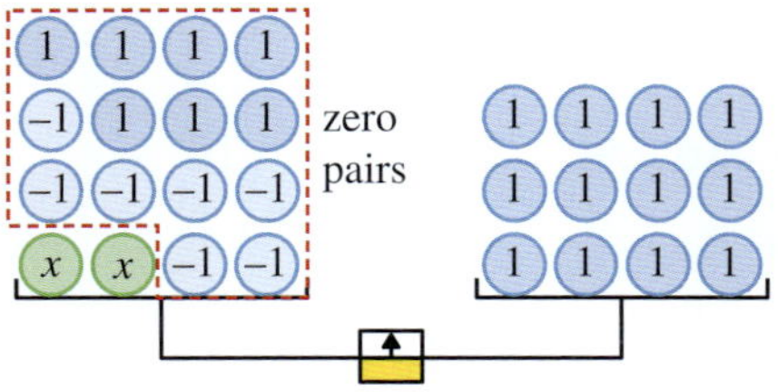

$2x - 7 + 7 = 5 + 7$

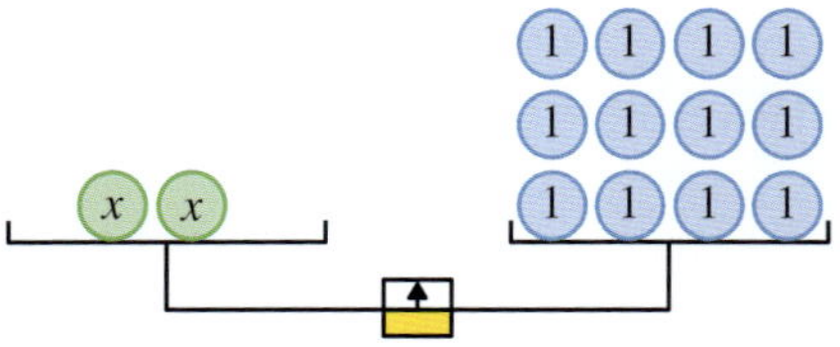

$2x = 12$

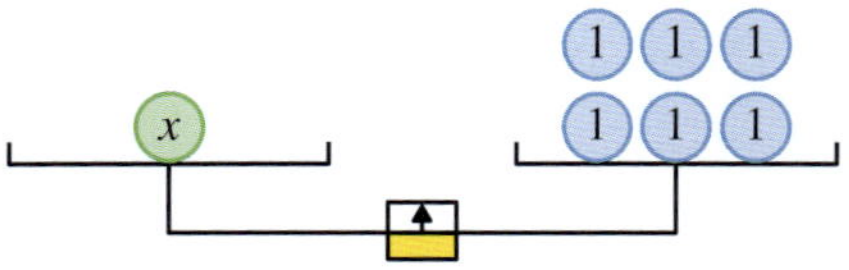

$x = 6$

You can also represent the equation $3x - 7 = x + 5$ using a bar model:

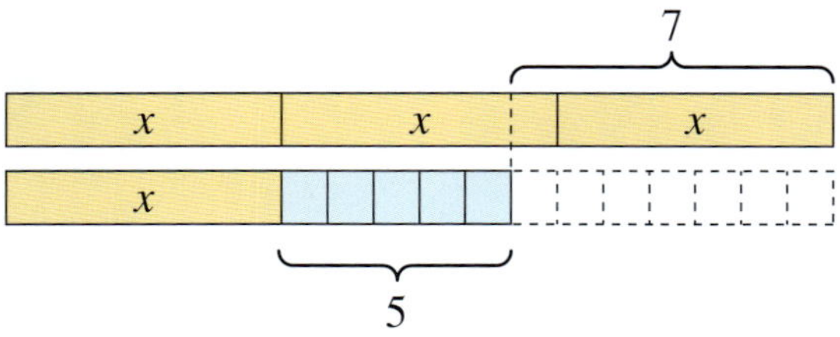

REMARK

You should check that your solution satisfies the equation.
When $x = 6$,
LHS $= 3(6) - 7$
$= 11$
RHS $= 6 + 5$
$= 11$
LHS = RHS
$\therefore$ the solution is correct.

From the bar model you can see that $3x - 7 = x + 5$

$$2x - 7 = 5$$
$$2x = 12$$
$$x = 6$$

You can also solve this using algebra:

$3x - 7 = x + 5$

$3x - x - 7 = x - x + 5$ Subtract x from both sides.

$2x - 7 = 5$

$2x - 7 + 7 = 5 + 7$ Add 7 to both sides.

$\frac{2x}{2} = \frac{12}{2}$ Divide both sides by 2.

$x = 6$

(b) You can represent the equation $5y + 1 = 15 - 2y$ using a bar model:

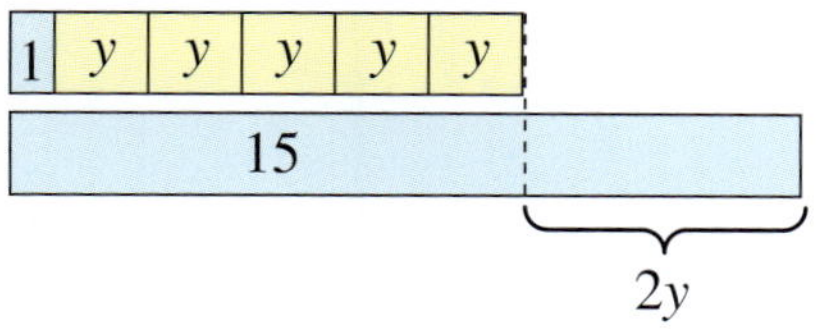

From the bar model you can see that

$5y + 1 = 15 - 2y$

$7y + 1 = 15$

$7y = 14$

$y = 2$

You can also solve this using algebra:

$5y + 1 = 15 - 2y$

$5y + 2y + 1 = 15 - 2y + 2y$ Add $2y$ to both sides.

$7y + 1 = 15$

$7y + 1 - 1 = 15 - 1$ Subtract 1 from both sides.

$7y = 14$

$\frac{7y}{7} = \frac{14}{7}$ Divide both sides by 7.

$y = 2$

Try It! 2

Solve these equations.

(a) $4x + 5 = 2x + 13$ **(b)** $3y + 1 = 21 - y$

DISCUSS

Work out this equation using algebra discs. What is the same and what is different when you use algebra discs?

REMARK

You should check that your solution satisfies the equation.

When $y = 2$,

$\text{LHS} = 5(2) + 1$
$= 11$

$\text{RHS} = 15 - 2(2)$
$= 11$

$\text{LHS} = \text{RHS}$

$\therefore$ the solution is correct.

DISCUSS

Use two different methods for Try It! 2 (algebra discs, bar model or algebra). Which method do you find easiest?

SPOT CHECK

Use substitution to check your answers.

Example 3

A book is £3 more than a pen. The total price of the book and the pen is £13. Find the price of the pen.

Solution

Let £x be the price of the pen.
Then, the price of the book is £$(x + 3)$.

This can be represented by a bar model.

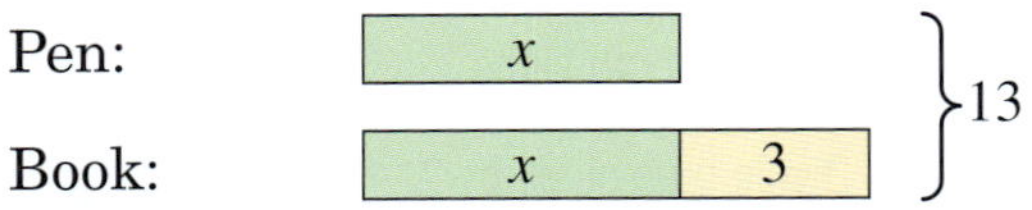

As the sum of the pen and the book is £13, you can form the equation

$$x + x + 3 = 13$$
$$2x + 3 = 13$$
$$2x + 3 - 3 = 13 - 3$$
$$2x = 10$$
$$\frac{2x}{2} = \frac{10}{2}$$
$$x = 5$$

Therefore, the price of the pen is £5.

REMARK

You should check your solution by substituting your answer into the original question.
Price of the pen = £5.
Price of the book
= £(5 + 3)
= £8
Total price
= £(5 + 8)
= £13
∴ the solution is correct.

Try It! 3

The number of red balloons is 14 less than the number of yellow balloons. The total number of these balloons is 32. Draw a bar model and find the number of yellow balloons.

B Equations Involving Brackets

If an equation involves brackets, you can expand the expression first then solve as usual, or in some cases you might not need to expand the brackets. Have a look at some examples.

Example 4

Solve these equations.

(a) $3(2x) = 18$
(b) $2(x + 5) = 23$
(c) $4(x - 3) + 5 = 29$

Solution

(a) $3(2x) = 18$

$$\frac{3(2x)}{3} = \frac{18}{3}$$ Divide both sides by 3 to remove the brackets.

$$2x = 6$$

$$\frac{2x}{2} = \frac{6}{2}$$ Divide both sides by 2.

$$x = 3$$

REMARK

$3(2x) = 3 \times 2x$
$= 6x$

Alternative method:

$$3(2x) = 18$$
$$6x = 18 \quad \text{Expand the brackets.}$$
$$\frac{6x}{6} = \frac{18}{6} \quad \text{Divide both sides by 6.}$$
$$x = 3$$

You can also represent the equation $3(2x) = 18$ using a bar model:

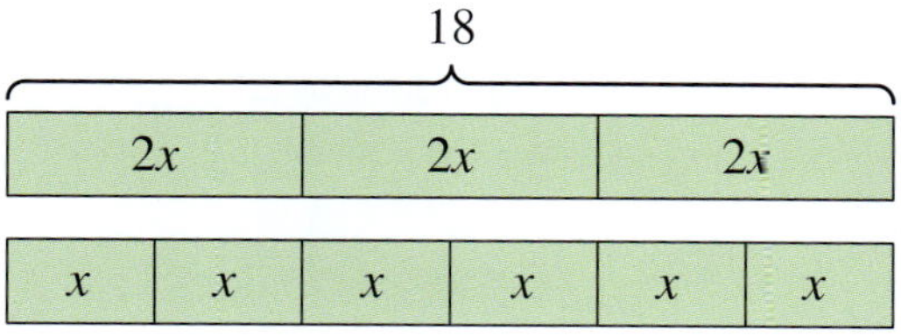

(b)

$$2(x + 5) = 23$$
$$2x + 10 = 23 \quad \text{Expand the brackets.}$$
$$2x + 10 - 10 = 23 - 10 \quad \text{Subtract 10 from both sides.}$$
$$2x = 13$$
$$\frac{2x}{2} = \frac{13}{2} \quad \text{Divide both sides by 2.}$$
$$x = 6\frac{1}{2} \text{ or } 6.5$$

You can also use a bar model to support your working for this question:

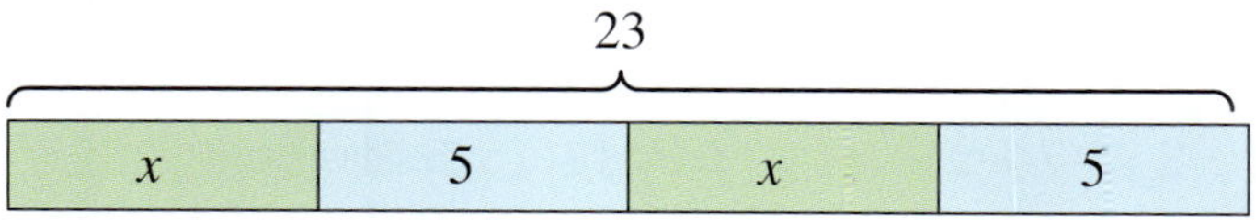

(c)

$$4(x - 3) + 5 = 29$$
$$4(x - 3) + 5 - 5 = 29 - 5 \quad \text{Subtract 5 from both sides.}$$
$$4(x - 3) = 24$$
$$\frac{4(x - 3)}{4} = \frac{24}{4} \quad \text{Divide both sides by the common factor 4.}$$
$$x - 3 = 6$$
$$x - 3 + 3 = 6 + 3 \quad \text{Add 3 to both sides.}$$
$$x = 9$$

Try It! 4

Solve these equations.

(a) $2(4x) = 24$ **(b)** $2(x - 4) = 15$

(c) $2(x + 3) - 1 = 11$

SPOT CHECK

Check:
LHS $= 3(2 \times 3)$
$= 3(6)$
$= 18 =$ RHS
$\therefore$ the solution is correct.

DISCUSS

What is the same and what is different about the methods in Example 4(a)? Would both methods always be appropriate? Can you use the bar model to explain both methods?

DISCUSS

Could you divide both sides by 2 on the top line rather than expanding the brackets? Discuss both methods with a classmate.

DISCUSS

Is there another way to work out Example 4(c)? Discuss the benefits of each method for this question.

Example 5

Solve these equations.

(a) $4(2y-3)=20$ **(b)** $-2(p-2)=14$

Solution

(a) $4(2y-3)=20$

$\frac{4(2y-3)}{4}=\frac{20}{4}$ Divide both sides by 4.

$2y-3=5$

$2y-3+3=5+3$ Add 3 to both sides.

$2y=8$

$\frac{2y}{2}=\frac{8}{2}$ Divide both sides by 2.

$y=4$

Alternative method:

$4(2y-3)=20$

$8y-12=20$ Expand the brackets.

$8y-12+12=20+12$ Add 12 to both sides.

$8y=32$

$\frac{8y}{8}=\frac{32}{8}$ Divide both sides by 8.

$y=4$

(b) $-2(p-2)=14$

$\frac{-2(p-2)}{-2}=\frac{14}{-2}$ Divide both sides by –2.

$p-2=-7$

$p-2+2=-7+2$ Add 2 to both sides.

$p=-5$

Alternative method:

$-2(p-2)=14$

$-2p+4=14$ Expand the brackets.

$-2p+4-4=14-4$ Subtract 4 from both sides.

$-2p=10$

$\frac{-2p}{-2}=\frac{10}{-2}$ Divide both sides by –2.

$p=-5$

REMARK

$4(2y-3)=4(2y)-4(3)$
$=8y-12$

SPOT CHECK

Check:
LHS $=-2(-5-2)$
$=-2(-7)$
$=14=$ RHS
$\therefore$ the solution is correct.

Try It! 5

Solve these equations.

(a) $3(3t-4)=6$

(b) $-4(5q+1)=16$

PRACTICE 3.1

LEVEL 1

1. Solve these equations.

(a) $3x + 2 = 14$ **(b)** $3x + 2 = 17$ **(c)** $3x - 1 = 14$ **(d)** $15 = 4x - 1$

2. Solve these equations.

(a) $2p + 5 = p + 11$ **(b)** $2p - 5 = p + 11$ **(c)** $3p - 5 = p + 11$ **(d)** $3p - 5 = 11 - p$

3. Solve these equations.

(a) $3(4a) = 24$ **(b)** $-24 = 3(4a)$ **(c)** $2(2a) = 11$

(d) $2(a + 1) = 10$ **(e)** $16 = 2(a - 1)$ **(f)** $2(a - 1) = 15$

4. Is $x = -3$ a solution of the equation $4(2x + 5) = -4$? Explain your answer.

5. Henry attempts to solve the equation $2y + 3 = y + 9$. His working is as shown.

$$2y + 3 = y + 9$$
$$3y + 3 = 9$$
$$3y = 6$$
$$y = 2$$

(a) Check the solution and show that it is wrong.

(b) Point out the wrong step and work out the correct solution.

LEVEL 2

6. Solve these equations.

(a) $3x + 7 = x + 5$ **(b)** $3x + 17 = 1 - x$ **(c)** $5x + 9 = 2x + 3$ **(d)** $2x - 6 = 19 - 3x$

7. Solve these equations.

(a) $2(3m + 4) = 14$ **(b)** $2(3m - 4) = 7$ **(c)** $36 = 3(2m + 4)$

(d) $-24 = 3(2m - 4)$ **(e)** $3(2m + 4) - 6 = 36$ **(f)** $2(m + 4) - 6 = 15$

8. Which of these equations have the same solution?

$2(3x - 1) = 16$ $3(2x - 1) = 15$ $2(1 - 2x) = 14$ $3(1 - 2x) = -15$

9. PROBLEM SOLVING A football club has 8 more members than a basketball club. The total number of members in the two clubs is 32. Represent this with a bar model and find the number of members in the basketball club.

10. PROBLEM SOLVING FINANCE The price for a VIP ticket is three times the price of an ordinary ticket for a show. The price of two VIP tickets and four ordinary tickets is £80. Find the price of a VIP ticket.

3.2 Manipulation of Formulae

For example, if a mobile phone contract costs £4 per month plus £2 per 1 GB of data, then

when $y = 1$, $x = 4 + 2(1) = £6$,
when $y = 2$, $x = 4 + 2(2) = £8$,
when $y = 3$, $x = 4 + 2(3) = £10$.

Here x represents the contract price and y represents the amount of data.
You can see x and y are connected by the **formula** $x = 4 + 2y$.

If you want to find the cost of a contract including 4 GB of data, you can substitute $y = 4$ into the formula:

$x = 4 + 2(4) = £12$

The cost is £12.

If you want to find the amount of data when the contract costs £24, you can substitute $x = 24$ into the formula:

$24 = 4 + 2y$
$20 = 2y$ Subtract 4 from both sides.
$10 = y$ Divide both sides by 2.

The amount of data is 10 GB.

A **formula** is an equation that connects two or more variables. You have met some formulae in Student Books 1A and 2A.

For example,

$C = 2\pi r$ is a formula connecting the circumference C and the radius r of a circle.

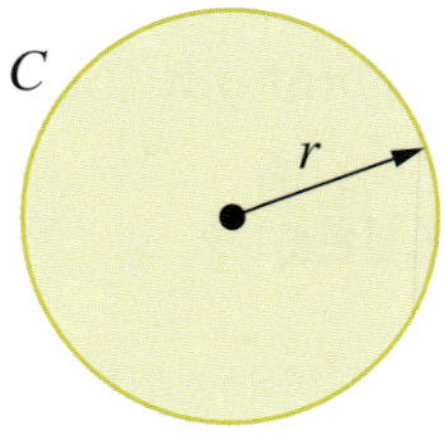

$A = \frac{1}{2}(a + b)h$ is a formula connecting the area A, the lengths of two parallel sides a and b, and the perpendicular height h of a trapezium.

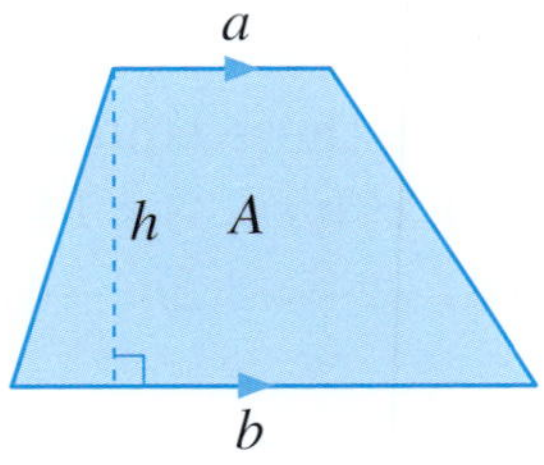

A variable that just appears as a single term on one side of a formula is called the **subject** of the formula. It is convention to put the subject on the LHS. For example,

the subject of the formula $x = 4 + 2y$ is x,
the subject of the formula $C = 2\pi r$ is C,
the subject of the formula is $A = \frac{1}{2}(a + b)h$ is A.

REMARK

In the formula
$x = \frac{(2y - x)}{7}$
x is not considered the subject, because it appears on both sides of the equation.

The value of the subject of a formula can be found by substitution if the values of other variables in the formula are known. However, if a variable is not the subject of a formula, you must solve an equation to get the value of that variable. If you want to calculate the value of that variable for several cases, it is more convenient to **change the subject of the formula** to that variable. Let us explore this.

CLASS ACTIVITY 2

Objective: To explore changing the subject of a formula.

1. The formula $x = y + 4$ is represented here using algebra discs.

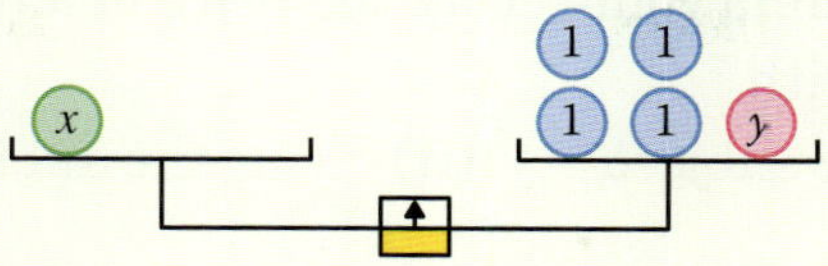

Use the techniques you have learnt for solving equations so that the y disc ends up on its own on one side of the balance. Then write down the formula with y as the subject.

2. **(a)** Use algebra discs to make y the subject of each of these formulae.

(i) $x = y + 6$ **(ii)** $x = y - 6$

(b) Using your answers in **(a)**, write down these formulae with y as the subject.

(i) $x = 2y + 6$ **(ii)** $x = 2y - 6$

(c) What do you notice about your answers?

3. Look at the following bar models. For each one, write a formula where x is the subject and write the same formula with y as the subject.

(a)

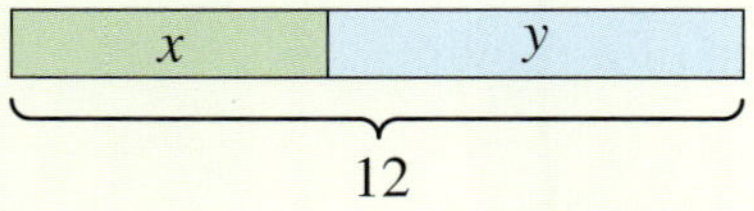

(b)

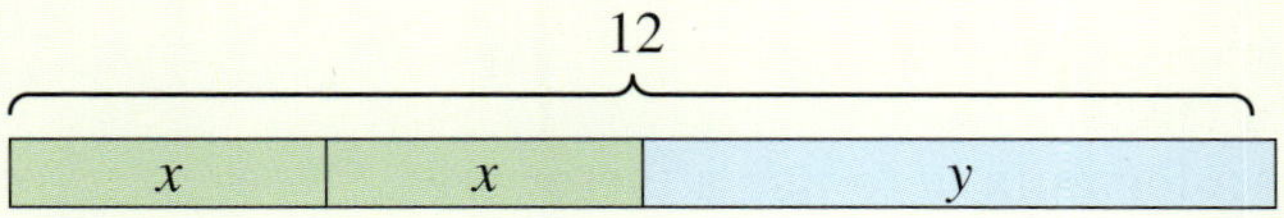

(c)

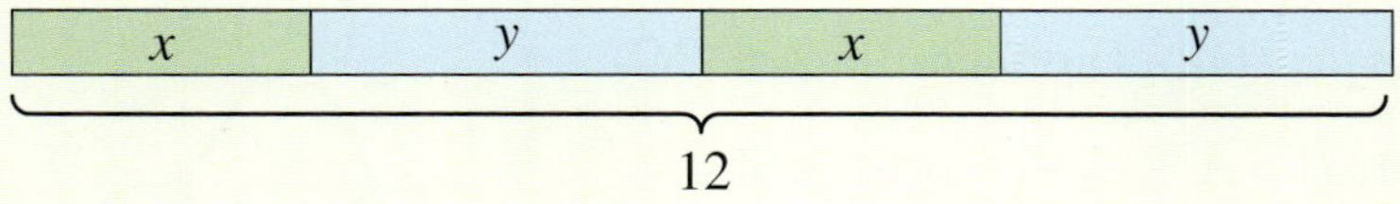

Explain your method of making x and y the subject of the formula for each bar model to a partner.

You can use algebra discs or bar models to represent and help you rearrange a formula.

For example, this bar model represents the formula $x + y = 20$.
From the bar model you can also see that $x = 20 - y$,
and $y = 20 - x$.

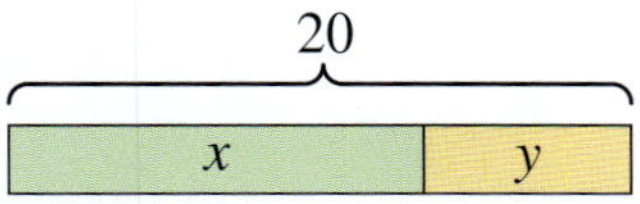

Example 6

The price of a book is £x. The price of a pen is £y.
The total price of the book and the pen is £8.

(a) Draw a bar model to represent this situation.

(b) Write a formula connecting the price of a book and a pen with

(i) x as the subject, **(ii)** y as the subject.

Solution

(a)

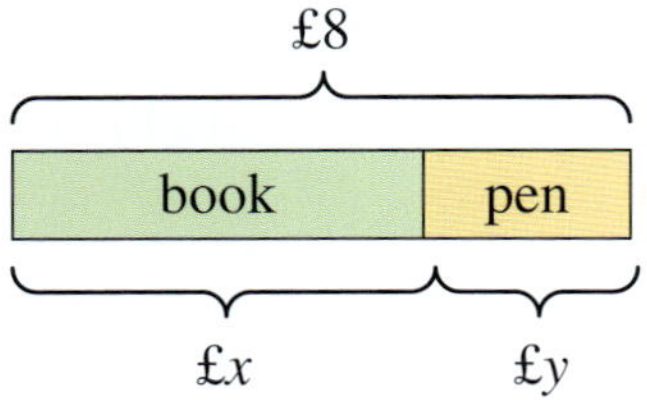

(b) From the bar model:

(i) $x = 8 - y$

(ii) $y = 8 - x$

DISCUSS

Paul tries to rearrange the formula $x + y = 10$ to make y the subject. He says the answer is $y = x - 10$.

Is he correct? Explain your answer?

Try It! 6

The price of a movie download is £m. The price of a bag of popcorn is £p. The total price of the movie and the popcorn is £11.

(a) Use a bar model to represent this situation.

(b) Write a formula connecting the price of a movie download and popcorn with

(i) m as the subject, **(ii)** p as the subject.

Another way to visualise rearranging a formula is to use a factor tree. You have already used these in Student Books 1A and 2A.

For example, this factor tree represents the formula $A = BC$.

But also, since you can see that $B = A \div C$, it represents $B = \frac{A}{C}$.

And since you can see that $C = A \div B$ it represents $C = \frac{A}{B}$.

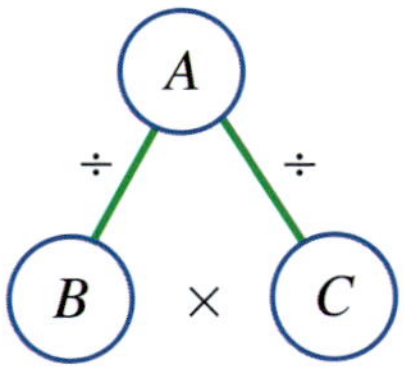

Can you see that by focusing on a different part of the factor tree, you can make different variables the subject?

Example 7

(a) Make x the subject of the formula $y = 5x$.

(b) Make T the subject of the formula $S = \frac{T}{3}$.

(c) Make P the subject of the formula $Q = \frac{7}{P}$

Solution

(a) You can use a factor tree to visualise the formula $y = 5x$.

You can see that $x = y \div 5$, which you write as $x = \frac{y}{5}$.

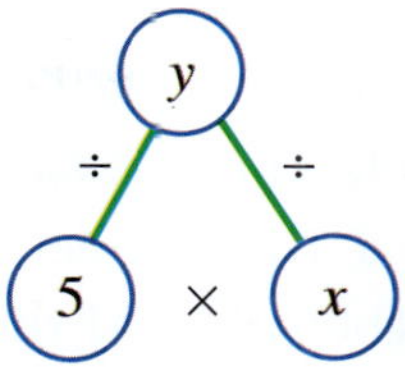

Alternatively,

$$y = 5x$$
$$5x = y$$
$$\frac{5x}{5} = \frac{y}{5} \quad \text{Divide both sides by 5.}$$
$$x = \frac{y}{5}$$

(b) You can use a factor tree to visualise the formula $S = \frac{T}{3}$.

You can see that $T = 3 \times S$, which you write as $T = 3S$.

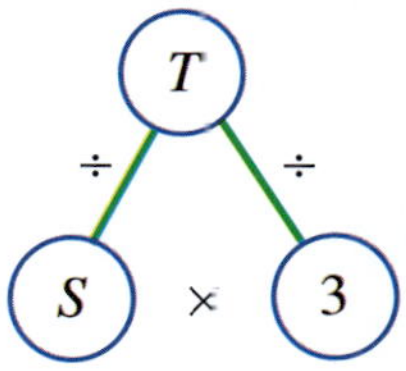

Alternatively,

$$S = \frac{T}{3}$$
$$\frac{T}{3} = S$$
$$\frac{T}{3} \times 3 = S \times 3 \quad \text{Multiply both sides by 3.}$$
$$T = 3S$$

(c) You can use a factor tree to visualise the formula $Q = \frac{7}{P}$.

You can see that $P = \frac{7}{Q}$.

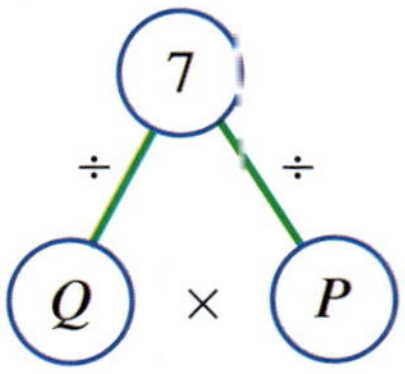

Using the balance method:

$$Q = \frac{7}{P}$$
$$Q \times P = \frac{7}{P} \times P \quad \text{Multiply both sides by } P.$$
$$QP = 7$$
$$\frac{QP}{Q} = \frac{7}{Q} \quad \text{Divide both sides by } Q$$
$$P = \frac{7}{Q}$$

REMARK

Writing $y = 5x$ implies that $5x = y$.

DISCUSS

Marie wants to make x the subject of the formula $y = \frac{x}{3}$. She says the answer is $x = \frac{y}{3}$. What mistake has she made?

Try It! 7

(a) Make p the subject of the formula $q = 8p$.

(b) Make R the subject of the formula $V = \frac{R}{4}$.

(c) Make b the subject of the formula $A = \frac{10}{b}$.

Example 8

The formula for the area, A cm^2, of a rectangle is $A = lw$, where l cm is the length and w cm is the width of the rectangle.

(a) Use a factor tree to represent this formula.

(b) Make w the subject of the formula.

(c) Find the width of the rectangle when $A = 80$ and $l = 4$.

Solution

(a)

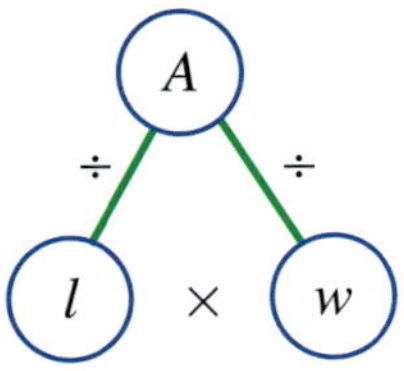

(b) Using the factor tree, you can see that $w = A \div l$.
Write this as $w = \frac{A}{l}$.

(c) When $A = 80$ and $l = 4$, $w = \frac{80}{4}$
$= 20$

Width of rectangle = 20 cm

RECALL

$A \div l$ is written as $\frac{A}{l}$.

Try It! 8

A car is at a constant speed of s km/h. The distance, d km, travelled by the car in t hours is given by the formula $d = st$.

(a) Use a factor tree to represent this formula.

(b) Make t the subject of the formula.

(c) Find t when $s = 70$ and $d = 210$.

DISCUSS

How else could this formula be expressed?

Example 9

(a) Make c the subject of the formula $p = 3c - 2$.

(b) Make x the subject of the formula $Y = \frac{x}{4} + 6$.

Solution

(a)

$$p = 3c - 2$$
$$3c - 2 = p$$
$$3c - 2 + 2 = p + 2 \quad \text{Add 2 to both sides.}$$
$$3c = p + 2$$
$$\frac{3c}{3} = \frac{p + 2}{3} \quad \text{Divide both sides by 3.}$$
$$c = \frac{p + 2}{3}$$

REMARK

You could represent $p = 3c - 2$ using a bar model:

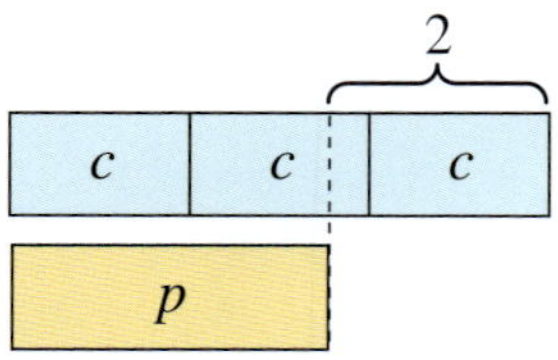

From the bar model, $3c = p + 2$.
Therefore, $c = \frac{p + 2}{3}$.

(b)

$$Y = \frac{x}{4} + 6$$

$$\frac{x}{4} + 6 = Y$$

$$\frac{x}{4} + 6 - 6 = Y - 6$$ Subtract 6 from both sides.

$$\frac{x}{4} = Y - 6$$

$$\frac{x}{4} \times 4 = (Y - 6) \times 4$$ Multiply both sides by 4.

$$x = 4(Y - 6)$$

DISCUSS

You could represent

$\frac{x}{4} = Y - 6$

using a factor tree:

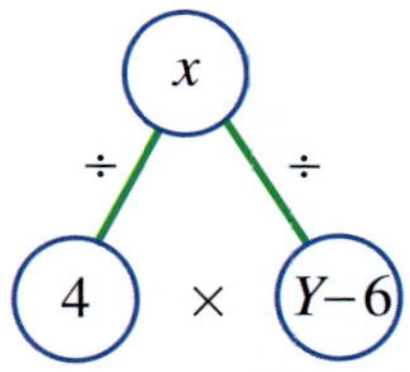

The expression '$Y - 6$' is in one circle because to make X on its own, you must multiply the whole of $Y - 6$ by 4, so $4(Y - 6)$.

Try It! 9

(a) Make r the subject of the formula $s = 5r + 3$.

(b) Make z the subject of the formula $y = \frac{z}{4} - 1$.

Example 10

The area, A cm², of a triangle is given by the formula

$$A = \frac{1}{2}bh,$$

where b cm is the length of the base and h cm is the perpendicular height.

(a) Change the subject of the formula to h.

(b) Find the perpendicular height of the triangle when $A = 15$ and $b = 6$.

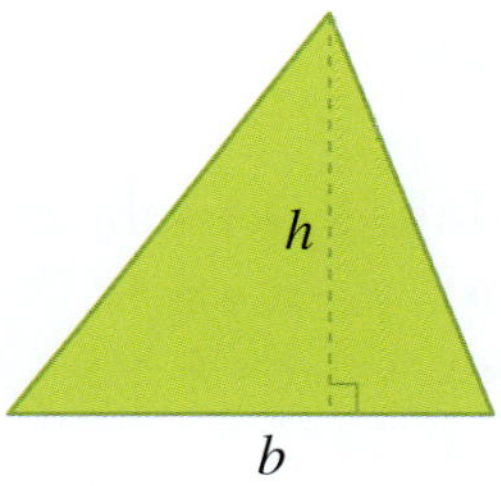

Solution

(a)

$$A = \frac{1}{2}bh$$

$$\frac{1}{2}bh = A$$

$$bh = 2A$$ Multiply both sides by 2.

$$h = \frac{2A}{b}$$ Divide both sides by b.

DISCUSS

Why do you multiply both sides by 2?

(b) When $A = 15$ and $b = 6$,

$$h = \frac{2A}{b}$$

$$= \frac{2 \times 15}{6}$$

$$= \frac{30}{6}$$

$$= 5$$

Perpendicular height of triangle = 5 cm

Try It! 10

The circumference, C cm, of the circle is given by the formula

$$C = 2\pi r$$

where r cm is the radius of the circle.

(a) Change the subject of the formula to r.

(b) Using $\pi = 3$, calculate the radius of a circle with $C = 24$.

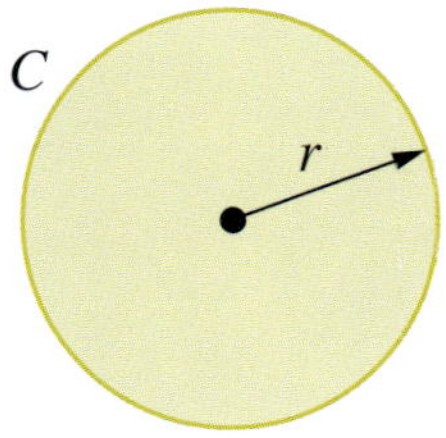

PRACTICE 3.2

LEVEL 1

1. Express the formula represented by each bar model in three different ways.

(a)

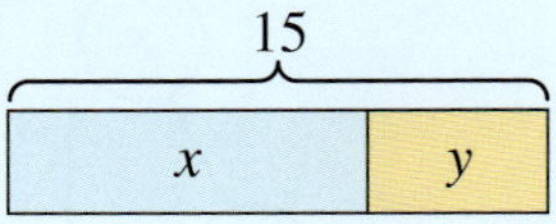

(b)

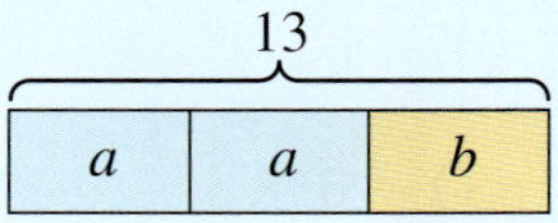

2. Express the formula represented by each factor tree in three different ways.

(a)

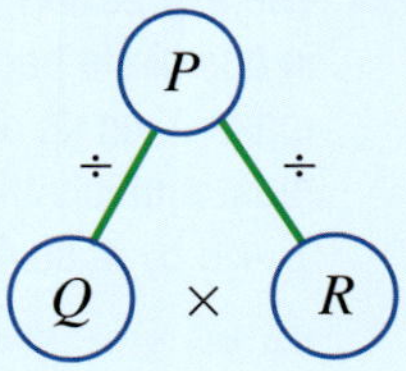

(b)

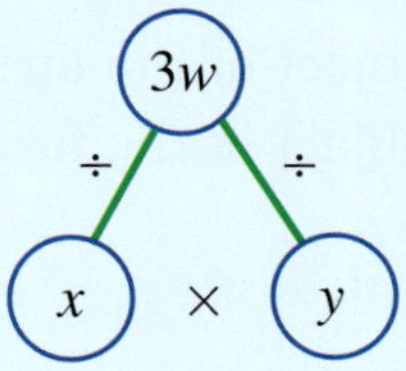

3. State the subject in each formula.

(a) $M = 2a + b$ **(b)** $b = 2a - M$ **(c)** $V = IR$ **(d)** $\frac{V}{R} = I$

4. Make x the subject of each formula.

(a) $y = x + 3$ **(b)** $y = x - 3$

(c) $y = x + k$ **(d)** $y = 7x$

(e) $y = \frac{x}{7}$ **(f)** $y = \frac{k}{x}$

5. Given the formula $P = 5R$, find

(a) the value of P when $R = 2$,

(b) the value of R when $P = 50$.

LEVEL 2

6. Make x the subject of each formula.

(a) $z = 2x + 1$ **(b)** $z = \frac{x}{2} - 1$ **(c)** $t = 1 - 3x$ **(d)** $2t = k + 3x$

7. Change the subject of each formula to m.

(a) $y = 2mx$ **(b)** $4r = 5ms$ **(c)** $3v = \frac{bm}{8}$ **(d)** $a = \frac{2}{m}$

8. Given the formula $y = \frac{x}{3} - 2$, find

(a) the value of y when $x = 6$,

(b) the value of x when $y = 4$.

9. When a substance has a mass of M grams and a volume of $V\text{cm}^3$, its density, $D\,\text{g/cm}^3$, is defined as $D = \frac{M}{V}$.

SCIENCE

(a) Represent this in a factor tree.

(b) Is it correct that $V = \frac{D}{M}$? Explain your answer.

(c) The density of a piece of bronze is $8\,\text{g/cm}^3$. Find the volume of the piece if its mass is 240 grams.

10. A car has an initial speed of u m/s. When it accelerates at a m/s^2 for t seconds its final speed, v m/s, is given by the formula

SCIENCE

$$v = u + at.$$

(a) Represent this with a bar model.

(b) Change the subject of the formula to a.

(c) Find the value of a when $t = 6$, $u = 11$ and $v = 29$.

REVIEW

Solving Equations Including Those with Unknowns on Both Sides

Use the balance method to solve equations by carrying out the same operations on the LHS and RHS.

For example,

$$3x - 5 = x + 1$$
$$3x - x - 5 = x - x + 1$$
$$2x - 5 = 1$$
$$2x - 5 + 5 = 1 + 5$$
$$2x = 6$$
$$\frac{2x}{2} = \frac{6}{2}$$
$$x = 3$$

You can check your solution is correct by substituting your answer back into the original equation.

Solving Equations Involving Brackets

When an equation has brackets, check to see if you can divide both sides by the number before the brackets to simplify the equation. If this does not work, expand the brackets and solve as normal.

For example,

$$5(2x) = 30$$
$$\frac{5(2x)}{5} = \frac{30}{5}$$

5 is a factor of 30.

$$2x = 6$$
$$x = 3$$

$$2(3x - 1) = 9$$
$$6x - 2 = 9$$
$$6x - 2 + 2 = 9 + 2$$
$$6x = 11$$
$$\frac{6x}{6} = \frac{11}{6}$$
$$x = 1\frac{5}{6}$$

Using and Rearranging Formulae

1. A formula is an equation connecting two or more variables. The variable that only appears as a single term on one side of the equation is called the subject of the formula.
2. The value of one variable can be found by substitution if the values of the other variables are known. For example,

   given the formula $y = 3x - 4$, when $x = 5$,

   $$y = 3(5) - 4 = 11.$$
3. The subject of a formula can be changed using algebraic manipulation. For example,

   make x the subject of the formula $y = 3x - 4$:

   $y = 3x - 4$ y is the subject.

   $y + 4 = 3x$

   $3x = y + 4$

   $x = \dfrac{y+4}{3}$ x is now the subject.

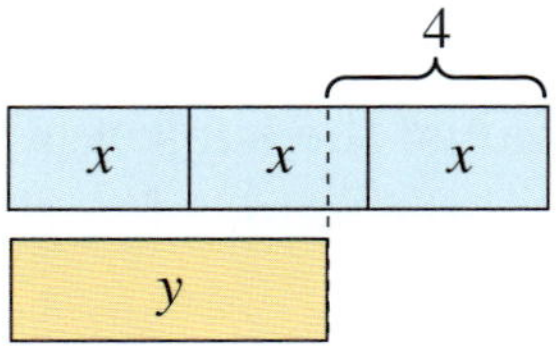

   make R the subject of the formula $V = IR$:

   $V = IR$ V is the subject.

   $IR = V$

   $R = \dfrac{V}{I}$ R is now the subject.

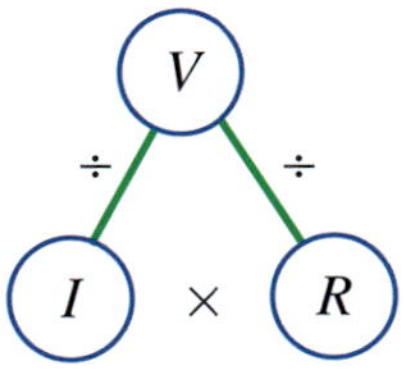

CHALLENGE 3

When an iron rod of length L cm is heated, its length will increase. The new length, y cm, is given by the formula

$$y = L(1 + kt),$$

where k is a constant (a value that does not change) and t °C is the temperature rise. Make k the subject of the formula.

REVISION EXERCISE 3

You may draw bar models, algebra discs or factor trees to help you with these questions.

1. Solve these equations.

(a) $x + 5 = 11$ **(b)** $x - 5 = 11$

(c) $3x + 5 = 11$ **(d)** $3x + 11 = 5$

2. Solve these equations.

(a) $2y - 7 = y + 5$ **(b)** $4y - 7 = y + 5$

(c) $4y + 7 = 2y - 5$ **(d)** $3y - 7 = 5 - y$

3. Solve these equations.

(a) $2(5p) = 20$ **(b)** $6(2q) = -24$

(c) $5(2a - 1) = 15$ **(d)** $4(3b + 1) = -20$

4. Which of these equations has a different solution from the others?

$3(2x - 1) = 15$ $4(2x - 1) = 20$

$4x = x + 9$ $4x - 1 = 6x + 5$

5. Find the pairs of formulae which are the same.
One of the formulae with y as the subject is missing. Can you work out what it is?

$x = 3y$ $y = x - 3$

$x = y + 3$ $y = 3x$

$x = \frac{3}{y}$ $y = 3 - x$

$x = y - 3$ $y = x + 3$

$x = 3 - y$ $y = \frac{x}{3}$

$x = \frac{y}{3}$

6. Make x the subject of each formula.

(a) $x + y = 50$ **(b)** $z = 3x + 5$

(c) $u = 1 - 2x$ **(d)** $v = \frac{x}{2} - 4$

(e) $p = Fx$ **(f)** $t = \frac{2r}{x}$

7. Given the formula $r = 4t - 7$, find

(a) the value of r when $t = 10$,

(b) the value of t when $r = 5$,

(c) the value of t when $r = -15$.

8. Given the formula $y = 5(2x + 3)$, find

(a) the value of y when $x = 4$,

(b) the value of x when $y = 35$,

(c) the value of x when $y = 15$.

9. The mass of a dog is 12 kg more than the mass of a cat. The total mass of the dog and the cat is 18 kg. Represent this with a bar model and find the mass of the cat.

10. John is three years older than his sister. The sum of their ages is 33 years. Represent this with a bar model and find John's age.

11. The charge, £C, for a job by a plumber is given by the formula $C = 30 + 25t$, where t is the number of hours of service.

FINANCE

(a) Represent this with a bar model.

(b) Make t the subject of the formula.

(c) If the charge for a job is £80, find the number of hours of service of the job.

12. The force of an object, F newtons, is written as

$$F = ma$$

SCIENCE

where m kilograms is the mass of the object and a m/s^2 is the acceleration.

(a) Draw a factor tree to show this formula.

(b) Make a the subject of the formula.

Write in Your Journal

What is the same and what is different about solving the equation $4x + 7 = 31$ and rearranging the formula $y = 4x + 7$ to make x the subject?

4 FUNCTIONS AND GRAPHS

WHAT IS IN THIS CHAPTER:

The seats in a cinema are arranged in a grid, the rows are labelled A, B, C, ... and each seat in a row is numbered. You can refer to each seat by its grid reference, for example B7 is the 7th seat in row B. Coordinates work in a similar way.

LET'S LEARN TO

- express coordinates using ordered pairs
- locate points on a Cartesian plane in two dimensions
- draw the graphs of linear functions given a table of values
- interpret and use linear graphs in practical situations
- identify and interpret the gradient of a graph
- recognise linear functions in the form of $y = mx + c$ and draw their graphs
- draw the graphs of quadratic functions given a table of values
- interpret real-life non-linear graphs

FLASHBACK

1. Lines

(a) A **plane** is a flat surface.

(b) Straight lines, or simply lines, can be drawn on a plane.

(c) *AB* and *DC* are **parallel lines** as they never meet. Parallel lines are indicated by arrows on the diagram.

(d) *BC* and *CD* are **perpendicular lines** as they intersect at right angles. This is denoted by $BC \perp CD$.

(e) The lines *AD* and *BC* are not parallel lines. They are also not perpendicular lines.

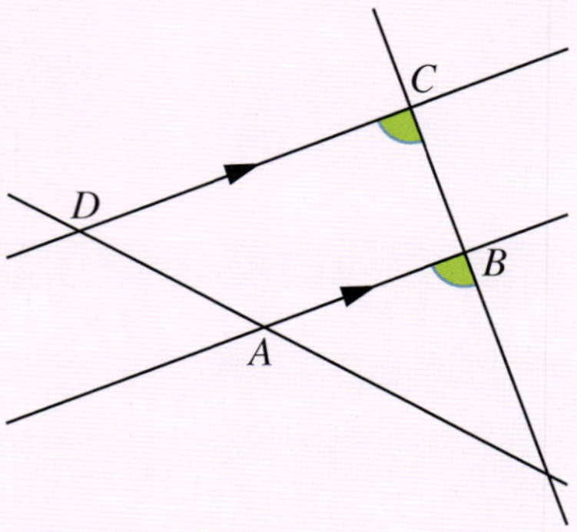

2. Number Lines

(a) A real number can be represented by a point on a number line. Consecutive integers are marked on a standard number line at equal intervals. The points *A*, *B* and *C* represent the numbers –3, 2 and 4.5 respectively.

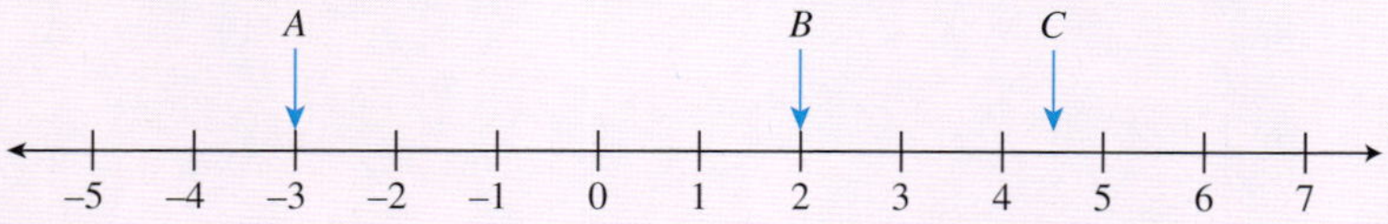

On a standard number line, negative numbers are written on the left and positive numbers on the right. Therefore:

(b) A number is less than any number to its right.
For example, –3 is less than –2, written as $-3 < -2$, because –2 is to the right of –3.

(c) A number is greater than any number to its left.
For example, –1 is greater than –5, written as $-1 > -5$, because –5 is to the left of –1.

3. Algebraic Expressions

(a) The expressions $2x + 3$ and $7 - 4x$ are examples of **linear algebraic expressions**. The power of the variable in each term is at most one.

(b) The expressions $x^2 - 2x$ and $-3x^2 + x - 4$ are examples of **quadratic algebraic expressions**. The highest power of the variable in any term is 2.

(c) When the value of x is given, the value of an expression can be found by substitution.
For example, when $x = 4$, $2x + 3 = 2(4) + 3 = 11$,
when $x = -3$, $x^2 - 2x = (-3)^2 - 2(-3) = 15$.

4. Formulae

(a) An equation connecting two or more variables is called a formula.
For example, let y be the total number of wheels that x bicycles have.
As each bicycle has two wheels, y is given by the formula $y = 2x$.

(b) The value of one variable in a formula can be found by substitution when the values of the other variables are known.
For example, when $x = 7$, $y = 2(7) = 14$,
so 7 bicycles have a total of 14 wheels.

4.1 Cartesian Coordinates in Two Dimensions

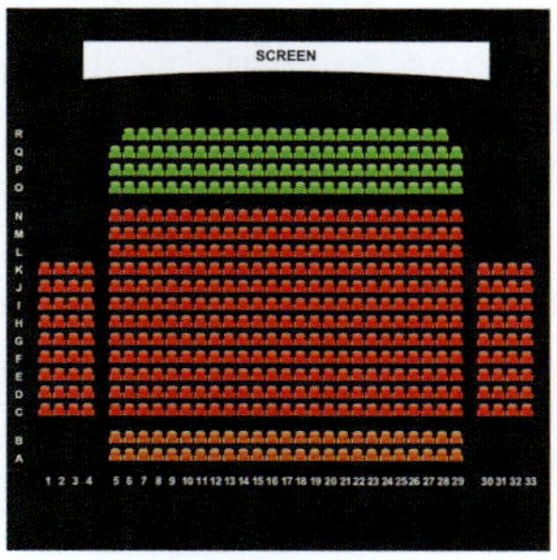

DISCUSS

What is the same and what is different about the coordinates of cinema seats and the ordered pairs?

How do you identify the chosen seat in a cinema ticket booking? You need to identify the row and the seat number, such as for example H8 or P17. In a similar way, you can describe the position of a point on a plane by using two numbers on a **Cartesian plane**.

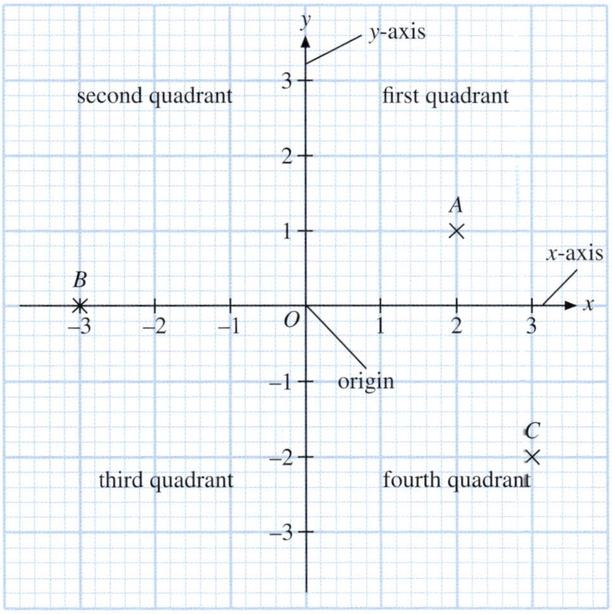

REMARK

René Descartes (1596 – 1650), a French mathematician, came up with the idea of the coordinate system when he wondered how to describe the position of a fly on the ceiling.

A Cartesian plane divides a plane into four **quadrants** by two perpendicular number lines intersecting at zero. The horizontal number line is called the ***x*-axis**. The vertical number line is called the ***y*-axis**. Their intersecting point is called the **origin**, denoted by the letter ***O***. We use **ordered pairs** to describe coordinates: the first number is the x-coordinate and the second number is the y-coordinate.

On this Cartesian plane, point A has coordinates (2, 1)
point B has coordinates (–3, 0)
point C has coordinates (3, –2)

REMARK

The four quadrants are called the **first**, **second**, **third** and **fourth quadrants**. They do not include any points on the x-axis or the y-axis.

RECALL

In Student Book 2A, you used coordinates in the 1st quadrant to plot scatter graphs.

CLASS ACTIVITY 1

Objective: To use ordered pairs on a Cartesian plane to play a game.

1. Draw your Cartesian plane. The values of x and y should both range from -2 to 2.

2. Place three counters on three points (with integer coordinates) on the grid. An example is shown. The counters are placed at (1, 2), (2, −1) and (0, −2).

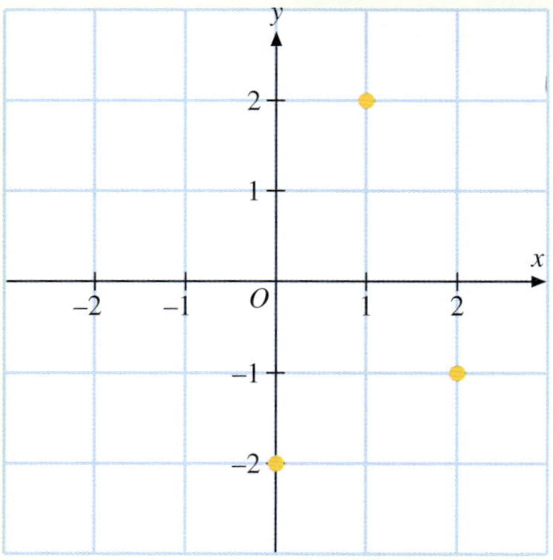

3. Imagine the counters are gold doubloons hidden on a treasure island. Your aim is to find all your partner's treasure before they find yours. Play the game with a classmate.

Keep track of all the calls					
Calls to opponent			Calls by opponent		
Coordinates	Found	Miss	Coordinates	Found	Miss
			(1, 2)	✓	

4. You and your classmate should take turns to call an ordered pair. If your classmate calls out an ordered pair where one of your counters is located, your classmate gets the counter. If not, it is a miss. For example, the call (2, 1) is a miss while the call (1, 2) is found. Remember the first coordinate is always the x-coordinate. You can use the given table to keep track of the calls. Copy it and add as many rows to the bottom as you need.

5. The first person who gets all three counters (gold doubloons) from the opponent is the winner.

Example 1

(a) State the coordinates of the points A and B on the Cartesian plane.

(b) State the quadrants in which A and B lie.

(c) Plot the points $C(2, 3)$, $D(0, 2)$, $E(-3, 0)$ and $F(-2, -3)$ on the plane.

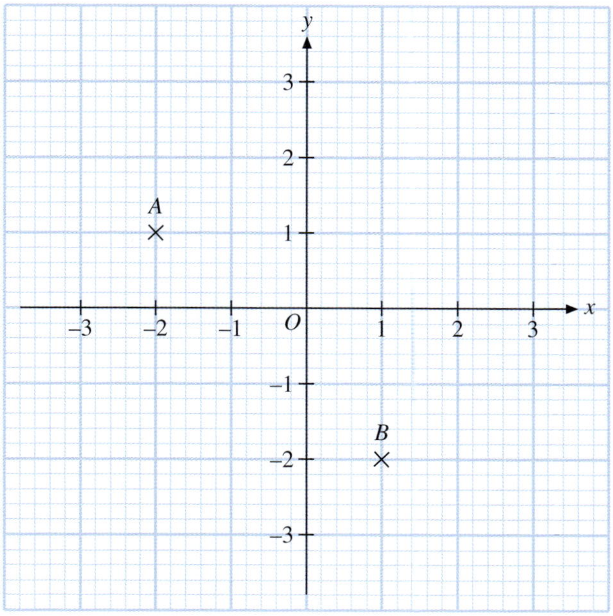

Solution

(a)

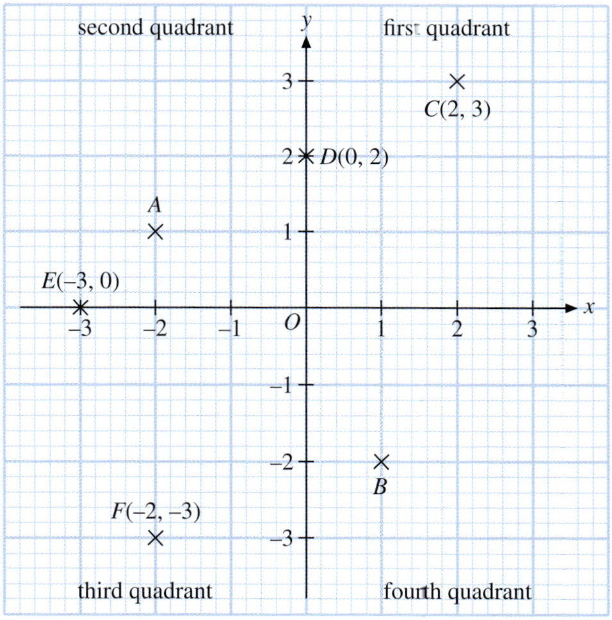

From the origin, count left 2 and up 1 to find A.
Therefore, the coordinates of A are $(-2, 1)$.
From the origin, count right 1 and down 2 to find B.
Therefore, the coordinates of B are $(1, -2)$.

(b) $A(-2, 1)$ lies in the second quadrant.

$B(1, -2)$ lies in the fourth quadrant.

(c) To plot the point $C(2, 3)$, you need to count right 2 and up 3.

DISCUSS

What is the same and what is different about the coordinates of points A and B?

DISCUSS

Which of the points is on the x-axis? Which of the points is on the y-axis?

How can you tell from their coordinates?

To plot the point $D(0, 2)$, you need to count up 2.
To plot the point $E(-3, 0)$, you need to count left 3.
To plot the point $F(-2, -3)$, you need to count left 2 and down 3.
The points are plotted on the diagram in part **(a)**.

Try It! 1

(a) State the coordinates of the points P and Q on the Cartesian plane.

(b) State the quadrants in which P and Q lie.

(c) Copy the plane and then plot the points $R(1, 3)$, $S(-2, 3)$, $T(0, -1)$ and $U(2, -2)$.

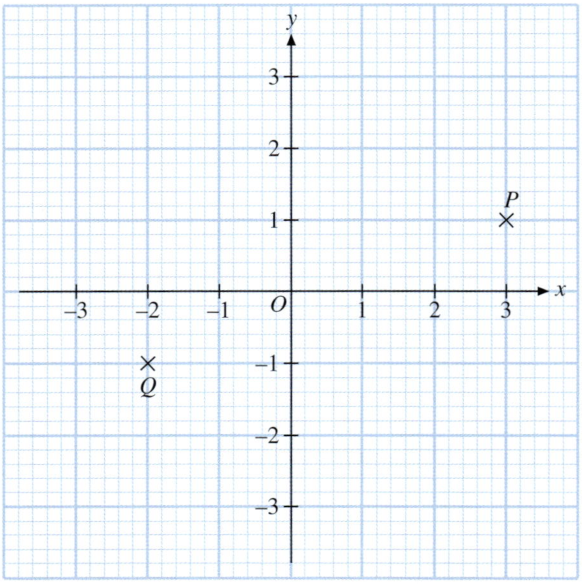

DISCUSS

Before you plot points, can you work out from their coordinates which quadrant they will be in?

Which of the points is not in any of the quadrants? How do you know?

Example 2

In the diagram, the points A, B and C are three vertices of a square. Mark a point D in the diagram to complete the square and write down the coordinates of D.

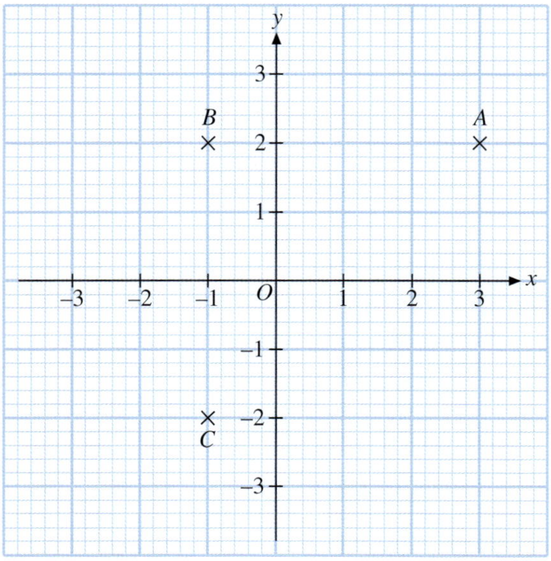

DISCUSS

What type of triangle is ABC? How do you know?

Solution The length of the square is 4 units. Hence, the length of CD should be 4 units. The coordinates of D are (3, –2)

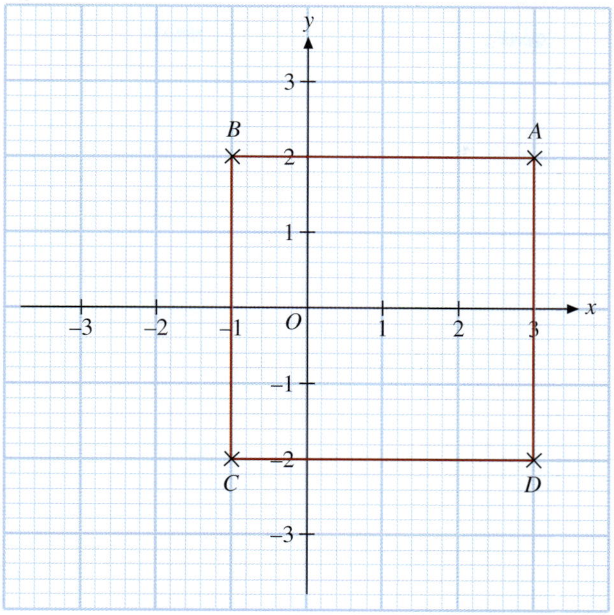

Try It! 2

In the diagram, the points A, B and C are three vertices of a parallelogram. Copy the diagram and mark a point D to complete the parallelogram. Write down the coordinates of D.

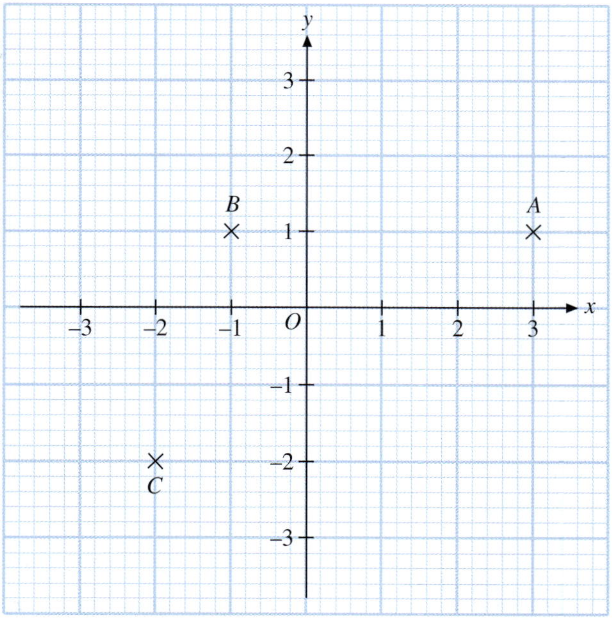

DISCUSS

Which quadrant is point D in?

DISCUSS

What could the coordinates of D be if $ABCD$ was a trapezium instead of a parallelogram?

Example 3

Three vertices of rectangle $ABCD$ are $A(4, 2)$, $B(-3, 2)$ and $C(-3, -1)$.

(a) Find the coordinates of D.

(b) Work out the area and the perimeter of the rectangle.

Solution

(a) Draw the rectangle. You can see that D must have coordinates $(4, -1)$.

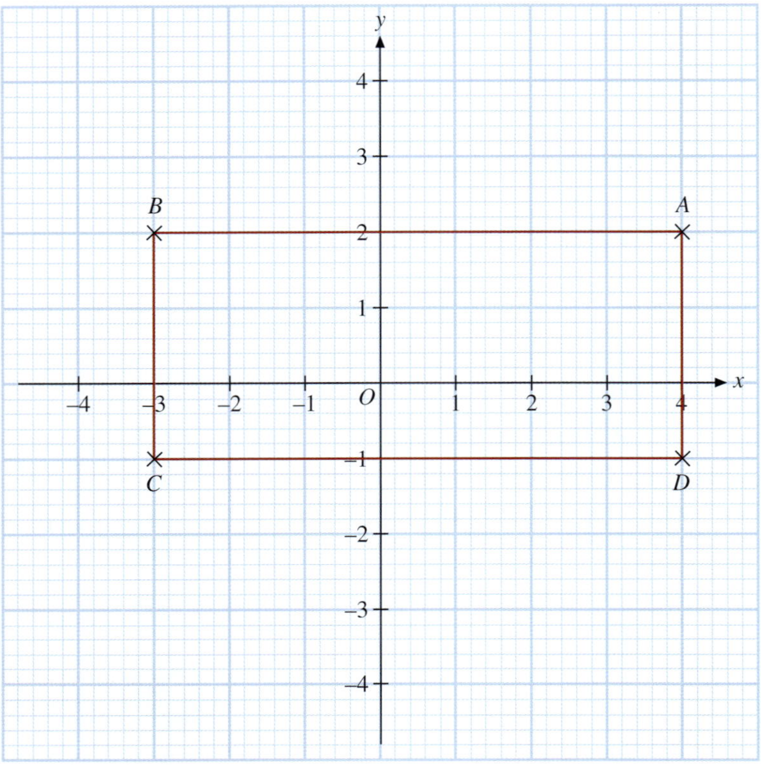

(b) Length of line segment $AB = 7$ units

Length of line segment BC = 3 units

Therefore,

Area of $ABCD = 7 \times 3 = 21$ square units

Perimeter of $ABCD = 2 \times (7 + 3)$

$= 20$ units

DISCUSS

Can you work out the coordinates of D by looking at the coordinates of A, B and C?

DISCUSS

If you have drawn the rectangle on a 1 cm grid, then what will the units of the perimeter and the area be?

Try It! 3

Three vertices of rectangle $ABCD$ are $A(3, 4)$, $B(-2, 4)$ and $C(-2, -3)$.

(a) Find the coordinates of D.

(b) Work out the area and the perimeter of the rectangle.

PRACTICE 4.1

LEVEL 1

1. **(a)** Write down the coordinates of the points A to G.

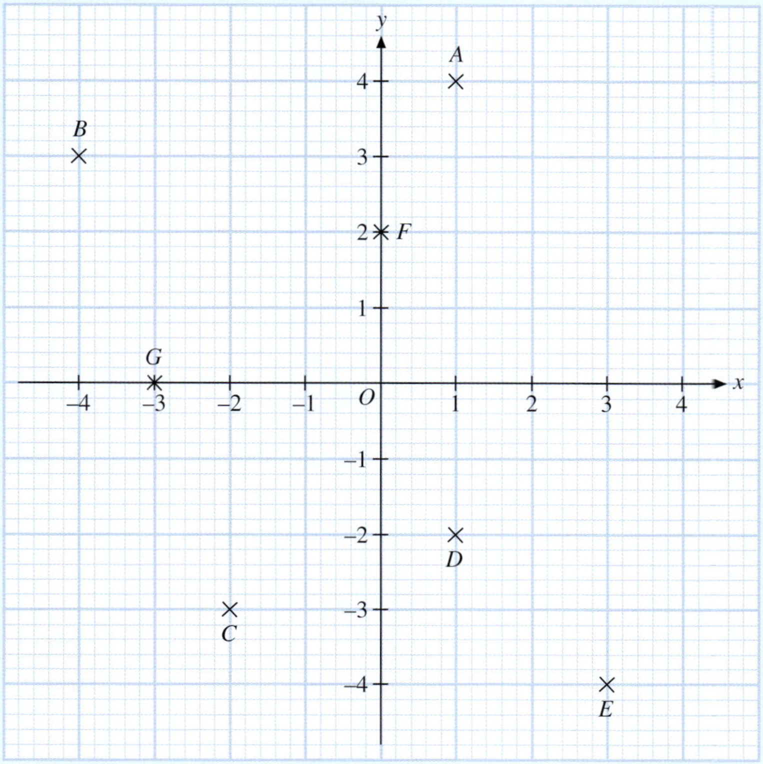

(b) Which point is

(i) in the 1st quadrant, **(ii)** in the 3rd quadrant,

(iii) on the x-axis, **(iv)** on the y-axis?

2. **(a)** Copy the Cartesian plane from **Question 1**. Plot and label these points on the plane.

$L(3, 0)$ $M(0, -3)$ $N(-3, 3)$ $P(3, -3)$

(b) In which quadrant is point

(i) N, **(ii)** P?

3. The point A has coordinates $(0, -7)$.

(a) Write down

(i) the x-coordinate of A, **(ii)** the y-coordinate of A.

(b) On which axis does the point A lie?

4. What is the same and what is different about these sets of points?

(a) $(5, -2)$, $(5, 0)$ and $(5, 8)$

(b) $(7, -4)$, $(0, -4)$ and $(4, -4)$

5. Which of these points might be the odd one out? Explain your answer.

$(-3, 7)$ $(-5, 2)$ $(-3, -4)$ $(-1, 3)$

LEVEL 2

6. A map of an island is shown on a Cartesian plane.

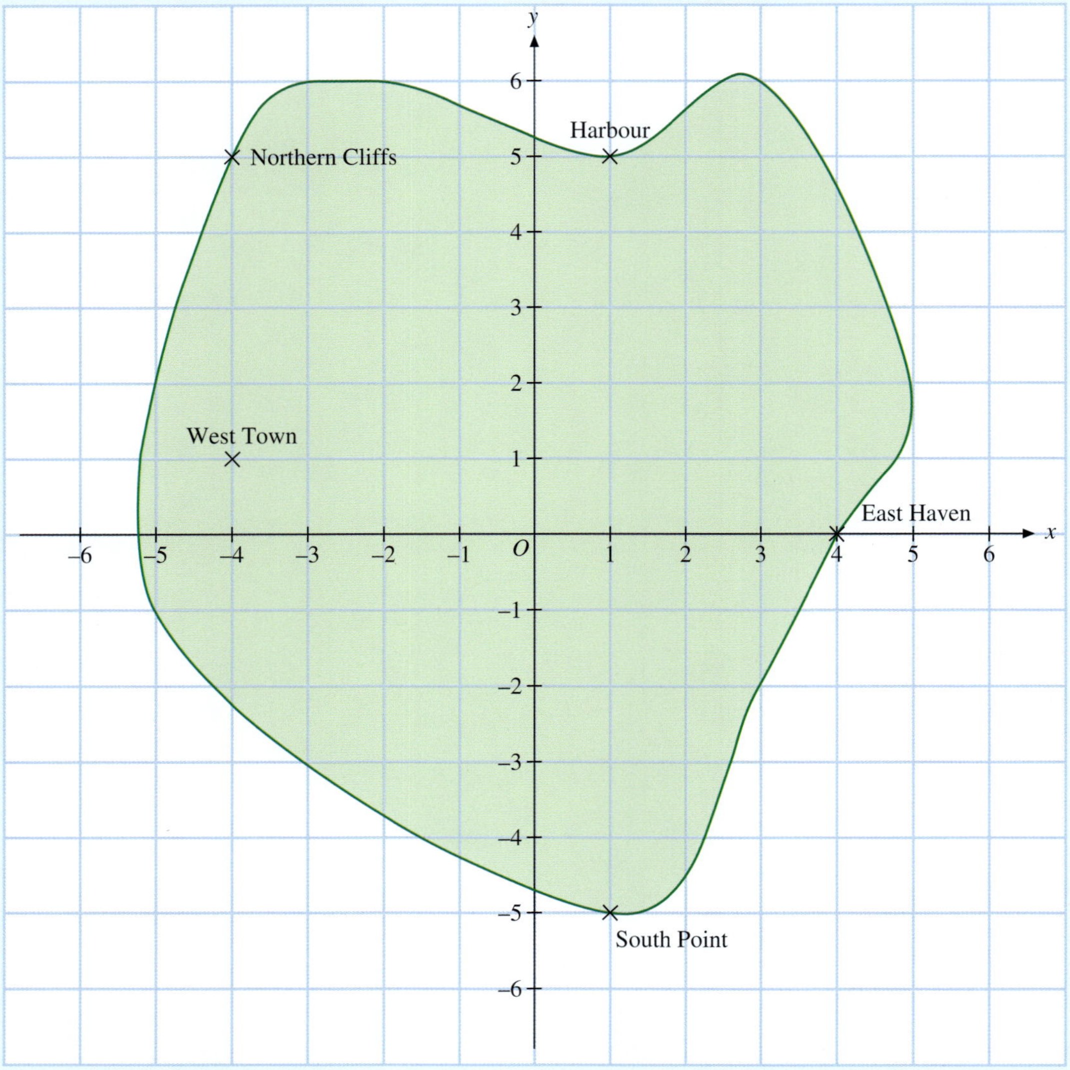

(a) Write down the coordinates of

(i) the Harbour, **(ii)** South Point.

(b) Name the places located at these coordinates.

(i) $(-4, 5)$ **(ii)** $(4, 0)$

(c) How many units apart are the Northern Cliffs and the Harbour?

There is a castle located 1 unit from West Town.

(d) Write down the coordinates for four possible locations of the castle.

7. The points $A(4, 3)$, $B(1, 3)$ and $C(-1, -2)$ are three vertices of the shape $ABCD$.

OPEN QUESTION

(a) If $ABCD$ is a parallelogram, write down the coordinates of D.

(b) Find another possible quadrilateral for $ABCD$. Write down the coordinates of D that would make this quadrilateral.

8. Three vertices of a rectangle $ABCD$ are $A(1, 4)$, $B(-4, 4)$ and $C(-4, -1)$. Find the coordinates of D and calculate the perimeter and area of the rectangle.

9. The points (3, 0) and (−3, 0) are two vertices of a square. Write down possible coordinates for the other two vertices.

OPEN QUESTION

4.2 Graphs of Linear Functions

A Idea of a Function

In real-life situations, two quantities may have a relationship between them. For instance, the price for a group of people to buy rail tickets will change according to the size of the group.

A **function machine** takes an input, applies a rule to it, then produces an output. For example, the rule could be 'add four' or 'subtract three' or 'multiply by two'.

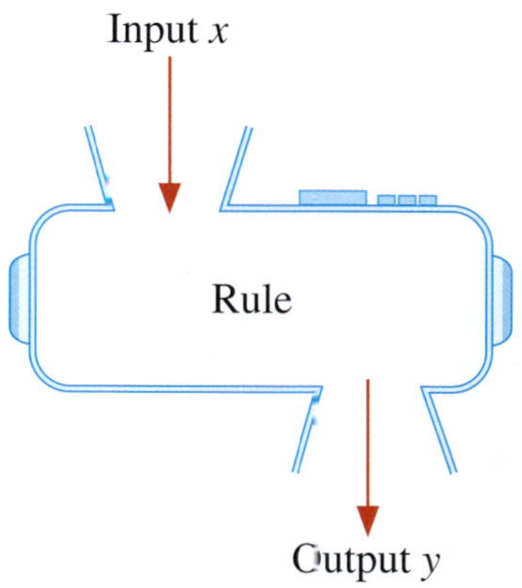

DISCUSS

Can you think of some different possible rules for the function machine?

CLASS ACTIVITY 2

Objective: To use a function machine to understand the concept of a function.

1. The rule for this function machine is 'add 4'.

If you input 5 into the machine, then

Output = 5 + 4

= 9

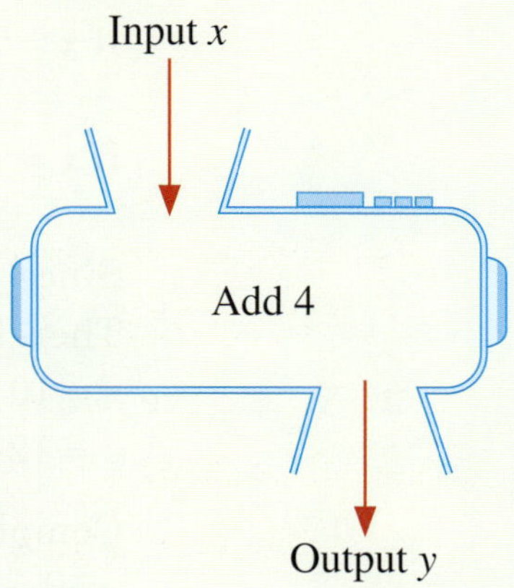

(a) Choose some more input values and write down their corresponding output values in a copy of the table.

Input, x	5			
Output, y	9			

(b) How many different values of the output, y, correspond to each value of the input, x?

2. (a) Make up three more different function machines.

(b) For each function machine, create a table like the one in **Question 1**, and fill it in to show four input values and their corresponding output values.

(c) Swap tables with a classmate and see if you can work out what the rule is for each of their function machines.

For the function machine given in Class Activity 2, you can see that there is exactly one value of the output, y, that corresponds to every value of the input, x. Therefore, y is said be a **function** of x:

> A variable y is a function of another variable x if each value of x corresponds to exactly one value of y.

The function from Class Activity 2 can be represented by

- a statement: 'y is 4 more than x',
- a table with corresponding values of x and y,
- the equation $y = x + 4$.

DISCUSS

The wage, y, earned by Oliver corresponds to the number of hours worked, x, multiplied by his hourly wage, £15. This is a real-life function. Can you write this function as an equation? Can you think of other real-life examples?

Example 4

A function y of x is given by the statement: 'y is two less than x'.

(a) Represent the function using an equation.

(b) Complete the table to show the corresponding values of x and y.

x	2	5	7	
y				10

Solution

(a) The equation is $y = x - 2$

(b) The value of y is two less than the value of x, so

If $x = 2$, $y = 2 - 2$
$= 0$

If $x = 5$, $y = 5 - 2$
$= 3$

If $x = 7$, $y = 7 - 2$
$= 5$

Since y is two less than x, x is two more than y.

Therefore, if $y = 10$,

$x = 10 + 2$
$= 12$

Complete the table:

x	2	5	7	12
y	0	3	5	10

RECALL

The equation $y = x - 2$ could also be called a formula.

DISCUSS

Can you rearrange $y = x - 2$ to make x the subject? How could this have helped you to fill in the table?

DISCUSS

Can you think of a real-life situation that could be represented by this function?

Try It! 4

A function y of x is given by the statement: 'y is three more than x'.

(a) Represent the function as an equation.

(b) Copy and complete the table to show the corresponding values of x and y.

x	1	4	8	
y				16

REMARK

Try rearranging the equation to make x the subject.

Example 5

The cost of a rail ticket is £25. Let £y be the total cost of buying x rail tickets.

(a) Write an equation that represents the relationship between x and y.

(b) Complete the table to show the corresponding values of x and y.

x	1	2	3	4	5
y					

Solution

(a) To find the total cost, y, you multiply the number of tickets, x, by 25.
Therefore, the equation is $y = 25x$.

(b) x is the number of rail tickets.
Cost of 1 rail ticket = £25
Cost of 2 rail tickets = 2 × 25
= £50
Cost of 3 rail tickets = 3 × 25
= £75
And so on.
Complete the table:

x	1	2	3	4	5
y	25	50	75	100	125

DISCUSS

Can you rearrange $y = 25x$ to make x the subject? Why might it be useful to do this? Can you give an example of how you could use the rearranged equation?

Try It! 5

The cost of a coach ticket is £10. Let £y be the total cost of buying x coach tickets.

(a) Write an equation that represents the relationship between x and y.

(b) Copy and complete the table to show the corresponding values of x and y.

x	1	2	3	4	5
y					

B Graphs of Linear Functions

A function can also be represented by its graph. You can draw the **graph of a function** by plotting the corresponding values of x and y onto a Cartesian plane.

CLASS ACTIVITY 3

Objective: To investigate how a linear function relates to its graph.

1. All students in your class need to be seated in chairs arranged in rows and columns that resemble a grid, for example, 5 rows by 5 columns.
2. Choose a student in the middle to represent the origin (0, 0).
3. Write down the coordinates you represent on a mini whiteboard or piece of paper, then hold it up for everyone to see.
4. Your teacher calls out linear functions as statements and if your coordinates satisfy the function, stand up.

   For example, if the function is 'x is double y' then all students whose x-coordinate is double their y-coordinate will stand up: (–4, –2), (–2, –1), (0, 0), (2, 1), (4, 2).
5. Your teacher will then call out some linear functions as equations and if your coordinates satisfy the function, stand up. For example, if the function is $y = x + 1$ then all the students whose y-coordinate is one more than their x-coordinate will stand up, for example, (–3, –2), (–2, –1), (–1, 0), (0, 1), (1, 2), (2, 3).
6. **(a)** Choose one of the linear functions your teacher called out in part **5** (or make up your own).

   (b) Write down the coordinates of three points that satisfy the function.

   (c) Draw a Cartesian plane with a scale of 1 cm to 1 unit on both axes. Both axes should run from –5 to 5. Plot your points on the plane.

   (d) Join the points using a ruler.

DISCUSS

Which students are on the x-axis?
Which students are on the y-axis?

DISCUSS

What do you notice about the students standing up each time?

REMARK

You can use substitution to check if your point satisfies the function.

RECALL

Expressions like $x + 3$ and $9 - 2x$ are called linear expressions.

In Class Activity 3, the functions connecting x and y were all **linear functions**. As you saw, all the points that satisfy a linear function lie on a straight line:

> A linear function y of x is a function of the form
> $$y = mx + c,$$
> where m and c are constants.

Let us see some more examples of linear functions and their graphs.

Example 6 Draw the graph of the function $y = x + 3$ for $-2 \le x \le 2$.

Solution First set up a table of values of x and y.

x	-2	-1	0	1	2
y	1	2	3	4	5

Draw the x-axis from -2 to 2 and the y-axis to cover the data.
Plot the points (x, y) from the table of values and join them with a straight line.

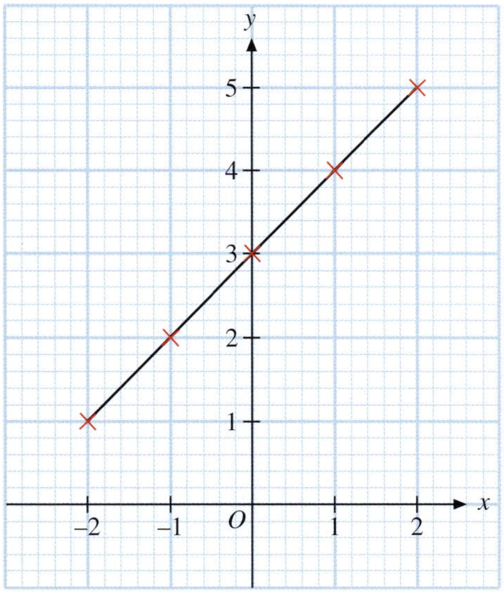

Try It! 6 Draw the graph of the function $y = x - 1$ for $-2 \le x \le 2$.

REMARK

A constant is a number. Its value does not change. For example, in the linear function $y = 2x + 1$, $m = 2$ and $c = 1$.

DISCUSS

Which of these are linear?

$y = 2x$ $\quad y = \frac{1}{2}x$

$y = x + 2$ $\quad y = x^2 - 2$

$y = x^2$ $\quad y = 2x - 2$

Explain your answers. How could you describe the non-linear examples?

RECALL

$-2 \le x \le 2$ means x is bigger than or equal to -2 and less than or equal to 2, so you use the values $-2, -1, 0, 1, 2$ in the table.

REMARK

When $x = -2$,
$y = x + 3$
$= (-2) + 3$
$= 1$
The other values of y in the table are worked out in this way.

DISCUSS

How do you decide what number the y-axis should go up to?

DISCUSS

As two points determine a straight line, can you just find the coordinates of two points to draw the linear graph? Is it a good idea?

Example 7

Draw the graph of the function $y = 2x - 1$ for $-1 \le x \le 3$.

Solution

First set up a table of values of x and y.

x	-1	0	1	2	3
y	-3	-1	1	3	5

Draw the x-axis from -1 to 3 and the y-axis to cover the data.

Plot the points (x, y) from the table and join them with a straight line.

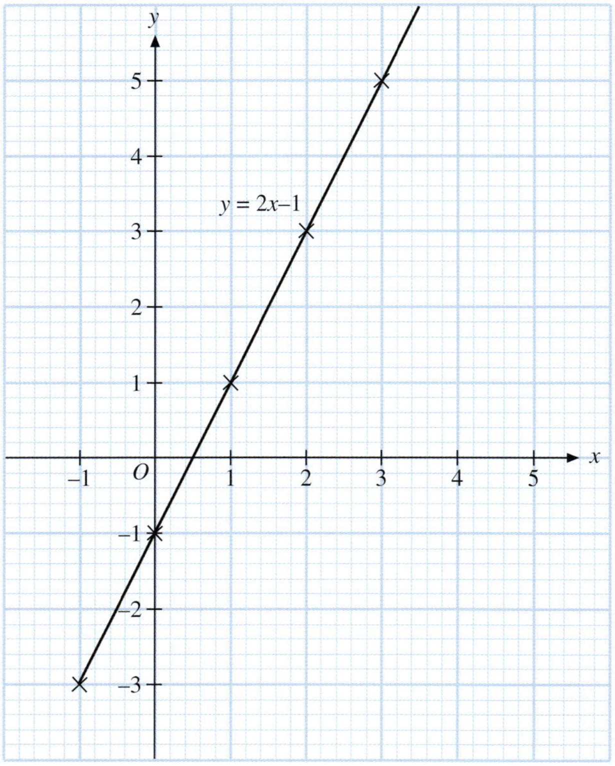

REMARK

When $x = -1$,

$y = 2x - 1$

$= 2(-1) - 1$

$= -3.$

The other values of y in the table are worked out in this way.

DISCUSS

What values of x could you use in your table of values? How many values should you use?

Try It! 7

Draw the graph of the function $y = 3x - 1$ for $-1 \le x \le 3$.

Example 8

A money box has £1 in it. £3 is put into the box each day. Let £y be the amount in the box at the end of x days. The table shows some corresponding values of x and y.

x	0	1	2	3	4
y	1	4	7	10	13

(a) Plot the points (x, y) on a Cartesian plane.

(b) What can you say about the plotted points?

DISCUSS

How were the values in the table worked out? Can you work out the value of y when $x = 5$?

Solution **(a)** The diagram shows the plotted points (x, y) from the table.

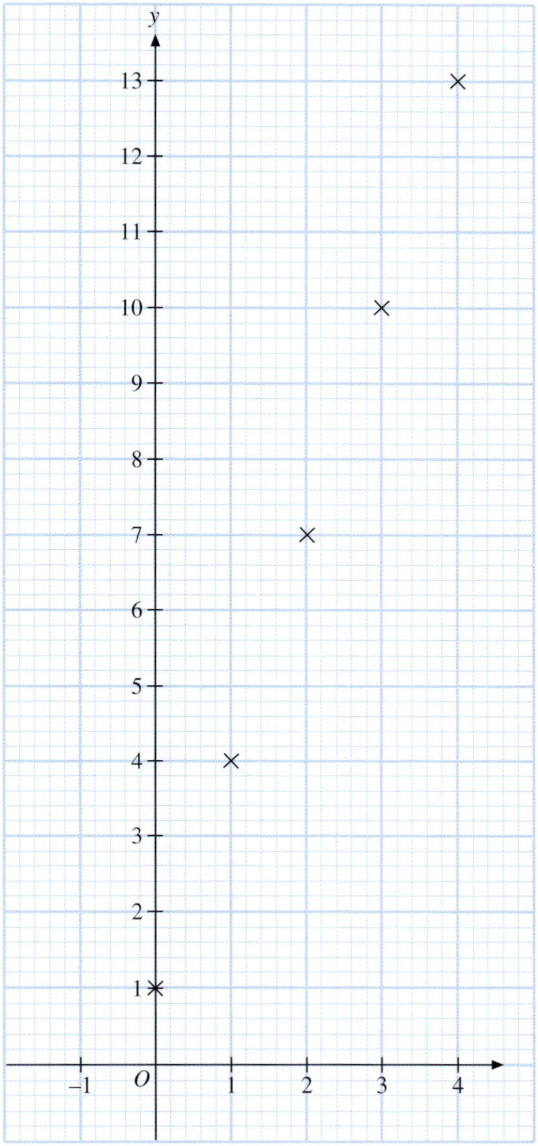

(b) The plotted points lie on a straight line.

REMARK

The scale on the y-axis needs to go up to at least 13 because that is the biggest value for y in the table.

DISCUSS

Ffion claims that if you join up the points, the equation of the line will be $y = 3x + 1$.
Is she correct? How could you check?

Try It! 8

A taxi driver charges £3 per ride plus £2 per km travelled. Let £y be the amount charged for travelling x km. The table shows some corresponding values of x and y.

x	0	1	2	3	4
y	3	5	7	9	11

(a) Plot the points (x, y) on a Cartesian plane.
(b) What can you say about the plotted points?

DISCUSS

John claims that if you join up the points, the equation of the line will be $y = 2x + 3$.
Is he correct? How could you check?

Example 9

The depth of water in a tank is 10 cm. Water is draining from the tank. Let y cm be the depth of water after t minutes. The table shows some corresponding values of t and y.

t	0	1	2	3	4	5
y	10	9	8	7	6	5

(a) Plot the points (t, y) on a Cartesian plane.

(b) Which of these equations connect t and y? Explain your answer.

$y = 10 + t$ $\quad$ $y = 10 - t$

DISCUSS

How much water is draining from the tank each minute?

REMARK

The horizontal axis is the t-axis in Example 9, because the variable is t.

Solution

(a) The points are plotted on the plane.

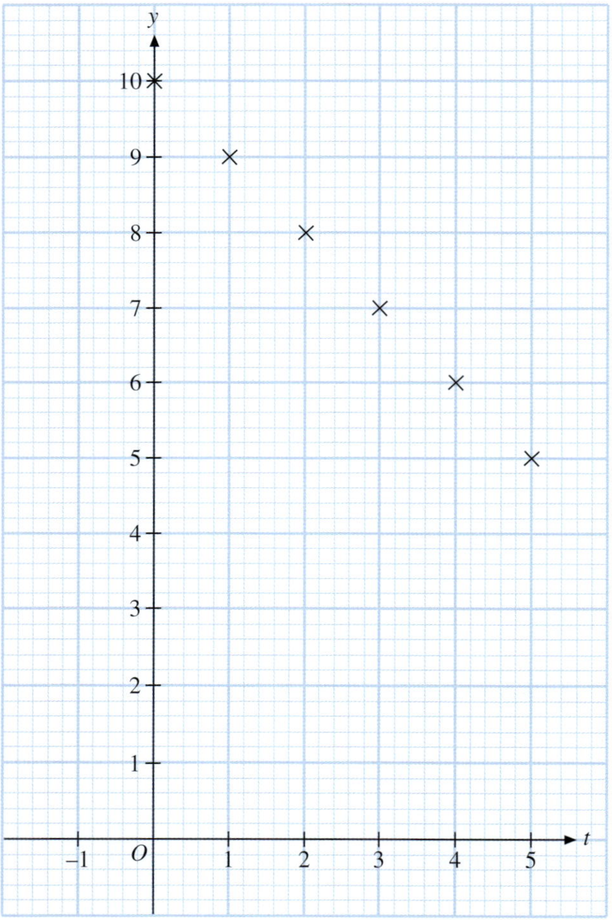

(b) Substitute into the equation $y = 10 + t$:

When $t = 0, y = 10 + 0$
$= 10$

However, when $t = 1, y = 10 + 1$
$= 11$

REMARK

Since two points determine a straight line you only need to substitute two values of t to confirm if the equation is correct.

Therefore, t and y are not connected by the equation $y = 10 + t$.
Substituting into the equation $y = 10 - t$:
When $t = 0$, $y = 10 - 0$
$= 10$
When $t = 1$, $y = 10 - 1$
$= 9$
When $t = 2$, $y = 10 - 2$
$= 8$
These match the corresponding values of y in the table.
Therefore, t and y are connected by the equation $y = 10 - t$.

DISCUSS

What would the depth of water be after
(a) 6 minutes,
(b) 8 minutes?

Try It! 9

Jake works in a nursery. There are 7 litres of milk in the fridge. The children drink milk during the day. Let y litres be the amount of milk remaining after t hours. The table shows some corresponding values of t and y.

t	0	1	2	3	4
y	7	6	5	4	3

(a) Plot the points (t, y) on a Cartesian plane.

(b) Which of these equations connect t and y? Explain your answer.
$y = 7 + t$ $\quad$ $y = 7 - t$

DISCUSS

After how many hours will the milk run out?

Example 10

The charge £y of a plumber for a job which took t hours to complete is given by $y = 20t + 30$.
(a) Using a scale of your choice, draw the graph of $y = 20t + 30$ from $t = 0$ to $t = 4$.
(b) Use the graph to find the time taken to complete the job where the charge for a job was £80.

Solution

(a)

t	0	1	2	3	4
y	30	50	70	90	110

The graph of $y = 20t + 30$ is shown, using a scale of 2 cm to 1 unit on the t-axis and 1 cm to 20 units on the y-axis.

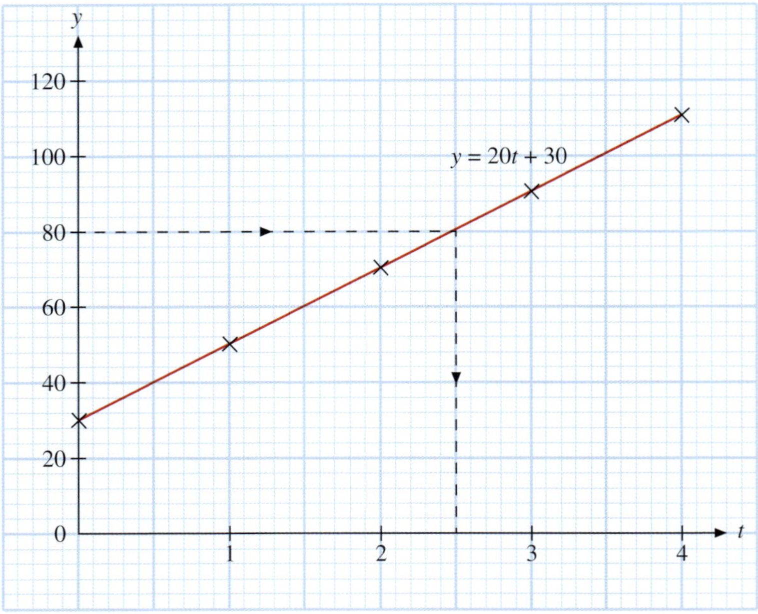

(b) Draw the horizontal line $y = 80$ to meet the graph and then drop a perpendicular line from the point of intersection with the graph to the t-axis. The value of t where the perpendicular meets the t-axis is the required value.

$\therefore$ the time taken to complete the job was 2.5 hours.

Try It! 10

The price £p for booking a function room for x guests is given by $p = 500 + 50x$.

(a) Using a scale of your choice, draw the graph of $p = 500 + 50x$ from $x = 0$ to $x = 50$.

(b) Use the graph to find the number of guests when the price is £2250.

REMARK

Draw a table of values, using these values of x: 0, 10, 20, 30, 40, 50. Then look at the values and work out a sensible scale that covers all the values.

Example 11

Draw the graph of the linear function $y = -2$ for $-3 \le x \le 3$.

Solution

Form a table of values of x and y.

x	−3	−2	−1	0	1	2	3
y	−2	−2	−2	−2	−2	−2	−2

For any value of x, y is always equal to −2.
The graph of $y = -2$ is as shown.

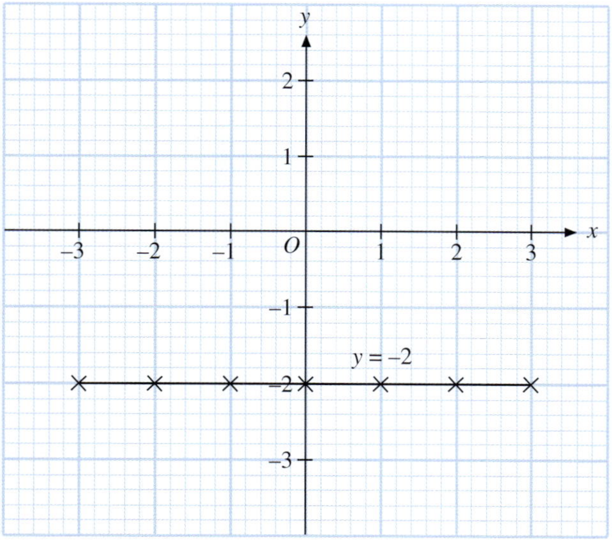

Note: In general, the function $y = c$, where c is a constant, is called a constant function. Its graph is a horizontal line cutting the y-axis at $y = c$.

Try It! 11 Draw the graph of the linear function $y = 1$ for $-3 \leq x \leq 3$.

Example 12 Draw the graph of $x = -2$.

Solution

You do not need to draw a table of values because x can only be –2.

Instead, write down some points with an x-coordinate of –2:

(–2, –4), (–2, –3), (–2, –2), (–2, –1), (–2, 0), (–2, 1), (–2, 2) (–2, 3), (–2, 4)

The graph of $x = -2$ is as shown.

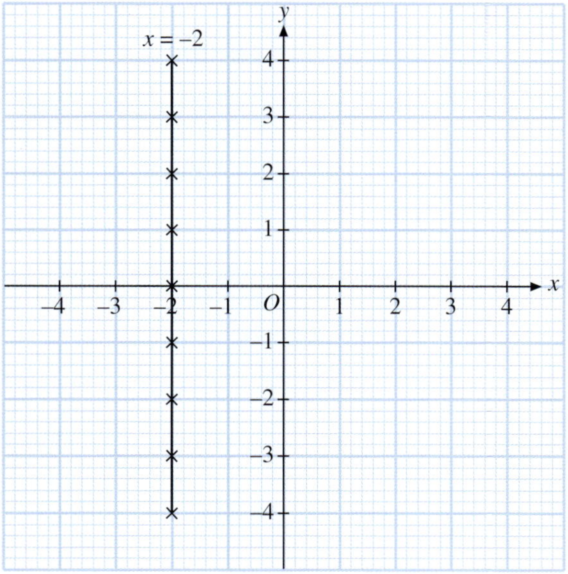

RECALL

Two lines on a plane that never meet are called **parallel** lines.

The line representing $y = -2$ is parallel to the x-axis.

DISCUSS

What is the relationship between the graphs of $y = -2$ and $y = 1$?

DISCUSS

Is $x = -2$ a function of x?

Remember, a variable y is a function of another variable x if each value of x corresponds to exactly one value of y.

DISCUSS

What is the same and what is different about the graphs of $y = -2$ and $x = -2$?

Note: In general, the graph of $x = c$, where c is a constant, is a vertical line cutting the x-axis at $x = c$.

Try It! 12 Draw the graph of $x = 1$.

DISCUSS

What is the same and what is different about the graphs of $y = 1$ and $x = 1$? What is the relationship between the graphs of $x = -2$ and $x = 1$?

PRACTICE 4.2

LEVEL 1

1. Match up the functions expressed as a statement with those represented by an equation. One of the equations is missing. Write down the missing equation.

'y is 5 more than x'	$y = x - 5$
'y is 5 less than x'	$y = 5x$
'y is 5 times x'	$y = 5 - x$
'y is x less than 5'	

2. Here are some functions:
   (a) $y = x$ **(b)** $y = 2x$
   (c) $y = x - 2$ **(d)** $y = x + 2$

   For each of these functions
   (i) copy and complete the table of values,

x	−3	−2	−1	0	1	2	3
y							

   (ii) draw the graphs, using the scale of 1 cm to 1 unit on both axes.

3. **(a)** Draw a Cartesian plane with $-4 \le x \le 4$ and $-4 \le y \le 4$, using the scale of 1 cm to 1 unit on both axes. On the plane draw the graphs of $x = 3$, $x = -3$, $y = 3$ and $y = -3$.
   (b) From your graph, write down the equation of
   (i) a horizontal line, **(ii)** a vertical line,
   (iii) a pair of parallel lines.

4. **(a)** Draw the graphs of the functions $y = 2$ and $y = -1$ for $-3 \le x \le 3$ on the same diagram, using the scale of 1 cm to 1 unit on both axes.
   (b) What is the relationship between the two graphs?

5. The table shows values of x and y for the function $y = 2x + 3$.

x	0	2	4	6
y	3		11	

(a) Fill in the missing values of y.

(b) Write down the ordered pairs of the function from the table.

(c) Plot the ordered pairs on a Cartesian plane with $0 \le x \le 6$ and $0 \le y \le 13$. Use a scale of 1 cm to 1 unit on both axes.

LEVEL 2

6. Draw the graphs of these functions for $-3 \le x \le 3$.

(a) $y = 3x + 1$ **(b)** $y = 4x + 1$

(c) $y = 3x - 2$ **(d)** $y = 4x - 2$

Hint: Start by drawing a table of values for each function.

7. The table shows the values of x and y for a function.

x	−2	−1	0	1	2
y	−4	−1	2	5	8

(a) Which of these functions could be the function for the table?

$y = 3x$ $y = 3x + 2$ $y = x + 2$ $y = 3x - 2$

(b) Draw the graph of the function using the scale of 1 cm to 1 unit for both axes.

(c) Is the point $A(3, 10)$ on the graph? Explain your answer.

8. The hourly wage, £y, of an electrician is four times the hourly wage, £x, of his apprentice.

£ FINANCE

(a) Write down the equation of the function connecting x and y.

(b) Draw the graph of the function for $0 \le x \le 10$ using the scale of 1 cm to 1 unit on the x-axis and 1 cm to 5 units on the y-axis.

9. A loaf of bread contains 16 slices. Three slices are eaten each day. Let y be the number of slices left at the end of x days. The table shows some corresponding values of x and y.

x	0	1	2	3	4	5
y	16	13	10	7	4	1

(a) Plot the points (x, y) on a coordinate plane.

(b) Josie claims that if you join up the points, the equation of the line will be $y = 16 - 3x$. Is she correct? Explain your answer.

10. The speed, y m/s, of a car at time t seconds after applying the brake is given by the function $y = 20 - 4t$, where $0 \le t \le 5$.

SCIENCE

(a) Draw the graph of the function using the scale of 1 cm for 1 unit on the t-axis and 1 cm for 5 units on the y-axis.

(b) Using the graph, find the time when the speed of the car is 6 m/s.

4.3 Gradients and Intercepts of Linear Functions

A Gradients

On some steep roads, there are road signs to indicate the steepness of the roads. In mathematics, the **gradient** is a measure of the steepness of a slope:

$$\text{Gradient} = \frac{\text{vertical change}}{\text{horizontal change}}.$$

Using this definition, the gradients of four slopes are shown.

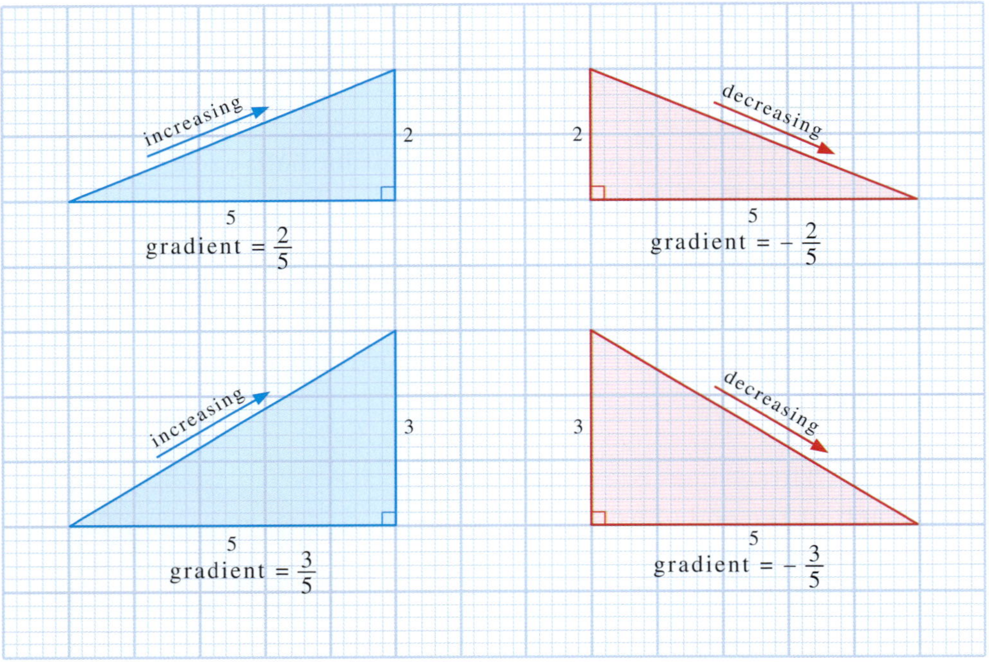

For the two blue slopes, y increases as x increases. The gradient is said to be positive. For the two red slopes, y decreases as x increases. The gradient is said to be negative.

CLASS ACTIVITY 4

Objective: To find the gradients of some slopes.

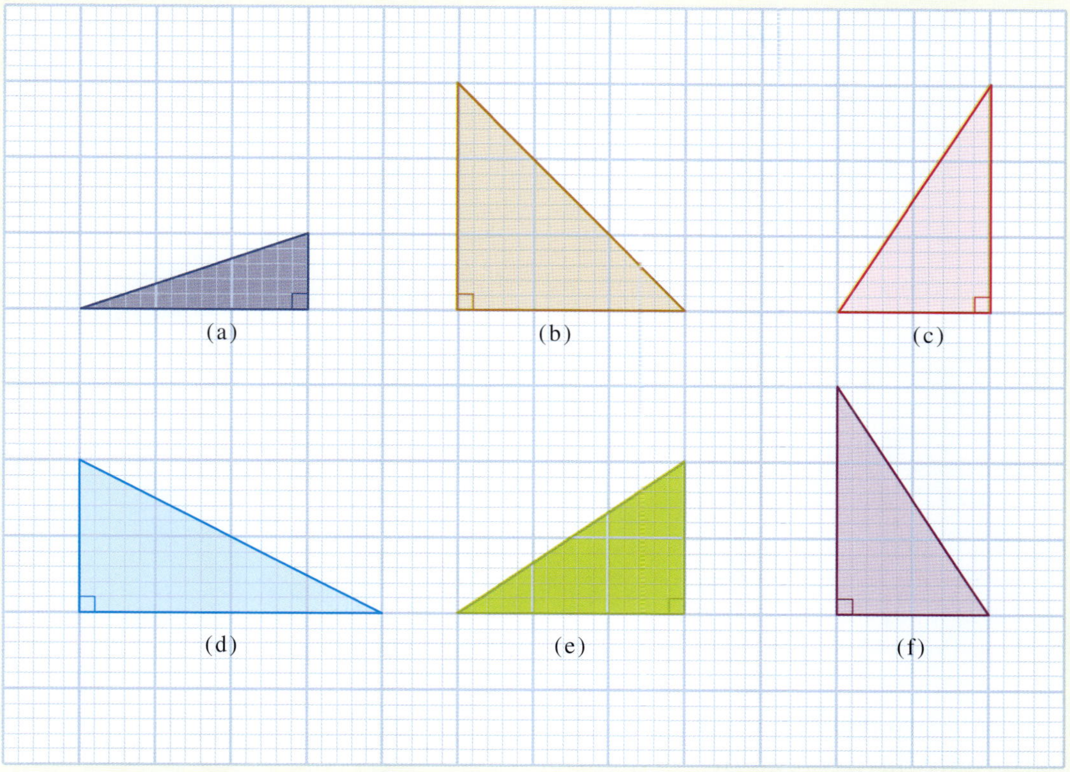

1. Find the gradient of each slope.
2. Look at the slopes with positive gradients. Which one is the steepest? What do you notice about the gradient of the steepest slope?
3. Look at the slopes with negative gradients. Which one is the steepest? What do you notice about the gradient of the steepest slope?
4. Draw slopes with these gradients.

   (a) 1 **(b)** $\frac{1}{2}$ **(c)** -2

From Class Activity 4, you see that steeper lines have a greater gradient when the gradients are positive. To find the gradient of a line in a Cartesian plane, choose two points on the line with integer coordinates and use them as vertices of your right-angled triangle.

Example 13

Find the gradient of the line L in the diagram.

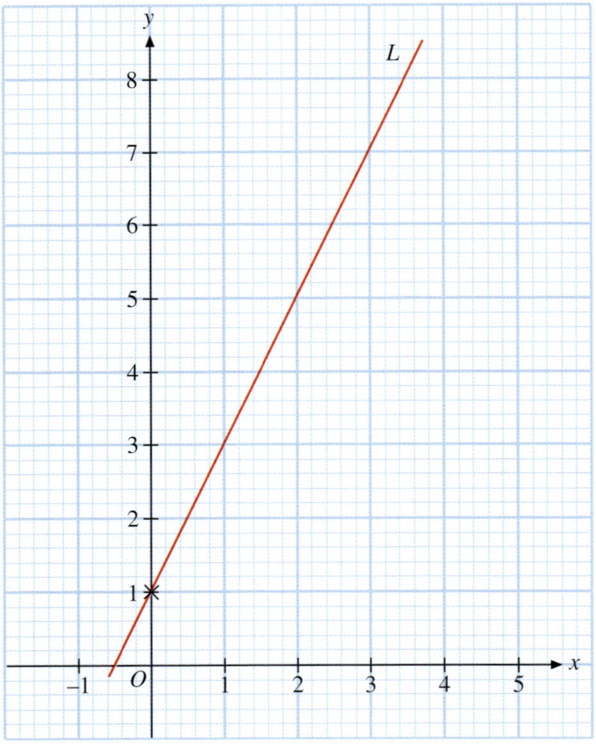

Solution

Locate two points with integer coordinates on the line.
Here we have chosen $A(1, 3)$ and $B(3, 7)$.
Draw a right-angled triangle ABC to find the vertical change and the horizontal change.

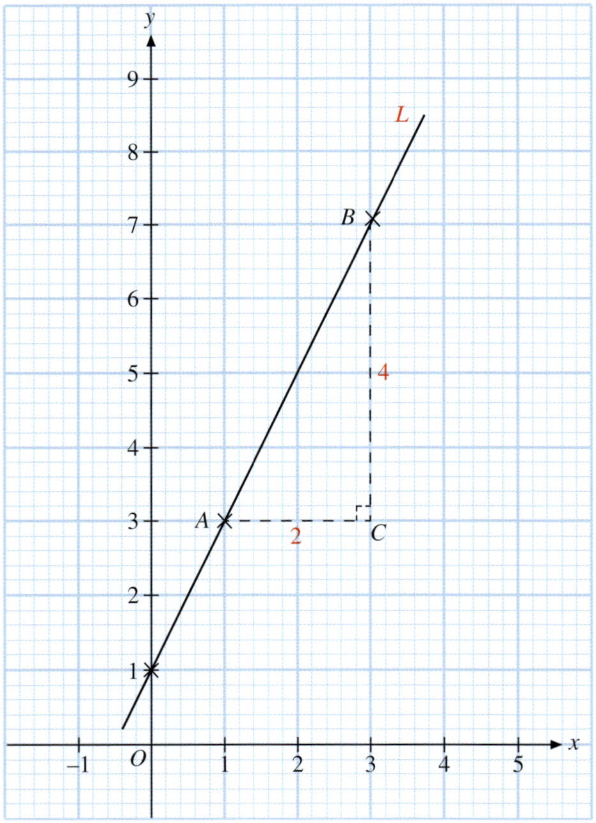

DISCUSS

Can you choose different points to find the gradient of the line L?

$$\text{Gradient of the line } L = \frac{\text{vertical change}}{\text{horizontal change}}$$
$$= \frac{4}{2}$$
$$= 2$$

DISCUSS

How do you know that the gradient is 2 not −2?

Try It! 13

Find the gradient of the line L in the diagram.

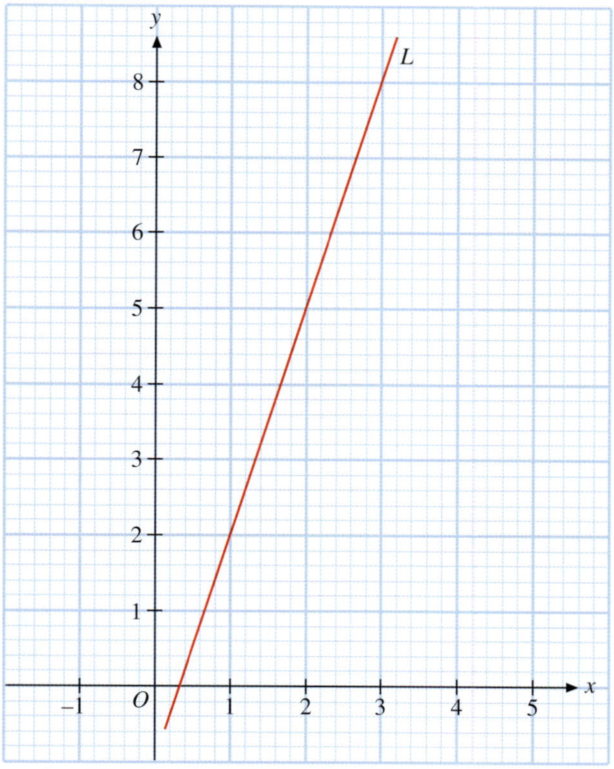

Example 14

Find the gradient of the line L in the diagram.

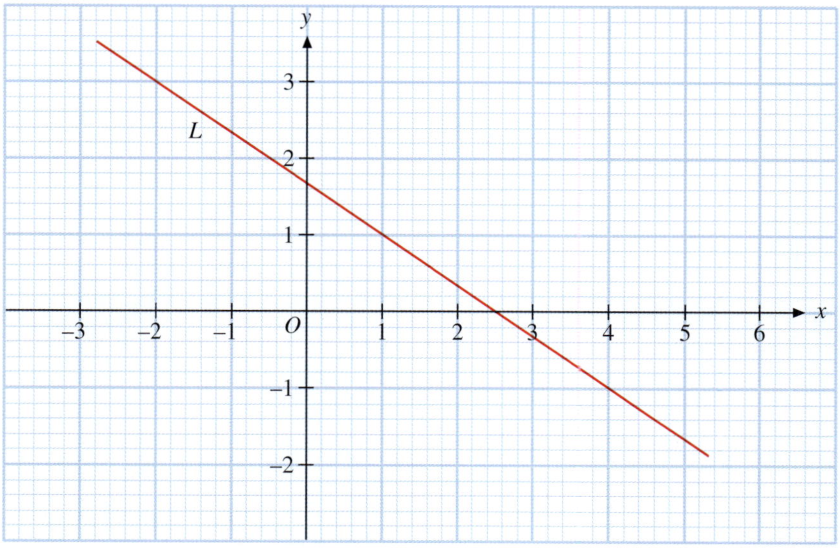

Solution Locate two points with integer coordinates on the line. Here we have chosen $A(1, 1)$ and $B(4, -1)$.
Draw a right-angled triangle ABC to find the vertical change and the horizontal change.

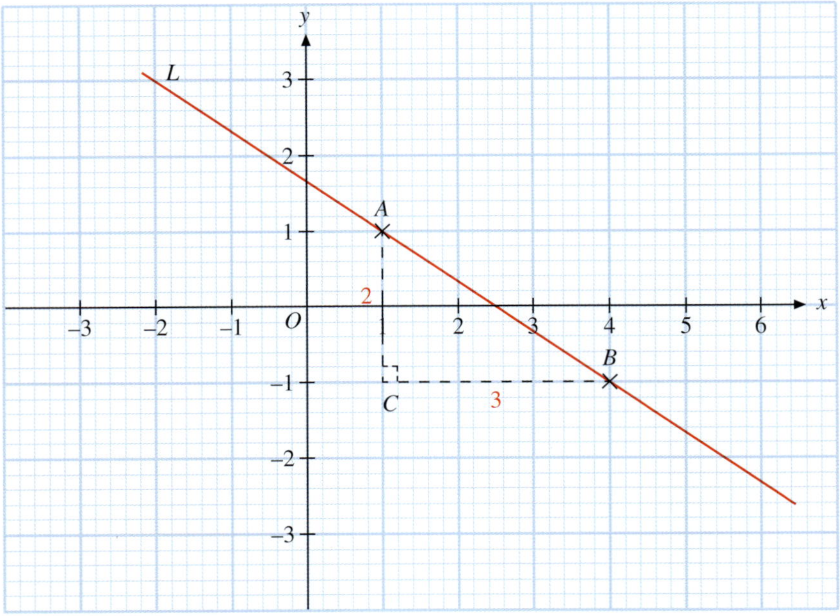

$$\text{Gradient of the line } L = \frac{\text{vertical change}}{\text{horizontal change}}$$
$$= -\frac{2}{3}$$

DISCUSS

The vertical change from A to B is –2.

How else can you tell that the gradient will be negative?

Try It! 14 Find the gradient of the line L in the diagram.

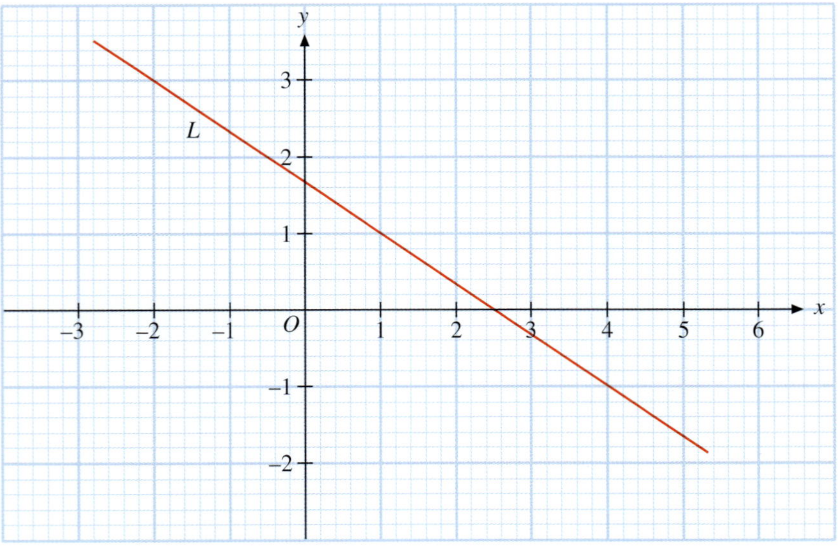

Example 15 Find the gradients of the lines $y = 3$ and $x = -3$.

Solution

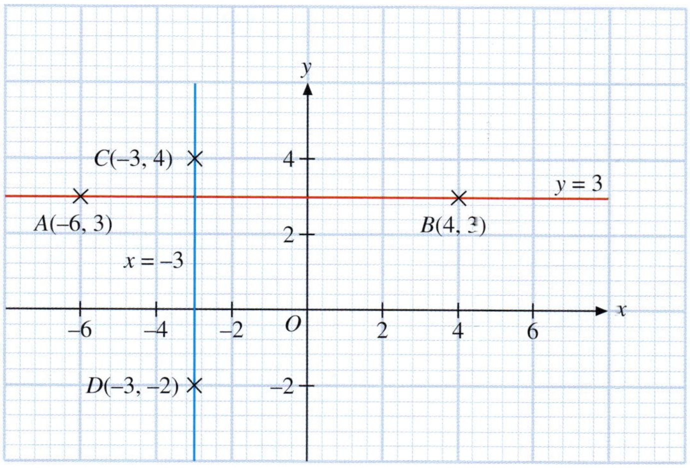

$y = 3$ is a horizontal line.

$A(-6, 3)$ and $B(4, 3)$ are two points on it.

Vertical change from A to $B = 3 - 3$

$= 0$

Horizontal change from A to $B = 4 - (-6)$

$= 10$

Gradient of the line AB $(y = 3) = \dfrac{\text{vertical change}}{\text{horizontal change}}$

$= \dfrac{0}{10}$

$= 0$

$x = -3$ is a vertical line. $C(-3, 4)$ and $D(-3, -2)$ are two points on it.

Vertical change from C to $D = 4 - (-2)$

$= 6$

Horizontal change from C to $D = (-3) - (-3)$

$= 0$

Gradient of the line CD $(x = -3) = \dfrac{6}{0}$

Since division by zero is undefined, the gradient of the line $x = -3$ is undefined.

DISCUSS

What happens if you choose two different points on the line?

Try It! 15 Find the gradients of the lines $y = -2$ and $x = 2$.

The results in Example 15 can be generalised:

The gradient of a horizontal line is 0.
The gradient of a vertical line is undefined.

B Intercepts and Equations of Straight Lines

The general equation of a linear function is $y = mx + c$. Let us explore what this means.

CLASS ACTIVITY 5

Objective: To investigate how the equation of a line relates to its graph.

1. **(a)** Draw a Cartesian plane with $-3 \le x \le 3$ and $-9 \le y \le 9$.

   Draw the graphs of $y = x$, $y = 2x$ and $y = 3x$ on the plane.

   (b) What is the same and what is different about the graphs in part **(a)**?

   (c) Work out the gradient of each line. What do you notice?

2. **(a)** Draw a Cartesian plane with $-3 \le x \le 3$ and $-9 \le y \le 9$.

   Draw the graphs of $y = x + 1$, $y = 2x + 1$ and $y = 3x + 1$ on the plane.

   (b) What is the same and what is different about the graphs in part **(a)**?

3. **(a)** Draw a Cartesian plane with $-3 \le x \le 3$ and $-9 \le y \le 9$.

   Draw the graphs of $y = 2x$, $y = 2x + 3$ and $y = 2x - 3$ on the plane.

   (b) What is the same and what is different about the graphs in part **(a)**?

   (c) What do you notice about the lines?

4. Write down the equation of two graphs with gradient 4.

DISCUSS

Can you predict what the graph of $y = -2x$ will look like?

DISCUSS

Can you predict what the graph of $y = 2x - 1$ will look like?

DISCUSS

Compare your answers to **Question 4** with a classmate. How many different equations can you think of?

The x-coordinate of the point of intersection of a graph with the x-axis is called the ***x*-intercept** of the graph. The y-coordinate of the point of intersection of a graph with the y-axis is called the ***y*-intercept** of the graph. In Class Activity 5 you may have noticed that:

The linear graph of $y = mx + c$ has
- gradient $= m$,
- y-intercept $= c$.

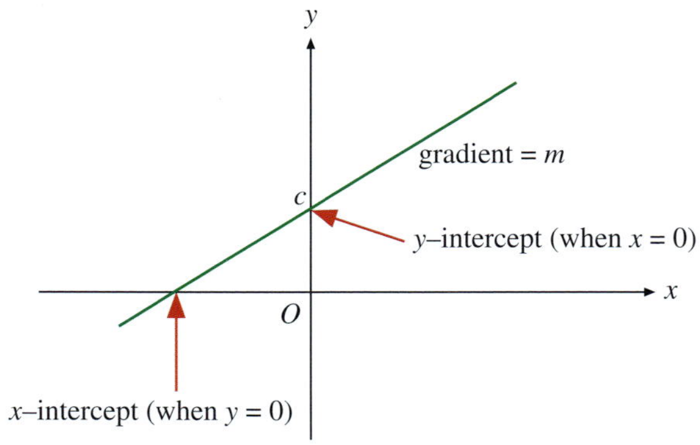

Example 16

State the gradient and the y-intercept of each linear graph.

(a) $y = 3x + 4$ **(b)** $y = 9 - x$

(c) $y = -8$ **(d)** $x + y = 8$

Solution

(a) Compare $y = 3x + 4$ with $y = mx + c$.

$m = 3$ and $c = 4$.

$\therefore$ gradient $= 3$ and y-intercept $= 4$.

(b) $y = 9 - x$ can be written as

$y = -x + 9$.

Hence, $m = -1$ and $c = 9$.

$\therefore$ gradient $= -1$ and y-intercept $= 9$.

(c) $y = -8$ can be written as

$y = 0 \times x + (-8)$.

Hence, $m = 0$ and $c = -8$

$\therefore$ gradient $= 0$ and y-intercept $= -8$.

(d) $x + y = 8$

Change the subject to y.

$$x - x + y = 8 - x$$

$$y = 8 - x$$

This can be written as $y = -x + 8$.

Hence, $m = -1$ and $c = 8$.

$\therefore$ gradient $= -1$ and y-intercept $= 8$.

Try It! 16

State the gradient and the y-intercept of each linear graph.

(a) $y = 2x + 5$ **(b)** $y = -4 - 6x$

(c) $y = 5$ **(d)** $x + y = 5$

RECALL

Parallel lines will never meet.

DISCUSS

Which of these graphs are parallel? What can you say about the gradients of parallel lines?

DISCUSS

What does the graph of $y = -8$ look like? Why is its gradient 0?

RECALL

A bar model can help you rearrange.

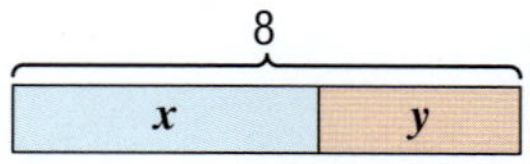

Example 17

The line L has gradient -4 and y-intercept 2.

(a) Write down the equation of L.

(b) Write down the equation of a line which is parallel to L.

Solution

(a) The equation of a straight line is $y = mx + c$, where m is the gradient and c is the y-intercept.

For L, $m = -4$ and $c = 2$.

Thus, the equation of L is

$$y = -4x + 2$$

(b) A line which is parallel to L will have the same gradient, $m = -4$, and c can be any value except 2.
For example, the line could have equation
$y = -4x + 5$ or $y = -4x - 3$

Try It! 17

The line L has gradient 3 and y-intercept -5.

(a) Write down the equation of L.

(b) Write down the equation of a line that is parallel to L.

Example 18

Which of these could be the equation of the given graph?

$y = 2x$ $y = -2x - 3$ $y = 2x + 3$ $y = -2x + 3$

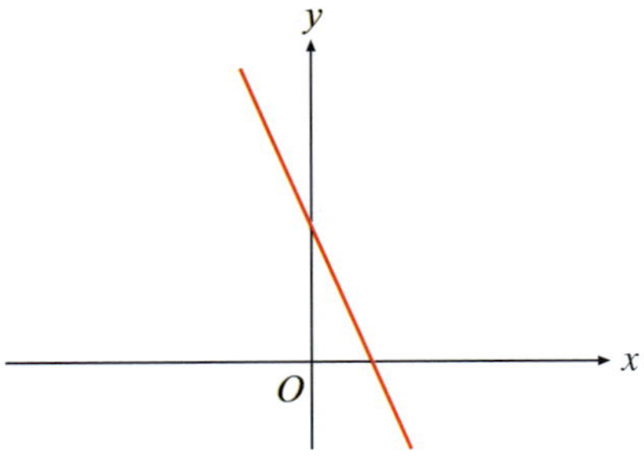

Solution

The given graph has negative gradient and positive y-intercept.

Let us look at the equations.

Equation	Gradient	y-intercept
$y = 2x$	2	0
$y = -2x - 3$	-2	-3
$y = 2x + 3$	2	3
$y = -2x + 3$	-2	3

Hence, the equation of the graph could be $y = -2x + 3$.

DISCUSS

Which of these given equations has the graph passing through the origin? Explain your answer.

Try It! 18

Which of these could be the equation of the given graph?

$y = -x + 2$ $y = x - 2$ $y = x + 2$ $y = -x$

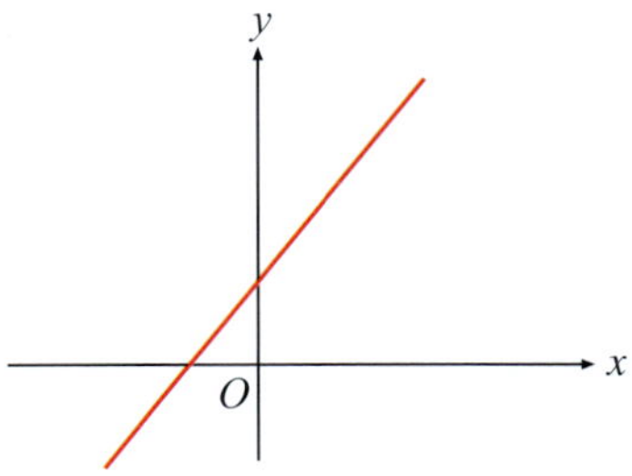

DISCUSS

Which of these given equations has the graph passing through the origin? Explain your answer.

Another way to think about the gradient of a line is as the change in y-variable for every increase in 1 unit of the x-variable. In other words, the gradient is the **rate of change** of y. For instance, the gradient of this line is 2. For every increase of 1 unit in the x-direction, there is an increase of 2 units in the y-direction.

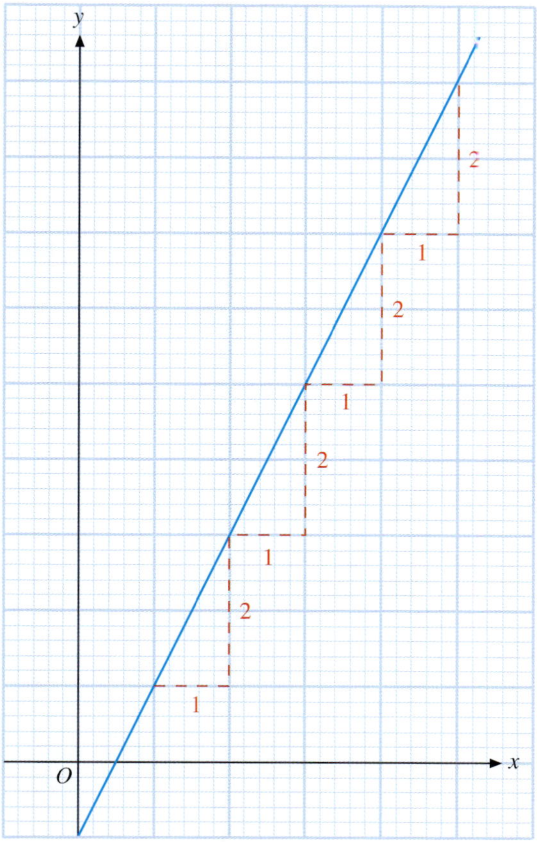

In Section 4.2, you saw that a graph can represent the relationship between variables in real-life contexts. The same principle can be applied here:

> The gradient of a line equals the change in the variable on the y-axis per 1 unit increase in the variable on the x-axis.

Example 19

Petrol is pumped into a tank. The volume, y litres, of petrol in the tank at time x minutes is given by the function $y = 50x + 40$ for $0 \le x \le 8$.

(a) Draw the graph of the function.

(b) Interpret the meaning of 40 in the equation.

(c) Interpret the meaning of 50 in the equation.

Solution

(a)

x	0	2	4	6	8
y	40	140	240	340	440

The graph of $y = 50x + 40$ is shown.

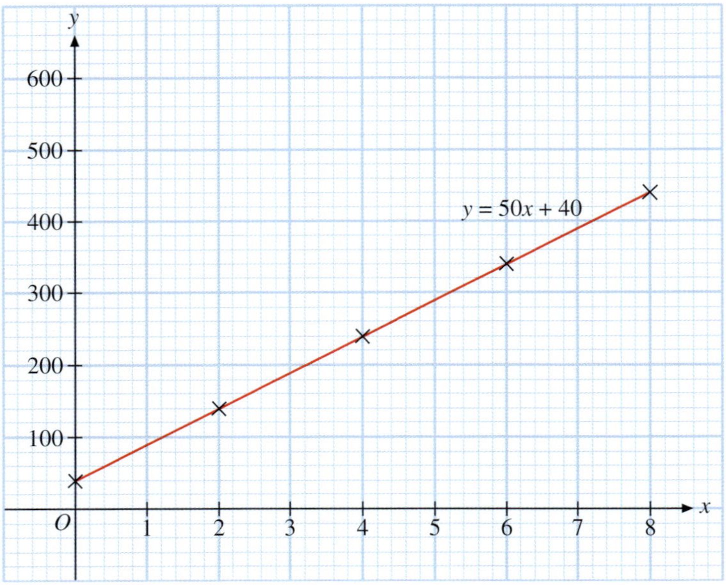

(b) 40 is the y-intercept of the graph.
It represents the volume of petrol in the tank when the time is zero.
So, the initial volume of petrol in the tank is 40 litres.

(c) 50 is the gradient of the graph.
It represents the increase of petrol in the tank per unit of time.
So, the increase in volume of petrol is 50 litres per minute.

DISCUSS

Explain why you do not need to use every value of x in your table.

Try It! 19

The height, h cm, of a plant after x days is given by the function $h = 10 + 2x$ for $0 \le x \le 30$.

(a) Draw the graph of the function using the scale of 1 cm to 5 units on the x-axis and 1 cm to 10 units on the h-axis.

(b) Interpret the meaning of 10 in the equation.

(c) Interpret the meaning of 2 in the equation.

Example 20

The battery charge, $y\%$, left on a mobile phone after x hours is given by the function $y = 100 - 5x$ for $0 \le x \le 10$.

(a) Draw the graph of the function.

(b) Interpret the meaning of 100 in the equation.

(c) Interpret the meaning of 5 in the equation.

Solution

(a)

x	0	2	4	6	8	10
y	100	90	80	70	60	50

The graph of $y = 100 - 5x$ is shown.

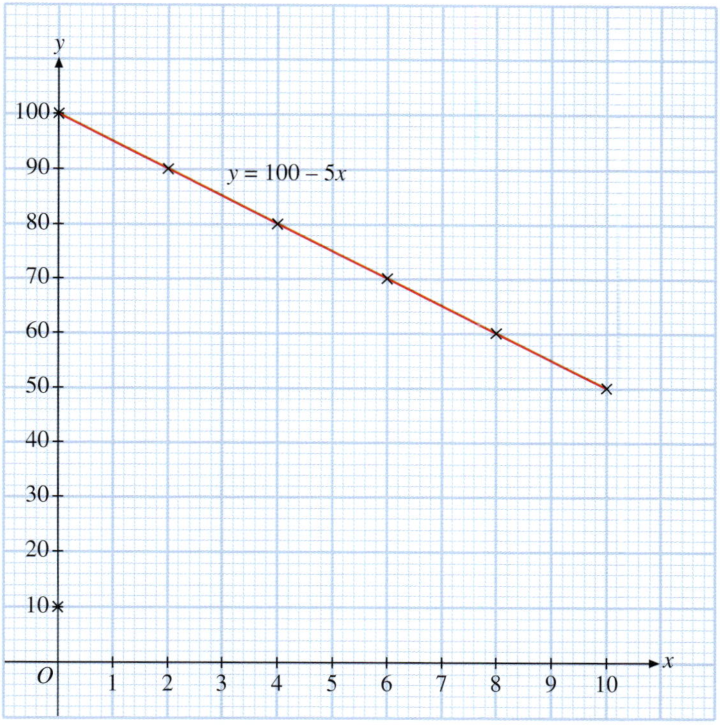

(b) 100 is the y-intercept. It is the value of y when $x = 0$.

$\therefore$ the charge of the battery is initially 100%.

(c) -5 is the gradient of the graph.

$\therefore$ the charge of the battery **decreases** by 5% per hour.

> **REMARK**
>
> The negative sign of the gradient indicates the battery charge is decreasing.

Try It! 20

Lyndsey is building a wall using bricks and cement. The amount of cement, y kg, left in the mixer after x hours is given by the function $y = 120 - 15x$ for $0 \le x \le 6$.

(a) Draw the graph of the function.

(b) Interpret the meaning of 120 in the equation.

(c) Interpret the meaning of 15 in the equation.

PRACTICE 4.3

LEVEL 1

1. What is the same and what is different about the two slopes in each part?

(a)

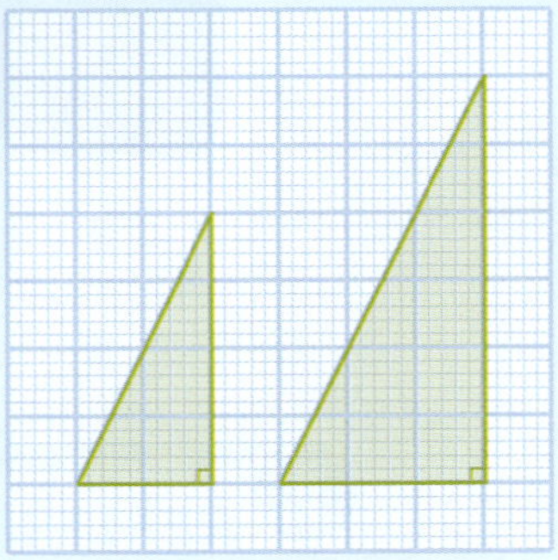

(b)

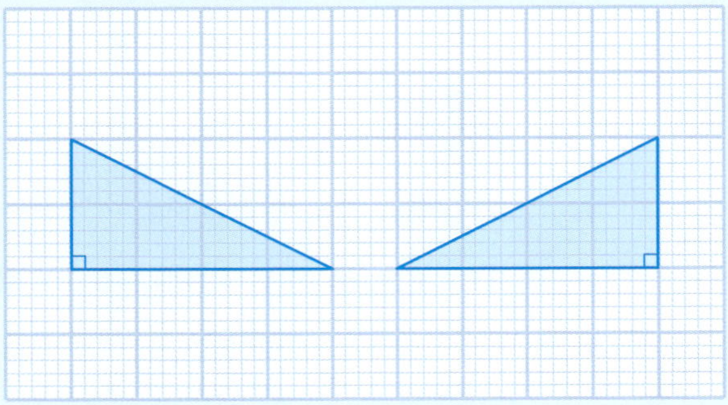

2. State whether the gradient of each of these red lines is positive, negative, zero or undefined.

(a)

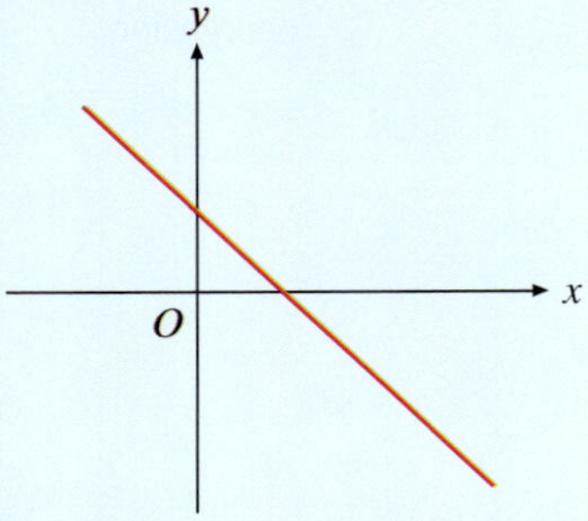

(b)

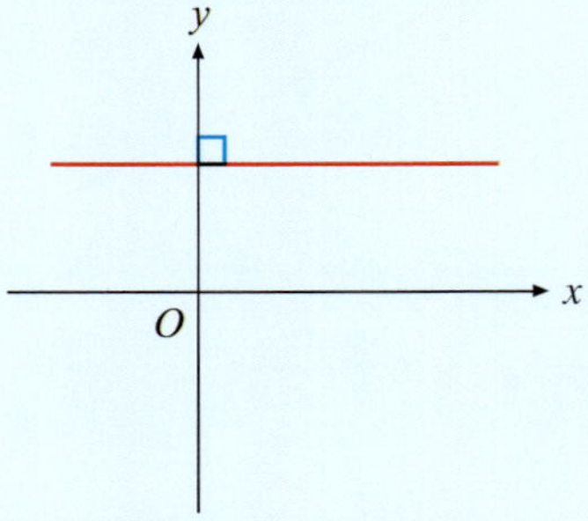

(c)

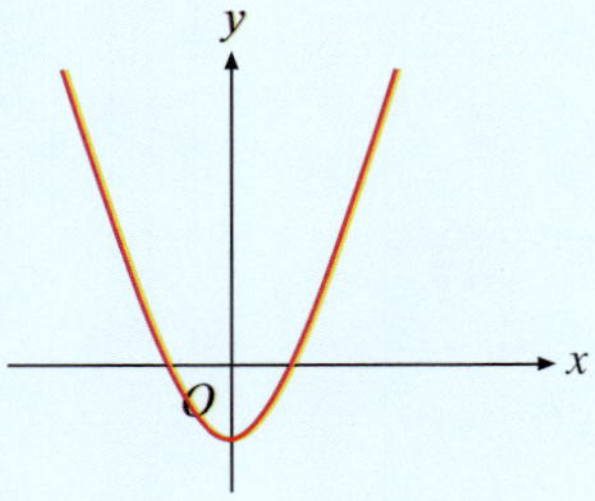

(d)

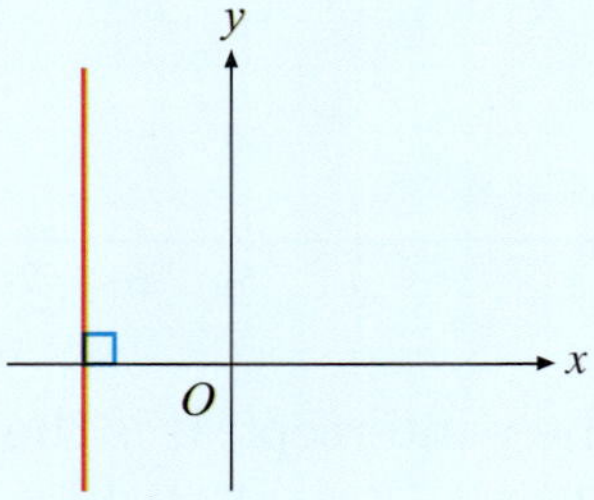

(e)

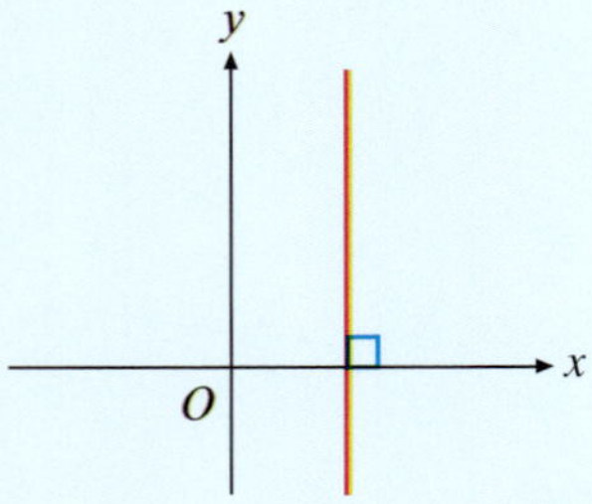

(f)

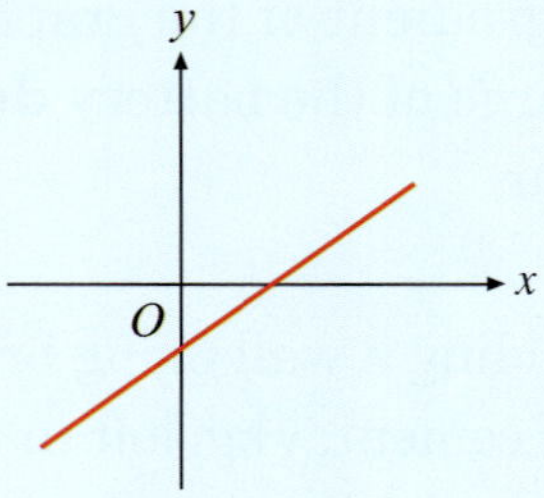

3. Find the gradient and y-intercept of each graph.

(a)

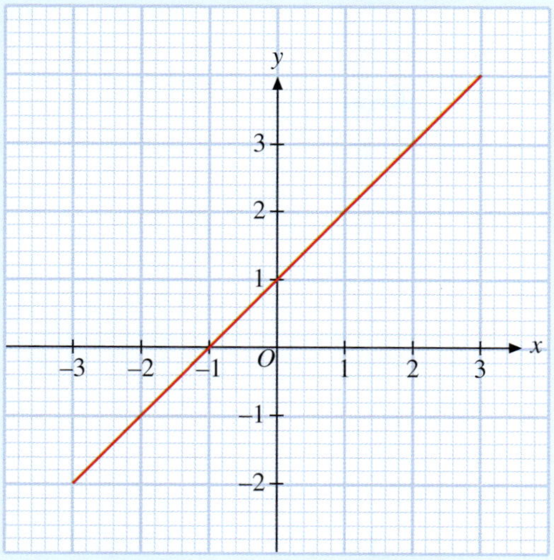

(b)

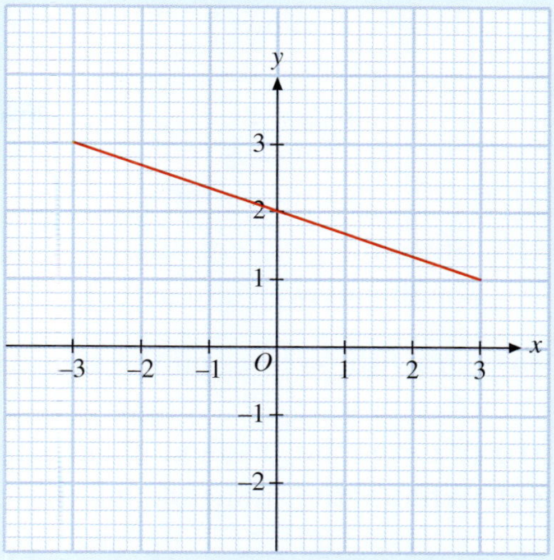

(c)

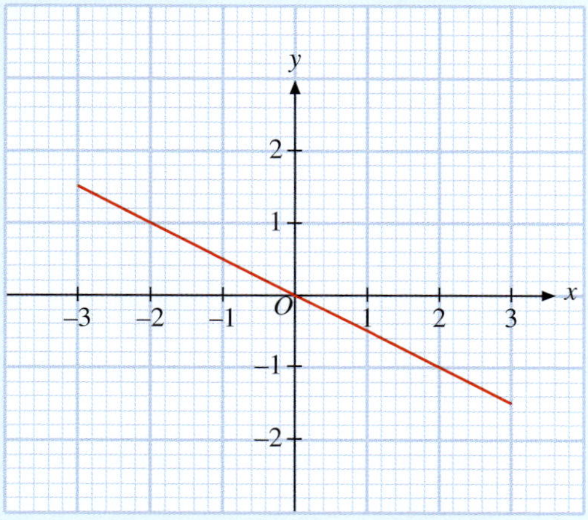

(d)

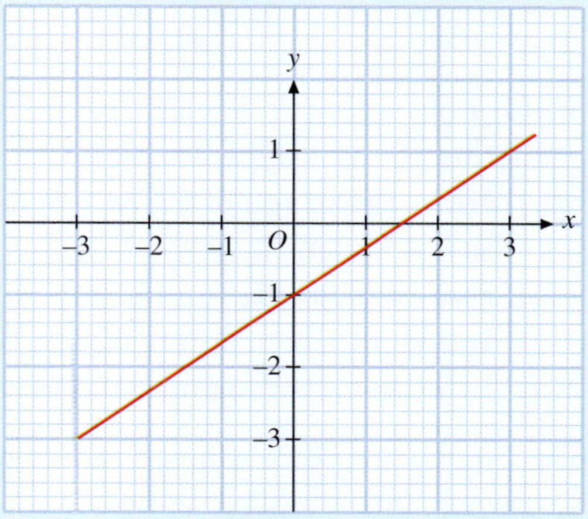

4. State the gradient and the y-intercept of the graph of each function.

(a) $y = 3x - 7$
(b) $y = 3x + 1$
(c) $y = 4x$
(d) $y = -2x - 5$
(e) $y = -5$
(f) $2x + y = 4$

LEVEL 2

5. Consider these six linear graphs.

(1) $y = 1 - 4x$
(2) $y = -4x$
(3) $y = 5x$
(4) $y = -5x + 3$
(5) $y = 3$
(6) $2x - y - 6 = 0$

(a) Which graphs have positive gradients?
(b) Which graphs have negative gradients?
(c) Which graphs have a positive y-intercept?
(d) Which graph does not intersect the x-axis?

Explain your reasoning for each question part.

6. (a) Which of these functions could have the graph shown?

$y = 2x + 2$

$y = 2x - 2$

$y = -2x + 2$

$y = -2x - 2$

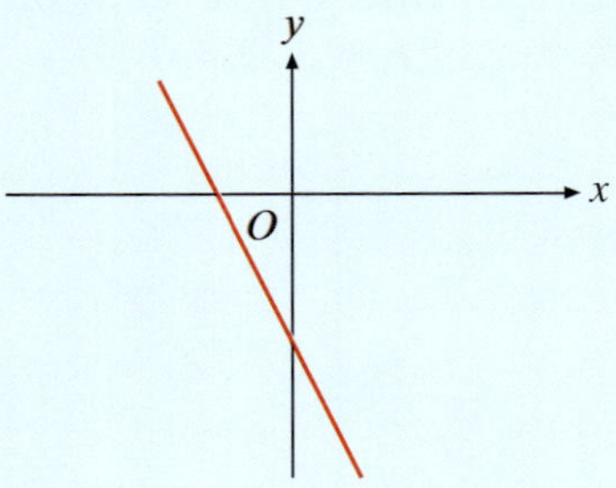

(b) State the gradient and the y-intercept for the answer in part **(a)**.

7. (a) Draw these lines on the same axes for $-3 \leq x \leq 3$.

$y = 3x + 2$ $\quad$ $y = 3x$ $\quad$ $y = 3x - 1$

(b) What is the gradient of each line?

(c) What is the same and what is different about these lines?

8. Write down three pairs of parallel lines from their equations.

$y = 6x + 3$	$y = -6x + 2$	$y = 3 - 6x$	$y = 3x + 1$
$y = 3x$	$y = -3x + 6$	$y = 1 - 3x$	$y = 6x + 2$

9. Laura is jogging on a trail. Her distance, y m, from a signpost at time x seconds is given by the function $y = 3x + 5$ for $0 \leq x \leq 10$.

PROBLEM SOLVING

(a) Draw the graph of $y = 3x + 5$, using the scale of 1 cm to 1 unit on the x-axis and 1 cm to 5 units on the y-axis.

(b) State the gradient and the y-intercept of the graph.

(c) Interpret the meaning of 5 in the function.

(d) Interpret the meaning of 3 in the function.

10. Mr Smith bought a sofa set to pay in monthly instalments. Let £y be the amount he owes after x months. y is given by the function $y = 1200 - 200x$ for $0 \leq x \leq 6$.

FINANCE

PROBLEM SOLVING

(a) Draw the graph of $y = 1200 - 200x$, using a scale of 1 cm to 1 unit on the x-axis and 1 cm to 200 units on the y-axis.

(b) Using the graph, find the value of x when $y = 400$.

(c) Interpret the meaning of 1200 in the function.

(d) Interpret the meaning of 200 in the function.

4.4 Non-linear Graphs

In the previous sections, you have learnt that the graph of the function $y = mx + c$, where m and c are constants, is a straight line. In this section, you will learn about some functions with graphs that are **not** straight lines.

CLASS ACTIVITY 6

Objective: To recognise some non-linear graphs.

1. Let $y\,\text{cm}^2$ be the area of a square of side x cm.

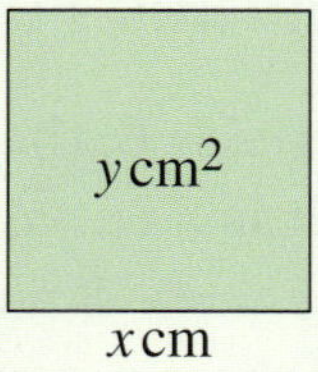

(a) Copy and complete the table of values of x and y.

x	0	1	2	3	4	5
y	0	1	4			

(b) Copy the axes shown and plot the points with the ordered pairs (x, y).

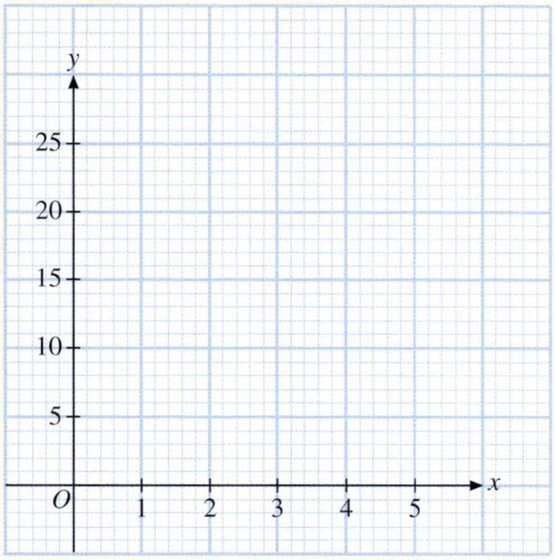

(c) Join the plotted points with a smooth curve.

2. A rectangle is x cm by y cm. The area of the rectangle is $36\,\text{cm}^2$.

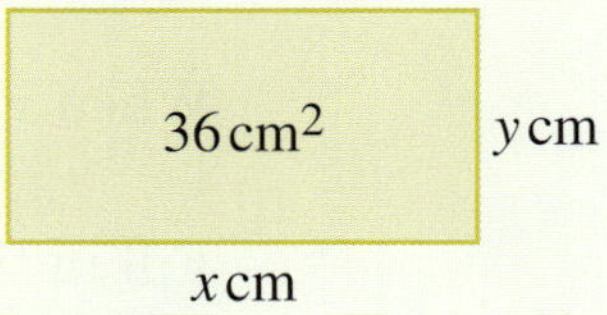

(a) Copy and complete the table of values of x and y.

x	1	2	4	9	18	36
y	36	18				

(b) Copy the axes shown and plot the points with the ordered pairs (x, y).

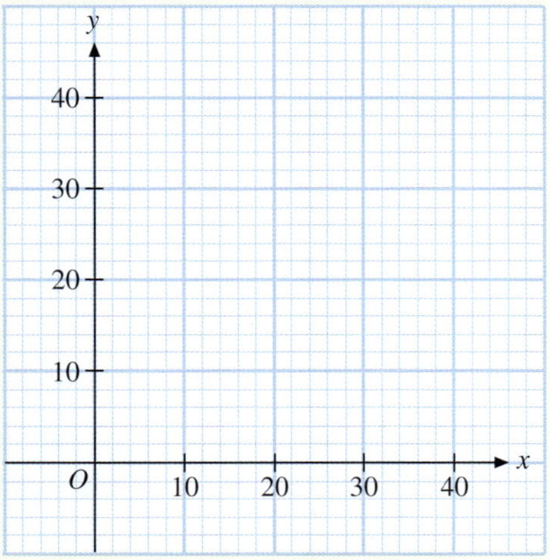

(c) Join the plotted points with a smooth curve.

3. Compare the shapes of the two curves in **Questions 1** and **2**. Write down any observations that you make.

The graphs in Class Activity 6 are curves, not lines. This is because they are the graphs of non-linear functions.

A Quadratic Functions

In Class Activity 6, the first graph is called a graph of a **quadratic function**. It is a curve called a **parabola**. The functions $y = x^2$, $y = x^2 - 3x$, $y = x^2 - 3$ and $y = -3x^2 + 3x - 4$ are **quadratic functions**, since the highest power of x is 2.

The graph of a quadratic function can be drawn by creating a table of values of x and y, plotting the points and joining them by a smooth curve.

DISCUSS

Which of these are quadratic functions?

$y = 3x$ $\quad$ $y = x^2 + 3$

$y = 3x^2$ $\quad$ $y = x^3$

$y = x^2 + 2x$ $\quad$ $y = x^2 - x^3$

Example 21

(a) Complete the table of values for the function $y = x^2 + 1$.

x	−2	−1	0	1	2
y		2			5

(b) Draw the graph of $y = x^2 + 1$ for $-2 \le x \le 2$.

Solution

(a) When $x = -2$, $y = (-2)^2 + 1$
$= 4 + 1$
$= 5$

$(-2) \times (-2) = 4$

When $x = 0$, $y = 0^2 + 1$
$= 1$
$= 5$

When $x = 1$, $y = 1^2 + 1$
$= 2$

Fill in the table of values:

x	−2	−1	0	1	2
y	5	2	1	2	5

(b) Plot these points and join them with a smooth curve.

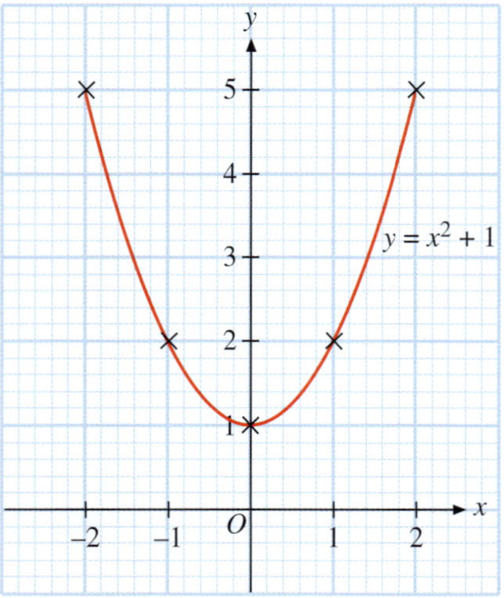

RECALL

In Chapter 2 you learnt about expanding brackets. The result of the expansion of $2x(x - 3)$ is a quadratic expression, $2x^2 - 6x$.

REMARK

You should always label graphs with the function they represent.

REMARK

Notice that the graph is symmetrical (about the y-axis).

Try It! 21

(a) Copy and complete the table of values for the function $y = x^2 + 4$.

x	−2	−1	0	1	2
y	8			5	

(b) Draw the graph of $y = x^2 + 4$ for $-2 \le x \le 2$.

Example 22

(a) Complete the table of values for the function $y = 4x^2$.

x	−2	−1	0	1	2
y	16		0		

(b) Draw the graph of $y = 4x^2$ for $-2 \le x \le 2$.

REMARK

You need to work out the squared term before multiplying by 4.

DISCUSS

What do you notice about the shapes of the quadratic functions you have seen so far?

Solution

(a) When $x = -1$, $y = 4(-1)^2$
$= 4(1)$
$= 4$

When $x = 1$, $y = 4(1)^2$
$= 4$

When $x = 2$, $y = 4(2)^2$
$= 16$

Fill in the table of values:

x	−2	−1	0	1	2
y	16	4	0	4	16

(b) Plot these points and join them by a smooth curve.

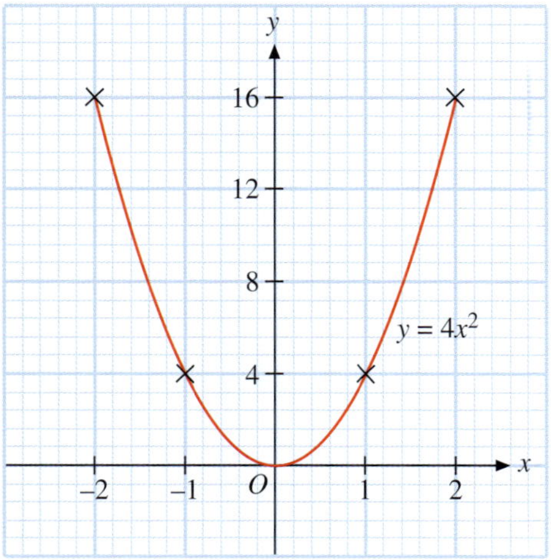

DISCUSS

What is wrong with this graph?

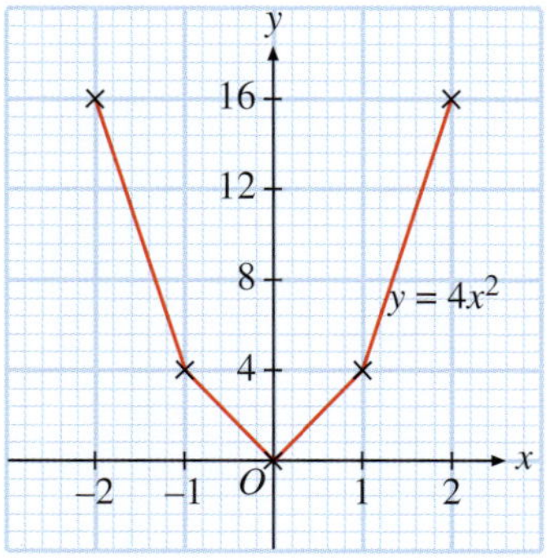

Try It! 22

(a) Copy and complete the table of values for the function $y = 2x^2$.

x	-2	-1	0	1	2
y		2			8

(b) Draw the graph of $y = 2x^2$ for $-2 \le x \le 2$.

Example 23

(a) Complete the table of values for the function $y = x^2 - 3x$.

x	-1	0	1	2	3	4
y			-2		0	4

(b) Draw the graph of $y = x^2 - 3x$ for $-1 \le x \le 4$.

Solution

(a) When $x = -1$, $y = (-1)^2 - 3(-1)$
$= 1 + 3$
$= 4$

When $x = 0$, $y = 0^2 - 3(0)$
$= 0$

When $x = 2$, $y = 2^2 - 3(2)$
$= 4 - 6$
$= -2$

Fill in the table of values:

x	-1	0	1	2	3	4
y	4	0	-2	-2	0	4

(b) Plot these points and join them by a smooth curve.

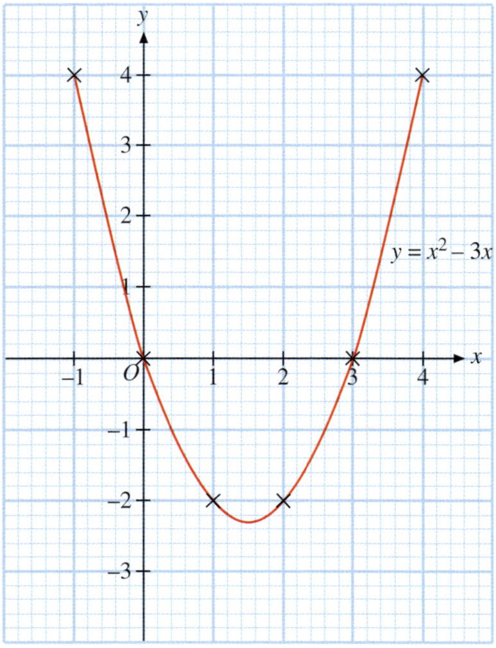

REMARK

You know that the graph of the function should be a parabola. Therefore, you must use a smooth curve to join all the points, including (1, –2) and (2, –2).

Try It! 23

(a) Copy and complete the table of values for the function $y = x^2 - x$.

x	−2	−1	0	1	2	3
y	6			0	2	

(b) Draw the graph of $y = x^2 - x$ for $-2 \le x \le 2$.

Example 24

(a) Complete the table of values for the function $y = -x^2 + 1$.

x	−2	−1	0	1	2
y	−3			0	

(b) Draw the graph of $y = -x^2 + 1$ for $-2 \le x \le 2$.

Solution

(a) When $x = -1$, $y = -(-1)^2 + 1$
$= -1 + 1$
$= 0$

When $x = 0$, $y = -0^2 + 1$
$= 1$

When $x = 2$, $y = -2^2 + 1$
$= -4 + 1$
$= -3$

Fill in the table of values:

x	−2	−1	0	1	2
y	−3	0	1	0	−3

(b) Plot these points and join them by a smooth curve.

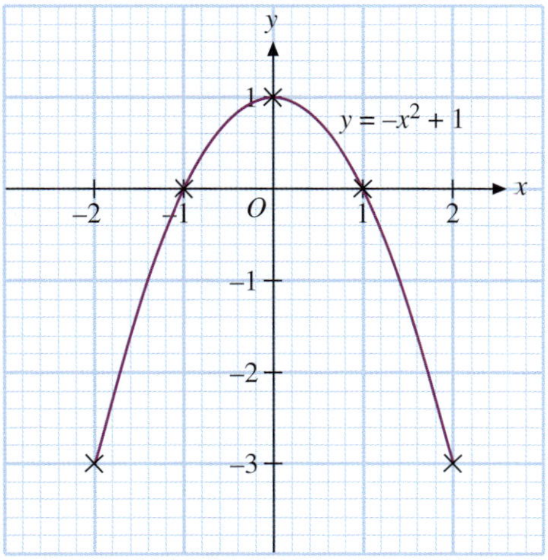

DISCUSS

Is it true that $-x^2 = (-x)^2$?

DISCUSS

Consider this graph and the graph of $y = x^2 + 1$ in Example 21. What is the same and what is different about the two graphs?

Try It! 24

(a) Complete the table of values for the function $y = -x^2 + 4$.

x	-2	-1	0	1	2
y		3			0

(b) Draw the graph of $y = -x^2 + 4$ for $-2 \leq x \leq 2$.

DISCUSS

Compare this graph with the graph of $y = x^2 + 4$ in Try It! 21. What is the same and what is different about the graphs?

From Examples 21–24 you have seen that a quadratic function is a symmetric curve.
It is either open upwards or open downwards.

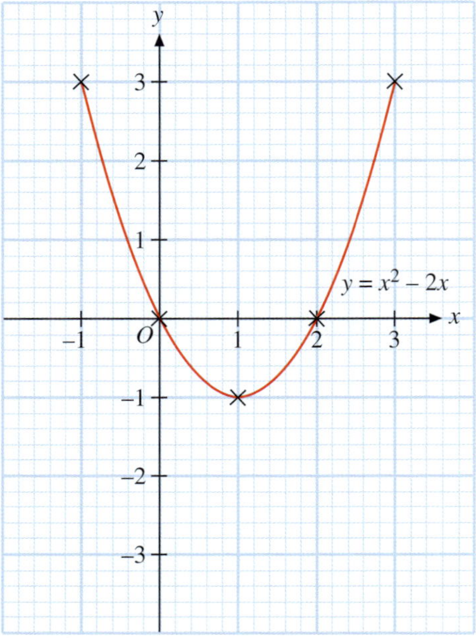

Open upwards

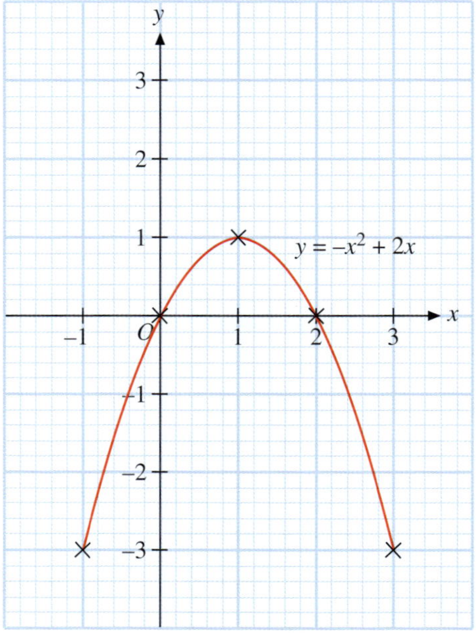

Open downwards

DISCUSS

Which of these quadratic functions have graphs that open upwards and which have graphs that open downwards?

$y = 3x^2$ $\quad y = x^2 + 3$

$y = -x^2$ $\quad y = x^2 - 3x$

$y = -x^2 + x$ $\quad y = -3x^2 + 1$

You could use graphing software to check.

In general:

> The graph of $y = ax^2 + bx + c$ where a, b and c are constants and $a \neq 0$ is a parabola.
> If $a > 0$ then the graph is open upwards.
> If $a < 0$ then the graph is open downwards.

Example 25

The height, y m of a ball x seconds after it is thrown is given by the quadratic function $y = -5x^2 + 20x + 2$. The graph of the function is shown.

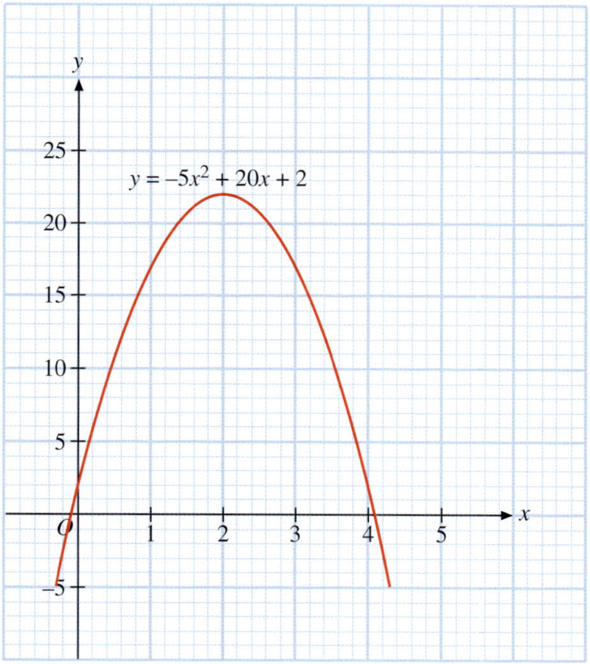

(a) Find the height of the ball after 3 seconds.

(b) What was the maximum height reached by the ball?

(c) Interpret the meaning of the 2 in the function.

Solution

(a) After 3 seconds, $x = 3$.

Draw a vertical line from 3 on the x-axis then across to the y-axis.

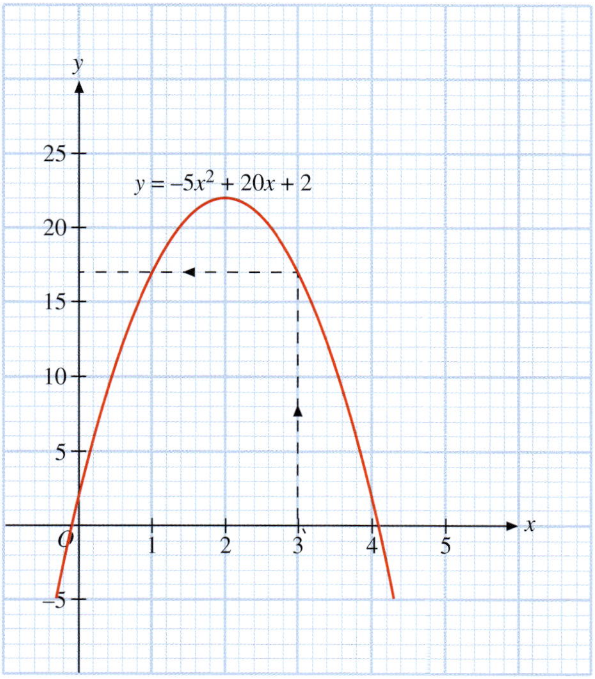

DISCUSS

The parabola here has a maximum point at (2, 22). Will a parabola always have a maximum? Explain your answer.

When $x = 3$, $y = 17$

$\therefore$ the height of the ball after 3 seconds = 17 m.

(b) The maximum value of y is 22.

$\therefore$ the maximum height of ball = 22 m.

(c) Initially (when $x = 0$), $y = 2$

$\therefore$ the ball is thrown from a height of 2 m.

Try It! 25

The height, y m of a ball x seconds after it is thrown from a tower is given by the quadratic function $y = -5x^2 + 10x + 30$.

The graph of the function is shown.

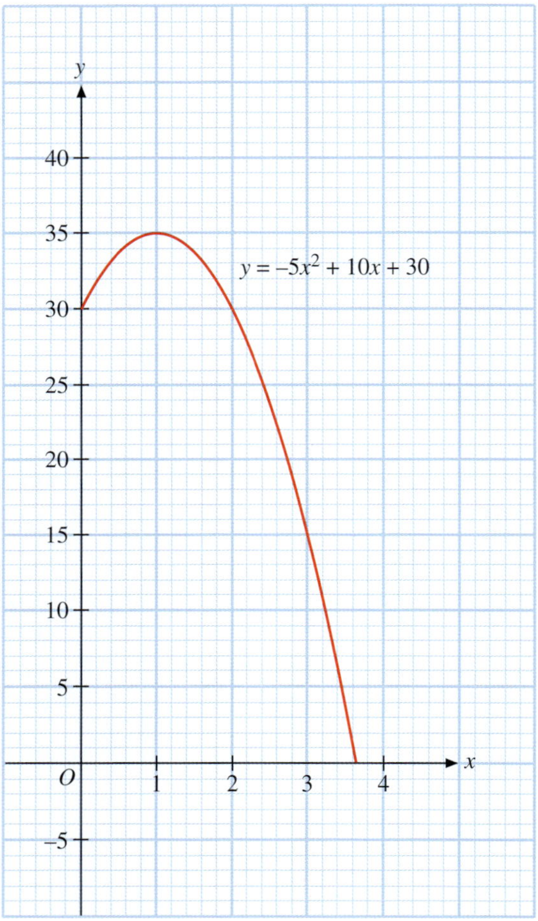

(a) Find the height of the ball after 2 seconds.

(b) What was the maximum height reached by the ball?

(c) Interpret the meaning of 30 in the function.

B Reciprocal Functions

In Class Activity 6, the second graph is the graph of a **reciprocal function**. It is a curve called a **hyperbola**. A function such as $y = \frac{1}{x}$, $y = \frac{2}{x}$ or $y = -\frac{3}{x}$ where $x \neq 0$ is called a **reciprocal function**, since it involves the reciprocal of x.

Example 26

The graph of $y = \frac{3}{x}$, $x \neq 0$ is shown.

(a) Find the value of x when $y = 3$.

(b) Find the value of y when $x = -1$.

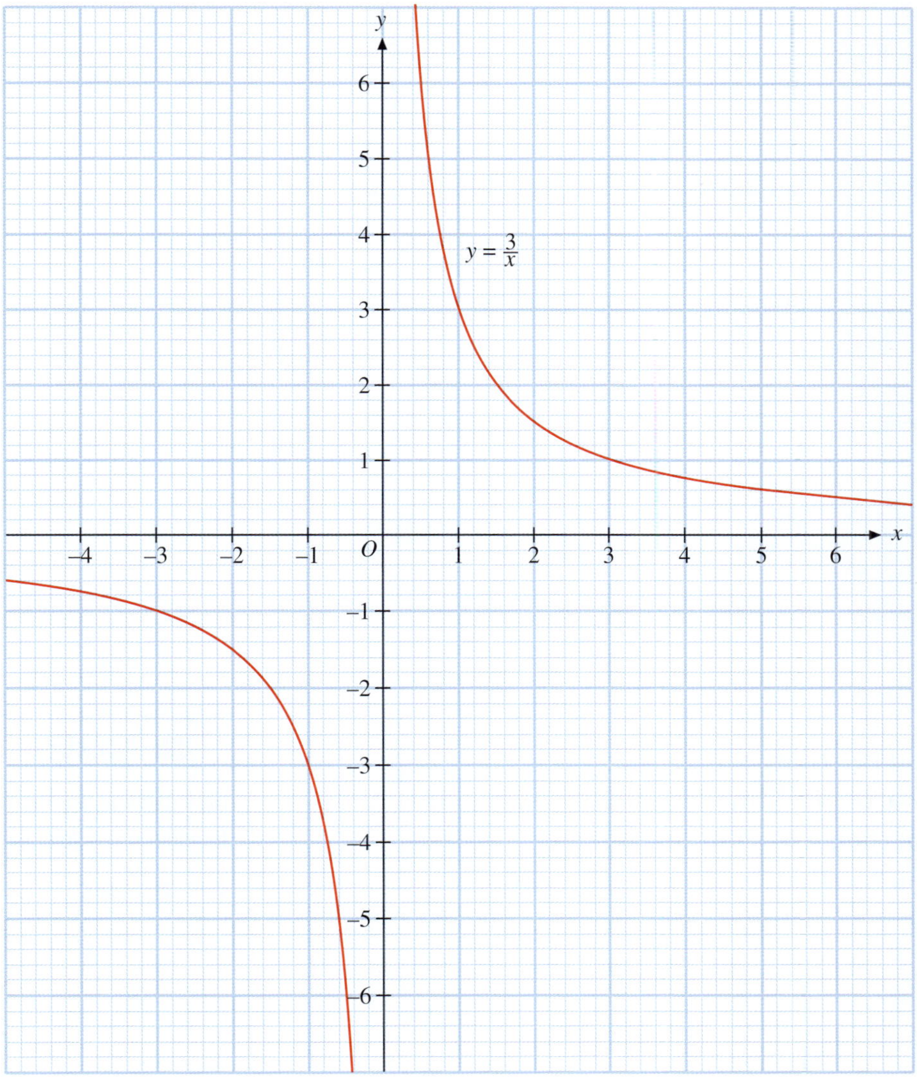

RECALL

The product of a number and its reciprocal is 1. For example,

The reciprocal of 2 is $\frac{1}{2}$ since $2 \times \frac{1}{2} = 1$.

The reciprocal of $\frac{1}{3}$ is 3 since $\frac{1}{3} \times 3 = 1$.

DISCUSS

What is the reciprocal of x? How can you check?

REMARK

When $x = 0$, $\frac{3}{x} = \frac{3}{0}$ which is undefined. Hence, you write $x \neq 0$ which means x cannot be zero for our function.

REMARK

When a graph gets closer and closer to a line but never meets it, the line is called an **asymptote**.

Solution

(a) Draw a horizontal line from 3 on the y-axis to the graph, then down to the x-axis.

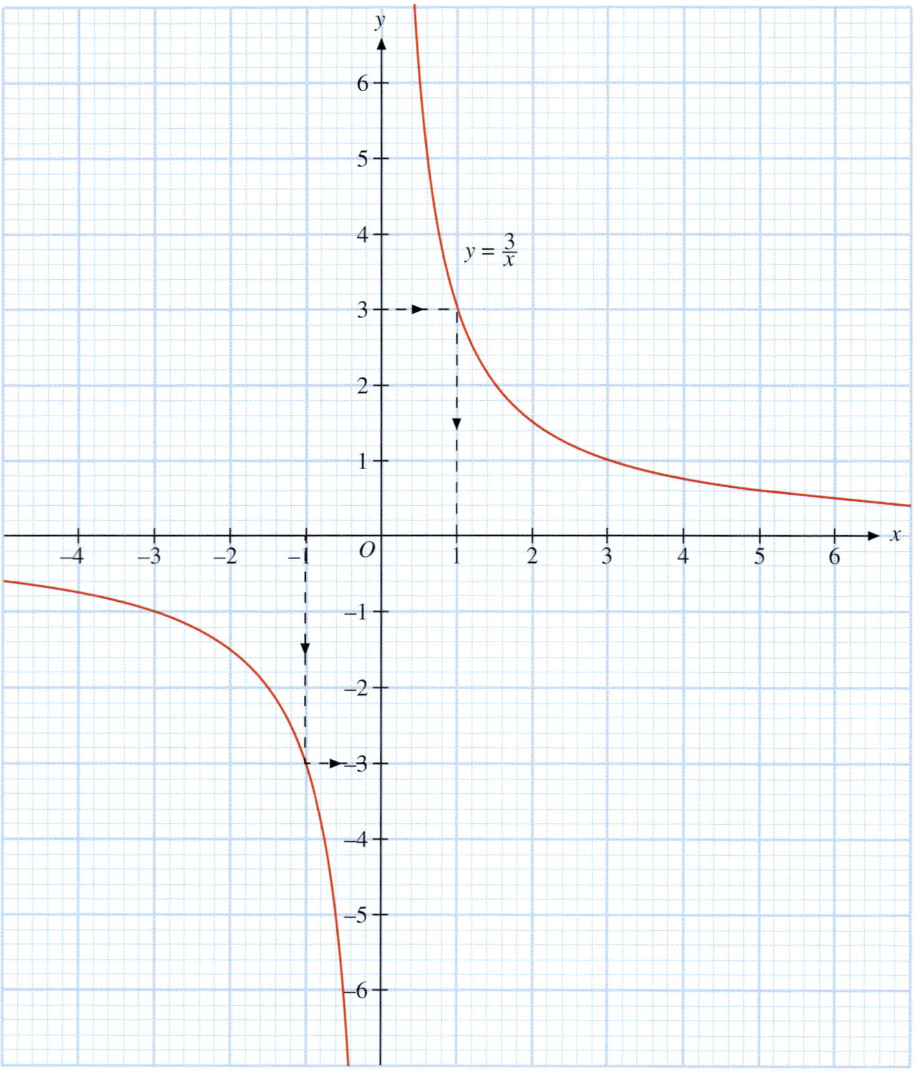

So, you see that, when $y = 3$, $x = 1$.

(b) Draw a vertical line from -1 on the x-axis to the graph, then across to the y-axis.
So, you see that, when $x = -1$, $y = -3$.

RECALL

A factor tree can be used to represent this function.

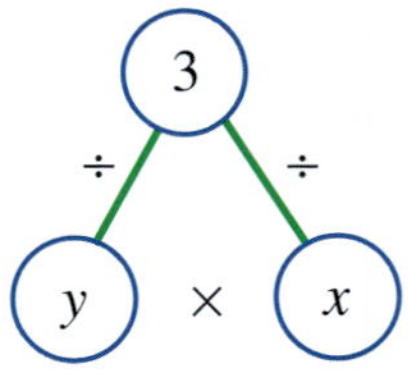

DISCUSS

How can you use the function $y = \frac{3}{x}$ to check your answers?

Try It! 26

The graph of $y = \frac{4}{x}$, $x \neq 0$ is shown.

(a) Find the value of x when $y = -4$.

(b) Find the value of y when $x = 8$.

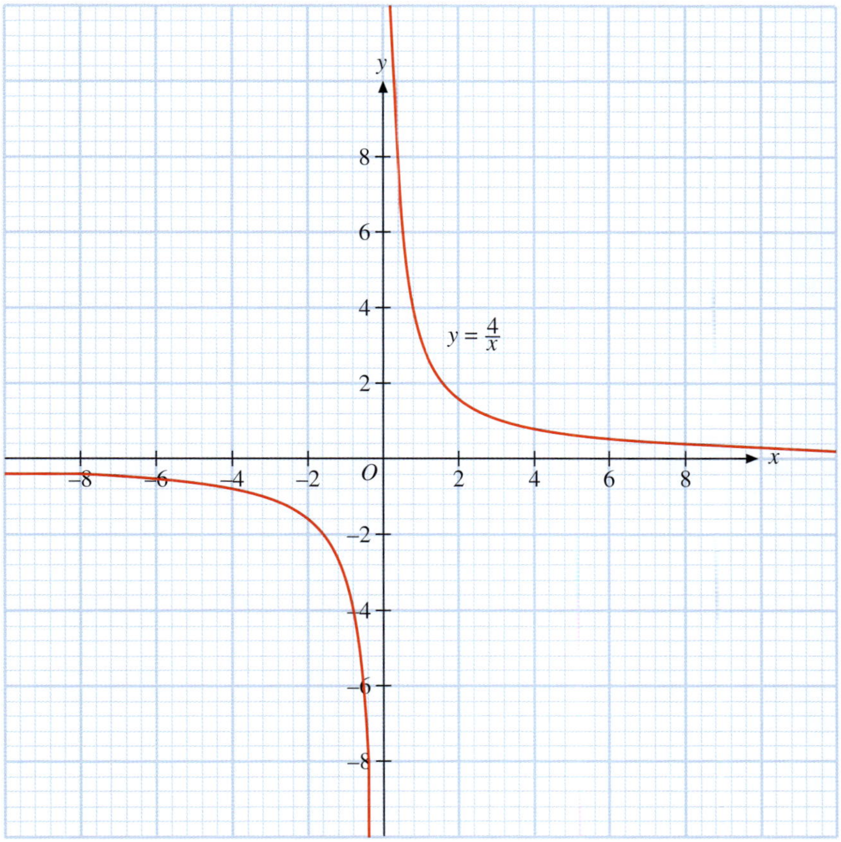

DISCUSS

Can you draw a factor tree to represent this function? Use the factor tree to check your answers.

PRACTICE 4.4

LEVEL 1

1. For each function, copy and complete the table of values, then draw the graph for the range of values of x in the table.

(a) $y = x^2 - 5$

x	−3	−2	−1	0	1	2	3
y		−1	−4		−4		4

(b) $y = 3x^2$

x	−2	−1	0	1	2
y	12			3	

(c) $y = x^2 + x$

x	−3	−2	−1	0	1	2
y	6		0		2	

(d) $y = -x^2 - 1$

x	−2	−1	0	1	2
y		−2			−5

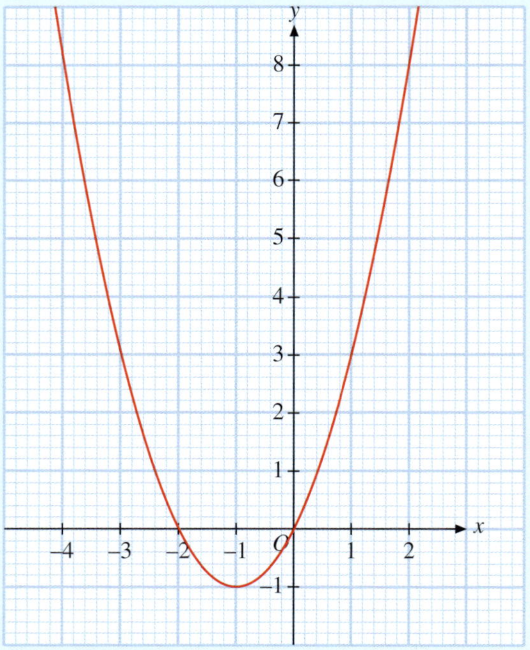

2. The graph of a quadratic function is shown.

(a) Find the value of y when $x = -3$.

(b) Which of these is a possible equation for the graph? Explain your answer.

$y = -2x^2$ $\qquad$ $y = x^2 + 2x$ $\qquad$ $y = -x^2 + 2x$

$y = \frac{2}{x}, x \neq 0$

3. Match each graph with one of these functions. Explain your answers.

$y = x^2 - 6$ $\qquad$ $y = -x^2 + 6$ $\qquad$ $y = \frac{6}{x}, x \neq 0$

(a)

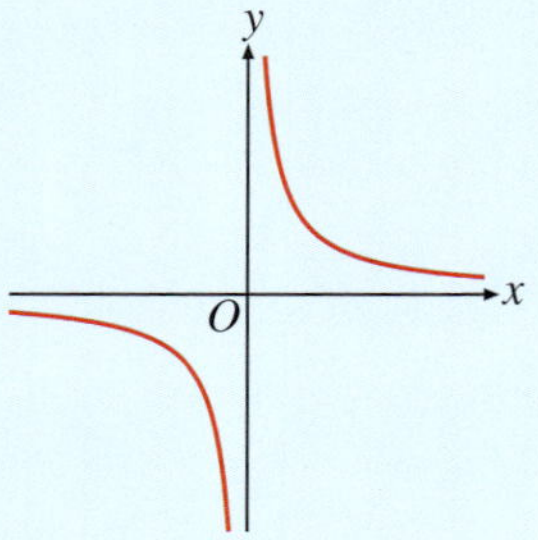

(b)

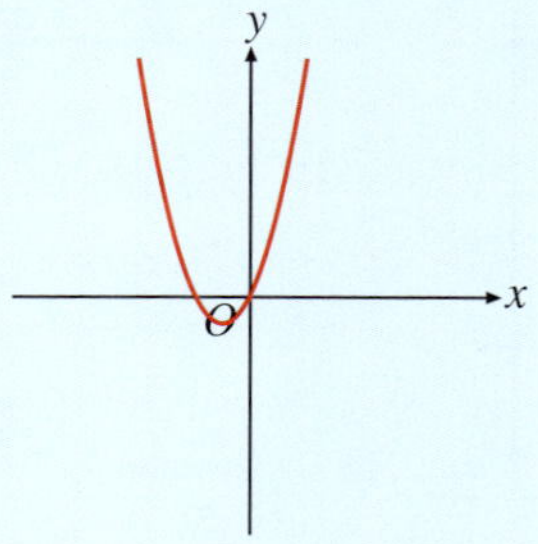

(c)

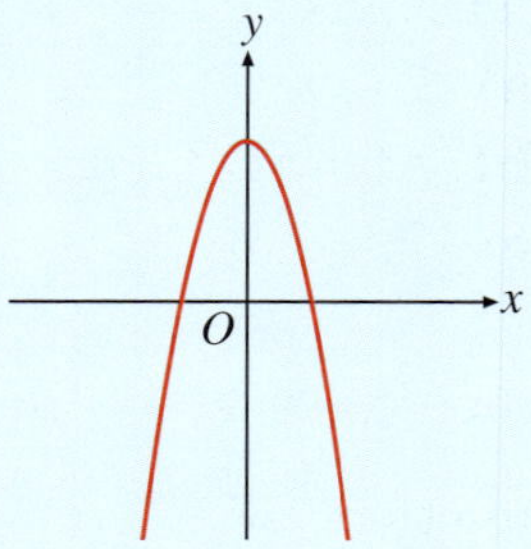

4. The graph of $y = \frac{24}{x}, x \neq 0$ is shown. Use the graph to find

(a) the value of y when $x = 4$,

(b) the value of x when $y = -2$.

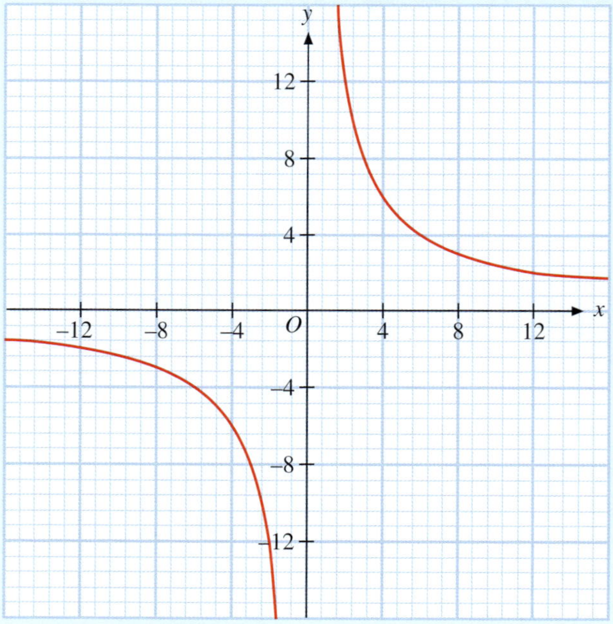

LEVEL 2

5. **(a)** Draw the graphs of $y = x^2 - 1$ and $y = 2x^2 - 1$ on the same diagram for $-3 \le x \le 3$, using the scale of 1 cm to 1 unit on the x-axis and 1 cm to 2 units on the y-axis.

(b) What is the same and what is different about the graphs?

6. **(a)** Draw the graphs of $y = -x^2 + 1$ and $y = -x^2 + 4$ on the same diagram for $-3 \le x \le 3$, using the scale of 1 cm to 1 unit on the x-axis and 1 cm to 2 units on the y-axis.

(b) What is the same and what is different about the graphs?

7. **(a)** Draw the graph of $y = x^2 - 4x + 4$ for $-1 \le x \le 5$ using the scale of 1 cm to 1 unit on both axes.

(b) Use the graph to estimate the value of x when $y = 1$.

(c) At which point(s) does the graph cut

(i) the x-axis,

(ii) the y-axis?

(d) State the coordinates of the minimum point of the graph.

8. A ball is dropped from the top of a building. The height, y m, of the ball above the ground, x seconds after being dropped is given by the quadratic function $y = 45 - 5x^2$.

(a) Draw the graph of the function for $0 \le x \le 3$.

(b) At what time is the ball 25 m above the ground?

(c) Interpret the meaning of 45 in the function.

9. The time taken, y hours, to travel by road from Northampton to Manchester is given by the function $y = \frac{240}{x}$, where x km/h is the average speed.

(a) Copy and complete the table of values.

x	10	20	40	60	120
y	24		6		2

(b) Draw the graph of the function for $10 \le x \le 120$, using a scale of 1 cm to 10 units on the x-axis and 1 cm to 2 units on the y-axis.

(c) Use your graph to estimate the value of x if $y = 5$.

(d) Interpret the meaning of 240 in the function.

REVIEW

Cartesian Coordinates in Two Dimensions

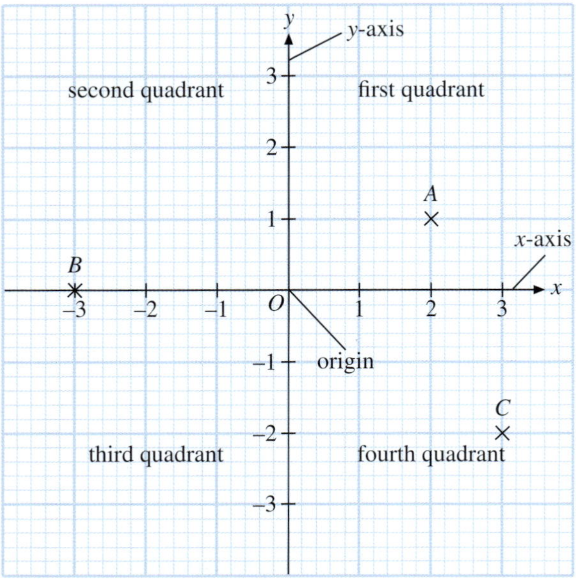

Coordinates can be given as ordered pairs.

x-coordinate *y*-coordinate

A has coordinates (2, 1)

B has coordinates (–3, 0)

C has coordinates (3, –2)

Idea of a Function

- A variable y is a function of another variable x if each value of x corresponds to exactly one value of y.
  For example, $y = 2x + 3$ is a function.
- A function can be represented by
  - a statement,
  - a table,
  - a graph,
  - an equation.

Graphs of Linear Functions

The line $y = mx + c$ has gradient $= m$, and y-intercept $= c$.

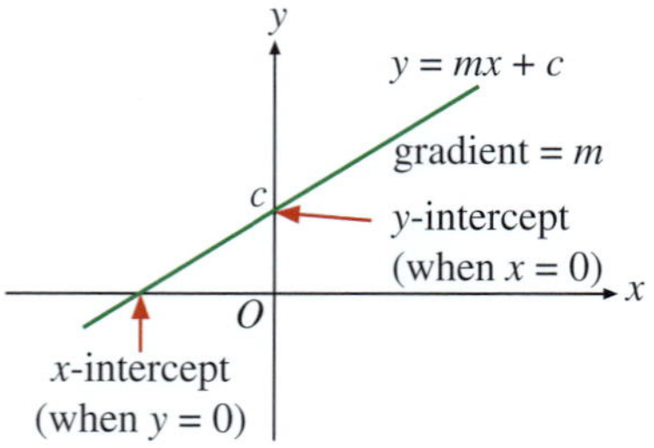

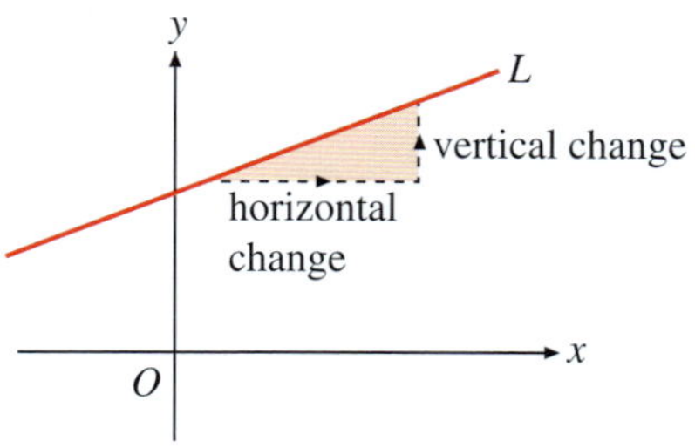

Gradient of the line $L = \dfrac{\text{vertical change}}{\text{horizontal change}}$

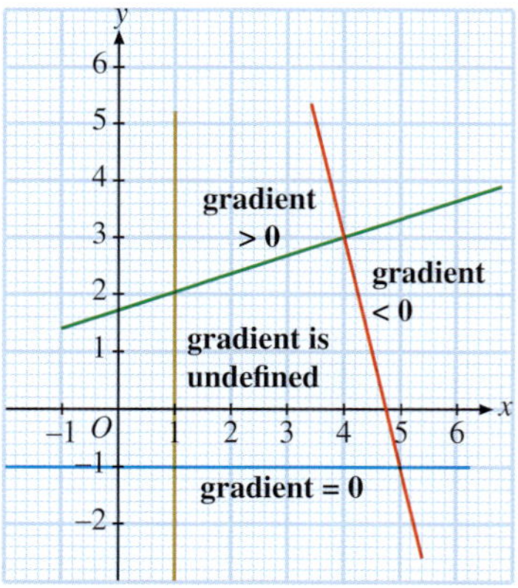

Graphs of Non-linear Functions

(a) Quadratic Functions

The graph of the quadratic function $y = ax^2 + bx + c$, where a, b and c are constants and $a \neq 0$, is a parabola.

If $a > 0$ then the graph is open upwards.

If $a < 0$ then the graph is open downwards.

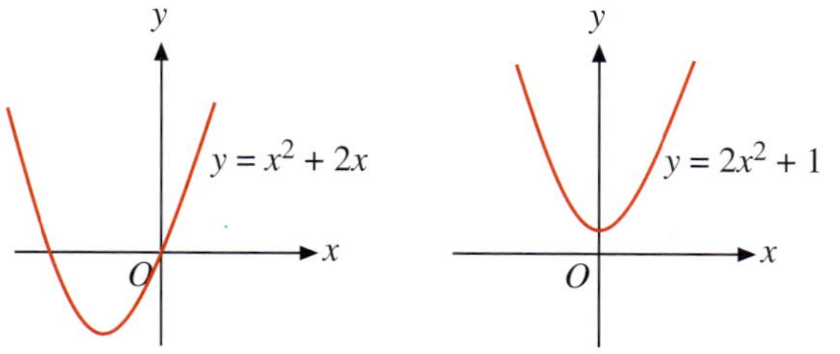

Open upwards

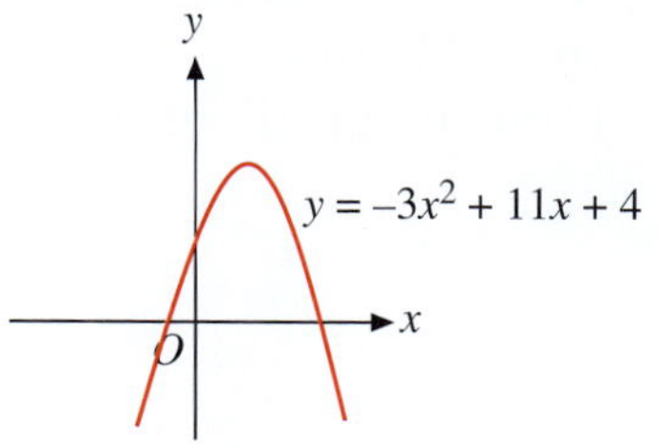

Open downwards

(b) Reciprocal Functions

A function such as $y = \frac{1}{x}$ or $y = \frac{2}{x}$ where $x \neq 0$ is called a reciprocal function.

The graph of a reciprocal function is called a hyperbola.

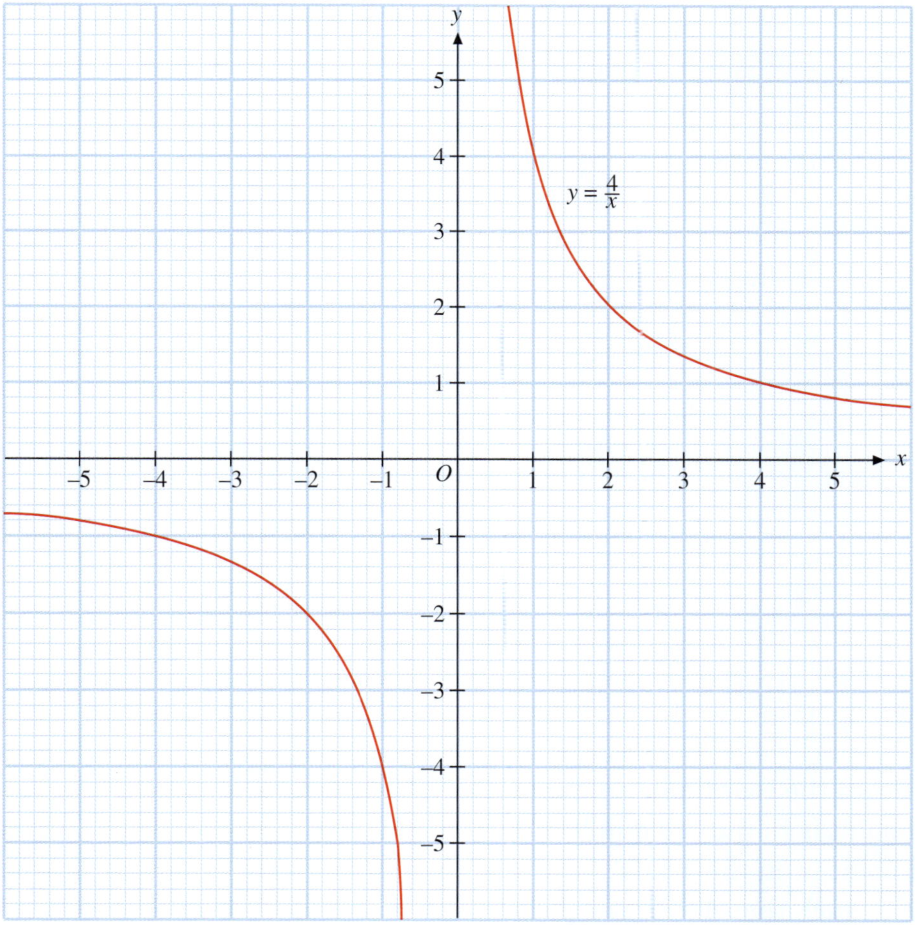

CHALLENGE 4

A plumber charges £y for an on-site maintenance job of x hours. The function of y of x is shown in the graph.

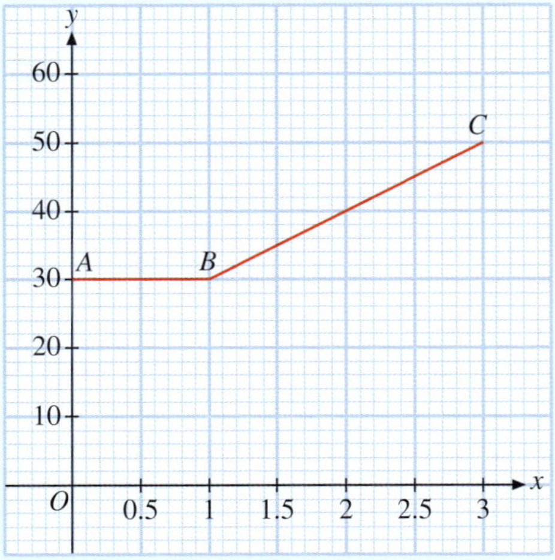

(a) Find the charge for a job taking

  (i) 30 minutes,

  (ii) 2 hours.

(b) Find the gradient and y-intercept of the line BC.

REVISION EXERCISE 4

1.

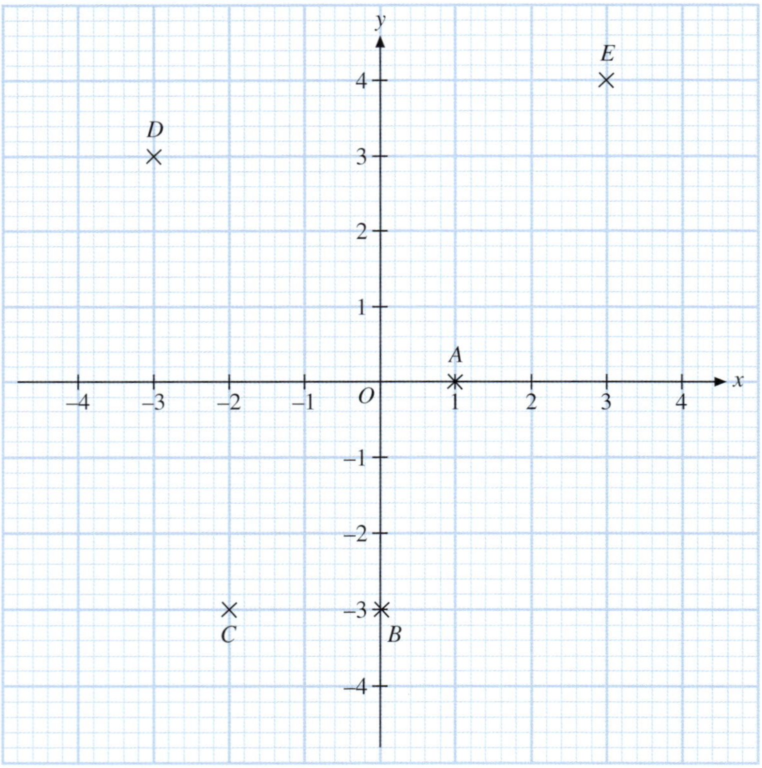

(a) Write down the coordinates of points A, B, C, D and E.

(b) Which point is in the 3rd quadrant?

(c) Which point is on the y-axis?

The point F is such that $ABCF$ is a parallelogram.

(d) Write down possible coordinates of F.

2. **(a)** Copy and complete the table of values of x and y for the function $y = 2x + 5$.

x	−4	−2	0	2	4
y	−3			9	

(b) Draw the graph of $y = 2x + 5$ for $-4 \le x \le 4$.

(c) Is the point $A(-1, 7)$ on the graph? Explain your answer.

3. **(a)** Find the gradient of each line.

(i)

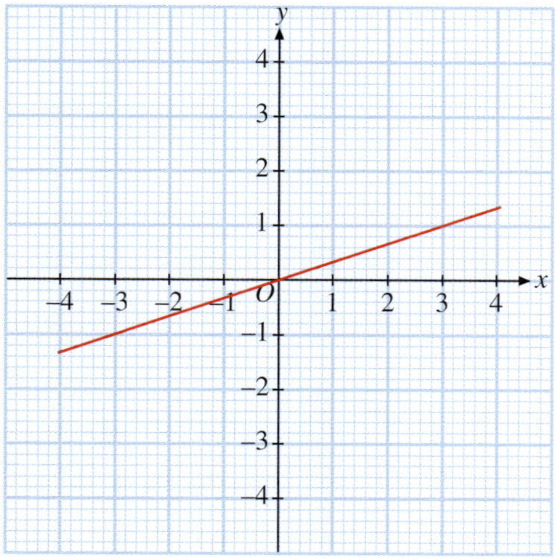

(ii)

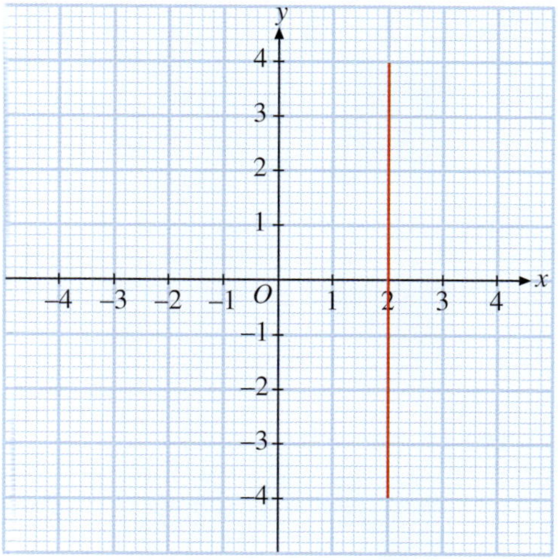

(iii)

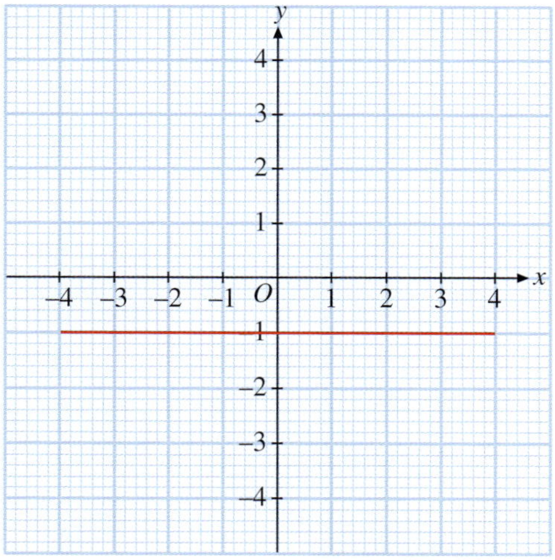

(iv)

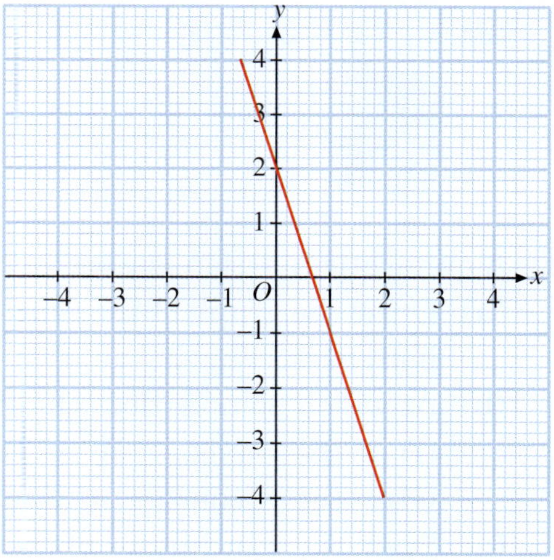

(b) Which of these functions could **(iv)** be the graph of?

$y = 3x + 2$ $\quad$ $y = -3x + 2$ $\quad$ $y = \frac{1}{3}x + 2$ $\quad$ $y = -3x - 2$

4. **(a)** Find the gradient and the y-intercept of the graph of each function.

(i) $y = 2x - 5$ $\quad$ **(ii)** $y = -3x + 1$ $\quad$ **(iii)** $y = 3x$

(iv) $y = -4x - 5$ $\quad$ **(v)** $y = -4$ $\quad$ **(vi)** $2x + y = 6$

(b) Which lines in part **(a)** are parallel? How do you know?

5. **(a)** Draw these lines on the same axes for $-3 \le x \le 3$, using a scale of 1 cm to 1 unit on both axes.

$y = 2x + 1$ $\quad$ $y = x + 1$ $\quad$ $y = -2x + 1$

(b) What is the same and what is different about these lines?

6. The total price, £y, of buying a watermelon and x mangoes is given by the function $y = 3x + 4$.

FINANCE

(a) Draw the graph of the function for $0 \le x \le 8$ using the scale of 1 cm to 1 unit on the x-axis and 1 cm to 5 units on the y-axis.
(b) State the gradient and y-intercept of the function.
(c) Interpret the meanings of 3 and 4 in the function.

7. For each function, copy and complete the table of values and then draw the graph for the range of values of x in the table.

(a) $y = x^2 - 4$

x	−4	−2	0	2	4
y	12			0	

(b) $y = -2x^2$

x	−2	−1	0	1	2
y		−2			−8

(c) $y = x^2 + 3x$

x	−4	−3	−2	−1	0	1
y	4			−2		4

(d) $y = -x^2 - 2$

x	−3	−2	−1	0	1	2
y		−6		−2	−3	

8. A quadratic function is $y = x^2 - 2x - 3$.
(a) Draw the graph of the function for $-2 \le x \le 4$ using the scale of 1 cm to 1 unit on both axes.
(b) At which point(s) does the graph cut
  (i) the x-axis,
  (ii) the y-axis?
(c) State the coordinates of the minimum point of the graph.

9. The height, y m of a golf ball, x seconds after it is hit, is modelled by the quadratic function $y = -5x^2 + 20x$. The graph of the function is shown.

SCIENCE

(a) What is the total time of flight of the golf ball?
(b) What is the maximum height of the ball?
(c) Estimate the height of the ball after 3 seconds.

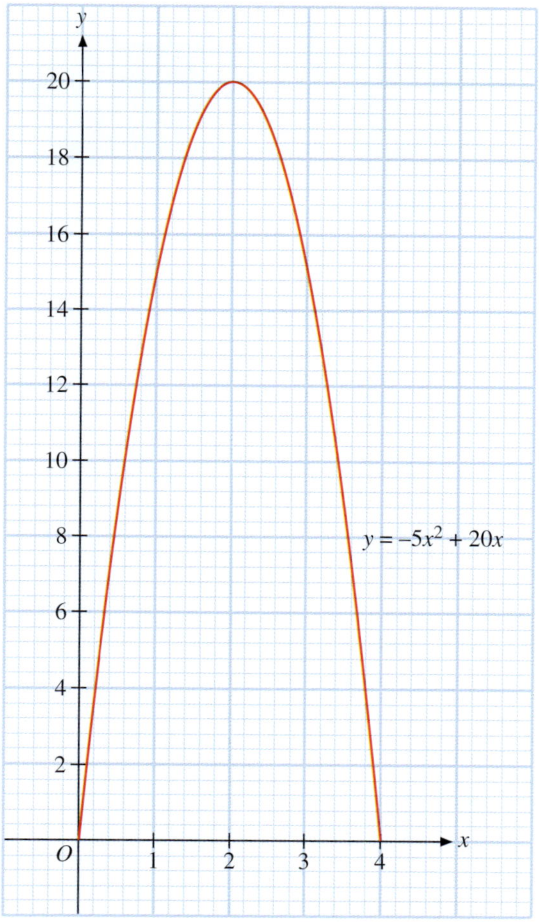

10. The cost of a minibus is shared equally between x people. The cost, £y, per person is given by the function $y = \frac{120}{x}$.

(a) Copy and complete the table of values:

x	5	6	8	10	15
y		20			8

(b) Draw the graph of the function for $5 \leq x \leq 15$.

(c) Use your graph to estimate the value of x when $y = 12$.

(d) Interpret the meaning of 120 in the function.

Write in Your Journal

Give some real-life examples of linear relationships. Explain whether the graphs representing the relationships will have positive or negative gradients.

INTEGRATED EXAMPLES AND REVIEW EXERCISE 1

Integrated Examples

Example 1

(a) Express 36 as a product of prime factors using index notation.

(b) Complete the table for the function $y = \frac{36}{x}, x \neq 0$.

x	2	4	6	9	18
y	18				

(c) Draw the graph of $y = \frac{36}{x}$ for $2 \leq x \leq 18$.

(d) Change the subject of the formula $y = \frac{36}{x}$ to x.

(e) Find the value of x in $y = \frac{36}{x}$ when $y = 9 \times 10^{-3}$.

Express your answer in standard form.

Solution

(a) Draw a factor tree.

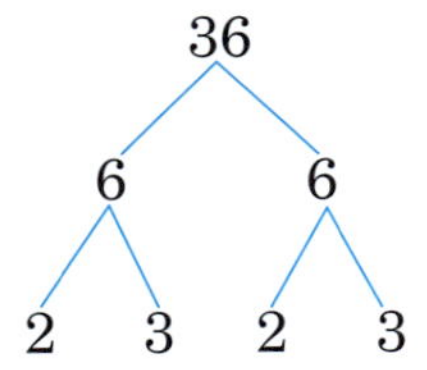

Hence, $36 = 2^2 \times 3^2$

(b) When $x = 4, y = \frac{36}{4} = 9$

When $x = 6, y = \frac{36}{6} = 6$ and so on.

x	2	4	6	9	18
y	18	9	6	4	2

REMARK

The table can be completed using the factors of 36 in part **(a)** as $xy = 36$.
For example,
$36 = 2 \times 2 \times 3 \times 3$
$= (3 \times 3) \times (2 \times 2)$
$= 9 \times 4$
So, when $x = 9, y = 4$.

(c) The graph shows $y = \frac{36}{x}$ for $2 \le x \le 18$.

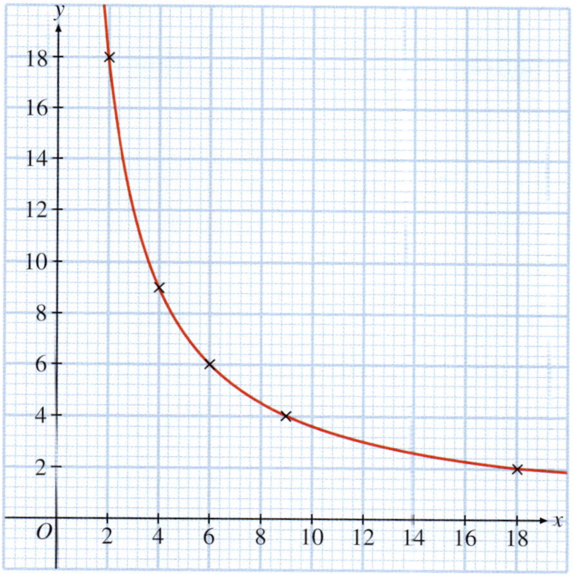

(d) A factor tree can be used to represent $y = \frac{36}{x}$.

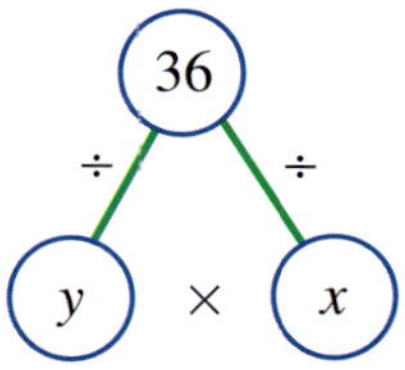

Using the factor tree, you can see that $x = \frac{36}{y}$.

You can also use algebra to rearrange this equation:

$$y = \frac{36}{x}$$

$$y \times x = \frac{36}{x} \times x \qquad \text{Multiply both sides by } x.$$

$$xy = 36$$

$$\frac{xy}{y} = \frac{36}{y} \qquad \text{Divide both sides by } y.$$

$$x = \frac{36}{y}$$

(e) Substituting $y = 9 \times 10^{-3}$ into $x = \frac{36}{y}$,

$$x = \frac{36}{9 \times 10^{-3}}$$

$$= \frac{36}{9} \times \frac{1}{10^{-3}}$$

$$= \frac{36}{9} \times 10^3 \qquad a^{-n} = \frac{1}{a^n}$$

$$= 4 \times 10^3$$

Note: The key sequence for working out the value of x on a calculator is:

[3] [6] [÷] [9] [$\times 10^x$] [(−)] [3] [=]

RECALL

You can use a factor tree in cases like this where one variable or number is equal to a number or variable divided by another number or variable.

REMARK

If you have a 'fraction' button $\frac{\square}{\square}$ on your calculator, you can use this to enter the calculation as it appears here.

Try It! 1

(a) Express 100 as a product of prime factors using index notation.

(b) Copy and complete the table for the function $y = \frac{100}{x}, x \neq 0$.

x	4	5	10	20	25
y					

(c) Draw the graph of $y = \frac{100}{x}$ for $4 \leq x \leq 25$, using a scale of 1 cm to 5 units on both axes.

(d) Change the subject of the formula $y = \frac{100}{x}$ to x.

(e) Find the value of x in $y = \frac{100}{x}$ when $y = 2 \times 10^4$. Express your answer in standard form.

Example 2

(a) Simplify $8(x + y) - 6(2x + y)$.
(b) Factorise the answer in part **(a)**.
(c) The equation of a straight line is $8(x + y) - 6(2x + y) = 12$. Find the value of y when $x = 4$.
(d) Make y the subject of the equation of the line.
(e) Write down the gradient and the y-intercept of the line.

Solution

(a) You can use multiplication frames to help expand the brackets.

$\times$	x	y
8	$8x$	$8y$

$\times$	$2x$	y
-6	$-12x$	$-6y$

$$\begin{aligned} 8(x + y) - 6(2x + y) &= 8(x + y) + -6(2x + y) \\ &= 8x + 8y - 12x - 6y && \text{Distributive law.} \\ &= 8x - 12x + 8y - 6y && \text{Collect like terms.} \\ &= -4x + 2y \end{aligned}$$

(b)
$$\begin{aligned} -4x + 2y &= (2)(-2x) + (2)(y) \\ &= 2(-2x + y) && \text{Extract the common factor 2.} \end{aligned}$$

(c)
$$\begin{aligned} 8(x + y) - 6(2x + y) &= 12 \\ -4x + 2y &= 12 && \text{From part (a).} \\ \frac{-4x + 2y}{2} &= \frac{12}{2} && \text{Divide both sides by 2.} \\ -2x + y &= 6 \end{aligned}$$

DISCUSS

Mia says the expression can also be factorised to $-2(2x - y)$. Is she correct?

When $x = 4$, substituting the value into the equation,

$$-2(4) + y = 6$$
$$-8 + y = 6$$
$$-8 + 8 + 2y = 6 + 8 \quad \text{Add 8 to both sides.}$$
$$2y = 14$$
$$\frac{2y}{2} = \frac{14}{2} \quad \text{Divide both sides by 2.}$$
$$y = 7$$

(d) Equation of the line is

$$-4x + 2y = 12 \quad \text{From part (c).}$$
$$-4x + 4x + 2y = 12 + 4x \quad \text{Add } 4x \text{ to both sides.}$$
$$2y = 4x + 12$$
$$\frac{2y}{2} = \frac{4x + 12}{2} \quad \text{Divide both sides by 2.}$$
$$y = 2x + 6$$

(e) The equation of the line is $y = 2x + 6$,
Therefore,
gradient = 2
y-intercept = 6

RECALL

A line with equation $y = mx + c$ has gradient m and y-intercept c.

Try It! 2

(a) Simplify $3(4x - y) - 2(x - 4y)$.
(b) Factorise the answer in part **(a)**.
(c) The equation of a straight line is $3(4x - y) - 2(x - 4y) = 15$. Find the value of y when $x = 2$.
(d) Make y the subject of the equation of the line.
(e) Write down the gradient and the y-intercept of the line.

Example 3

$ABCD$ is a rectangle. The length of AB is x cm and the length of BC is $(10 - x)$ cm. The area of $ABCD$ is y cm^2.
(a) Show that $y = -x^2 + 10x$.
(b) Draw the graph of $y = -x^2 + 10x$ for $0 \le x \le 10$.
(c) Find the maximum area of the rectangle.

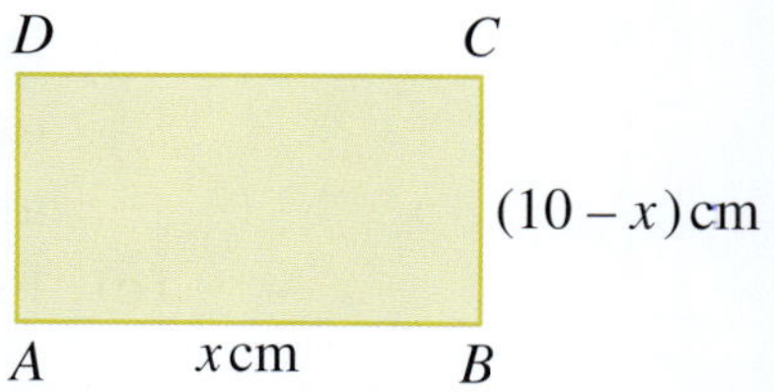

Solution

(a) Area of $ABCD = AB \times BC$

$$\therefore \quad y = x(10 - x)$$
$$= 10x - x^2 \quad \text{Distributive law.}$$
$$\text{So} \quad y = -x^2 + 10x$$

REMARK

You could have used a multiplication frame:

×	10	$-x$
x	$10x$	$-x^2$

(b) Draw a table of values:

x	0	2	4	5	6	8	10
y	0	16	24	25	24	16	0

The graph shows the function:

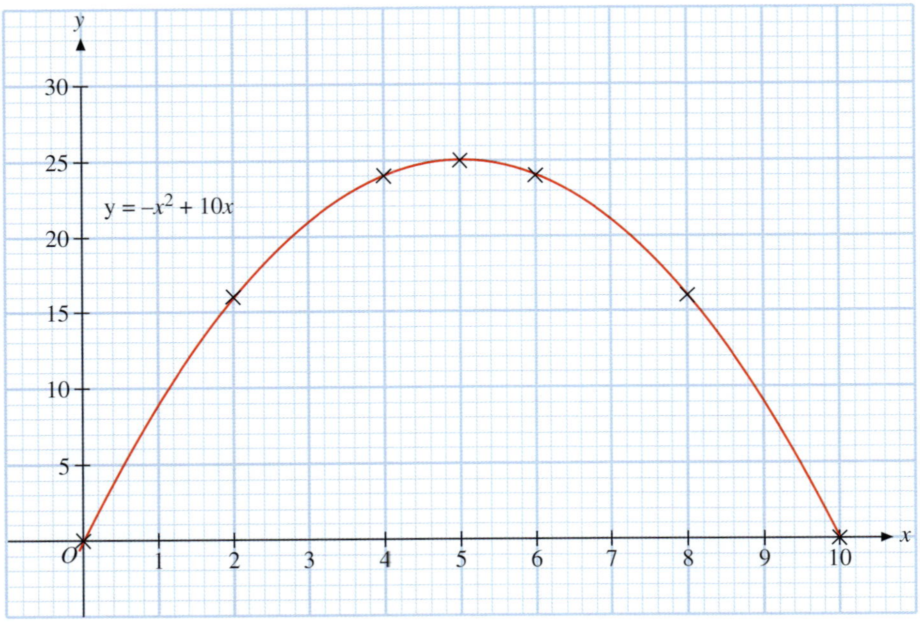

(c) Reading from the graph, the maximum value of y is 25.

Therefore,

maximum area $= 25\,\text{cm}^2$

REMARK

Substitute into $y = x(10 - x)$:

When $x = 2$,

$y = 2(10 - 2)$
$= 2(8)$
$= 16$

When $x = 4$,

$y = 4(10 - 4)$
$= 4(6)$
$= 24$

And so on.

DISCUSS

What are the dimensions of the rectangle when the area is $25\,\text{cm}^2$?

Try It! 3

$PQRS$ is a rectangle of perimeter 16 cm. The length of PQ is x cm and the length of QR is $(8 - x)$ cm. The area of $PQRS$ is $y\,\text{cm}^2$.

(a) Show that $y = -x^2 + 8x$.

(b) Draw the graph of $y = -x^2 + 8x$ for $0 \le x \le 8$ using the scale of 1 cm to 1 unit on the x-axis and 1 cm to 5 units on the y-axis.

(c) Find the maximum area of the rectangle.

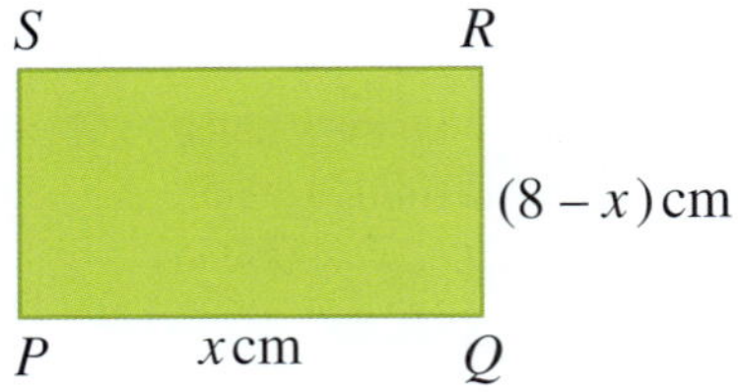

REVIEW EXERCISE 1

1. (a) Express 125 as a product of prime factors in index notation.
   (b) Express 250 as a product of prime factors in index notation.
   (c) Find the HCF and LCM of 125 and 250.

2. (a) Find the value of $5^0 - 3^{-2}$.
   (b) Is it true that $(-99)^0 = 9^0$? Explain your answer.
   (c) Is it true that $(-a)^{-4} = -\frac{1}{a^4}$? Explain your answer.

3. (a) Express the number of seconds in 10 hours in standard form.
   SCIENCE
   (b) The diameter of an influenza virus is 85×10^{-9} m. The diameter of an atmospheric dust particle is 0.000 000 25 m.
      (i) Express these two diameters in standard form.
      (ii) Which one has a smaller diameter?

4. Expand and simplify these expressions.
   (a) $5(3x + 7) + 2x - 3$
   (b) $4(x - 2y) - 3(2x - 7y)$
   (c) $x(x - 1)$
   (d) $2x(3x + 5)$

5. Factorise these expressions fully.
   (a) $9a + 6$
   (b) $5p - 15q$
   (c) $12x + 24y$
   (d) $-6p + 18r$

6. Solve these equations.
   (a) $3p + 7 = 2p - 4$
   (b) $q - 5 = 3q - 13$
   (c) $4(r - 3) = 12$
   (d) $3(2s + 1) = -9$

7. Make x the subject of each formula.
   (a) $y = x + 7$
   (b) $y = 7x$
   (c) $3y = \frac{k}{x}$
   (d) $2y = \frac{x}{3} + k$

8. A formula is $I = 2v - 10$.
   (a) Change the subject of the formula to v.
   (b) Find the value of v when $I = 20$.

9. A rectangle is bounded by the lines $y = 3$, $y = -2$, $x = -1$ and $x = 4$.
   (a) Draw all four lines for $-3 \le x \le 6$ on the same diagram using the scale of 1 cm to 1 unit on both axes.
   (b) Find the area of the rectangle.

10. Find the gradient and the y-intercept of each line.
   (a) $y = 5x - 4$
   (b) $y = -2x - 3$
   (c) $y = 3$
   (d) $3x + y = 9$

11. For each function, copy and complete the table of values and then draw the graph for the range of values of x in the table.
   (a) $y = 3x - 3$

x	−2	−1	0	1	2
y					

   (b) $y = -3x + 2$

x	−2	−1	0	1	2
y					

(c) $y = x^2 - 9$

x	-4	-3	0	3	4
y					

(d) $y = -x^2 - 2x$

x	-4	-2	0	2	4
y					

12. Blue ribbon is sold in lengths of 270 cm. Yellow ribbon is sold in lengths of 120 cm. Andy wants to tie a piece of yellow ribbon and a piece of blue ribbon onto some balloons. The pieces of ribbon must all be the same length, and he wants to use all the ribbon. What is the longest possible length of each piece?

13. (a) Draw the lines $y = -2x + 6$ and $y = 2x + 6$ for $-2 \leq x \leq 2$ on the same axes using the scale of 1 cm to 1 unit on both axes.

(b) What is the same and what is different about the graphs?

(c) Make x the subject of the formula $y = -2x + 6$.

14. SCIENCE A bottle of solution is divided into x equal parts for an experiment. The volume, y ml, of each part is given by the function $y = \frac{80}{x}$, $x > 0$.

(a) Use a table of values to draw the graph of the function $y = \frac{80}{x}$.

(b) Interpret the meaning of 80 in the function.

(c) Make x the subject of the formula $y = \frac{80}{x}$.

15. PROBLEM SOLVING The height, y cm of a football x seconds after it is kicked is given by the function $y = -5x^2 + 10x$.

(a) Draw the graph of the function for $0 \leq x \leq 2$.

(b) Use your graph to estimate the maximum height reached by the ball.

(c) The ball is kicked directly towards the goal. It reaches the goal after 1.5 seconds. Given that the goal is 2.4 m tall, could it have gone in? Explain your answer.

5 PROPORTION

WHAT IS IN THIS CHAPTER:

A photo of a puppy is printed in two sizes. One is 14 cm by 10 cm. The other is 21 cm by 15 cm. Work out the ratio of the length of the smaller photo to that of the larger photo and simplify the ratio. Work out the ratio of the width of the smaller photo to that of the larger photo and simplify the ratio. What do you think will happen to the picture if only the length is increased?

LET'S LEARN TO

- understand the ideas of direct proportion and inverse proportion
- determine whether two quantities are in direct or inverse proportion
- solve problems involving proportion

FLASHBACK

1. Ratios

The ratio of a quantity p to a quantity $q = p:q$.
You can find equivalent ratios by multiplying or dividing both sides of the ratio by the same number.
For example, if there are 8 cats and 6 dogs,

number of cats : number of dogs

$$8:6 \xrightarrow{\div 2} 4:3$$

Cats	:	Dogs
8	:	6
4	:	3

4:3 is the ratio in its simplest form. It cannot be simplified further since the HCF of 4 and 3 is 1.

Note that the order of the parts in a ratio is important. For example, the ratio of cats to dogs in the example is 4:3 not 3:4. The ratio of dogs to cats, however, is 3:4.

2. Graphs of Functions

(a) The graph of the linear function $y = mx + c$ is a straight line with gradient m and y-intercept c.

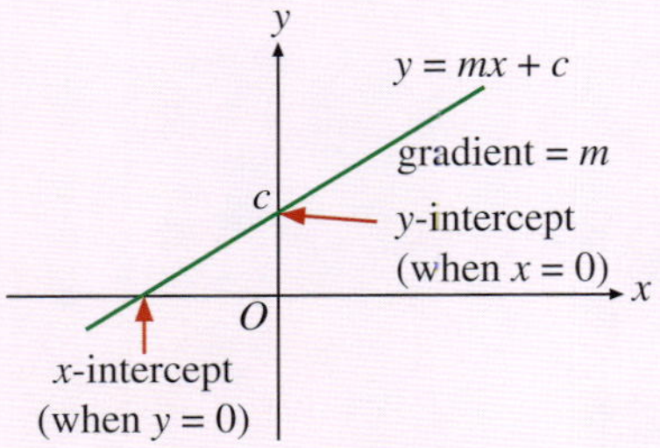

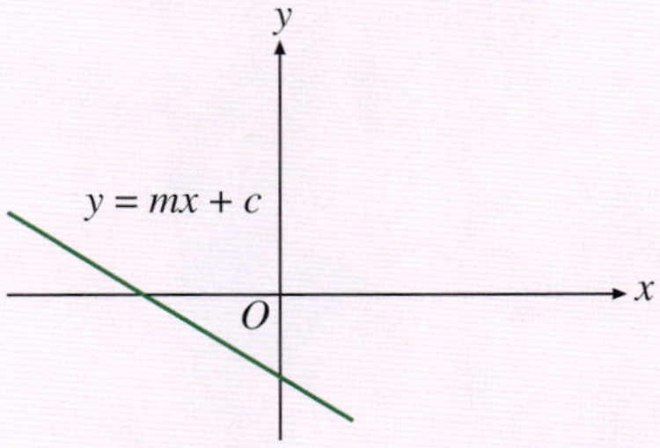

DISCUSS

What is the same and what is different about these two graphs? What might the values of m and c be in each?

(b) The graph of the reciprocal function $y = \frac{k}{x}, x \neq 0$ is a hyperbola as shown when $k > 0$.

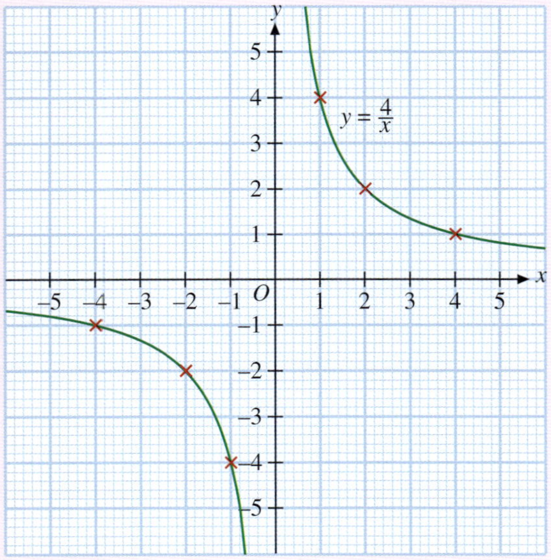

5.1 Direct Proportion

On a market stall, two apples are sold for £1. The price for four apples will be £2. The price for six apples will be £3. The price is related to the number of apples bought and it follows a certain pattern. You will learn about this type of relationship between two quantities in this chapter.

DISCUSS

What would be the price for

(a) three apples,

(b) five apples,

(c) seven apples?

CLASS ACTIVITY 1

Objective: To represent direct proportion relationships between two quantities using tables, double number lines, graphs and equations.

The market stall sells three plums for £1.

1. Copy and complete the table.

Number of plums (x)	3	6	9		15
Price (£y)	1	2			
$\frac{y}{x}$	$\frac{1}{3}$				

2. The values of x and y can be represented with a **double number line** as shown. It consists of two number lines, aligned at 0. The scales on the lines are aligned so that the corresponding values of x and y are aligned vertically.

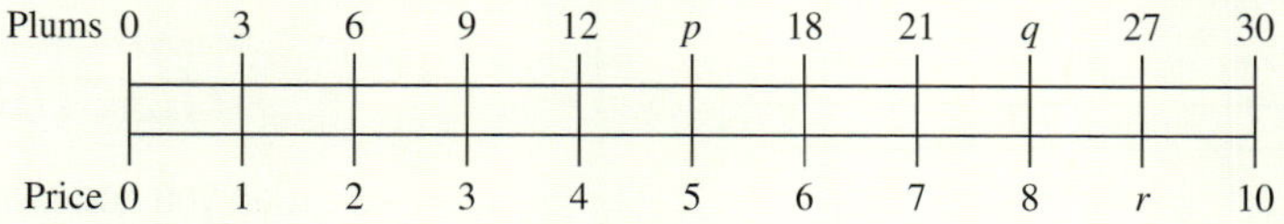

DISCUSS

Why are the number lines aligned at 0?

(a) What are the values of p, q and r on the double number line? Explain your reasoning to a partner.

(b) Use the double number line to work out

(i) the price of 21 plums,

(ii) the number of plums that can be bought for £6.

(c) Describe what happens to the price when the number of plums

(i) doubles, (ii) halves,

(iii) is multiplied by 4, (iv) increases by 3,

(v) decreases by 3.

(d) Describe what happens to the number of plums when the price

(i) doubles, (ii) halves,

(iii) is multiplied by 4, (iv) increases by 1,

(v) decreases by 3.

3. Copy the Cartesian plane and mark the ordered pairs (x, y) from your completed table on it.

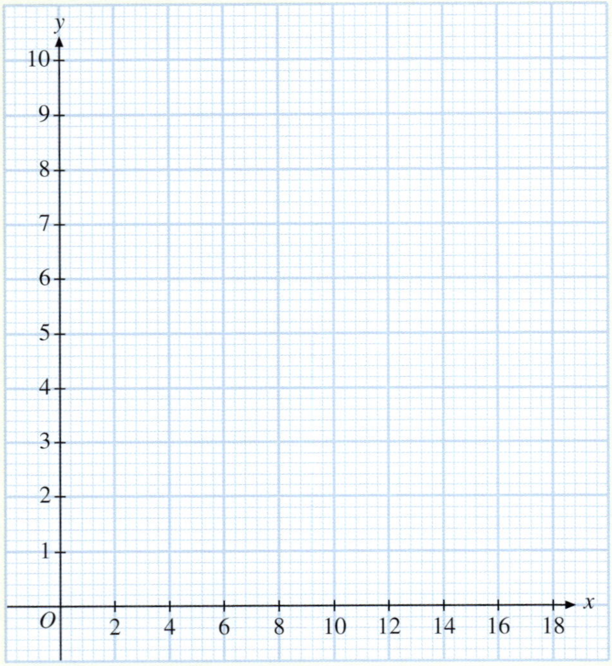

DISCUSS

What do you notice about the points you have marked? Can you join them up to form a line?

Do you recall what type of function is represented by a straight line? Do you know what the equation of the line is?

4. The market stall also sells melons. It sells two melons for £3.

(a) Copy and complete the double number line to represent the relationship between the number of melons sold and the price charged.

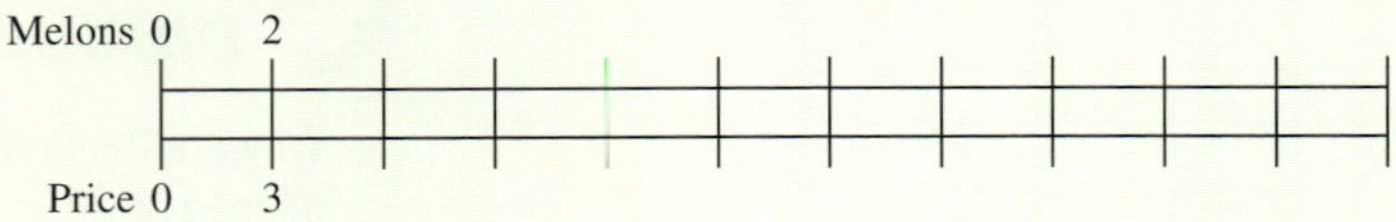

(b) Use your double number line to work out

(i) the price of 18 melons,

(ii) the number of melons that can be bought for £12.

(c) Complete these sentences:

(i) When the number of melons doubles, the price charged ______.

(ii) When the number of melons _____, the price charged _____.

DISCUSS

Can you add a line onto your Cartesian plane for **Question 3** to represent the relationship between the number of melons and the cost?

In Class Activity 1, the number of plums (x) and the price (£y) are said to be in **direct proportion**. You can see that the points (x, y) lie on a straight line passing through the origin. The equation of this line is $y = \frac{1}{3}x$. You can also see that this rearranges to $\frac{y}{x} = \frac{1}{3}$. Here $\frac{1}{3}$ is a constant.

In general:

> Two quantities, x and y, are in direct proportion if, when x changes by a multiplicative scale factor (for example, '$\times 2$'), y changes by the same multiplicative scale factor.

For example, if 3 plums cost £1, and you multiply 3 plums by two then the price will also be multiplied by two. Therefore, 6 plums will cost £2.

DISCUSS

Which of these double number lines represents direct proportion relationships? Explain how you know.

(a)
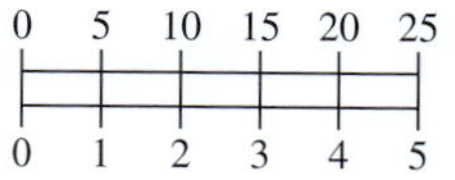

(b)
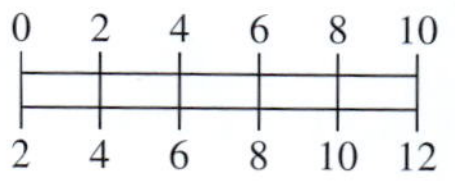

(c)
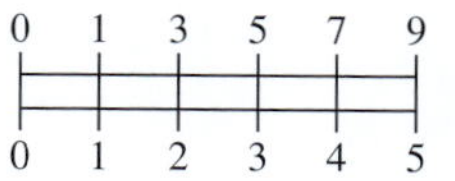

Example 1

Identical nails are aligned in a straight line.

(a) Copy and complete the table for the number, x, of nails on a line and the length, y cm, of the line.

Number of nails (x)	1	2	3	4	5
Length (y cm)	3				

(b) Draw a double number line to represent the relationship between x and y.

(c) Are x and y in direct proportion? Explain your reasoning.

(d) Plot the coordinate pairs (x, y) on a Cartesian plane and join with a line.

Solution

(a)

From the given table, the length of 1 nail = 3 cm.
The length of 2 nails = $3 \times 2 = 6$ cm, and so on.
The completed table is shown.

Number of nails (x)	1	2	3	4	5
Length (y cm)	3	6	9	12	15

(b) The double number line is shown.
Note that $x = 1$ is aligned with $y = 3$, as in the table.

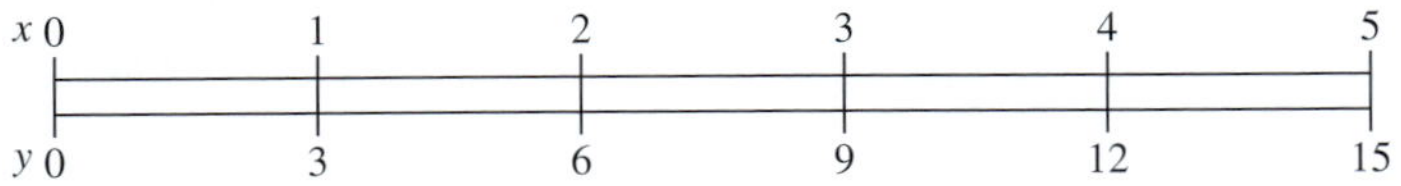

(c) When the number of nails, x, changes by a multiplicative scale factor then the length, y, changes by the same multiplicative scale factor. For example, when the number of nails doubles from 2 to 4, the length doubles from 6 to 12. Therefore, the number of nails and their length are in direct proportion.

(d)

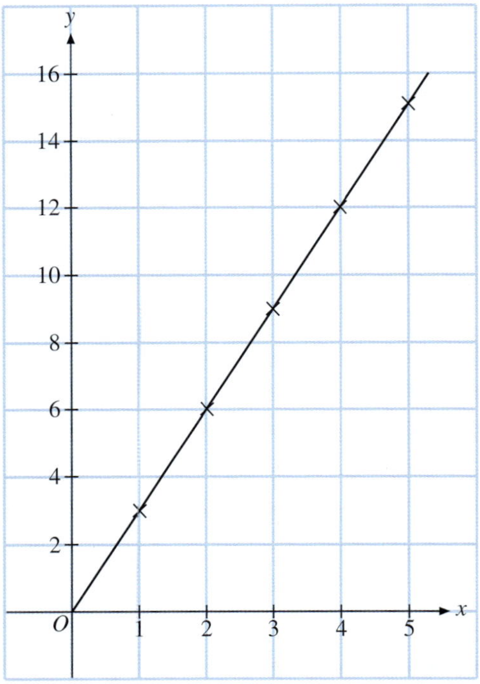

> **DISCUSS**
> What is the constant, $\frac{y}{x}$, in Example 1?

> **DISCUSS**
> What is the gradient of this line? How does this relate to the context of the question? Can you write down the equation of the line?

Try It! 1

Identical copies of a book are stacked up into a pile.

(a) Copy and complete the table for the number (x) of copies on a pile and the height, y cm, of the pile.

Number of copies (x)	2	4	6	8	10
Height (y cm)	5				

(b) Draw a double number line to represent the relationship between x and y.

(c) Are x and y in direct proportion? Explain your reasoning.

(d) Plot the coordinate pairs (x, y) on a Cartesian plane and join with a line.

Example 2

The price charged by a taxi firm for different length journeys is shown in the table.

Length of journey (km)	1	2	3	4
Price (£)	6	8	10	12

(a) Is the price charged in direct proportion to the length of the journey? Explain your answer.

(b) Draw a graph showing the price, £P, of a journey of x km.

Solution

(a) Consider what happens to the price when the length of journey varies.

When the length of the journey is doubled, is the price of the journey doubled?
Price of 1 km journey = £6
Price of 2 km journey = £8
So, the price does not double, since $2 \times$ £6 = £12 not £8.

When the length of the journey is multiplied by 3 from 1 to 3, is the price of the journey also multiplied by 3?
Price of 1 km journey = £6
Price of 3 km journey = £10
So, the price is not multiplied by 3, since
$3 \times$ £6 = £18 not £10.

Therefore, the price of the journey is **not** in direct proportion to the length of the journey.

(b)

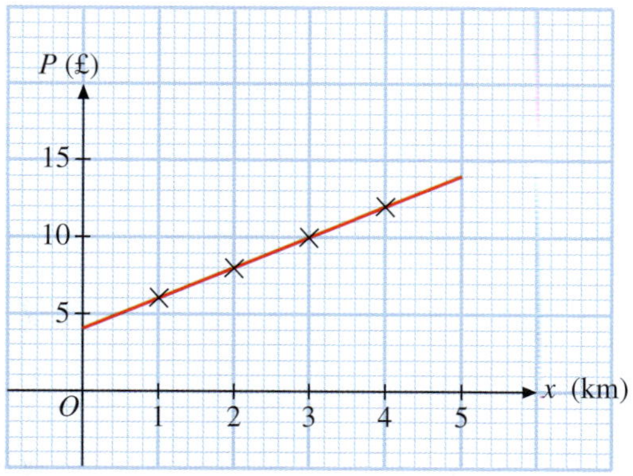

DISCUSS

What is the same and what is different about this graph and the graph in Example 1?

Try It! 2

A teenager does odd-jobs to earn some money. The table shows the price they charge for jobs of different durations.

Duration of job (hours)	1	2	3	4
Price (£)	7	12	17	22

(a) Is the price charged in direct proportion to the number of hours worked? Explain your answer.

(b) Draw a graph showing the price, £P, of a job of x hours.

From Class Activity 1 and Example 1 you can see that if x and y are in direct proportion, then:

- the corresponding values of x and y lie on a straight line passing through the origin,
- x and y are linked by the function $y = kx$ for some constant k.

DISCUSS

Consider the equation $y = x + 2$.

Tim says, 'x and y are in direct proportion since the graph of $y = x + 2$ is a straight line.' Is Tim correct? Explain your answer.

As you saw, the price and distance in Example 2 were not in direct proportion.

Ratios can also be used to represent relationships between variables in direct proportion. You can solve problems by 'scaling up' or 'scaling down' the ratio. For example, in Class Activity 1, the price of two melons is £3, so to find the price of 8 melons:

melons : price

$$2:3 \quad \xrightarrow{\times 4} \quad 8:12$$

(×4 on both sides)

You could also draw a table:

Melons	Price (£)
2	3
8	12

(×4 down both columns)

Therefore, the price of 8 melons is £12.

Example 3

A recipe for 12 Yorkshire puddings requires three eggs.

(a) How many Yorkshire puddings can be made using five eggs?

(b) Draw a double number line to represent the relationship between the number of Yorkshire puddings and the number of eggs.

(c) Use your double number line to find the number of eggs needed to make 16 Yorkshire puddings.

(d) Which of these functions describes the relationship between the number of eggs, e, and the number of Yorkshire puddings, y, for $e > 0$?

$y = 3e$ $\quad$ $y = 4e$ $\quad$ $y = \frac{1}{4}e$ $\quad$ $y = \frac{4}{e}$

Solution

(a) Draw a table:

	Yorkshire puddings	Eggs	
$\div 3$	12	3	$\div 3$
$\times 5$	4	1	$\times 5$
	20	5	

Find the number that can be made with 1 egg (scale down).

Find the number that can be made with 5 eggs (scale up).

Number of Yorkshire puddings made with five eggs = 20

(b)

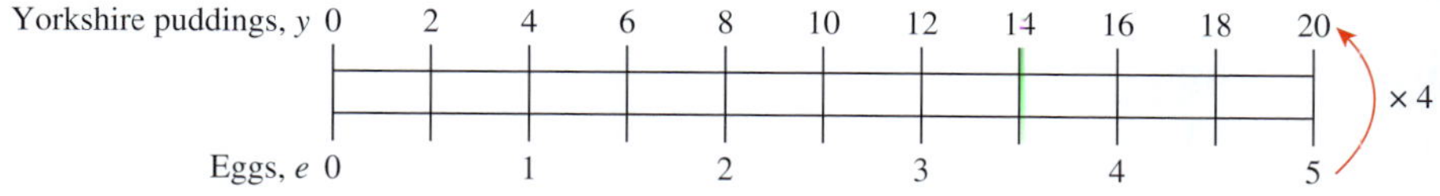

(c) Using the double number line, 16 puddings correspond to 4 eggs.
Number of eggs required to make 16 Yorkshire puddings = 4

(d) Number of eggs, e, and number of Yorkshire puddings, y, are in direct proportion because when e doubles, y doubles. Therefore, the relationship between them is of the form $y = ke$ where k is a constant. The correct function is $y = 4e$.
Since, for example, when $e = 1$, $y = 4 \times 1 = 4$ ✓
and when $e = 5$, $y = 4 \times 5 = 20$ ✓

DISCUSS

Morris works out the answer to part **(a)** as follows:

	Yorkshire puddings	Eggs	
$\times 5$	12	3	$\times 5$
$\div 3$	60	15	$\div 3$
	20	5	

What is the same and what is different about the two methods? In both methods can you get from the top row of the table to the bottom row in one step?

REMARK

Once you have found the number of Yorkshire puddings that can be made with 1 egg, you can really easily scale this up by multiplying to find the number made with any number of eggs.

Try It! 3

A recipe for curry for 6 people uses 3 teaspoons of curry powder.

(a) How many people can you make the curry for with 4 teaspoons of curry powder?

(b) Draw a double number line to represent the relationship between the amount of curry powder and number of people.

(c) Use your double number line to find the amount of curry powder that should be used to make the curry for 18 people.

(d) Which of these functions describes the relationship between the number of teaspoons of curry powder, c, and the number of people the curry can serve, y, for $c > 0$?

$y = 3c \qquad y = 2c \qquad y = \frac{1}{2}c \qquad y = \frac{2}{c}$

Example 4

The daily wage of a worker is directly proportional to the number of hours worked. When the worker does 6 hours of work, the salary is £90. Find the wage for 8 hours of work.

Solution

Draw a table.

	Hours	Wage		
	6	90		
÷6	1	15	÷6	Find wage for 1 hour.
×8	8	120	×8	Find wage for 8 hours.

Wage for working 8 hours = £120

Alternatively, use a double number line to represent the relationship.

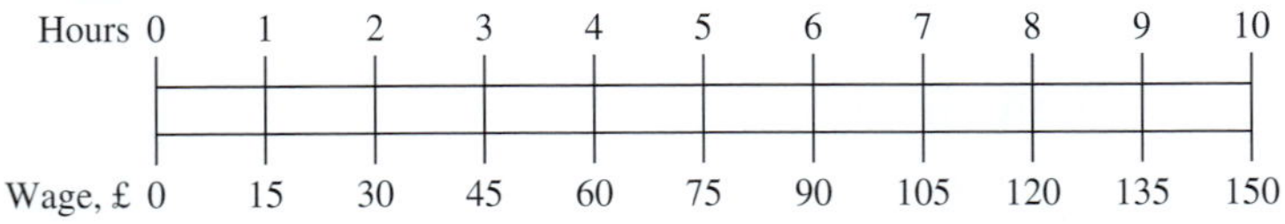

On the double number line, 8 hours is aligned with £120. Therefore,

Wage for working 8 hours = £120

REMARK

The method of scaling down so that one of the variables is 1 is called the **unitary method**. Here you are working out the wage for one **unit** of time (one hour).

REMARK

Start by aligning 6 on the top with 90 on the bottom then work out what the scale must be on each line.

Try It! 4

The price of some milkshakes is directly proportional to the number bought. The price of 4 milkshakes is £12. Find the price for 7 milkshakes.

Example 5

A type of crisps can be bought in small bags of 6 packs for £1.50 or in large bags of 20 packs for £4. Which is better value?

£1.50 £4

Solution

There are two methods you can use. You can use the unitary method ('scaling down') to find the price for one pack in each case.

Small bag

	Packs	Price	
÷6	6	1.50	÷6
	1	0.25	

Price of 1 pack = £0.25 (25p)

Large bag

	Packs	Price	
÷20	20	4	÷20
	1	0.2	

Price of 1 pack = £0.20 (20p)

Therefore, the bag of 20 is better value because the price of one packet is lower than the price for one packet in the bag of 6 packs.

Or you can use 'scaling up' to find the cost of a larger number of packs:

Small bag

	Packs	Price	
÷10	6	1.50	÷10
	60	15	

Price of 60 packs = £15

Large bag

	Packs	Price	
×3	20	4	×3
	60	12	

Price of 60 packs = £12

Therefore, the bag of 20 is better value because 60 packs will cost less if you buy them in bags of 20 packs than in bags of 6 packs.

DISCUSS

Why would you calculate the cost of 60 packs? How does this relate to the pack sizes of 6 and 20?

Try It! 5

Tins of fruit salad can be in bought in small packs of 4 tins for £1.60 or in large packs of 10 tins for £4.50. Which is better value?

DISCUSS

Use the two different methods to calculate your answer. Which method do you find easier?

PRACTICE 5.1

LEVEL 1

1. The tables show the prices of mangoes in two shops.

Shop A

Number of mangoes (x)	1	2	3	4
Price (£ y)	2	3	4	5

Shop B

Number of mangoes (x)	2	4	6	8
Price (£ y)	4	8	12	16

(a) In which shop is the number of mangoes and the price in direct proportion? Explain your answer.

(b) Draw a double number line to represent the relationship between x and y for the answer in part **(a)**, and work out

(i) the price for 10 mangoes, **(ii)** the price for 7 mangoes,

(iii) the number of mangoes you can get for £10.

2. The two graphs show the distance, y km, of two cyclists from a church at time x hours.

(a) Which graph represents a relationship between the distance, y, and the cycling time, x, that is in direct proportion? Explain your answer.

(b) Draw a double number line to represent the relationship between x and y for the answer in **(a)**.

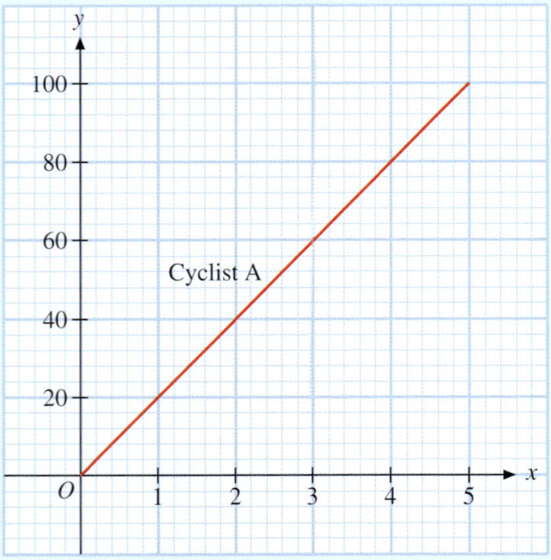

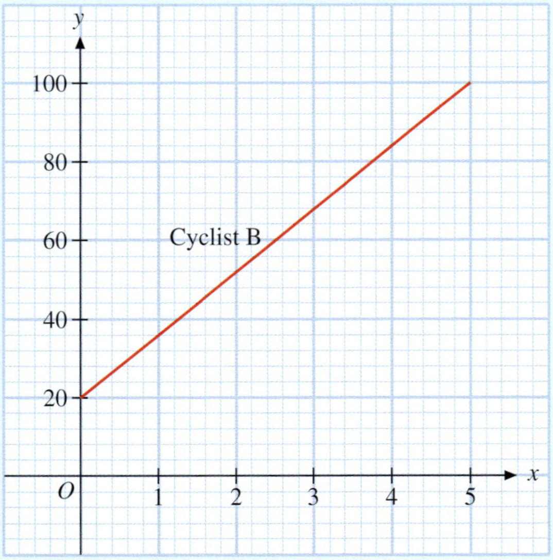

3. The total mass, T grams, of beads is directly proportional to the number, x, of beads.

Number of beads (x)	5	10	q	20
Total mass (T grams)	20	p	56	80

(a) Draw a double number line to represent the relationship between x and T.
(b) Find the values of p and q in the table.
(c) Plot the corresponding values of x and T on a Cartesian plane and join with a line.
(d) Which of these is the equation of the line in part **(c)** for $x > 0$?

$T = 5x$ $\quad$ $T = 4x$ $\quad$ $T = \frac{1}{4}x$ $\quad$ $T = \frac{4}{x}$

4. A supermarket sells tins of tomatoes either as single tins or in packs of 4. The cost of a single tin of tomatoes is 60p and the cost of a pack of 4 tins is £2. Is the price of the tins of tomatoes in direct proportion to the number of tins? Explain your answer.

£ FINANCE

5. **(a)** The price of sandwiches is directly proportional to the number bought. The price of two sandwiches is £6. Find the price of

£ FINANCE

(i) 4 sandwiches, **(ii)** 6 sandwiches.

(b) The price of pears is directly proportional to the number bought. The price of four pears is £2. Find the price of

(i) 8 pears, **(ii)** 10 pears.

6. The distance run by a person is directly proportional to the time taken. Given that they run 640 m in 4 minutes, how far can they run in 9 minutes? Work out your answer in two different ways.

LEVEL 2

7. The time, y minutes, taken to paint x tables is directly proportional to the number of tables. Given that it takes 26 minutes to paint 2 tables

(a) represent this relationship on a double number line,
(b) find the time taken to paint 5 tables,
(c) explain which of these functions represents the relationship between x and y for $x > 0$.

$y = 26x$ $\quad$ $x = 26y$ $\quad$ $y = 13x$ $\quad$ $y = \frac{13}{x}$

8. Here is a basic muffin recipe for 20 muffins. Base your answers on this recipe.

- 2 eggs
- 125 ml vegetable oil
- 250 ml milk
- 250 grams sugar
- 400 grams self-raising flour
- 1 teaspoon salt

(a) Represent the relationship between the number of muffins made and the volume of milk needed on a double number line. How much milk is needed to make 30 muffins?

(b) Represent the relationship between the number of muffins made and the mass of flour needed on a double number line. How many muffins can you make with 760 grams self-raising flour?

(c) Represent the relationship between the mass of sugar used and the mass of flour needed on a double number line. If 375 grams of sugar are used, how many grams of flour are needed?

(d) Write an equation connecting the number of eggs, e, with the number of muffins, m.

9. A type of paint can be bought in a 2 litre tub for £12 or in a 5 litre tub for £28. Show that the bigger tub is better value than the smaller tub. Show your reasoning in two different ways.

£ FINANCE

10. There are two different brands of orange juice in a shop. Brand X costs £1.40 for 700 ml and Brand Y costs £1.25 for 500 ml. Which is better value? Show your reasoning in two different ways.

£ FINANCE

5.2 Inverse Proportion

shared between 2 people

shared between 8 people

When two quantities x and y are in direct proportion, you have learnt that y increases by the same scale factor as x increases. However, in some real-life situations, quantities are not in direct proportion, but are in inverse proportion. This is where one value decreases proportionally as the related value increases. For instance, when a sum of money is shared equally between x people, the share, £y, that each person gets decreases as the number of people increases.

CLASS ACTIVITY 2

Objective: To represent inverse proportion relationships between two quantities using tables and graphs.

A sum of £36 is divided equally between some people. Each person gets the same share. Every person receives a whole number of pounds.

1. How many ways can you find to share the money equally between different numbers of people? Copy and complete the table to show different possibilities. One has been done for you.

Number of people (x)	**Share of each person (£y)**
3	12

2. Complete these sentences.
   When the number of people doubles, each person's share ______
   When the number of people ______, each person's share ______

3. Copy the axes and plot the corresponding points (x, y) from the table.

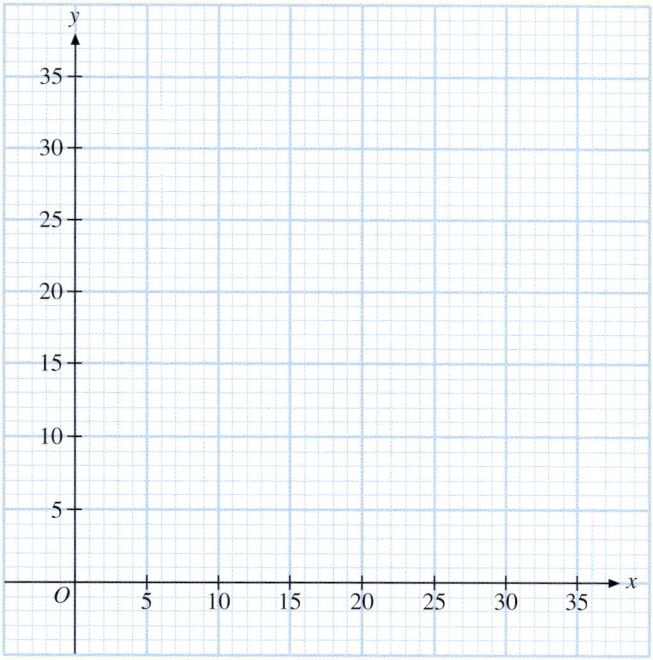

4. What can you say about the points plotted in **Question 3**? Are they on a straight line?

DISCUSS

Do you recognise the graph? What type of function has a graph like this?

In Class Activity 2, the number (x) of people and the share for each person $(£y)$ are said to be in **inverse proportion**. You can see that the points (x, y) lie on a hyperbola. The equation of the hyperbola is $y = \frac{36}{x}$ when $x > 0$.

DISCUSS

Can you verify that the equation $y = \frac{36}{x}$ is correct? How might you do this with the information in Class Activity 2?

When you multiply (or divide) the number of people by a scale factor, you must divide (or multiply) the share each person gets by the same scale factor. For example

	Number of people (x)	Share of each person (£y)	
	2	18	
$\times 3$	6	6	$\div 3$
$\div 2$	3	12	$\times 2$

In general:

Two variables x and y are in inverse proportion if, when there is a multiplicative scale factor change in x (for example '$\times$ 3'), there is the inverse multiplicative scale factor change in y (for example, '$\div$ 3').

REMARK

A 'multiplicative scale factor change' simply means multiplying (or dividing) by a constant, for example '$\times$ 3'. The inverse of '$\times$ 3' is '$\div$ 3'.

For example, if x and y are in inverse proportion, when x is multiplied by 2, y is divided by 2 and when x is divided by 3, y is multiplied by 3.

Example 6

A rectangle has a length of x cm and a width of y cm. The area of the rectangle is always 40 cm^2.

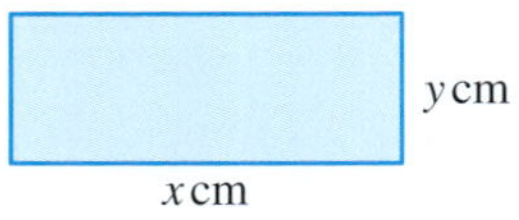

(a) Copy and complete the table of values of x and y.

x	2	4	10	20
y	20			

(b) Are x and y in inverse proportion? Explain your answer.

(c) Plot the coordinate pairs (x, y) on a Cartesian plane. Join the points with a smooth curve. What type of graph have you drawn?

Solution

(a) Area of the rectangle $= x \times y$

As the area $= 40$ cm^2,

when $x = 4, y = 10$ since $4 \times 10 = 40$

when $x = 10, y = 4$ since $10 \times 4 = 40$

when $x = 20, y = 2$ since $20 \times 2 = 40$

This is the completed table.

x	2	4	10	20
y	20	10	4	2

(b) When x changes by a multiplicative scale factor then y changes by the inverse multiplicative scale factor. For example, when x is doubled (such as from 2 to 4), y is halved (from 20 to 10). Therefore, x and y are in inverse proportion.

(c)

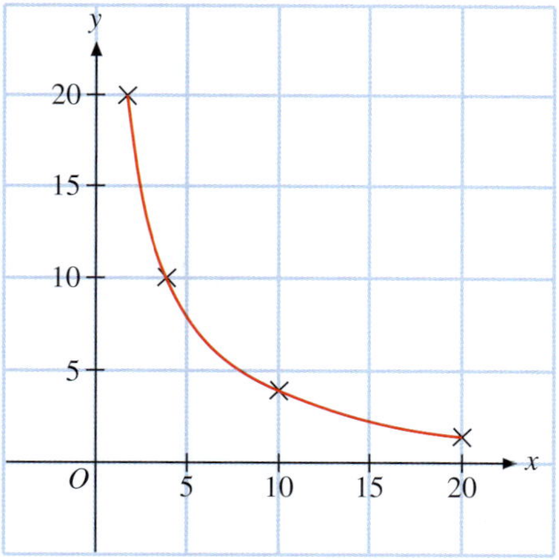

The graph is a hyperbola.

DISCUSS

How would you join up the points? Which of these could be the equation of the graph?

$y = 40x \qquad y = \frac{40}{x}$

DISCUSS

Is it possible for x or y to be equal to 0 in Example 6?

Try It! 6

The lengths of the two adjacent sides of a rectangle are x cm and y cm. The area of the rectangle is always $70\,\text{cm}^2$.

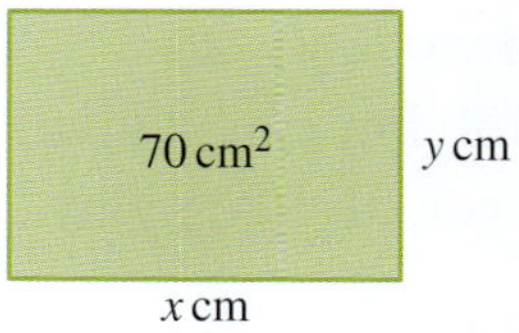

(a) Copy and complete the table of values of x and y.

x	5	7	14	35
y	14			

(b) Are x and y in inverse proportion? Explain your answer.

(c) Plot the coordinate pairs (x, y) on a Cartesian plane.

DISCUSS

Which of these could be the equation of the graph?

$y = 70x \qquad y = \frac{70}{x}$

Example 7

A rectangle has a length of x cm and a width of y cm. The perimeter of the rectangle is always 60 cm.

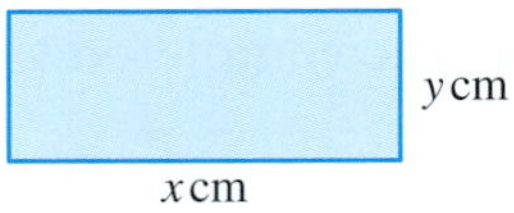

(a) Copy and complete the table of values of x and y.

x	5	10	15	20
y	25			

(b) Are x and y in inverse proportion? Explain your answer.

Solution

(a) Perimeter of rectangle $= (x + y) \times 2$

Therefore, $(x + y) \times 2 = 60$

$\Rightarrow x + y = 30$

Since the perimeter is always 60 cm.

Thus, when $x = 10, y = 20$ since $10 + 20 = 30$

when $x = 15, y = 15$ since $15 + 15 = 30$

when $x = 20, y = 10$ since $20 + 10 = 30$

x	5	10	15	20
y	25	20	15	10

(b) Consider what happens to y when x varies.

If x and y are in inverse proportion then when x is multiplied by a scale factor, y will be divided by the same scale factor.

When $x = 5, y = 25$.
Multiplying x by 2 gives 10.
However, dividing y by 2 gives 12.5 not 20.

When $x = 5, y = 25$.
Multiplying x by 4 gives 20.
However, dividing y by 4 gives 6.25 not 10.

Therefore, x and y are not in inverse proportion.

DISCUSS

Jamie says that x and y must be in inverse proportion since y increases when x decreases. What do you think?

DISCUSS

What happens if you consider the value of y when x varies from 10 to 20?

Why should you always do more than one check?

Try It! 7

A necklace must have 20 beads. The beads can be either blue or green.

(a) Copy and complete the table to show the number of each colour of bead.

Blue	5	10	15	20
Green	15			

(b) Are the number of blue beads and the number of green beads in inverse proportion? Explain your answer.

From Class Activity 2 and Example 6, you can see that if x and y are in inverse proportion:

- the corresponding values of x and y lie on a hyperbola,
- x and y are linked by the function $y = \frac{k}{x}$, $x \neq 0$ for some constant k.

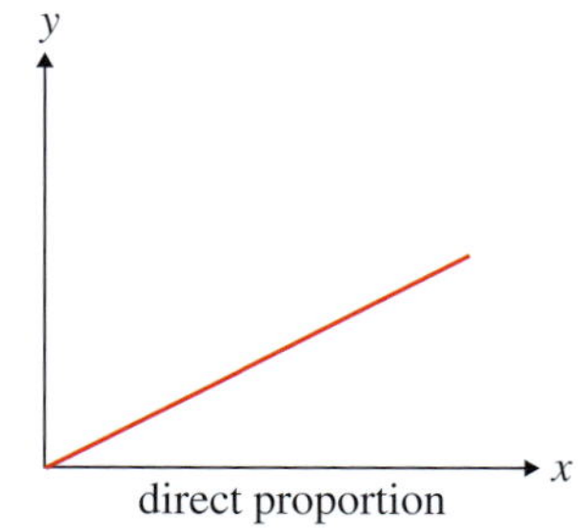

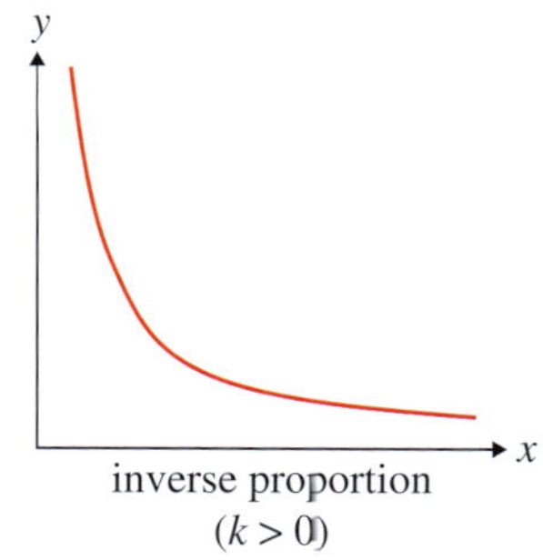

DISCUSS

For each of these equations, discuss whether x and y are in direct proportion, inverse proportion or neither.

$y = 5x$ $\quad$ $y = x + 5$

$y = \frac{5}{x}$ $\quad$ $y = \frac{x}{5}$

As you saw in Example 7, the length and width of the rectangle with perimeter 60 cm were not in inverse proportion. Their corresponding values do not lie on a hyperbola.

Recall that if two variables are in inverse proportion, then when you multiply one variable by a scale factor, you must divide the other variable by the same scale factor. For example, in Class Activity 2:

	Number of people (x)	Share of each person (£y)	
×3	2	18	÷3
÷2	6	6	×2
	3	12	

Example 8

The time taken for a train to complete a journey between two towns is inversely proportional to its average speed. When the average speed is 30 km/h, the journey takes 24 minutes.

(a) Work out the time for the journey if the average speed is 90 km/h.

(b) Work out the average speed required to give a journey time of 48 minutes.

Solution

(a) Draw a table:

	Speed (km/h)	Time (min)	
×3	30	24	÷3
	90	8	

When the speed is multiplied by 3 the time will be divided by 3.

Time for journey = 8 minutes

(b) Draw a table:

	Speed (km/h)	**Time (min)**	
÷2	30	24	×2
	15	48	

When the time is multiplied by 2 the speed will be divided by 2.

Average speed = 15 km/h

Try It! 8

The time taken by a rambler to walk between two landmarks is inversely proportional to their average speed. When the average speed is 6 km/h, the walk takes 2 hours.

(a) Work out the time for the journey if the average speed is 4 km/h.

(b) Work out the average speed required to give a journey time of 6 hours.

Example 9

The time taken to paint a wall is inversely proportional to the number of workers. Five workers would take 32 minutes. How long will it take eight workers to paint the wall?

Solution

Draw a table:

	Workers	**Time (min)**	
÷5	5	32	×5
×8	1	160	÷8
	8	20	

Work out the time for one worker.

When the number of workers is multiplied by 8 the time is divided by 8.

Time taken for 8 workers = 20 minutes.

Try It! 9

A carton of juice is divided into equal parts. The volume of each part is inversely proportional to the number of parts. When there are nine parts, the volume of each part is 50 ml. Find the volume of each part when there are 10 parts.

Example 10

Some prize money is shared between all the people who win a competition. The amount of prize money per person, £m, is inversely proportional to the number of people who win the competition, p.

(a) Which of these could be a function linking m and p for $p > 0$?

$m = \frac{600}{p}$ $\quad m = 600p$ $\quad m = \frac{p}{600}$

(b) Use your answer from part **(a)** to find the amount received per person when there are

(i) 5 people, **(ii)** 10 people.

Solution

(a) The function could be $m = \frac{600}{p}$ since m and p are inversely proportional.

(b) **(i)** When $p = 5$, $m = \frac{600}{5} = 120$.
Each person received £120.

Substitute into the function from part **(a)**.

(ii) When $p = 10$, $m = \frac{600}{10} = £60$.
Each person received £60.

REMARK

The constant, k, in this equation is 600.

Try It! 10

Some tasks are shared equally between the students in a group. The number of tasks per student, t, is inversely proportional to the number of students in the group, s.

(a) Which of these could be a function linking t and s for $s > 0$?

$t = \frac{s}{12}$ $\quad t = 12s$ $\quad t = \frac{12}{s}$

(b) Use your answer from **(a)** to find the number of tasks per student when there are

(i) 3 students in each group,

(ii) 4 students in each group.

DISCUSS

What is the constant in this equation?

PRACTICE 5.2

LEVEL 1

1. The cost of a minibus and the number of people on the minibus are in inverse proportion. When there are 12 people the cost is £10 each.

FINANCE

(a) What is the cost per person if there are

(i) 24 people, **(ii)** 6 people?

(b) How many people are there if the cost is £12 per person?

2. Paul shares 24 snack bags equally between some friends. The table shows how many snack bags each friend will receive depending on the number of friends he shares with.

Number of friends	1	2	3	4	6	8	12
Number of snack bags	24			6		3	2

(a) Copy and complete the table.

(b) Are the number of friends and the number of snack bags in inverse proportion? Explain your answer.

3. The tables show the time taken, t hours, by x students to finish two projects.

Project A

x	1	2	3	4
t	8	6	4	2

Project B

x	2	4	6	8
t	12	6	4	3

(a) In which project are x and t in inverse proportion? Explain your answer.

(b) Draw the graph of t against x using the scale of 1 cm to 1 unit on both axes for your answer in part **(a)**.

(c) Using your graph in part **(b)**, work out how many hours it would take 10 students to finish the project.

4. Which of these graphs shows a relationship of inverse proportion between the variables x and y? Explain your answer.

Graph A

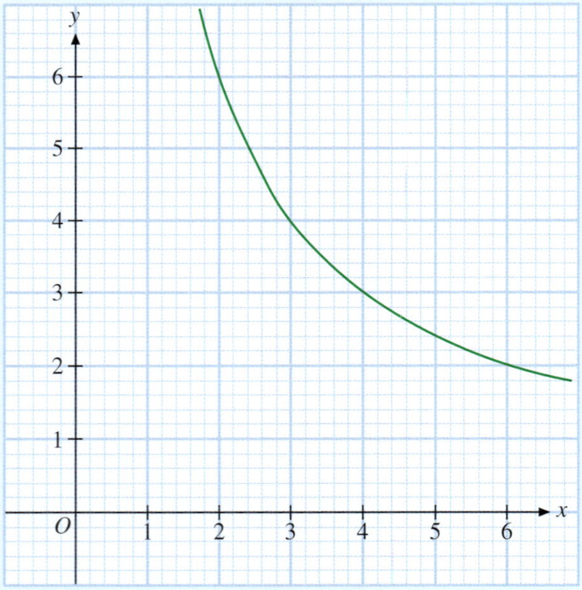

Graph B

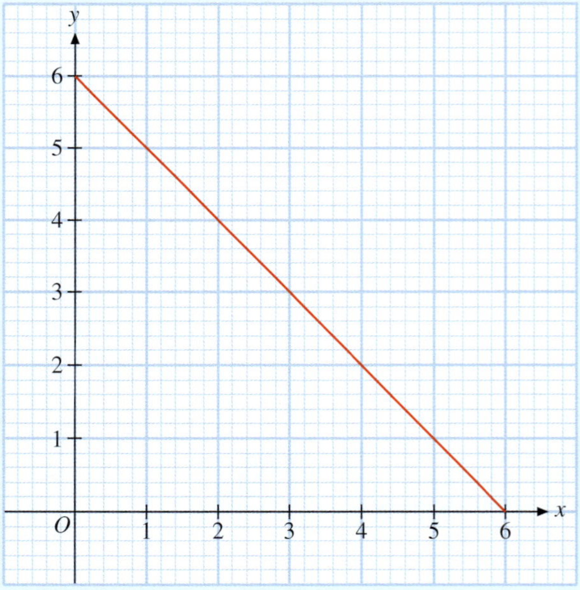

5. The cost per person of a coach for a school trip is inversely proportional to the number of people on it. If there are 20 people on the coach, then it costs £30 per person.

(a) How much will it cost per person if there are 60 people on the coach?
(b) If the cost per person is £15, how many people must be on the coach?
(c) Which of these could be a function linking the cost per person, £C, and the number of people on the coach, p, for $p > 0$?

$C = 30p$ $\quad C = \frac{p}{30}$ $\quad C = \frac{600}{p}$ $\quad C = \frac{p}{600}$

LEVEL 2

6. A parallelogram has a base of x cm and a perpendicular height of h cm. The area of the parallelogram is always equal to 30 cm². Give some possible values of x and h.
Are x and h in inverse proportion? Explain your reasoning.

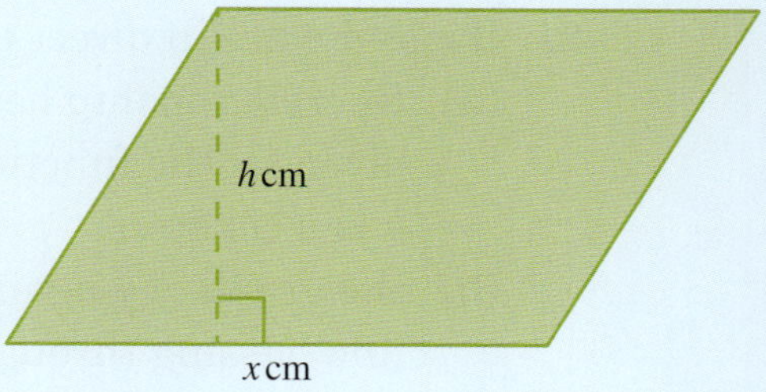

7. Exercise books are cheaper when bought in large quantities. The price per exercise book for different quantities is shown in the table.

Number of books	10	20	100	200
Cost per book (p)	60	50	40	20

Are the cost per book and the number of books bought in inverse proportion?
Explain your answer.

8. The time taken to fix a roof is inversely proportional to the number of roofers working on it. If there are 3 roofers, then it will take 8 hours. How long will it take if there are 4 roofers? Work out your answer in two different ways.

9. It takes 12 workers 30 days to build a swimming pool. Is it true that 60 workers can build the pool in 6 days? Explain your answer.
OPEN QUESTION

10. It takes 12 musicians 30 minutes to play a piece of music. Is it true that 60 musicians can play the same piece of music in 6 minutes? Explain your answer.
OPEN QUESTION

REVIEW

Direct Proportion

1. Two quantities x and y are in direct proportion if, when x changes by a multiplicative scale factor, y changes by the same multiplicative scale factor.
2. If x and y are in direct proportion then
   (a) the relationship between them is given by the function $y = kx$, where k is a constant,
   (b) the graph of y against x is a straight line passing through the origin.

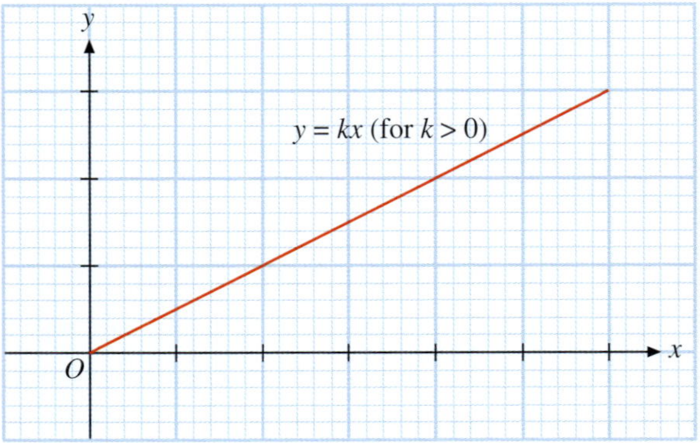

For example, the total price, £T, of n jackets is directly proportional to the number, n, of jackets.
The price for 2 jackets is £90. You can work out the price for 6 jackets:

	n	T	
×3	2	90	×3
	6	270	

So, the total price for 6 jackets is £270.

You can represent two quantities in direct proportion with each other using a double number line:

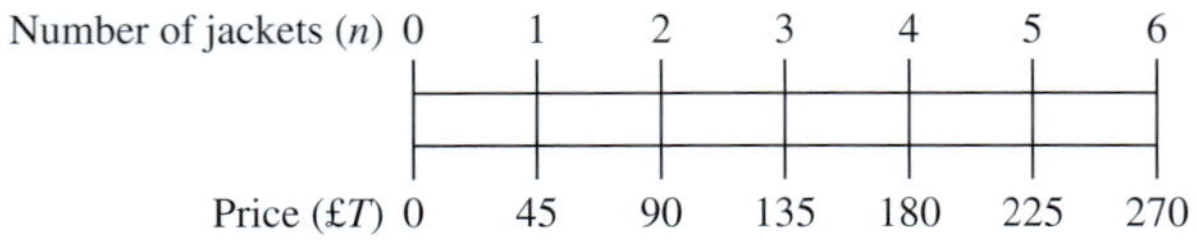

From the double number line, you can quickly see that the price for 3 jackets is £135, or see that you could buy 4 jackets for £180.

Inverse Proportion

1. Two quantities x and y are in inverse proportion if when x changes by a multiplicative scale factor, y changes by the inverse of that multiplicative scale factor.
2. If x and y are in inverse proportion then
   (a) the relationship between them is given by the function $y = \frac{k}{x}, x \neq 0$, where k is a constant,
   (b) the graph of y against x is a hyperbola.

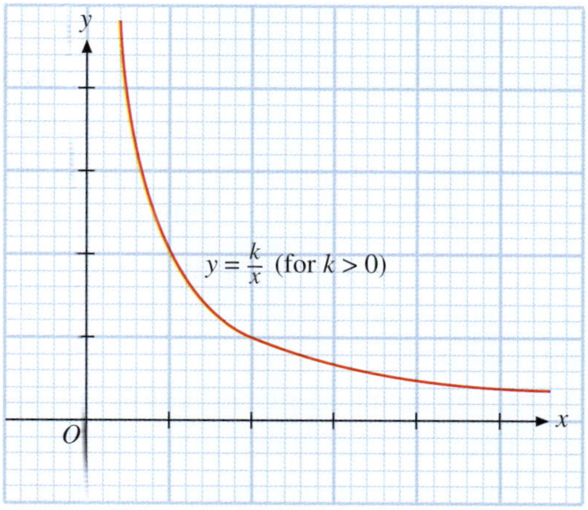

For example, the time, y hours, of cleaning all the rooms in a hotel is inversely proportional to the number, x, of cleaners. If 6 cleaners can clean all the rooms in 8 hours, you can work out how quickly 12 cleaners can clean them all.

	x	y	
$\times 2$	6	8	$\div 2$
	12	4	

So, the time taken for 12 cleaners to clean is 4 hours.

CHALLENGE 5

The cost per person to hire a canal boat is inversely proportional to the number of people hiring the boat.

If x people hire the boat, the cost is £30 per person. What will be the cost per person if $3x$ people hire the boat?

REVISION EXERCISE 5

1. **(a)** The price of potatoes is directly proportional to the mass. The price of 2 kg of potatoes is £3. What is the cost of

(i) 4 kg of potatoes, **(ii)** 6 kg of potatoes?

(b) The time taken for a rambler to complete a trail is inversely proportional to their speed. If their speed is 6 km/h then they complete the trail in 2 hours. How long do they take to complete the trail if their speed is

(i) 3 km/h, **(ii)** 2 km/h?

2. The table shows some corresponding values of the length, x metres, and the price, £y, of a ribbon.

Length (x metres)	2	4	6	8
Price (£ y)	3	6	9	12

(a) Are x and y in direct proportion? Explain your answer.

(b) Draw a double number line to represent the relationship between x and y.

(c) Find the price of a ribbon that is 14 m long.

3. In a department store sale, the selling price of an item is directly proportional to the marked price.

£ FINANCE

When the marked price is £60, the selling price is £48.

(a) Draw a double number line to represent the relationship between the marked price and the selling price of an item. Include five values for x and y of your choice.

(b) What is the selling price of a watch if its marked price is £30?

(c) What is the marked price of a dress if its selling price is £8?

4. The table shows the currency exchange between British pounds and Euros.

£ FINANCE

British pound (£x)	10	20	30	40
Euro (€ y)	11	22	33	44

(a) Draw a double number line to represent the relationship between x and y.
Are x and y in direct proportion? Explain your answer.

(b) How many Euros can you exchange with £80?

(c) Which of these functions describes the relationship between x and y?

$y = \frac{x}{11}$ $\quad y = x + 10$ $\quad y = 1.1x$ $\quad y = \frac{11}{x}$

5. For each graph, explain whether it shows a relationship between x and y that is directly proportional, inversely proportional, or neither.

(a)

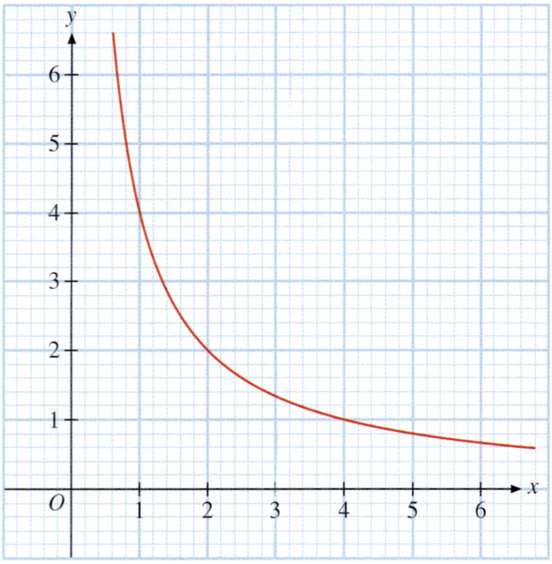

(b)

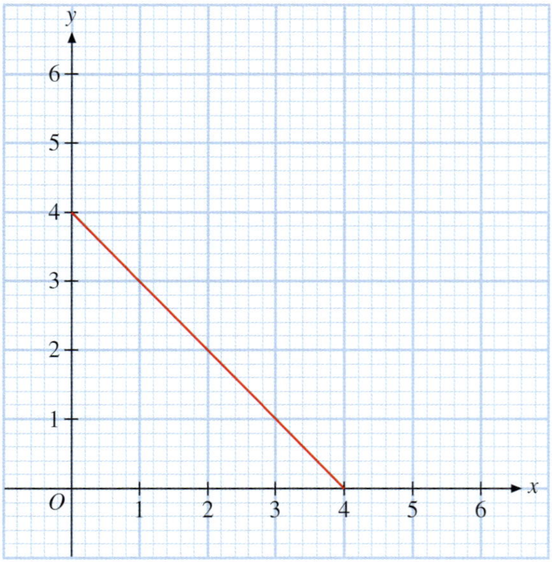

(c)

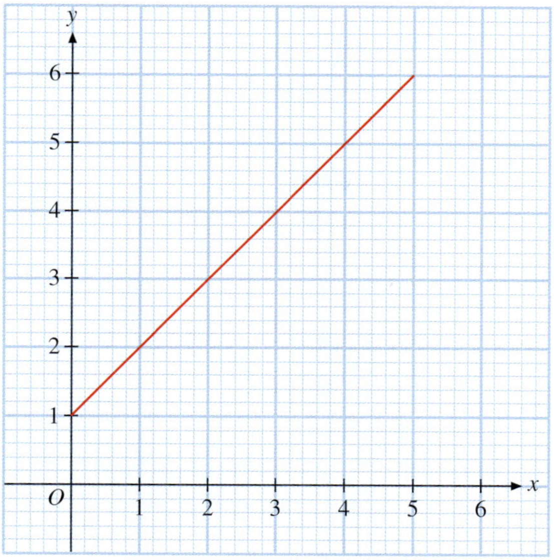

(d)

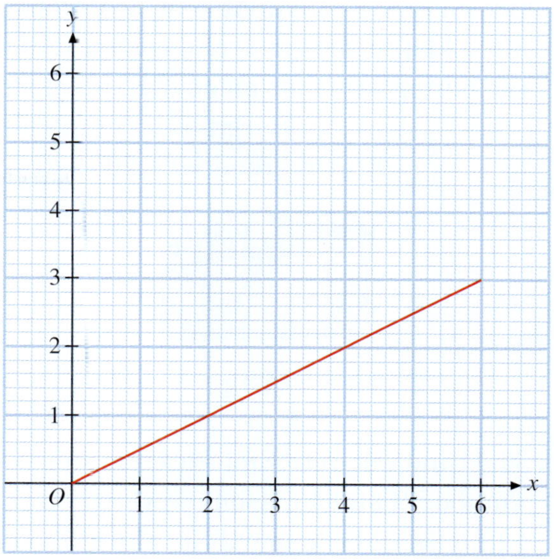

6. The cost, £C, of paint is directly proportional to the area, $a\,\text{m}^2$, to be painted. An area of $8\,\text{m}^2$ costs £12 to paint.

(a) Draw a double number line to represent the relationship between the cost of paint and the area to be painted. Calculate the cost of painting an area of $6\,\text{m}^2$.

(b) Calculate the area that can be painted with £21 of paint.

(c) Draw the graph of C against a.

7. A jug of juice is shared equally into some glasses. The table shows the volume, V ml, of each glass when there are n glasses.

Number of glasses (n)	2	3	5	6
Volume (V ml)	450	300	180	150

(a) Show that n and V are in inverse proportion.

(b) Draw the graph of V against n for $2 \le n \le 8$ using the scale of 1 cm to 1 unit on the n-axis and 1 cm to 100 units on the V-axis.

(c) Which of these functions describes the relationship between n and V for $n > 0$?

$V = n + 448$ $\qquad$ $V = 900n$ $\qquad$ $V = \frac{900}{n}$ $\qquad$ $V = \frac{n}{900}$

(d) Use your answer to part **(c)** to find the value of V when $n = 9$.

8. Here is an easy basic biscuit recipe:

Makes: 30

- 230 g butter
- 110 g caster sugar
- 275 g plain flour

Base your answers on the easy basic biscuit recipe. Use double number lines to represent your reasoning.

(a) How much butter is required for making 42 biscuits?

(b) How much caster sugar is required for 660 grams of plain flour?

9. Brown bread is available in two shops: Bargains and Budget. Brown bread costs £1.20 for a 500 g loaf in Bargains and costs £1.40 for a 600 g loaf in Budget. In which shop is brown bread the better value for money? Explain your reasoning in two different ways.

£ FINANCE

Bargains
Brown bread = £1.20

500 g

Budget
Brown bread = £1.40

600 g

10. The time taken to replace some stonework around a window is inversely proportional to the number of stone masons working on the project. If 2 masons work on the project, it will take 21 hours. How long will it take if 5 masons work on the project?

Write in Your Journal

When you are given a table of values of two quantities x and y, describe how you would determine whether x and y are in direct proportion, inverse proportion or otherwise. Give some examples of direct and inverse proportion occurring in everyday life. Give some examples of relationships that are not in direct and inverse proportion.

6 RATE AND SPEED

WHAT IS IN THIS CHAPTER:

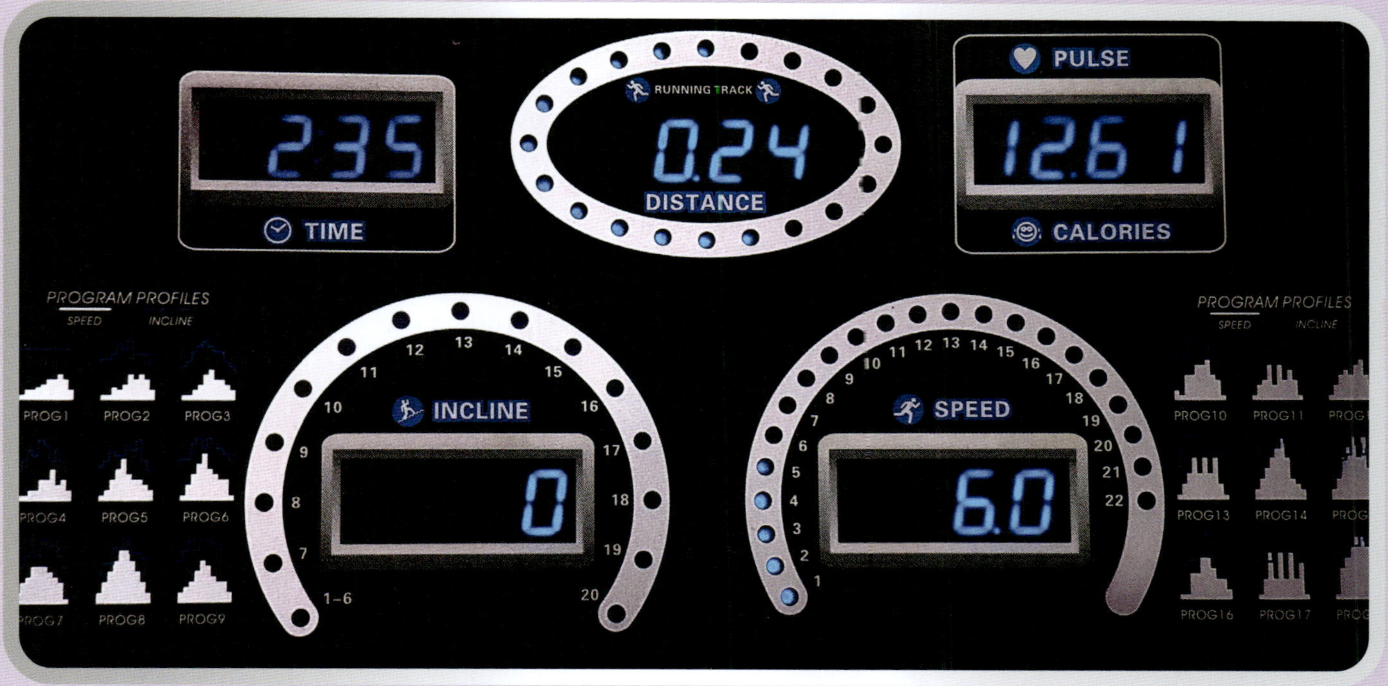

The display panel of a treadmill shows your running speed and heartbeat. What do these two quantities measure? What are their units?

LET'S LEARN TO

- define rate and apply it to everyday situations
- understand the concepts of rate and average rate
- solve problems involving rate
- calculate and use exchange rates
- calculate simple interest
- understand the concepts of speed and average speed
- solve problems involving speed

FLASHBACK

1. Inverse Relationship between Multiplication and Division

If $a \times b = c$, then $a = \frac{c}{b}$ and $b = \frac{c}{a}$.

For example, as $6 \times 8.5 = 51$, this gives $6 = \frac{51}{8.5}$ and $8.5 = \frac{51}{6}$.

REMARK

This can be seen in a factor tree:

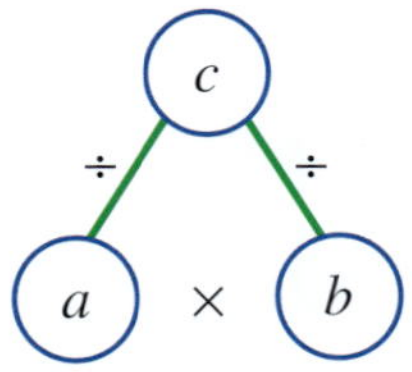

2. Direct Proportion

If two quantities are in direct proportion then when one quantity changes by a multiplicative scale factor, then the other variable changes by the same multiplicative scale factor.
For example, the amount a person is paid is in direct proportion to the number of hours worked.

× 11

Time (hours)	Pay (£)
1	11
7	77

× 7 (Time, 1 → 7) × 7 (Pay, 11 → 77)

× 11

The person is paid £11 for 1 hour and £77 for 7 hours.

3. Percentages of Amounts

(a) A percentage can be written as a fraction with 100 as the denominator.

For example, $13\% = \frac{13}{100}$

(b) To find a percentage of an amount, multiply the amount by the percentage.

For example, $30\% \text{ of } 600 = \frac{30}{\cancel{100}_1} \times \cancel{600}^6$ Cancel the common factor 100.

$= 30 \times 6$

$= 180.$

You can also present this calculation using a bar model.

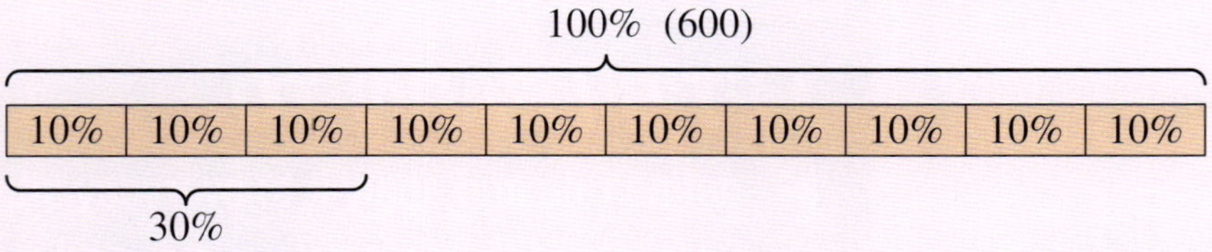

$10\% \text{ of } 600 = 600 \div 10$

$= 60$

$30\% \text{ of } 600 = 60 \times 3$

$= 180$

REMARK

There are other ways of working this out. $\frac{30}{100}$ is equivalent to the fraction $\frac{3}{10}$, therefore you could work out three tenths of 600. One tenth of 600 is 60, so three tenths would be 180.

6.1 Rate and Average Rate

David earns £36 for working 3 hours. Simon earns £50 for working 5 hours. How can you decide who has the better rate of pay?

David's pay for one hour = £36 ÷ 3

= £12

Simon's pay for one hour = £50 ÷ 5

= £10

Therefore, David has the better rate of pay since he is paid £12 per hour, whereas Simon is only paid £10 per hour.

David

Pay (£)	No. hours
36	3
12	1

(÷ 3 on both columns)

Simon

Pay (£)	No. hours
50	5
10	1

(÷ 5 on both columns)

In general:

> Rate is the amount of one quantity per single unit of another quantity.

For example, if the rate of pay of a worker is £15 per hour, this means they earn £15 in an hour. If a person's heart rate is 72 beats per minute, this means their heart beats 72 times in one minute.

REMARK

You need to find the pay received in 1 hour. The pay and the number of hours are in **direct proportion**. Therefore, you can use the same method as in Section 5.1.

REMARK

£15 per hour can also be written as £15/hour. 72 beats per minute can also be written 72 beats/min.

DISCUSS

What other rates can you think of? What would the unit of measurement of each rate be?

CLASS ACTIVITY 1

Objective: To calculate heart rate before and after exercise.

Work in pairs for this activity. Label yourselves A and B.

1. Person A should find their pulse by placing two fingers on the inside of their wrist. Person B should use a stopwatch to time 15 seconds whilst person A counts how many beats they feel.
2. Multiply the number of beats in 15 seconds by 4 to give the number of beats per minute.
3. Person A should now jog on the spot for 1 minute whilst Person B times them.
4. Repeat steps **1** and **2** and compare the two heart rates. What do you notice about the two heart rates?
5. Swap over and follow steps **1** to **4** again.

DISCUSS

Why do you multiply the number of beats by 4?

Example 1

(a) Jane types 150 words in 3 minutes. Find her typing rate in words per min.

(b) A car uses 6 litres of petrol when travelling 60 km. Find the petrol consumption rate in km per litre.

Solution

(a) Using a table:

Words	Time (min)
150	3
50	1

(÷ 3 down each column; ÷ 50 across)

Jane's typing rate = 150 words ÷ 3 min

= 50 words per min

Using a double number line:

Align 150 words on the top line with 3 minutes on the bottom line, then work out how to complete each of the scales.

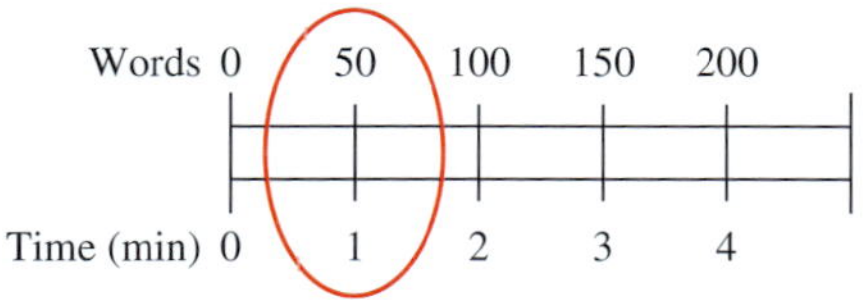

You can see that 50 words aligns with 1 minute.

∴ Jane's typing rate = 50 words per min.

(b) Using a table:

Distance (km)	Petrol (litres)
60	6
10	1

(÷ 6 down each column; ÷ 10 across)

Petrol consumption rate = 60 km ÷ 6 litres

= 10 km per litre

Using a double number line:

Align 60 km on the top line with 6 litres on the bottom line, then work out how to complete each of the scales.

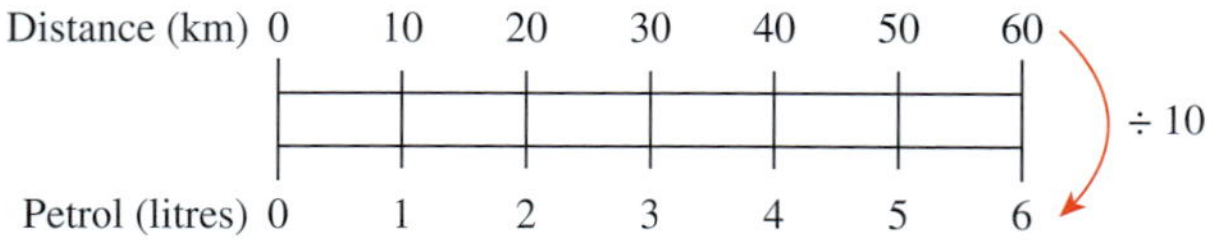

You can see that 10 km aligns with 1 litre.

∴ petrol consumption rate = 10 km per litre.

DISCUSS

Can you see that each ratio table also shows the same relationship between the two columns in every row as well?

DISCUSS

How could you work out the number of words Jane can type in 30 seconds? Will she always type exactly that amount?

DISCUSS

Divide both quantities by 6 since the quantities are in direct proportion and you need the distance travelled for 1 litre of petrol.

Try It! 1

(a) David packs 20 boxes in 5 minutes. Find his packing rate in boxes per min.

(b) The price for four cans of pineapple is £8. Find the price rate in £ per can.

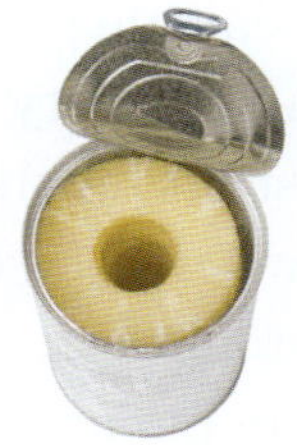

Example 2

Georgia mows $60\,\text{m}^2$ of lawn in five minutes. Find

(a) her mowing rate in m^2 per min,

(b) the area of lawn Georgia can mow in 11 minutes,

(c) the time it would take her to mow an area of $96\,\text{m}^2$.

Solution

(a) Using a table:

	Area (m^2)	Time (min)	
	60	5	
÷ 5	12	1	÷ 5

Georgia's mowing rate $= 60\,\text{m}^2 \div 5$ min

$= 12\,\text{m}^2$ per min

(b) The rate means $12\,\text{m}^2$ of lawn is mowed in one minute.

Area of lawn mowed in 11 minutes $= 12 \times 11$

$= 132\,\text{m}^2$

You could also add a row to your table:

	Area (m^2)	Time (min)	
	60	5	
÷ 5	12	1	÷ 5
× 11	132	11	× 11

(c) Using the factor tree from the Remark box:

time = area ÷ rate

∴ time taken to mow $96\,\text{m}^2 = 96 \div 12$

$= 8$ min

DISCUSS

Why did you divide both quantities by 5?

REMARK

The relationship between the area, time and rate can be shown using a factor tree.

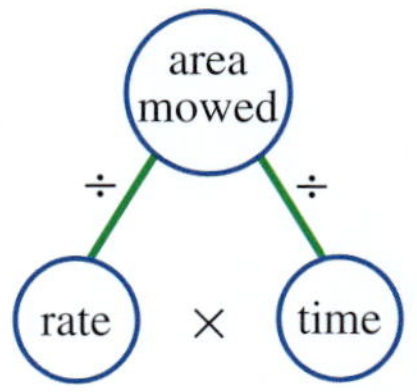

DISCUSS

Can you create a factor tree with the correct numbers for parts **(b)** and **(c)**?

Try It! 2

A tap releases 10 litres of water in two minutes. Find

(a) the release rate in litres per min,

(b) the volume of water that could be released in 12 minutes,

(c) the time taken to release 65 litres of water.

In some real-life situations, the rate is likely to be constant throughout. For example, in Try It! 2, the release rate of water from the tap could have been constant for the whole time being considered. In some situations, the rate will not be constant throughout. For example, a coffee shop may serve customers at a rate of 50 customers per hour. However, this does not necessarily mean that they serve exactly 50 customers every hour of the day. It is likely that certain times will be busier than others, so strictly speaking, this is an **average rate**. The term 'rate' is often used even if you are really speaking about an 'average rate'.

REMARK

Some important rates include exchange rate and speed. You will learn about these later in the chapter. Another rate you will come across in science is **density**. The density of a substance is the mass per unit of volume of the substance.

Example 3

A worker earns £160 for working 8 hours.

(a) Find the rate of pay in £ per hour.

(b) Draw the graph of wage, £y, against working hours, x hours, for $0 \le x \le 8$.

(c) Work out the gradient of the graph. What does it represent?

Solution

(a) Using a table:

	Pay (£)	Time (hours)	
÷ 8	160	8	÷ 8
	20	1	

Rate of pay = £160 ÷ 8 hours
= £20 per hour

(b) When working for 2 hours,
the wage = £20 × 2
= £40.

So, when $x = 2$, $y = 40$.

Hence, a table of values of x and y can be set up in this way.

Time, x (hours)	0	2	4	6	8
Wage, y (£)	0	40	80	120	160

The graph shows y against x.

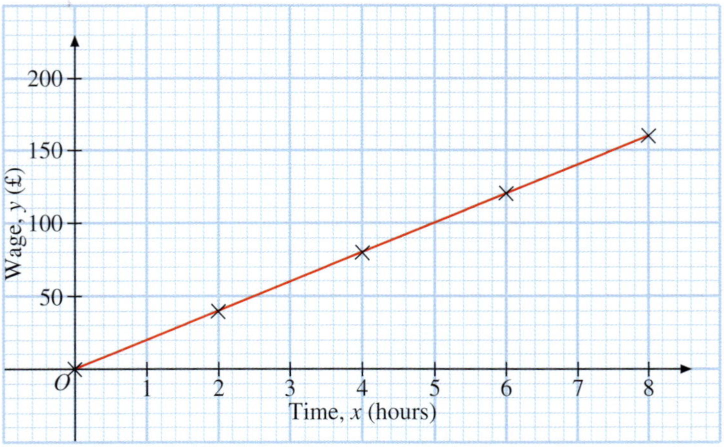

DISCUSS

What will the worker earn for working 0 hours? How many points should you work out in order to draw this graph? Do you necessarily need a table of values? Why do you put time on the horizontal axis?

DISCUSS

What are the features of this graph?

(c) Take the points (0, 0) and (8, 160) on the graph.

$$\text{Gradient of the graph} = \frac{\text{vertical change}}{\text{horizontal change}} = \frac{160 - 0}{8 - 0} = 20$$

Hence, the gradient of the graph represents the rate of pay.

> **DISCUSS**
>
> Why is the gradient of the line the same as the rate of pay?

Try It! 3

Amy spends £84 in 7 days.

(a) Find her spending rate in £ per day.

(b) Draw the graph of spending, £y, against the number of days, x, for $0 \leq x \leq 7$. Use a scale of 1 cm to 1 unit on the x-axis and 1 cm to 20 units on the y-axis.

(c) Work out the gradient of the graph. What does it represent?

Example 4

Washing powder A sells at £7 for 4 kg. Washing powder B sells at £12 for 5 kg. Compare the price rate of each.

Solution

Price rate of washing powder A = £7 ÷ 4 kg
= £1.75 per kg

Price rate of washing powder B = £12 ÷ 5 kg
= £2.40 per kg

Therefore, washing powder A is the better value for money.

Alternatively, you could 'scale up' the quantities:

Cost of powder A (£)	Mass (kg)
7	4
35	20

(× 5 on both columns)

Cost of powder B (£)	Mass (kg)
12	5
48	20

(× 4 on both columns)

Price of 20 kg of powder A = £35

Price of 20 kg of powder B = £48

∴ washing powder A is cheaper.

> **DISCUSS**
>
> $7 \div 4 = \frac{7}{4} = 1\frac{3}{4} = 1.75$
>
> $12 \div 5 = \frac{12}{5} = 2\frac{2}{5} = 2\frac{4}{10} = 2.40$

> **DISCUSS**
>
> Why did you scale up to 20 kg? Could you scale up to make the costs the same instead of the mass? How would this be different?

> **DISCUSS**
>
> If there were horizontal arrows running from the left column to the right column for each table, what would these arrows show? Think about the relationship between the cost and the mass.

Try It! 4

An iron bar costs £24 for 2 m. A copper bar costs £45 for 3 m. Compare the price rate of each.

PRACTICE 6.1

LEVEL 1

1. Find the rate in each case. Use tables or double number lines to work out the answers.
   (a) 2 litres of olive oil cost £8. The price rate is £______ per litre.
   (b) A machine produces 200 clips in 5 minutes. The production rate is ______ clips per min.
   (c) The height of a plant increases 30 cm in 6 days. The rate of growth is ______ cm per day.

2. A wheel rotates 48 times in 16 minutes.
   (a) Draw a double number line to show the time in minutes and the number of revolutions.
   (b) Find the rate of rotation in revolutions per min.
   (c) Work out the number of revolutions in 14 minutes.
   (d) Work out the time taken for 9 revolutions.

3. A carpenter works 8 hours in a day. She makes 16 chairs and earns £200. Find
   £ FINANCE
   (a) the production rate in chairs per hour,
   (b) the pay rate in £ per hour,
   (c) the pay rate in £ per chair.

4. A car mechanic takes 10 minutes to change a tyre.
   (a) Work out the rate of work in tyres per hour.
   (b) Copy and complete the factor tree and put the terms 'time' and 'tyres' in the correct places.
   (c) Work out how many tyres the mechanic can change in 3 hours.

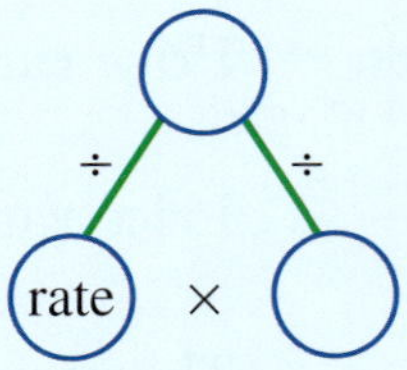

5. A shop assistant serves 15 customers in 30 minutes. He wants to work out how long it will take for him to serve 100 customers. Find the mistake in his calculation.

   Rate of serving customers = 30 ÷ 15
   = 2 customers per minute.

   Time to serve 100 customers = 100 ÷ 2
   = 50 minutes.

LEVEL 2

6. A rectangular carpet is 5 m by 3 m. Its price is £375.
   £ FINANCE
   (a) Find the price rate of the carpet in £ per m^2.
   (b) What is the price of the carpet for a room of 6 m by 4 m?

7. The price for 4 kg of apples is £10.

FINANCE

(a) Find the price rate of apples in £ per kg.

(b) Find the price for 3 kg of apples.

(c) Find the mass of apples that can be bought with £12.

(d) Draw the graph of the price, £y, against the mass, x kg for $0 \le x \le 6$. Use a scale of 1 cm to 1 unit on the x-axis and 1 cm to 2 units on the y-axis.

(e) What does the gradient of the graph represent?

8. The density of a substance is defined as the rate of mass per unit of volume of the substance. A piece of copper has a volume of 40 cm^3 and a mass of 360 grams.

SCIENCE

(a) Copy and complete the factor tree with the terms 'mass' and 'volume'.

(b) Find the density of copper in g per cm^3 from these measurements.

(c) A copper cube has edges of 2 cm long. What is its mass?

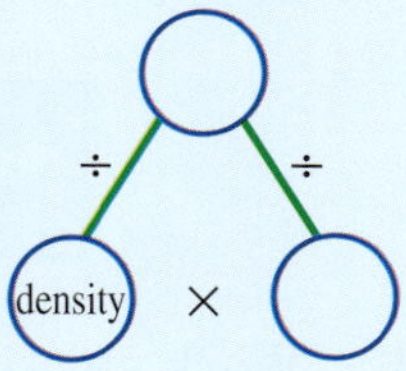

9. A car consumes 5 litres of petrol for 100 km. John says the petrol consumption rate is 20 km per litre. Nazia says the petrol consumption rate is 0.05 litres per km.

(a) Is John correct?

(b) Is Nazia correct?

(c) What is the same and what is different about their statements?

10. In supermarket A, a 3 kg bag of rice costs £13.50. In supermarket B, a 7 kg bag of rice costs £28. Which supermarket's offer is better value for money? Explain your answer.

PROBLEM SOLVING

6.2 Exchange Rate

When you go on a trip to another country, you often need to exchange some money to a foreign currency. An exchange rate shows how much foreign currency you can exchange using Great British Pounds (GBP) or British Pound Sterling and vice versa. Note that exchange rates change every second, depending on financial situations in the world.

CLASS ACTIVITY 2

Objective: To find the exchange rates between British pounds and other foreign currencies on the Internet.

1. Using a search engine on the Internet, find the exchange rate between British pounds and some foreign currencies. For example, you may type '1 GBP to USD' in the search box to obtain the rate between British pounds and US dollars. Find at least five different exchange rates.

   British pounds (GBP) £1 —exchange→ US dollars (USD) $

2. Work out the price in each of these two currencies of

   (a) a DVD costing £10,

   (b) a deposit of £100 for a holiday.

Exchange rates change all the time, but on a particular day, the exchange rate from British pounds to Australian dollars (AUD) was 1 GBP = 2 AUD.

The two amounts are in direct proportion, so you can use the same methods as in Section 5.1 and Section 6.1 to convert between currencies. To find the exchange rate from Australian dollars to British pounds, you need to find the number of British pounds that are equal to 1 Australian dollar.

REMARK

Exchange rates are usually represented as an equation, not in the rate form: '2 AUD per GBP'.

Using a table:

	GBP	AUD	
$\div 2$	1	2	$\div 2$
	0.5	1	

Therefore, the exchange rate from Australian dollars to British pounds was 1 AUD = 0.5 GBP.

Example 5 The exchange rate one day between British pounds (GBP) and US dollars (USD) is 1 GBP = 1.25 USD.

(a) How many US dollars can be exchanged for 12 GBP?

(b) How many British pounds can be exchanged for 8 USD?

Solution

(a) Using a table:

	GBP	USD	
× 12	1	1.25	× 12
	12	15	

× 1.25

$$1 \text{ GBP} = 1.25 \text{ USD}$$
$$\therefore \quad 12 \text{ GBP} = 1.25 \times 12 \text{ USD}$$
$$= 15 \text{ USD}$$

You can also see from the table that you can find the answer by multiplying the British pounds by the exchange rate, 1.25, to find the equivalent number of US dollars:

$$12 \text{ GBP} \times 1.25 = 15 \text{ USD}$$

(b) Using a table:

	GBP	USD	
÷ 1.25	1	1.25	÷ 1.25
× 8	0.8	1	× 8
	6.4	8	

$$1.25 \text{ USD} = 1 \text{ GBP}$$
$$\therefore \quad 1 \text{ USD} = 1 \text{ GBP} \div 1.25$$
$$1 \text{ USD} = 0.8 \text{ GBP}$$
$$\therefore \quad 8 \text{ USD} = 0.8 \times 8 \text{ GBP}$$
$$= 6.40 \text{ GBP}$$

Try It! 5

The exchange rate one day between British pounds (GBP) and Euros (EUR) is 1 GBP = 1.12 EUR. Use a calculator to find

(a) the amount in Euros that can be exchanged for 25 GBP,

(b) the amount in British pounds that can be exchanged for 20 EUR.

DISCUSS

What type of proportion are the two quantities in for exchange rates?

RECALL

Remember that it is often easier to scale the quantity to 1 first, and then scale it up to 8. This is the Unitary Method.

DISCUSS

Can you add a horizontal arrow to the table and work out the answer in a different way?

REMARK

The answers for money should be given to two decimal places. This is because legal tender is usually up to a hundredth of a unit. Likewise, the exchange rates are usually given with two decimal places.

Example 6

The graph shows British pounds (GBP) against Chinese yuan (CNY).

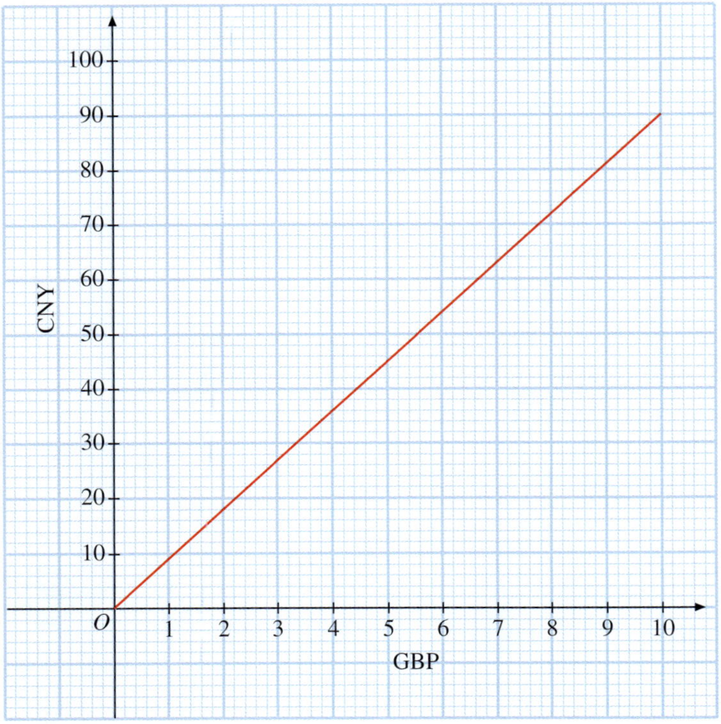

Use the graph to estimate

(a) the amount in Chinese yuan that can be exchanged for 6 GBP,

(b) the amount in British pounds that can be exchanged for 80 CNY.

Solution

(a)

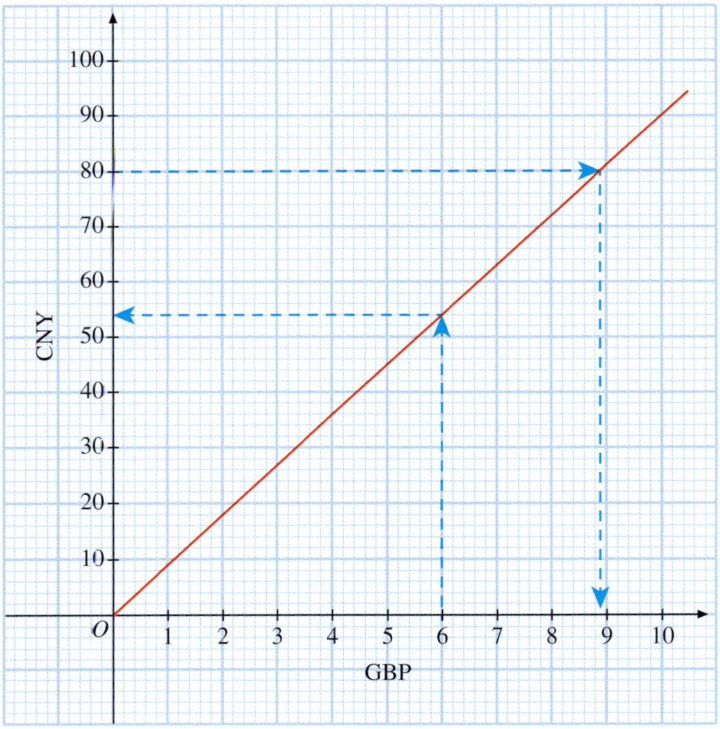

REMARK

In the UK (and most of Europe) a place where you can exchange currency is commonly called a 'Bureau de change'.

Draw a vertical line up from 6 GBP then across.
The value on the vertical axis is approximately 54.
$\therefore$ 6 GBP = 54 CNY

(b) Draw a horizontal line from 80 CNY then down.
The value on the horizontal axis is approximately 8.9.
$\therefore$ 80 CNY $\approx$ 8.90 GBP

DISCUSS

What is the gradient of the graph and its meaning? Are the two quantities in direct proportion?

Try It! 6

The graph shows British pounds (GBP) against Russian rubles (RUB).

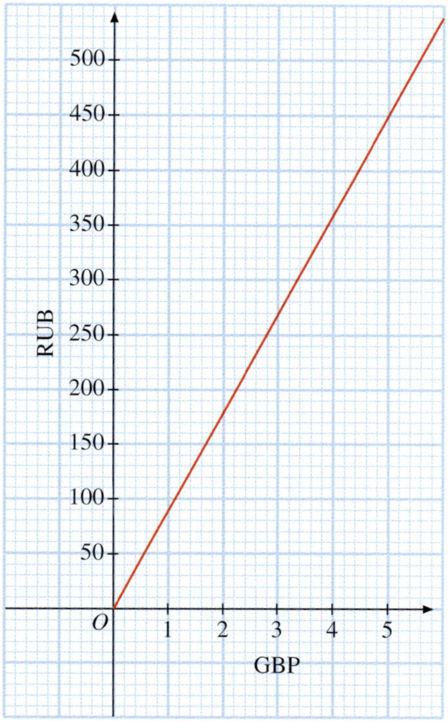

Use the graph to estimate

(a) the amount in Russian rubles that can be exchanged for 4 GBP,

(b) the amount in British pounds that can be exchanged for 200 RUB.

PRACTICE 6.2

Use a calculator and give your answers to two decimal places in this exercise.

LEVEL 1

1. The exchange rate on a certain day between British pounds and Euros is 1 GBP = 1.13 EUR.

FINANCE

(a) Draw a double number line showing British pounds (GBP) and Euros (EUR).

(b) How many Euros can you exchange for 12 GBP?

2. The exchange rate on a certain day of US dollars to Euros was 1 USD = 0.90 EUR.

FINANCE

(a) Sadie says that the exchange rate from Euros to US dollars is equal to $1 \div 0.9 = 1.11$ (to 2 dp). Is she correct? Explain your answer.

(b) How many US dollars could you exchange for 60 EUR?

3. The exchange rate one day between British pounds (GBP) and Danish krone (DKK) is 1 GBP = 8.41 DKK. Terry has 60 DKK to convert to British pounds. They do this calculation to work out how much they should receive:

FINANCE

60 DKK = 60 × 8.41 GBP
= 504.60 GBP

Do you agree with Terry's calculation? Explain your answer.

4. The graph shows British pounds (GBP) against Thai baht (THB)

FINANCE

Use the graph to estimate

(a) the amount in Thai baht that can be exchanged for 4 GBP,

(b) the amount in British pounds that can be exchanged for 200 THB.

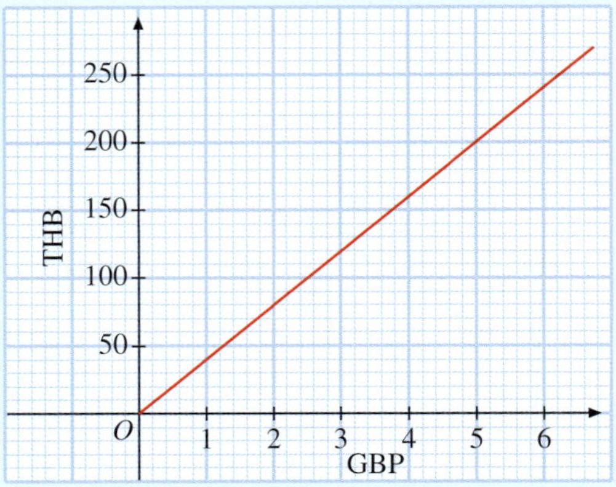

5. Currency exchange shop A offers 1 GBP = 1.69 SGD (Singapore dollars).

FINANCE

Currency exchange shop B offers 1 GBP = 1.67 SGD.

If you want to exchange 300 GBP to Singapore dollars,

(a) which shop should you exchange with,

(b) how many Singapore dollars can you get from that shop?

LEVEL 2

6. The exchange rate between British pounds (GBP) and Hong Kong dollars (HKD) is 1 GBP = 9.58 HKD. A tourist bought a handbag for 7000 HKD in Hong Kong. How much is the handbag worth in British pounds?

7. On a certain day, 1 GBP = 1.11 EUR and 1 GBP = 1.22 USD. The price of a computer is 1000 USD on a US website. The price of the same computer is 950 EUR on a French website. Which site's offer is cheaper? Explain your answer.

PROBLEM SOLVING

8. The graph shows the exchange of x British pounds (GBP) for y Swiss francs (CHF). Use the graph to estimate
   (a) the number of Swiss francs you can exchange for 3 GBP,
   (b) the exchange rate of GBP to CHF.

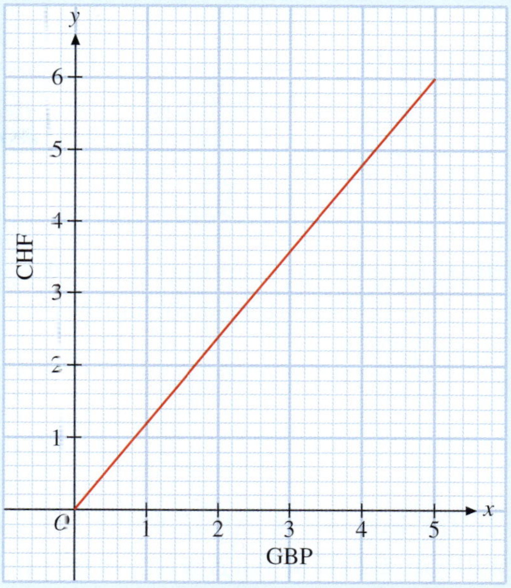

9. PROBLEM SOLVING On one day, £500 can be exchanged for 910 Australian dollars (AUD). The price for a hotel room for one night in Australia is 130 AUD. What is the total price for the hotel room for 12 nights in pounds?

10. PROBLEM SOLVING When you buy US dollars from a bank, the exchange rate is 1 GBP = 1.22 USD. When you sell US dollars to the bank and exchange for British pounds, the exchange rate is 1 USD = 0.81 GBP. If you exchange £1000 to US dollars in the bank and then exchange the US dollars back to British pounds, will you get back exactly £1000? Explain your answer.

6.3 Simple Interest

When you deposit money in a bank for a period of time, the bank will pay you extra money, called **interest**, for the use of your money. On the other hand, when you borrow money from a bank, you must pay back extra money, the interest, on the loan.

The amount initially invested or borrowed is called the **principal**. Interest is calculated using an **interest rate** per year. The interest rate is a percentage of the principal.

REMARK

To deposit means 'to put into'. The opposite, in terms of money, is to **withdraw**.

For example, if £3000 is borrowed and the interest rate is 10% per year,

$$\begin{aligned}\text{the interest for one year} &= 10\% \text{ of } £3000\\ &= 10\% \times £3000\\ &= \frac{10}{\cancel{100}_1} \times £\cancel{3000}^{30}\\ &= 10 \times £30\\ &= £300\end{aligned}$$

You can also use a bar model to find the interest:

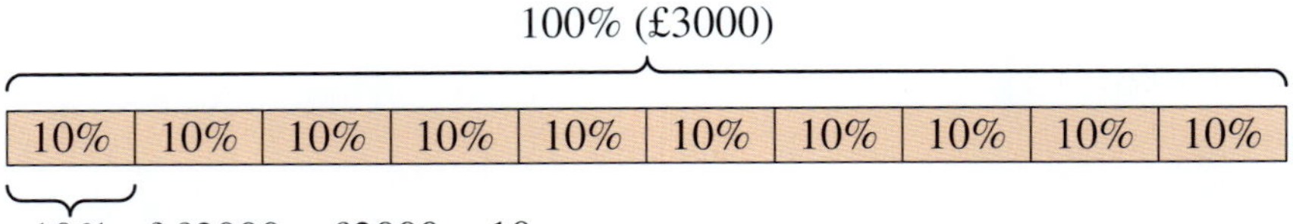

$10\% \text{ of } £3000 = £3000 \div 10$
$= £300$

RECALL

'Per cent' means 'out of 100', therefore 10% can be written as $\frac{10}{100}$.

If £3000 is put into a savings account with an interest rate of 5% per year,

$$\begin{aligned}\text{the interest for one year} &= 5\% \text{ of } £3000 \\ &= 5\% \times £3000 \\ &= \frac{5}{\cancel{100}} \times \cancel{£3000}^{30} \\ &= 5 \times £30 \\ &= £150\end{aligned}$$

DISCUSS

Interest rates for borrowing money tend to be higher than interest rates for investments. Why do you think this might be?

When the interest is calculated only based on the principal (the amount initially invested or borrowed), it is called **simple interest**. The interest for each of the following years is the same as the interest for the first year. Hence,

After 1 year:

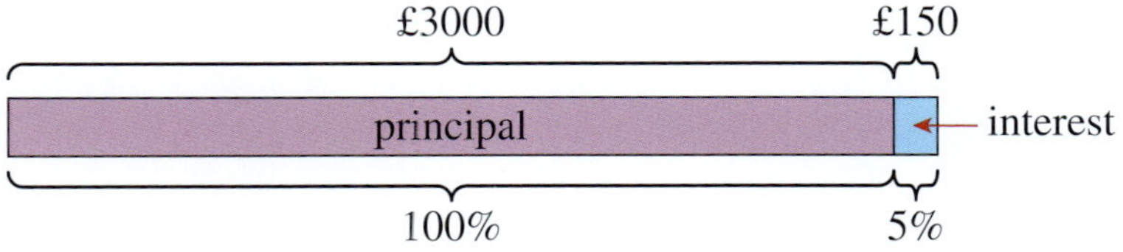

After 2 years:

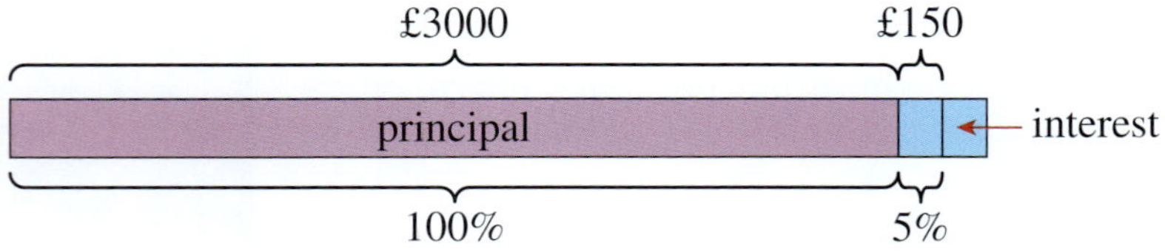

After 3 years:

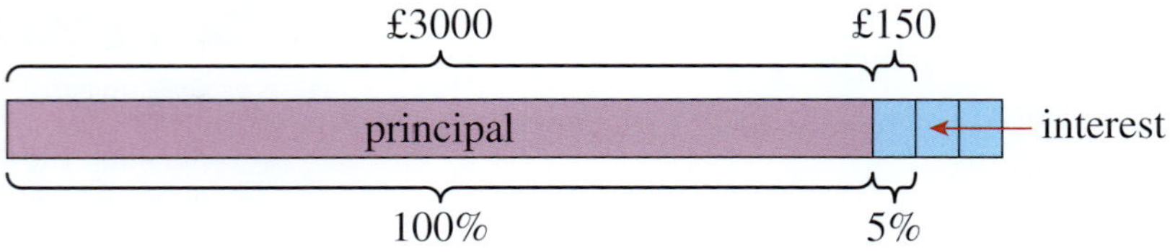

Example 7

The Green family borrows £2000 from a bank for three years. The interest rate is 8% per annum and they pay off only the interest each year. Find the total amount of simple interest.

Solution

Interest for one year = 8% of £2000

$= 8\% \times £2000$

$= \frac{8}{100} \times £2000$ (cancelled: 100_1, $£2000^{20}$)

$= 8 \times £20$

$= £160$

Simple interest for three years = $3 \times £160$

$= £480$

You can see this in the bar model.

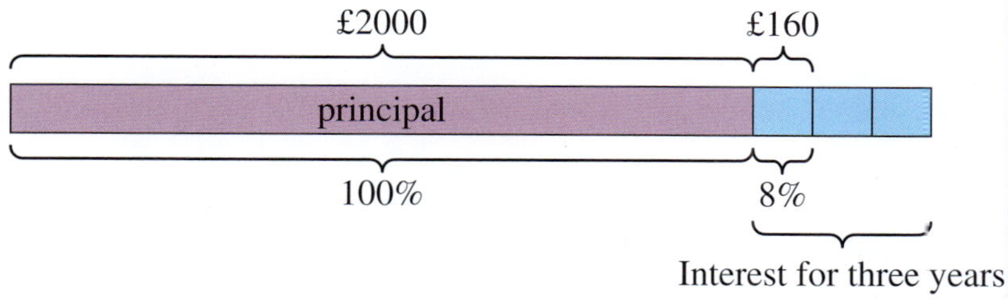

Try It! 7

The Red family borrows £1000 from a bank for two years. The interest rate is 7% per annum and they pay off only the interest each year. Find the total amount of simple interest.

REMARK

'8% per annum' means an interest rate of 8% each year.

DISCUSS

This is an example of **simple interest** since they are paying off the interest each year, so at the start of each year they still owe £2000.

If they do not pay anything off each year what will happen to the interest?

Example 8

A sum of £1800 is invested at an interest rate of 4% per annum for five years. At the end of each year the interest is withdrawn. Work out the simple interest earned.

Solution

Interest for one year = 4% of £1800

$= 4\% \times £1800$

$= \frac{4}{100} \times £1800$ (cancelled: 100_1, $£1800^{18}$)

$= 4 \times £18$

$= £72$

Simple interest for five years = $5 \times £72$

$= £360$

Try It! 8

A sum of £1500 is invested at an interest rate of 3% per annum for 4 years. At the end of each year the interest is withdrawn. Work out the simple interest earned.

REMARK

This is an example of **simple interest** since the interest earned is withdrawn at the end of each year.

DISCUSS

What would a bar model for Example 8 look like?

Example 9

A sum of £4000 is deposited in a bank. The simple interest rate of 10% per annum is earned only on the original investment. Find the amount in the account after two years.

Solution

Method 1

Interest for one year = 10% of £4000

$= \frac{10}{100} \times £4000$

$= £400.$

Simple interest for two years = £400 × 2

$= £800.$

Amount after two years = principal + interest

$= £4000 + £800$

$= £4800.$

Method 2

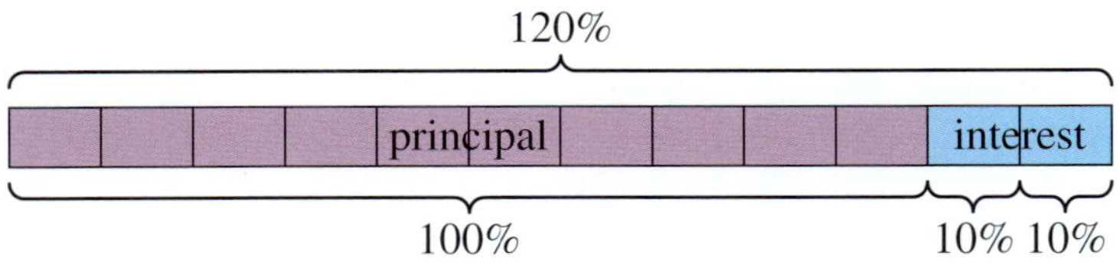

From the bar model you can see that after two years the total in the account is 120% of the principal.

∴ amount after 2 years = 120% of £4000

$= \frac{120}{100} \times £4000$

$= 120 \times £40$

$= £4800$

DISCUSS

Which method do you prefer? Why?

Try It! 9

A sum of £6000 is deposited in a bank. The simple interest rate of 5% per annum is earned only on the original investment. Find the amount in the account after 2 years.

PRACTICE 6.3

LEVEL 1

1. Work out the value of

FINANCE

(a) 5% of £300, **(b)** 1% of £9200, **(c)** 9% of £2000, **(d)** 8% of £2500.

2. Which is the odd one out? Explain your answer.

FINANCE

3% of £2000 2% of £3000 3% of £1000 1% of £6000

3. Mandy wants to deposit £500 in a bank. In Bank A, the interest rate is 4% per annum.

FINANCE

(a) Find the simple interest in

(i) one year, **(ii)** two years.

(b) Bank B offers an interest rate of 5% per annum. Which bank should Mandy choose to get a better interest rate? Explain your answer.

4. Alan needs to borrow a loan of £8000 from a bank. The interest rate at Bank A is 7% per annum. Find the simple interest in

FINANCE

(a) **(i)** one year, **(ii)** two years.

(b) The interest rate at Bank B is 8% per annum. Which loan do you suggest Alan chooses? Explain your answer.

5. The simple interest rate on a loan of £6400 is 9% per annum. At the end of three years, what is

FINANCE

(a) the total interest, **(b)** the amount to repay?

6. Peter calculates the simple interest for a sum of £300 at the interest rate of 8% for five years.

FINANCE

Simple interest $= £300 \times 8 \times 5$

$= £1200$

What is wrong in his calculation? Correct it and work out the right answer.

LEVEL 2

7. Which could be the odd one out? Explain your answer.

6% simple interest for 4 years 5% simple interest for 6 years

2% simple interest for 12 years 3% simple interest for 8 years

8. If you wanted to invest some money in a savings account, which of the following would you choose and why? Assume that the interest rate after the years specified drops to 0%.

4% simple interest for 8 years 2% simple interest for 16 years

4% simple interest for 11 years 1% simple interest for 32 years

9. A sum of £4800 is to be deposited for five years. How much more interest will be earned if the simple interest rate is 2.5% compared to if it is 2%?

10. Lawrence deposits £2400 into an account that pays 3.5% simple interest per annum. Malik deposits £2800 into an account that pays 3% simple interest per annum.

(a) Who receives the most interest per year?

(b) After three years, what is the difference between the amounts in their accounts?

6.4 Speed and Average Speed

Speed is the rate of change of distance per unit of time.

$$\text{Speed} = \frac{\text{distance}}{\text{time taken}}$$

Brighton half-marathon 2017

When a ball rolls 10 metres in 5 seconds,

its speed = 10 metres ÷ 5 seconds

= 2 metres per second

When a man takes 2 hours to run a half-marathon of 21 km,

his speed = 21 km ÷ 2 hours

= 10.5 km per hour

Note that the unit of speed depends on the units of the distance and the time. The common units are metres per second and km per hour. These are often abbreviated to m/s and km/h.

REMARK

The relationship between speed, distance and time can be represented as a factor tree.

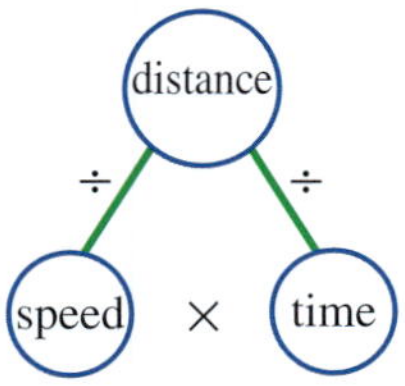

CLASS ACTIVITY 3

Objective: To calculate speeds in real life.

1. Measure a straight distance of 10 m on a school playground or in your classroom.
2. Use a stopwatch to record the time taken for three of your classmates to walk or jog 10 m.
3. Work out their speeds in metres per second.
4. Identify who is the fastest.

When an object maintains the same speed throughout the movement, it is moving at a **constant speed**. This is sometimes referred to as a **uniform speed**. In everyday life, the speed of an object may vary over time. For instance, a cyclist may have a slower speed when pedalling uphill and a faster speed going downhill. The speeds obtained in Class Activity 3 are actually **average speeds**.

$$\text{Average speed} = \frac{\text{total distance travelled}}{\text{total time taken}}$$

REMARK

The notation for the units is helpful because it reminds you to divide the first quantity by the second quantity. For example, 'km/h' reminds you that to find speed you can divide the number of km by the number of hours.

Example 10

A train takes 3 hours to travel from London to Liverpool. The distance covered is 285 km. Find the average speed of the train.

Solution

You can use a table as you did in Sections 6.1 and 6.2:

	Distance (km)	Time taken (hours)	
÷ 3	285	3	÷ 3
	95	1	

You can see from the table that the speed is 95 km per hour. Alternatively you can use the formula:

$$\text{Average speed} = \frac{\text{total distance travelled}}{\text{total time taken}}$$
$$= \frac{285}{3}$$
$$= 95\,\text{km/h}.$$

RECALL

Here is the relationship between speed, distance and time in a factor tree.

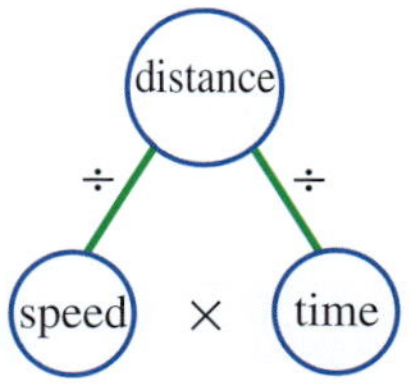

Try It! 10

A car takes 4 hours to travel from Southampton to Manchester. The distance travelled is 360 km. Find the average speed of the car.

Example 11

A cyclist travels at an average speed of 19 km/h. What is the distance travelled in 3 hours?

Solution

You can use the table method:

	Distance (km)	Time taken (hours)	
× 3	19	1	× 3
	57	3	

Therefore, the cyclist can travel 57 km in three hours.

Or you can use a factor tree:

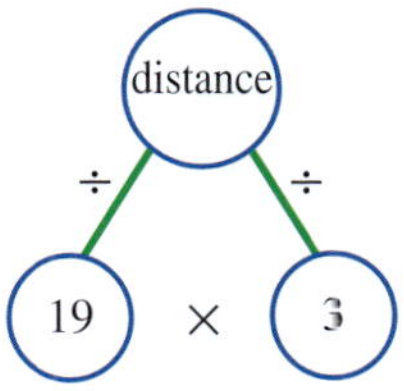

Since $\text{speed} = \frac{\text{distance}}{\text{time taken}}$,

$$\text{distance} = \text{speed} \times \text{time taken}$$
$$= 19 \times 3$$
$$= 57\,\text{km}$$

So, the distance travelled is 57 km.

Try It! 11

An athlete runs at an average speed of 11 km/h. Find the distance travelled in 2 hours.

Example 12

A student runs a 21 km half-marathon at an average speed of 10 km/h. How long would they take to complete the half-marathon?

Solution

Using the factor tree:

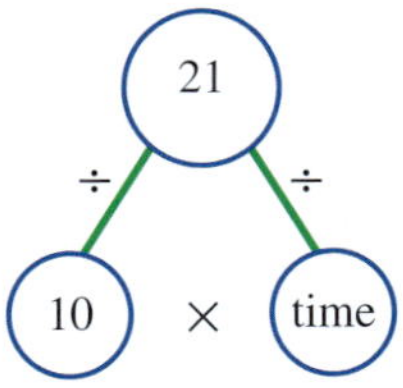

Since $\text{speed} = \dfrac{\text{distance}}{\text{time taken}}$,

$$\text{time taken} = \frac{\text{distance}}{\text{speed}}$$

$$= \frac{21}{10}$$

$$= 2.1 \text{ hours.}$$

So, the student would take 2.1 hours to complete the half-marathon.

> **DISCUSS**
>
> Can you also use the table method for this question? Work through it with a partner. Which do you prefer?

> **DISCUSS**
>
> How many minutes is 0.1 hours?

Try It! 12

A train travels 120 km at an average speed of 80 km/h. How long would it take to complete the journey?

Example 13

A racecar travels 1000 m in 15 seconds. It covers the first 600 m in 10 seconds. Find the average speed of the car

(a) during the first 10 seconds,
(b) during the last 5 seconds,
(c) for the whole course.

Solution

(a)

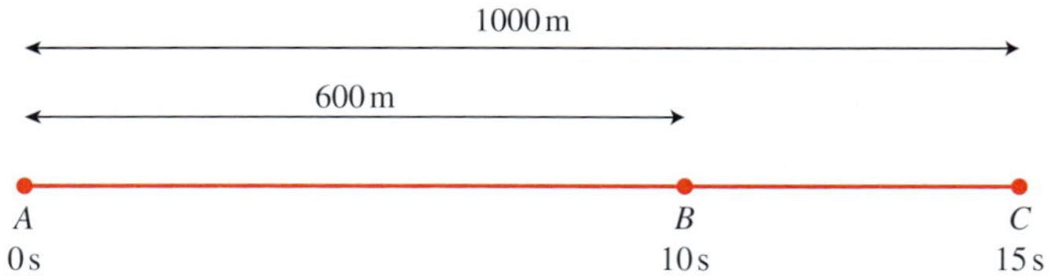

The diagram shows the situation. AB is the first part of the course and BC is the remaining part of the course.

In the first 10 seconds, the racecar covers 600 m.

$\therefore$ average speed in the first 10 seconds $= \dfrac{600}{10}$

$= 60 \text{ m/s}$

(b) $BC = 1000 - 600$

$= 400 \text{ m}$

In the last 5 seconds, it covers 400 m.

$\therefore$ average speed in the last 5 seconds $= \dfrac{400}{5}$

$= 80 \text{ m/s}$

(c) In the whole course, 1000 m is covered in 15 seconds.

$\therefore$ average speed in the whole course $= \frac{1000}{15}$

$= 66\frac{2}{3}$ m/s

DISCUSS

Why is the average speed of the whole course not $(60 + 80) \div 2 = 70$ m/s?

Try It! 13

A cheetah runs 900 m in 40 seconds. It covers the first 600 m in 30 seconds. Find the average speed of the cheetah

(a) during the first 30 seconds,

(b) during the last 10 seconds,

(c) for the whole distance.

To convert between common units of speed:

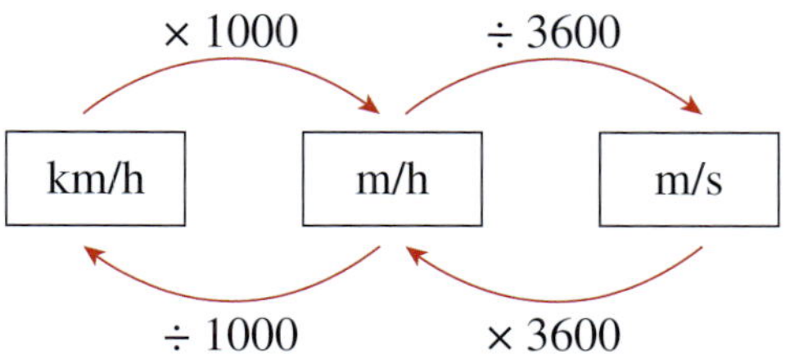

DISCUSS

Why must you multiply by 1000 to convert from km/h to m/h? Why must you divide by 3600 to convert from m/h to m/s?

Example 14

(a) Express 72 km/h in m/s.

(b) Express 15 m/s in km/h.

Solution

(a)

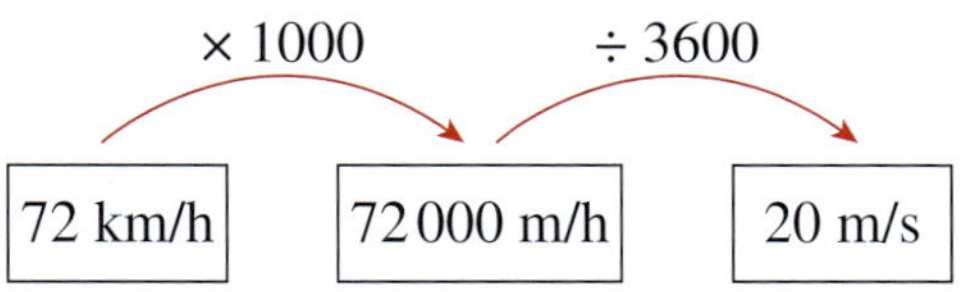

72 km/h $= (72 \times 1000)$ m/h — Since 1 km = 1000 m.

$= 72\,000$ m/h

$= (72\,000 \div 3600)$ m/s — Since 1 hour = 3600 s.

$= 20$ m/s

(b)

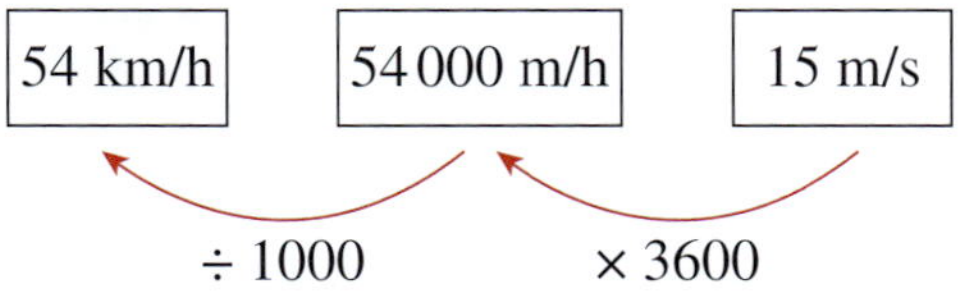

15 m/s $= (15 \times 3600)$ m/h — Since 1 hour = 3600 s.

$= 54\,000$ m/h

$= (54\,000 \div 1000)$ km/h — Since 1 km = 1000 m.

$= 54$ km/h

MATHS

k stands for 'kilo', which is a Greek prefix meaning 'thousand'. Think about words such as 'kilogram', 'kilometre' and 'kilobyte' and their meanings.

Try It! 14

(a) Express 96 km/h in m/s.

(b) Express 5 m/s in km/h.

PRACTICE 6.4

LEVEL 1

1. **(a)** A car travels 240 km in three hours. The average speed of the car is ☐ km/h.
   (b) Dan takes 80 seconds to swim 100 m. Dan's average speed is ☐ m/s.

2. Helen cycles at an average speed of 32 km/h. Work out
   (a) how far she travels in two hours,
   (b) how long it takes her to travel 96 km.

3. Paul drives at an average speed of 60 km/h for 20 minutes. He works out his distance travelled.

   $$\text{Distance travelled} = 60 \times 20$$
   $$= 1200\,\text{km}$$

   What is wrong in his calculation? Find the correct answer.

4. Erica drives 120 km from Swindon to Cardiff. Her time taken is $1\frac{1}{2}$ hours.
   (a) What is her average speed?
   (b) How long does it take her to travel 20 km?
   (c) What assumption have you made in part **(b)**?

LEVEL 2

5. **(a)** Convert each speed into m/s.
   (i) 54 km/h　　**(ii)** 90 km/h
   (b) Convert each speed into km/h.
   (i) 25 m per second　　**(ii)** 20 m/s

6. An athlete in an 800 m race ran the first 200 m in 24 s and the rest of the race in 77 s. What was their average speed for the whole race?

7. Which is the odd one out? Explain your answer.
   20 m/s　　55 km/h　　1200 m/min　　72 km/h

8. A standard triathlon course consists of 1.5 km swimming, 40 km cycling and 10 km running. An athlete can swim at an average speed of 3 km/h, cycle at 32 km/h and run at 12 km/h. What is the time taken for the athlete to complete the course? Give your answer in hours and minutes.

9. PROBLEM SOLVING
   Lance drives from Birmingham to Reading in two hours. In one hour on the M40, he drives at an average speed of 65 miles per hour (mph). In the remaining time, he drives a distance of 40 miles. Find his average speed for the whole journey in miles per hour.

10. Susan drives from Oxford to Cambridge at an average speed of 70 km/h. She then drives back to Oxford along a different route at an average speed of 60 km/h. Is her average speed for the whole trip equal to 65 km/h? Explain your answer.

REVIEW

Rate

Rate expresses one quantity per unit of another quantity.

For example, fish costs £30 for 2 kg.

Price rate = £30 ÷ 2 kg
= £15 per kg

Wage is £72 for 4 hours.

Wage rate = £72 ÷ 4 hours
= £18 per hour

When the rate is not a constant, average rate is often used.

Exchange Rate

An exchange rate shows the conversion of one currency to another currency.

For example, 1 GBP = 1.11 EUR means £1 can be exchanged for 1.11 Euros.

Then, 300 GBP = 1.11 × 300 EUR
= 333 EUR

$1 \text{ EUR} = \frac{1}{1.11} \text{ GBP}$
= 0.90 GBP (to 2 dp)

$400 \text{ EUR} = \frac{1}{1.11} \times 400 \text{ GBP}$
= 360.36 GBP (to 2 dp)

Simple Interest

Simple interest is calculated as a percentage of the principal (the amount initially borrowed or deposited).

For example, a sum of £2500 is deposited at an interest rate of 3% for 4 years.

Interest in one year = 3% of £2500
$= \frac{3}{100} \times £2500$
= £75

Simple interest for four years = £75 × 4
= £300

Total in account = £2500 + £300
= £2800

Speed and Average Speed

$$\text{Speed} = \frac{\text{distance travelled}}{\text{time taken}}$$

$$\text{Average speed} = \frac{\text{total distance travelled}}{\text{total time taken}}$$

For example, a ball moves 45 m in 9 seconds.

Speed of the ball $= \frac{45}{9}$
= 5 m/s

A car drives 110 km in 2 hours and 70 km in 1 hour.

Average speed $= \frac{110 + 70}{2 + 1}$
= 60 km/h

CHALLENGE 6

The distance between London and Leeds is 320 km. Peter took 4 hours to drive from London to Leeds. He returned to London using the same route. His average speed for the whole journey is 75 km/h. Find his average speed during the trip

(a) from London to Leeds,

(b) from Leeds to London.

REVISION EXERCISE 6

1. (a) The price of three boxes of chocolate is £18. Find the price rate in £ per box.
   (b) A worker earns £160 for working 8 hours. Find the wage rate in £ per hour.
   (c) A machine produces 15 vases in 5 minutes. Find the production rate in vases per min.
   (d) Water level in a tank drops by 28 cm in 4 hours. Find the rate of decrease in cm per hour.

2. A wheel turns 180 revolutions in 5 minutes.
   (a) Draw a double number line to show the time in minutes and the number of revolutions.
   (b) Find the rate of rotation in revolutions per min.
   (c) Work out the number of revolutions in 9 minutes.
   (d) Work out the time taken for 108 revolutions.

3. Batteries are sold in different packs. A pack of 12 batteries is £15. A pack of 8 batteries is £9. Which pack is a better deal? Explain your answer.

FINANCE

4. The exchange rate between British pounds (GBP) and US dollars (USD) on a certain day is 1 GBP = 1.27 USD. How many US dollars can you exchange with £500?

FINANCE

5. The exchange rate between British pounds (GBP) and Swiss francs (CHF) on a certain day is 1 GBP = 1.21 CHF. A tourist bought a watch for 2300 CHF in Switzerland. How much is the watch worth in British pounds?

FINANCE

6. The graph shows British pounds (GBP) against Singapore dollars (SGD).

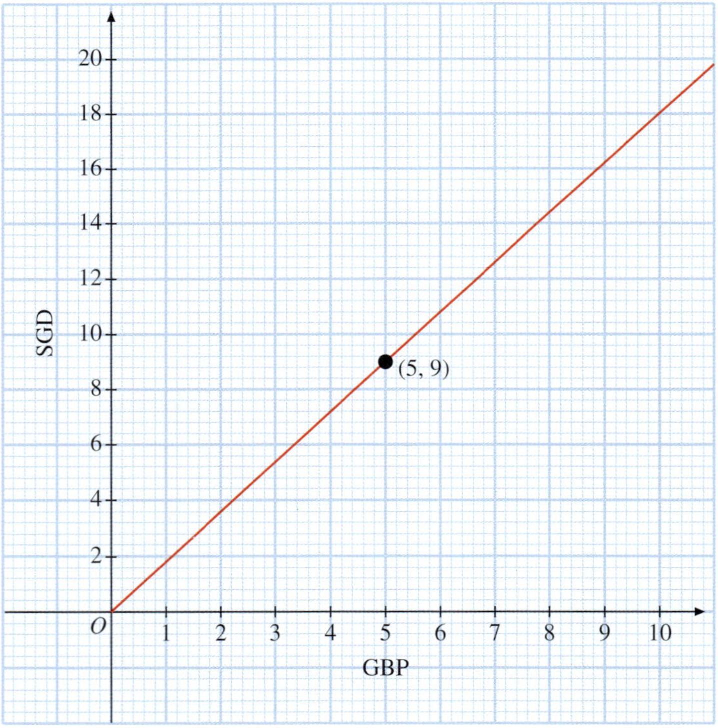

   (a) Use the graph to estimate the number of British pounds that can be exchanged for 14 SGD.
   (b) Use the fact that the point (5, 9) lies on the line to work out the gradient of the line.
   (c) What does the gradient of the line represent?

7. Florence deposits £3500 in a bank. The interest rate is 4% per annum.

£ FINANCE

Find

(a) the simple interest in two years,

(b) the amount in the account after two years.

8. Frank wants to borrow some money. He has the option of two deals. Which deal would charge the most interest? Explain your answer.

£ FINANCE

Deal A	**Deal B**
8% simple interest per annum for 4 years	10% simple interest per annum for 3 years

9. Tanya takes 20 minutes to walk 2 km at a constant speed.

(a) What is Tanya's speed in

(i) km/h,   (ii) m/s?

(b) How long will it take her to walk 15 km at the same speed?

10. The athlete Mo Farah ran 10 000 m in 27 minutes. He sped up near the end and took only 2.5 minutes to run the final 1000 m. What was his average speed for the first 9000 m? State the units of your answer.

PROBLEM SOLVING

Write in Your Journal

On a motorway, the speed limit is 70 miles per hour. A car journey from Newcastle to Leicester takes 3 hours. The cities are 180 miles apart. Do you think the speed limit was broken? Explain your reasoning carefully, using the keywords 'speed' and 'average speed'.

PROBLEM-SOLVING PROCESSES AND HEURISTICS

A 20th-century mathematician, George Pólya (1887–1985), developed a classic four-step problem-solving process to help students become good problem solvers. A summary of the steps from his book *How to Solve It* is given below.

STEP 1 Understanding the Problem

(a) Can you restate the problem in your own words?
(b) What are you going to do or what is the goal?
(c) What are the given pieces of information and unknowns?
(d) Is there sufficient information or redundant information?

STEP 2 Devising a Plan

(a) Find the connection between the given information, the unknowns and the goal.
(b) Consider some possible actions or heuristics.

Heuristics are simple and efficient strategies that people use to solve problems. Here is a list of some useful heuristics.

- Use guess and check
- Draw a diagram
- Use a variable
- Think of a related problem
- Work backwards
- Look for a pattern
- Make a table
- Write an equation
- Examine a simpler problem
- Identify subgoals

STEP 3 Carrying Out the Plan

(a) Implement the strategy or strategies that you have chosen.
(b) Carry out the necessary actions or computations.
(c) Modify your plan and choose a new strategy if necessary until the problem is solved.

STEP 4 Looking Back

(a) Check that the solution is reasonable and satisfies the original problem.
(b) Examine whether there is an easier method to find the solution.
(c) Extend the solution to solve other problems or more general problems.

The following examples illustrate some of the problem-solving strategies.

Example 1

(Make a Table)

Let $P = (a^b)^c$, where a, b and c are equal to –2, –3 and –4 in any order without repetition. What is the largest value of P?

Solution

STEP 1 Understanding the Problem

The numbers –2, –3 and –4 are used to form an expression P, for example

$((-2)^{-3})^{-4}$, $((-3)^{-4})^{-2}$, and so on,

where –2, –3 and –4 appear in any order.

You need to find the largest value possible.

STEP 2 Devising a Plan

The value of $(a^b)^c$ can be evaluated by first working out the value of a^b, and then calculating this value to the power of c.

e.g.
$$((-2)^{-3})^{-4} = \left(\frac{1}{(-2)^3}\right)^{-4} = \left(\frac{1}{-8}\right)^{-4} = (-8)^4 = 4096$$

To solve this problem systematically, a table of possible values of a, b and c can be formed. The value of P for each set of values of a, b and c is evaluated. Then you can find the largest possible value of P.

STEP 3 Carrying Out the Plan

The required table of values is shown.

a	b	c	a^b	$P = (a^b)^c$
–2	–3	–4	$-\frac{1}{8}$	4096
–2	–4	–3	$\frac{1}{16}$	4096
–3	–2	–4	$\frac{1}{9}$	6561
–3	–4	–2	$\frac{1}{81}$	6561
–4	–2	–3	$\frac{1}{16}$	4096
–4	–3	–2	$-\frac{1}{64}$	4096

From the table, the largest possible value of $P = (a^b)^c$ is 6561.

This corresponds to $a = -3$, $b = -2$ and $c = -4$, or $a = -3$, $b = -4$ and $c = -2$.

DISCUSS

What does a negative number in a power indicate?

DISCUSS

What is the difference between $-x^y$ and $(-x)^y$?

DISCUSS

Which of these statements are true? Explain how you know.

$(-2)^3 = 2^3$ $\quad (-2)^{-3} = 2^{-3}$

$(-2)^4 = 2^4$ $\quad (-2)^{-4} = 2^{-4}$

DISCUSS

Can you find these values without using a table? What is the advantage of using a table?

STEP 4 Looking Back

You can check the values in the table using a calculator.

From the table, you can observe that

$(a^b)^c = (a^c)^b$.

In fact, this is valid for any values of a, b and c as

$(a^b)^c = (a^c)^b = a^{bc}$.

You will learn about this property in the future.

As $(-2)^{-4} = (-4)^{-2} = \frac{1}{16}$,

the values of P are equal in the second and the fifth rows of values in the table.

This strategy of making a table can be applied to other situations where some of the variables have a finite number of possible values.

DISCUSS

Is $((-2)^{-3})^{-1}$ equal to $((-2)^{-1})^{-3}$?

Is $((-2)^{-3})^{-1}$ equal to $((-1)^{-3})^{-2}$?

Explain your answers.

Example 2

(Identify a Subgoal and Write an Equation)

A bath can be filled by a cold water tap and a hot water tap. The cold water tap alone can fill the bath in 15 minutes. The hot water tap alone can fill the bath in 20 minutes. If both taps fill together, how long would it take to fill the bath?

DISCUSS

What units could you use for the rate of filling?

Solution

STEP 1 Understanding the Problem

There are two taps to fill a bath.
The cold water tap alone takes 15 minutes.
The hot water tap alone takes 20 minutes.
It is required to find the time to fill the bath with two taps together.

STEP 2 Devising a Plan

You may consider the rate of filling the bath of each tap.

The cold water tap can fill the bath in 15 minutes. Rate of filling by the cold water tap $= \frac{1}{15}$ bath per min.

The hot water tap can fill the bath in 20 minutes.

DISCUSS

Look carefully at the question. Do you think that it will take more, less, or equal to 15 minutes to fill the bath in this way?

Rate of filling by the hot water tap $= \frac{1}{20}$ bath per min.

At this point, you may observe that if both taps can fill the tap in n minutes, then

rate of filling by both taps $= \frac{1}{n}$ bath per min.

Thus, if you could find the rate of filling by both taps, you can get the value of n.

Hence, this is a sub-goal of solving the problem.

From the above working,

the rate of filling by both taps $= \frac{1}{15} + \frac{1}{20}$ bath per min.

This will help you solve the problem.

STEP 3 Carrying Out the Plan

Rate of filling by the cold water tap $= \frac{1}{15}$ bath per min.
Rate of filling by the hot water tap $= \frac{1}{20}$ bath per min.

$\therefore$ rate of filling by both taps $= \frac{1}{15} + \frac{1}{20}$

$= \frac{4}{60} + \frac{3}{60}$ Equivalent fractions.

$= \frac{7}{60}$ bath per min

Time taken to fill the bath by both taps $= 1 \div \frac{7}{60}$

$= \frac{60}{7}$

$= 8\frac{4}{7}$ min.

STEP 4 Looking Back

The time taken for the hot water tap to fill $\frac{1}{2}$ bath $= 15 \div 2$

$= 7.5$ min.

The time taken for the cold water tap to fill $\frac{1}{2}$ bath $= 20 \div 2$

$= 10$ min.

The required answer should be between 7.5 min and 10 min.
Thus, the answer $8\frac{4}{7}$ min is reasonable.

This problem can be solved using equations.
Let n min be the time taken to fill the bath with both taps.

DISCUSS

Can you work out $\frac{1}{15} + \frac{1}{20}$?

DISCUSS

Why is the answer given by $1 \div \frac{7}{60}$?

Can you draw a factor tree to link rate of filling with the time and the number of baths?

DISCUSS

Why is the answer between 7.5 min and 10 min?

Then, the rate of filling the bath by both taps $= \frac{1}{n}$ bath per min.

This gives the equation

$$\frac{1}{n} = \frac{1}{15} + \frac{1}{20}$$

$$\frac{1}{n} = \frac{7}{60}$$

$$n = \frac{60}{7}$$

$$= 8\frac{4}{7}$$

$\therefore$ the time taken to fill the bath by both taps is $8\frac{4}{7}$ min.

The strategy of solving this problem can be applied to solve working problems. For example, a painting job can be done by a team of workers in 8 days or another team of workers in 6 days. If both teams work together, in how many days can they complete the job?

DISCUSS

With a partner, draw a bar model to present this question.

DISCUSS

Can you solve this problem?

Example 3

(Use a Variable and Write an Equation)

Naz and Vincent cycle from Gloucester to Bristol along the same route. Naz takes four hours. Vincent takes one hour less than Naz. The speed of Vincent is 6 km/h faster than that of Naz. Find the distance they cycled.

Gloucester ——— ? km ———→ Bristol

Solution

STEP 1 Understanding the Problem

Naz and Vincent cycle from one city to the other.

Their times taken are 4 hours and 3 hours respectively.

Vincent's speed is 6 km/h faster than Naz's speed.

You need to find their distance travelled.

STEP 2 Devising a Plan

This is a speed problem. The formula

Average speed $= \frac{\text{total distance travelled}}{\text{total time taken}}$

should be applied.

If Naz's speed is x km/h,

then Vincent's speed is $(x + 6)$ km/h.

DISCUSS

Can you make 'total distance travelled' the subject of the average speed formula?

You should identify a common part of Naz and Vincent's data to set up an equation. You know that they both travel the same distance.

Naz takes 4 hours. Her distance travelled $= 4x$ km.

Vincent takes 3 hours. His distance travelled $= 3(x + 6)$ km.

Thus, you can formulate the equation

$$4x = 3(x + 6)$$

to solve the problem.

> **DISCUSS**
>
> What do you get when you solve the equation $4x = 3(x + 6)$?

STEP 3 Carrying Out the Plan

Let x km/h be Naz's cycling speed. She takes 4 hours.

Then Vincent's cycling speed $= (x + 6)$ km/h.

He takes 3 hours.

They travel the same distance:

$$4x = 3(x + 6)$$

$$4x = 3x + 18 \quad \text{Expand the brackets.}$$

$$4x - 3x = 3x - 3x + 18 \quad \text{Subtract } 3x \text{ from both sides.}$$

$$x = 18$$

Their cycling distance $= 4x$

$= 4 \times 18$

$= 72$ km

STEP 4 Looking Back

Check whether the distance agrees with the given information.

Naz's time taken is 4 hours.

Her cycling speed $= \frac{72}{4}$

$= 18$ km/h.

Vincent's time taken is 3 hours.

His cycling speed $= \frac{72}{3}$

$= 24$ km/h

Difference between their speeds $= 24 - 18$

$= 6$ km/h.

This matches the information given in the question.

To solve this type of problem involving two objects, you can follow these general steps:

1. Let x be one of the unknown variables.
2. Identify which quantity related to the two objects is equal. (In this example, the quantities are time, distance or speed and the equal quantity is the distance).

> **DISCUSS**
>
> Can you solve this problem by letting the cycling distance be y km as the unknown? Explain your answer.

3. Express that quantity for each object in terms of the variable.
4. Set the two expressions equal to form an equation.
5. Solve the equation.

7 TRIANGLES, QUADRILATERALS AND POLYGONS

WHAT IS IN THIS CHAPTER:

Many buildings around the world make use of geometric shapes. The buildings in Machu Picchu in Peru were built using stone blocks cut into precise shapes. The faces of many of these stones are quadrilaterals.

LET'S LEARN TO

- classify different types of triangles
- explore the angle properties of triangles
- calculate unknown angles in triangles
- identify different types of quadrilaterals
- explore the properties of different types of quadrilaterals
- calculate unknown angles in quadrilaterals
- identify different types of polygons
- explore the properties of different types of polygons
- calculate unknown angles in polygons

FLASHBACK

1. Types of Angle

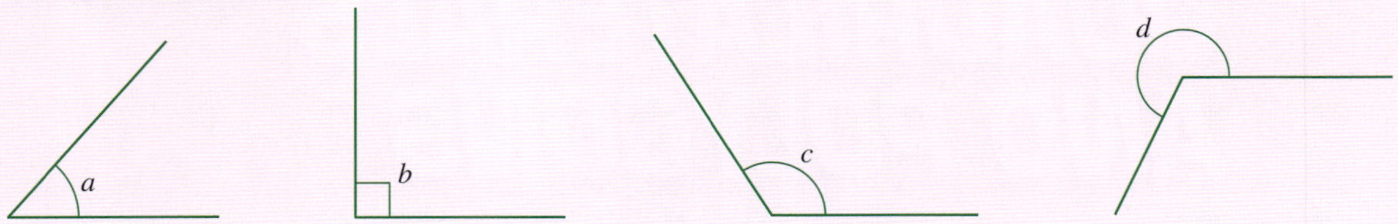

acute angle $\angle a < 90°$ | right angle $\angle b = 90°$ | obtuse angle $90° < \angle c < 180°$ | reflex angle $180° < \angle d < 360°$

2. Angle Properties

(a) Angles on a straight line add up to 180°.

AOB is a straight line.

$\angle a + \angle b = 180°$

(Angles on a straight line add up to 180°.)

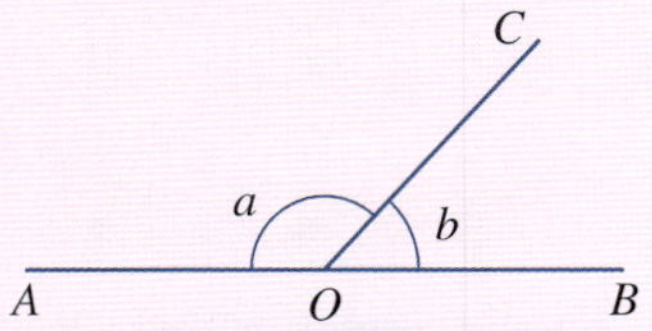

You can illustrate this using a bar model:

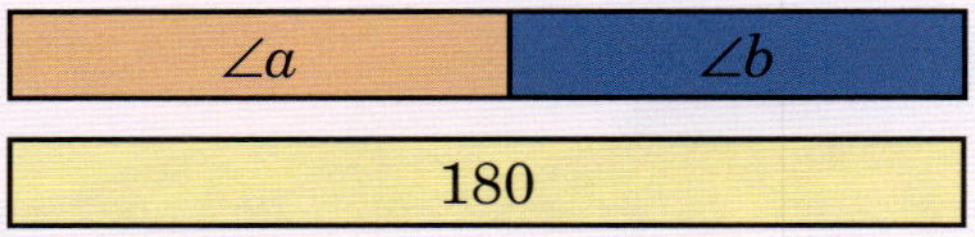

(b) Vertically opposite angles are equal.

AB and CD are straight lines intersecting at O.

$\angle a = \angle b$ (Vertically opposite angles are equal.)

$\angle x = \angle y$ (Vertically opposite angles are equal.)

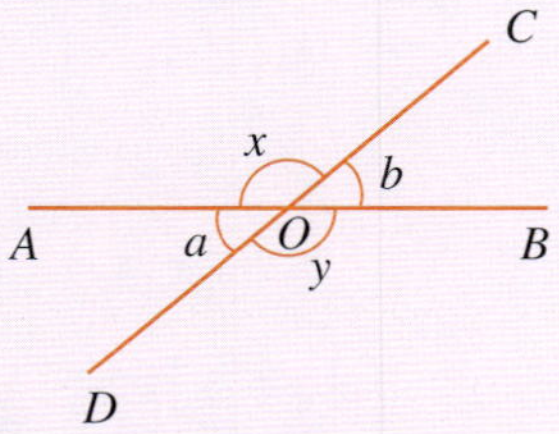

(c) Angles at a point add up to 360°.

$\angle a + \angle b + \angle c + \angle d = 360°$

(Angles at a point add up to 360°.)

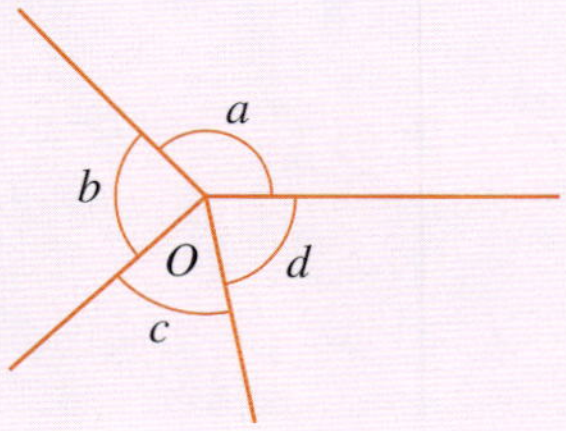

3. Angles between Parallel Lines

Since $AB \,//\, CD$:

(a) Corresponding angles are equal.

So, $\angle a = \angle p$ and $\angle c = \angle r$

(b) Alternate angles are equal.

So, $\angle c = \angle p$ and $\angle d = \angle q$

(c) Co-interior angles add up to 180°.

So, $\angle d + \angle p = 180°$ and $\angle c + \angle q = 180°$

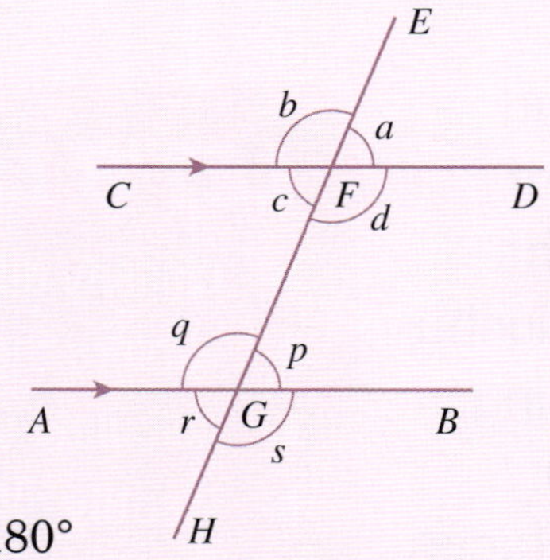

DISCUSS

Name two more pairs of angles that are corresponding angles.

7.1 Triangles

You can find triangles in many objects you see every day. A triangle has three straight sides and three angles. The point at which two sides meet is called a **vertex** (plural: **vertices**). In triangle ABC, A, B and C are the vertices. The sides are AB, BC and CA. The angles are $\angle BAC$, $\angle ABC$ and $\angle ACB$. Remember that triangle ABC can be labelled as ΔABC.

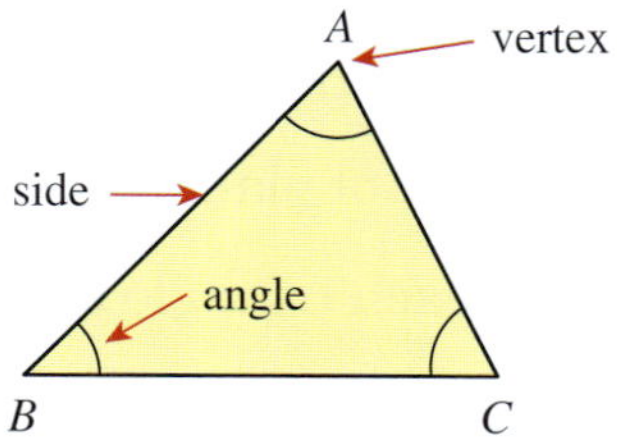

DISCUSS

Is this a triangle?

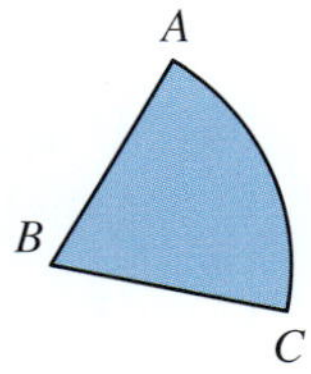

Triangles can be classified based on their sides or angles. Class Activity 1 will explore how much you already know about different types of triangles.

CLASS ACTIVITY 1

Objective: To classify triangles based on their sides and angles.

Use these six triangles for this activity.

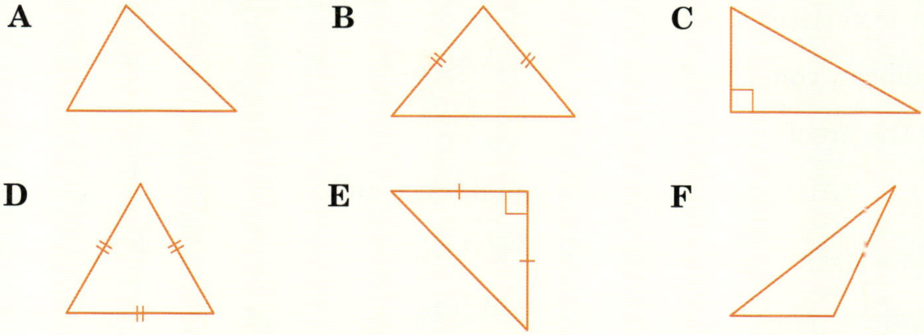

DISCUSS

What do the dashes marked at the centre of some of the sides of the triangles indicate?

1. Can you think of a way to group the triangles? Can you think of another way to group the triangles?
2. What is the same and what is different about their side lengths?

3. What is the same and what is different about their angles?

4. Copy the table and write the letter for each triangle in the correct part of the table.

	Scalene	Isosceles	Equilateral
Acute-angled (all angles acute)			
Right-angled (one right angle)			
Obtuse-angled (one obtuse angle)			

DISCUSS

1. Can an isosceles triangle be obtuse-angled?
2. Can an equilateral triangle be right-angled?

Draw an example to illustrate your answers if possible.

CLASS ACTIVITY 2

Objective: To explore the angle sum of angles in a triangle.

1. (a) Use a ruler to draw three triangles on a sheet of plain paper.
   (b) Use a protractor to measure the angles in each triangle and label each with its size.
   (c) Work out the sum of the angles in each of the triangles.
   (d) What conclusion can you draw from the results in part **(c)**?

2. Choose one of your triangles from **Question 1**.
   (a) Colour in the vertices.
   (b) Cut out the triangle.
   (c) Make three cuts as shown.
   (d) Arrange the cut-out pieces with the coloured vertices together.
   (e) What conclusion can you draw?

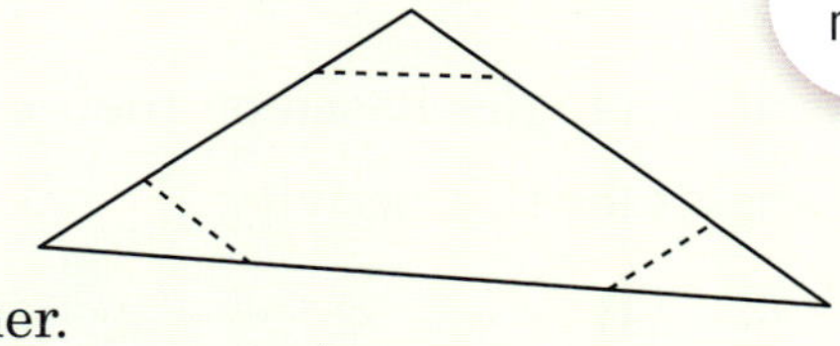

3. Copy and complete the proof.

$\angle p = \angle b$ (Alternate angles are equal, $PQ \,//\, BC$.)

$\angle q =$ ________ (________ are equal, $PQ \,//\, BC$.)

$\angle a + \angle p + \angle q =$ ________ (Angles on a straight line add up to 180°.)

$\therefore \angle a + \angle b + \angle c =$ ________ (Substitution.)

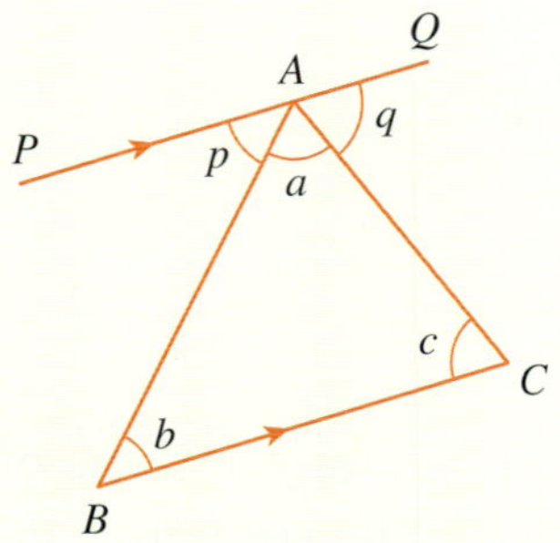

DISCUSS

What units do you use to give the size of an angle?

DISCUSS

Compare your results to **Question 1** with another person's. If they are different, check the accuracy of each other's measuring.

In Class Activity 2, you derived this property of a triangle:

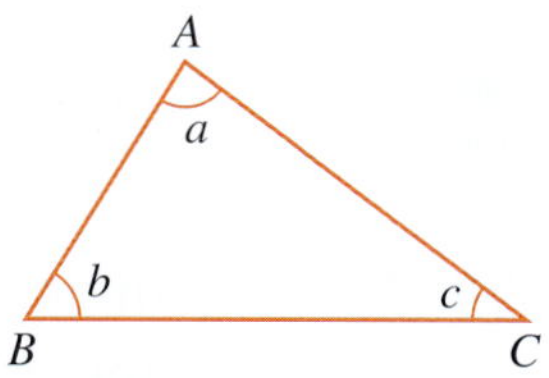

Angles in a triangle add up to 180°.

In ΔABC,

$\angle a + \angle b + \angle c = 180°$. (Angles in a triangle add up to 180^{c}.)

$\angle a$, $\angle b$ and $\angle c$ are called the **interior angles** of the triangle.

Example 1

Name the type of triangle based on the angles and find the size of the unknown angle in each triangle.

(a)

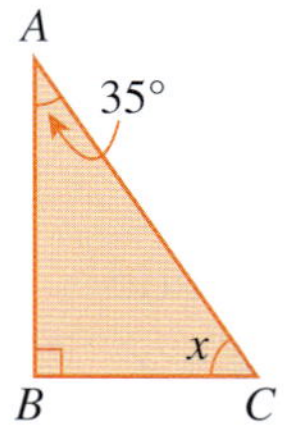

(b)

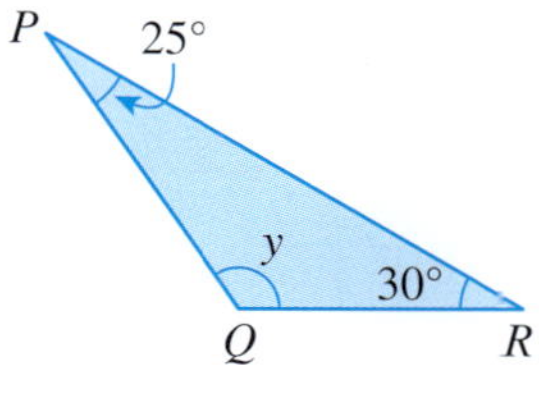

Solution

(a) Using a bar model:

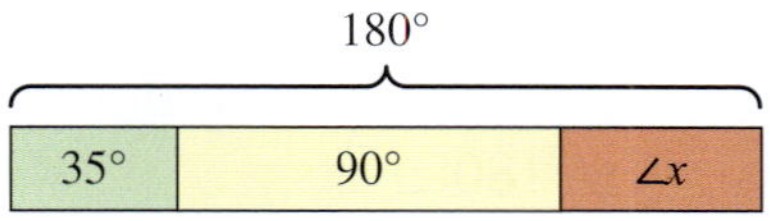

The square at $\angle ABC$ means this angle is a right angle. Therefore, ΔABC is a right-angled triangle.

$35° + 90° + \angle x = 180°$ (Angles in a triangle add up to 180°.)

$125° + \angle x = 180°$

$\angle x = 180° - 125°$

$= 55°$

(b) Using a bar model:

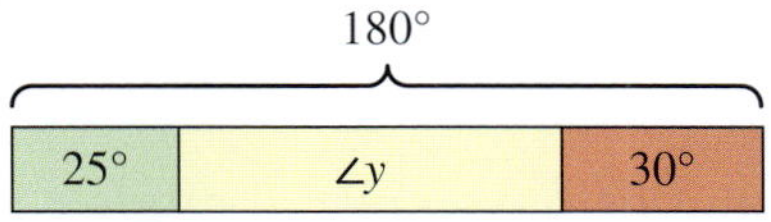

ΔPQR is an obtuse-angled triangle.

$25° + \angle y + 30° = 180°$ (Angles in a triangle add up to 180°.)

$55° + \angle y = 180°$

$\angle y = 180° - 55°$

$= 125°$

Try It! 1

Name the type of triangle based on the angles and find the size of the unknown angle in each triangle.

(a)

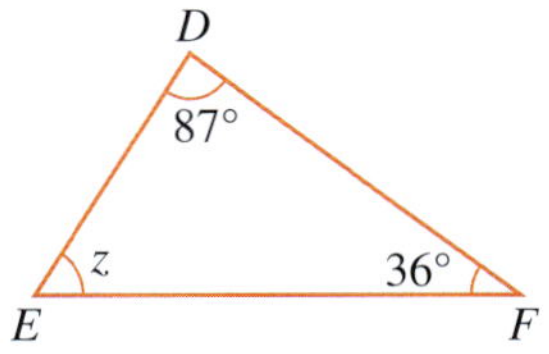

(b)

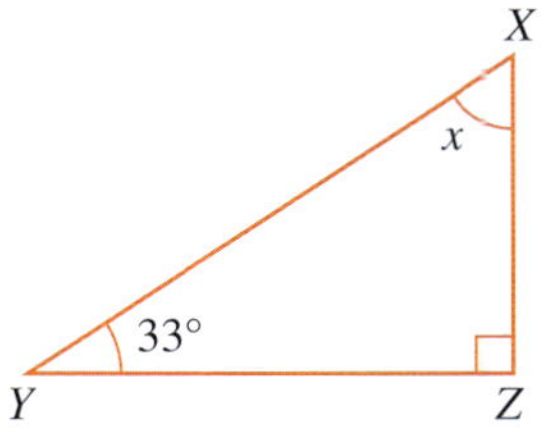

REMARK

The diagrams in this section are not drawn to scale. You need to work out the missing angles. You should **not** use a protractor.

REMARK

You must state the geometric reasoning in your working.

RECALL

Remember your efficient methods for addition and subtraction by hand. Here you can split up 35 + 90 into 30 + 5 + 90 = 120 + 5 = 125. You can also split up 180 − 125 into 180 − 120 − 5 = 60 − 5 = 55. You can also draw a number line to help you.

REMARK

You should use column addition and subtraction if you need to.

Example 2 *ACD* is a straight line. Find the size of angle x.

Solution

In order to find the size of angle x using the angles of ΔABC, you need to find $\angle ACB$ first. This can be done as $\angle ACB$ and $\angle BCD$ are angles on a straight line.

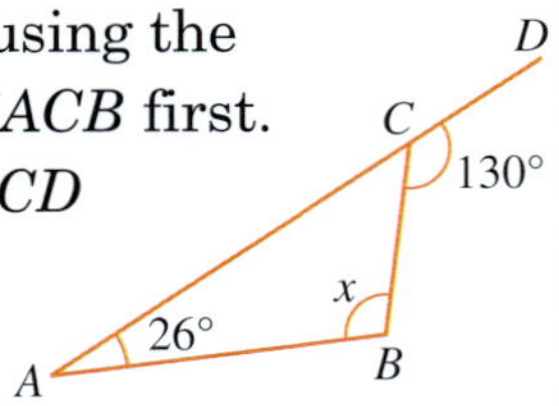

Using bar models:

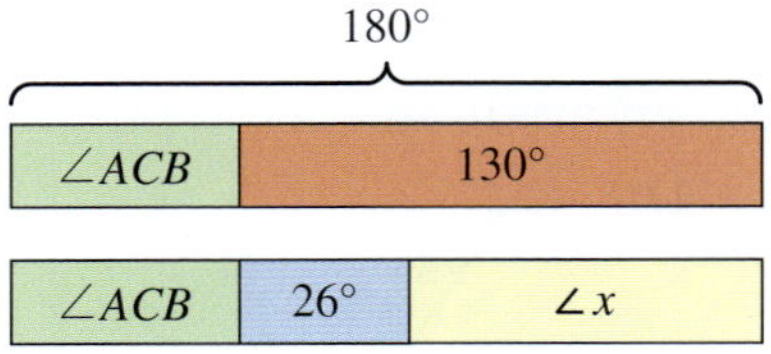

$\angle ACB + 130° = 180°$ (Angles on a straight line add up to 180°.)

$\angle ACB = 180° - 130°$

$= 50°$

$26° + \angle x + \angle ACB = 180°$ (Angles in a triangle add up to 180°.)

$26° + \angle x + 50° = 180°$ Substitute in your value for $\angle ACB$.

$76° + \angle x = 180°$

$\angle x = 180° - 76°$

$= 104°$

Try It! 2 *QRS* is a straight line. Using a bar model, find the size of angle y.

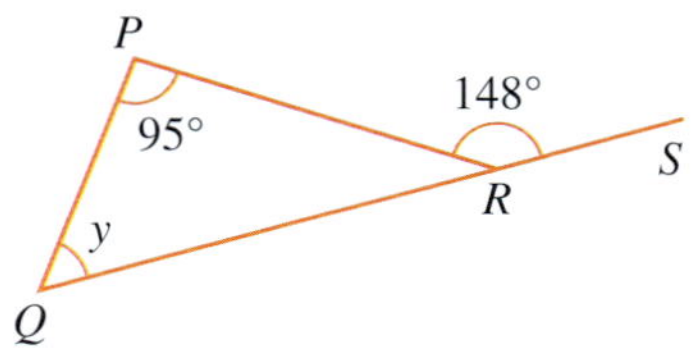

REMARK

Use column subtraction if you need to:

$$\begin{array}{r} 180 \\ -130 \\ \hline 50 \end{array}$$

DISCUSS

What is the relationship between 26°, $\angle x$ and 130°? Can you generalise the result? Use the bar model to help you.

Isosceles triangles and equilateral triangles have special angle properties.

CLASS ACTIVITY 3

Objective: To explore properties of isosceles triangles and equilateral triangles.

1. **(a)** Use a pair of compasses to draw a circle of any size.

   (b) Label the centre of the circle *A* and mark two points, *B* and *C*, on the circumference of the circle as shown.

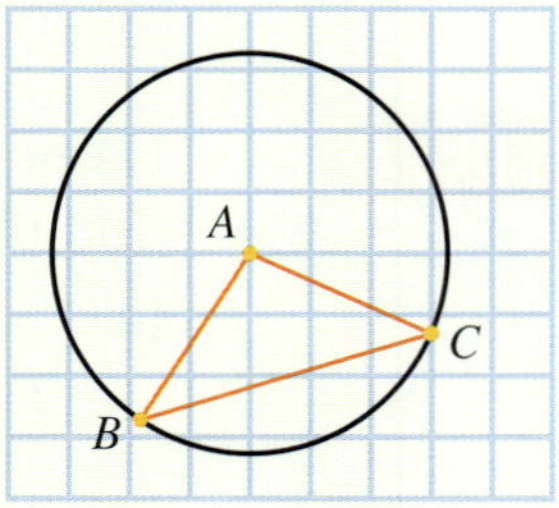

   (c) Explain why ΔABC is an isosceles triangle.

   (d) Measure the angles of the triangle.

   (e) Compare your answer to part **(d)** with the answers of your classmates. What can you say about the angles of an isosceles triangle?

2. **(a)** Draw an equilateral triangle of any size on isometric dotted paper.

(b) Measure the angles of the triangle.

(c) Compare your answer to part **(b)** with the answers of your classmates. What can you say about the angles of an equilateral triangle?

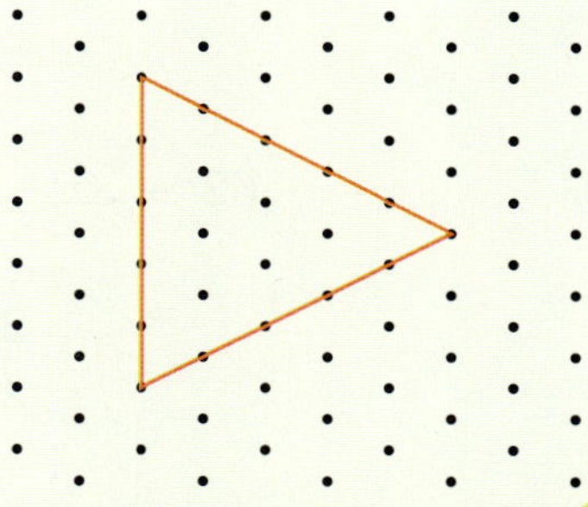

In an isosceles triangle, the angles opposite the equal sides are called base angles. From Class Activity 3 you have evidence that:

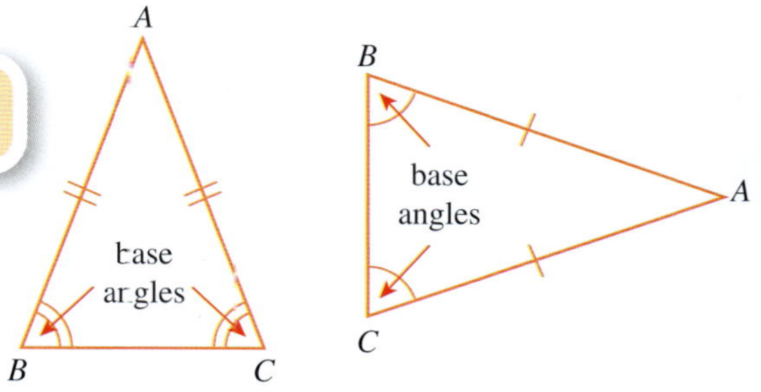

The two base angles of any isosceles triangle are equal.

In ΔABC, if $AB = AC$,

then $\angle ABC = \angle ACB$

(Base angles of an isosceles triangle are equal.)

Class Activity 3 also reveals that:

All three angles in any equilateral triangle are equal.

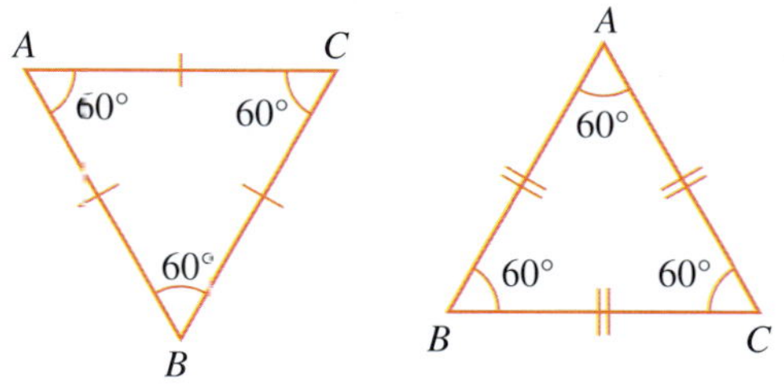

Using a bar model:

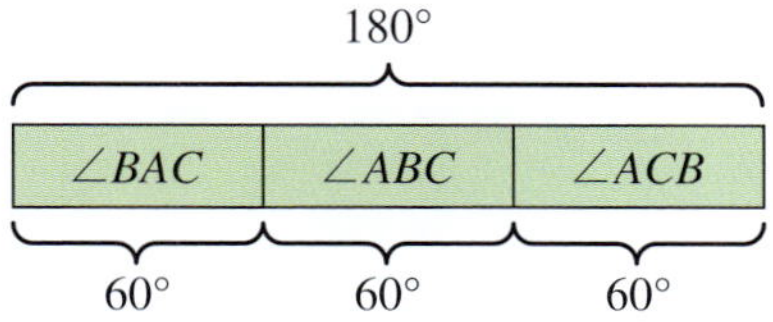

If ΔABC is equilateral,

then $\angle BAC = \angle ABC = \angle ACB = 60°$ (Angles in an equilateral triangle are equal.)

Example 3

Name the type of triangle based on its sides and find the size of the unknown angle.

(a) **(b)**

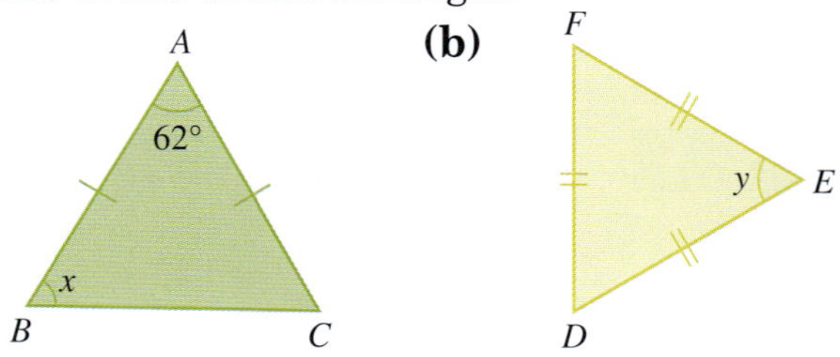

Solution

(a) Since $AB = AC$, ΔABC is an isosceles triangle.

Therefore, $\angle ABC = \angle ACB = \angle x$

Using a bar model:

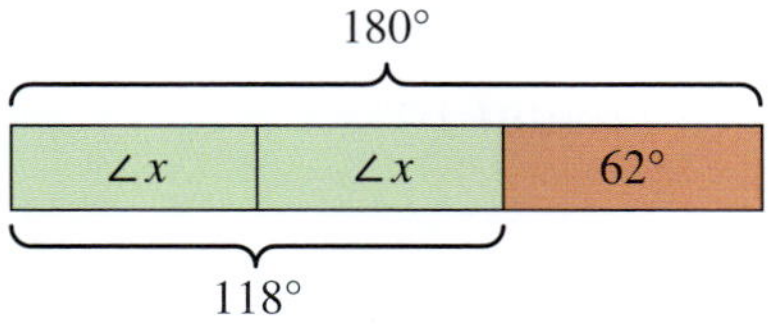

REMARK

Use column subtraction if you need to:

$$\begin{array}{r} {}^{7}{}^{1} \\ 180 \\ -\ 62 \\ \hline 118 \end{array}$$

To work out 118 ÷ 2, you can use short division:

$$\begin{array}{r} 0\,5\,9 \\ 2\,\overline{)\,1\,{}^{1}1\,{}^{1}8} \end{array}$$

$\angle ACB = \angle x$ (Base angles of an isosceles triangle are equal.)

$62° + \angle x + \angle x = 180°$ (Angles in a triangle add up to 180°.)

$2\angle x = 180° - 62°$ $2\angle x$ means two equal angles x.

$2\angle x = 118°$

$\angle x = 59°$ Divide both sides by 2.

(b) Since $DE = EF = FD$, ΔDEF is an equilateral triangle.

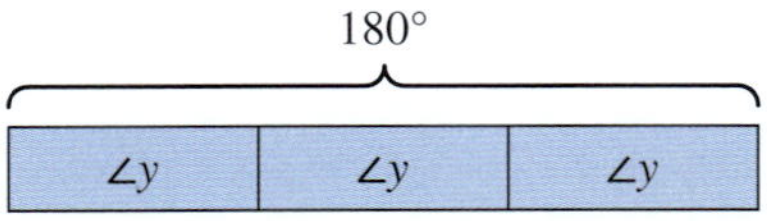

$3\angle y = 180°$ (Angles in an equilateral triangle are equal.)

$\angle y = 180° \div 3$

$= 60°$

Try It! 3

Name the type of triangle based on its sides and find the size of the unknown angle.

(a)

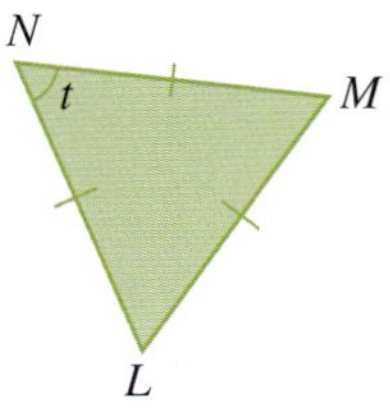

(b)

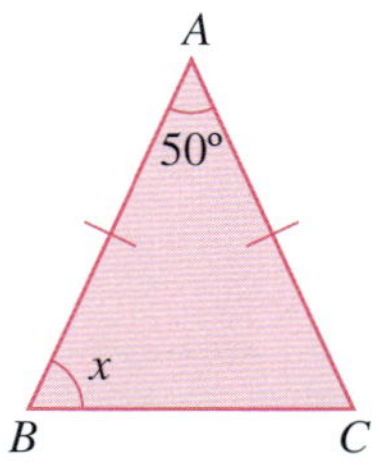

REMARK

The base angles of an isosceles triangle may not be at the bottom of the triangle.

Example 4

$AB = AC$, BCD is a straight line and $\angle ACD = 113°$.
Find the sizes of angles x and y.

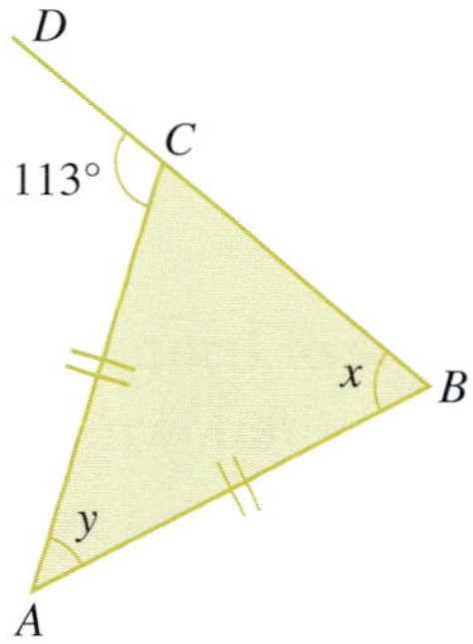

Solution

Using bar models:

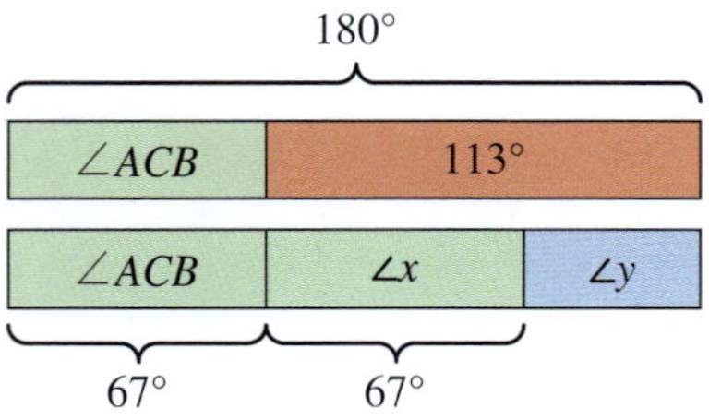

$\angle ACB + 113° = 180°$ (Angles on a straight line add up to 180°.)

$\angle ACB = 180° - 113°$

$= 67°$

$\angle x = \angle ACB$ (Base angles of an isosceles triangle are equal.)

$= 67°$

DISCUSS

Roberta says that y and x must be equal. Do you agree?

REMARK

Use column subtraction if you need to:

```
 7 1
–180
 113
  67

 7 1
–180
 134
  46
```

$$\angle y + \angle x + \angle ACB = 180^\circ \quad \text{(Angles in a triangle add up to 180°.)}$$
$$\angle y + 67^\circ + 67^\circ = 180^\circ \quad \text{Substitution.}$$
$$\angle y + 134^\circ = 180^\circ$$
$$\angle y = 180^\circ - 134^\circ$$
$$= 46^\circ$$

Try It! 4

$PQ = PR$, QRS is a straight line and $\angle PRS = 117^\circ$.
Using bar models, find the sizes of angles u and v.

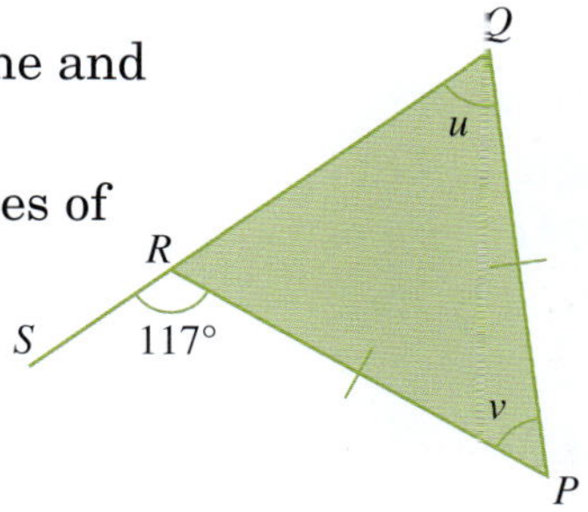

PRACTICE 7.1

You should state the geometric reasoning in your working. Diagrams not drawn to scale. You can draw bar models to explain how you solved each problem.

LEVEL 1

1. State the type of each triangle based on
(i) its sides, **(ii)** its angles.

(a)

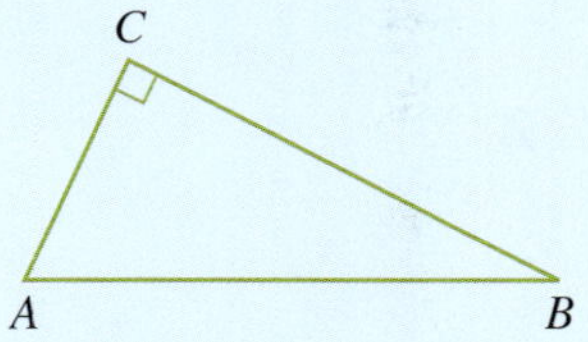

(b)

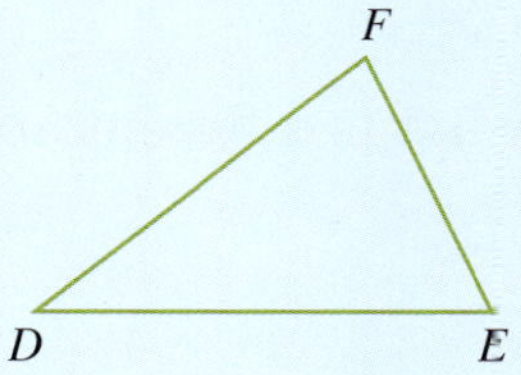

(c)

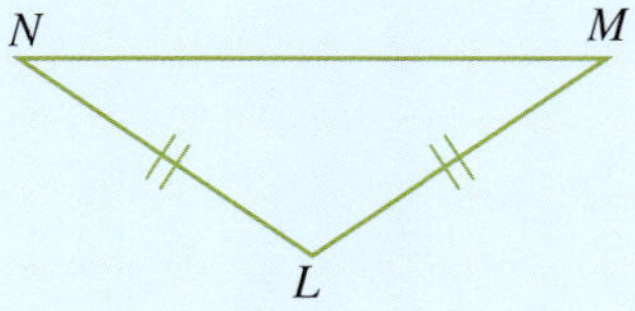

(d)

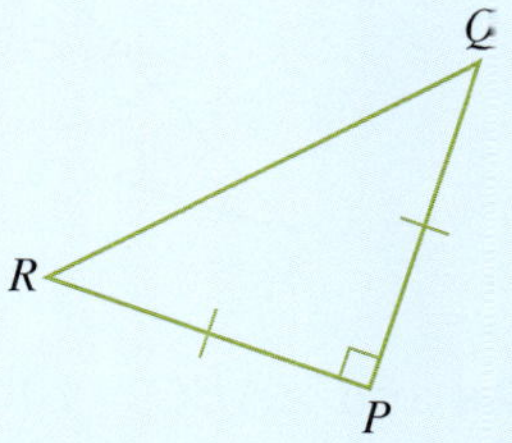

2. Find the size of angle x in each triangle.

(a)

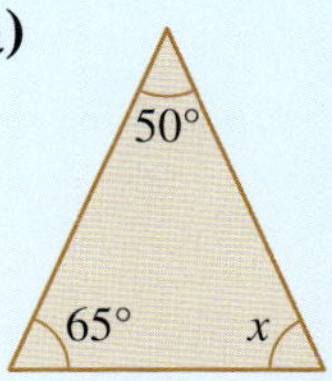

(b)

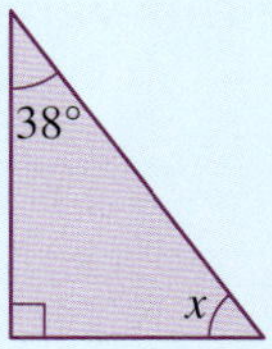

(c)

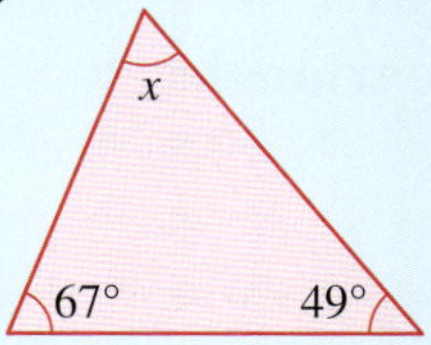

(d)

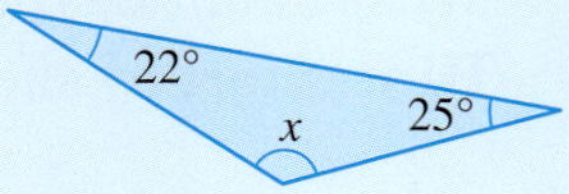

3. Find the size of angle x in each triangle.

(a)

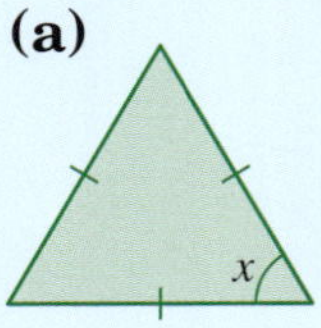

(b)

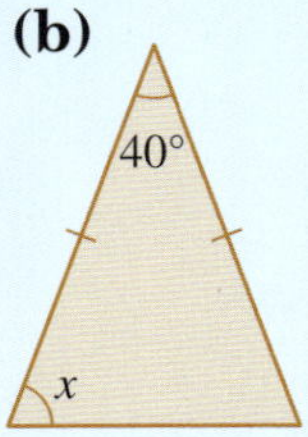

(c)

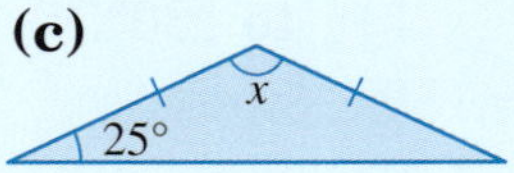

4. The sign board ABC has $AB = BC = CA = 20$ cm.
   (a) What type of triangle is ABC?
   (b) Find the size of $\angle BAC$.

5. In the wooden hanger, $HX = HY$ and $\angle HXY = 28°$.
   Find the size of $\angle XHY$.

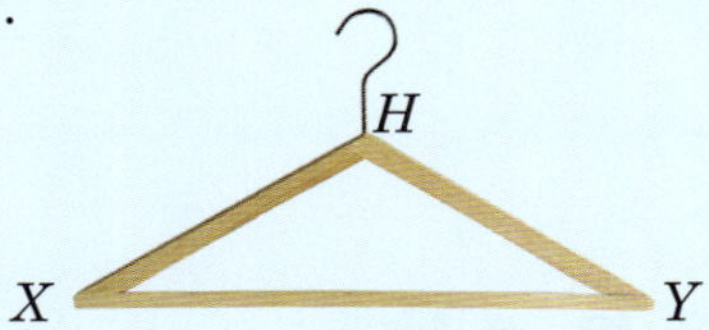

LEVEL 2

6. **(a)** What is the same and what is different about ΔABC and ΔDEF?

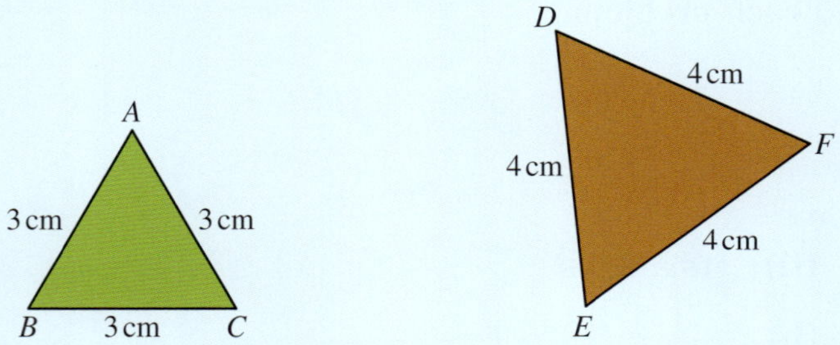

   (b) What is the same and what is different about ΔPQR and ΔXYZ?

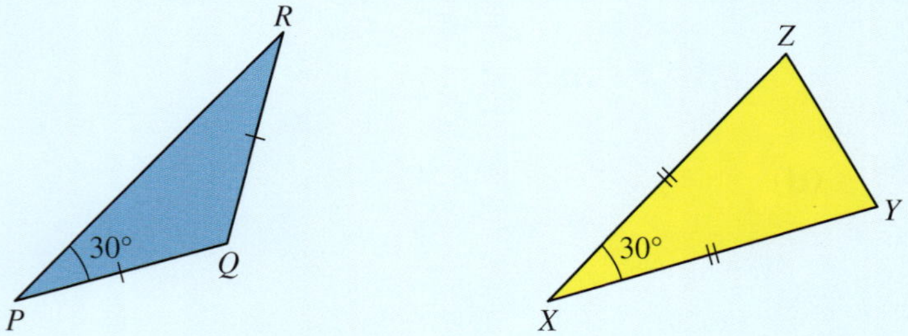

7. **(a)** Triangle ABC is isosceles and $\angle ABC = 70°$.
   What might be the size of $\angle BCA$? Does it have to be this value?
   (b) Triangle PQR is isosceles and $\angle PQR = 100°$.
   What might be the size of $\angle QRP$? Does it have to be this value?
   Hint: Start by sketching the triangles.

8. Find the size of angle x in each diagram.

(a) BCD is a straight line.

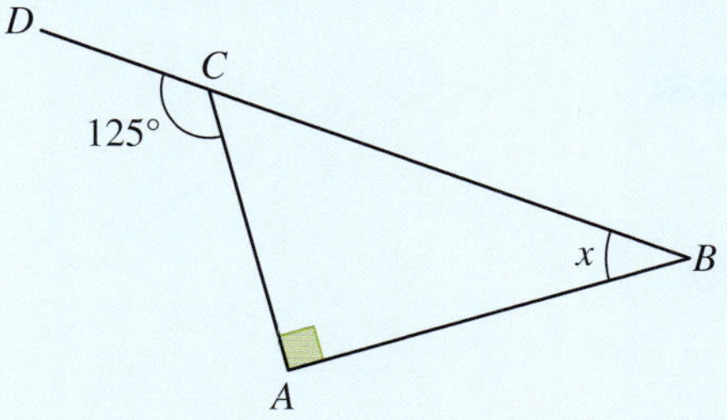

(b) $ABCD$ is a straight line.

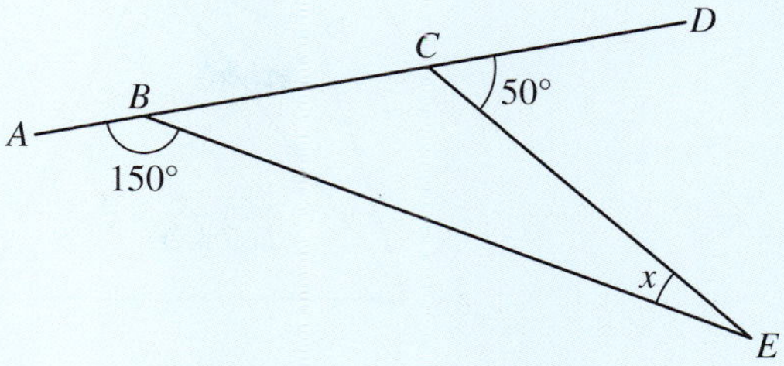

9. Find the sizes of angles x and y in each diagram.

(a) QRS is a straight line.

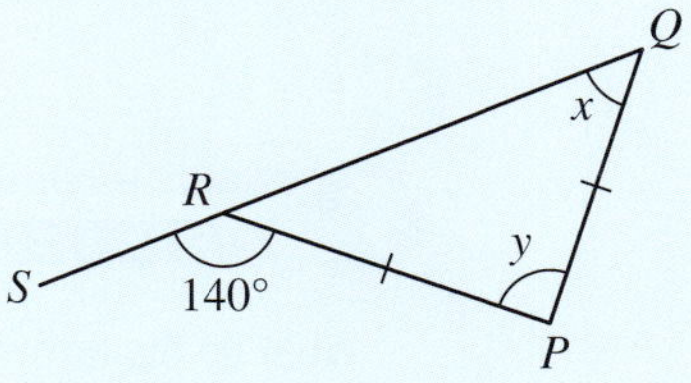

(b) BCD is a straight line.

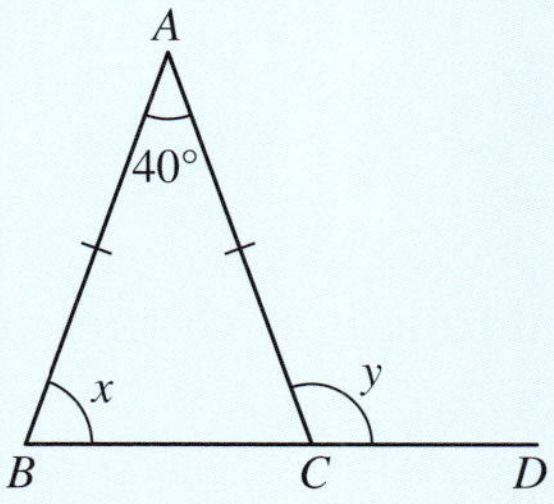

10. In the diagram, BCD is a straight line.

(a) Given that angle $a = 50°$ and angle $b = 70°$, Sam works out that $x = 120°$. Do you agree? Explain your reasoning.

(b) Sam then says that x will always equal $a + b$. Do you agree? Explain your reasoning.

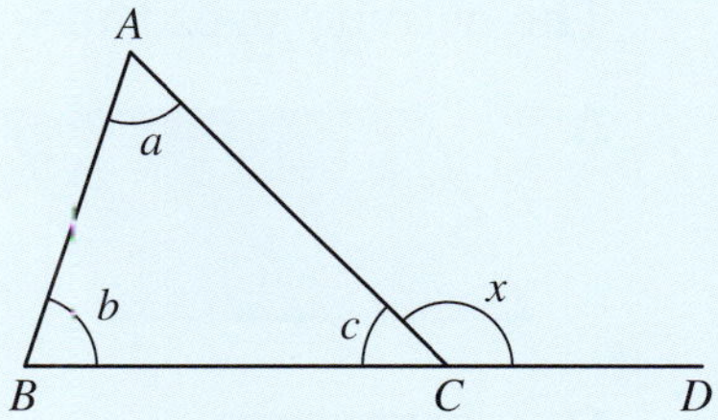

7.2 Quadrilaterals

A Types of Quadrilaterals and the Angle Sum of a Quadrilateral

DISCUSS

Which quadrilaterals can you find in these photos?

A closed plane figure with four straight sides is called a **quadrilateral**. It is a common shape in everyday life.

The diagram shows a quadrilateral $ABCD$. The points A, B, C and D are its **vertices**. AB, BC, CD and DA are its sides.

RECALL

A closed plane figure is a two-dimensional shape.

The line segments AC and BD joining the opposite vertices are called the **diagonals**.

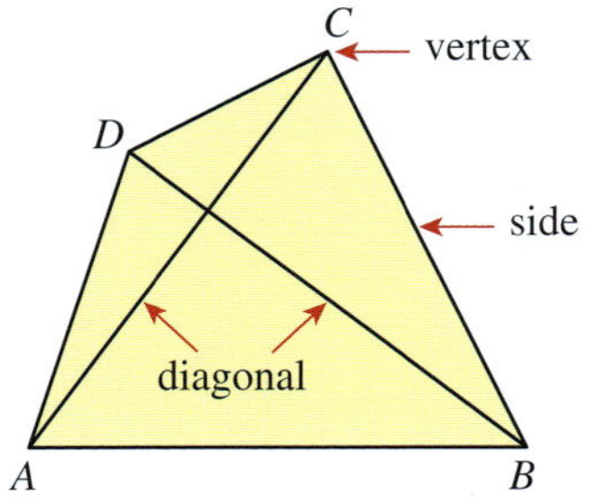

> **DISCUSS**
>
> Are these quadrilaterals? Explain your answers.

Some quadrilaterals have special names, and you will already be familiar with many of them. Class Activity 4 will explore how much you already know about different types of quadrilaterals.

CLASS ACTIVITY 4

Objective: To match up quadrilaterals with their names and descriptions.

> **DISCUSS**
>
> What do the arrows on some of the sides indicate?

The activity uses these quadrilaterals.

A

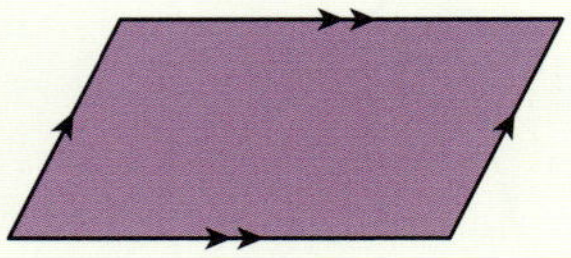

B

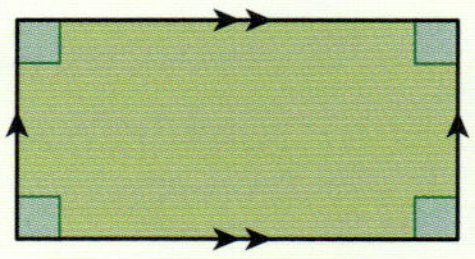

C

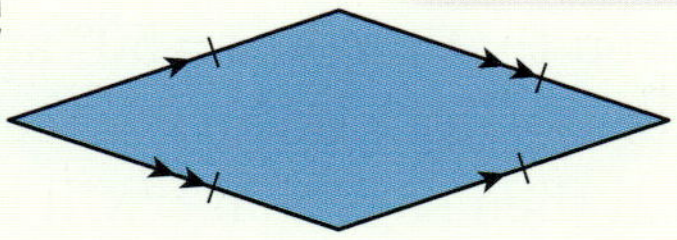

D

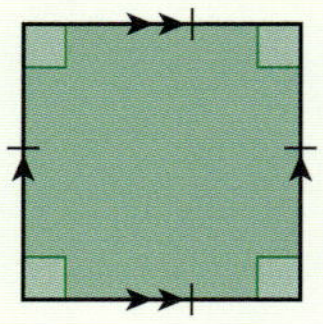

E

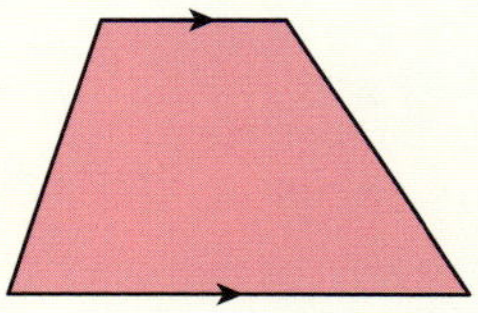

F

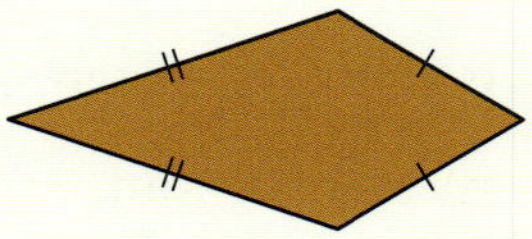

1. Can you group the shapes into categories using the number of parallel sides they have?
2. Can you group the shapes into categories using the number of equal sides they have?
3. Match each quadrilateral with its name, then copy and complete the description.

Parallelogram
A quadrilateral with
____ pairs of parallel sides.

Rectangle
A quadrilateral with
____ pairs of parallel sides,
____ right angles.

Rhombus
A quadrilateral with
____ pairs of parallel sides,
____ equal sides.

Square
A quadrilateral with
____ pairs of parallel sides,
____ right angles,
____ equal sides.

Trapezium
A quadrilateral with
____ pairs of parallel sides.

Kite
A quadrilateral with
____ pairs of equal adjacent sides.

> **DISCUSS**
>
> Use the definitions to decide if each statement is true or false.
>
> 1. A rectangle is a parallelogram.
> 2. A square is a rectangle.
> 3. A parallelogram is a rhombus.
> 4. A rhombus is a parallelogram.
> 5. A rhombus is a kite.

4. Which of these shapes are trapezia? Which are kites?

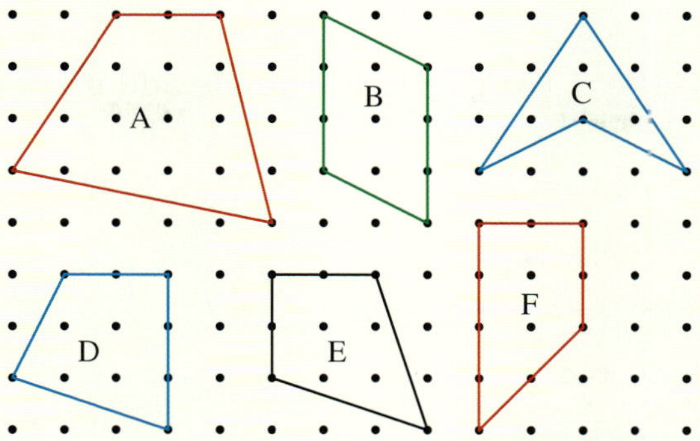

CLASS ACTIVITY 5

Objective: To explore the angle sum in a quadrilateral.

1. **(a)** Draw three different types of quadrilateral on a piece of paper. For example, you could draw a parallelogram, a trapezium and a kite.

   (b) Use a protractor to measure the angles in your quadrilaterals and label each with its size.

   (c) Work out the sum of all the angles for each quadrilateral.

   (d) What do you notice about your answers in part **(c)**?

2. **(a)** Draw another quadrilateral and label it *ABCD*.

   (b) Split your quadrilateral into two triangles as shown.

   (c) Measure the angles in the two triangles and label each with its size.

   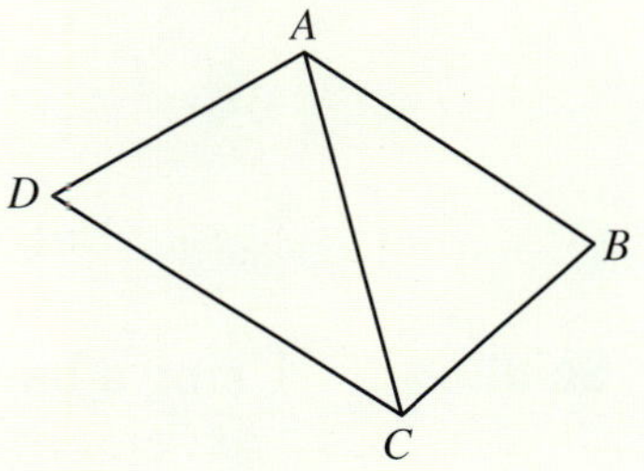

   (d) Copy and complete the following for your diagram.

   Angle sum of triangle *ABC* = ________ + ________ + ________

   = 180°

   Angle sum of triangle *ACD* = ________ + ________ + ________

   = ________

   Angle sum of quadrilateral *ABCD* = angle sum of triangle *ABC* + angle sum of triangle *ACD*

   = ________ + ________

   = ________

3. Copy and complete the proof for the angle sum of a quadrilateral.

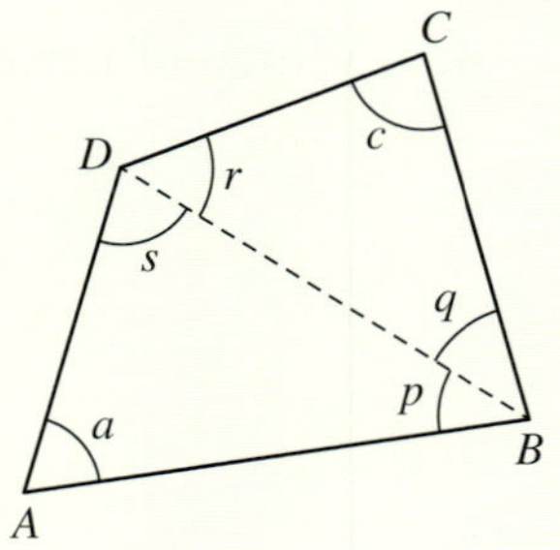

In ΔABD,

$\angle a + \angle p + \angle s = 180°$ (Angles in a triangle add up to 180°.)

In ΔBCD,

$\angle c + \angle q + \angle r =$

(____________________________)

$\angle a + \angle p + \angle s + \angle c + \angle q + \angle r =$ __________

$\angle a + (\angle p + \angle q) + \angle c + (\angle r + \angle s) =$ __________

So, $\angle DAB + \angle ABC + \angle BCD +$ ______ = ________

From Class Activity 5, you have evidence that:

The four angles in any quadrilateral add up to 360°.

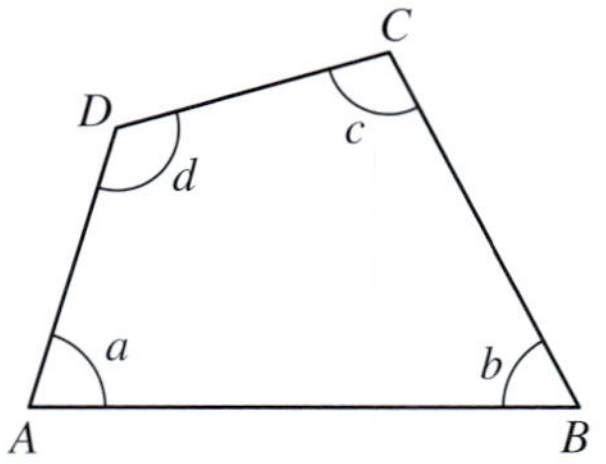

In the quadrilateral $ABCD$,

$\angle a + \angle b + \angle c + \angle d = 360°$.

(Angles in a quadrilateral add up to 360°.)

Example 5 Find the size of $\angle c$ in the quadrilateral $ABCD$.

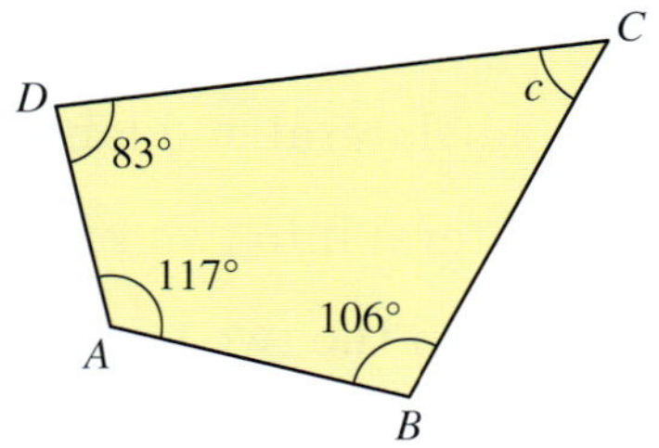

Solution Using a bar model:

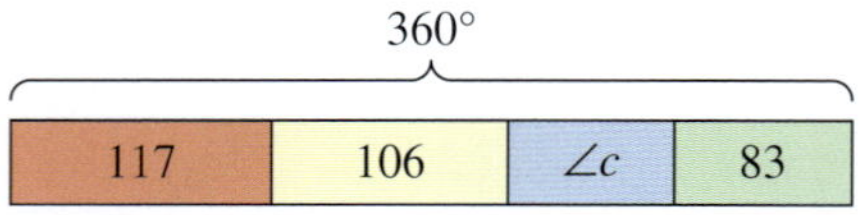

$117° + 106° + \angle c + 83° = 360°$ (Angles in a quadrilateral add up to 360°.)

$\angle c + 306° = 360°$

$\angle c = 360° - 306°$

$= 54°$

Try It! 5 Find the size of $\angle q$ in the quadrilateral $PQRS$.

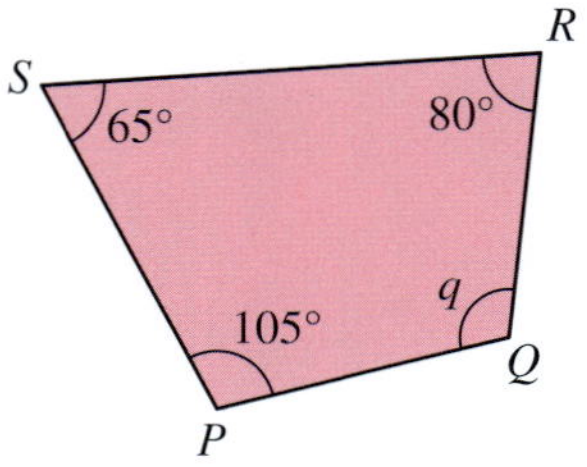

DISCUSS

Draw a quadrilateral that has a reflex angle. Do the four angles still add up to 360°? For example, you could draw a shape like this:

REMARK

Remember to use your efficient methods for calculating by hand, such as partitioning, or you can use column addition and subtraction.

B Properties of Parallelograms

The sides and angles of a parallelogram have some interesting properties.

CLASS ACTIVITY 6

Objective: To explore some properties of a parallelogram.

1. Draw three different parallelograms on dotted paper.

2. **(a)** Measure each of the angles in your parallelograms and label each with its size.

(b) What do you notice about the sizes of the angles in your parallelograms?

3. **(a)** Add diagonals onto your parallelograms as shown.

(b) Measure the lengths of

AE and *ED*,

BE and *EC*.

(c) What do you notice about these pairs of lengths?

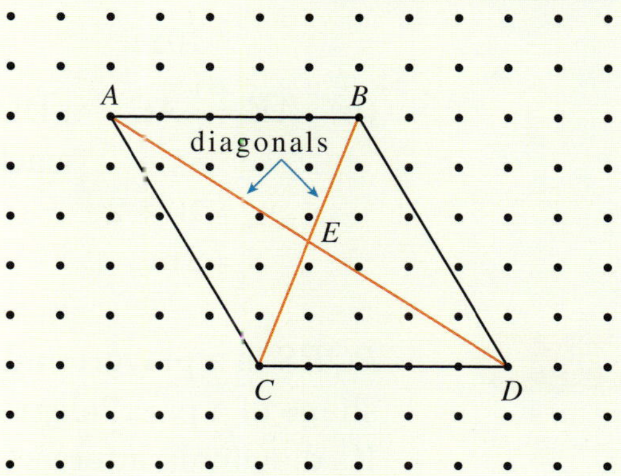

DISCUSS

How can you ensure your shapes are parallelograms?

A line segment **bisects** another line segment if it cuts it into two equal line segments.
So *AB* bisects *CD* since $CM = MD$.
M is the **midpoint** of *CD*.

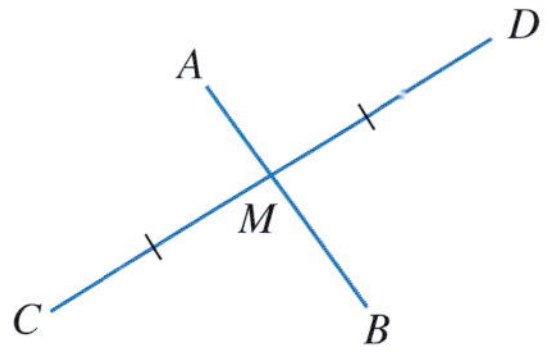

From Class Activity 6, you have evidence that any parallelogram has these properties:

The opposite sides of a parallelogram are equal.

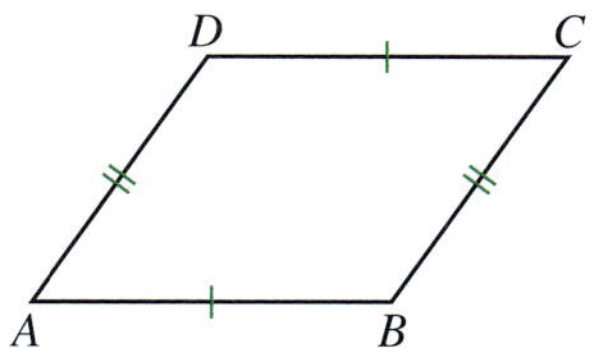

$AB = DC$ (Opposite sides of a parallelogram are equal.)
$AD = BC$ (Opposite sides of a parallelogram are equal.)

The opposite angles of a parallelogram are equal.

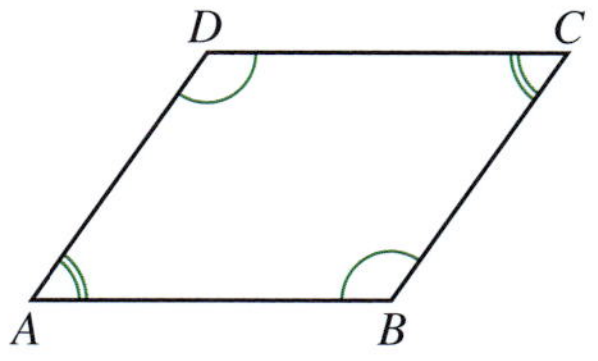

$\angle BAD = \angle BCD$ (Opposite angles of a parallelogram are equal.)
$\angle ABC = \angle ADC$ (Opposite angles of a parallelogram are equal.)

The diagonals of a parallelogram bisect each other.

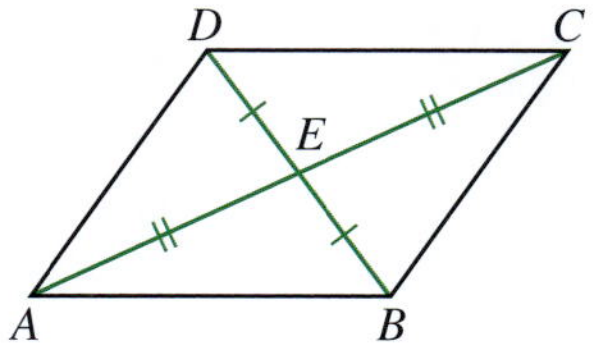

$AE = CE$ (Diagonals of a parallelogram bisect each other.)
$BE = DE$ (Diagonals of a parallelogram bisect each other.)

Example 6

ABCD is a field in the shape of a parallelogram. Its diagonals intersect at *E*. $AB = 10$ m and $AC = 16$ m. The farmer wants to build two footpaths. Find the length of

(a) *DC*,

(b) *AE*.

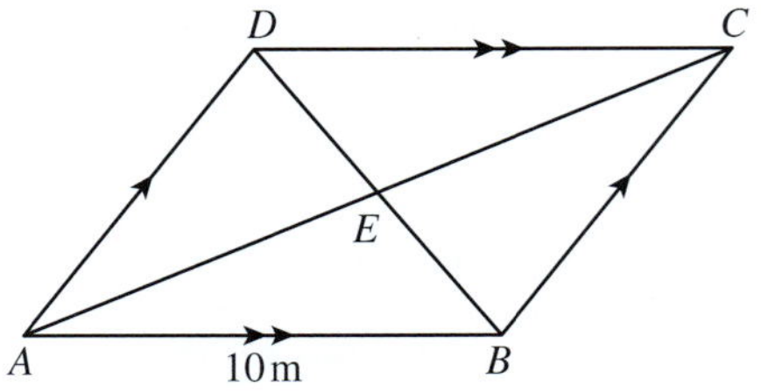

Solution

(a) $DC = AB$ (Opposite sides of a parallelogram are equal.)

$= 10$ m

(b) $AE = \frac{1}{2}AC$ (Diagonals of a parallelogram bisect each other.)

$= 16 \div 2$

$= 8$ m

Try It! 6

PQRS is a playground in the shape of a parallelogram. Its diagonals intersect at *T*. $QR = 8$ m and $ST = 6$ m. The headteacher wants to put up two fences. Find the length of

(a) *PS*,

(b) *QT*.

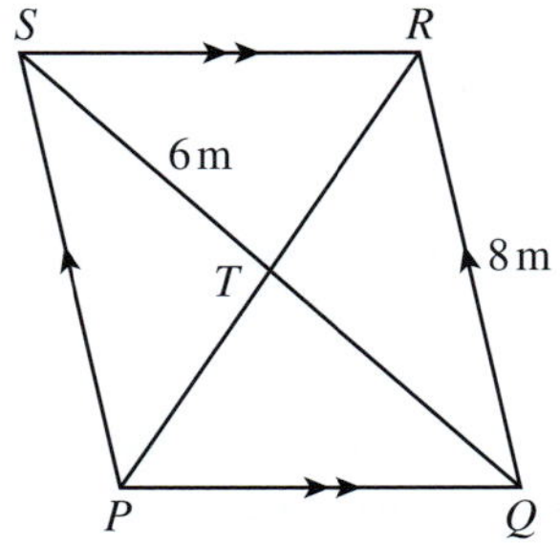

Example 7

EFGH is a tile in the shape of a parallelogram. Find the sizes of angles *x* and *y*.

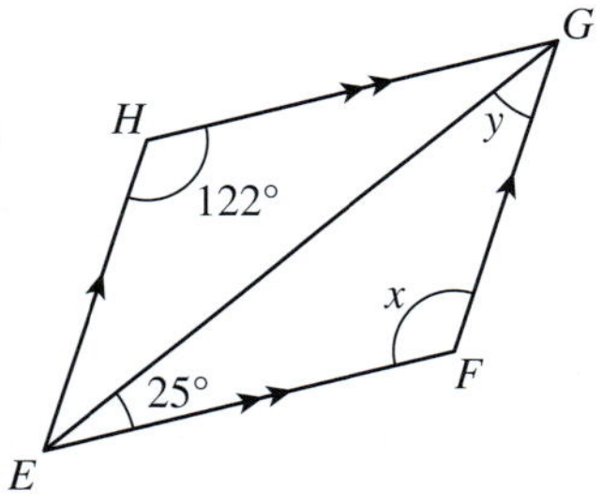

Solution

$\angle x = 122°$ (Opposite angles of a parallelogram are equal.)

$\angle x + \angle y + 25° = 180°$ (Angles in a triangle add up to 180°.)

$122° + \angle y + 25° = 180°$

$147° + \angle y = 180°$

$\angle y = 180° - 147°$

$\angle y = 33°$

DISCUSS

Is there another way to find the size of $\angle y$ without using $\angle x$?

Try It! 7

TXYZ is a paving stone in the shape of a parallelogram. Find the sizes of angles *u* and *v*.

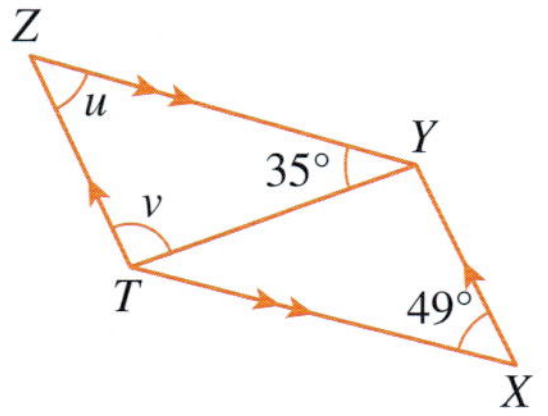

C Properties of Rectangles, Rhombuses and Squares

Rectangles, rhombuses and squares are parallelograms. In addition to the properties of parallelograms, each shape also has its own special properties.

CLASS ACTIVITY 7

Objective: To explore some properties of rectangles, rhombuses and squares.

1. (a) Draw one or more rectangles, rhombuses and squares on dotted paper.
   (b) Add diagonals onto each of your quadrilaterals.
2. Use your diagrams to decide if the statements are true or false for each shape.

Statement	Square	Rectangle	Rhombus
The diagonals are always equal in length.	True		
The diagonals are always perpendicular to each other.			
The diagonals always bisect the interior angles.			

REMARK

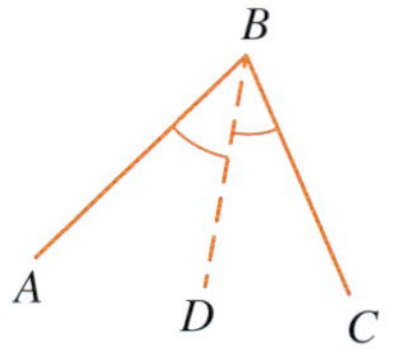

A line BD bisects $\angle ABC$ if it divides the angle into two equal angles, $\angle ABD$ and $\angle CBD$.

From Class Activity 7, you have evidence for some special properties of all squares, rhombuses and rectangles.

> The diagonals of a rectangle are equal.

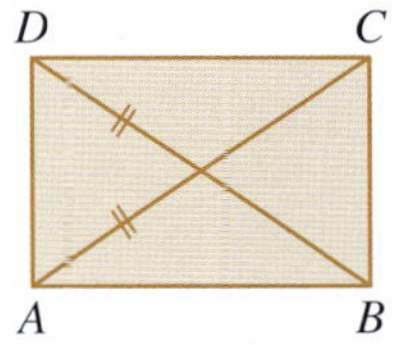

If $ABCD$ is a rectangle
then $AC = BD$. (Diagonals of a rectangle are equal.)

> The diagonals of a rhombus are perpendicular to each other.
> The interior angles of a rhombus are bisected by the diagonals.

RECALL

The notation $AC \perp BD$ means AC is perpendicular to BD. That means they intersect at right angles.

If $ABCD$ is a rhombus
then $AC \perp BD$, (Diagonals of a rhombus are perpendicular to each other.)
$\angle BAC = \angle DAC$, (Interior angles of a rhombus are bisected by the diagonals.)
$\angle ABD = \angle CBD$. (Interior angles of a rhombus are bisected by the diagonals.)

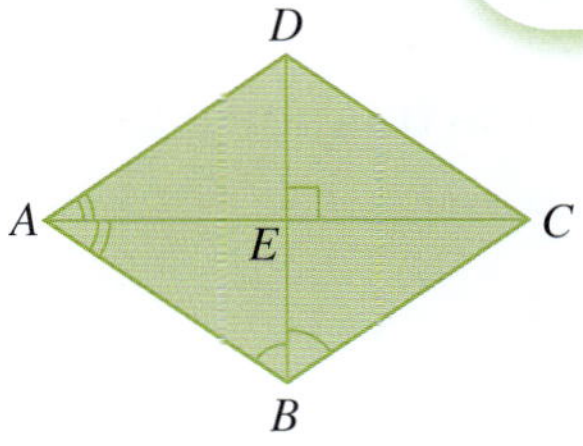

> The diagonals of a square are equal and are perpendicular to each other.
> The angle between each diagonal of a square and a side is 45°.

If $ABCD$ is a square,

then $AC = BD$, (Diagonals of a square are equal.)

$AC \perp BD$, (Diagonals of a square are perpendicular to each other.)

$\angle CAB = 45°$. (The angle between each diagonal of a square and a side is 45°.)

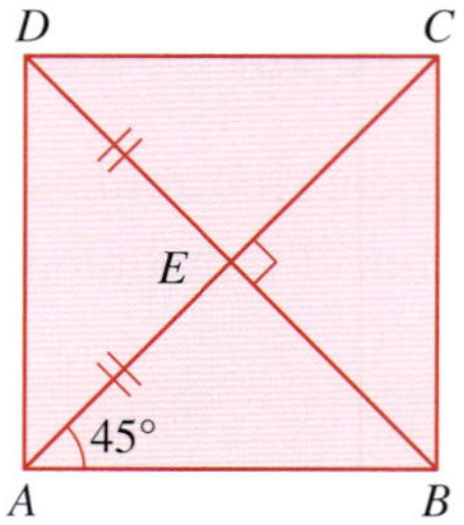

Example 8

$EFGH$ is a rhombus. Find the sizes of angles x and y.

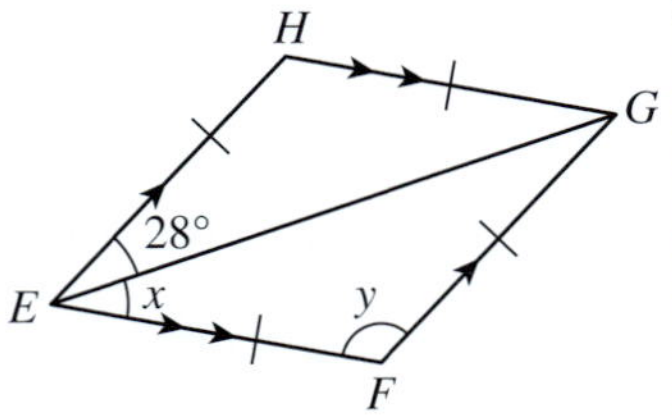

Solution

$\angle x = \angle HEG$ (Interior angles of a rhombus are
$= 28°$ bisected by the diagonals.)

$28° + \angle x + \angle y = 180°$ (Co-interior angles, $EH \mathbin{//} FG$.)

$28° + 28° + \angle y = 180°$

$56° + \angle y = 180°$

$\angle y = 180° - 56°$

$\angle y = 124°$

DISCUSS

Can $\angle y$ be found in another way? If so, explain your method.

Try It! 8

$TXYZ$ is a rhombus. Find the size of the angles a and b.

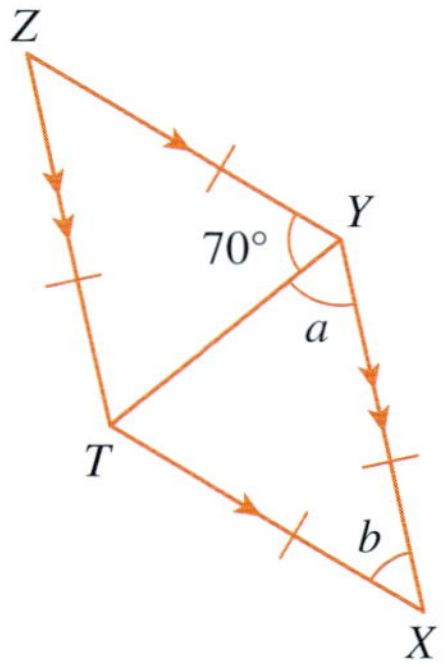

PRACTICE 7.2

Diagrams not drawn to scale. You should state the geometric reasoning in your working.

LEVEL 1

1. Find the size of the unknown angle in each quadrilateral.

(a)

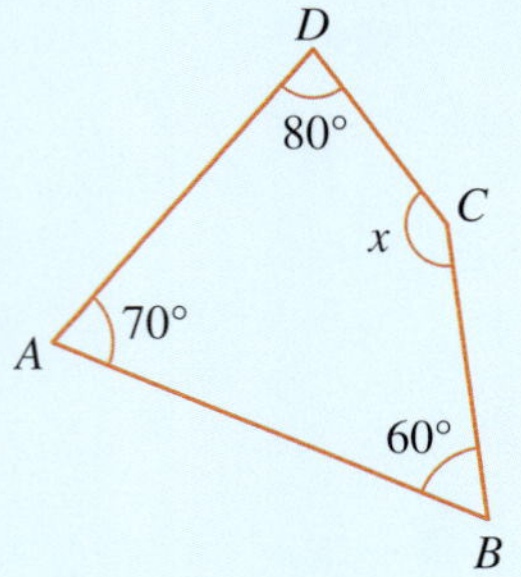

(b)

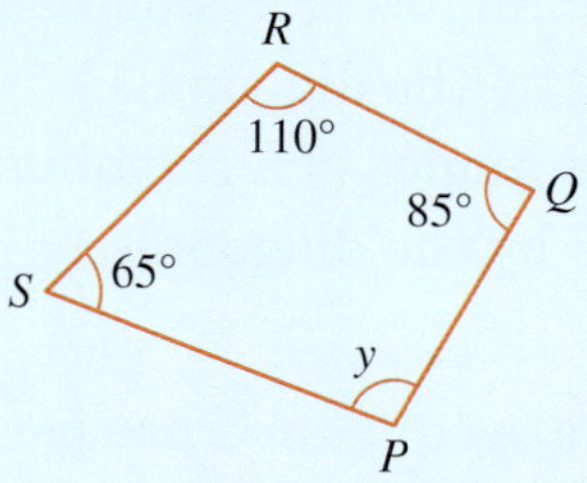

2. *PQRS* is a rectangle. $ST = 6$ cm.
Find the length of *PR*.

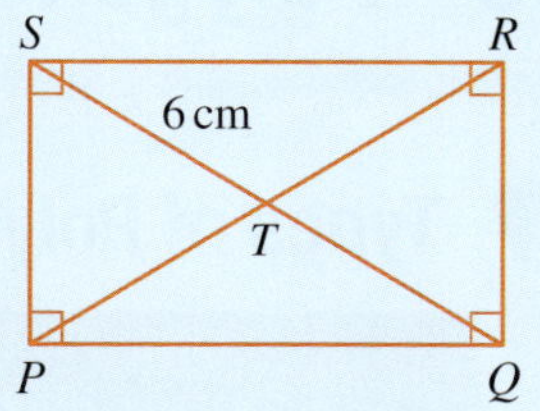

3. *TXYZ* is a rhombus. $YZ = 13$ cm and $TS = 10$ cm.
Find the lengths of *XY* and *TY*.

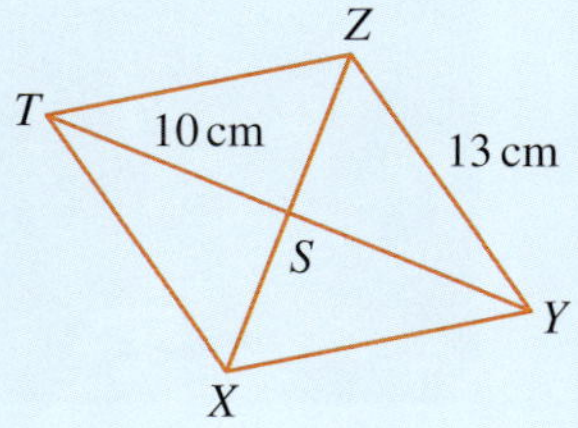

4. **(a)** What is the same and what is different about a rectangle and a rhombus?
(b) What is the same and what is different about a parallelogram and a trapezium?

5. This toy is called a kite. Does the kite shown in the picture satisfy the mathematical definition of the quadrilateral called a kite? Explain your answer.

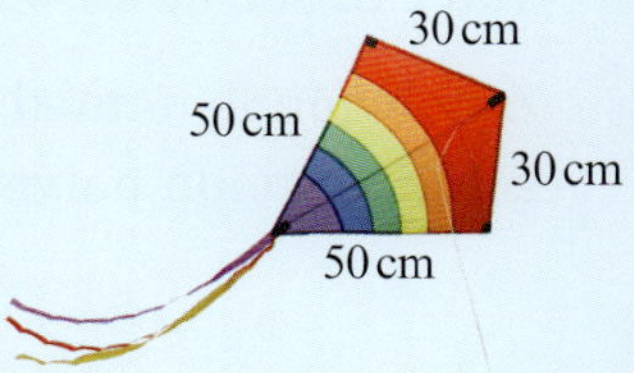

LEVEL 2

6. *ABCD* is a parallelogram. Find the sizes of angles x and y.

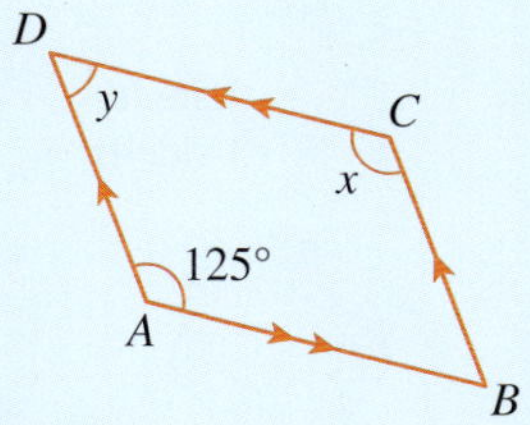

7. In the diagram, *ABCD* is a square photo frame. *AEC* is a straight line.
Find the sizes of angles x and y.

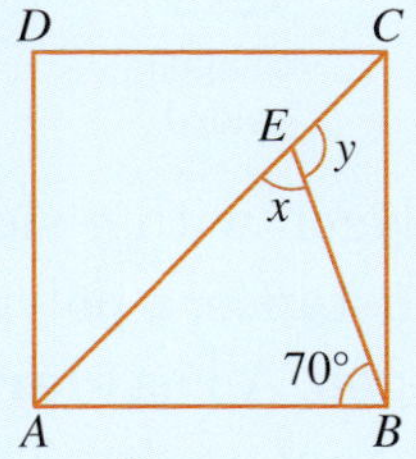

8. *ABCD* is a rhombus. Find the sizes of angles x and y.

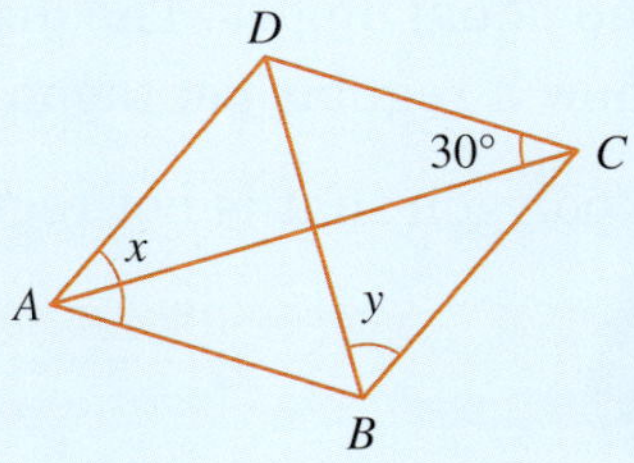

9. Is this quadrilateral a rhombus? Explain your reasoning.

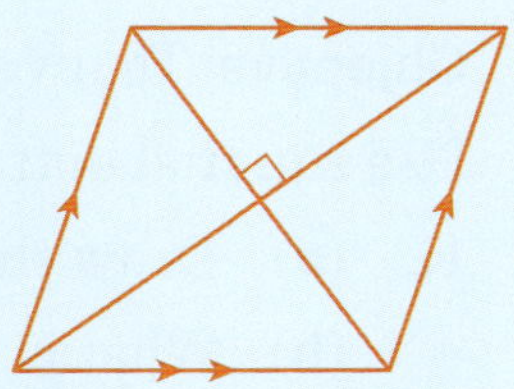

10. *ABCD* is a quadrilateral. Can you tell what sort of quadrilateral it is if
(a) $\angle ABC = 50°$, $\angle BCD = 130°$, $\angle CDA = 50°$,
(b) $\angle ABC = 50°$, $\angle BCD = 50°$, $\angle CDA = 130°$,
(c) $\angle ABC = 50°$, $\angle BCD = 140°$, $\angle CDA = 30°$?

7.3 Polygons

A Types of Polygons

A **polygon** is a closed plane figure formed by three or more line segments. Triangles and quadrilaterals are polygons. Apart from them, you can see other objects in the shapes of polygons in everyday life.

A polygon is named according to the number of sides it has. Here are some common polygons.

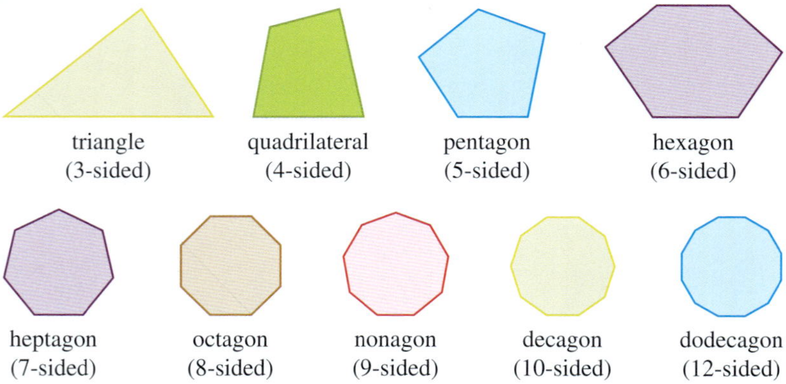

A polygon with n sides can be called an n-gon. For instance, a polygon with 17 sides is called a 17-gon. A **regular polygon** has equal sides and equal angles. The diagrams on the right show a regular pentagon and hexagon.

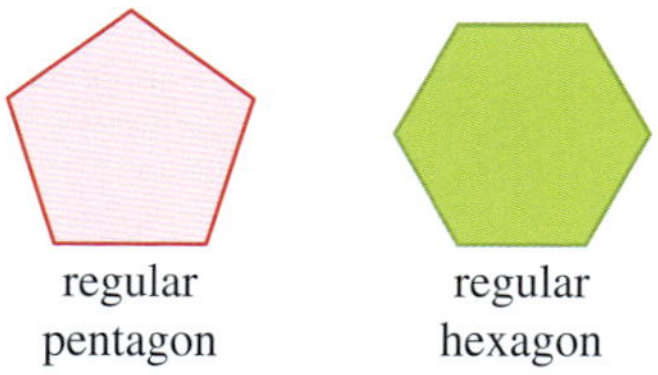

A polygon that is not regular is called **irregular**.

DISCUSS

What polygons can you see in the photographs?

DISCUSS

Are these hexagons? Explain your answers.

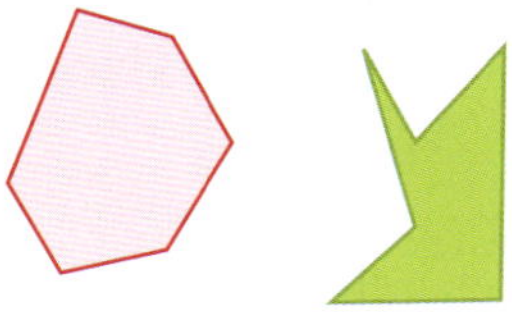

CLASS ACTIVITY 8

Objective: To investigate polygons.

Use squared dotted paper for this activity.

1. **(a)** Draw three different hexagons.

(b) What is the same and what is different about your hexagons?

Try to use some of these key words in your descriptions:

acute, obtuse, reflex, right angle
equal
regular, irregular
vertex, vertices

RECALL

A reflex angle is an angle that is greater than 180°.

2. (a) Draw a pentagon with three right angles.

(b) Draw a pentagon with two reflex angles.

3. (a) Can you draw a pentagon with four right angles?

(b) Can you draw a pentagon with three reflex angles?

(c) Can you draw a hexagon with five right angles?

DISCUSS

Are these regular polygons?

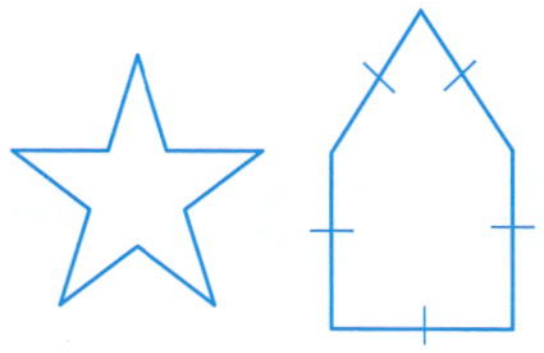

Are they convex or concave?

A polygon is **convex** if all of its interior angles are less than 180°. If one or more of its angles is more than 180° then it is **concave**.

B Sum of Exterior Angles of a Polygon

When a side of a polygon is extended, an exterior angle is formed at a vertex. Here, $\angle x$, $\angle y$ and $\angle z$ are the exterior angles of ΔABC at the vertices A, B and C. $\angle p$, $\angle q$, $\angle r$, $\angle s$ and $\angle t$ are the exterior angles at the vertices E, F, G, H and K of the pentagon $EFGHK$.

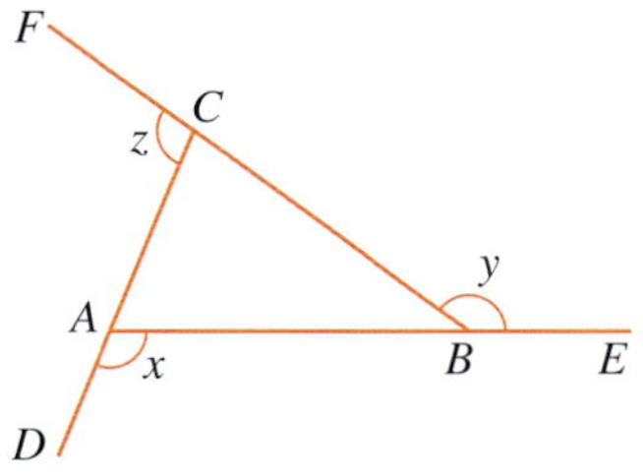

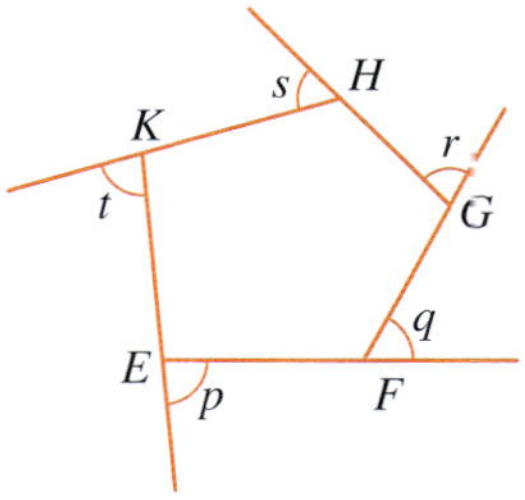

REMARK

Notice that the exterior angles are **not** the whole reflex angle.

CLASS ACTIVITY 9

Objective: To investigate exterior angles of polygons.

Use squared dotted paper for this activity.

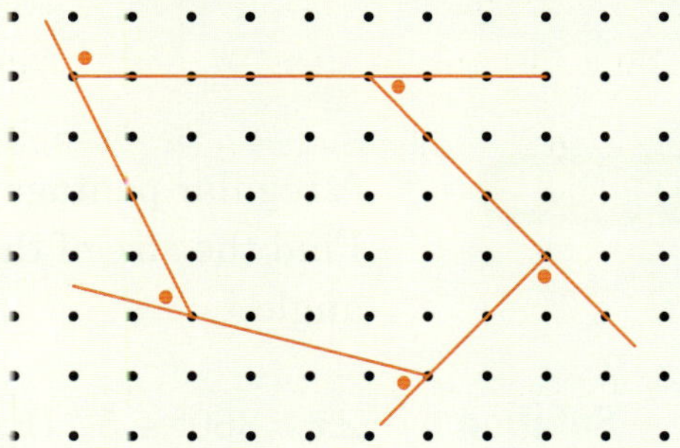

1. (a) Draw four different convex polygons.

(b) Extend each side and mark the exterior angles as shown.

(c) Use a protractor to measure the size of the exterior angles.

(d) Find the sum of the exterior angles for each of your polygons.

(e) What do you notice about your answers to part **(d)**?

2. (a) Draw a polygon with a reflex interior angle.

(b) What happens if you extend each side and mark on the exterior angles?

From Class Activity 9 you have evidence that:

The exterior angles of any polygon add up to 360°.

Example 9

Write down the name of the polygon, then work out the size of angle x.

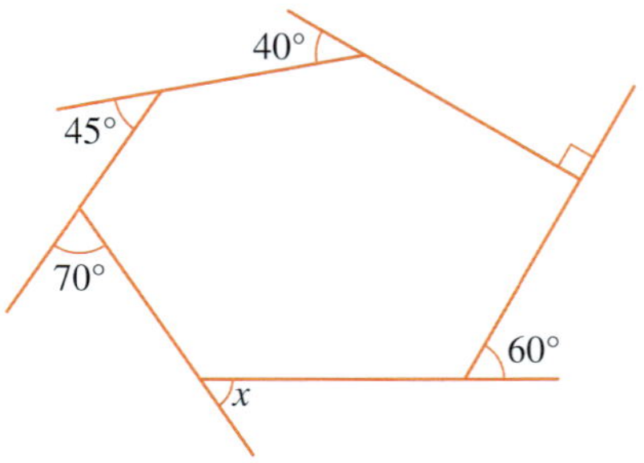

Solution

The polygon is an irregular hexagon.

$\angle x + 70° + 45° + 40° + 90° + 60° = 360°$

(Exterior angles of polygon add up to 360°.)

$\angle x + 305° = 360°$

$\angle x = 360° - 305°$

$= 55°$

Try It! 9

Write down the name of the polygon, then work out the size of angle x.

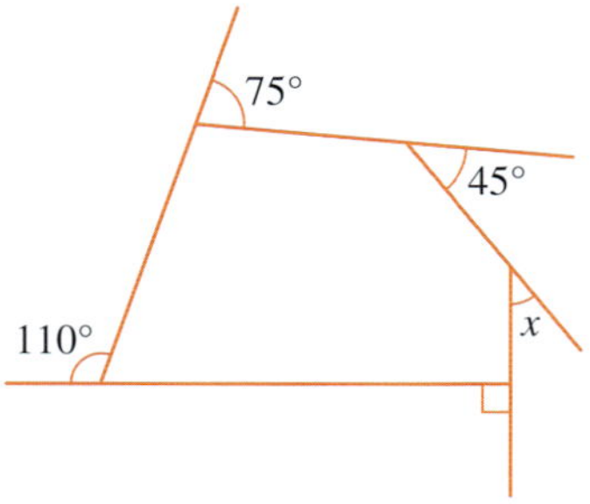

The exterior angles of a regular polygon are equal. Therefore, in general:

The size of each exterior angle of a regular n-sided polygon = $360 \div n$.

REMARK

Here n is the number of sides of the polygon.

Example 10

A regular pentagon is shown. Find the size of the exterior angle x.

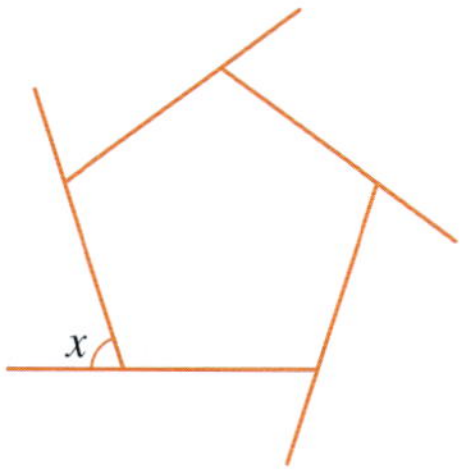

Solution

$\angle x = 360° \div 5$ (Exterior angles of a regular polygon are equal.)

$= 72°$

Try It! 10

What is the size of an exterior angle of a regular hexagon?

DISCUSS

What will be the size of each interior angle? Can you complete this rule?

At any vertex of a convex polygon, interior angle + exterior angle = ☐

Example 11 Each exterior angle of a polygon is 30°. Find the number of sides of the polygon.

Solution

$360° \div n = 30°$

$n = 360 \div 30$

$= 12$

Try It! 11 Each exterior angle of a polygon is 36°. Find the number of sides of the polygon.

REMARK

You can use a factor tree:

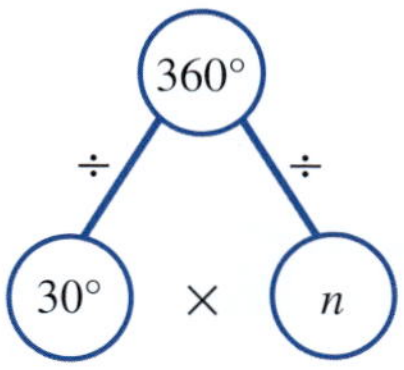

REMARK

You can use a calculator for this sub-section.

C Sum of Interior Angles of a Polygon

CLASS ACTIVITY 10

Objective: To derive the formula for the sum of interior angles of a polygon.

Polygon	Triangle 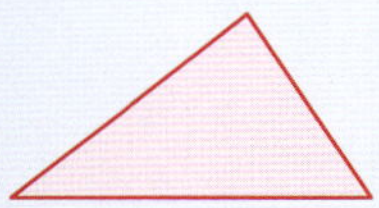	Quadrilateral 	Pentagon 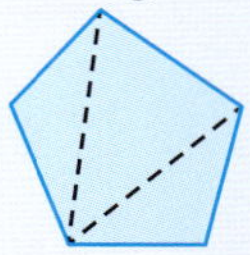	Hexagon 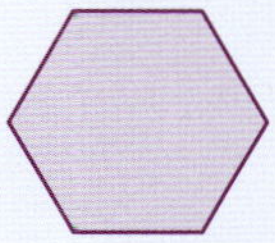	Heptagon 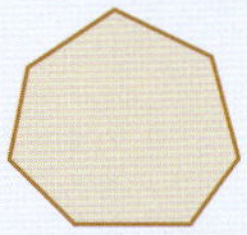
Number of sides	3	4			
Number of dissected triangles	1	2			
Sum of interior angles	$180° = (3-2) \times 180°$	$2 \times 180° = (4-2) \times 180°$			

1. Copy the table and draw dotted lines on the hexagon and heptagon by joining one vertex to every other vertex to divide each shape into non-overlapping triangles.
2. Complete the table.
3. (a) Predict the sum of the interior angles of an octagon.
   (b) Draw an octagon.
   (c) How many non-overlapping triangles can it be divided into?
   (d) What is the sum of its interior angles? Was your prediction correct?
4. Predict the sum of the interior angles of
   (a) a 9-sided polygon,
   (b) a 12-sided polygon.
5. Can you generalise the rule for a polygon with n sides?

From Class Activity 10, you have evidence that:

> Angles in an n-sided polygon add up to $(n - 2) \times 180°$.

Example 12

Find the size of angle x in the heptagon.

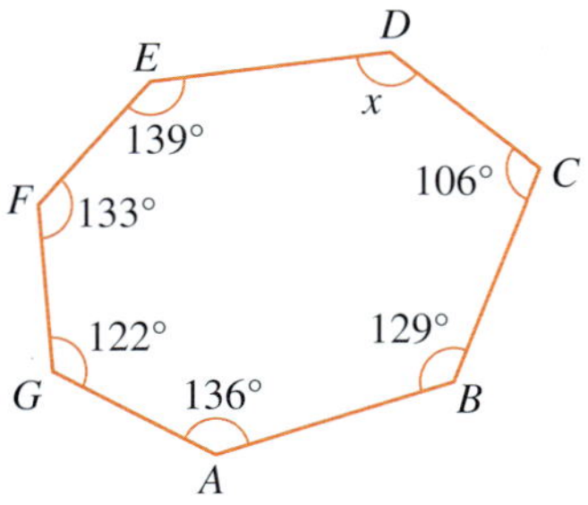

Solution

Sum of interior angles of a heptagon

$= (7 - 2) \times 180°$ (Angles in an n-sided polygon add up to $(n - 2) \times 180°$.)

$= 900°$

$136° + 129° + 106° + \angle x + 139° + 133° + 122° = 900°$

$765° + \angle x = 900°$

$\angle x = 135°$

Try It! 12

Find the size of angle y in the pentagon. You may use a calculator.

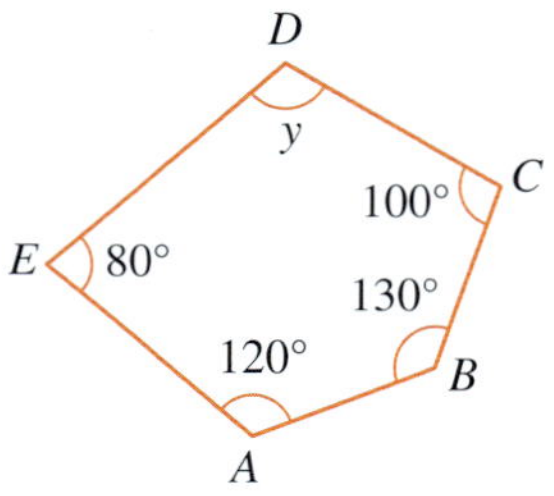

Example 13

The size of each interior angle of a polygon is 140°. Find the number of sides of the polygon.

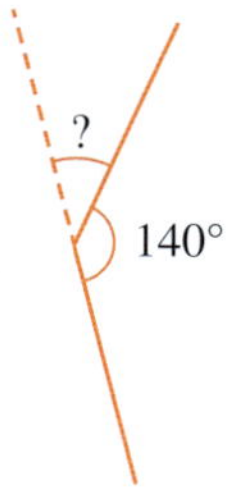

Solution

Let n be the number of sides of the polygon.

Exterior angle + interior angle = 180°
(Angles on a straight line add up to 180°.)

Each exterior angle $= 180° - 140°$
$= 40°$

$360 \div n = 40°$ (Exterior angles of a polygon add up to 360°.)

$n = 9$

$\therefore$ the polygon has 9 sides.

REMARK

You can use a factor tree:

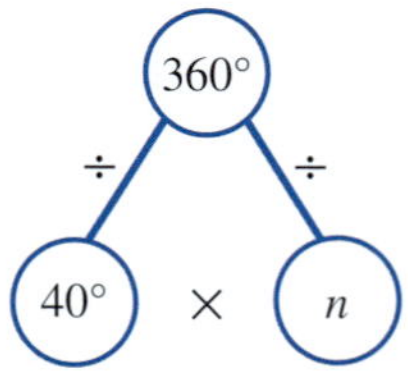

Try It! 13

The size of each interior angle of a polygon is 135°. Find the number of sides of the polygon.

PRACTICE 7.3

LEVEL 1

1. Find the sum of the interior angles of a polygon which has

(a) 8 sides, **(b)** 9 sides, **(c)** 15 sides.

2. Find the size of angle x in each diagram.

(a)

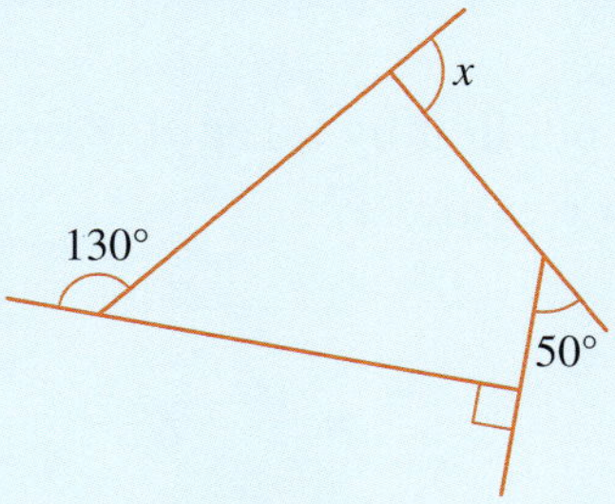

(b)

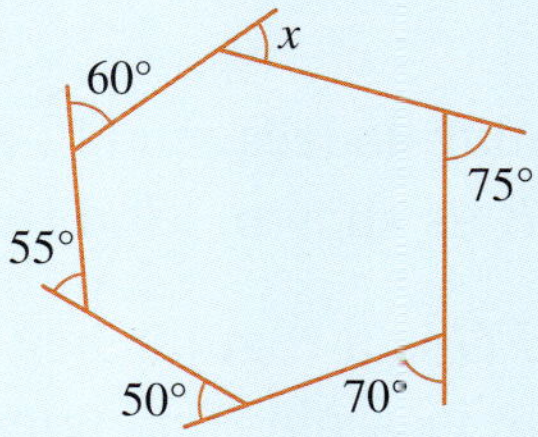

3. Find the size of angle x in each shape.

(a)

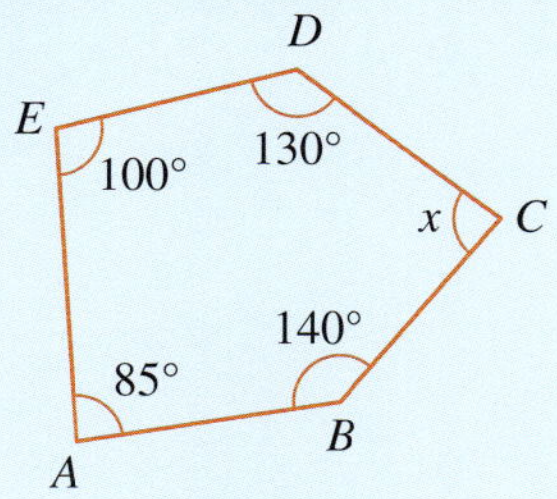

(b)

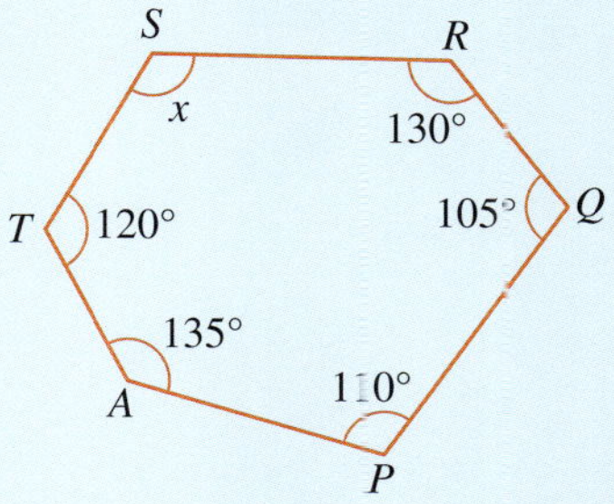

4. Ava measures the interior angles in a heptagon. She claims the size of her angles are 100°, 125°, 140°, 120°, 125°, 130° and 150°. Could her measurements be correct? Explain your answer.

5. Find the size of each interior angle and the size of each exterior angle of a regular

(a) pentagon, **(b)** octagon, **(c)** nonagon.

LEVEL 2

6. Find the number of sides of a regular polygon if all of its

(a) exterior angles are 40°, **(b)** exterior angles are 20°,

(c) interior angles are 108°, **(d)** interior angles are 156°.

7. Dennis said the exterior angle of a regular polygon is 75°. Is he correct? Explain your answer.

8. *ABCDE* is a regular pentagon. *FAB* and *FED* are straight lines.
Find the sizes of angles x, y and z.

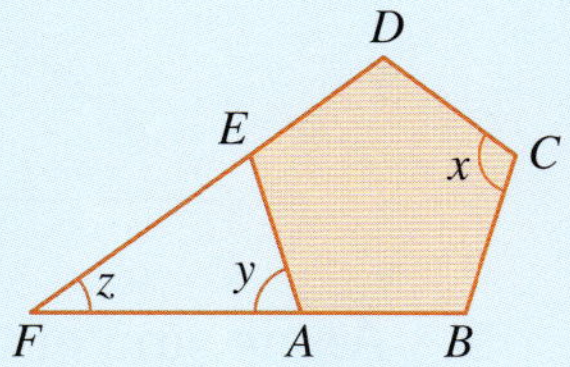

9.

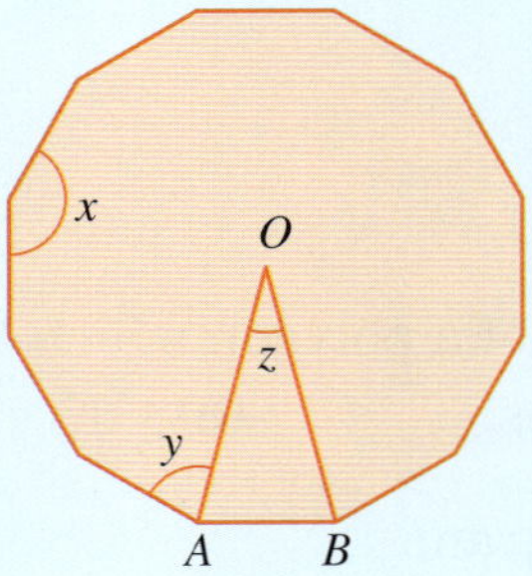

A one-pound coin is a regular dodecagon (12-gon). It can be modelled by a regular dodecagon with centre O and edge AB as shown. Find the sizes of angles x, y and z.

10. $ABGH$ is a square. $BCDEFG$ is a regular hexagon.

(a) Show that ΔFGH is an isosceles triangle.

(b) Find the size of $\angle HGF$.

(c) Find the size of $\angle FHG$.

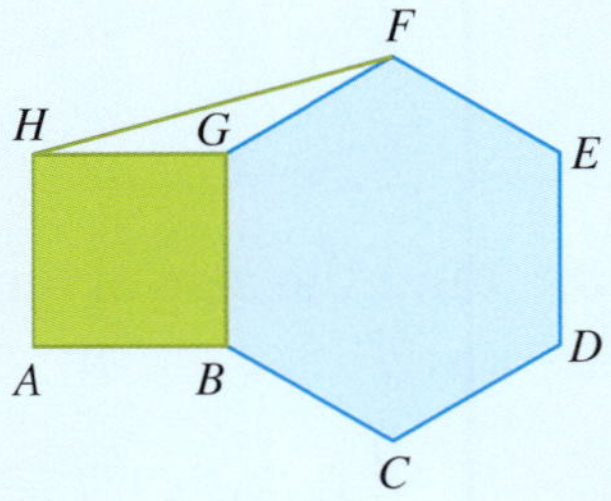

REVIEW

Triangles

1. Types of triangles

(a) Based on sides:

Scalene triangle | Isosceles triangle | Equilateral triangle

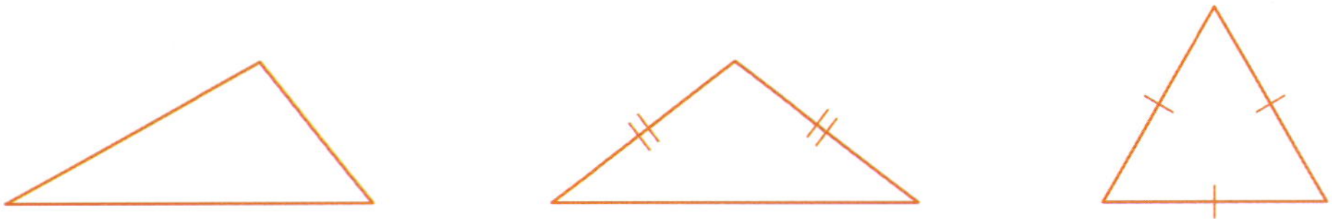

(b) Based on angles:

Acute-angled triangle | Right-angled triangle | Obtuse-angled triangle

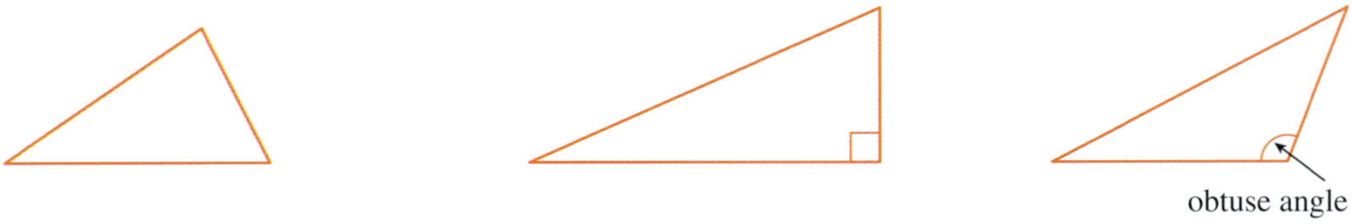

2. Angle sum of triangles:

(a) The three angles in any triangle add up to 180°.

(b) The two base angles of any isosceles triangle are equal.

(c) All three angles in an equilateral triangle are equal. Each angle is 60°.

Quadrilaterals

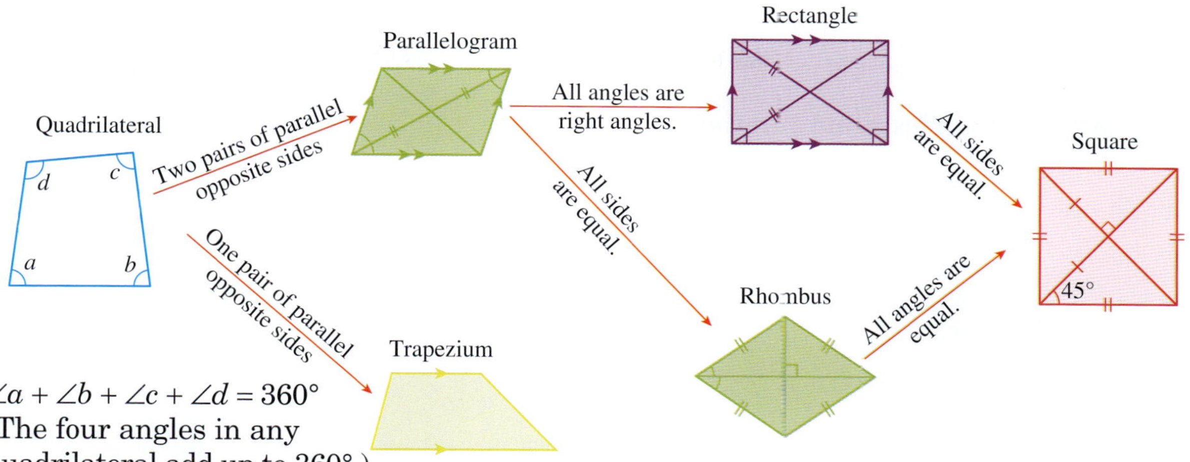

$\angle a + \angle b + \angle c + \angle d = 360°$
(The four angles in any quadrilateral add up to 360°.)

Angle Properties of Polygons

- A regular polygon has equal sides and equal angles.
- Interior angles in an n-sided polygon add up to $(n - 2) \times 180°$.
- Exterior angles of any polygon add up to 360°.

CHALLENGE 7

In the diagram, a star is drawn using the vertices of the regular pentagon $ABCDE$. Find the sizes of the angles x and y.

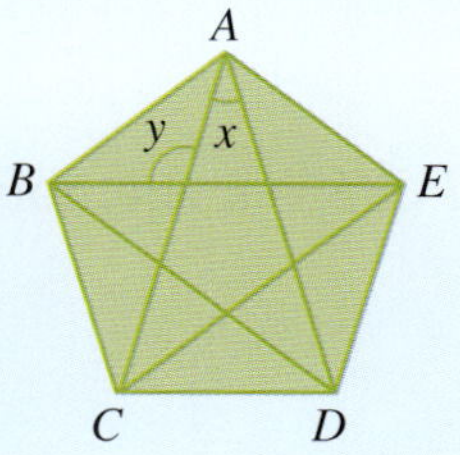

REVISION EXERCISE 7

You should state the geometric reasoning in your working. Diagrams are not drawn to scale.

1. Find the size of angle x in each triangle. Name the type of the triangle based on its angles.

(a)

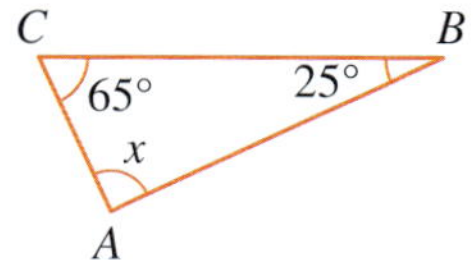

(b)

2. Which of these triangles might be the odd one out? Explain your answer.

(a)

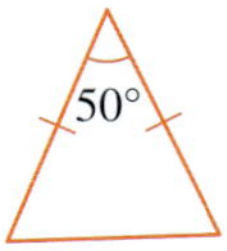

(b)

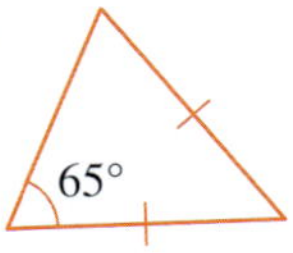

(c)

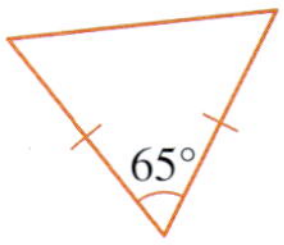

(d)

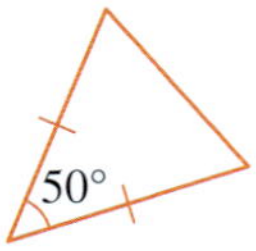

3. Find the sizes of angles x and y in the diagram.

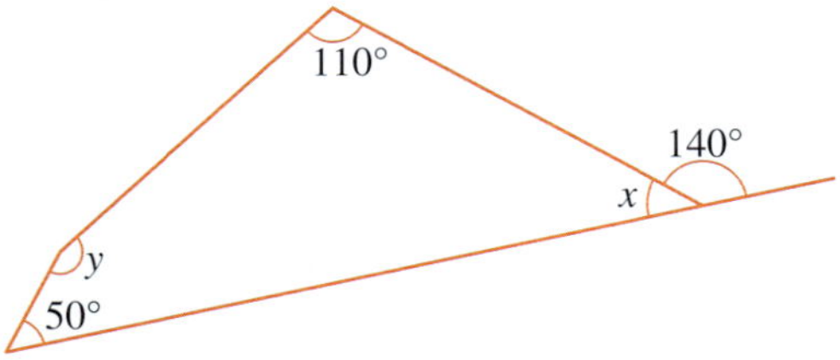

4. $ABCD$ is a parallelogram.
$AD = 12$ cm and $AE = 4$ cm.
Work out the length of
(a) BC,
(b) AC.

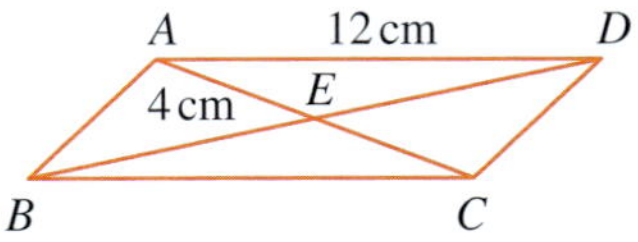

5. **(a)** Can the angles of a triangle be 56°, 120° and 24°? Explain your answer.
(b) Can the angles of a quadrilateral be 39°, 100°, 127° and 94°? Explain your answer.

6. $ABCD$ is a rectangle, $AE = 8$ cm and $\angle ABD = 30°$.
(a) Find the length of BD.
(b) Find the sizes of angles x and y.

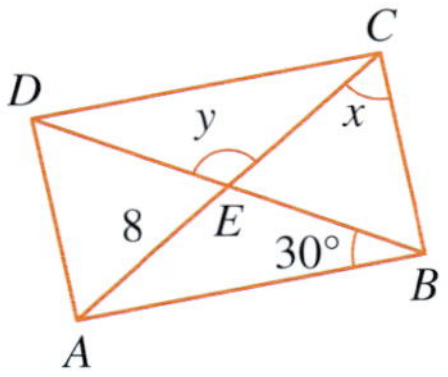

7. $EFGH$ is a rhombus. Find the sizes of angles x and y.

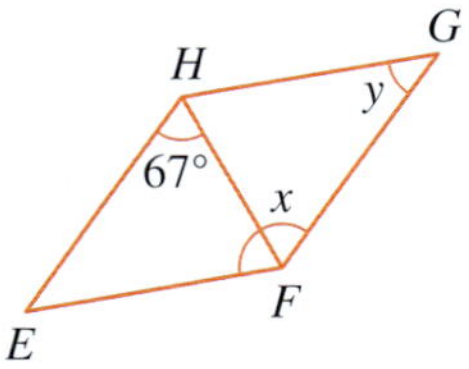

8. In the pentagon $ABCDE$, is it true that $\angle x = 90°$? Explain your answer.

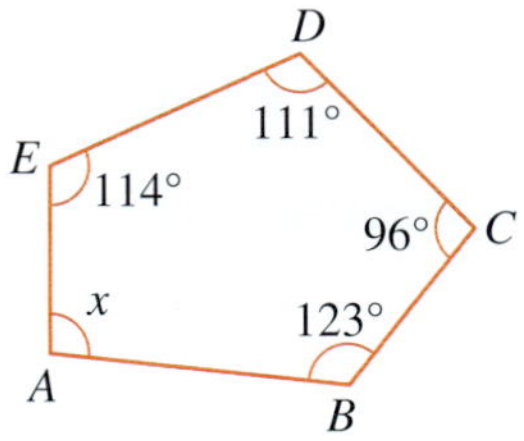

9. A metal nut is a regular hexagon.
Calculate the size of angles x, y and z.

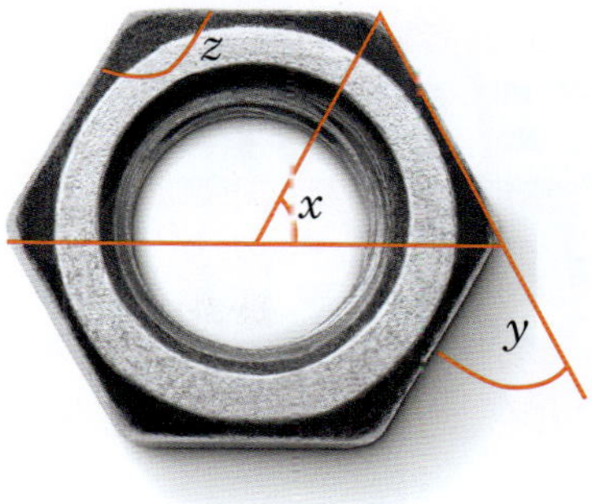

10. The interior angle of a regular polygon is 144°. Work out how many sides the polygon has.

11. Can the size of each exterior angle of a regular polygon be 50°? Explain your answer.

Write in Your Journal

Does every exterior angle of a regular polygon have to be an acute angle? Explain your answer.

8 GEOMETRIC CONSTRUCTIONS

WHAT IS IN THIS CHAPTER:

Plans for buildings involve perpendicular lines, triangles and different angles which must all be accurately drawn so that the design can be followed correctly.

LET'S LEARN TO

- construct triangles using geometrical instruments
- identify perpendicular and angle bisectors
- construct perpendicular bisectors and angle bisectors
- construct a perpendicular to a line from a point or at a given point

FLASHBACK

1. Drawing Angles

You can draw an angle using a protractor. For example, to draw an angle of 140°:

(a) Draw a line segment AB.

(b) Align the base of the protractor with AB so the centre of the protractor is at B. Mark point C at 140°.

(c) Draw the line segment BC. Then $\angle ABC = 140°$.

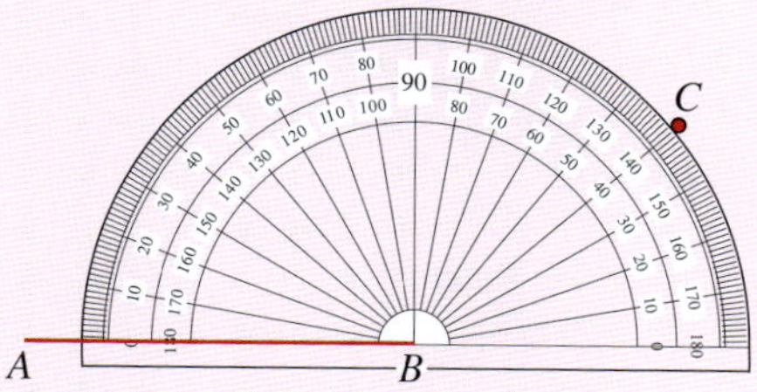

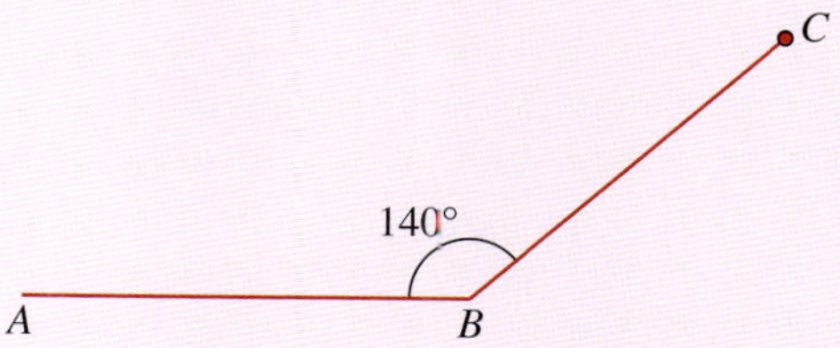

2. Types of Triangles

(a) Scalene
(no equal sides)

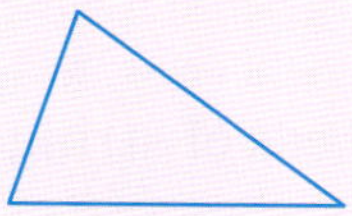

(b) Isosceles
(two equal sides)

c) Equilateral
(three equal sides)

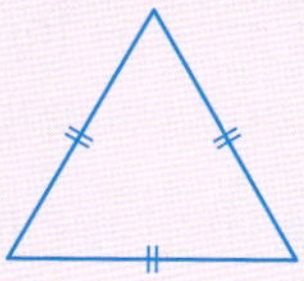

(d) Acute-angled
(All angles are acute.)

(e) Right-angled
(One of the angles is a right angle.)

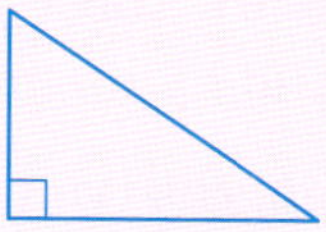

(f) Obtuse-angled
(One of the angles is an obtuse angle.)

3. Perpendicular Lines

Two lines are perpendicular if they intersect at right angles.
In the diagram, AB is perpendicular to CD.
This is written as $AB \perp CD$.

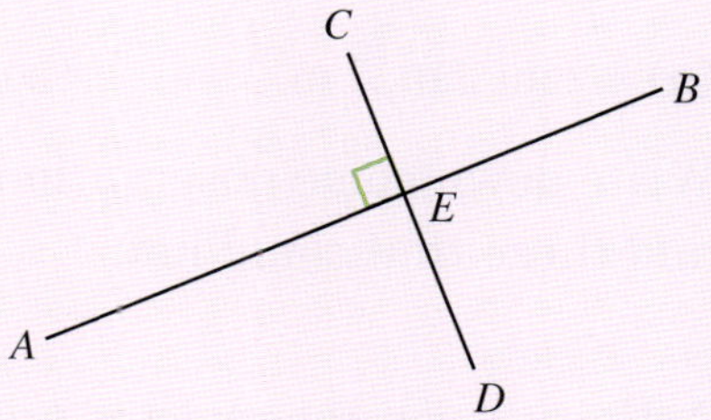

4. Compasses and Circles

The legs of a pair of compasses can be set to a certain distance.
The compasses can be used to draw a circle with the distance as the radius.

STEP 1

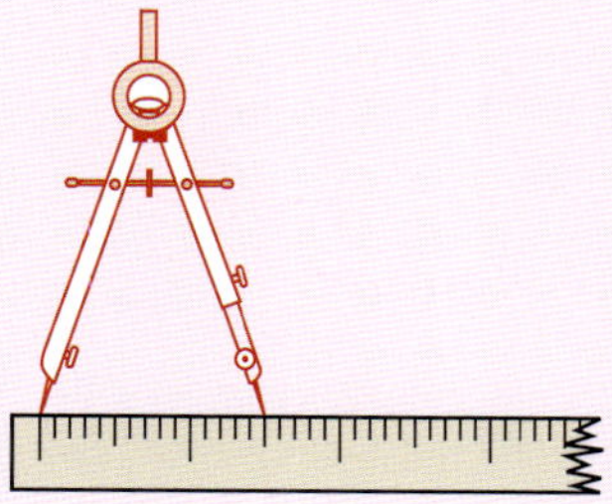

STEP 2

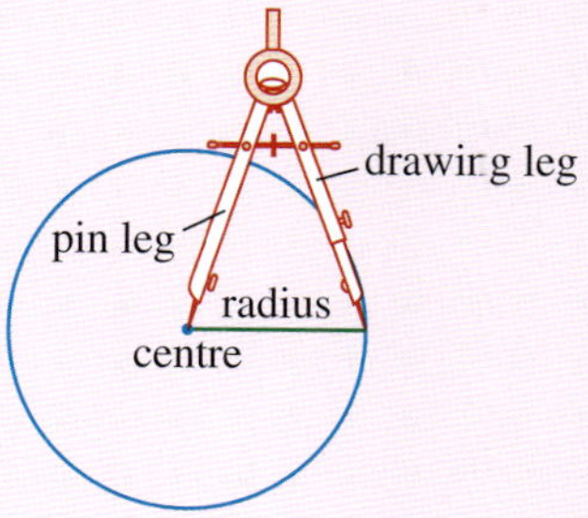

REMARK

Compasses may look like this, with the pencil included, or they will have a grip to hold the pencil. Both are used in the same way.

8.1 Constructing Triangles

In Chapter 7, you learnt some properties of triangles. You will learn to construct some geometric shapes such as triangles, using a pair of compasses, a protractor and a ruler in this chapter.

Compasses

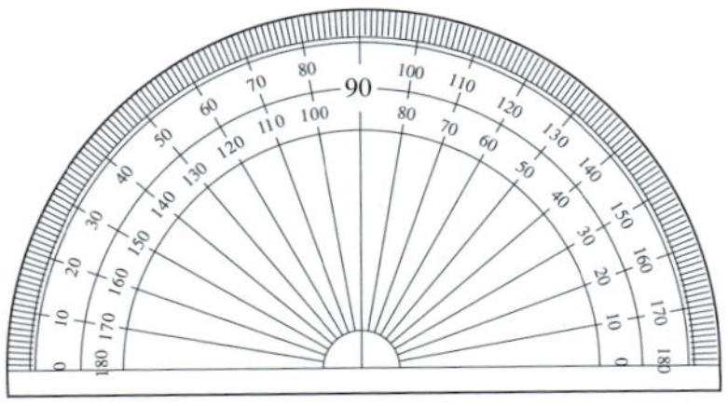
Protractor

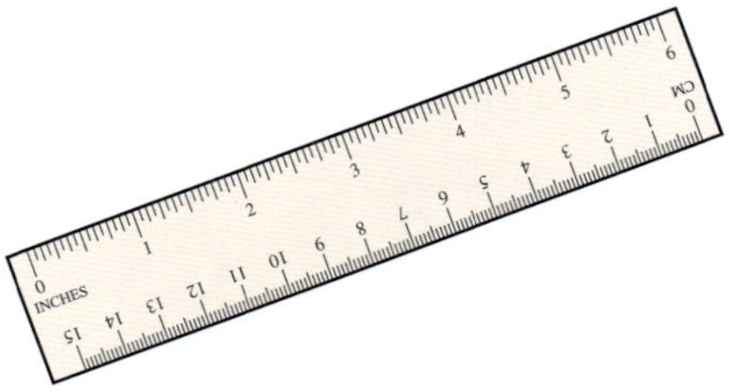

Ruler

CLASS ACTIVITY 1

Objective: To construct triangles using string and a tape measure.

Work in groups for this activity. Each group will need a tape measure, 6 m of string or wool and scissors.

1. Use the tape measure and scissors to measure and cut three pieces of string with lengths 2 m, 2 m and 2 m.
2. Attempt to form a triangle, with one person at each vertex holding the end of two pieces of string.
3. Is it possible to form a triangle with these lengths? If not, why? If so, can you classify the triangle by its sides and by its angles?
4. Repeat tasks **1–3** for these side lengths (you can cut down your existing pieces of string or wool).

   (a) 2 m, 2 m, 1 m **(b)** 2 m, 1 m, 1.5 m **(c)** 2 m, 1 m, 0.5 m
5. Write down some observations about the side lengths that could form a triangle, and those that could not.

In Class Activity 1 you constructed triangles given the lengths of all three sides. Let us look at how you can construct triangles on paper given different combinations of sides and angles.

A Given the Lengths of Three Sides

Example 1

Construct a triangle ABC such that $AB = 7$ cm, $BC = 5$ cm and $AC = 6$ cm. Measure $\angle ABC$.

Solution

STEP 1

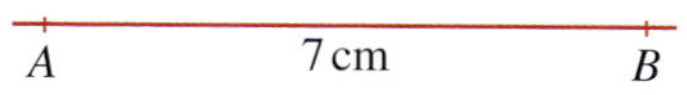

Draw line segment $AB = 7$ cm.

STEP 2

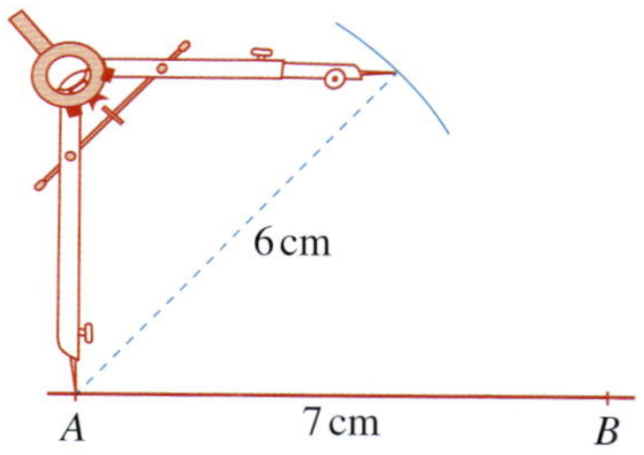

Draw an arc with centre A and radius 6 cm.

STEP 3

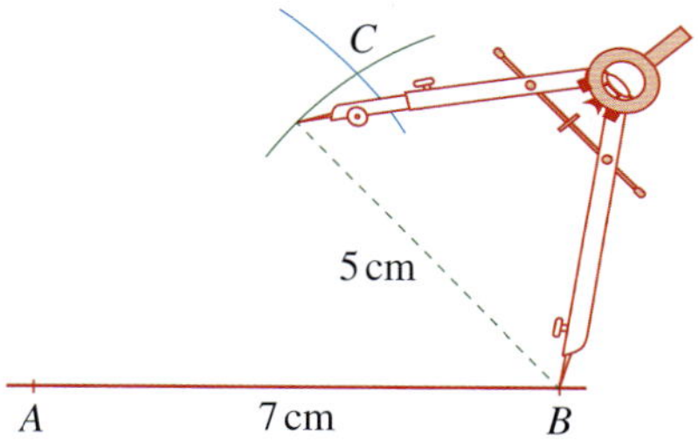

Draw an arc with centre B and radius 5 cm to cut the first arc at C.

STEP 4

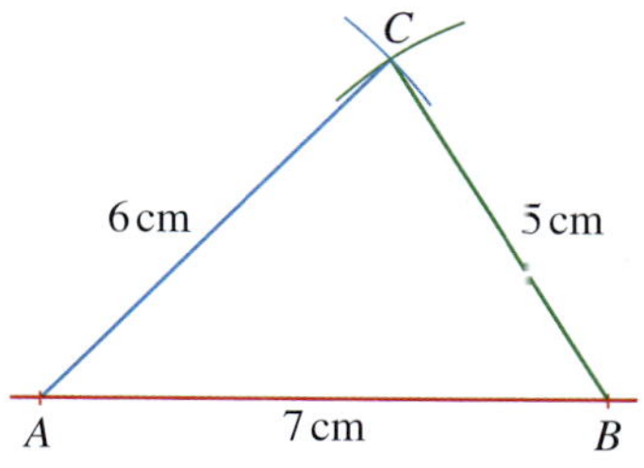

Draw the line segments AC and BC. ΔABC is the required triangle.

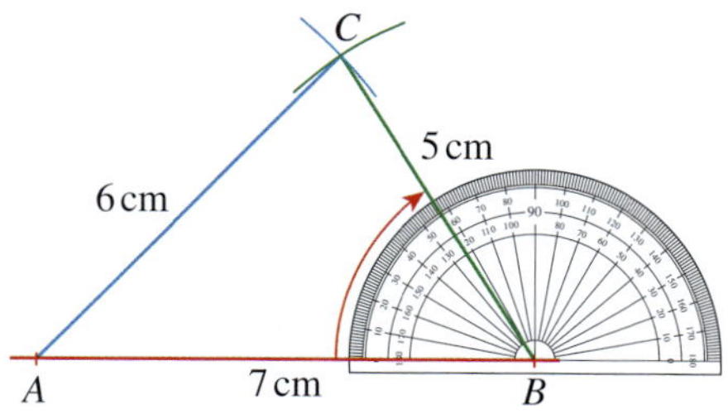

Measure $\angle ABC$ using a protractor. This gives $\angle ABC = 57°$.

Try It! 1

Construct a triangle ABC such that $AB = 6$ cm, $BC = 4$ cm and $AC = 7$ cm. Measure $\angle BAC$.

DISCUSS

Which angle in the triangle is $\angle ABC$?

REMARK

It is good practice to sketch ΔABC to give yourself a clearer picture before constructing it.

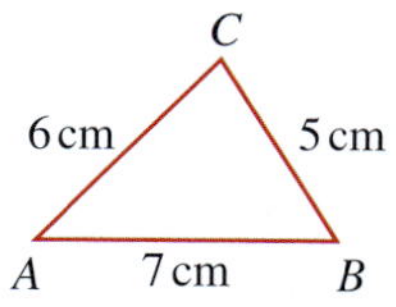

DISCUSS

What happens if you draw AC first? Do you get a different triangle?

REMARK

In geometric constructions, the construction lines should be thin and should not be erased after drawing a diagram. These lines indicate the working steps in constructing the diagram.

B Given Two Sides and an Included Angle

Example 2

Construct a triangle ABC such that $\angle ABC = 45°$, $AB = 6\,\text{cm}$ and $BC = 5\,\text{cm}$. Measure $\angle BAC$.

Solution

STEP 1

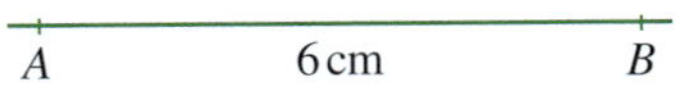

Draw a line segment $AB = 6\,\text{cm}$.

STEP 2

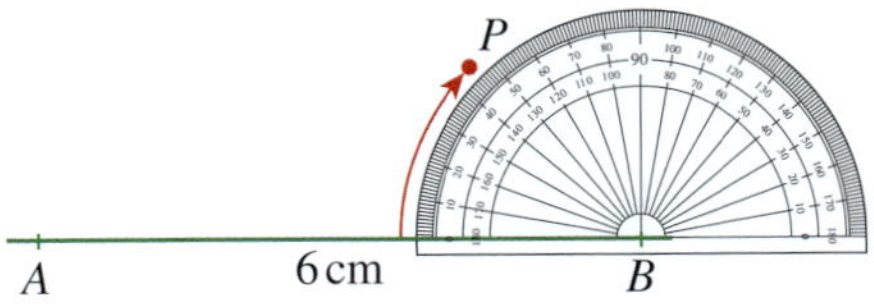

Draw an angle ABP at B of $45°$.

STEP 3

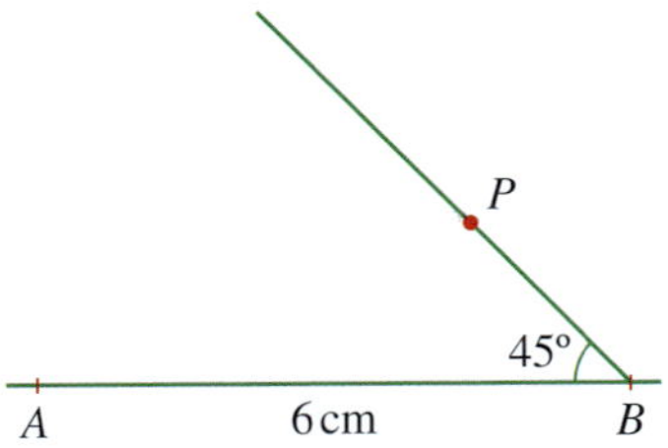

Draw the ray BP.

STEP 4

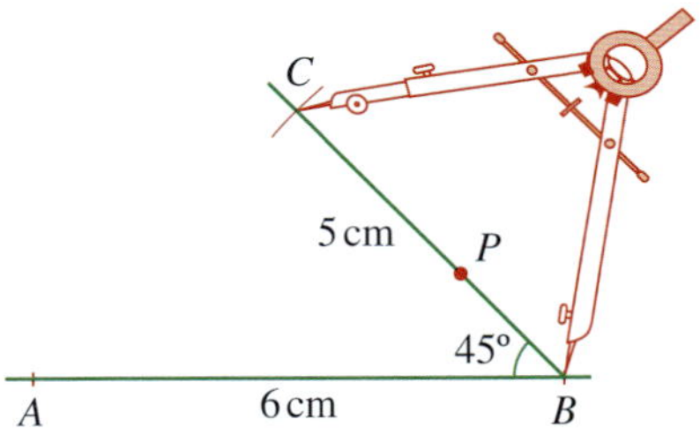

Draw an arc with centre B and radius $5\,\text{cm}$ to cut the ray at C.

STEP 5

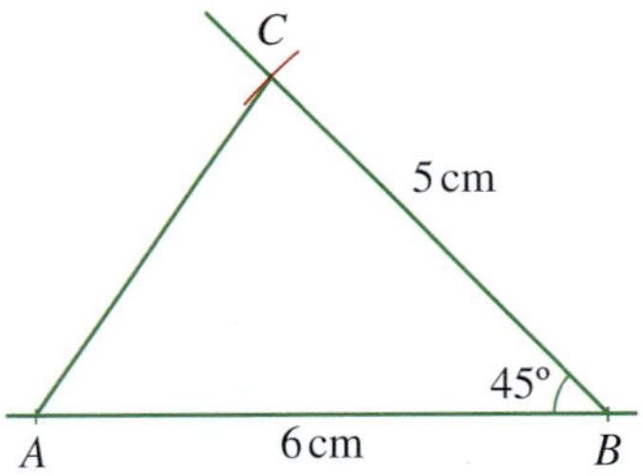

Draw the line segment AC. Then ΔABC is the required triangle.

STEP 6

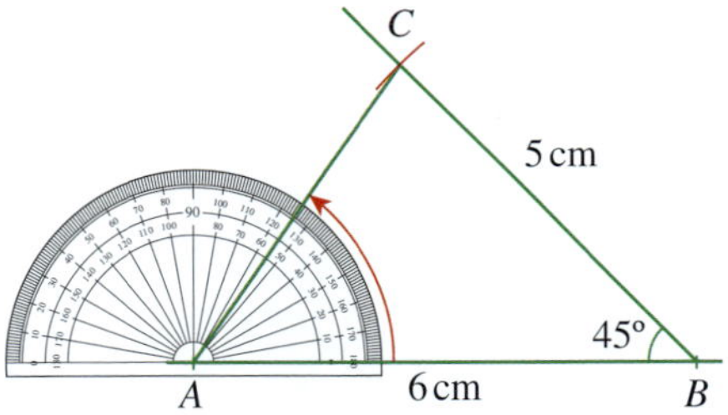

Use a protractor to measure $\angle BAC$. This gives $\angle BAC = 55°$.

Try It! 2

Construct a triangle ABC such that $\angle ABC = 35°$, $AB = 5\,\text{cm}$ and $BC = 4\,\text{cm}$. Measure $\angle ACB$.

REMARK

An **included angle** is the angle between two sides. Here $\angle ABC$ is between AB and BC.

REMARK

Sketch ΔABC before constructing it.

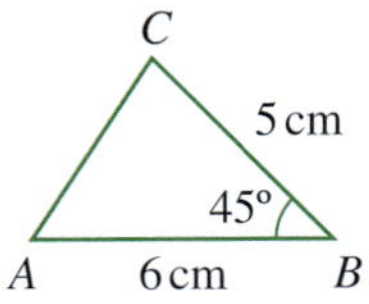

DISCUSS

Could you draw this triangle in a different way with the given information?

DISCUSS

What if you were given AB, BC and $\angle CAB$ instead? Would it be the same triangle or different?

C Given Two Angles and One Side

Example 3

Construct a triangle ABC such that $AB = 5\,\text{cm}$, $\angle ABC = 30°$ and $\angle BAC = 40°$.

Solution

STEP 1

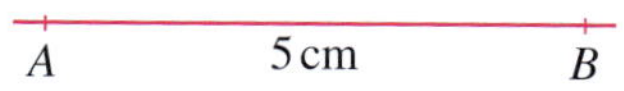

Draw a line segment $AB = 5\,\text{cm}$.

STEP 2

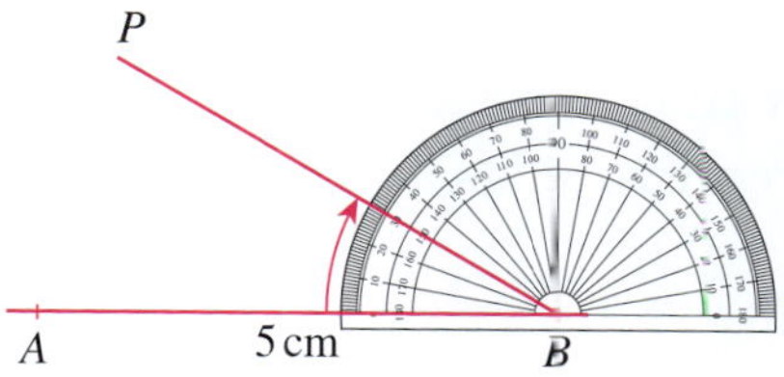

Draw the line BP such that $\angle ABP = 30°$.

STEP 3

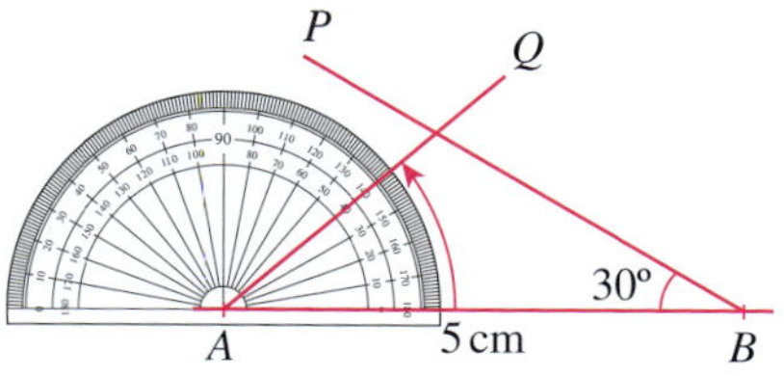

Draw the line AQ such that $\angle BAQ = 40°$.

STEP 4

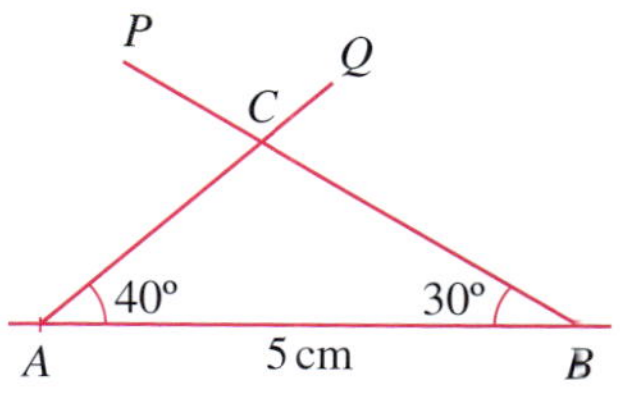

Label the point of intersection of AQ and BP as C. Then ΔABC is the required triangle.

DISCUSS

Could you draw this triangle in a different way with the given information?

DISCUSS

What is the size of $\angle ACB$? How could you construct the triangle if you knew AC instead of AB?

Try It! 3

Construct a triangle ABC such that $AB = 6\,\text{cm}$, $\angle ABC = 50°$ and $\angle BAC = 70°$.

D Given Two Sides and a Non-included Angle

CLASS ACTIVITY 2

Objective: To construct triangles given two sides and a non-included angle.

1. Draw a 7 cm line using a ruler and label AB.
2. Measure an angle of 50° at A.

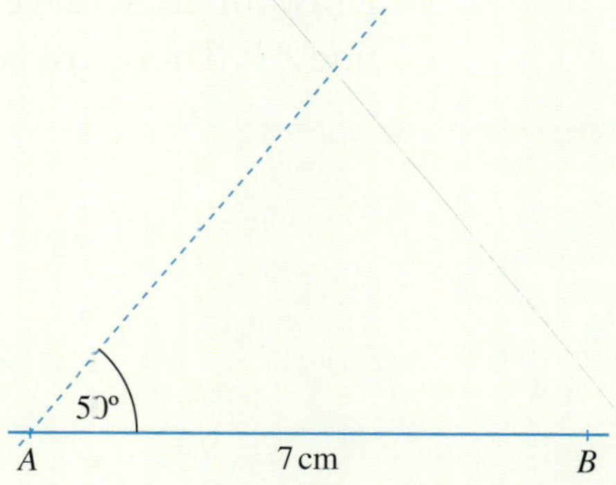

3. Complete triangle ABC with $BC = 6\,\text{cm}$ such that

(a) AC is longer than BC,

(b) AC is shorter than BC.

4. Measure $\angle BCA$ for each of your triangles in **Question 3**. What do you notice?

REMARK

A **non-included** angle is an angle that is not between the two sides you are given.

In Class Activity 2 you saw that there are sometimes two possible triangles when you are given two sides and a non-included angle.

Example 4

Construct a triangle ABC with $AB = 6\,\text{cm}$, $BC = 4\,\text{cm}$ and $\angle BAC = 40°$.

REMARK

Sketch $\triangle ABC$ before constructing it.

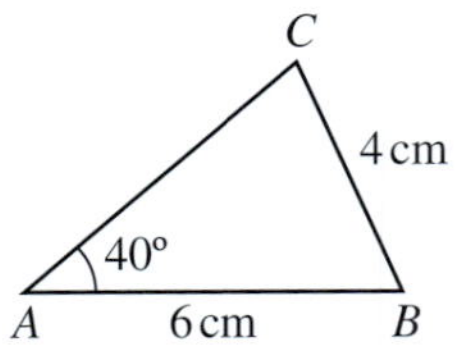

Solution

STEP 1

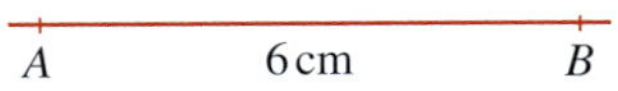

Draw a line segment $AB = 6\,\text{cm}$.

STEP 2

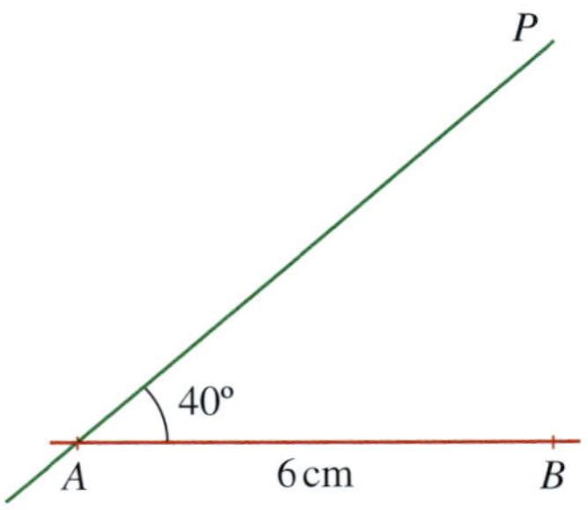

Draw a line AP which makes an angle of $40°$ with AB.

STEP 3

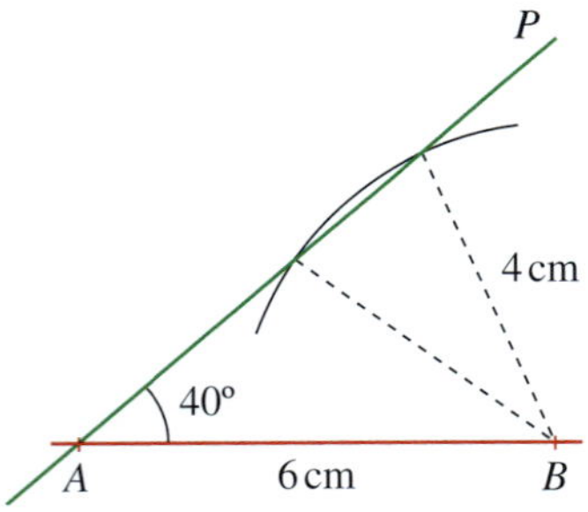

Draw an arc with centre B and radius $4\,\text{cm}$ to cut the line AP. There are two intersecting points.

STEP 4

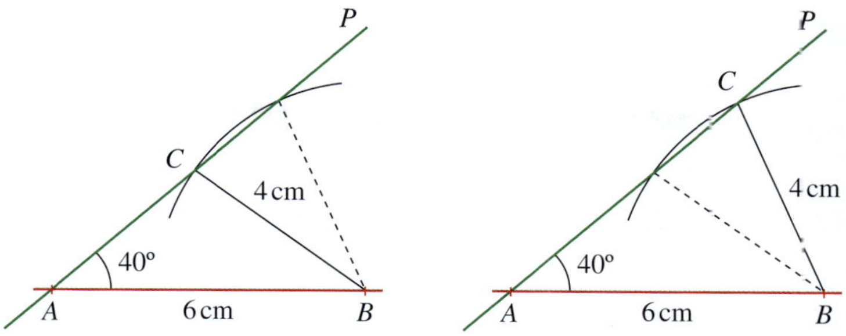

There are two possible positions for point C, so two possible triangles for ΔABC.

Note: Unlike other given conditions, when the given angle is not included between the given sides, there may be two possible triangles.

Try It! 4 Draw two different triangles ABC with $AB = 8$ cm, $AC = 5$ cm and $\angle ABC = 30°$.

DISCUSS

Will there always be two possible triangles when given two sides and a non-included angle? Does it matter what size the non-included angle is?

PRACTICE 8.1

LEVEL 1

1. Construct a triangle ABC such that
   (a) $AB = 12$ cm, $BC = 10$ cm and $AC = 9$ cm,
   (b) $AB = 8$ cm, $BC = 10$ cm and $AC = 5$ cm.

2. **(a)** Construct a triangle ABC such that
   (i) $\angle ABC = 40°$, $AB = 6$ cm and $BC = 14$ cm,
   (ii) $\angle ACB = 70°$, $AB = 12$ cm and $AC = 11$ cm.
   (b) Measure $\angle BAC$ in each triangle.

3. Construct a triangle XYZ such that $\angle XYZ = 50°$, $\angle YZX = 60°$ and $YZ = 7$ cm.

4. Construct a triangle PQR such that $\angle QPR = 30°$, $PR = 8$ cm, $QR = 5$ cm and
   (a) $\angle PQR$ is acute, **(b)** $\angle PQR$ is obtuse.

5. Which of these triangles can be constructed in only one way? Explain your answer.
   (a) $AB = 5$ cm, $BC = 7$ cm and $\angle ABC = 45°$
   (b) $AB = 5$ cm, $\angle BCA = 70°$ and $\angle ABC = 45°$
   (c) $AB = 5$ cm, $AC = 7$ cm and $\angle ABC = 45°$

LEVEL 2

6. Construct a triangle XYZ such that $XY = 6$ cm, $\angle XYZ = 40°$ and $\angle XZY = 30°$.

7. Construct an isosceles triangle PQR such that $PQ = PR = 6$ cm and $\angle QPR = 30°$.

8. Construct an equilateral triangle ABC such that $AB = 5$ cm.

9. Construct a right-angled triangle ABC such that $AB = 7$ cm, $\angle BAC = 90°$ and $\angle ABC = 55°$.

10. Explain why these triangles cannot be constructed.

PROBLEM SOLVING

(a) ΔABC with $AB = 8$ cm, $BC = 4$ cm and $AC = 3$ cm

(b) ΔPQR with $PQ = 6$ cm, $\angle QPR = 120°$ and $\angle PQR = 70°$

(c) ΔXYZ with $YZ = 9$ cm, $XZ = 7$ cm and $\angle XYZ = 90°$

8.2 Constructing Perpendicular and Angle Bisectors

A Perpendicular Bisector

CLASS ACTIVITY 3

Objective: Investigate a line of points that are the same distance from two points.

Work in pairs and use tracing paper for this activity.

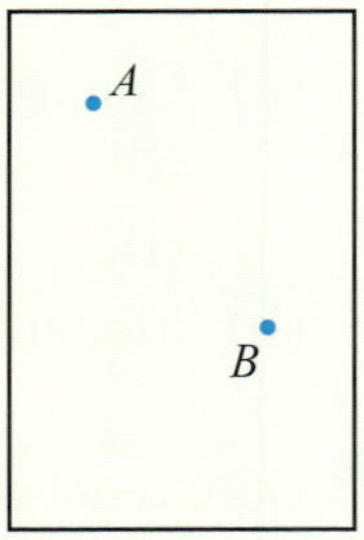

1. Each of you mark a point on the tracing paper and label them A and B.
2. Imagine you are going to share a flat with a friend and these are the locations of your places of work. You want to find a location for the flat which is the same distance from both your places of work, so the same distance from A as it is from B.
3. Fold the paper so that A is on top of B. Then open out the paper and use a ruler to draw along the crease line.

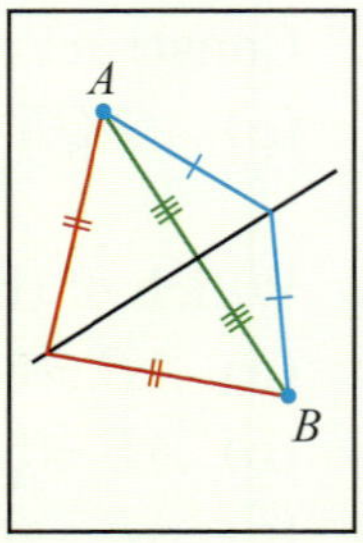

4. Measure the distance of some points on the line to both A and B.

   What do you notice about the distances between A and a point and B and the same point?
5. Draw the line segment AB. What do you notice about the angle where AB meets the crease line?

In Class Activity 3, you saw that the line of points that are the same distance from A as from B is perpendicular to the line AB and bisects the line AB (cuts it in half).

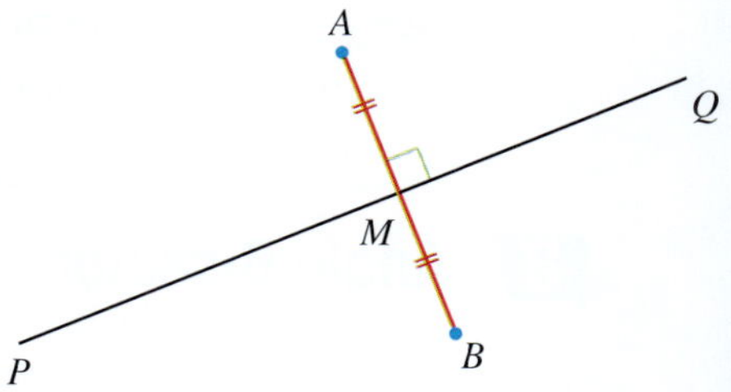

In the diagram, PQ is a line passing through the midpoint M of the line segment AB. It is said to **bisect** AB as $AM = MB$. PQ is also perpendicular to AB. It is called the **perpendicular bisector** of AB.

The perpendicular bisector of a line segment can be constructed using a pair of compasses and a ruler.

Example 5

Draw a line segment AB of 6 cm long. Construct the perpendicular bisector of AB.

Solution

STEP 1

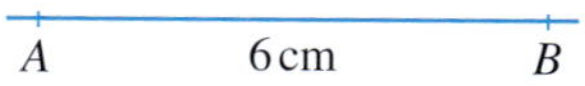

Draw $AB = 6$ cm.

STEP 2

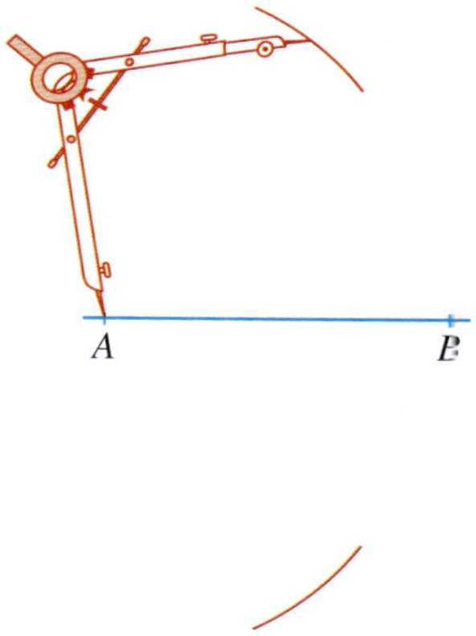

Draw an arc with centre A and equal radii greater than $\frac{1}{2}AB$ on each side of AB.

STEP 3

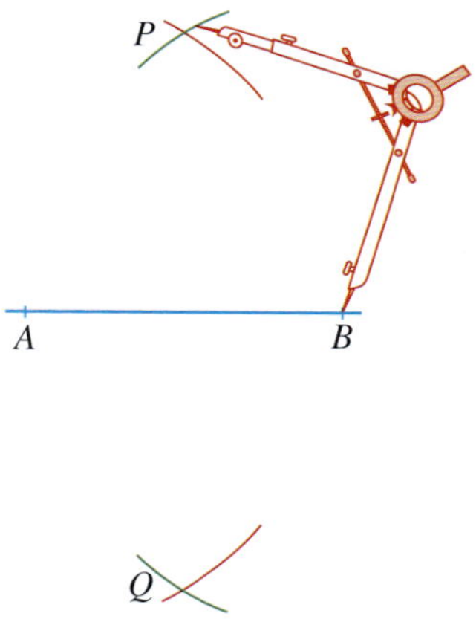

Draw two arcs with centre B and equal radii as *Step 2* to cut the first two arcs at P and Q.

STEP 4

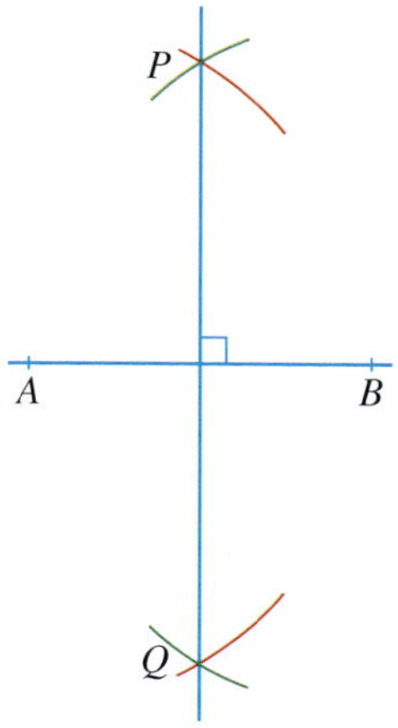

Draw the line PQ. Then PQ is the perpendicular bisector of AB.

Try It! 5

Draw a line segment CD of 5 cm long. Construct the perpendicular bisector of CD.

DISCUSS

In constructing the perpendicular bisector of AB, why must the radius of the two arcs be greater than $\frac{1}{2}AB$?

DISCUSS

What would be the same and what would be different if you used a different compass length?

You can observe the following property from Example 5:

Any point on the perpendicular bisector of a line segment is equidistant from the end points of the line segment.

REMARK

'Equidistant' means 'at an equal distance'.

B Angle Bisector

CLASS ACTIVITY 4

Objective: Investigate a line of points which are the same distance from two lines.

Work in pairs and use tracing paper for this activity.

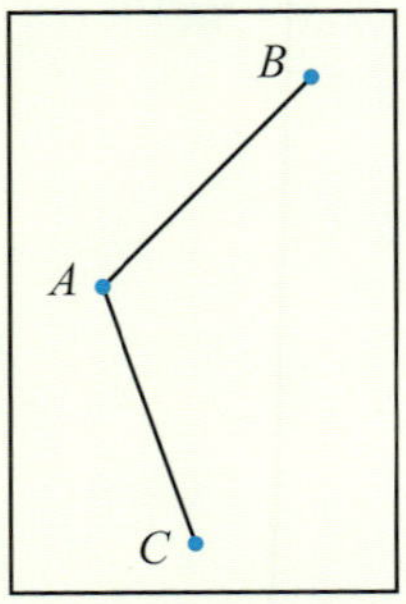

1. Mark three points on a sheet of paper and label them A, B and C. Draw the lines AB and AC.
2. Imagine these are the walls of a garden you are designing and you want to find a location for a water feature which is the same distance from each of the walls.
3. Fold the paper so that AB is on top of AC. Then open out the paper and use a ruler to draw along the crease line.
4. Measure the angles between AB and AC and the crease line. What do you notice?

In Class Activity 4, you saw that the line of points that were the same distance from AB as from AC bisected $\angle BAC$.

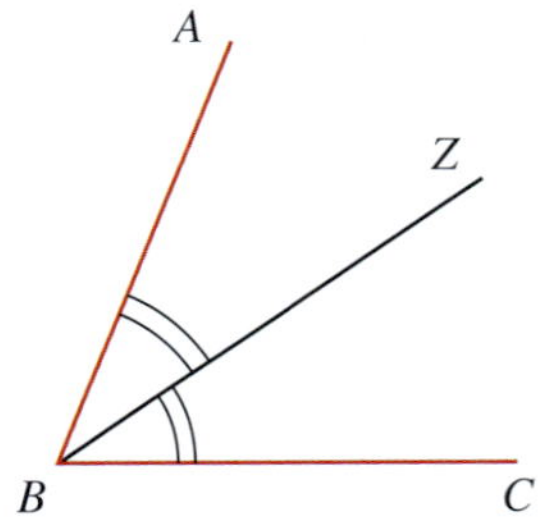

In the diagram, the line BZ divides $\angle ABC$ into two equal angles, $\angle ABZ$ and $\angle CBZ$. It is called the **angle bisector** of $\angle ABC$.

An angle bisector can be constructed using a pair of compasses and a ruler.

Example 6

Draw an angle ABC of 60°. Use a ruler and a pair of compasses to construct the angle bisector of $\angle ABC$.

Solution

STEP 1

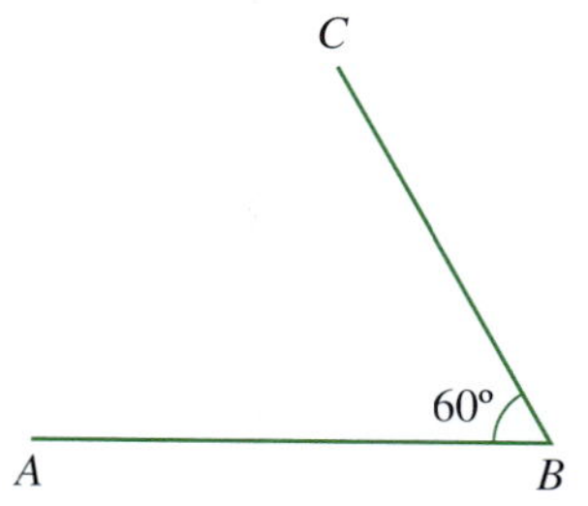

Draw $\angle ABC = 60°$ using a protractor.

STEP 2

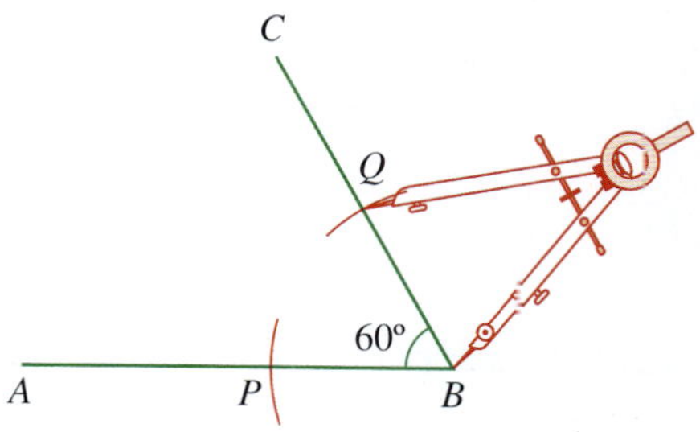

Draw an arc with centre at B to cut AB at P and BC at Q.

STEP 3

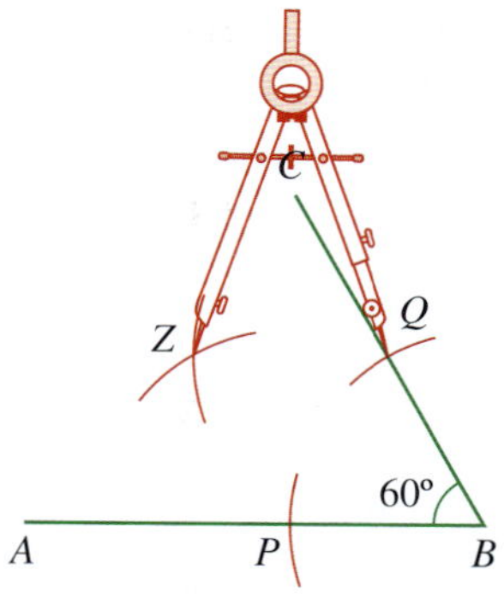

With centres at P and Q, draw two arcs with equal radii to intersect at a point Z.

STEP 4

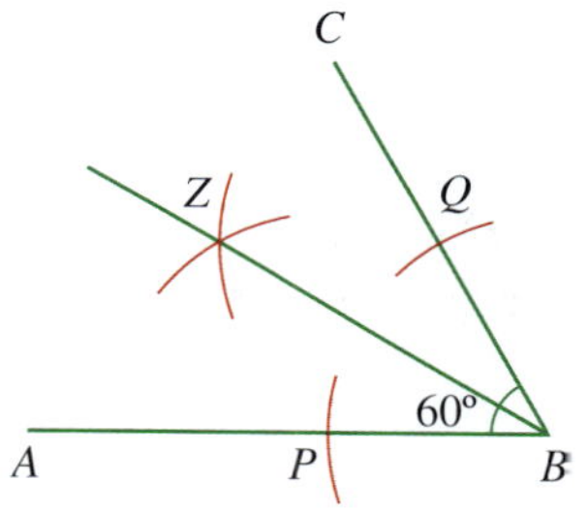

Draw the line BZ. Then BZ is the angle bisector of $\angle ABC$.

DISCUSS

Must the radii *BP* and *PZ* be equal?

Try It! 6

Draw an angle PQR of 70°. Use a ruler and a pair of compasses to construct the angle bisector of $\angle PQR$. Then check that you have two 35° angles.

From Example 6, you can observe the following property:

Any point on the angle bisector of an angle is equidistant from the sides of the angle.

PRACTICE 8.2

LEVEL 1

1. Draw a horizontal line segment AB of 8 cm long. Construct the perpendicular bisector of AB.

2. Draw a vertical line segment HK of 7 cm long. Construct the perpendicular bisector of HK.

3. Draw an angle ABC of 80°. Construct the angle bisector of $\angle ABC$.

4. Draw an angle XYZ of 120°. Construct the angle bisector of $\angle XYZ$.

LEVEL 2

5. The location of two friends' offices is shown on the map. They want to share a flat that is the same distance from both their offices.
   - **(a)** Trace their relative locations onto a sheet of paper.
   - **(b)** Use a pair of compasses and a ruler to construct a line of possible locations for their flat.

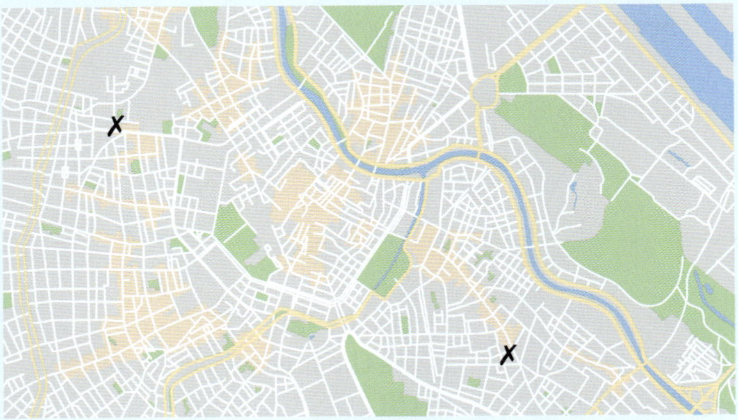

6. Draw a reflex angle PQR of 230°. Divide the angle into four equal angles using a pair of compasses and a ruler.

7. Using a pair of compasses and a ruler
   - **(a)** copy the line segment XYZ in the diagram,
   - **(b)** construct the perpendicular bisector of XY to intersect XY at M,
   - **(c)** construct the perpendicular bisector of YZ to intersect YZ at N.
   - **(d)** What is the relationship between MN and XZ? Explain your answer.

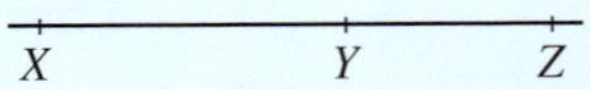

8. **(a)** Draw a triangle ABC with $AB = 9$ cm, $BC = 8$ cm and $CA = 7$ cm.
   PROBLEM SOLVING
   - **(b)** Construct the perpendicular bisectors of AB, BC and CA.
   - **(c)** What can you say about the perpendicular bisectors in part **(b)**?

9. **(a)** Draw a triangle PQR with $PQ = 6\,\text{cm}$, $\angle QPR = 45°$ and $\angle PQR = 60°$.

PROBLEM SOLVING **(b)** Construct the angle bisectors of $\angle QPR$, $\angle PQR$ and $\angle PRQ$.

(c) What can you say about the angle bisectors in part **(b)**?

10. **(a)** Draw a trapezium $ABCD$ with $AB \parallel DC$.

PROBLEM SOLVING **(b)** Construct the angle bisector of $\angle BAD$.

(c) Construct the angle bisector of $\angle ADC$.

(d) Let E be the point of intersection of the angle bisectors in parts **(b)** and **(c)**. What is the size of $\angle AED$?

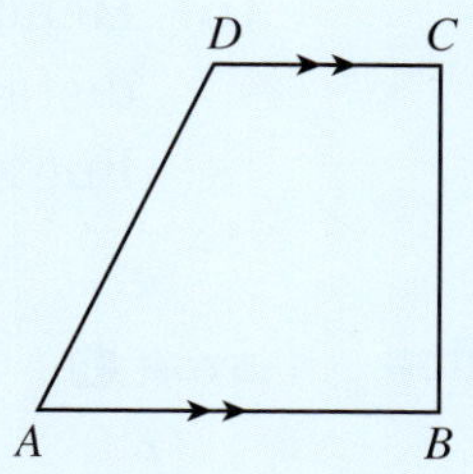

8.3 Constructing Perpendicular Lines

CLASS ACTIVITY 5

Objective: Investigate the distance from a point to a line.

1. Copy the diagram showing line AB and points C, D and E.
2. Imagine AB is the finish line of a race and three runners are currently at points C, D and E.
3. Which runner is closest to the finish line? Which runner is furthest away?
4. Draw the paths that each of the runners should follow to get to the finish line in the shortest possible distance.
5. What do you notice about the paths of the runners and the finish line?

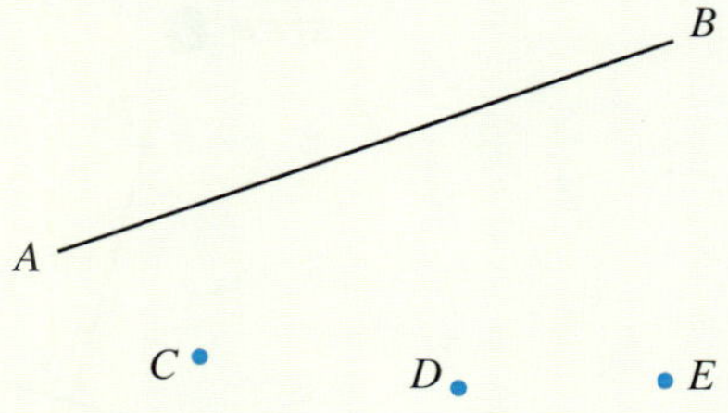

In Class Activity 5 you saw that the shortest distance from a point to a line is along a perpendicular to the line.

If P is a point not on a line AB, the distance of P from the line is the perpendicular distance PN. This is the shortest distance from the point to the line. The perpendicular PN can be constructed using a pair of compasses and a ruler. If Q is a point on the line, the perpendicular RQ to the line AB at Q can also be constructed in a similar way.

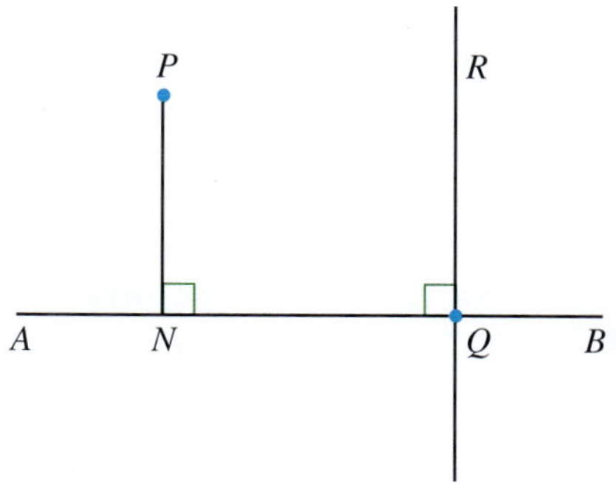

Construction of perpendicular lines is important in everyday life, particularly in architecture and construction of furniture. You also see perpendiculars in the markings on tennis courts and football pitches.

Example 7

(a) Construct the perpendicular line from the point P to the line AB in the diagram.

(b) Hence measure the distance of P from the line AB.

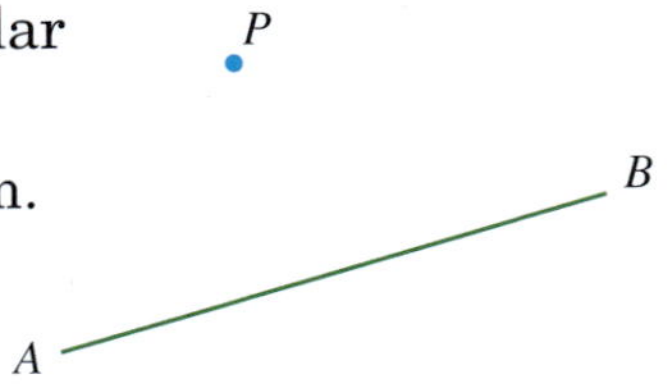

Solution

STEP 1

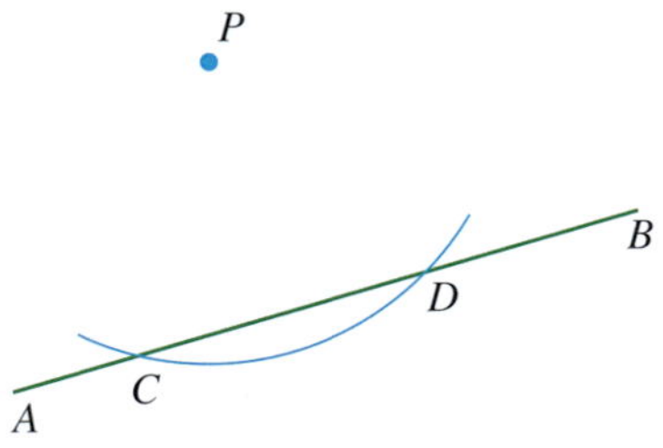

With centre at P, draw an arc to cut the line AB at C and D.

STEP 2

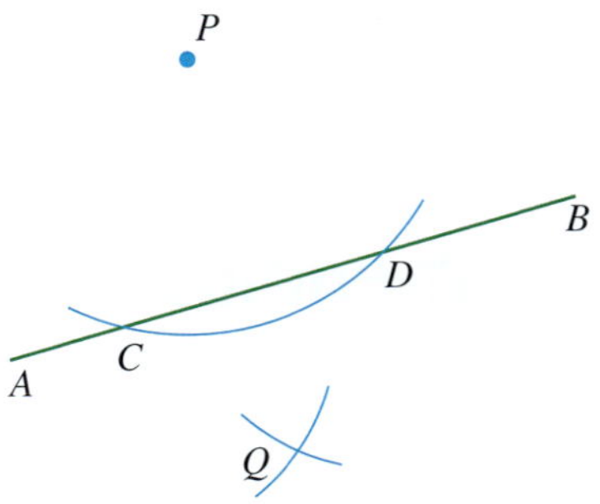

With centres at C and D draw two arcs of equal radius to intersect at Q.

STEP 3

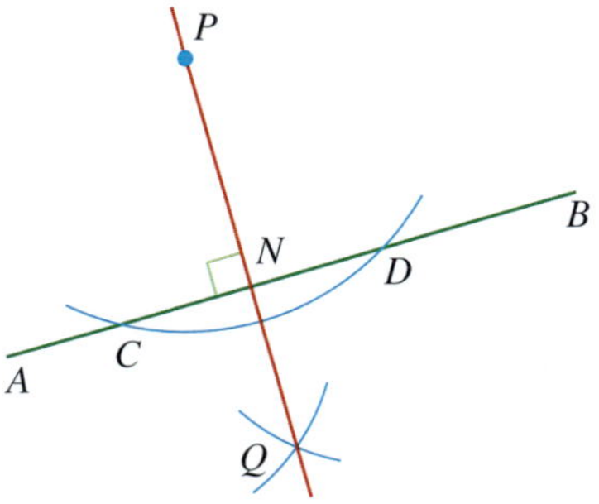

Draw the line PQ. Then $PQ \perp AB$.

(b) Distance of P from the line AB

$= PN$

$= 2\,\text{cm}$ (by measurement)

REMARK

The radii CQ and DQ must be equal, but they may be different from the radius PC.

Try It! 7

(a) Copy the diagram. Construct the perpendicular line from the point R to the line XY.

(b) Hence measure the distance of R from the line XY.

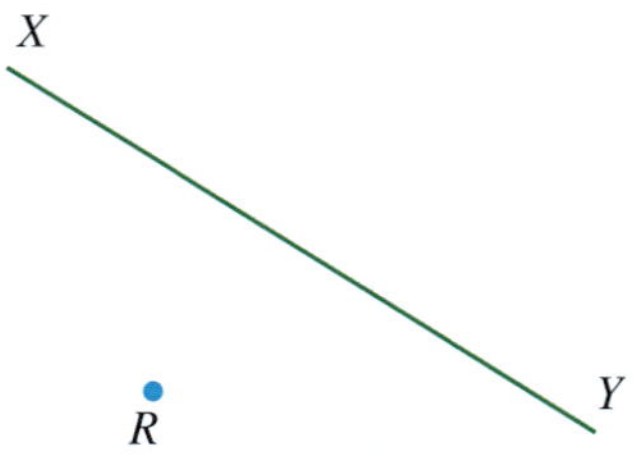

Example 8

P is a point on the line segment XY. Construct a line through P perpendicular to XY.

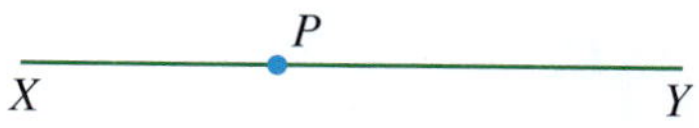

Solution

STEP 1

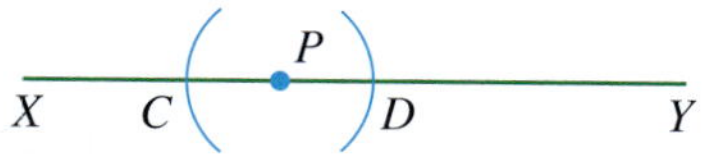

With centre at P, draw two arcs of equal radius to cut the line XY at C and D.

STEP 2

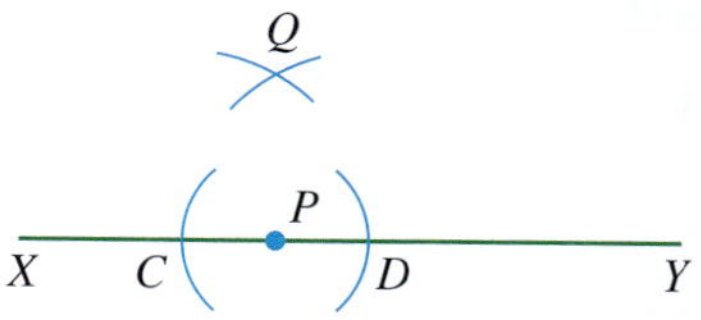

With centres at C and D, draw two arcs of equal radius to intersect at a point Q.

STEP 3

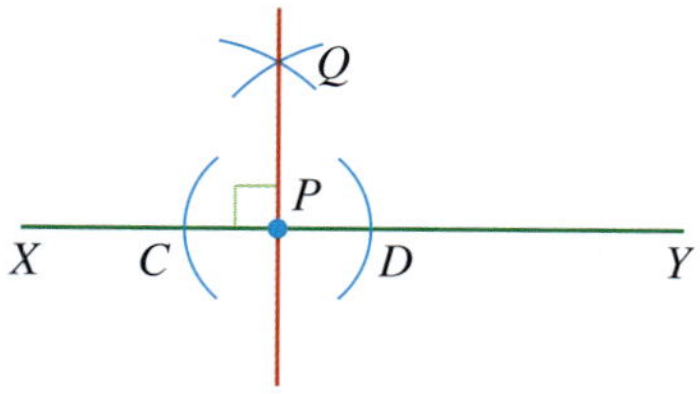

Draw a line through P and Q. Then $PQ \perp XY$.

REMARK

The radii PC and PD must be equal and the radii CQ and DQ must be equal, but these two pairs of radii may be different from each other.

Try It! 8

Draw a line segment HK and mark a point L on it as shown in the diagram. Construct a line through L perpendicular to HK.

PRACTICE 8.3

LEVEL 1

1. Draw a line segment AB and a point P as shown. Construct the perpendicular from P to AB.

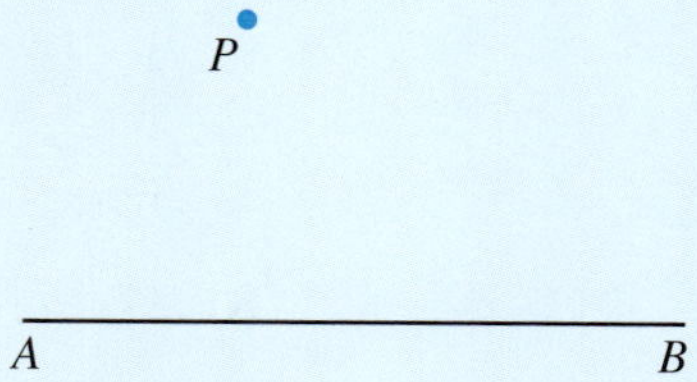

2. Draw a line segment CD and a point T as shown. Construct the perpendicular from T to CD.

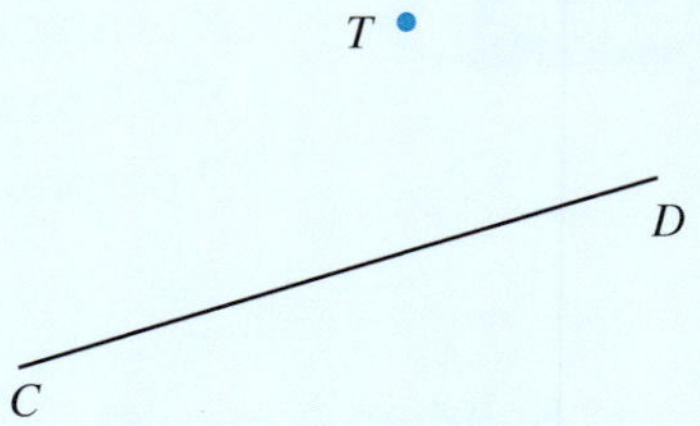

3. Draw a line segment AB with a point P on it as shown. Construct the perpendicular to the line AB at P.

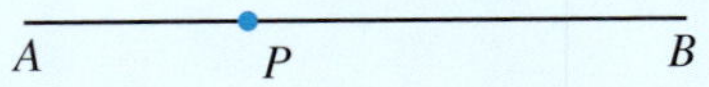

4. Draw a line segment CD with a point N on it as shown. Construct the perpendicular to the line CD at N.

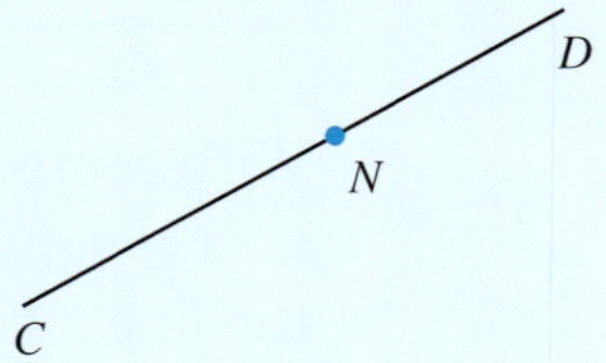

LEVEL 2

5. **(a)** Construct an equilateral triangle ABC with side length 6 cm.
(b) Construct the perpendicular from A to BC.
(c) Measure the distance from A to BC.

6. **(a)** Construct an isosceles triangle PQR with $PQ = PR = 7$ cm and $\angle RPQ = 110°$.
(b) Construct the perpendicular from P to QR.
(c) Measure the distance from P to QR.

7. **(a)** Draw a parallelogram $ABCD$.
PROBLEM SOLVING
(b) Construct a perpendicular to AB at B to meet DC at N.
(c) Construct a perpendicular to CD at D to meet AB at P.
(d) What is the relationship between BN and PD?

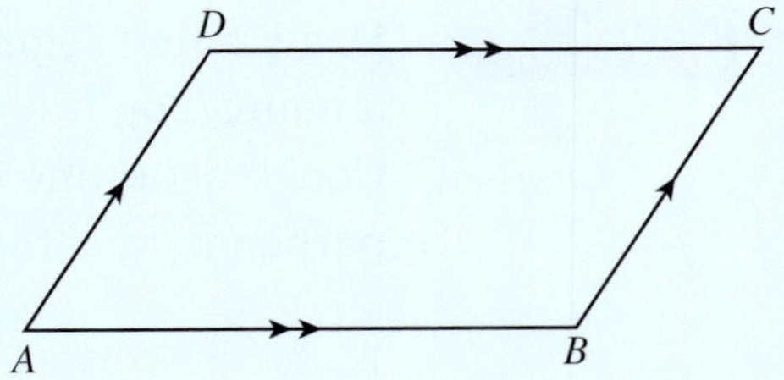

8. **(a)** Draw a triangle ABC.
PROBLEM SOLVING
(b) Construct the perpendicular AD from A to BC.
(c) Construct the perpendicular BE from B to AC.
(d) Construct the perpendicular CF from C to AB.
(e) What can you say about the perpendiculars AD, BE and CF?

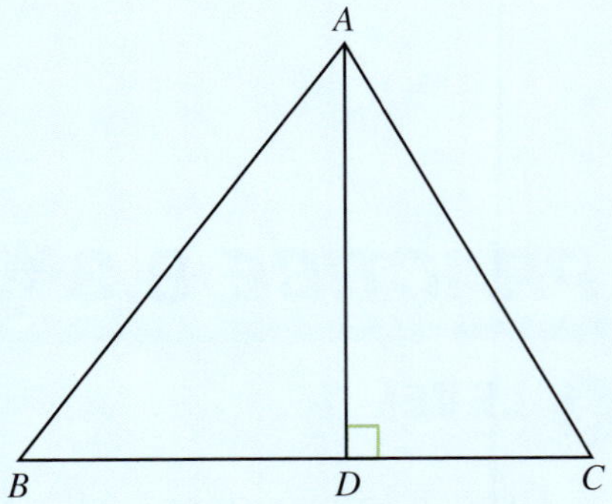

REVIEW

Constructing Triangles

A triangle can be constructed using a pair of compasses and a ruler when given the lengths of all three sides.

A triangle can be constructed using a ruler and protractor when given one side and two angles or two sides and the angle between them.

Constructing Perpendicular Lines

(a) From a point P to the line AB

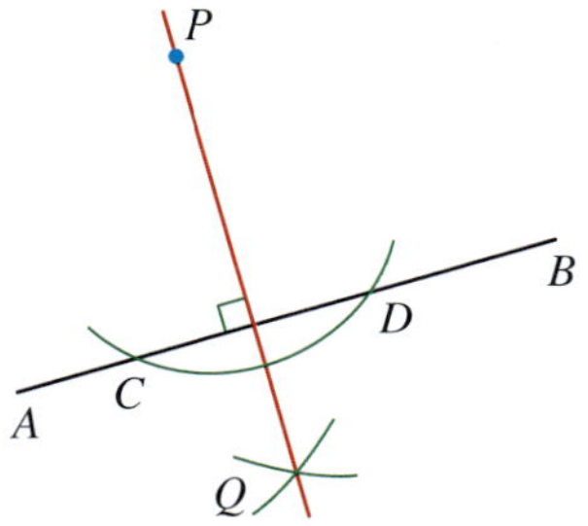

$CQ = DQ$

(b) Through a point P on the line XY

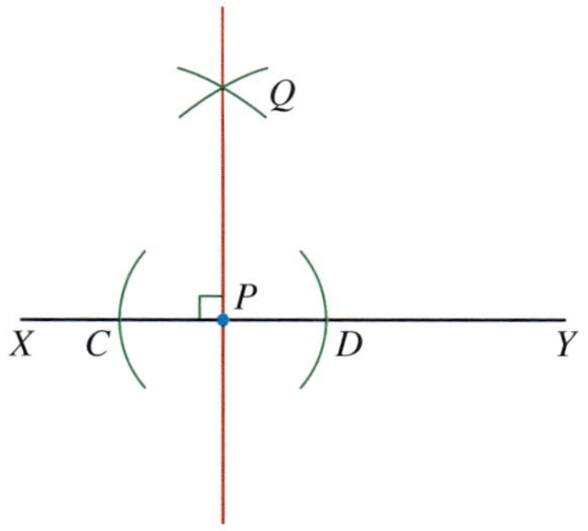

$CP = DP$ and $CQ = DQ$

Constructing Perpendicular Bisectors

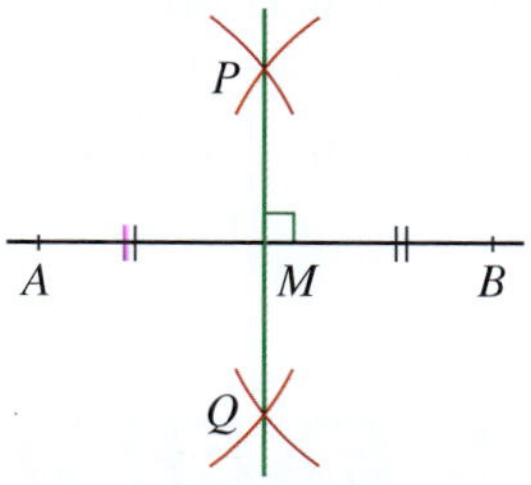

Construct arcs with centres at A and B and equal radii to mark P and Q.

PQ is the perpendicular bisector of AB. $AM = MB$ and $PQ \perp AB$.

Constructing Angle Bisectors

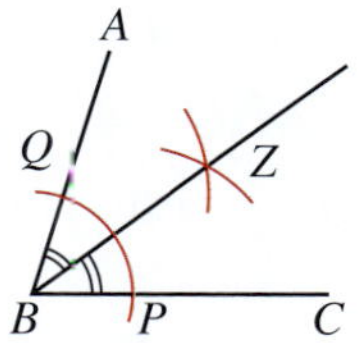

Arc PQ has centre at B. Arcs with centres at P and Q and equal radii intersect at Z.

BZ is the angle bisector of $\angle ABC$.
$\angle ABZ = \angle CBZ$

CHALLENGE 8

Using only a pair of compasses and a ruler, copy the line AB and construct

(a) a right angle at B on the line AB,

(b) an angle of $60°$ at B.

Hint: Where do you always find $60°$ angles?

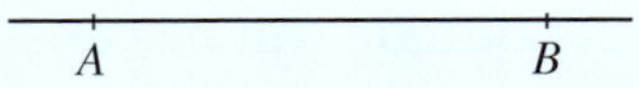

REVISION EXERCISE 8

1. Construct a triangle ABC such that $\angle ABC = 40°$, $AB = 6$ cm and $BC = 12$ cm. Measure $\angle ACB$.

2. Construct a triangle PQR such that $\angle QPR = 50°$, $PR = 10$ cm and $QR = 11$ cm.

3. Construct a triangle XYZ such that $XY = 9$ cm, $\angle XYZ = 30°$ and $\angle YXZ = 55°$. Measure the length of YZ.

4. Is it possible to construct a triangle ABC with the given conditions? Explain your answer.

(a) $AB = 10$ cm, $BC = 6$ cm and $CA = 3$ cm

(b) $BC = 9$ cm, $\angle ABC = 45°$ and $\angle ACB = 140°$

(c) $AC = 8$ cm, $BC = 3$ cm and $\angle BAC = 30°$

5. Draw a line segment AB of 7 cm long. Construct the perpendicular bisector of AB.

6. Draw an angle PQR of $130°$. Construct the angle bisector of $\angle PQR$.

7. **(a)** Draw a triangle ABC with $AB = 13$ cm, $BC = 5$ cm and $\angle ACB = 90°$.

PROBLEM SOLVING

(b) Measure the length of AC.

(c) Construct the perpendicular bisectors of BC and AC.

(d) What can you say about the point of intersection of the lines in part **(c)**?

8. **(a)** Draw a triangle PQR with $PQ = 6$ cm, $\angle RPQ = 110°$ and $\angle PQR = 40°$.

PROBLEM SOLVING

(b) Construct the angle bisectors of $\angle RPQ$ and $\angle PQR$.

(c) Let I be the point of intersection of the angle bisectors in part **(b)**. Find $\angle PIQ$.

9. On a map of a triangular field ABC, $AB = 8$ cm, $AC = 10$ cm and $\angle BAC = 70°$.

(a) Draw ΔABC.

(b) A treasure T is on the angle bisector of $\angle BAC$ and on the perpendicular bisector of AC. Use construction to mark the point T on your diagram.

10. **(a)** Construct a triangle ABC with $AB = 8$ cm, $BC = 7$ cm and $CA = 5$ cm.

PROBLEM SOLVING

(b) Construct the midpoint D of BC, the midpoint E of CA and the midpoint F of AB.

(c) Draw the lines AD, BE and CF.

(d) What can you say about the lines in part **(c)**?

Write in Your Journal

Jordan says, 'If you give me any three numbers, I'll be able to construct a triangle with sides the same lengths as your numbers'. Do you agree with Jordan? Explain your answer.

9 CONGRUENCE, SIMILARITY AND ENLARGEMENT

WHAT IS IN THIS CHAPTER:

The photo shows a car assembly factory. In this factory, the workers assemble cars that are of the same shape and size. This is an example of the application of congruence.

LET'S LEARN TO

- translate, reflect and rotate 2D shapes
- identify congruent figures
- match the sides and angles of two congruent figures
- find the sides and angles of congruent figures
- enlarge and reduce a plane figure by a scale factor
- identify similar figures
- find the sides and angles of similar triangles
- find the sides and angles of similar quadrilaterals and other polygons

FLASHBACK

1. Parallel and Perpendicular Lines

(a) Two lines in the same plane are parallel if they never intersect. Parallel lines are indicated with the same number of arrows on each line.
In the diagram, AB and CD are parallel.
This is denoted by $AB \parallel CD$.

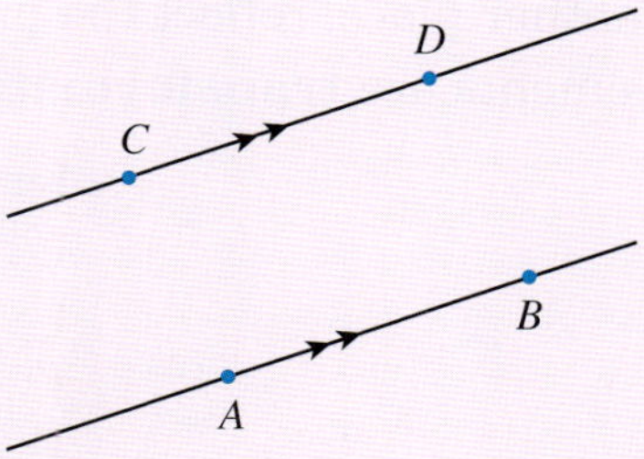

Real-world examples of parallel lines include train tracks, parallel bars in gymnastics, zebra crossing marks, and the lines in lined notepads.

(b) Two lines are perpendicular if they intersect at right angles.
In the diagram, PQ and RS are perpendicular at T.
This is denoted by $PQ \perp RS$.

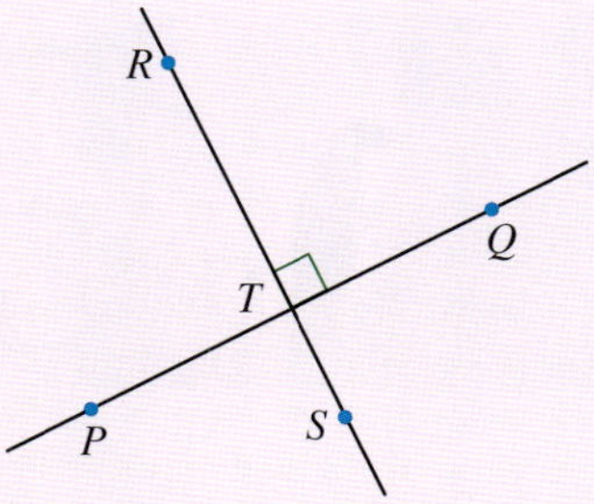

Real-world examples of perpendicular lines include in furniture and building work where lines meet at right angles, for example in a rectangular window frame.

2. Angle Sum of Triangles and Quadrilaterals

(a) Angles in a triangle add up to 180°. For example, in triangle ABC

$\angle a + 65° + 75° = 180°$
(Angles in a triangle add up to 180°.)
$\angle a = 180° - 65° - 75°$
$= 40°$

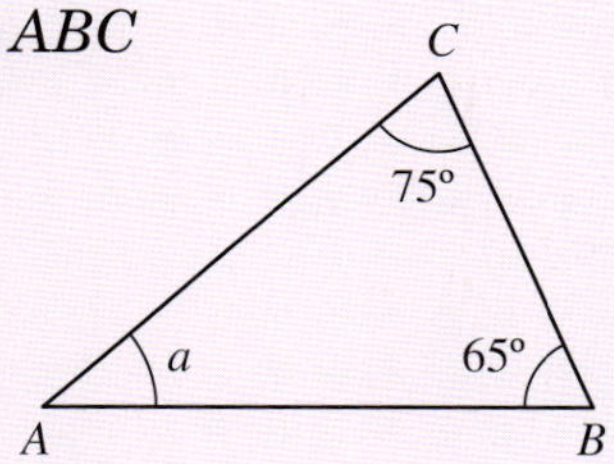

(b) Angles in a quadrilateral add up to 360°. For example, in quadrilateral $PQRS$

$67° + 72° + 88° + \angle s = 360°$
(Angles in a quadrilateral add up to 360°.)
$\angle s = 360° - 67° - 72° - 88°$
$= 133°$

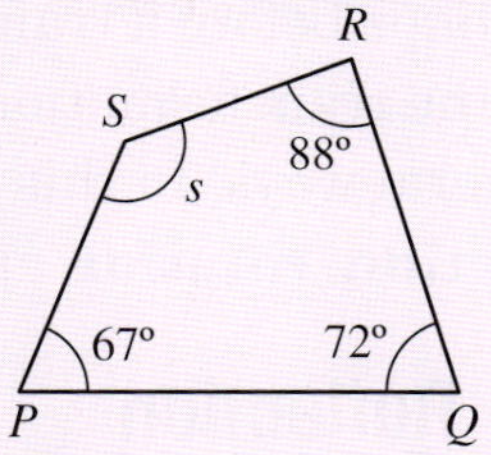

3. Symmetry

(a) The isosceles triangle has one line of symmetry. Each half is the mirror image of the other in the line.

(b) The regular pentagon has rotation symmetry of order 5. It maps onto itself 5 times in a 360° rotation.

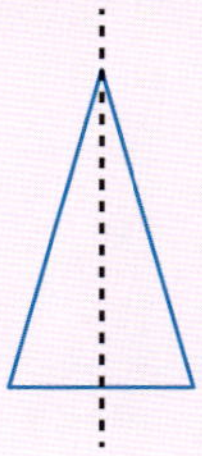

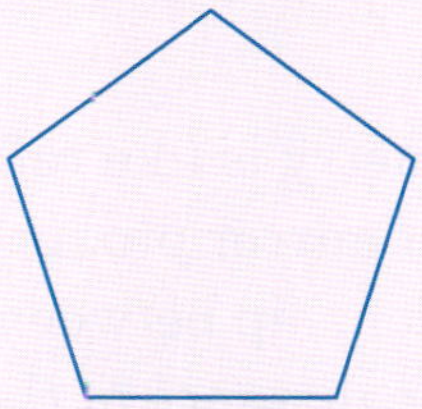

9.1 Transformations

When you edit a picture in a document you often need to drag the picture to another place, reflect the picture and rotate the picture. These kinds of movements are **transformations**.

The shape before a transformation is called the **object** and the shape after the transformation is called the **image**. A shape can be transformed in several ways. In this section you will study three transformations: **reflection**, **rotation** and **translation**.

A Reflection

In Student Book 1A, you learnt about reflective symmetry and were able to complete patterns so that they had lines of symmetry. You did this by reflecting part of the pattern in a mirror line.

Reflection in geometry is like reflection in a real mirror. An object in front of a mirror produces an image behind the mirror. What is the relationship between the distance of the object from the mirror and the distance of the image behind the mirror?

CLASS ACTIVITY 1

Objective: To explore the relationship between an object and its image under a reflection.

You will need a small mirror and squared paper.

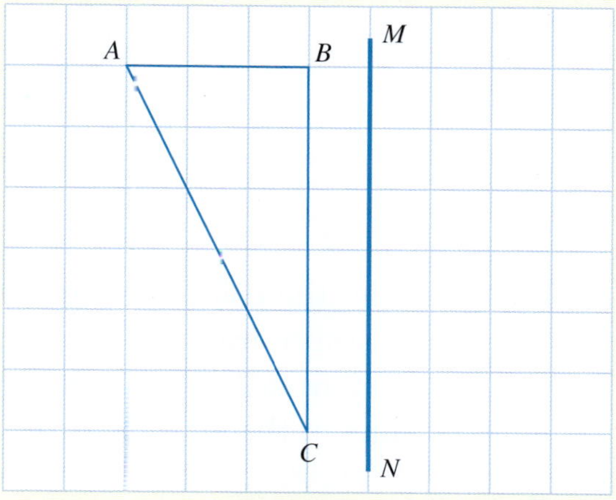

1. Draw any triangle ABC and a vertical line MN.

2. Place a mirror along MN.

The image of ΔABC in the mirror is $\Delta A'B'C'$.

3. What is the relationship between the sides and angles of ΔABC and $\Delta A'B'C'$?

4. By counting squares, find the distance from

(a) A to the mirror and A' to the mirror in the reflection,

(b) B to the mirror and B' to the mirror in the reflection,

(c) C to the mirror and C' to the mirror in the reflection.

What do you notice?

5. Draw the same triangle, but this time put the line MN in a different location. Place the mirror along MN. Repeat **Questions 3** and **4**.

In Class Activity 1, you see that the object ΔABC and its image $\Delta A'B'C'$ under a reflection have the same shape and size. Further, the reflection line bisects AA', BB' and CC' perpendicularly.

So $AA' \perp MN$, $BB' \perp MN$, $CC' \perp MN$

and $AP = A'P$, $BQ = B'Q$, $CR = C'R$.

You can use these properties to draw the image of an object under a reflection.

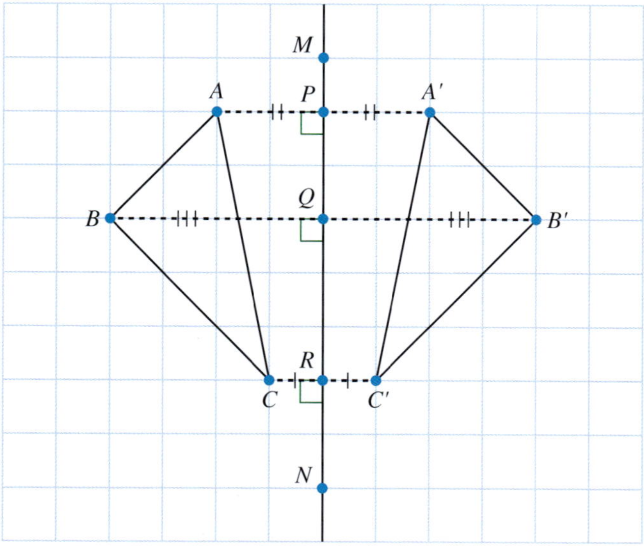

RECALL

Bisects means cuts in half.

REMARK

Here you can see that each point and its reflection are the same distance from the mirror line. For example, A is two units from the mirror line and A' is two units from the mirror line in the other direction.

Example 1

Reflect $ABCDE$ in the line XY.

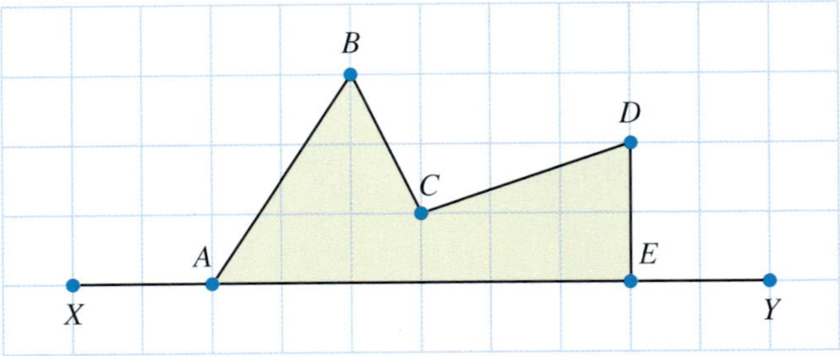

Solution

Plot the point B' such that B and B' are at the same distance from XY, so count three squares to the mirror line from B, so B' will be three squares from the mirror line in the opposite direction.

The images of other vertices can be constructed in the same way.

Note that the image A' and the point A are the same point. E and E' are also the same. This is because these points lie on the mirror line.

In the diagram, $A'B'C'D'E'$ is the image of $ABCDE$.

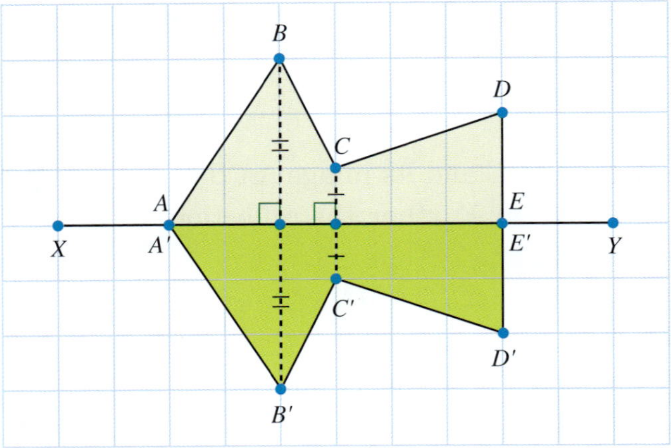

REMARK

In some books, 'reflecting in a mirror line' is described as 'reflecting about a mirror line'. They both mean the same thing.

Try It! 1

Copy the diagram. Reflect ΔABC in the line PQ.

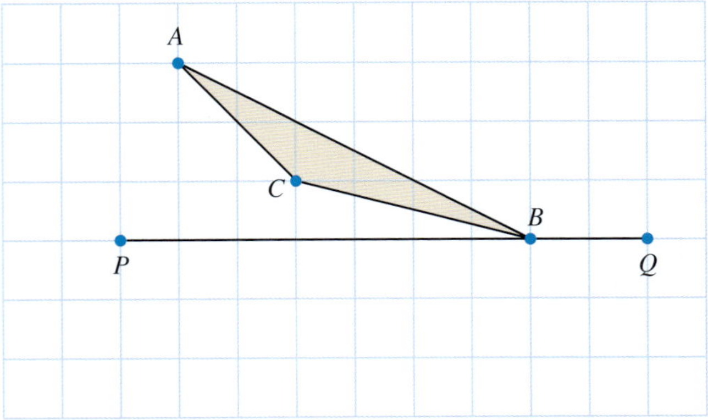

DISCUSS

With a partner, make a list of real-life examples of why you might want to reflect an image.

B Rotation

In Student Book 1A you learnt about rotation symmetry. You worked out the order of rotation symmetry of a shape by rotating it and counting the number of times it maps onto itself in a 360° rotation.

CLASS ACTIVITY 2

Objective: To explore the relationship between an object and its image under a rotation.

You will need squared paper and tracing paper for this activity.

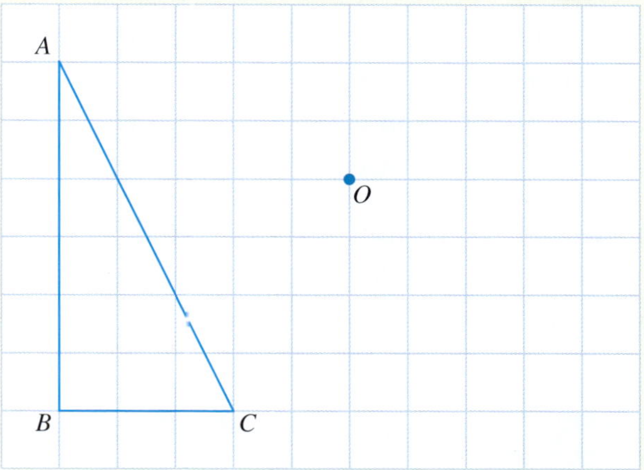

1. Draw any triangle ABC and a point O.

2. Copy ΔABC onto tracing paper.

3. Put the point of your pencil on the tracing paper at O, then rotate the paper 90° anticlockwise (quarter of a turn).

The image of ΔABC on the tracing paper is $\Delta A'B'C'$.

4. What is the relationship between the object ΔABC and the image $\Delta A'B'C'$?

5. Draw lines OA and OA' on the tracing paper and measure $\angle AOA'$.

6. Repeat tasks **2–5** with a rotation of 180°.

7. What do you notice about the angle $\angle AOA'$ and the angle of rotation in each case?

From Class Activity 2, you see that the object and the image under a rotation have the same shape and size. Moreover,

$$OA = OA', \qquad OB = OB', \qquad OC = OC',$$
$$\angle AOA' = \angle BOB' = \angle COC' = \text{angle of rotation.}$$

You can use these properties to draw the image under a rotation.

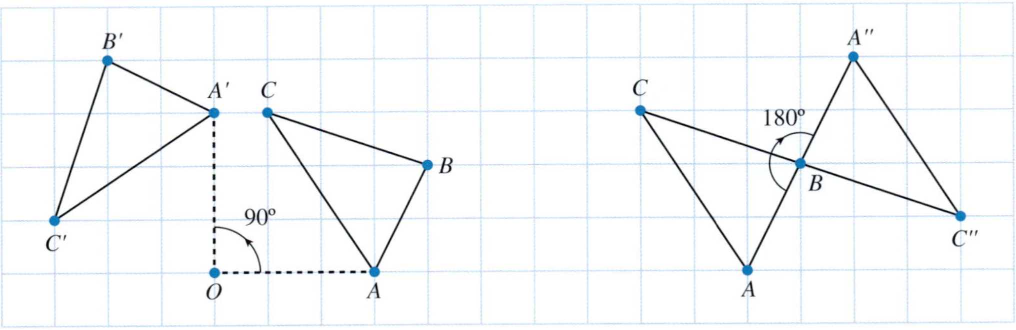

In rotating an object, you must specify three things:

1. The point at which the object is rotated about. This is called the **centre of rotation**.
2. The direction of rotation, either clockwise or anticlockwise.
3. The angle of rotation.

In the left diagram, ΔABC is rotated 90° anticlockwise about O. In the right diagram, ΔABC is rotated 180° clockwise about B. Note that the centre of rotation can be a point outside, inside or on the object.

Example 2

ΔABC is rotated 180° anticlockwise about O. Draw its image.

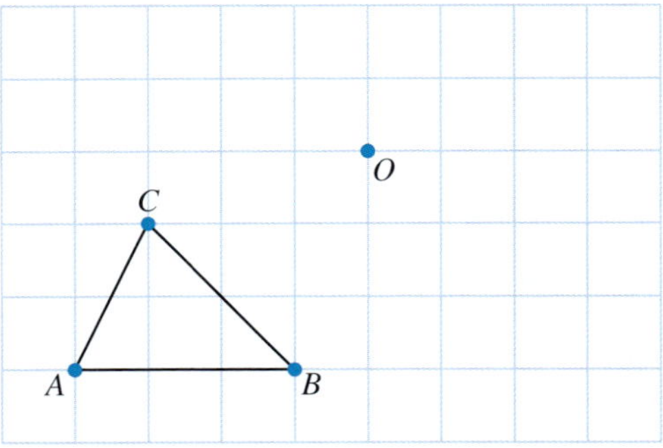

Solution

Copy ΔABC onto tracing paper. Rotate the paper 180° anticlockwise about O.

Copy the image on the tracing paper onto the grid and label $A'B'C'$.

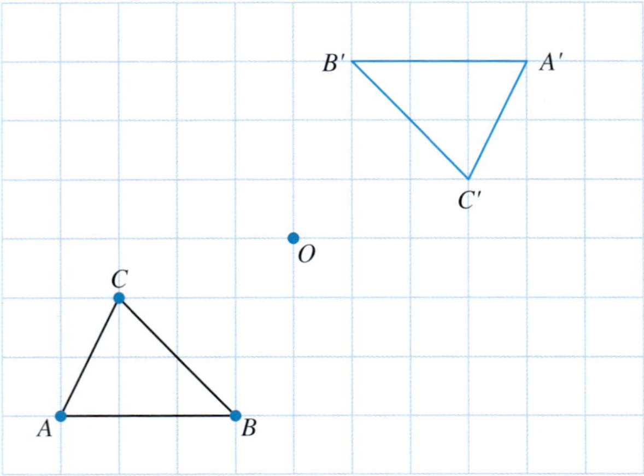

DISCUSS

What is the relationship between a rotation of 180° anticlockwise and a rotation of 180° clockwise?

Try It! 2

Copy the diagram. Draw the image of ΔABC when it is rotated 90° anticlockwise about the point B.

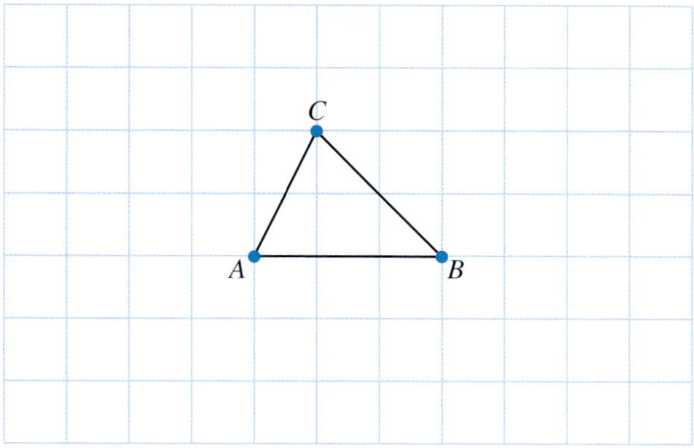

DISCUSS

With a partner, make a list of real-life examples of why you might want to rotate an image.

C Translation

Translation is the movement of an object from its original position to a new position. The translation on a plane can be described by the number of units to the right or left, and the number of units upwards or downwards.

CLASS ACTIVITY 3

Objective: To explore the relationship between the object and its image in a translation.

You will need a dice for this activity.

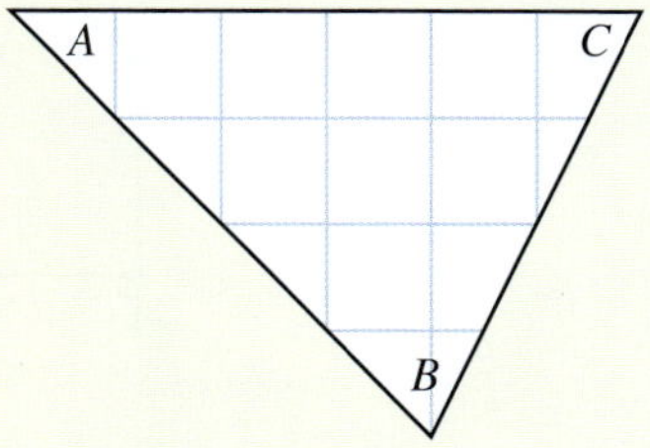

1. Draw any triangle ABC on squared paper and cut it out.
2. Place the triangle on another piece of squared paper so that the squares line up. Draw around it and label it.
3. Roll the dice twice and write down the two numbers.
4. Move the triangle to the right by the first number of squares and upwards to the second number of squares. For example, if your numbers were 2 and 5 you would move the triangle 2 squares to the right and 5 squares upwards.
5. Draw around the triangle in its new position and label $A'B'C'$.
6. What is the relationship between the object ΔABC and its image $\Delta A'B'C'$?
7. Draw lines AA', BB' and CC' on your diagram. Measure each line.
8. What is the relationship between the line segments AA', BB' and CC'?

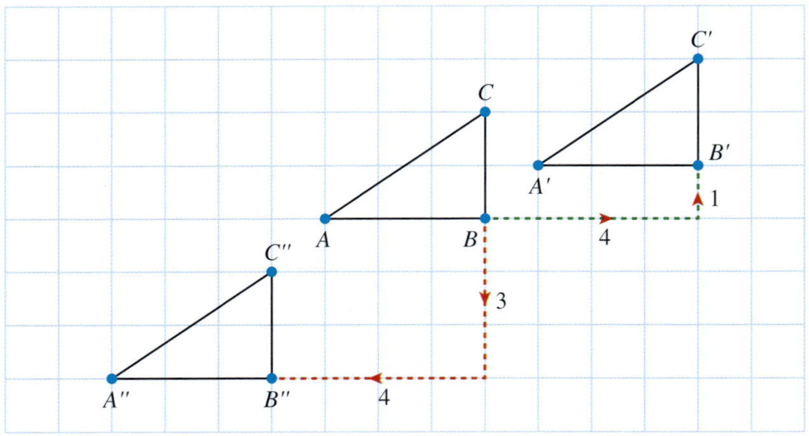

In the diagram, ΔABC is translated 4 units to the right and 1 unit upwards to become the image $\Delta A'B'C'$. ΔABC is translated 4 units to the left and 3 units downwards to become the image $\Delta A''B''C''$.

In Class Activity 3, you saw that an object and its image under a translation have the same orientation, shape and size. Moreover, the translation of each vertex is the same.

$AA' = BB' = CC'$

Example 3 Draw the image of $ABCD$ under a translation of 6 units to the right and 1 unit downwards.

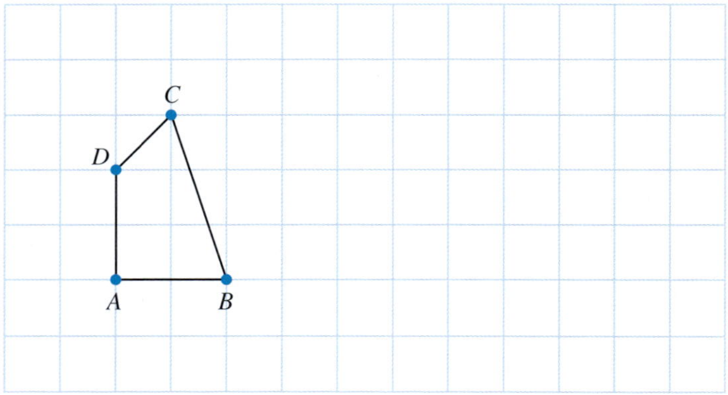

Solution Translate each vertex 6 units to the right and 1 unit downwards to get the image as shown.

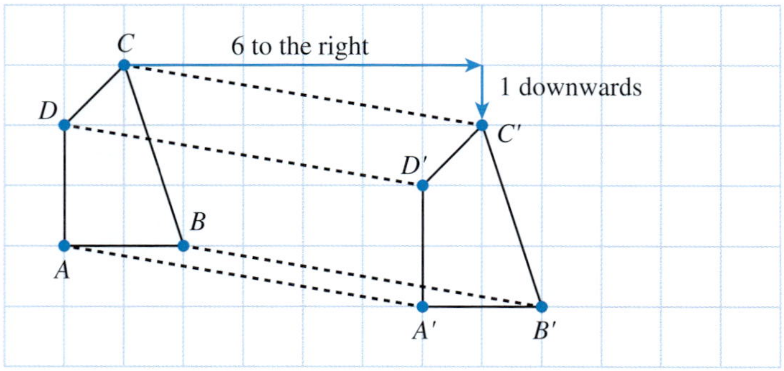

Try It! 3

Copy the diagram. Draw the image of $ABCD$ under a translation of 4 units to the left and 2 units upwards.

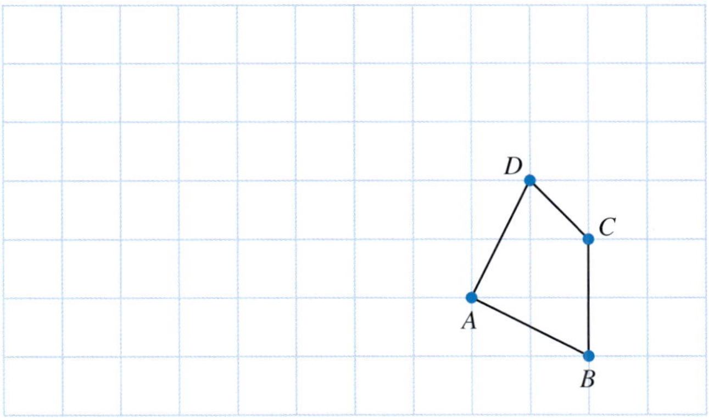

PRACTICE 9.1

LEVEL 1

1. Copy the shaded object and reflect it in the mirror line MN in each part. Label the vertices of the image using A', B', and so on.

(a)

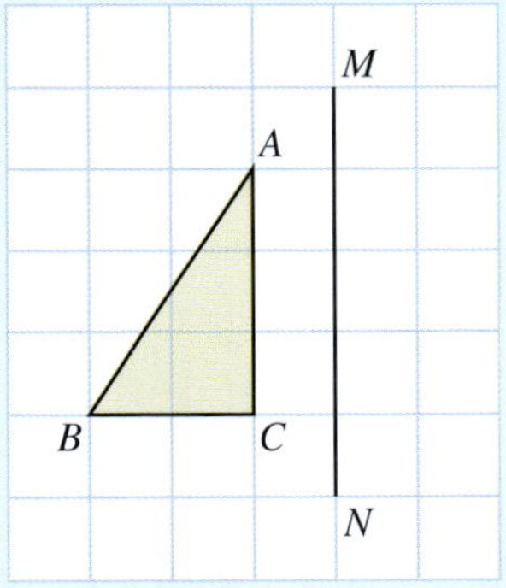

(b)

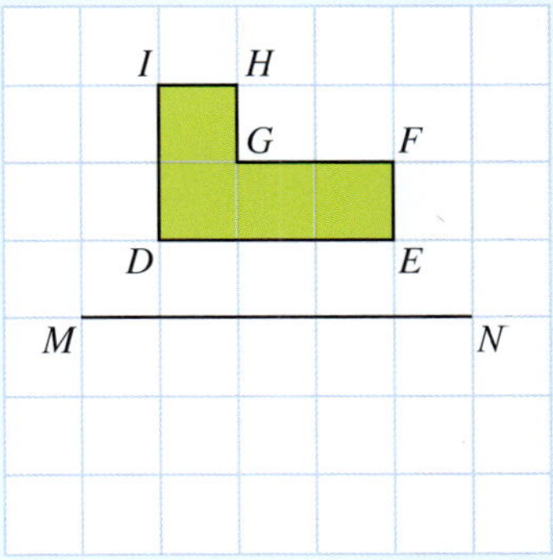

(c)

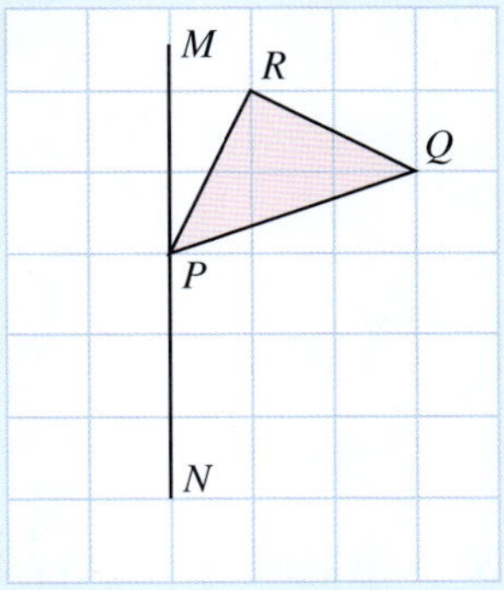

2. Copy the shaded object and rotate it as specified in each part. Label the vertices of the image using A', B', and so on.

(a) 90° clockwise about O

(b) 90° anticlockwise about D

(c) 180° clockwise about P

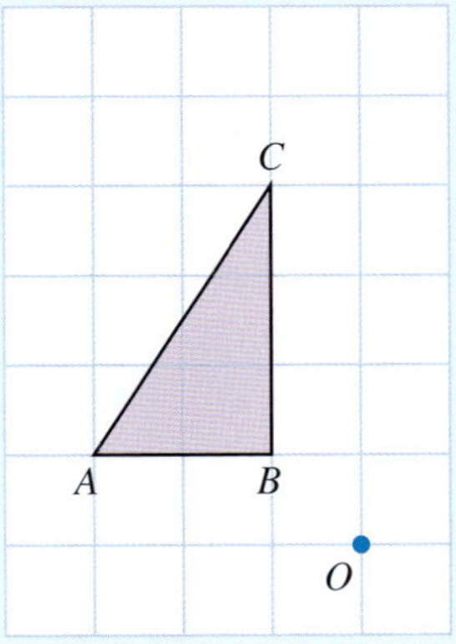

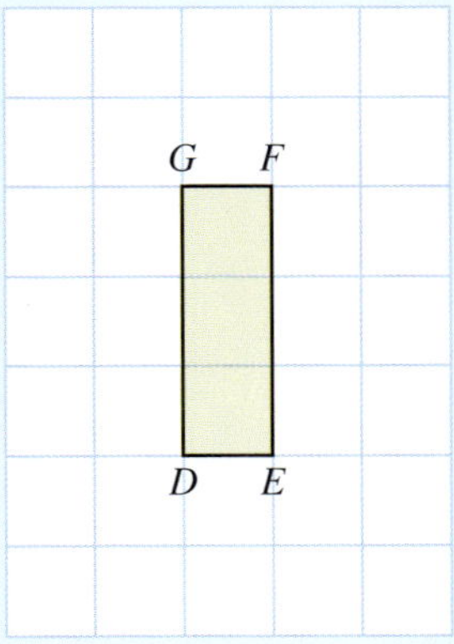

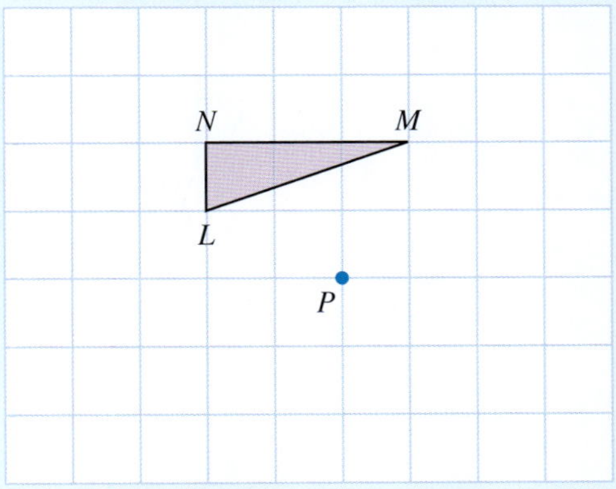

3. Copy the shaded object and translate it as specified in each part. Label the vertices of the image using A', B', and so on.

(a) 2 units to the right

(b) 3 units to the left and 2 units upwards

(c) 4 units to the right and 3 units downwards

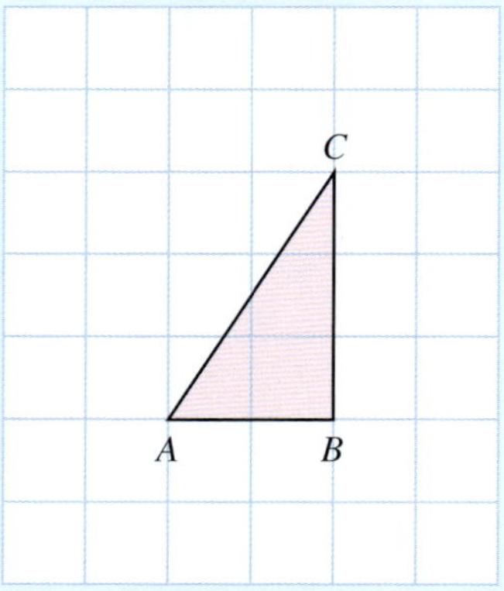

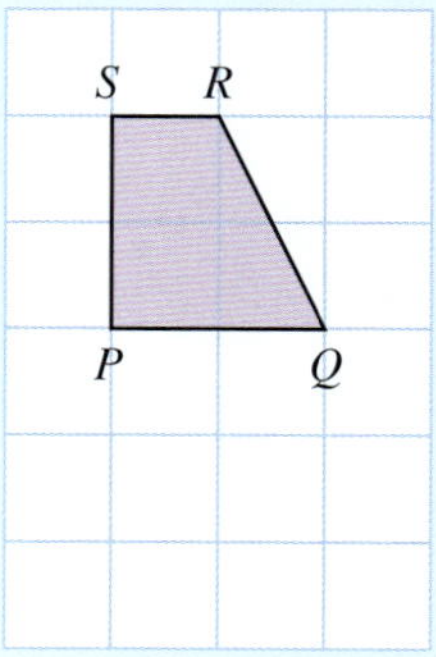

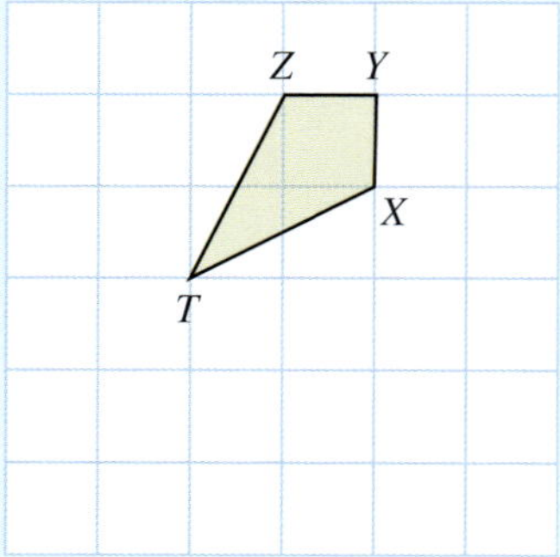

4. Copy each diagram and draw a mirror line so that the patterned shape is the reflected image of the other shape about the line.

(a)

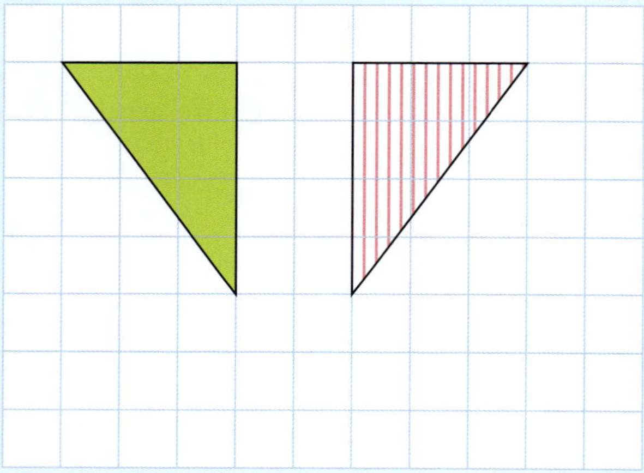

(b)

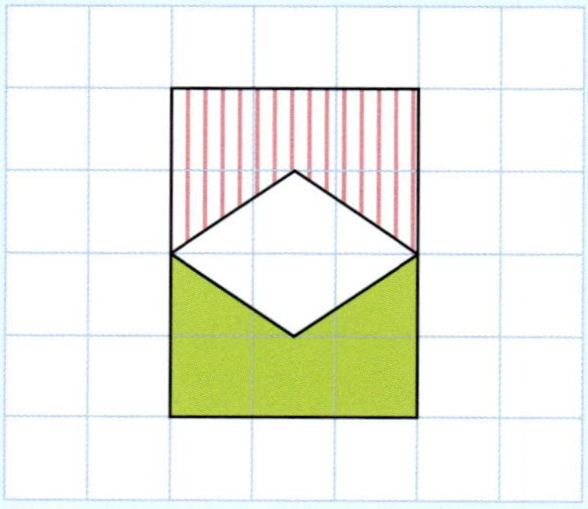

5. In each part, triangle $A'B'C'$ is the image of triangle ABC under a transformation. Is the transformation a reflection, rotation or translation? Explain your answer.

(a)

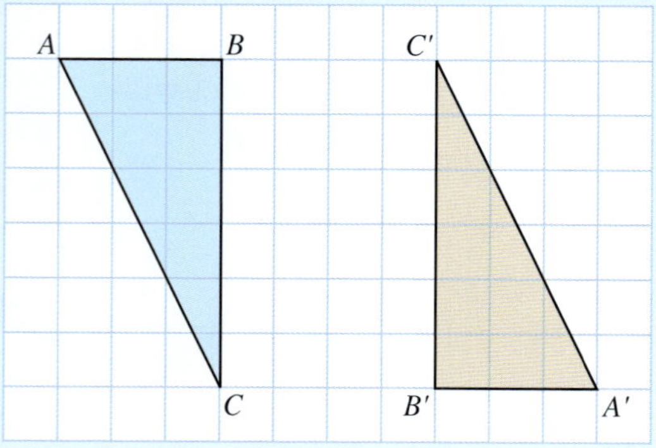

(b)

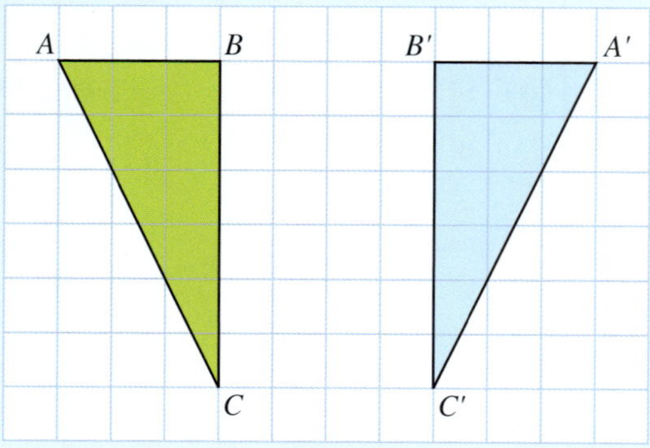

LEVEL 2

6. Describe the translation that maps

(a) triangle ABC to triangle $A'B'C'$,

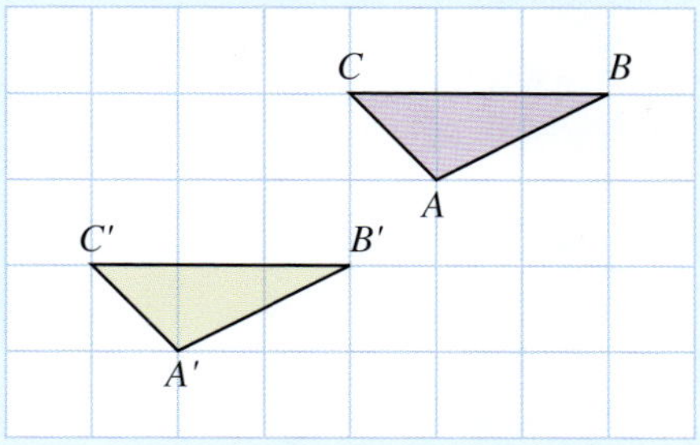

(b) rectangle $XYZT$ to rectangle $X'Y'Z'T'$.

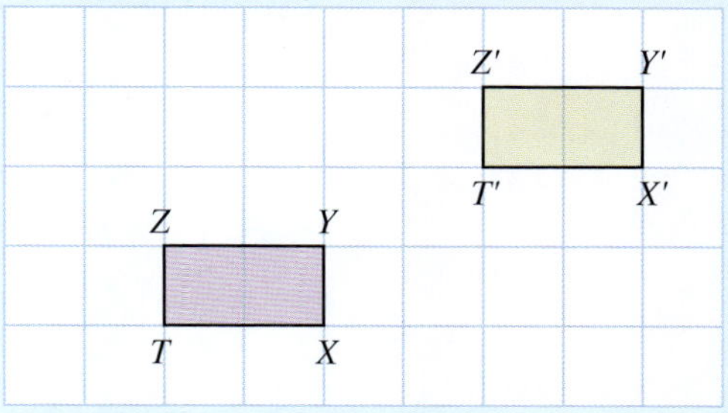

7. Write down the angle of rotation for the transformation that maps

(a) triangle ABC to triangle $A'B'C'$,

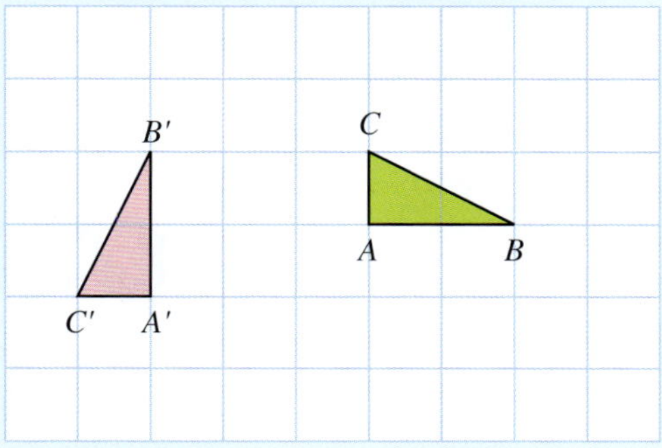

(b) triangle PQR to triangle $P'Q'R'$.

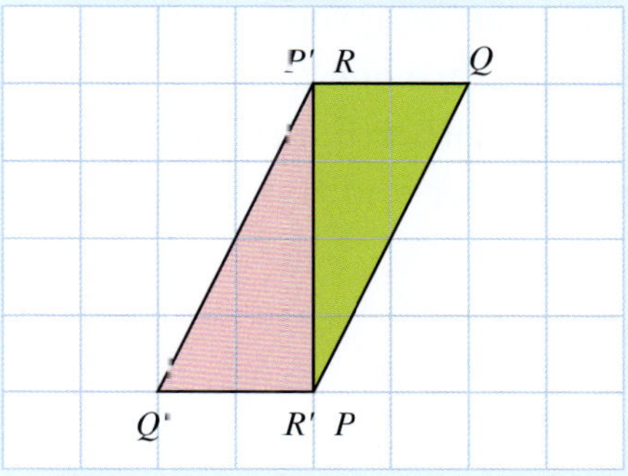

8. **(a)** Fill in the blanks to describe the transformation that transforms quadrilateral $ABCD$ to the shaded quadrilateral.

'A ________ of ________° about the point with coordinates ________ , ________.)'

(b) Copy the diagram and label the vertices of the shaded quadrilateral $A'B'C'D'$.

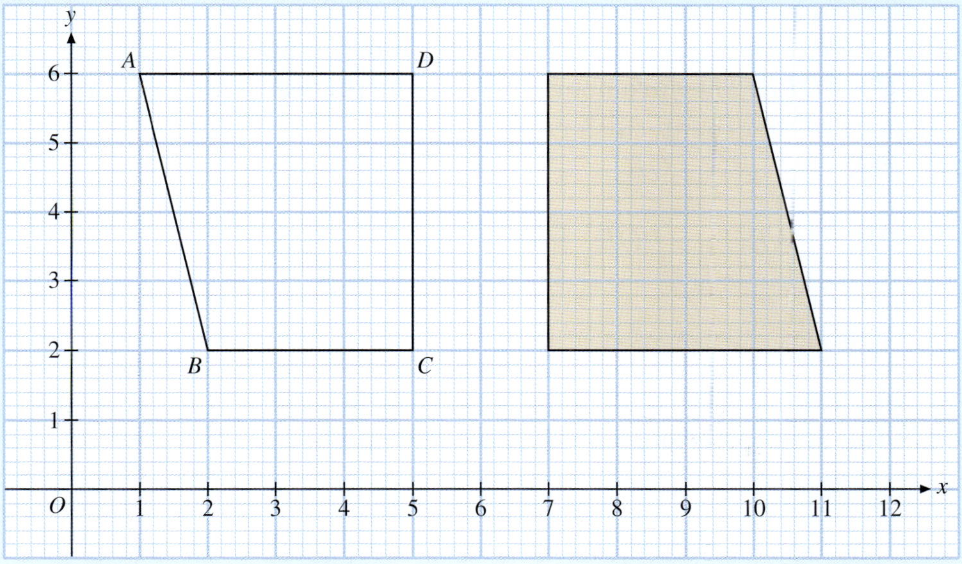

9.2 Congruent Figures

Two figures are **congruent** if they are of the same shape and size. Stamps and floor tiles are examples of congruent figures in everyday life.

One way to test for congruence of two figures is to check whether they fit exactly. You can trace one figure on a sheet of tracing paper or clear plastic and place it on another figure. If the two figures are congruent, the outline on the tracing paper and the other figure will fit exactly.

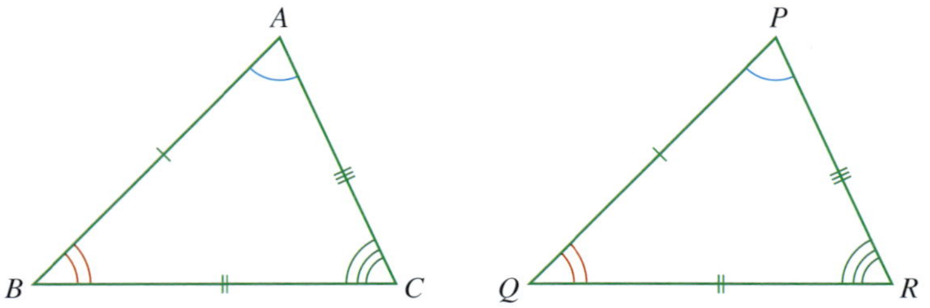

REMARK

When ΔABC is placed on ΔPQR, they will fit exactly.

Here, ΔABC and ΔPQR are congruent triangles. This is denoted by

$$\Delta ABC \equiv \Delta PQR.$$

Note that the order of the vertices of one figure must **correspond** to that of the other figure in writing a **congruence statement**. In the diagram, you can write $\Delta BCA \equiv \Delta QRP$ and $\Delta CAB \equiv \Delta RPQ$ but not $\Delta ABC \equiv \Delta QPR$. This is because $\angle ABC \neq \angle QPR$. They are not corresponding angles.

When the two triangles are congruent, this gives

$$AB = PQ, \qquad BC = QR, \qquad CA = RP,$$

$$\angle BAC = \angle QPR, \quad \angle ABC = \angle PQR \quad \text{and} \quad \angle ACB = \angle PRQ.$$

This means:

> Corresponding sides of congruent figures are equal.
> Corresponding angles of congruent figures are equal.

DISCUSS

Are ΔABC and ΔPQR, congruent triangles?

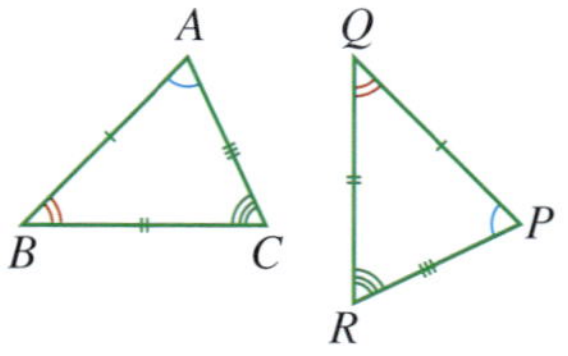

Example 4 Identify the different groups of congruent figures.

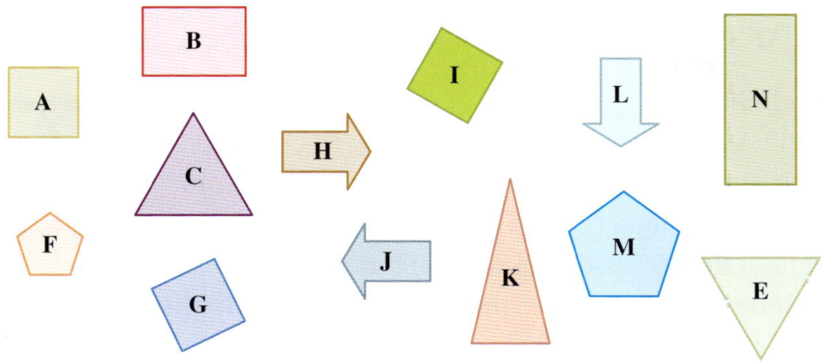

Solution You can use a tracing paper to check whether two figures are congruent.

There are three groups of congruent figures.

(1) Figures A, G and I

(2) Figures H, J and L

(3) Figures C and E

Try It! 4 Identify the different groups of congruent figures.

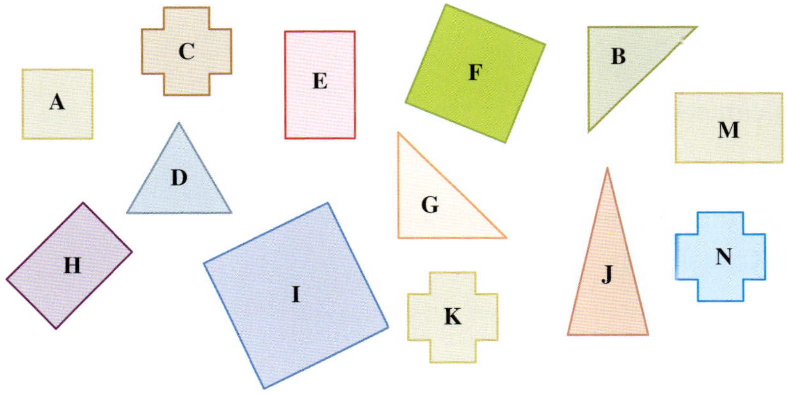

CLASS ACTIVITY 4

Objective: To determine the relationship of an object and its image under a reflection, rotation or translation.

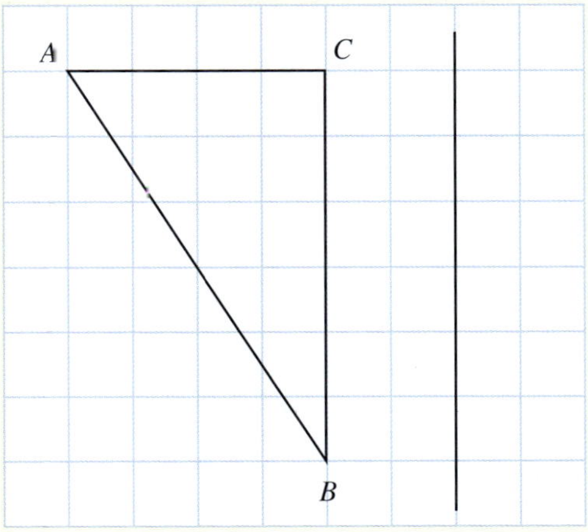

1. Draw any triangle ABC on squared paper, measure the lengths of the sides and the sizes of the angles.

2. **(a)** Draw a vertical line and reflect triangle ABC in it.

   (b) Measure the lengths of the sides and the sizes of the angles in the image. Are the object and the image congruent?

(c) Draw a horizontal line and reflect triangle ABC in it.
(d) Measure the lengths of the sides and the sizes of the angles in the image. Are the object and the image congruent?

3. Copy your triangle ABC.
(a) Rotate triangle ABC 180° about point B.
(b) Measure the lengths of the sides and the sizes of the angles in the image. Are the object and the image congruent?
(c) Rotate triangle ABC 90° anticlockwise about point A.
(d) Measure the lengths of the sides and the sizes of the angles in the image. Are the object and the image congruent?

REMARK

You can use tracing paper for **Questions 3** and **4**.

4. Copy your triangle ABC.
(a) Translate triangle ABC 8 units to the right.
(b) Measure the lengths of the sides and the sizes of the angles in the image. Are the object and the image congruent?
(c) Translate triangle ABC 2 units to the left and 3 units downwards.
(d) Measure the lengths of the sides and the sizes of the angles in the image. Are the object and the image congruent?

From Class Activity 4, you can see that:

An object and its image under a reflection, rotation or translation are congruent.

Example 5

The quadrilaterals $ABCD$ and $PQRS$ are congruent. Write down all the lengths and angles of $PQRS$.

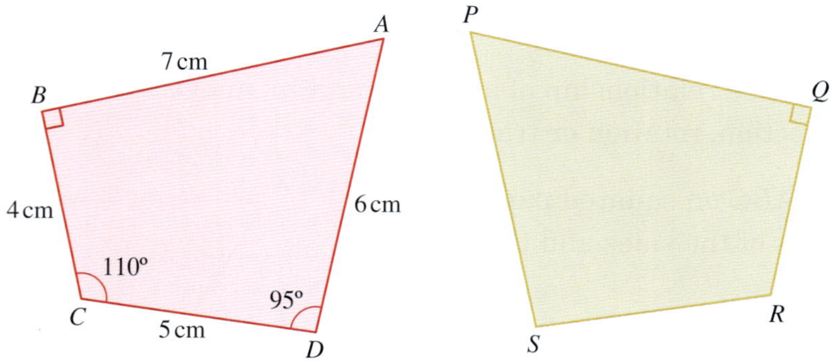

Solution Quadrilateral $PQRS$ is the image of $ABCD$ following a reflection.

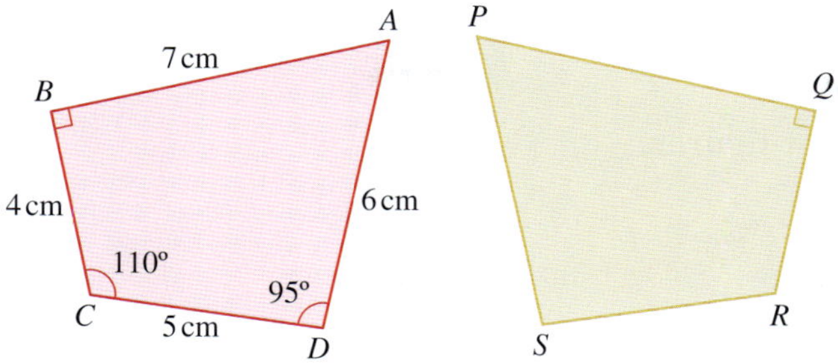

DISCUSS

Can you say $BCDA \equiv QRSP$? Explain your answer.

As $ABCD \equiv PQRS$,

$PQ = AB$ (Corresponding sides of congruent quadrilaterals.)
$= 7\text{ cm}$

$QR = BC$ (Corresponding sides of congruent quadrilaterals.)
$= 4\text{ cm}$

$RS = CD$ (Corresponding sides of congruent quadrilaterals.)
$= 5\text{ cm}$

$SP = DA$ (Corresponding sides of congruent quadrilaterals.)
$= 6\text{ cm}$

$\angle PQR = \angle ABC$ (Corresponding angles of congruent quadrilaterals.)
$= 90°$

$\angle QRS = \angle BCD$ (Corresponding angles of congruent quadrilaterals.)
$= 110°$

$\angle RSP = \angle CDA$ (Corresponding angles of congruent quadrilaterals.)
$= 95°$

$90° + 110° + 95° + \angle SPQ = 360°$ (Angles in a quadrilateral add up to 360°.)

$295° + \angle SPQ = 360°$

$\angle SPQ = 360° - 295°$

$\angle SPQ = 65°$

Try It! 5 The trapezia $ABCD$ and $PQRS$ are congruent. Write down all the lengths and angles of $PQRS$.

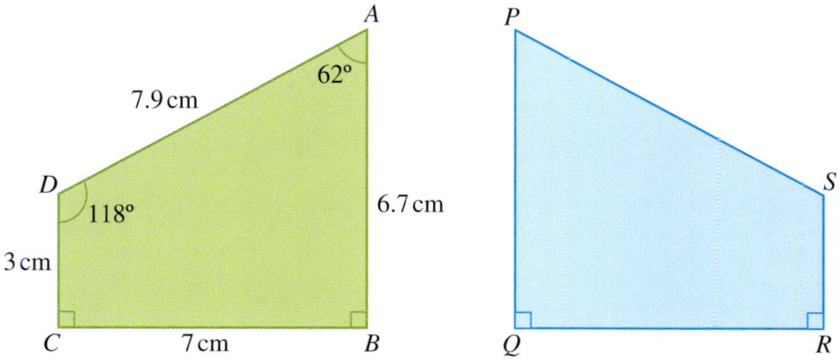

PRACTICE 9.2

LEVEL 1

1. Identify the groups of congruent figures.

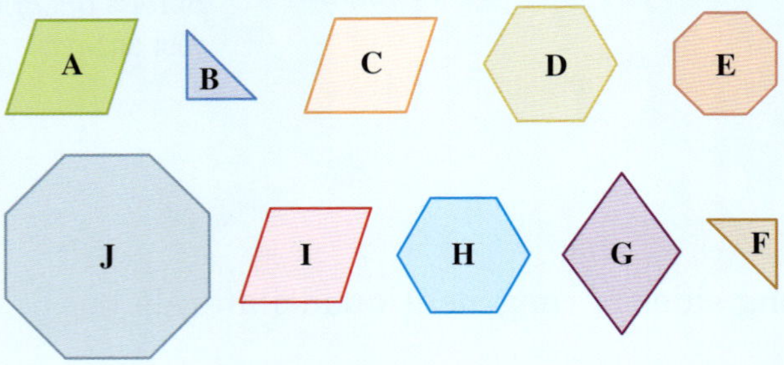

2. Write down the corresponding sides of each pair of congruent figures.

(a)

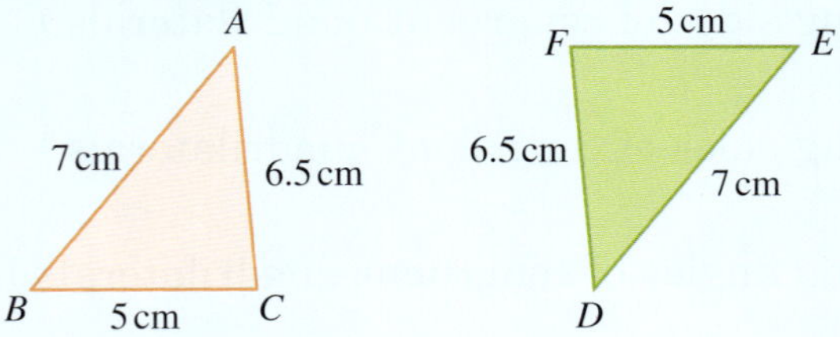

(b)

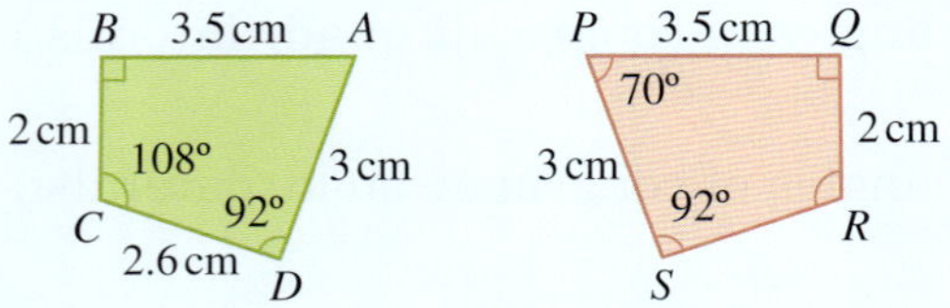

3. These three triangles are congruent. Is it true that

(a) $\Delta ABC \equiv \Delta DEF$,

(b) $\Delta ABC \equiv \Delta GHK$?

Explain your answers.

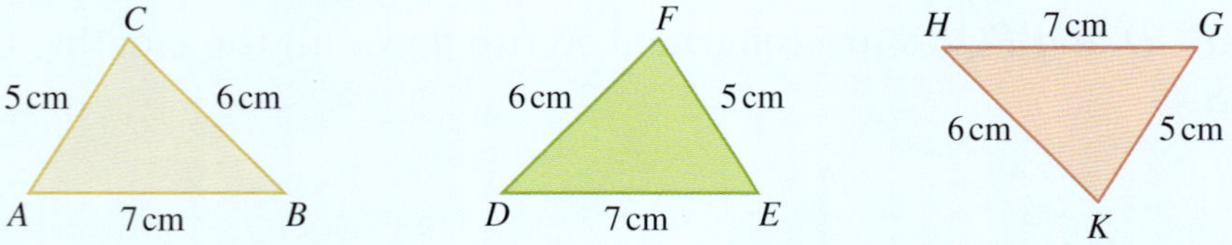

4. Two of the triangular tiles below are congruent. Write down the congruence statement. Explain your answer.

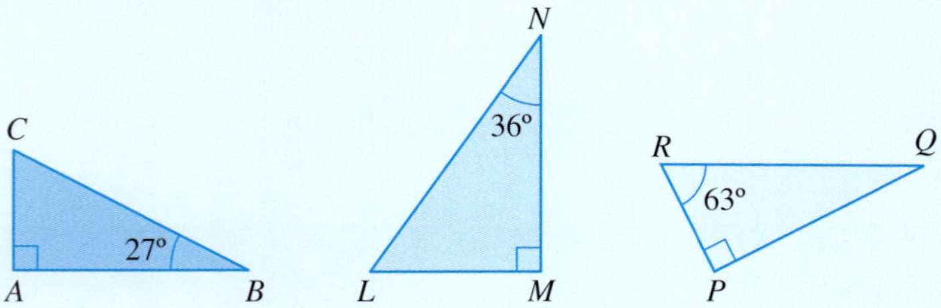

5. State whether $ABCD$ and $PQRS$ are congruent in each case. Explain your answer.

(a)

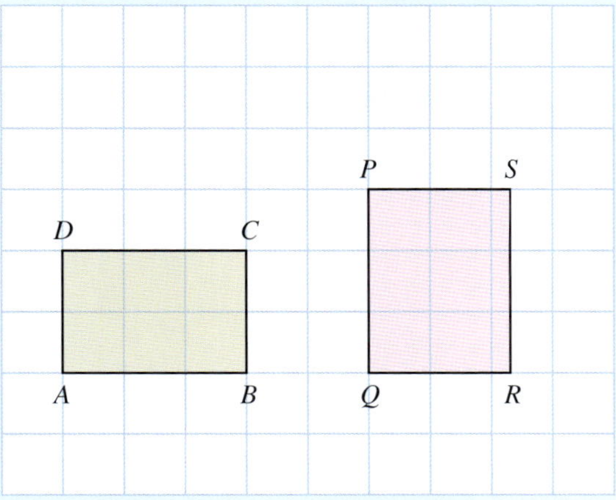

(b)

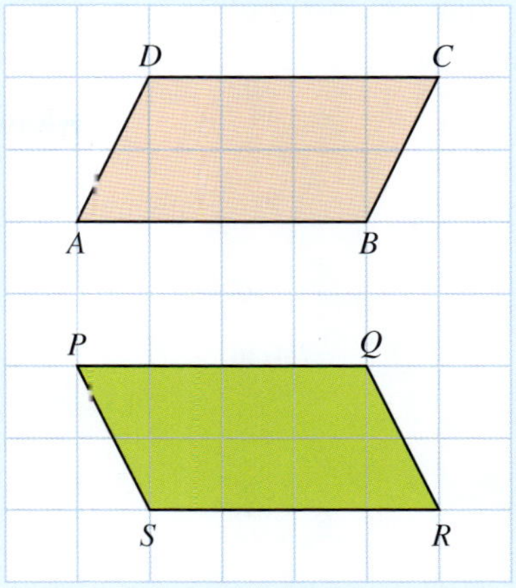

LEVEL 2

6. The earrings are congruent.

(a) Find the values of x and y.

(b) Is the small triangle at the top of each earring congruent to the larger triangle at the bottom of each earring? Explain your answer.

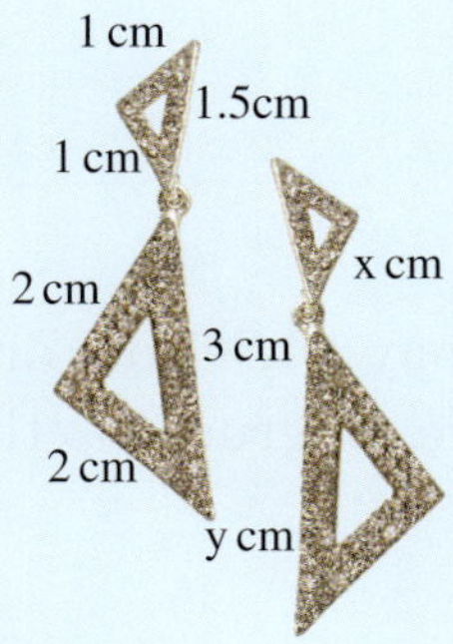

7. The figures in each part are congruent. Find the angles x and y.

(a)

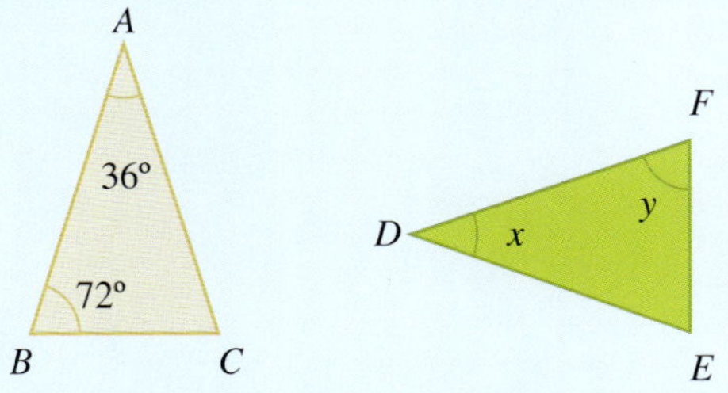

(b)

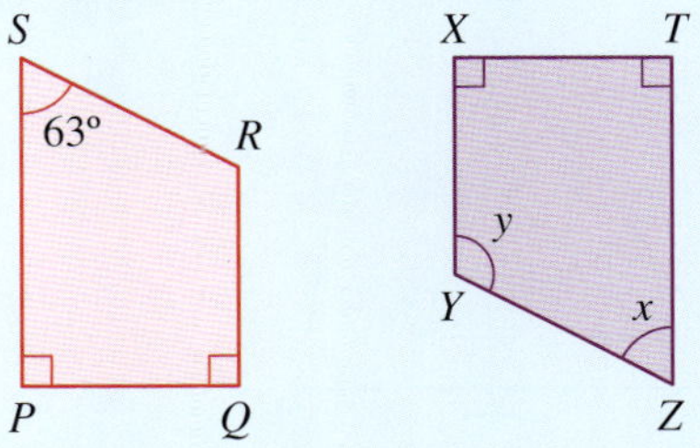

8. ΔABC and ΔPQR are congruent. Find the sizes of the angles x and y.

(a)

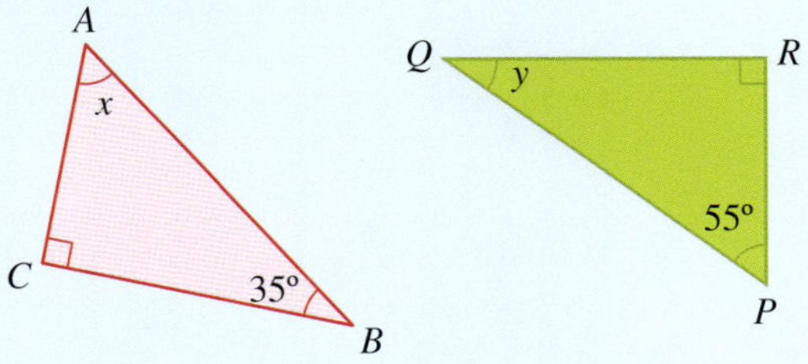

(b)

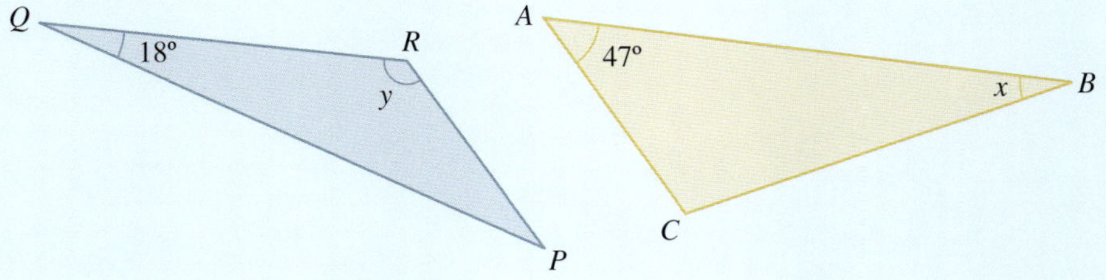

9. The two tiles in each part are congruent. Find the value of x and the size of angle y.

(a)

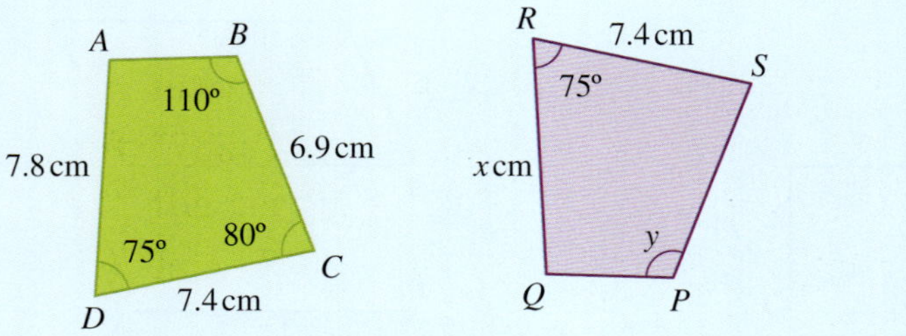

(b)

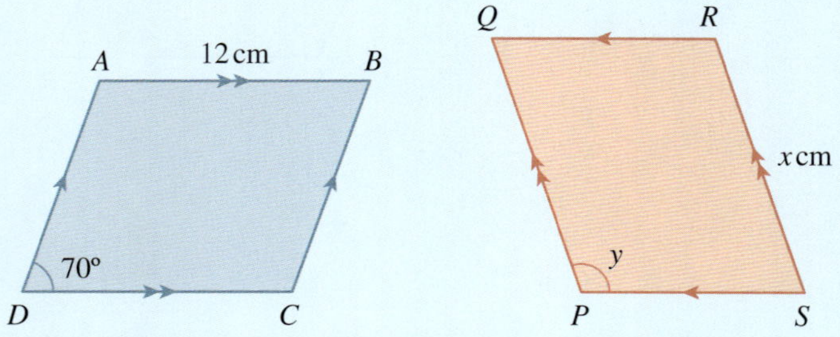

10. Copy $\triangle ABC$ and draw two triangles in different orientations that are congruent to this triangle.

OPEN QUESTION

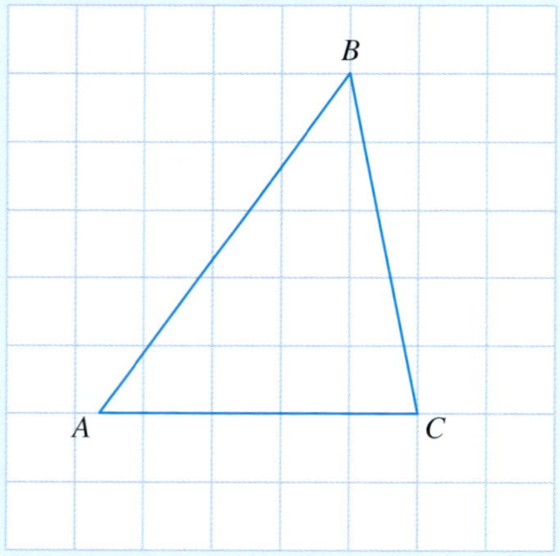

9.3 Enlargement and Scale Factor

When you want to include a photo in a project or presentation, you will often need to change the size of the photo to fit the layout of the page or slide. In mathematics, an **enlargement** is a type of transformation in which the shape of the object remains the same, but it is increased or decreased in size to create the image.

The photo *PQRS* is an enlarged image of the object photo *ABCD*. All the dimensions of *PQRS* are twice as big as the dimensions of *ABCD*.

$PQ = AB \times 2$ and $QR = BC \times 2$

$= 8\text{ cm}$ $= 6\text{ cm}$

Therefore, you say that the **scale factor** of the enlargement is 2.

> **DISCUSS**
>
> Is the wingspan of the eagle in *PQRS* divided by the wingspan of the eagle in *ABCD* equal to the scale factor?

CLASS ACTIVITY 5

Objective: Investigate enlargements of triangles.

1. In these pairs of triangles, $A'B'C'$ is the image of ABC following an enlargement. Copy and complete each part.

(a)

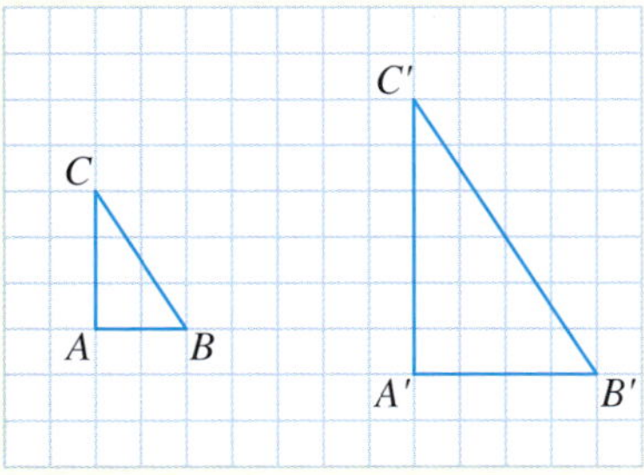

$AB = 2\text{ cm}$

$A'B' = 4\text{ cm}$

Scale factor of AB to $A'B'$ = ______

AC = ______

$A'C'$ = ______

Scale factor of AC to $A'C'$ = ______

> **RECALL**
>
> The shape before a transformation is called the object and the shape after the transformation is called the image.

(b)

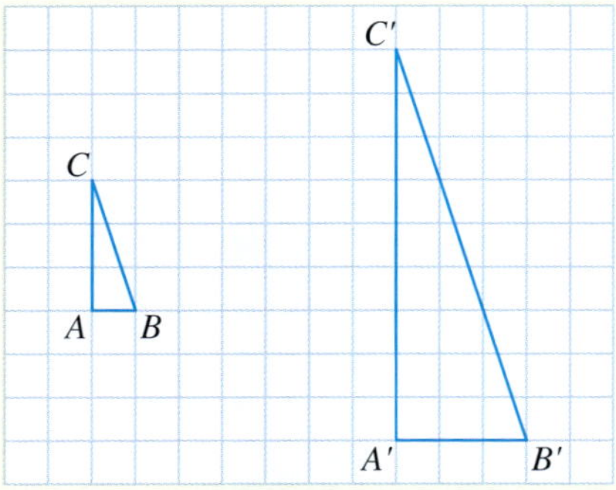

$AB =$ ______

$A'B' =$ ______

Scale factor of AB to $A'B' =$ ______

$AC =$ ______

$A'C' =$ ______

Scale factor of AC to $A'C' =$ ______

2. What do you notice about the scale factor of AB to $A'B'$ and of AC to $A'C'$ in each part of **Question 1**?

3. In these pairs of triangles, $A'B'C'$ is **not** the image of ABC following an enlargement. Copy and complete each part.

(a)

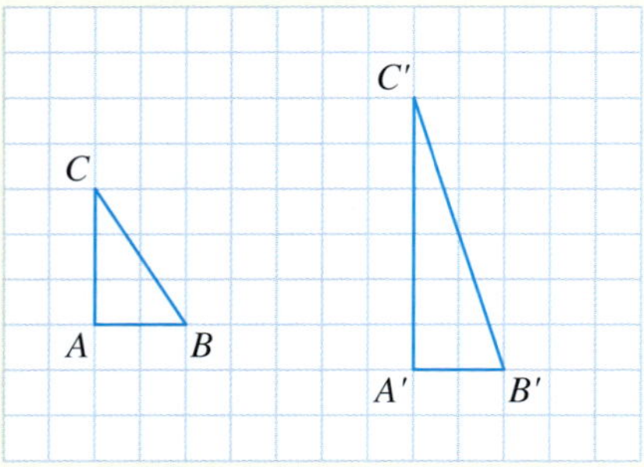

$AB =$ ______

$A'B' =$ ______

Scale factor of AB to $A'B' =$ ______

$AC =$ ______

$A'C' =$ ______

Scale factor of AC to $A'C' =$ ______

(b)

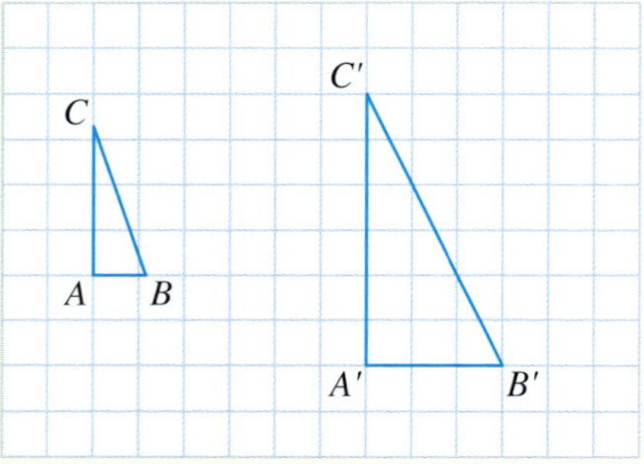

$AB =$ ______

$A'B' =$ ______

Scale factor of AB to $A'B' =$ ______

$AC =$ ______

$A'C' =$ ______

Scale factor of AC to $A'C' =$ ______

4. What do you notice about the scale factor of AB to $A'B'$ and of AC to $A'C'$ in each part of **Question 3**?

5. Draw one enlargement and one **non**-enlargement of each triangle.

(a)

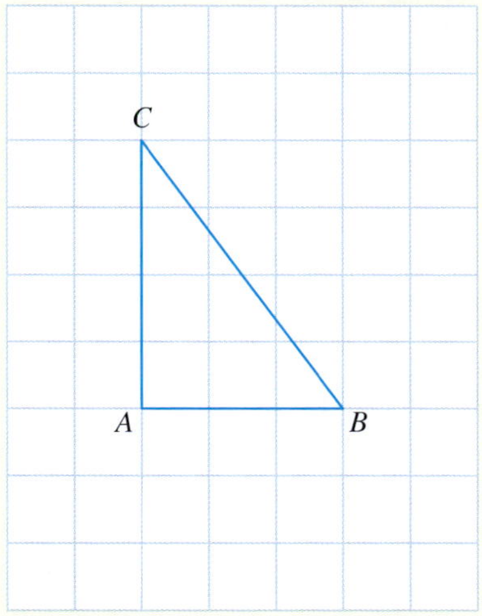

(b)

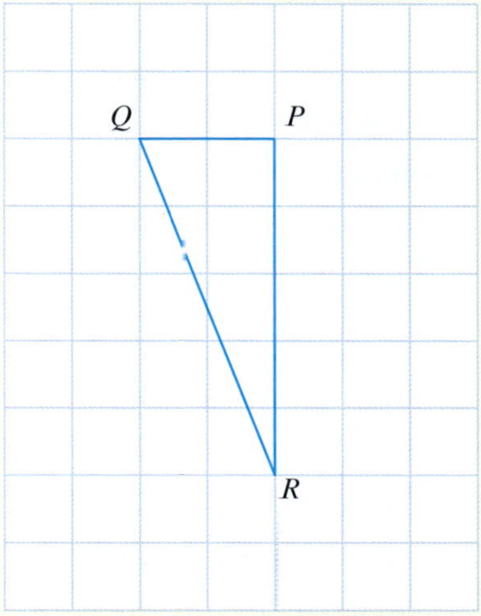

From Class Activity 5, you can see that for an enlargement, all lengths in the object must be multiplied by the same scale factor in the image.

Therefore:

$$\text{Scale factor} = \frac{\text{length of a side of the image}}{\text{length of the corresponding side of the object}}$$

Example 6

(a) Is ΔDEF an enlargement of ΔABC? If so, state the scale factor.

(b) Is ΔPQR an enlargement of ΔABC? If so, state the scale factor.

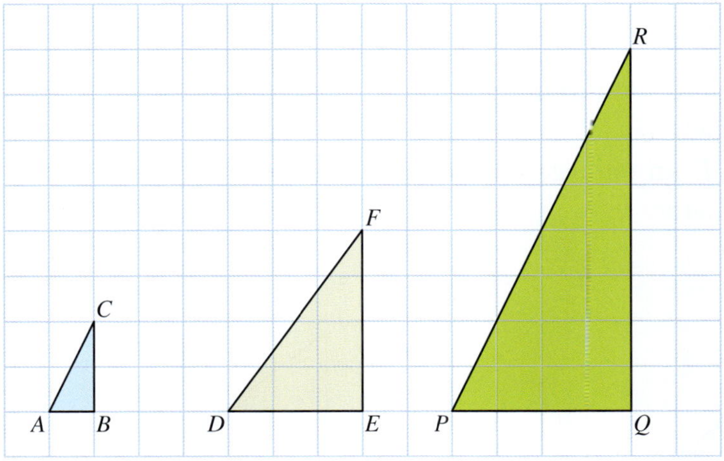

Solution

(a) $AB = 1\text{cm}$ and $DE = 3\text{cm}$

The scale factor of the enlargement of AB to $DE = \frac{3}{1}$

$= 3$

The base of the image is 3 times the length of the object.

$BC = 2\text{cm}$ and $EF = 4\text{cm}$

The scale factor of the enlargement of BC to $EF = \frac{4}{2}$

$= 2$

The height of the image is 2 times the length of the object.

Therefore, the scale factor enlargement of each corresponding side of the triangle is different, so ΔDEF is not an enlargement of ΔABC.

(b) $AB = 1\text{cm}$ and $PQ = 4\text{cm}$

The scale factor of the enlargement from AB to $PQ = \frac{4}{1}$

$= 4$

The base of the image is 4 times the length of the object.

$BC = 2\text{cm}$ and $QR = 8\text{cm}$

The scale factor of the enlargement from BC to $QR = \frac{8}{2}$

$= 4$

The height of the image is 4 times the length of the object.

The scale factors of the enlargements of the corresponding sides of the triangle are equal.

The angles of ΔPQR are also the same as the corresponding angles of ΔABC.

Thus, ΔPQR is an enlargement of ΔABC.

Scale factor = 4.

REMARK

$\angle CAB$ and $\angle RPQ$, $\angle ABC$ and $\angle PQR$, $\angle BCA$ and $\angle QRP$ are pairs of corresponding angles as they have the same relative positions in ΔABC and ΔPQR.

DISCUSS

Is ΔABC an enlargement of ΔDEF? If so, what is the scale factor?

Try It! 6

(a) Is ΔDEF an enlargement of ΔABC? If so, state the scale factor.

(b) Is ΔPQR an enlargement of ΔABC? If so, state the scale factor.

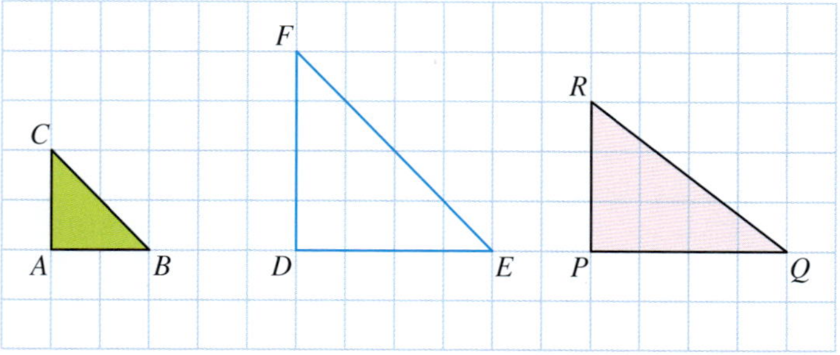

Example 7

Draw an enlargement of the given figure using a scale factor of 2.

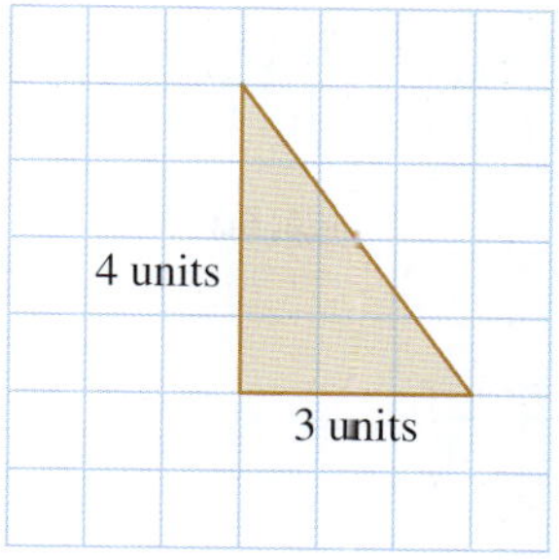

Solution

Since the scale factor is 2, all the lengths of the sides of the enlargement are 2 times the lengths of those in the original triangle.

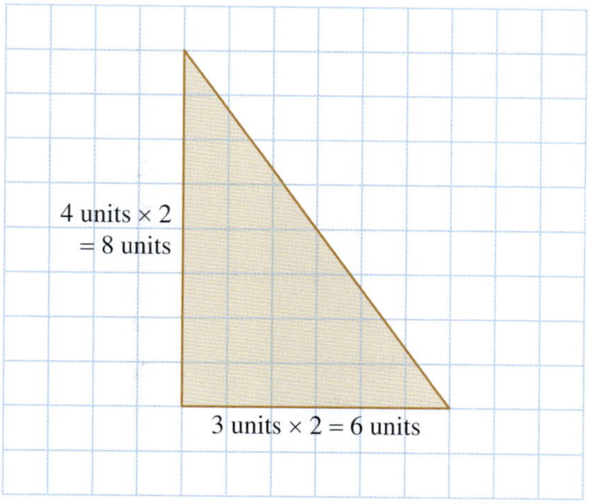

Try It! 7

Draw an enlargement of the given figure using a scale factor of 3.

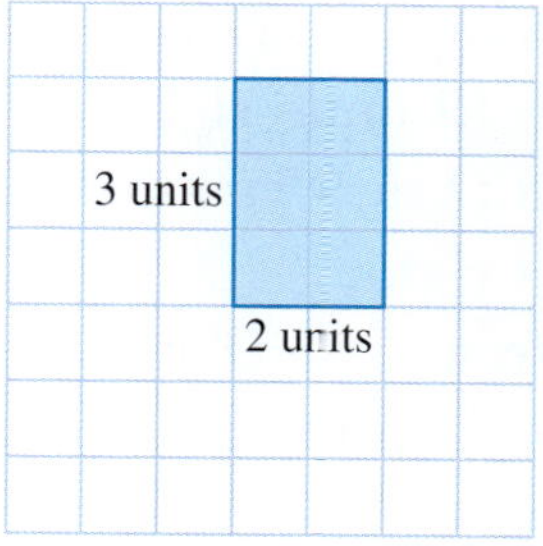

The image of an enlargement for a given scale factor can be drawn using a **centre of enlargement**. As well as all the lengths of the sides being multiplied by the scale factor, the distance from the centre of enlargement to each vertex must also be multiplied by the scale factor.

Example 8

Enlarge the quadrilateral $ABCD$ with a scale factor of 3, using the point O as the centre of enlargement.

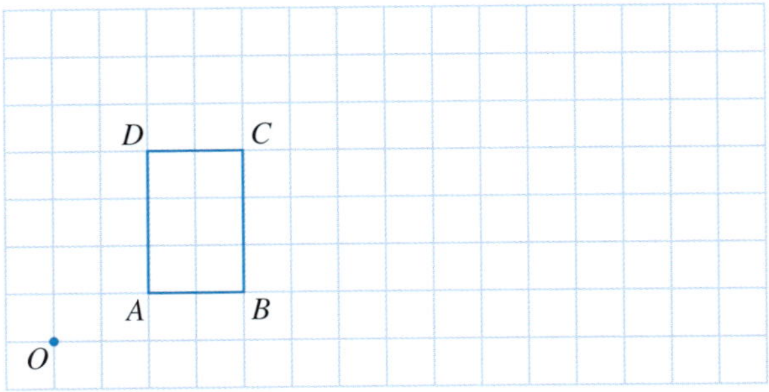

Solution

Multiply the vertical and horizontal distances from the centre of enlargement, O, to each vertex by the scale factor, 3.

To get from O to A you move
2 units right, 1 unit up.

So, to get from O to A' on the image you move
$2 \times 3 = 6$ units right, $1 \times 3 = 3$ units up.

To get from O to B you move
4 units right, 1 unit up.

So, to get from O to B' on the image you move
$4 \times 3 = 12$ units right, $1 \times 3 = 3$ units up.

To get from O to C you move
4 units right, 4 units up.

So, to get from O to C' on the image you move
$4 \times 3 = 12$ units right, $4 \times 3 = 12$ units up.

To get from O to D you move
2 units right, 4 units up.

So, to get from O to D' on the image you move
$2 \times 3 = 6$ units right, $4 \times 3 = 12$ units up.

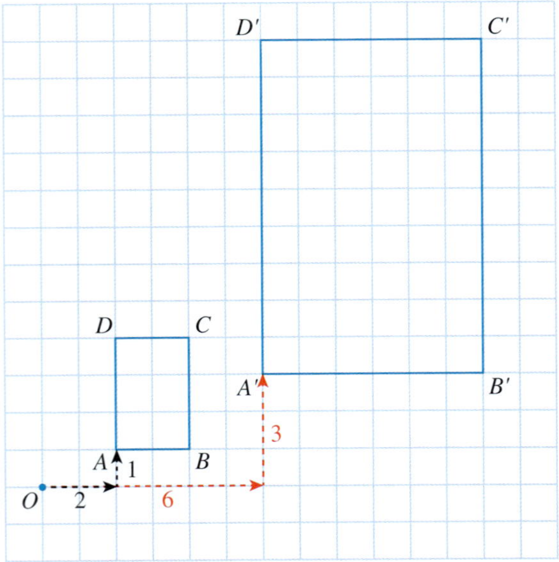

DISCUSS

Once you find the position of one of the vertices of the image, you can draw the rest of the image using the method in the Remark box for Example 9.

Try both methods. Which do you find easier?

Try It! 8

Enlarge the quadrilateral $ABCD$ with a scale factor of 2, using the point O as the centre of enlargement.

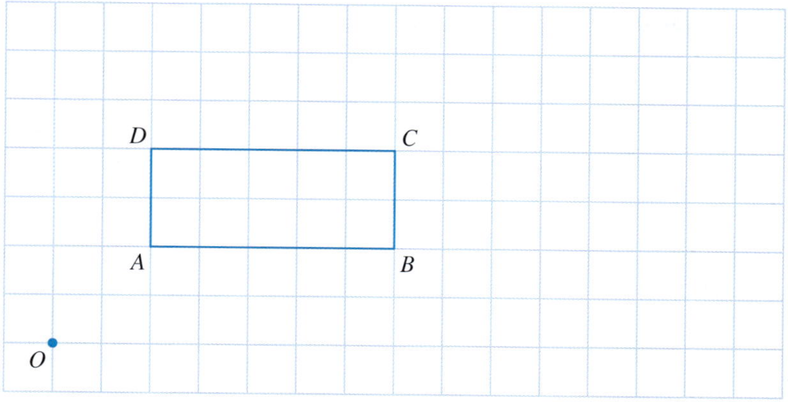

Example 9

Enlarge the triangle ABC with a scale factor of 3, using the point O as the centre of enlargement.

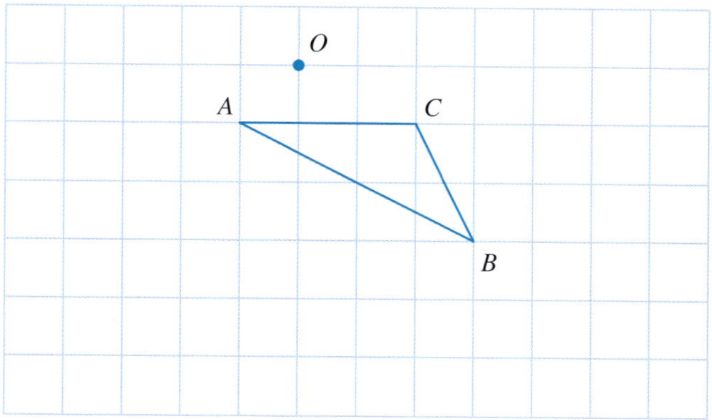

Solution

Multiply the vertical and horizontal distances from the centre of enlargement, O, to each vertex by the scale factor, 3.

To get from O to A you move

1 unit left, 1 unit down.

So, to get from O to A' on the image you move

$1 \times 3 = 3$ units left, $1 \times 3 = 3$ units down.

And so on.

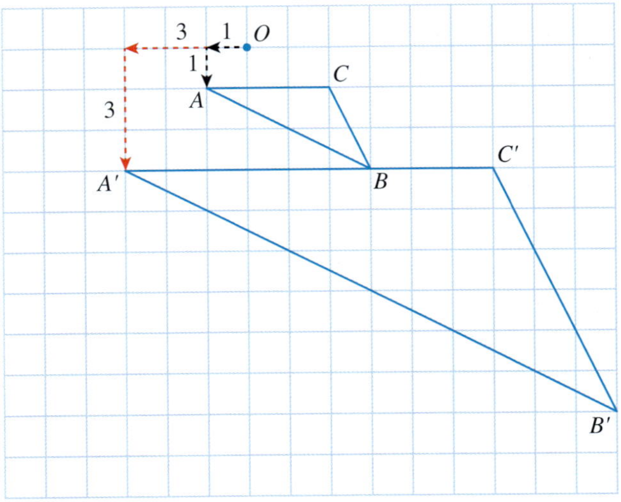

REMARK

Check your answer by counting squares, for example, to get from C to B on the object you move 1 unit right and 2 units down.
So, to get from C' to B' on the image you should move 3 units right and 6 units down since $C'B' = 3 \times CB$.

Try It! 9

Enlarge the triangle ABC with a scale factor of 2, using the point O as the centre of enlargement.

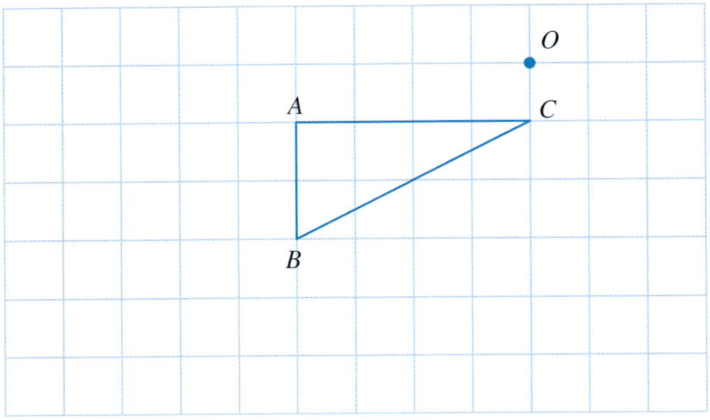

Example 10

Enlarge the quadrilateral $ABCD$ with a scale factor of $\frac{1}{2}$ using the point A as the centre of enlargement.

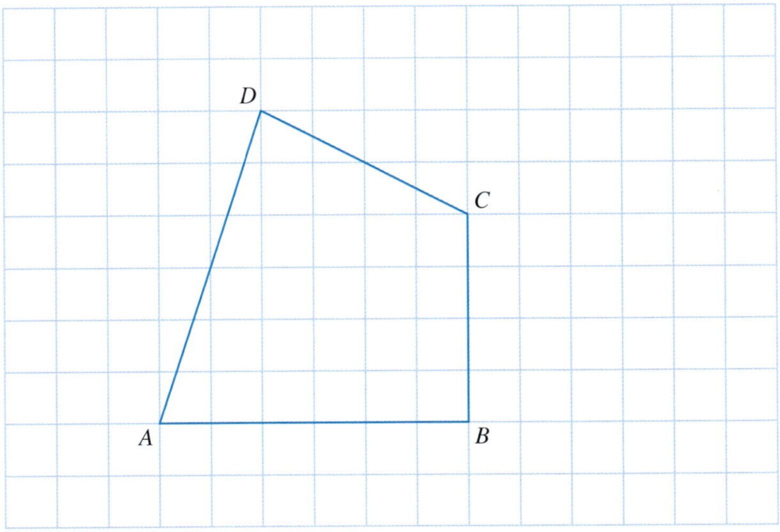

Solution Here, the centre of the enlargement is the vertex A on the object.

As the distance between A and itself, $AA = 0$, the image of A is A.

The scale factor is $\frac{1}{2}$.

To get from A to B you move 6 units right.
So, to get from A to B' on the image you move

$6 \times \frac{1}{2} = 3$ units right.

To get from A to C you move
6 units right, 4 units up.
So, to get from A to C' on the image you move

$6 \times \frac{1}{2} = 3$ units right, $4 \times \frac{1}{2} = 2$ units up.

To get from A to D you move
2 units right, 6 units up.
So, to get from A to D' on the image you move

$2 \times \frac{1}{2} = 1$ unit right, $6 \times \frac{1}{2} = 3$ units up.

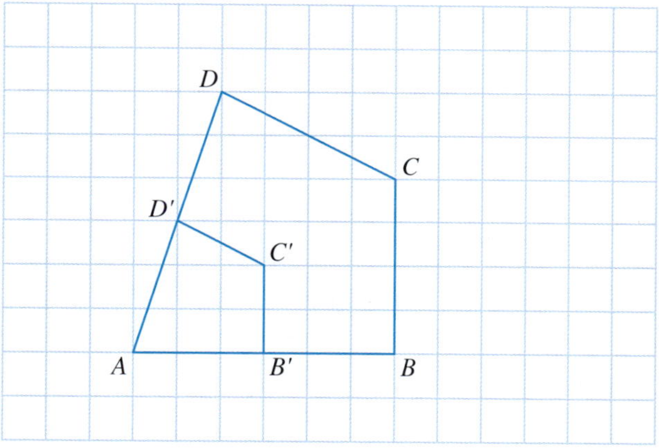

REMARK

When scale factor is a proper fraction, the image is smaller than the object. But the transformation is still called an enlargement.

DISCUSS

You might also see enlargements with a scale factor that is an improper fraction, for example $\frac{3}{2}$. What would the enlargement of $ABCD$ with scale factor $\frac{3}{2}$ look like?

Would it be bigger or smaller than $AB'C'D'$ and $ABCD$?

Try It! 10

Enlarge the quadrilateral $ABCD$ with a scale factor of $\frac{1}{2}$ using the point O as the centre of enlargement.

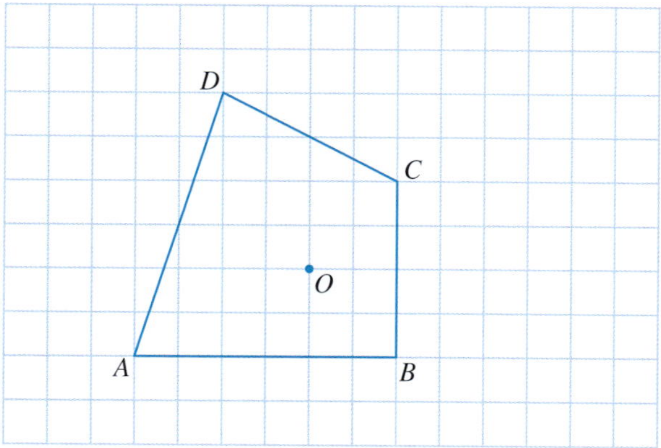

DISCUSS

What is the same and what is different about the image of Try It! 10 and the image of Example 10?

PRACTICE 9.3

LEVEL 1

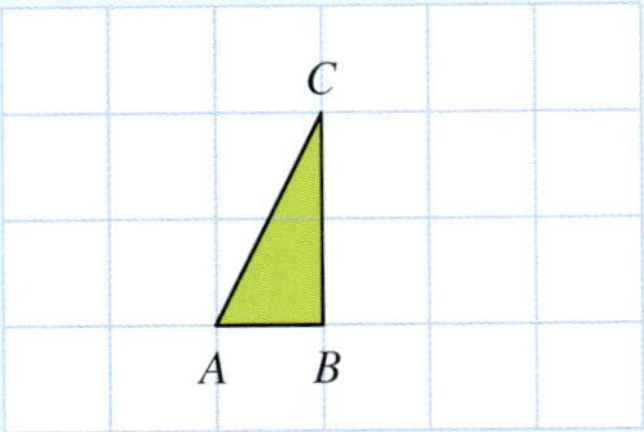

1. **(a)** Copy ΔABC and enlarge it with a scale factor of
   (i) 2, **(ii)** 3.
   (b) What is the same and what is different about the images in part **(a)**?

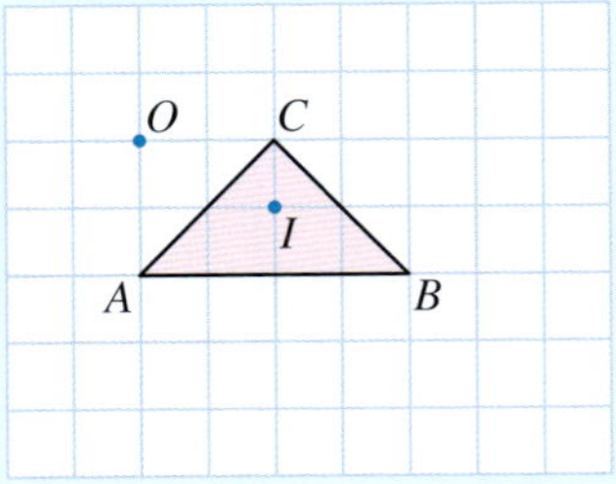

2. **(a)** Copy the diagram and enlarge ΔABC with a scale factor of 2 using
   (i) the point O as the centre of enlargement,
   (ii) the point I as the centre of enlargement.
   (b) What is the same and what is different about the images in part **(a)**?

3. Which triangle, ΔDEF or ΔPQR, is an enlargement of ΔABC? Explain why and state the scale factor of the enlargement.

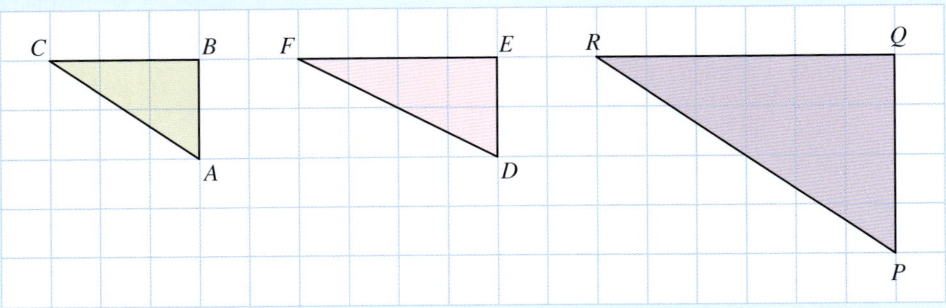

4. Which parallelogram, $EFGH$ or $PQRS$, is an enlargement of $ABCD$? State the scale factor of the enlargement.

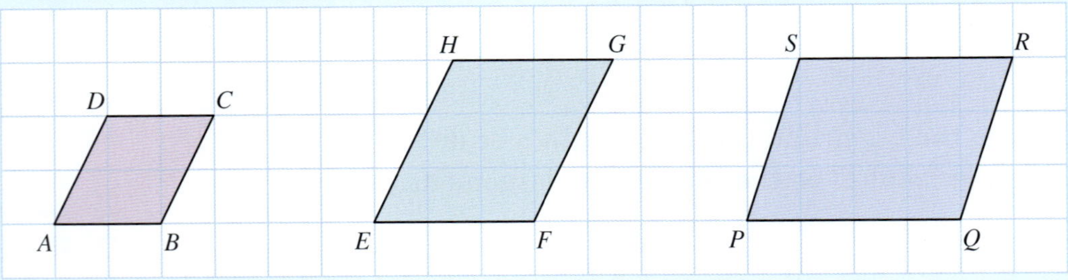

5. $ABCD$ is a square of sides 2 cm. $TXYZ$ is a rhombus of sides 3 cm. Is $TXYZ$ an enlargement of $ABCD$? Explain your answer.

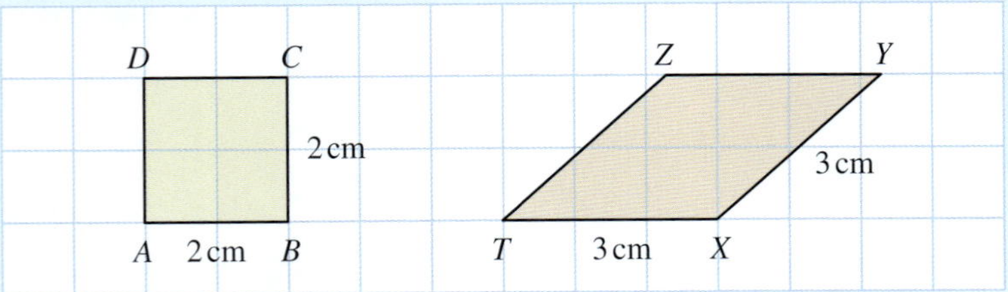

LEVEL 2

6. $ABCD$ is a rhombus. O is the point of intersection of its diagonals. Copy the diagram.
   (a) Enlarge $ABCD$ with a scale factor of 4 using the point C as the centre of enlargement.
   (b) Enlarge $ABCD$ with a scale factor of 4 using the point O as the centre of enlargement.

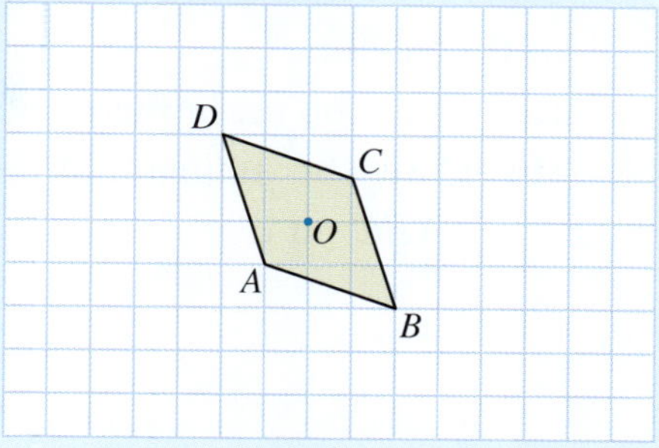

7. (a) Enlarge the quadrilateral $PQRS$ to its image $P'Q'R'S'$ using a scale factor of $\frac{1}{2}$.
   (b) Is $\angle Q'P'S'$ equal to 90°? Explain your answer.

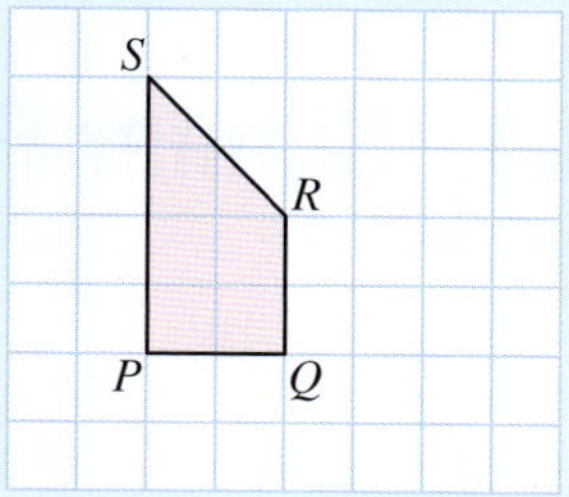

8. (a) Enlarge ΔABC with a scale factor of $\frac{1}{3}$ about
   (i) point O, (ii) point B.
   (b) What is the same and what is different about your images in part (a)?

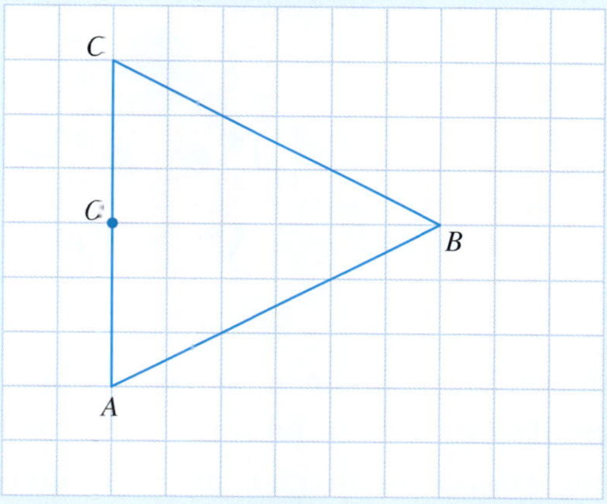

9. The shape $ABCD$ is enlarged. The image of $ABCD$ is $A'B'C'D'$.
   (a) What is the scale factor?
   (b) Which of the points, X, Y or Z, is the centre of enlargement?

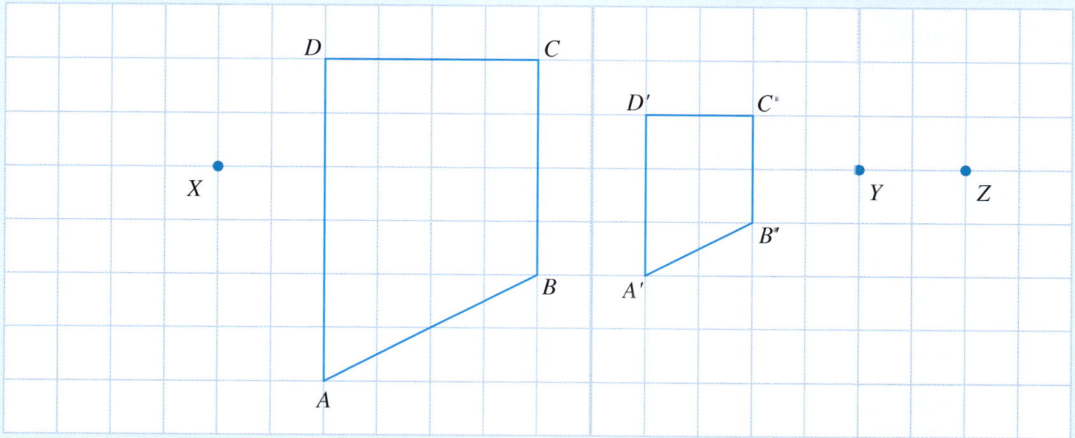

10. When $\triangle ABC$ is enlarged with the point O as the centre of enlargement, the point A' is the image of the vertex A.

(a) Find the scale factor of the enlargement.

(b) Copy the diagram and draw the image of $\triangle ABC$ on it.

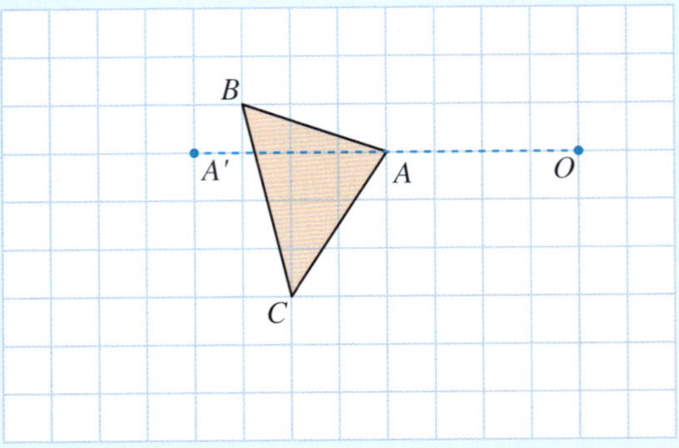

9.4 Similar Figures

A magnifying glass can be used to 'zoom in' on an insect. The image in the magnifying glass is the same shape as the object, but a different size. In other words, the image is an enlargement.

In the diagram, $\triangle ABC$ and $\triangle PQR$ are of the same shape but they are different sizes. You say that '$\triangle ABC$ is similar to $\triangle PQR$'. Note that the vertices in one triangle should correspond to the vertices in the other triangle. Therefore, you should **not** say '$\triangle ABC$ is similar to $\triangle QRP$' in this diagram or '$\triangle ABC$ is similar to $\triangle RPQ$'.

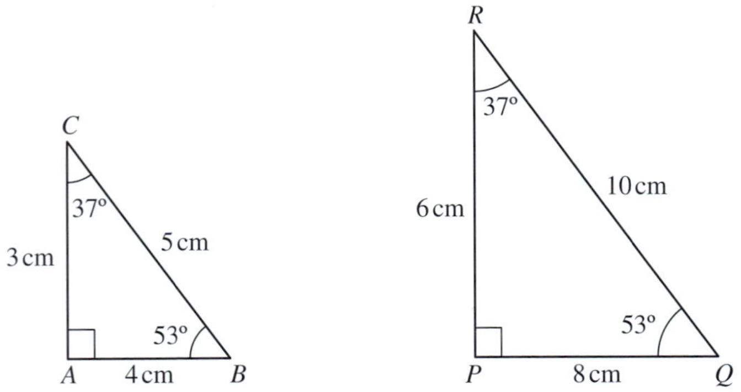

Observe that

$\angle ABC = \angle PQR = 53°$ $\quad \angle BCA = \angle QRP = 37°$ $\quad \angle CAB = \angle RPQ = 90°$

$PQ = AB \times 2$ $\quad QR = BC \times 2$ $\quad RP = CA \times 2$

That is, corresponding angles in both these triangles are equal and the scale factor of each pair of corresponding sides is 2.

In general, if two shapes are similar, then:

1. All their corresponding angles are equal.
2. The scale factors of their corresponding sides are equal.

CLASS ACTIVITY 6

Objective: To identify similar triangles/rectangles from cut-outs of triangles/rectangles and explain why they are similar.

1. **(a)** From observation, can you guess which pairs of triangles are similar?

(b) Trace and cut out the triangles.

(c) How can you verify that the triangles are similar? Explain your answer.

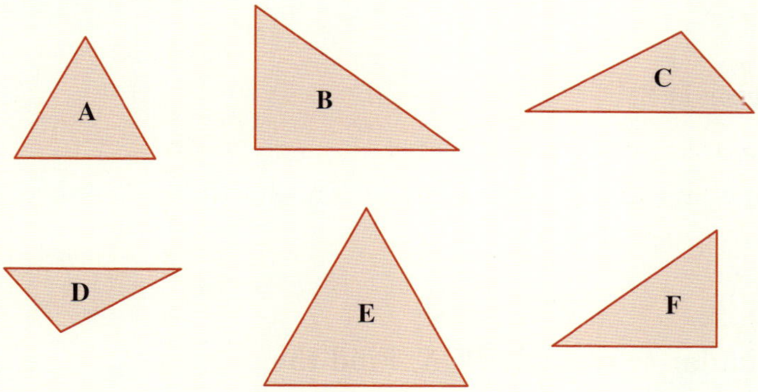

2. **(a)** Trace and cut out the rectangles.

(b) Identify the pairs of similar rectangles.

(c) Explain why they are similar.

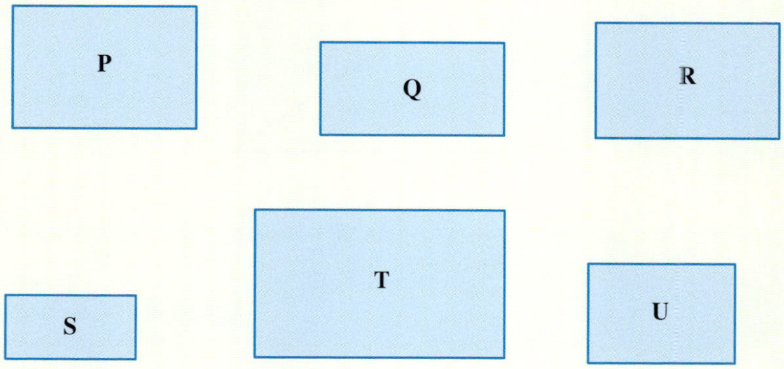

Example 11

The rectangular playground, $ABCD$, is similar to the rectangular playing field, $PQRS$. Find the length of PQ.

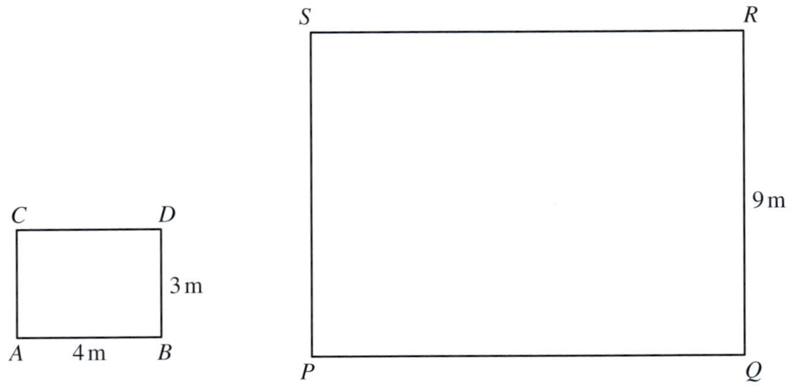

Solution

The rectangles are similar, so one must be an enlargement of the other. You need to find the scale factor of the enlargement to find the missing length.

$$\text{Scale factor} = \frac{\text{length of a side of the image}}{\text{length of the corresponding side of the object}}$$

$$= \frac{QR}{BD}$$

$$= \frac{9}{3}$$

$$= 3$$

Thus, the scale factor is 3.

Therefore,

$$PQ = AB \times 3$$

$$= 4 \times 3$$

$$= 12\,\text{m}$$

Try It! 11

Triangle ABC is similar to triangle PQR. Find the length of PQ.

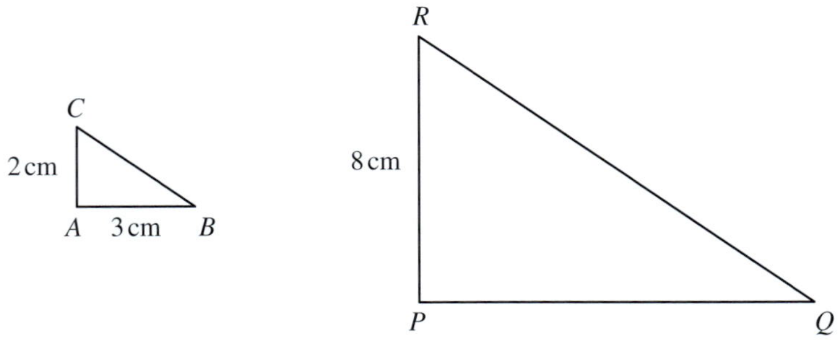

Example 12

The quadrilaterals *ABCD* and *PQRS* are similar. Find the values of x and y.

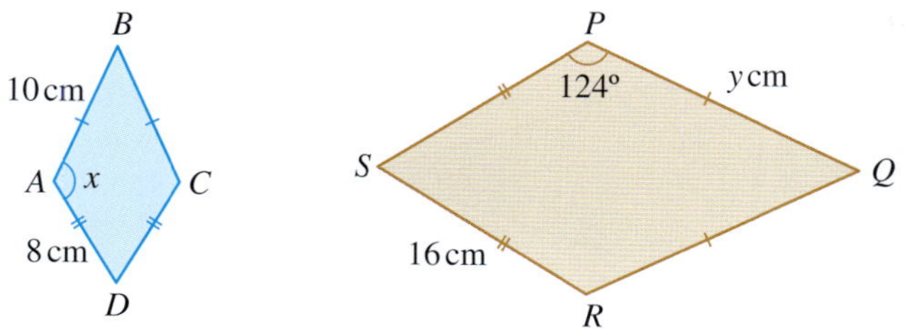

Solution

First draw *ABCD* in the same orientation as *PQRS*.

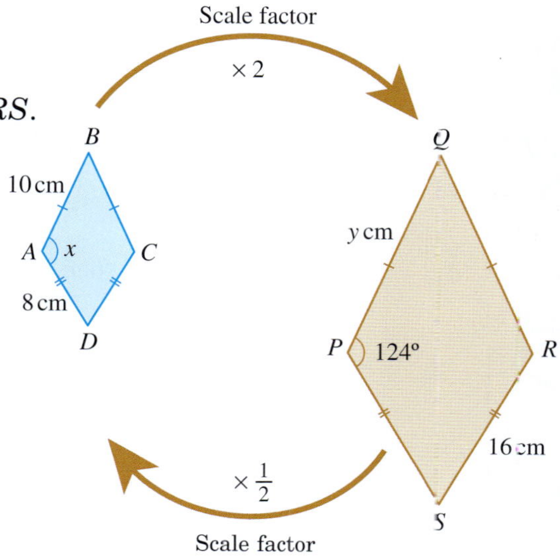

ABCD is similar to *PQRS*.

$\angle x = \angle SPQ$ (Corresponding angles of similar figures are equal.)

$= 124°$

So, $x = 124$

SR and *DC* are corresponding sides. $DC = DA = 8$ cm.

$$\text{Scale factor} = \frac{\text{length of a side of the image}}{\text{length of the corresponding side of the object}}$$

$$= \frac{SR}{DC}$$

$$= \frac{16}{8}$$

$$= 2$$

Thus, the scale factor from small quadrilateral to large quadrilateral is 2.

$PQ = AB \times 2$

$= 10 \times 2$

$= 20$ cm

$\therefore y = 20$

DISCUSS

How do you know that the scale factor of the large quadrilateral to the small quadrilateral is $\frac{1}{2}$?

Try It! 12

The quadrilaterals $ABCD$ and $PQRS$ are similar. Find the values of x and y.

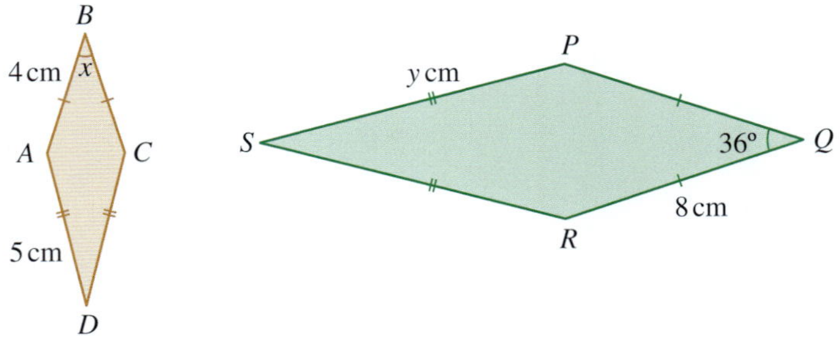

Example 13

Triangle ABC is similar to triangle PQR. Find the values of x and y.

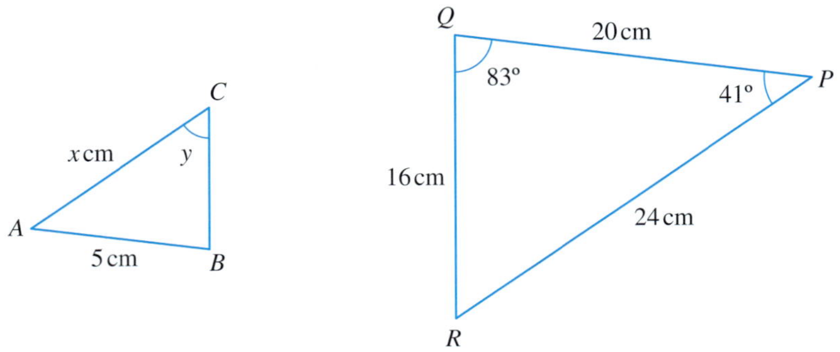

Solution Draw ΔPQR in the same orientation as ΔABC.

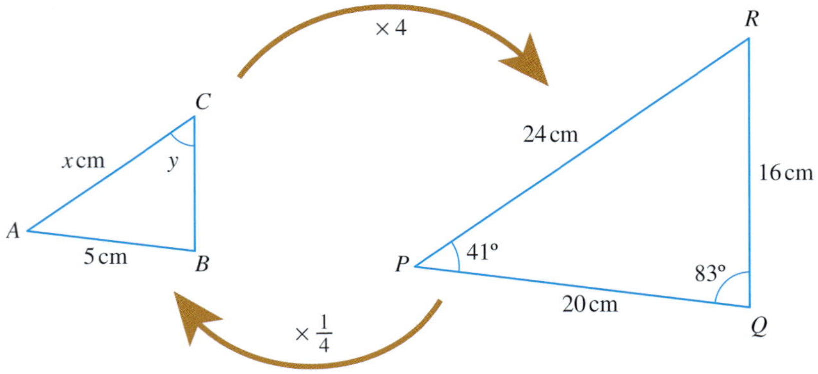

PQ and AB are corresponding sides.

$$\text{Scale factor} = \frac{\text{length of a side of the image}}{\text{length of the corresponding side of the object}}$$

$$= \frac{PQ}{AB}$$

$$= \frac{20}{5}$$

$$= 4$$

Thus, the scale factor from the small triangle to the big triangle is 4.

Therefore,

$AC \times 4 = PR$

$AC \times 4 = 24$

$AC = 24 \div 4$

$= 6\,\text{cm}$

So, $x = 6$

$41° + 83° + \angle PRQ = 180°$ (Angles in a triangle add up to 180°.)

$124° + \angle PRQ = 180°$

$\angle PRQ = 180° - 124°$

$= 56°$

$\angle ACB = \angle PRQ = 56°$ (Corresponding angles of similar triangles are equal.)

So, $y = 56$

REMARK

To get from the small triangle to the large triangle you multiply by a scale factor of 4 and to get from the large triangle to the small triangle you multiply by $\frac{1}{4}$. Remember that multiplying by $\frac{1}{4}$ is the same as dividing by 4, so you could also work out $AC = PR \div 4$ or $AC = PR \times \frac{1}{4}$.

Try It! 13

Figure $ABCD$ is similar to figure $PQRS$. Find the values of x and y.

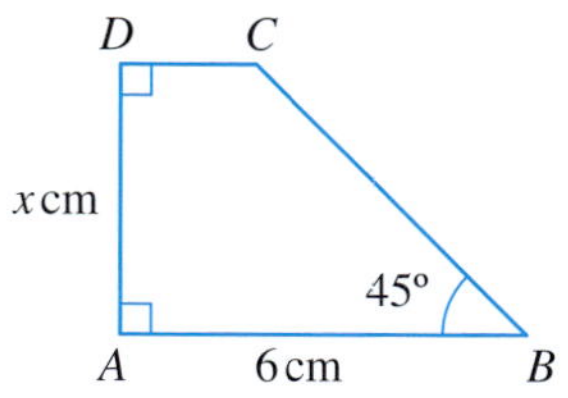

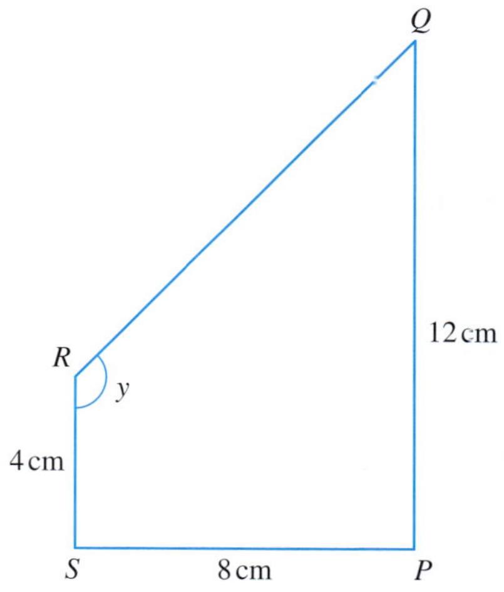

Example 14

In the diagram, triangle PBC is similar to triangle PQR. Find the value of x.

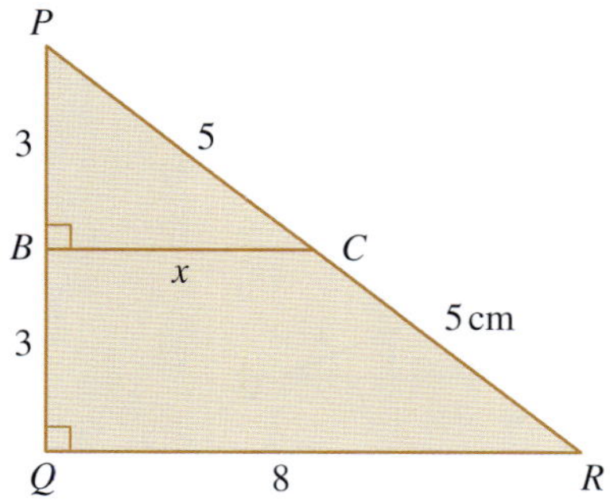

Solution First draw as two separate triangles:

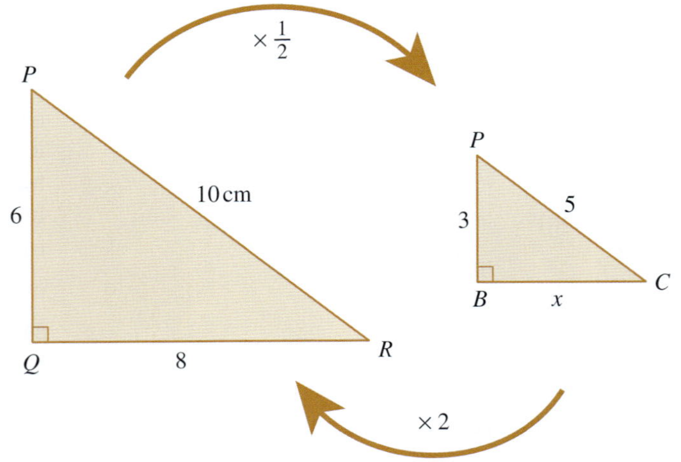

PQ and PB are corresponding sides.

$$\text{Scale factor} = \frac{\text{length of a side of the image}}{\text{length of the corresponding side of the object}}$$
$$= \frac{PQ}{PB}$$
$$= \frac{6}{3}$$
$$= 2$$

Thus, the scale factor from small triangle to big triangle is 2.

Therefore,

$$BC \times 2 = QR$$
$$BC \times 2 = 8$$
$$BC = 8 \div 2$$
$$= 4\,\text{cm}$$

So, $x = 4$

REMARK

In the same way as Example 13, you could alternatively work out $BC = QR \times \frac{1}{2}$.

Try It! 14

In the diagram, triangle PBC is similar to triangle PQR. Find the value of x.

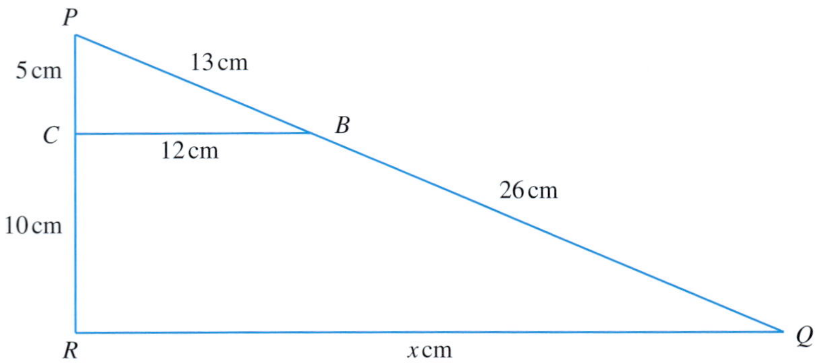

PRACTICE 9.4

LEVEL 1

1. Name the pairs of similar figures.

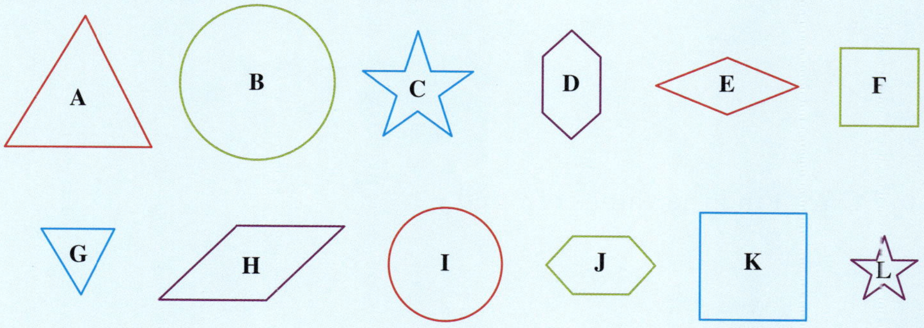

2. Which rectangle is similar to *ABCD*? Explain your answer.

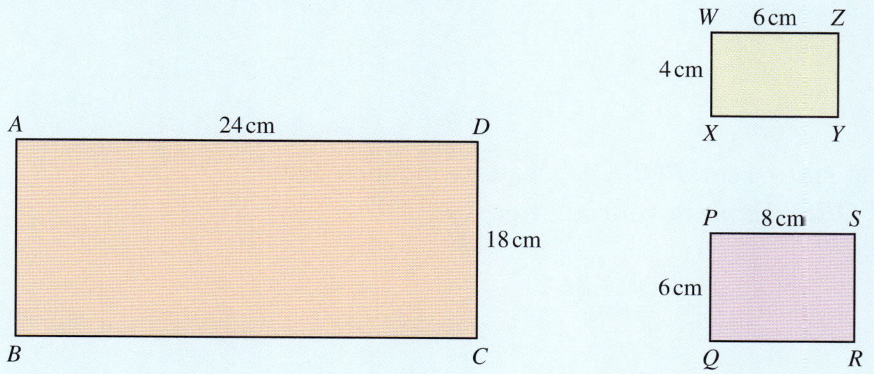

3. **(a)** Rectangle *WZYX* is similar to rectangle *PQRS*. Find the length of *PQ*.

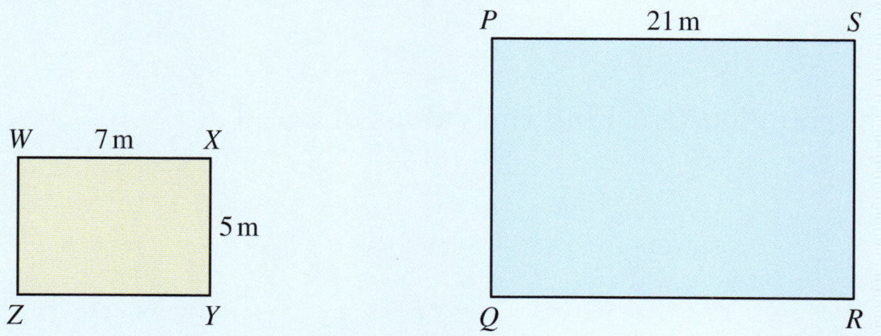

(b) Triangle *ABC* is similar to triangle *LMN*. Find the length of *LM*.

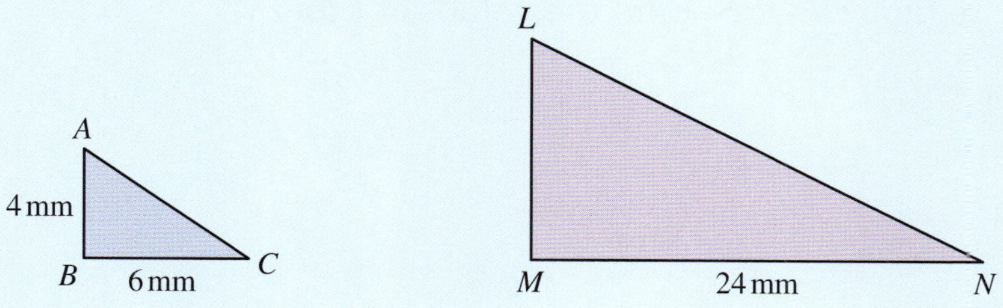

4. Triangle ABC is similar to triangle PQR. Find the values of x and y.

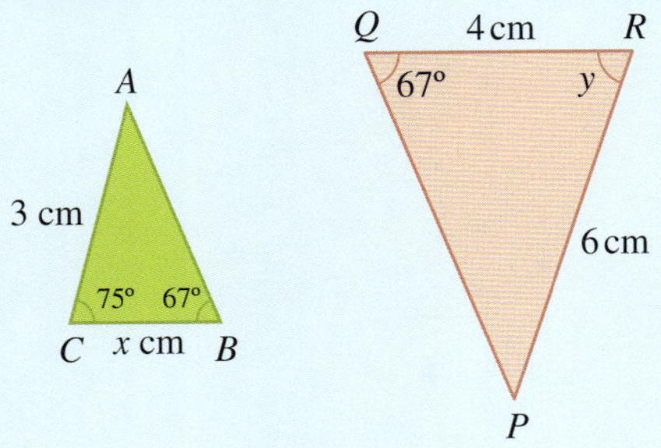

5. $ABCD$ is similar to $PQRS$. Find the values of x and y.

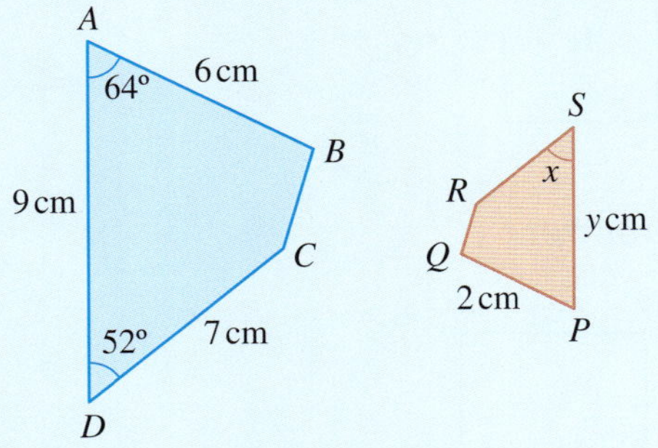

6. $ABCD$ is a rhombus of sides 4 cm. $PQRS$ is a square of sides 3 cm. Is $ABCD$ similar to $PQRS$? Explain your answer.

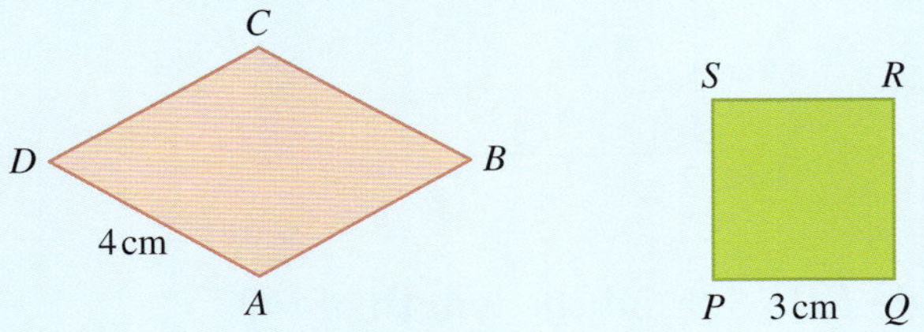

LEVEL 2

7. Triangle ABC is similar to triangle PQR. Find the values of x and y.

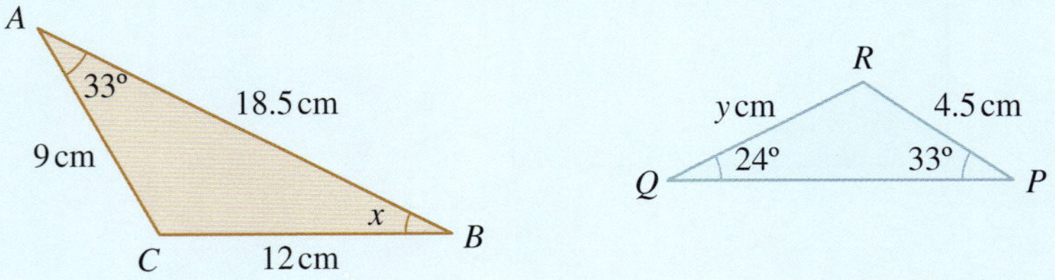

8. Figure $ABCD$ is similar to figure $PQRS$. Find the values of x and y.

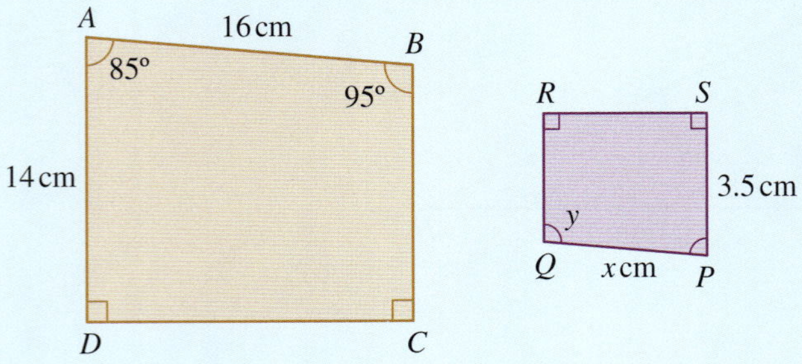

9. A man, AB, of 2 m tall casts a shadow BC of 3 m on horizontal ground HK. At the same time, a tree, TP, casts a shadow PQ of 6 m. ΔABC is similar to ΔTPQ. Find the height of the tree.

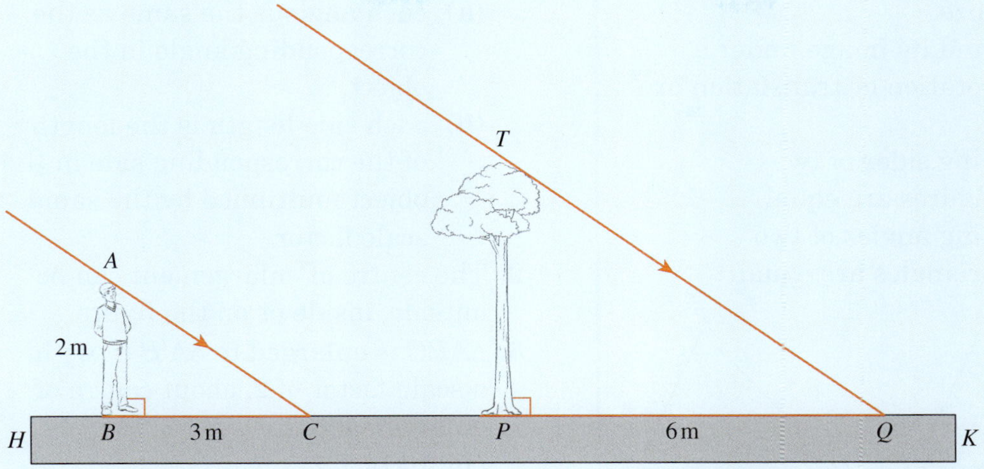

10. $ABCDE$ is a regular pentagon and $AB = 2$ cm.

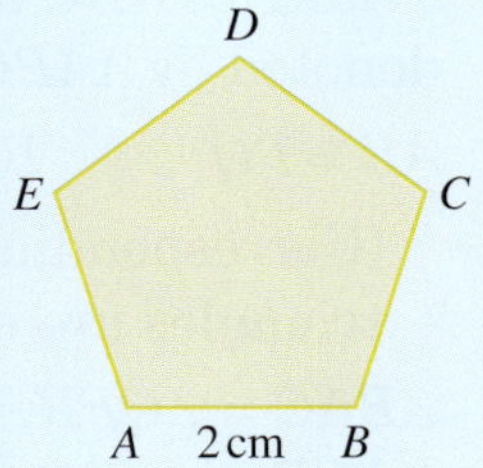

PROBLEM SOLVING

(a) Find the size of $\angle ABC$.

(b) Enlarge the pentagon with a scale factor of 2, using the point A as the centre of enlargement, to its image $AB'C'D'E'$.

(c) Are the pentagons $ABCDE$ and $AB'C'D'E'$ similar? Explain your answer.

REVIEW

Transformation

1. Reflection **2.** Rotation **3.** Translation

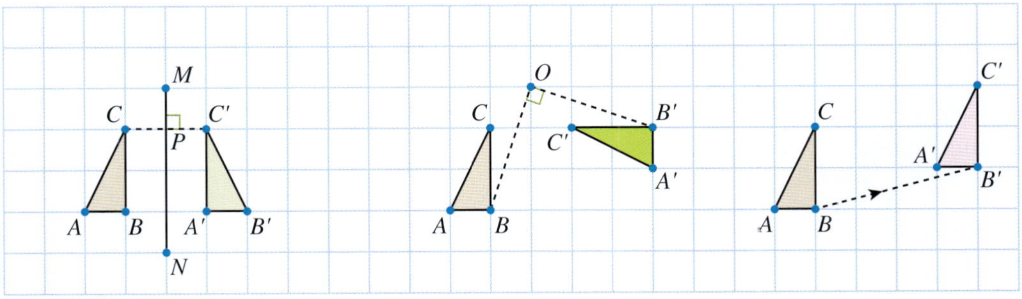

Reflect about the line MN.
$CC' \perp MN$
$CP = C'P$

Rotate 90° anticlockwise about O.
$\angle BOB' = 90°$

Translate 4 units to the right and 1 unit upwards.

Congruence

1. Two figures are congruent to each other if they have exactly the same shape and size.
2. The object and its image under a reflection, rotation or translation are congruent.
3. Corresponding sides of two congruent figures are equal.
4. Corresponding angles of two congruent triangles are equal.

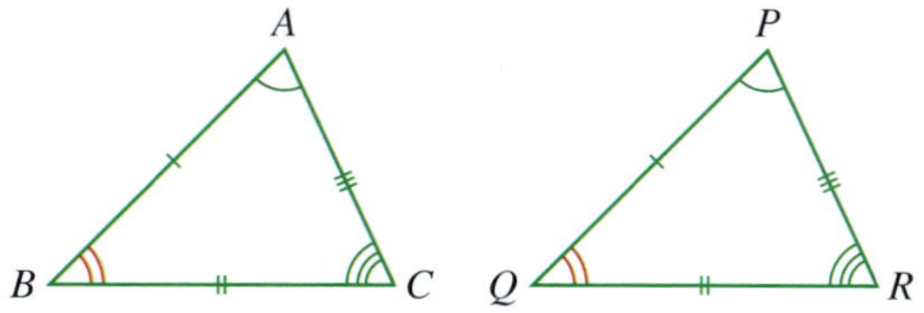

Triangles ABC and PQR are congruent, denoted by $\Delta ABC \equiv \Delta PQR$. This gives

$AB = PQ$, $BC = QR$, $CA = RP$,

(Corresponding sides of congruent triangles are equal.)

$\angle BAC = \angle QPR$, $\angle ABC = \angle PQR$ and $\angle ACB = \angle PRQ$.

(Corresponding angles of congruent triangles are equal.)

Enlargement and Scale Factor

1. If an object is enlarged then in the image
   (a) each angle is the same as the corresponding angle in the object,
   (b) each side length is the length of the corresponding side in the object multiplied by the same scale factor.
2. The centre of enlargement can be outside, inside or on the figure.
3. ΔABC is enlarged to $\Delta A'B'C'$ with a scale factor of 2, about centre of enlargement O.

   $OA' = OA \times 2$

   $OB' = OB \times 2$

   $OC' = OC \times 2$

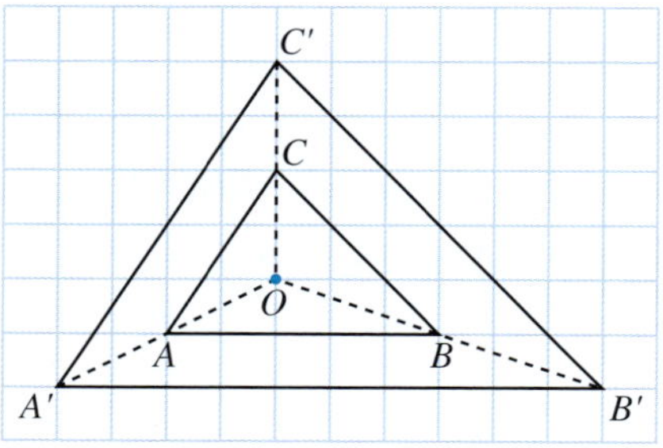

Similar Figures

1. Corresponding angles of similar figures are equal.
2. The scale factors of corresponding sides of similar figures are equal.
3. ΔABC is similar to ΔPQR,

   $\angle CAB = \angle RPQ$, $\angle ABC = \angle PQR$ and $\angle BCA = \angle QRP$.

   $PQ = AB \times 2$

   $QR = BC \times 2$

   $RP = CA \times 2$

   The scale factor is 2.

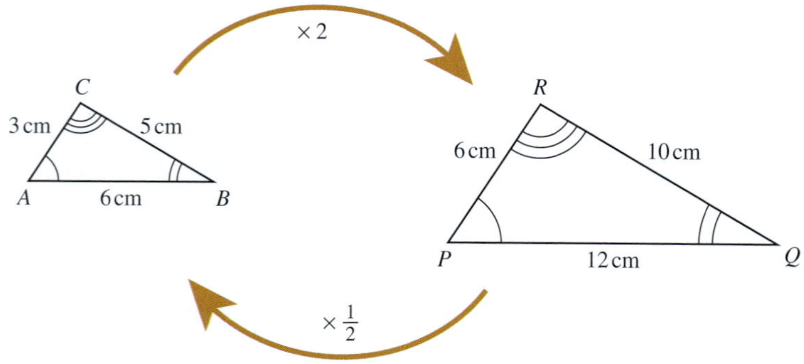

CHALLENGE 9

The diagram shows a playground. The quadrilaterals *ABCD* and *ADEF* are similar.

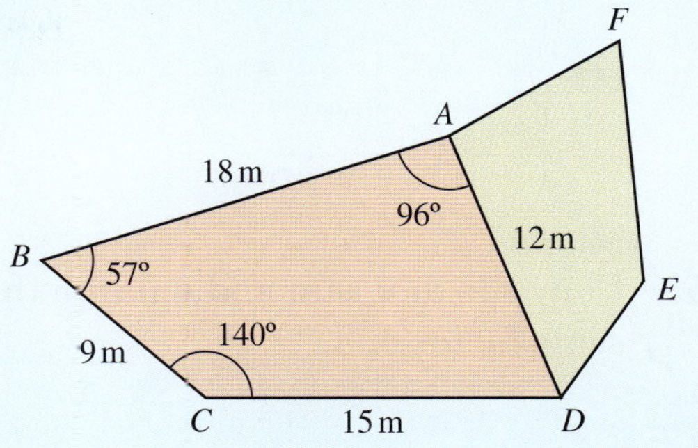

(a) Which type of transformation will change the orientation of the quadrilateral *ADEF* to be the same as *ABCD*?

(b) Find $\angle CDE$.

(c) Find the lengths of *DE*, *EF* and *FA*.

REVISION EXERCISE 9

1. Copy the diagram.

(a) Reflect $\triangle ABC$ about the line *TX*.

(b) Reflect $\triangle ABC$ about the line *YZ*.

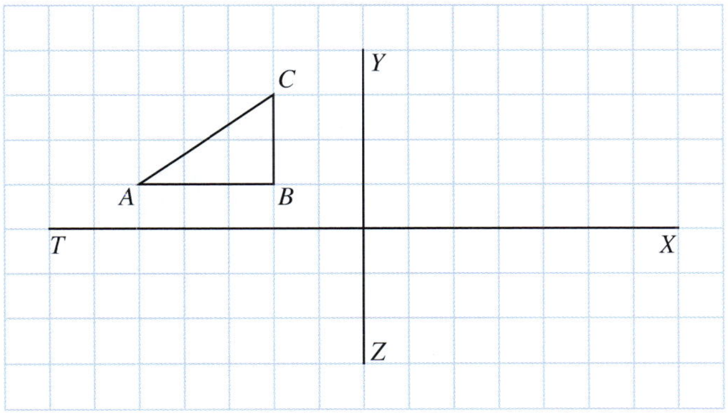

2. Copy the diagram.

(a) Rotate *ABCD* 90° anticlockwise about *A*.

(b) Rotate *ABCD* 180° clockwise about *O*.

(c) Translate *ABCD* 5 units to the right and 1 unit upwards.

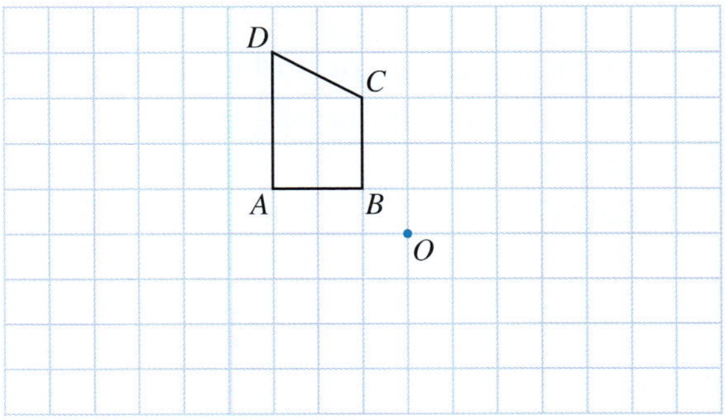

3. Given that the triangular tiles *ABC* and *PQR* are congruent, find the values of *x* and *y*.

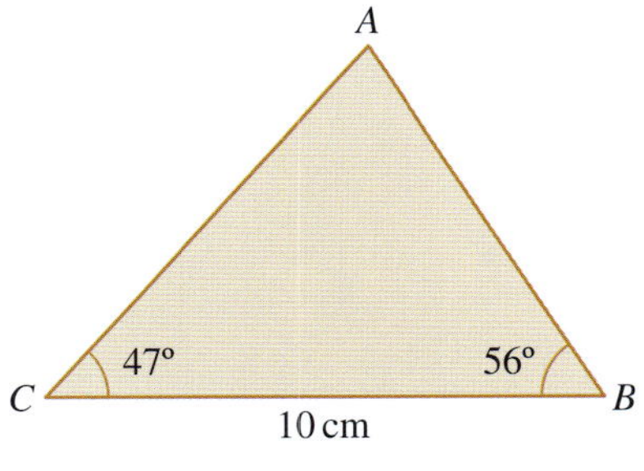

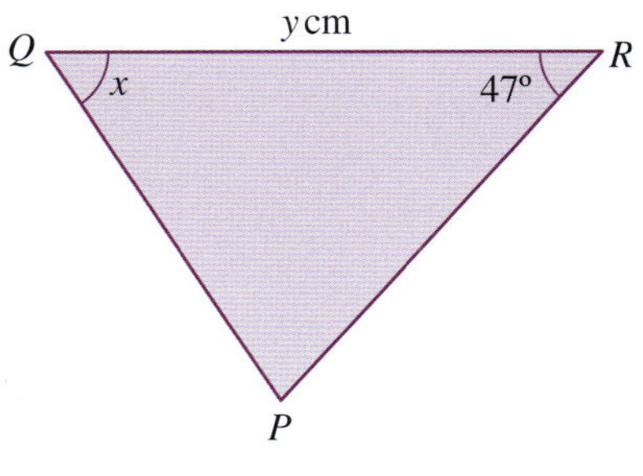

4. Given that the quadrilaterals $ABCD$ and $PQRS$ are congruent, find the values of x and y.

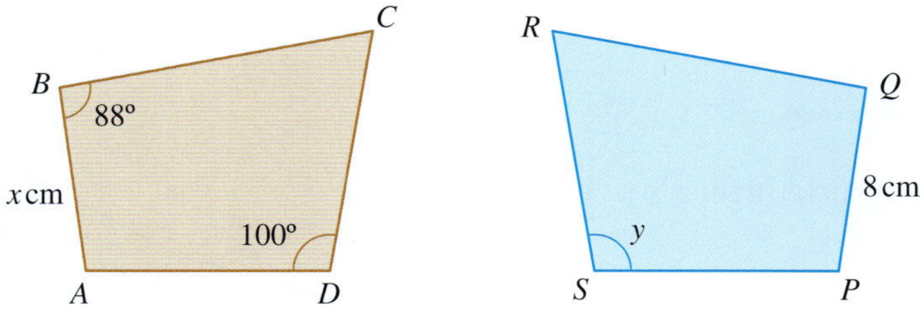

5. Copy the diagram and enlarge the quadrilateral $ABCD$ using a scale factor of 3.

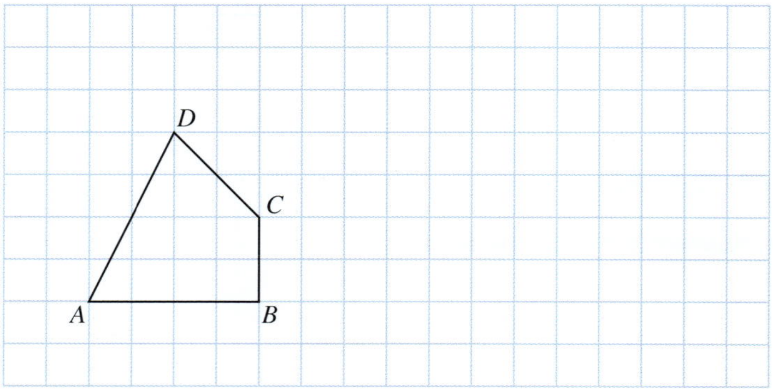

6. Copy the diagram and enlarge the triangle LMN with a scale factor of 2 using centre of enlargement
(a) L,
(b) O,
(c) P.

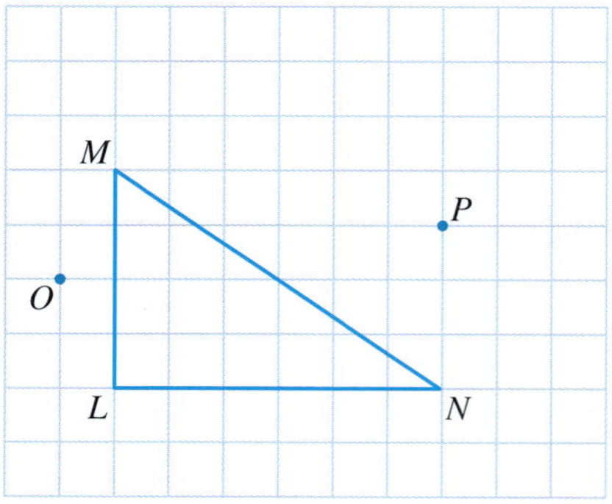

7. Copy the diagram and enlarge the quadrilateral $WXYZ$ with a scale factor of $\frac{1}{2}$ using centre of enlargement
(a) X,
(b) O.

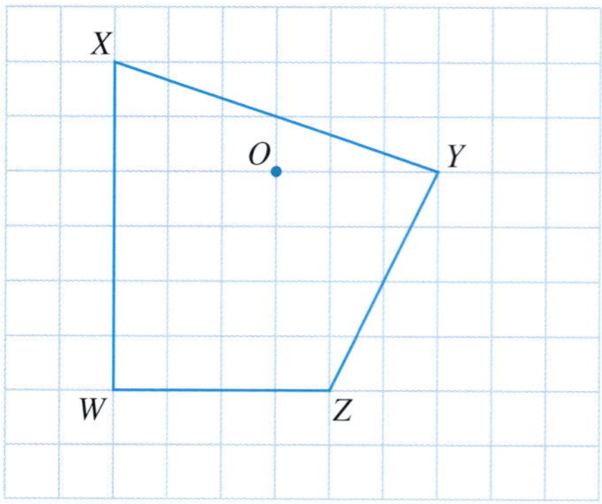

8. Given that each pair of figures are similar, find the value of x in each part. You may use a calculator.

(a)

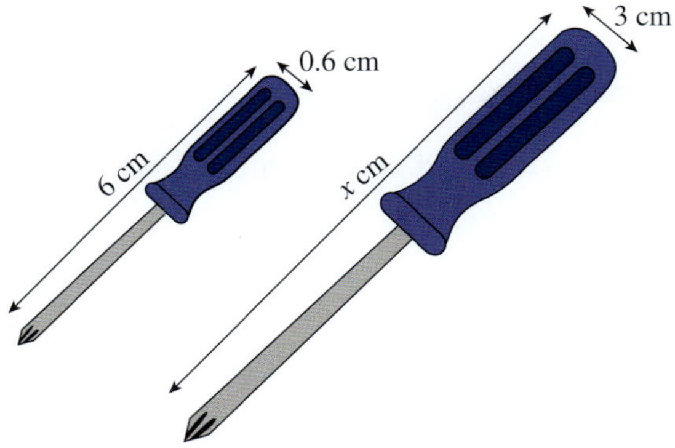

(b)

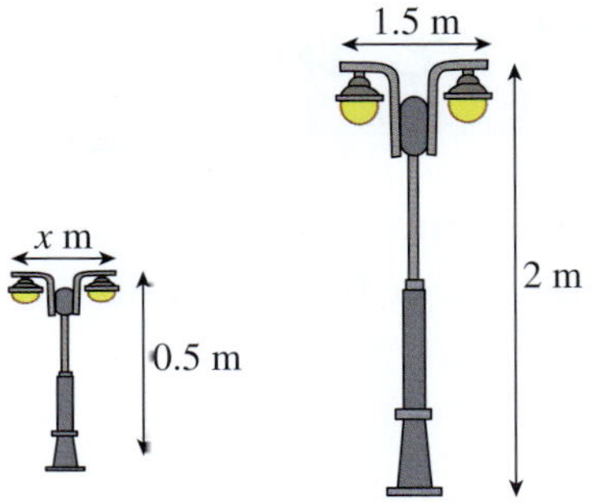

9. When a triangle is rotated 90° clockwise about the point O, the image is triangle $A'B'C'$ as shown in the diagram.

(a) Copy the diagram and draw the triangle ABC.

(b) Are ΔABC and $\Delta A'B'C'$ congruent? Explain your answer.

(c) Translate ΔABC 4 units to the left and 2 units downwards.

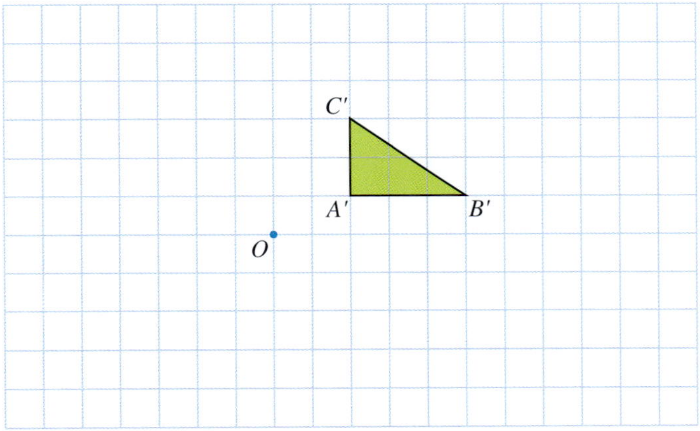

10. When a triangle ABC is enlarged with a scale factor of 2 using the point O as the centre of enlargement, the image is triangle $A'B'C'$ as shown on the diagram.

(a) Copy the diagram and draw the triangle ABC on it.

(b) If $A'C' = 5.4\,\text{cm}$, find the length of AC.

(c) If $\angle B'A'C' = 57°$ and $\angle A'C'B' = 59°$, find $\angle ABC$.

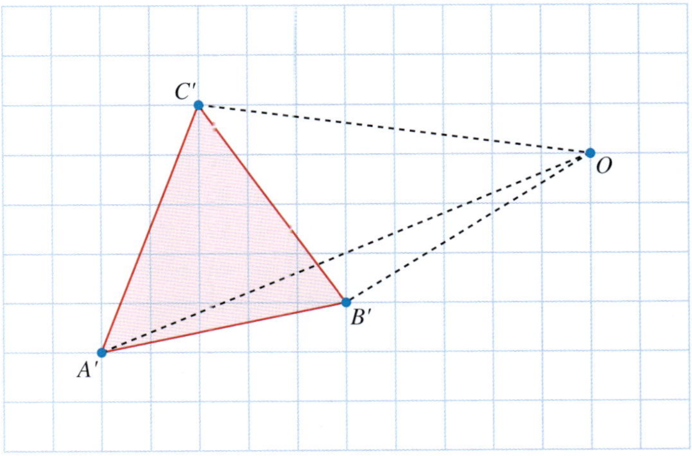

Write in Your Journal

Give examples of reflection, translation, rotation and enlargement from your other subjects or from real life.

INTEGRATED EXAMPLES AND REVIEW EXERCISE 2

Integrated Examples

Example 1 An American tourist drives at a constant speed v km/h along a straight road from town P to town Q. The time taken is t hours.

(a) Show that v and t are in inverse proportion.

(b) If they travel at a speed of 60 km/h, the time taken is 3 hours. Find the time taken if the speed they travel at is 90 km/h.

(c) The fuel consumption rate of the car is 8 litres per 100 km. Assume the price rate of the petrol is £1.25 per litre and the exchange rate is £1 = USD1.35. Use a calculator to find the price of the petrol in US dollars (USD) for the journey, to two decimal places.

Solution

(a) Let D km be the distance from town P to town Q along the road.

Then $v = \frac{D}{t}$ speed = $\frac{\text{distance}}{\text{time taken}}$

The distance, D, between the towns is fixed. Therefore, since D is a constant, v and t are in inverse proportion.

(b) At 60 km/h,

distance driven by tourist = 60×3

= 180 km

At 90 km/h,

time to travel 180 km = $\frac{180}{90}$

= 2 hours

Alternatively, you can use a table:

Speed (km/h)	Time (h)
60	3
30	6
90	2

(Speed: 60 → 30 ÷ 2, 30 → 90 × 3; Time: 3 → 6 × 2, 6 → 2 ÷ 3)

The required time taken is 2 hours.

REMARK

You can show the relationship between speed, distance and time in a factor tree.

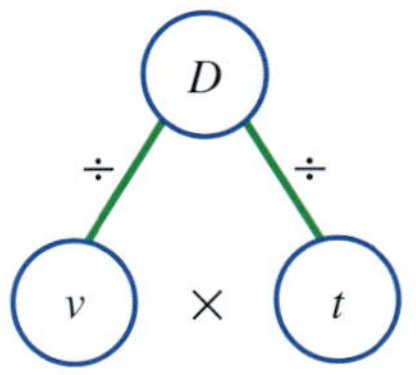

DISCUSS

Can you describe the relationship between

(a) the distance travelled and the volume of petrol required,

(b) price of petrol in GBP and price of petrol in USD?

(c) Using a table:

	Petrol (litres)	Distance (km)	
	8	100	
$\div 5$	1.6	20	$\div 5$
$\times 9$	14.4	180	$\times 9$

Amount of petrol to travel 20 km $= 8 \div 5$
$= 1.6$ litres

Amount of petrol for the journey $= 1.6 \times 9$
$= 14.4$ litres

Price of the petrol $= £1.25 \times 14.4$
$= £18$

Using a table:

	GBP	USD	
	1	1.35	
$\times 18$	18	24.3	$\times 18$

Price of the petrol $= 24.30$ USD

DISCUSS

Why did you $\div 5$ first in the table?

REMARK

Why do you give the answer as 24.30 USD instead of 24.3 USD?

Try It! 1

A French tourist drives at a constant speed v km/h along a motorway. The distance travelled is D km in t hours.

(a) Show that D and t are in direct proportion.

(b) The time taken for a journey of 240 km is 3 hours. Find the time taken for a journey of 320 km at the same speed.

(c) The fuel consumption rate of the car is 7.5 litres per 100 km. Assume the price rate of the petrol is £1.30 per litre and the exchange rate is £1 = EUR1.20. Use a calculator to find the price of the petrol in Euros (EUR) for the journey of 320 km, to two decimal places.

Example 2

Let n be the number of sides of a regular polygon and y be the size of an interior angle of the regular polygon.

(a) Complete the table.

n	4	5	8
y	90		

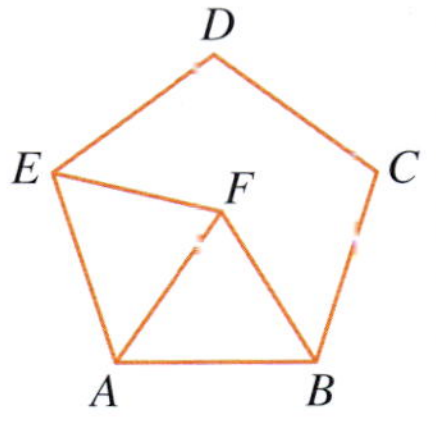

(b) Are n and y in direct proportion? Explain your answer.

(c) $ABCDE$ is a regular pentagon. ABF is an equilateral triangle. Find $\angle AEF$.

Solution

(a) Angle sum of a pentagon $= (5 - 2) \times 180°$

(Angles of an n-gon add up to $(n - 2) \times 180°$.)

$= 540°$

Interior angle of a regular pentagon $= 540° \div 5$

$= 108°$

Similarly,

angle sum of an octagon $= (8 - 2) \times 180°$

$= 1080°$

Interior angle of a regular octagon $= 1080° \div 8$

$= 135°$

$\therefore$ the completed table is:

n	4	5	8
y	90	108	135

(b)

n	4	5	8
y	90	108	135

If n and y were in direct proportion then when the value of n doubles from 4 to 8, the value of y should double from 90 to 180. This is not the case. Hence, n and y are **not** in direct proportion.

(c) $\angle x = 60°$

(Angles of an equilateral triangle are equal.)

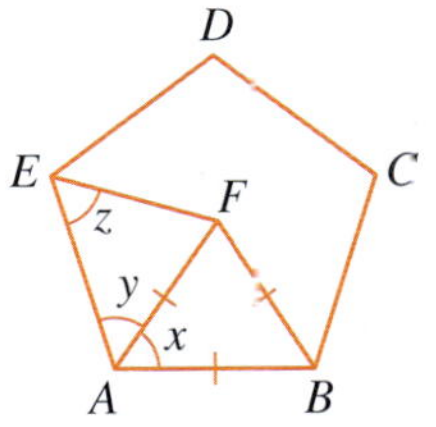

$\angle x + \angle y = 108°$

(Interior angle of a regular pentagon.)

$\angle y = 108° - 60°$

$= 48°$

$AE = AB$ (Sides of a regular pentagon.)

$AF = AB$ (Sides of an equilateral triangle.)

$\therefore AE = AF$

$\angle z = \angle AFE$ (Base angles of an isosceles triangle are equal.)

$\angle y + \angle z + \angle AFE = 180°$ (Angles in a triangle add up to 180°.)

$48° + \angle z + \angle z = 180°$

$2\angle z = 180° - 48°$

$2\angle z = 132°$

$\therefore \quad \angle z = 66°$

So, $\quad \angle AEF = 66°$

Try It! 2

Let n be the number of sides of a polygon and S be the sum of the interior angles of the polygon.

(a) Copy and complete the table.

n	3	6	10
S	180		

(b) Are n and S in direct proportion? Explain your answer.

(c) $ABCDEF$ is a regular hexagon. $ABGH$ is a square. Find $\angle BCG$.

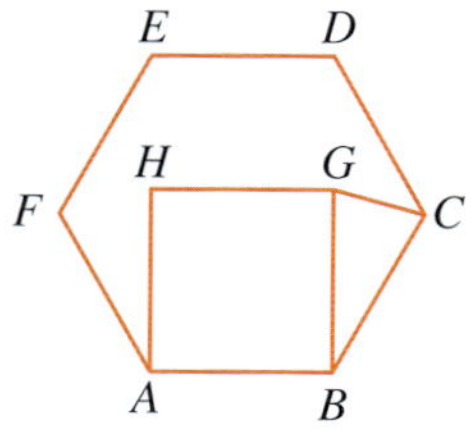

REMARK

Remember to state all your reasoning for part **(c)**.

Example 3

The diagram shows a rhombus $ABCD$.

(a) Construct the angle bisector of $\angle BAD$ using a pair of compasses and a ruler.

(b) What can you say about the angle bisector in part **(a)**?

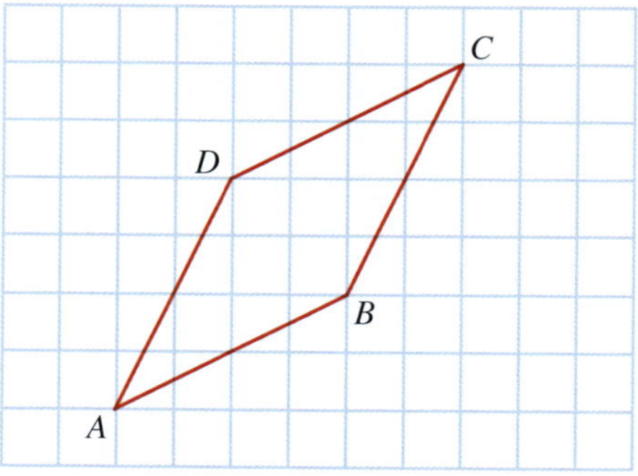

(c) Is ΔABC congruent to ΔADC? Explain your answer.

(d) Draw an enlargement of $ABCD$ using a scale factor of 2 and A as the centre of enlargement.

Solution

(a)

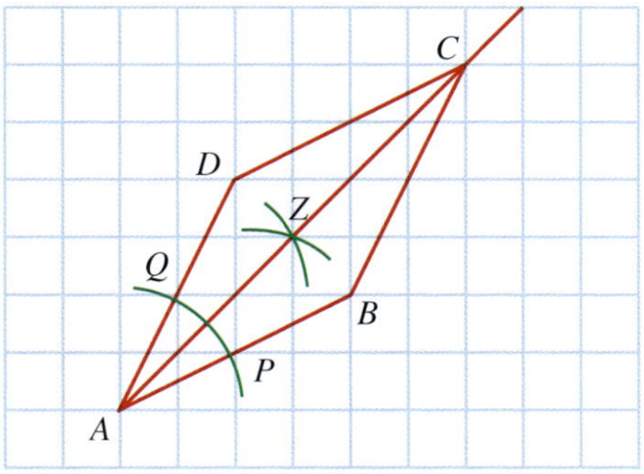

Steps

1. Draw an arc with A as centre to cut AB at P and AD at Q.
2. Draw arcs with equal radii at centres at P and Q to intersect at Z.
3. Draw the ray AZ.
4. Then AZ is the angle bisector of $\angle BAD$.

(b) The angle bisector AZ of $\angle BAD$ passes through the vertex C.

So, the diagonal AC of the rhombus bisects $\angle BAD$.

(c) If the rhombus is folded along AC, ΔABC and ΔADC overlap each other and are exactly the same size and shape.

Therefore, ΔABC and ΔADC are congruent.

(d) Since the centre of enlargement is A, the image of point A after the enlargement is A. The scale factor is 2.

To get from A to B you move

4 units right, 2 units up.

So, to get from A to B' on the image you move

$4 \times 2 = 8$ units right, $2 \times 2 = 4$ units up.

And so on.

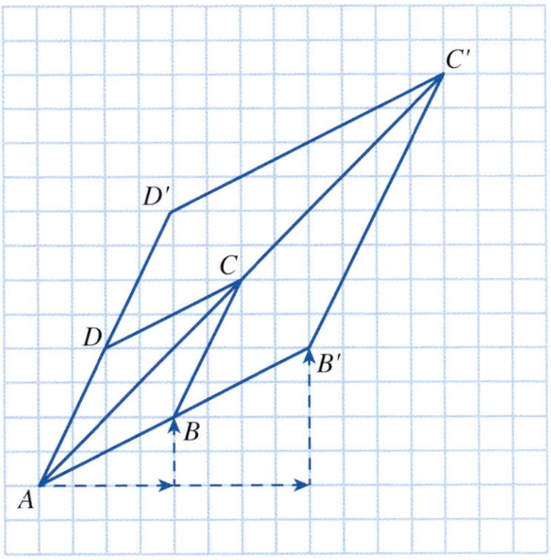

REMARK

You must leave your construction lines visible.

DISCUSS

How are the lengths of AC and AC' related?

Try It! 3

The diagram shows a rectangle $ABCD$. The diagonal, AC, is shown.

(a) Copy the rectangle and construct the perpendicular bisectors of AB and BC.

(b) What can you say about the point of intersection of the perpendicular bisectors in part **(a)**?

(c) Is ΔABC congruent to ΔCDA? Explain your answer.

(d) Enlarge $ABCD$ using a scale factor of 2 and the midpoint of AC as the point of enlargement.

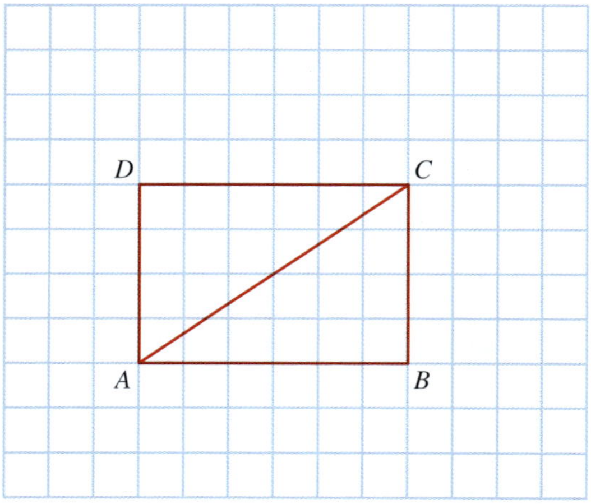

REVIEW EXERCISE 2

1. The height of a wall is directly proportional to the number of layers of bricks. When there are 20 layers, the wall is 150 cm high. When there are 30 layers, what is the height of the wall?

2. A box of oranges is distributed equally among some families. The number of oranges that each family gets is inversely proportional to the number of families. If there are 8 families, each family gets 12 oranges. If there are 24 families, how many oranges does each family get?

3. Peter is running at a constant speed. He covers 30 m in 6 seconds. Find
   (a) his speed in metres per second (m/s),
   (b) his distance covered in 10 seconds at the same speed.

4. 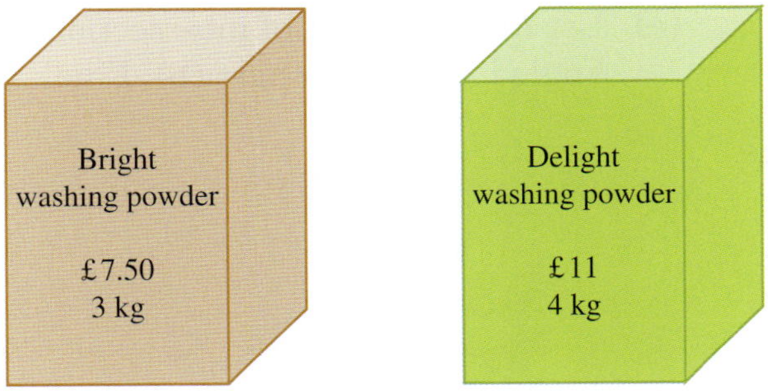

   Which of the washing powder packages is the better value? Explain your answer.

5. FINANCE A sum of £2500 is deposited at an interest rate of 3% per annum for 4 years. Find the simple interest earned.

6. *ABCD* is a straight line.
   (a) Find the size of angle *x*.
   (b) Classify triangle *BCE* by its sides and by its angles.

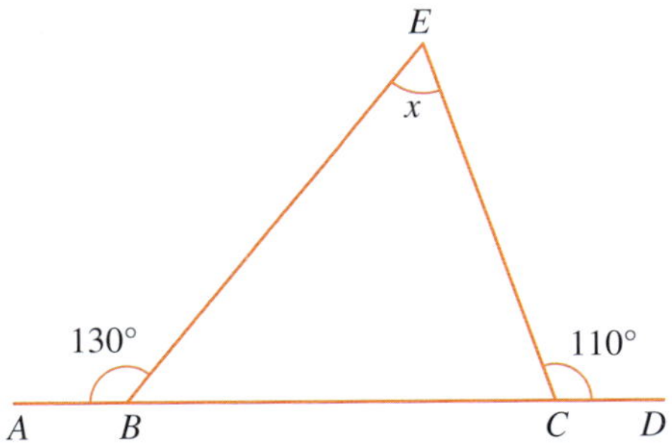

7. *ABCD* is a rectangle. Its diagonals intersect at *E*.
   $BE = 7$ cm and $\angle DAE = 55°$. Find
   (a) the length of *AC*,
   (b) the size of angle *y*.

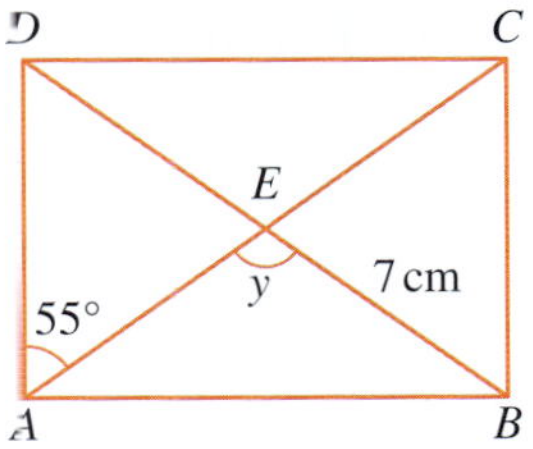

8. *BDC* is a straight line. ΔABD and ΔACD are congruent. $AC = 9$ cm and $\angle ABD = 65°$. Find
   (a) the length of *AB*,
   (b) the size of $\angle ADB$,
   (c) the size of $\angle CAD$.

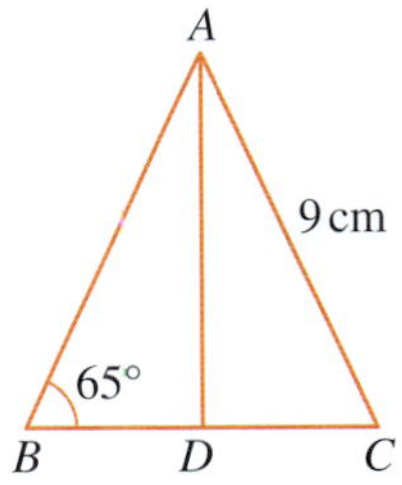

9. FINANCE A high-speed train takes 2 hours 30 minutes to travel a distance of approximately 500 km from London to Paris. The fare of a return ticket is £78.
   (a) Estimate the average speed of the train for the journey.
   (b) If £1 = 1.20 EUR, express the fare for a return ticket in Euros.
   (c) Assume the number of passengers carried by a train is directly proportional to the number of carriages. If a train with 12 carriages can take 672 passengers, how many passengers can a train with 18 carriages take?

10. Is it possible for the size of each exterior angle of a regular polygon to be 25°? Explain your answer.

11. The interior angle of a regular polygon is 160°. Work out how many sides the polygon has.

12. Copy triangle XYZ and then

(a) reflect in XY,
(b) rotate 90° clockwise about Z,
(c) translate 4 units right and 1 unit up,
(d) enlarge by scale factor $\frac{1}{2}$ using X as the centre of enlargement.

Label each image with the correct part: **(a)**, **(b)**, **(c)** or **(d)**.

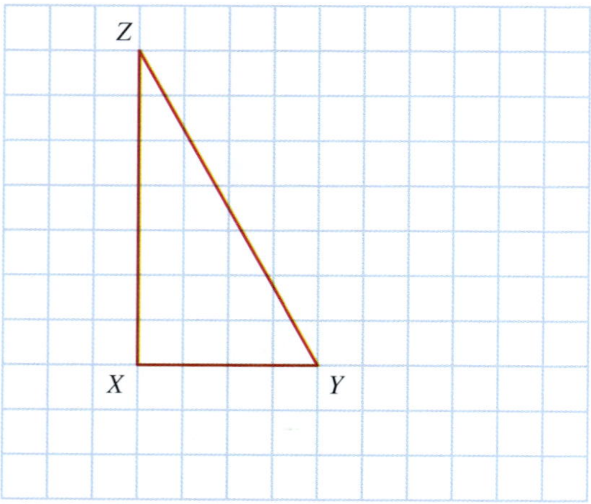

13. ΔABC and ΔADE are similar. $AD = 14$ cm, $DE = 15$ cm and $BC = 30$ cm. Find the length of AB.

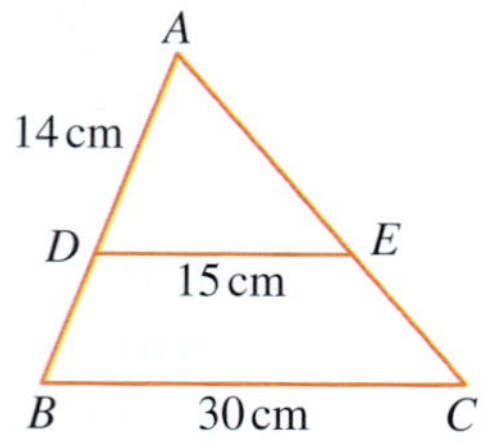

14. 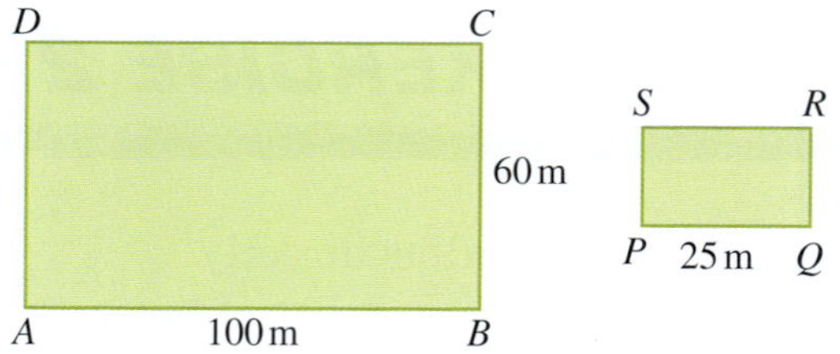

Two fields $ABCD$ and $PQRS$ are similar rectangles. $AB = 100$ m, $BC = 60$ m and $PQ = 25$ m. Jenny runs at a constant speed. She takes 80 seconds to run a loop along the boundary of $ABCD$.

(a) Find the length of QR.
(b) Find Jenny's running speed.
(c) How long would Jenny take to run a loop along the boundary of $PQRS$?

15. (a) Draw a triangle ABC with $BC = 7$ cm, $\angle ABC = 48°$ and $\angle ACB = 60°$ using a protractor and a ruler.
(b) Construct the angle bisectors of $\angle ABC$ and $\angle ACB$ using a pair of compasses and a ruler.
(c) Let I be the point of intersection of the angle bisectors in part **(b)**. Find $\angle BIC$.

10 PYTHAGORAS' THEOREM

WHAT IS IN THIS CHAPTER:

Right-angled triangles are often used in construction and engineering. A zip wire construction runs from a platform 20 m high to a platform 13 m high. Given that the horizontal distance between the platforms is 24 m, what is the length of the taut zip wire cable? If you know the lengths of two sides of a right-angled triangle, you can find the length of the third side using Pythagoras' Theorem.

LET'S LEARN TO

- identify the hypotenuse of a right-angled triangle
- state Pythagoras' Theorem
- determine whether a triangle is right-angled given the lengths of three sides
- use Pythagoras' Theorem to solve problems

FLASHBACK

1. Squares and Square Roots

The **square** of a number n, $n^2 = n \times n$.

For example, $3^2 = 3 \times 3 = 9$ is the square of 3,

$8^2 = 8 \times 8 = 64$ is the square of 8.

If $r^2 = n$, then r is called a **square root** of n. The positive square root of n is denoted by $\sqrt{n}$.

For example, $\sqrt{36} = 6$ since $6^2 = 36$,

$\sqrt{49} = 7$ since $7^2 = 49$.

RECALL

Can you write down all the square numbers from 1^2 to 15^2?

2. Right-angled Triangles

If an interior angle of a triangle is 90°, then the triangle is called a **right-angled triangle**.

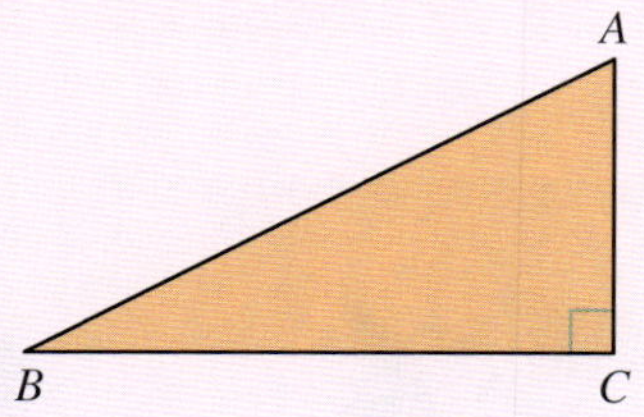

ΔABC is a right-angled triangle with $\angle ACB = 90°$. AC is also said to be perpendicular to BC, denoted by $AC \perp BC$.

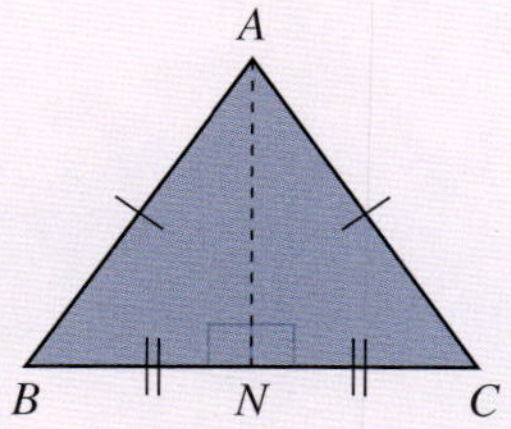

You can divide an isosceles triangle into two mathematically similar right-angled triangles as shown. The perpendicular line AN bisects BC.

3. Area

(a) Area of a triangle $= \frac{1}{2} \times$ base $\times$ perpendicular height.

In the diagram,

$$\text{area of } \Delta XYZ = \frac{1}{2} \times XY \times ZN$$
$$= \frac{1}{2} \times 20 \times 12$$
$$= 120\,\text{cm}^2$$

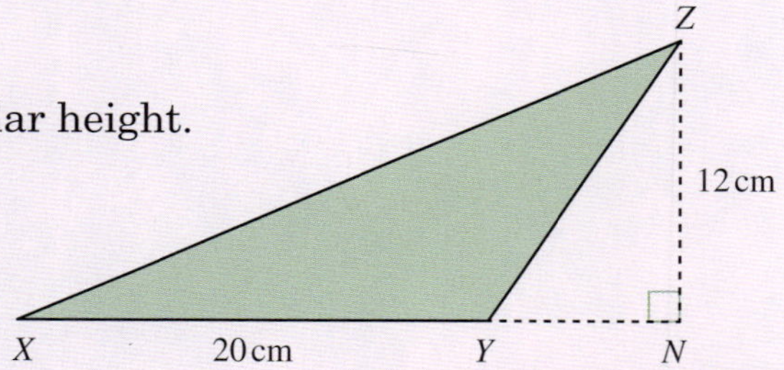

DISCUSS

Why is the length ZN used for the area of ΔXYZ instead of the length YZ?

(b) Area of a square = (side length)^2

In the diagram,

$$\text{area of square} = 8^2$$
$$= 64\,\text{cm}^2$$

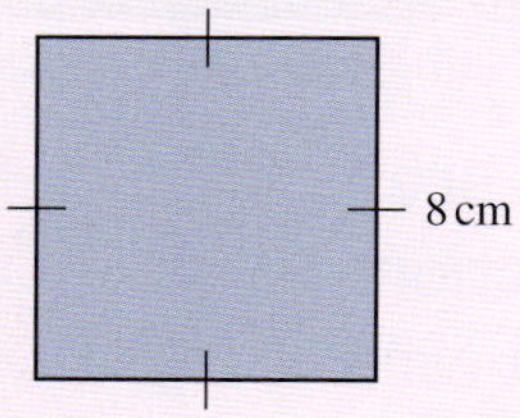

Conversely, if a square has area $64\,\text{cm}^2$, then

$$\text{side length} = \sqrt{64}$$
$$= 8\,\text{cm since } 8^2 = 64$$

DISCUSS

What would be the side length of a square with an area of $144\,\text{cm}^2$?

10.1 Pythagoras' Theorem

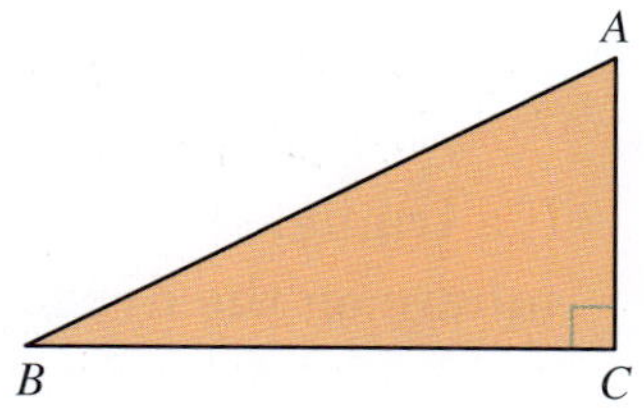

A triangle with a right angle is called a **right-angled triangle**.

The lengths of a right-angled triangle's three sides have a special relationship.

CLASS ACTIVITY 1

Objective: Investigate the areas of squares on the sides of right-angled triangles.

1. Draw squares of side lengths 3 cm, 4 cm and 5 cm on squared paper, shade each a different colour, then cut them out.

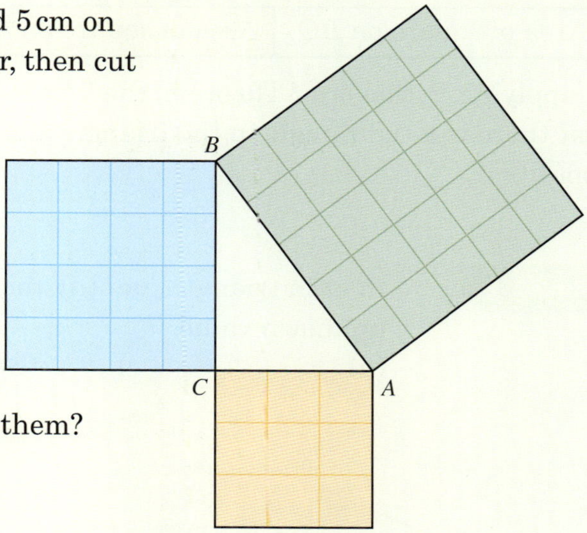

2. **(a)** Arrange the pieces so there is a triangle ABC in between them as shown.

(b) What type of triangle appears to be formed?

(c) Is there another way to arrange the squares so there is a triangle between them?

3. Copy and complete:

Area of square on BC = ☐ cm^2.

Area of square on AC = ☐ cm^2.

Area of square on BC + area of square on AC = ☐ cm^2.

Area of square on AB = ☐ cm^2.

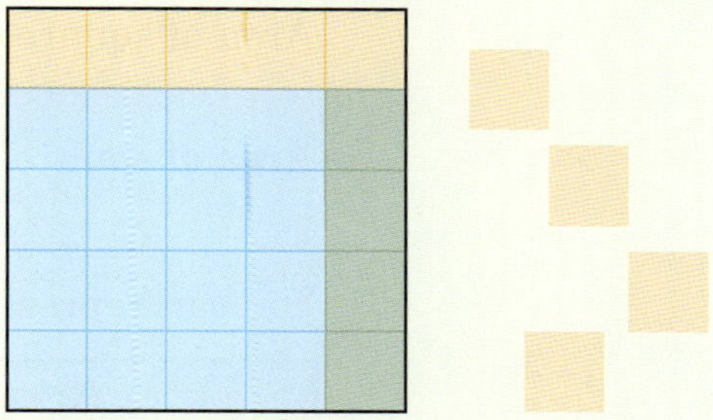

4. **(a)** Cut the smallest square into 1 cm squares.

(b) Place the largest square on the table then arrange all the other pieces on top of it to show that area of square on BC + area of square on AC = area of square on AB.

5. Repeat tasks **1**–**4** for squares with side lengths

(a) 12 cm, 5 cm and 13 cm,

(b) 6 cm, 8 cm and 10 cm.

From Class Activity 1, you can deduce that,

for a right-angled triangle,

area of the square on AB = area of the square on BC + area of the square on AC.

This relationship is called **Pythagoras' Theorem**. It is named after the Greek mathematician, Pythagoras.

In a right-angled triangle, the side opposite the right angle is the longest side. It is called the **hypotenuse** of the triangle. Pythagoras' Theorem states that:

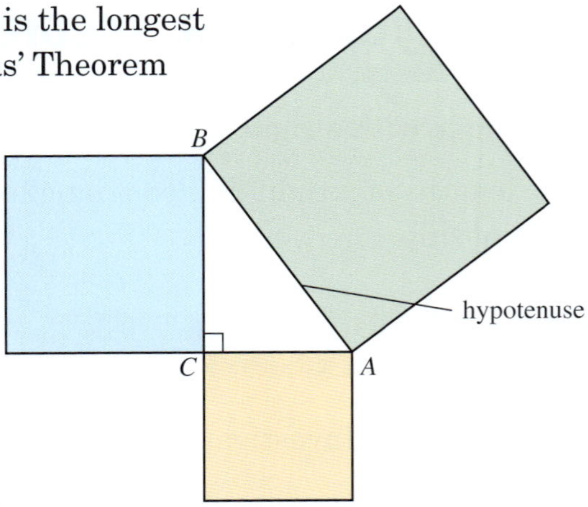

> If a triangle is right-angled, then the area of the square on the hypotenuse is equal to the sum of the areas of the squares on the other two sides.

You can represent the situation using a bar model.

Area of square on hypotenuse	
Area of square on BC	Area of square on AC

In applying Pythagoras' Theorem, the first thing to do is to check that there is a right angle in the triangle and identify the hypotenuse opposite it.

Example 1

In each triangle, identify the hypotenuse and find the unknown value.

(a)

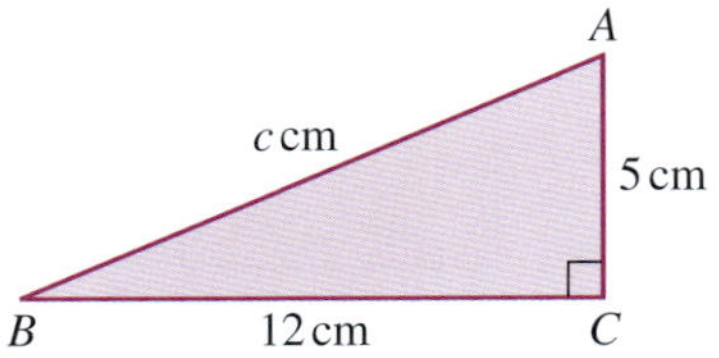

(b)

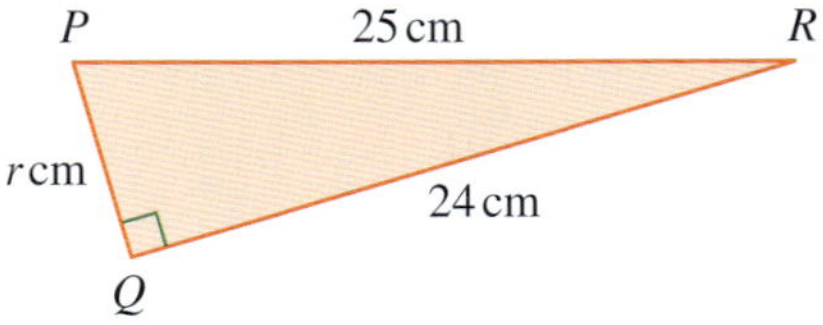

DISCUSS

Which side of a right-angled triangle is always the longest?

Solution

(a) ΔABC is right-angled since $\angle ACB = 90°$.

The hypotenuse is AB since it is opposite the 90° angle, $\angle ACB$.

Area of square on $BC = 12^2$

$= 144\text{ cm}^2$

Area of square on $AC = 5^2$

$= 25\text{ cm}^2$

You can represent the situation using a bar model.

Area of square on AB	
144	25

Area of square on AB = area of square on BC + area of square on AC (Pythagoras' Theorem)

$= 144 + 25$

$= 169\text{ cm}^2$

Therefore,

side length of square on $AB = \sqrt{169}$

$= 13\text{ cm}$

since $13^2 = 169$

$\therefore c = 13$

REMARK

You should know the square numbers up to 15^2. You can use a calculator for larger numbers.

REMARK

When you find the square root of a number you get two answers, one positive and one negative. This is because $13^2 = 169$ and $(-13)^2 = 169$. Here, you are looking for a length so you must use the positive answer.

(b) ΔPQR is right-angled since $\angle PQR = 90°$.
The hypotenuse is PR since it is opposite the $90°$ angle, $\angle PQR$.

Area of square on $PR = 25^2$
$= 625\,\text{cm}^2$

Area of square on $QR = 24^2$
$= 576\,\text{cm}^2$

You can represent the situation using a bar model.

625	
Area of square on PQ	576

Area of square on PR = area of square on PQ + area of square on QR (Pythagoras' Theorem)

625 = area of square on $PQ + 576$

$625 - 576$ = area of square on PQ

Area of square on $PQ = 49\,\text{cm}^2$

Therefore,

side length of square on $PQ = \sqrt{49}$
$= 7\,\text{cm}$ since $7^2 = 49$
$\therefore r = 7$

Try It! 1

In each triangle, identify the hypotenuse and find the unknown value.

(a)

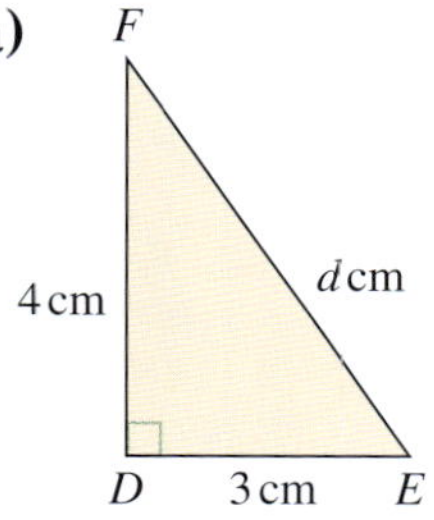

(b)

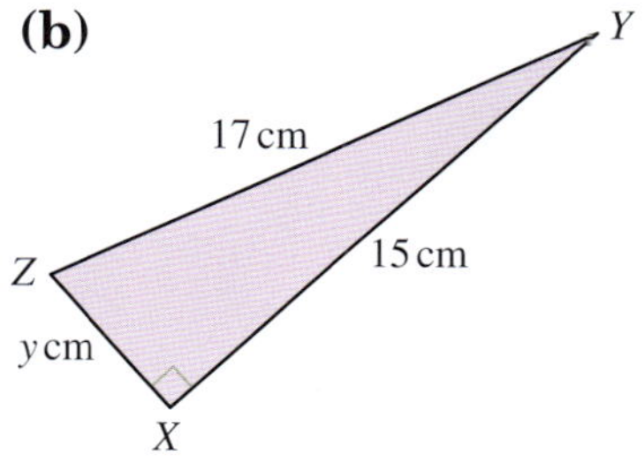

REMARK

You can use a calculator for these questions if you need to. Or, you can use the fact that $17^2 = 289$ for part **(b)**.

So far, all the side lengths of the triangles you have seen have been integers. In general, this will not be the case and you will need to use your calculator to work out the missing length.

There is also another common way of writing down Pythagoras' Theorem, that you may find useful:

In ΔABC,
if $\angle ACB = 90°$,
then $AB^2 = BC^2 + AC^2$
or $c^2 = a^2 + b^2$ (Pythagoras' Theorem)

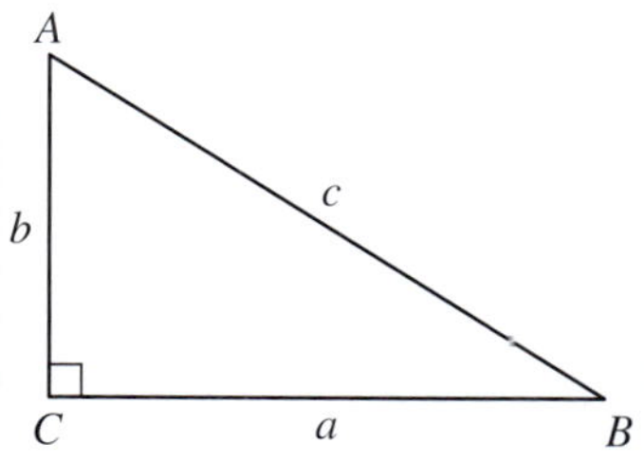

You can see that this is a simpler way of writing out the area of the square on AB equals area of the square on BC add area of square on AC. This is because the area of each square is the same as the side length of that square (side length of the triangle) to the power of two.

REMARK

Line AB on a right-angled triangle will not always be the hypotenuse. Make sure you check carefully which side is the hypotenuse before applying the theorem.

REMARK

Here AB denotes a side length of the triangle. AB^2 means the square of the side length AB.

Example 2

Find the unknown value in each triangle to three significant figures.

(a)

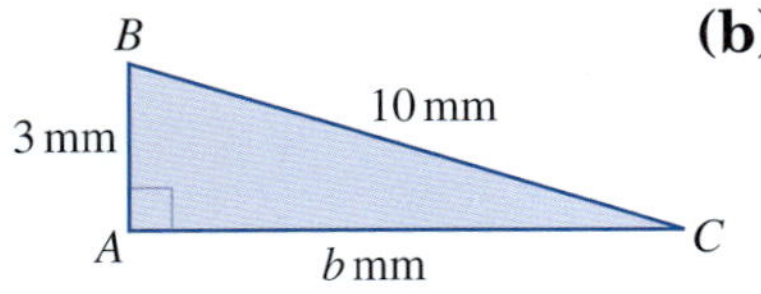

(b)

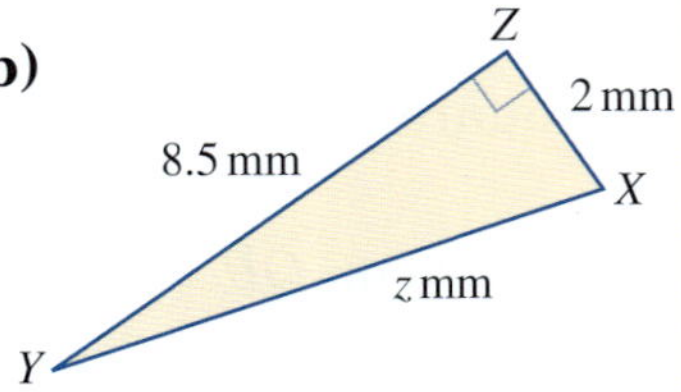

Solution

(a) The triangle is right-angled since $\angle BAC$ is a right angle.

The hypotenuse is BC, which is 10 mm, because this side is opposite the right angle.

Area of square on hypotenuse (BC) $= 10^2$
$= 100\,\text{mm}^2$

Area of smaller square $= 3^2$
$= 9\,\text{mm}^2$

You can represent the situation using a bar model.

100	
Area of square on AC	9

Area of square on hypotenuse, BC
= area of square on AC + area of square on AB (Pythagoras' Theorem)

$$100 = 9 + b^2$$
$$b^2 = 100 - 9$$
$$= 91$$

Therefore,

$$b = \sqrt{91}$$
$$= 9.54 \text{ (to 3 sf)}$$

Alternatively, you can apply the formula:

$$BC^2 = AC^2 + AB^2 \quad \text{(Pythagoras' Theorem)}$$
$$10^2 = b^2 + 3^2$$
$$100 = b^2 + 9$$
$$b^2 = 100 - 9$$
$$b = \sqrt{91}$$
$$= 9.54 \text{ (to 3 sf)}$$

(b) The triangle is right-angled since $\angle XZY$ is a right angle.

The hypotenuse is XY or z mm because this side is opposite the right angle.

Area of square on $YZ = 8.5^2$
$= 72.25\,\text{mm}^2$

Area of square on $XZ = 2^2$
$= 4\,\text{mm}^2$

RECALL

A number rounded to 3 significant figures (sf) will have 3 digits not including any leading or trailing zeros, for example,
4.2517 is 4.25 to 3 sf
25.851 is 25.9 to 3 sf
0.06841 is 0.0684 to 3 sf.
What about
21.63, 1.925, 0.38291?

DISCUSS

What is the same and what is different about the formula used here and the formula in the key point box? Why are they different?

You can represent the situation using a bar model.

Area of square on hypotenuse, XY	
72.25	4

Area of square on hypotenuse, XY
= area of square on YZ + area of square on XZ
(Pythagoras' Theorem)

$$z^2 = 72.25 + 4$$
$$= 76.25$$

Therefore,

$$z = \sqrt{76.25}$$
$$= 8.73 \text{ (to 3 sf)}$$

Alternatively, you can apply the formula:

$XY^2 = XZ^2 + YZ^2$ (Pythagoras' Theorem)

$$z^2 = 2^2 + 8.5^2$$
$$z^2 = 76.25$$
$$z = \sqrt{76.25}$$
$$z = 8.73 \text{ (to 3 sf)}$$

DISCUSS

Can you write down a calculation that you could put straight into your calculator in one go?

Try It! 2

Find the unknown value in each triangle to three significant figures.

(a)

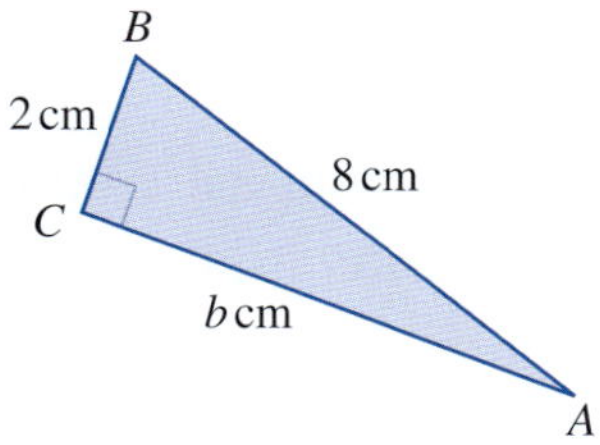

(b)

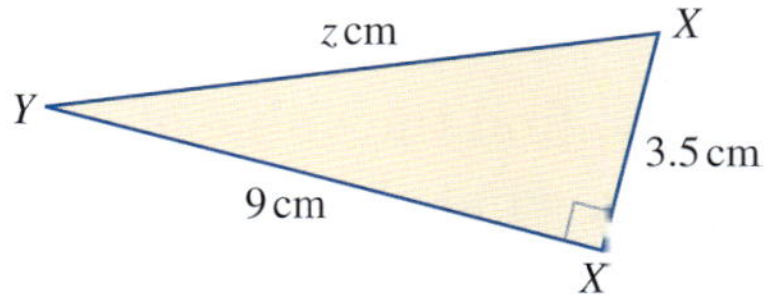

PRACTICE 10.1

LEVEL 1

1. Could Pythagoras' Theorem be applied to each of these triangles? Explain your answer.

(a)

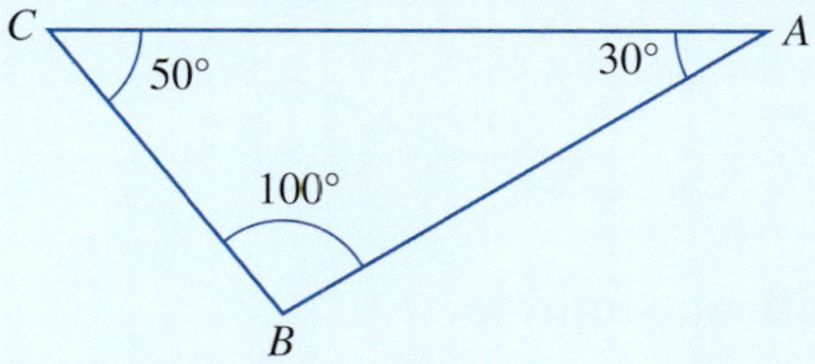

(b)

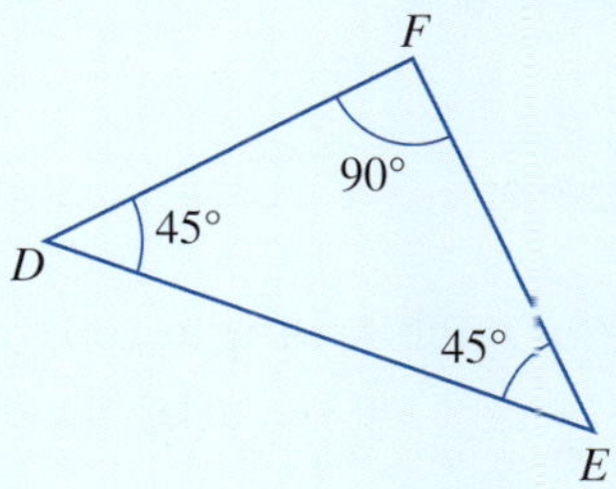

2. Work out

(a) the area of the square on BC,

(b) the area of the square on AC,

(c) the area of the square on AB,

(d) the length of AB.

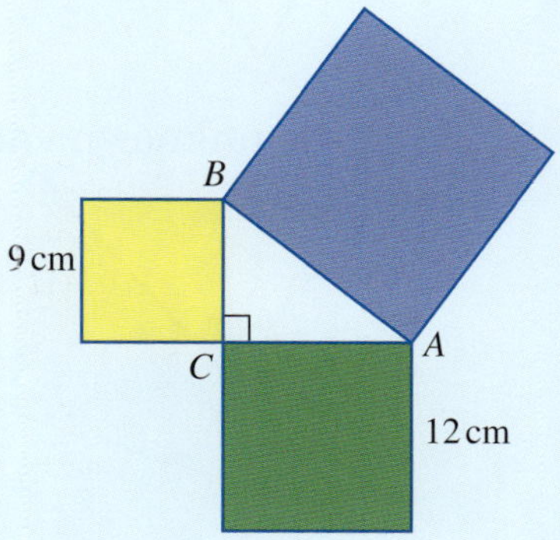

3. Find the unknown value in each triangle.

(a)

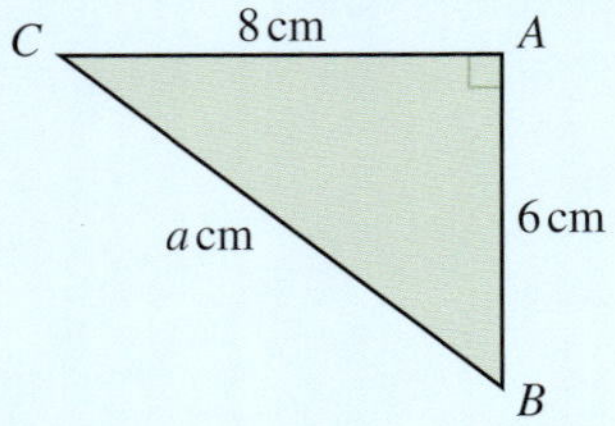

(b)

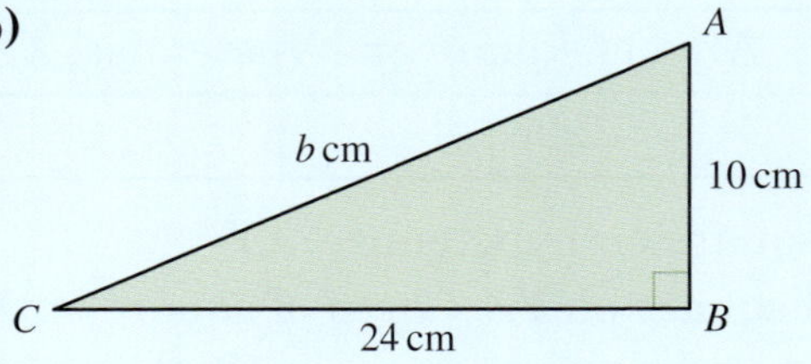

4. Find the unknown value in each triangle.

(a)

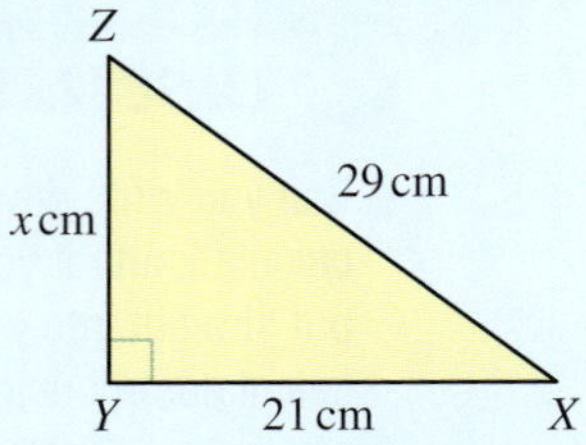

(b)

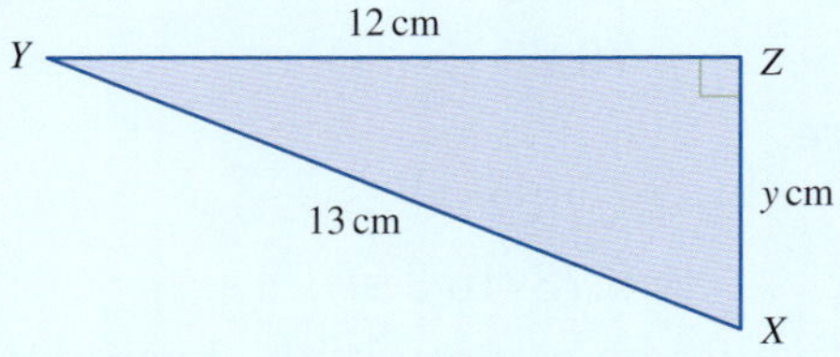

5. What is the same and what is different about these triangles?

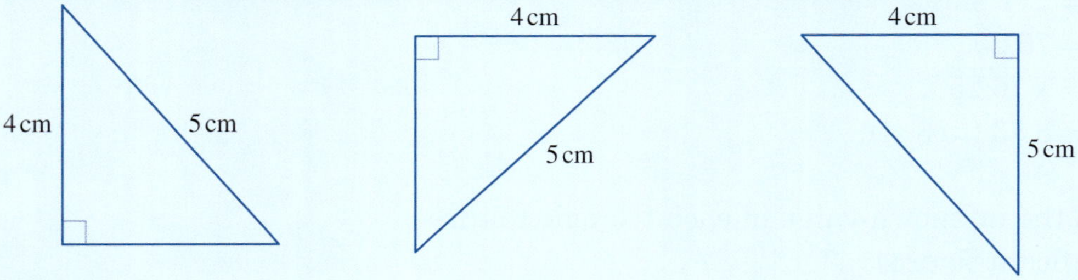

LEVEL 2

6. Ryan and Rosie are trying to find the value of x in this right-angled triangle. Their workings are shown. Explain what they have each done wrong and work out the correct answer.

Ryan

$x + 6 = 10$ (Pythagoras' Theorem)

$x = 10 - 6$

$x = 4$

Rosie

$x + 6^2 = 10^2$

$x + 36 = 100$

$x = 100 - 36$

$x = 64$

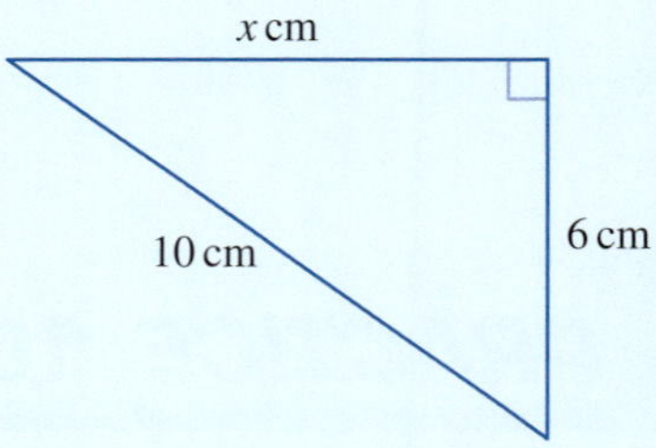

7. Find the unknown value in each triangle to three significant figures.

(a)

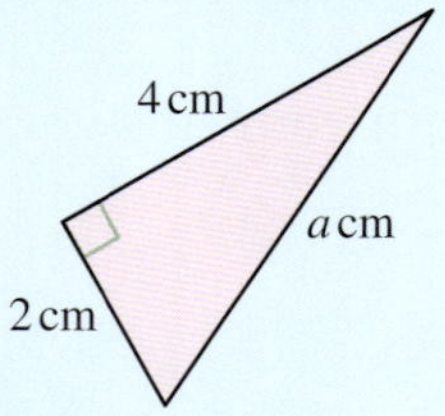

(b)

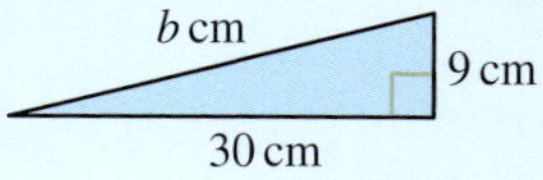

(c)

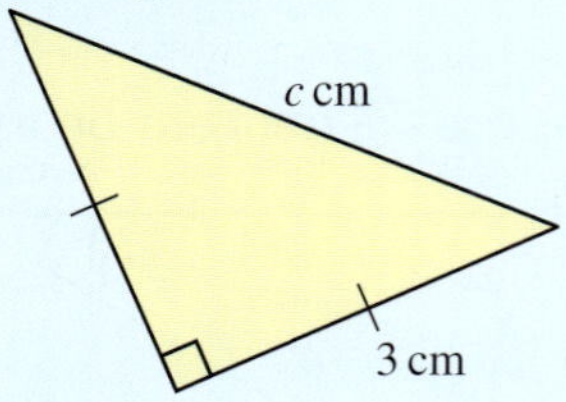

8. Find the unknown value in each triangle to three significant figures.

(a)

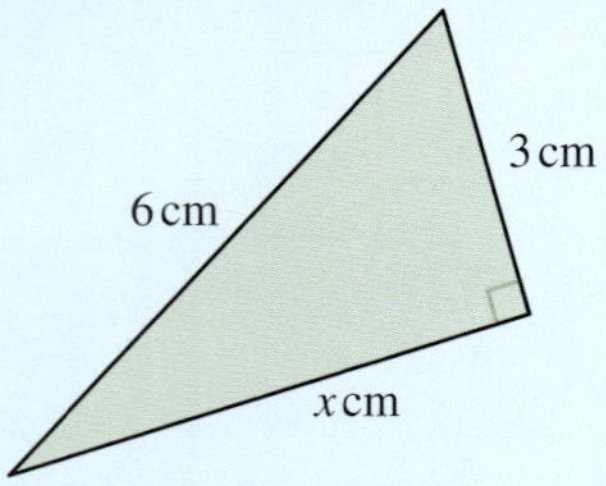

(b)

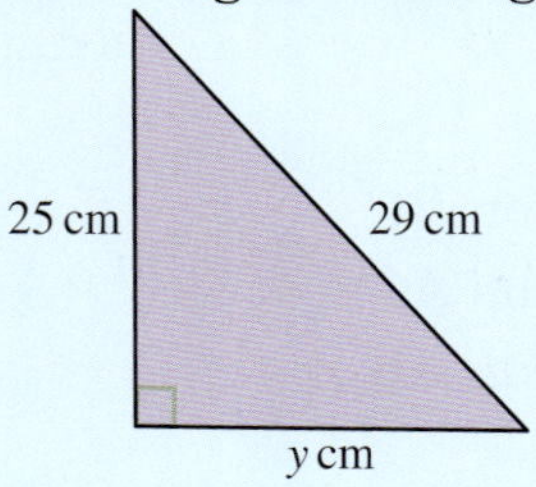

9. Find the unknown value in each triangle to three significant figures.

(a)

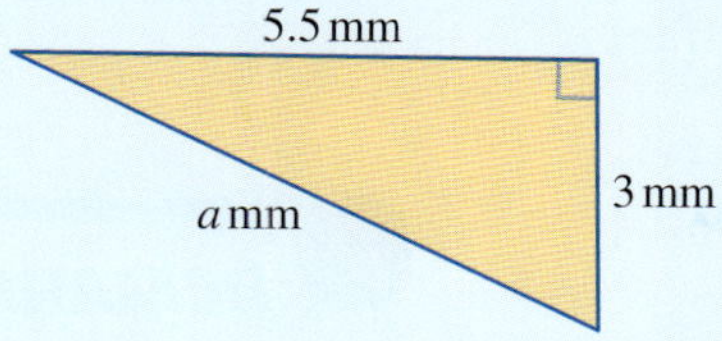

(b)

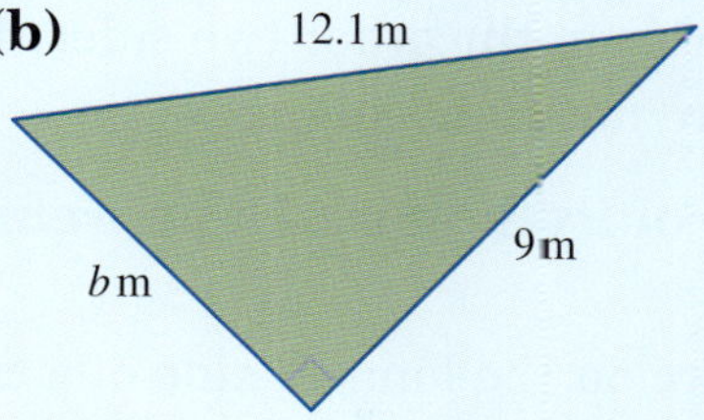

10. PQR is a right-angled triangle. $PR = 8$ cm, $PQ = 17$ cm and $\angle PRQ = 90°$. Find

(a) the length of QR,

(b) the perimeter of the triangle,

(c) the area of the triangle.

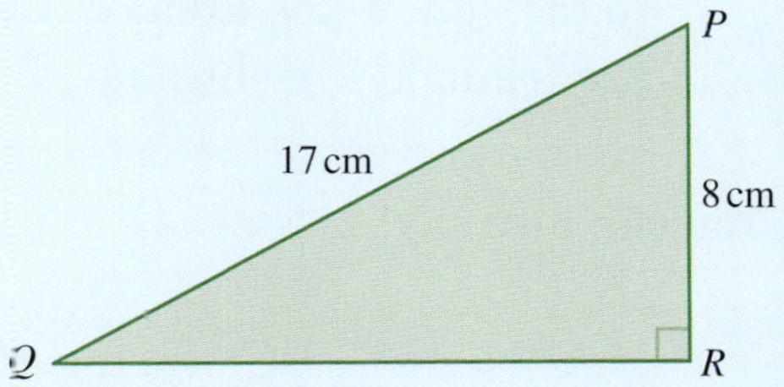

10.2 Applications of Pythagoras' Theorem

A Converse of Pythagoras' Theorem

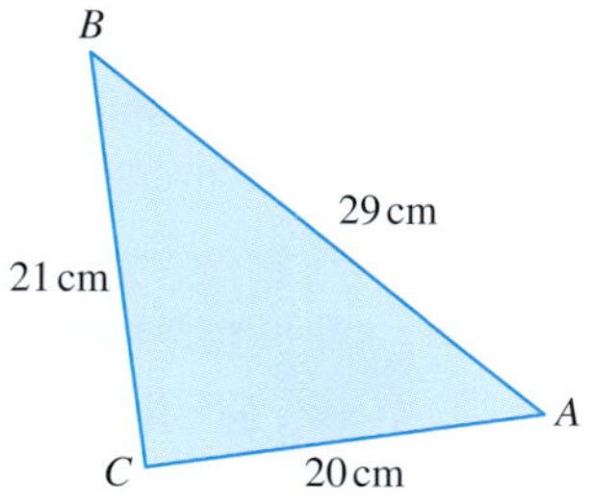

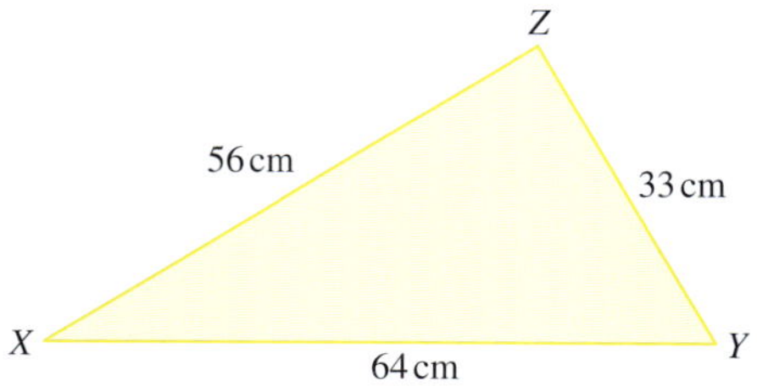

Here are two triangles whose three sides are given. How do you determine whether they are right-angled triangles or not?

CLASS ACTIVITY 2

Objective: Investigate the areas of squares on the sides of a non-right-angled triangle.

1. Copy the diagram onto centimetre squared paper.
2. Measure the side lengths of the triangle and label these on your diagram.
3. Measure the angles of the triangle and use these to classify the triangle.
4. Copy and complete:

   Area of square on BC = ☐ cm²

   Area of square on AC = ☐ cm²

   Area of square on AB = ☐ cm²

   Area of square on BC + area of square on AC = ☐ cm²

5. Does Pythagoras' Theorem hold for this triangle?

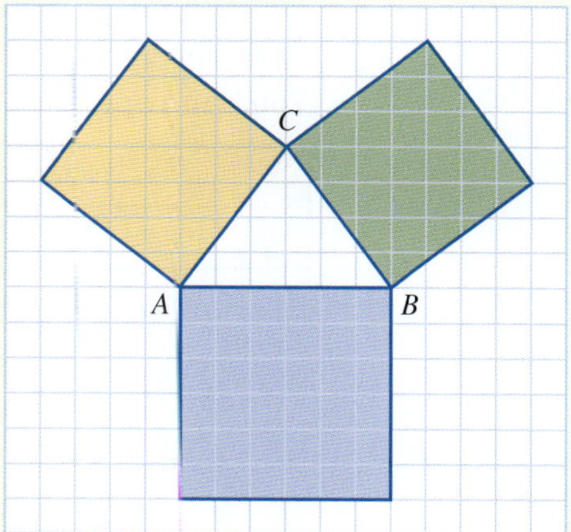

You found in Class Activity 2, that for a triangle that was not right-angled, the area of the square on the longest side was **not** equal to the sum of the area of the squares on the other two sides. This is, in fact, true for all triangles that are not right-angled.

This leads to the **converse of Pythagoras' Theorem**:

> If the area of the square on the longest side of a triangle is equal to the sum of the areas of the squares on the other two sides then the triangle is right-angled.

You can also say:

> If $AB^2 = AC^2 + BC^2$, then $\angle ACB = 90°$.

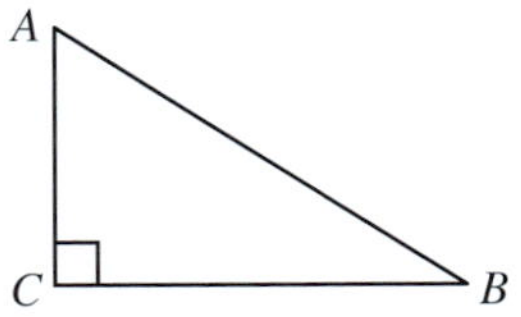

REMARK

When a statement is 'If P then Q', its converse is 'If Q then P'. When a statement is true, its converse may not be true. For example, the statement 'If an animal is a dog, then it has 4 legs.' is true. Its converse 'If an animal has 4 legs, then it is a dog' is not true.

DISCUSS

Think of some other true statements and write down their converses. Discuss whether or not the converse is also true.

Example 3

Determine whether triangles *ABC* and *XYZ* are right-angled triangles.

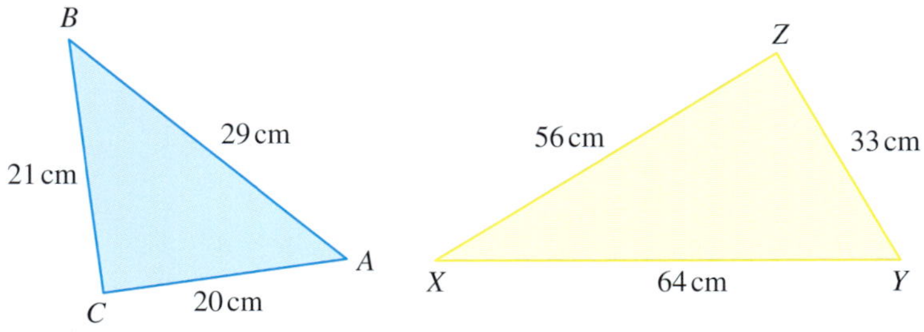

Solution

In triangle *ABC*, the longest side is *AB*.

Area of square on $AB = 29^2$

$= 841\text{ cm}^2$

Area of square on $BC = 21^2$

$= 441\text{ cm}^2$

Area of square on $AC = 20^2$

$= 400\text{ cm}^2$

Area of square on *BC* + area of square on *AC*

$= 441 + 400$

$= 841\text{ cm}^2$

= area of square on *AB*

Therefore, triangle *ABC* is right-angled with $\angle ACB = 90°$.

You can represent the situation using a bar model.

841	
441	400

In triangle *XYZ*, the longest side is *XY*.

$XY^2 = 64^2$

$= 4096$

$XZ^2 = 56^2$

$= 3136$

REMARK

If the triangle is right-angled then 29 cm would have to be the hypotenuse since the hypotenuse is always the longest side in a right-angled triangle.

REMARK

When three integers form the sides of a right-angled triangle, they are called a **Pythagorean triple**.

20, 21 and 29 is an example of a Pythagorean triple.

DISCUSS

Can you name some other Pythagorean triples?

$$ZY^2 = 33^2$$
$$= 1089$$
$$XZ^2 + ZY^2 = 3136 + 1089$$
$$= 4225$$
$4225 \neq 4096 \rightarrow XZ^2 + ZY^2 \neq XY^2$

Therefore, triangle XYZ is not right-angled.

DISCUSS

The methods for *ABC* and *XYZ* are slightly different. What is different about them? Which method do you prefer?

Try It! 3

Determine whether triangles ABC and XYZ are right-angled triangles.

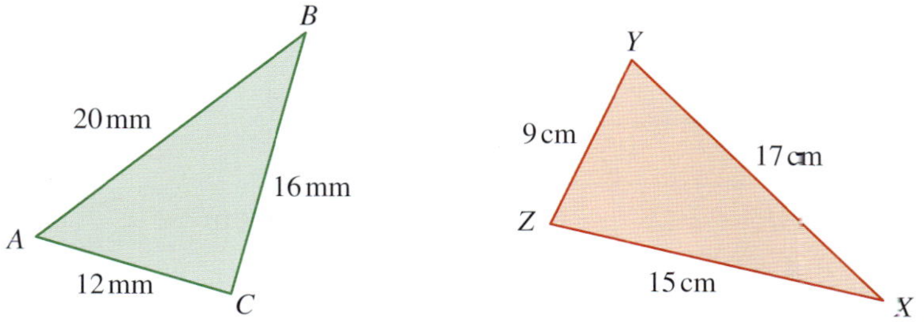

B Applications of Pythagoras' Theorem

Pythagoras' Theorem is used a lot in construction, architecture and engineering. You can see in the photographs a carpenter using a right-angled triangle called a set square to make sure some furniture is constructed at right angles, and a staircase which uses right-angled triangles in its construction. Pythagoras' Theorem is really useful when working out how long the sides of a triangle need to be in order to form a right angle.

Take a look at some examples.

Example 4

PQRS is a rectangular wall. Find the length of the diagonal *SQ*.

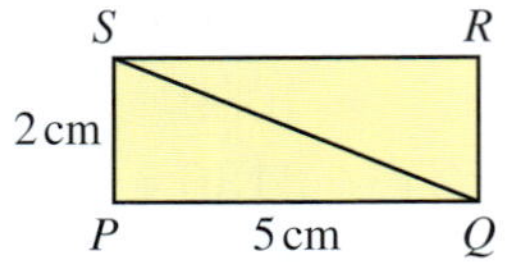

Solution

In ΔPQS, $\angle SPQ = 90°$ (*PQRS* is a rectangle.)

Therefore, *SQ* is the hypotenuse

$$SP^2 = 2^2$$
$$= 4$$
$$PQ^2 = 5^2$$
$$= 25$$

You can represent the situation using a bar model.

SQ^2	
4	25

$$SQ^2 = SP^2 + PQ^2 \quad \text{(Pythagoras' Theorem)}$$
$$= 4 + 25$$
$$= 29$$

Therefore, $SQ = \sqrt{29}$

$= 5.39\,\text{m}$ (to 3 sf)

Try It! 4

TXYZ is a square garden with sides 5 m. Find the length of the diagonal path *ZX*. Give your answer to three significant figures.

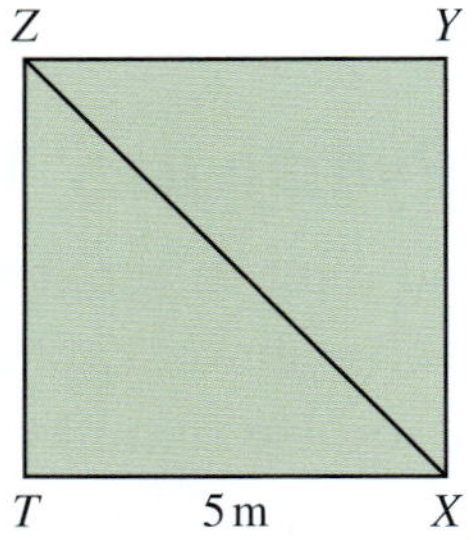

Example 5

The diagram shows a cross-section of a roof. The roof is an isosceles triangle *ABC* with *AB* = *AC*. *AB* = 5 m and *BC* = 7.6 m. *AN* is a supporting beam. Find the length of *AN* to three significant figures.

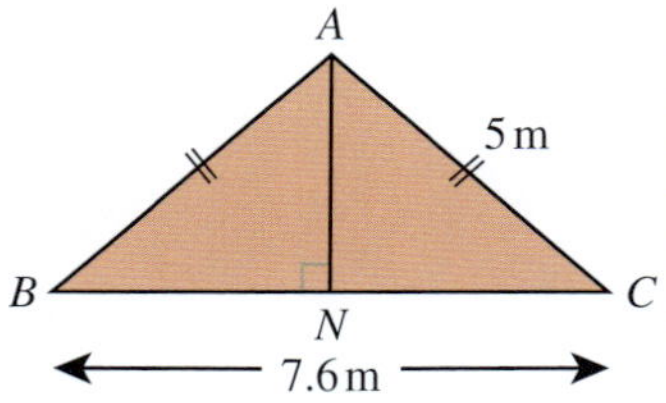

Solution

As *ABC* is an isosceles triangle, the perpendicular *AN* bisects *BC*.

$$\therefore \quad BN = \frac{1}{2}BC$$
$$= \frac{1}{2} \times 7.6$$
$$= 3.8\,\text{m}$$

In ΔABN, $\angle ANB = 90°$.

Therefore, *AB* is the hypotenuse.

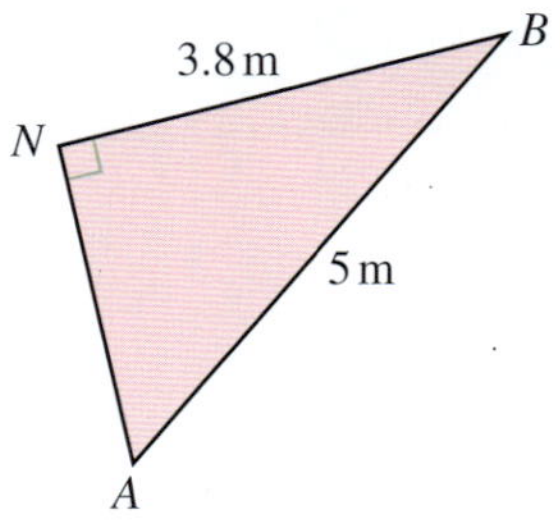

$$AB^2 = 5^2$$
$$= 25$$
$$BN^2 = 3.8^2$$
$$= 14.44$$

You can represent the situation using a bar model.

25	
AN^2	14.44

$$AB^2 = AN^2 + BN^2 \quad \text{(Pythagoras' Theorem)}$$
$$25 = AN^2 + 14.44$$
$$AN^2 = 25 - 14.44$$
$$= 10.56$$

Therefore, $AN = \sqrt{10.56}$

$= 3.25\,\text{m}$ (to 3 sf)

Try It! 5

PQR is a template for material bunting. PQR is an isosceles triangle with $PQ = PR$.
$PR = 6\,\text{cm}$ and $PT = 5.6\,\text{cm}$.
Find the length of QR.
Give your answer to three significant figures.

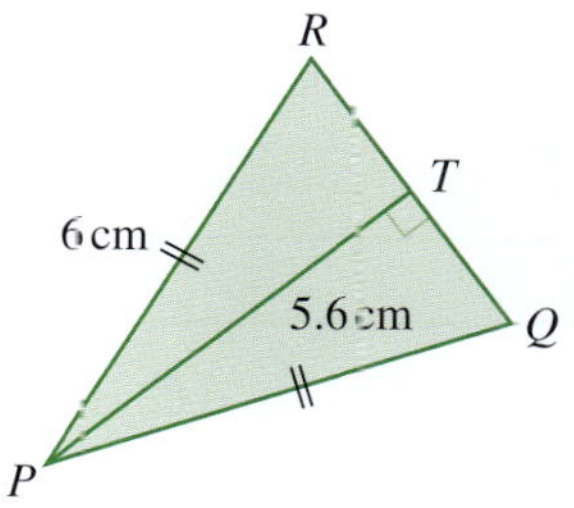

Example 6

$ABCD$ is a rectangle and E is a point on AB.
$BC = 4\,\text{cm}$, $CD = 10\,\text{cm}$ and $BE = 8\,\text{cm}$.

(a) Find the length of CE.

(b) Find the length of DE.

(c) Show that CDE is a right-angled triangle.

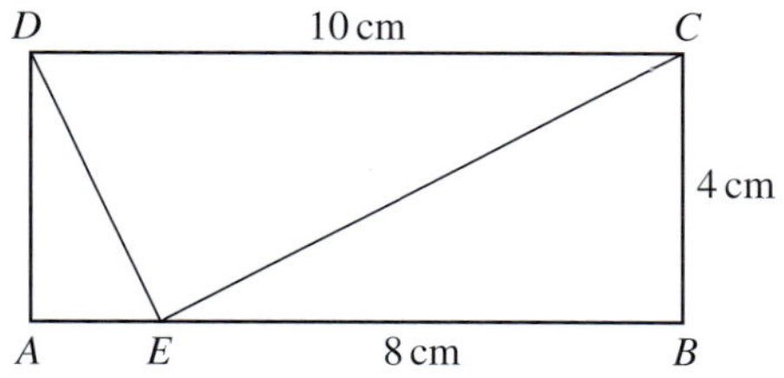

Solution

(a) In ΔBCE, $\angle CBE = 90°$. ($ABCD$ is a rectangle.)
Therefore, CE is the hypotenuse.

$$EB^2 = 8^2$$
$$= 64$$
$$BC^2 = 4^2$$
$$= 16$$

You can represent the situation using a bar model.

CE^2	
64	16

$$CE^2 = EB^2 + BC^2 \quad \text{(Pythagoras' Theorem)}$$
$$= 64 + 16$$
$$= 80$$

Therefore, $CE = \sqrt{80}$

$= 8.94\,\text{cm}$ (to 3 sf)

(b) In ΔADE, $\angle DAE = 90°$. (*ABCD* is a rectangle.)
Therefore, *DE* is the hypotenuse.

$DA = BC$ (Opposite sides of a rectangle are equal.)
$= 4\text{ cm}$

$AE = AB - BE$
$= 10 - 8$
$= 2\text{ cm}$

$DA^2 = 4^2$
$= 16$

$AE^2 = 2^2$
$= 4$

You can represent the situation using a bar model.

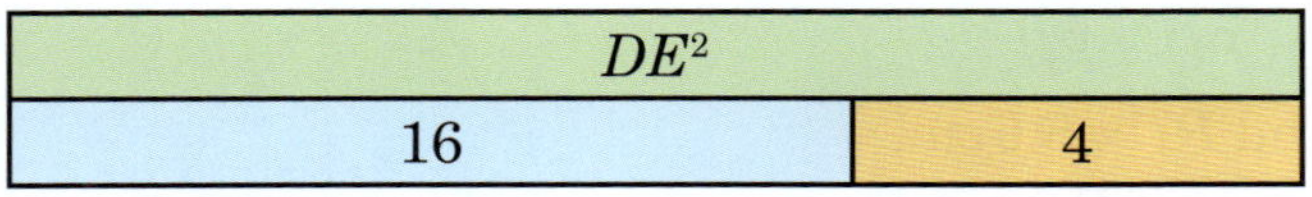

$DE^2 = DA^2 + AE^2$ (Pythagoras' Theorem)
$= 16 + 4$
$= 20$

Therefore, $DE = \sqrt{20}$
$= 4.47\text{ cm}$ (to 3 sf)

(c) In ΔCDE, the longest side is *CD*.

$CD^2 = 10^2$
$= 100$

$CE^2 = 80$ (From part **a**)

$DE^2 = 20$ (From part **b**)

$CE^2 + DE^2 = 80 + 20$
$= 100$
$= CD^2$

$\therefore \angle CED = 90°$ (Converse of Pythagoras' Theorem)

So *CDE* is a right-angled triangle.

Try It! 6

PQRS is a rectangle and *T* is a point on *SP*.
$SR = 12\text{ cm}$, $ST = 16\text{ cm}$ and $TP = 9\text{ cm}$.

(a) Find the length of *RT*.
(b) Find the length of *QT*.
(c) Show that *QRT* is a right-angled triangle.

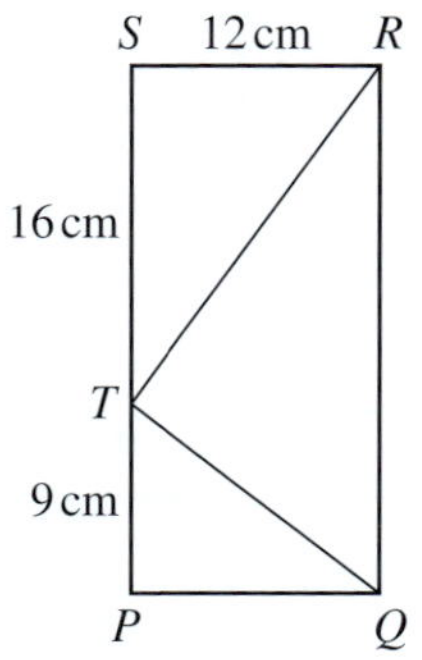

PRACTICE 10.2

In this exercise, give your answers to three significant figures if they are not integers.

LEVEL 1

1. Determine whether each of these triangles is a right-angled triangle. If so, state the right angle.

(a)

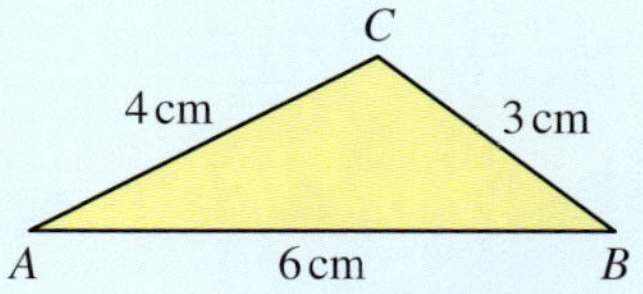

(b)

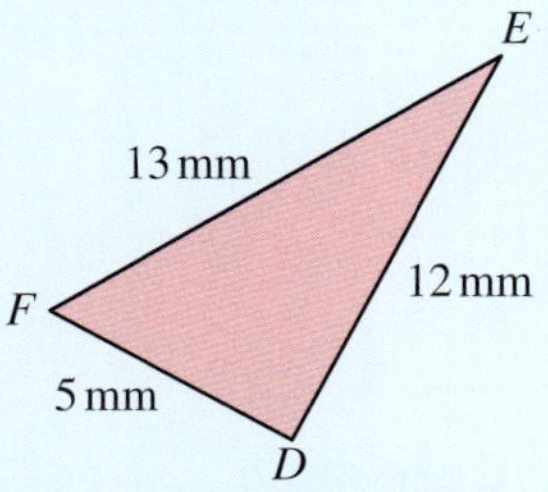

(c)

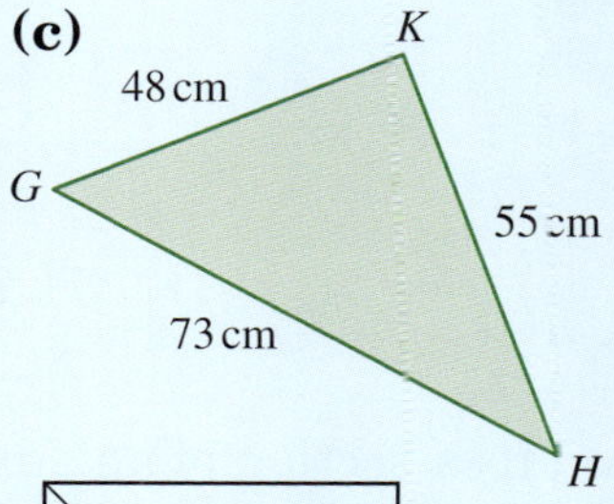

(d)

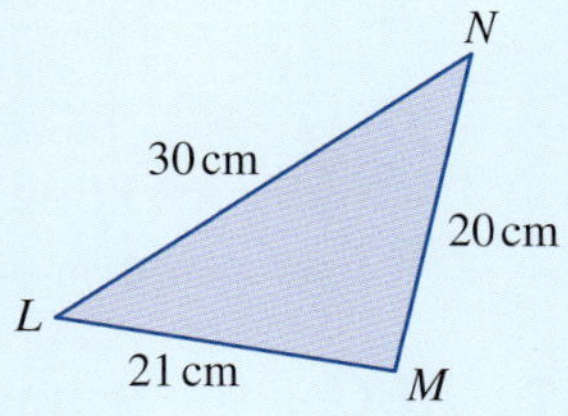

2. A square windowpane has side length 10 cm. Find the length of a diagonal of the square.

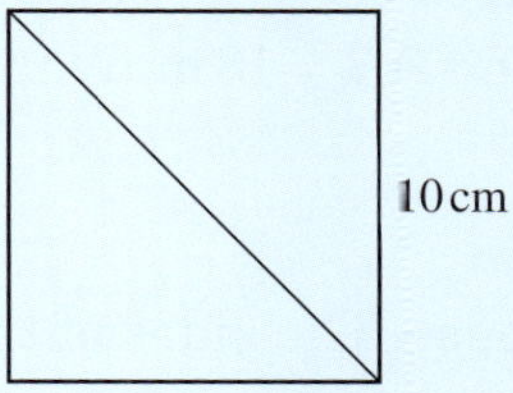

3. A rectangular picture frame is 45 cm by 30 cm. Find the length of a diagonal of the frame.

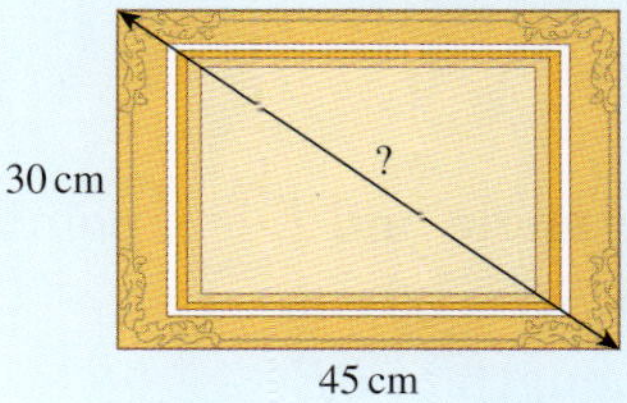

4. The measurements of the sides and a diagonal of a chopping board, *ABCD*, are as shown.
   (a) Is the board a rectangle? Explain your answer.
   (b) If you decide the board is not a rectangle, what shape do you think it is? Explain your answer.

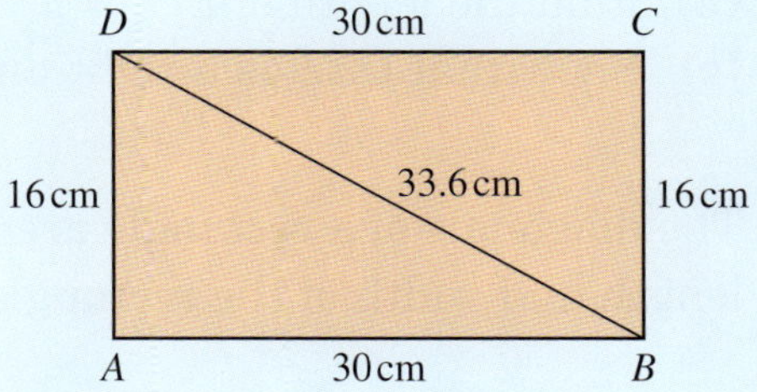

5. *ABCD* is a rectangle of 6 cm by 5 cm. *PQRS* is a rectangle of 7 cm by 4 cm.
   PROBLEM SOLVING
   (a) Predict which rectangle has a longer diagonal.
   (b) Check whether your prediction in part **(a)** was correct.

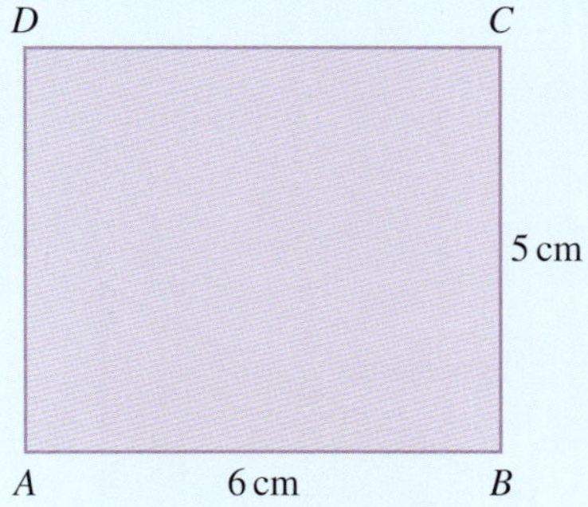

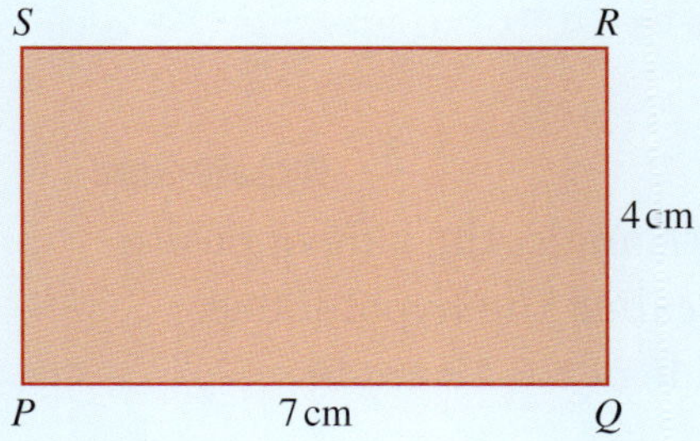

LEVEL 2

6. Triangles ABC and PQR are isosceles triangles. Find

(a) AN,

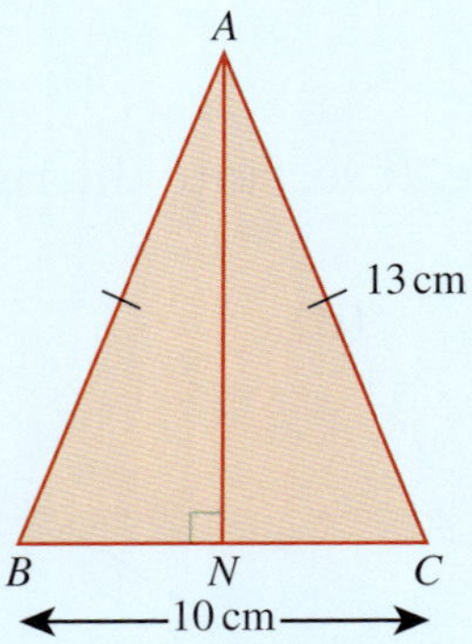

(b) PR.

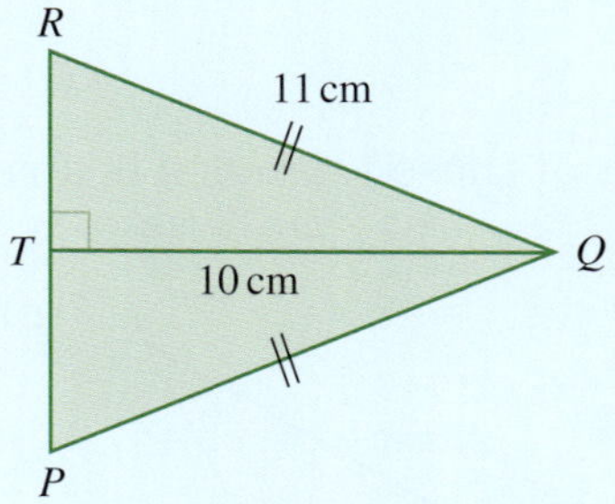

7. ABC is the triangular cross-section of an adventure slide. $\angle ACB = 90°$, $BC = 5$ m and $AB = 13$ m. What is the area of the triangle?

PROBLEM SOLVING

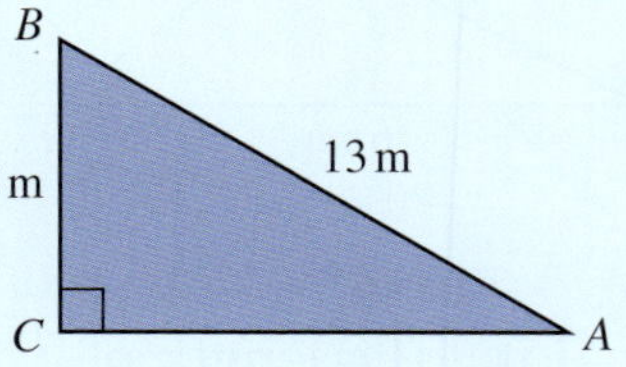

8. The diagram shows a house. The sides of the roof have lengths 4.2 m. Calculate the height of the house to the nearest metre.

PROBLEM SOLVING

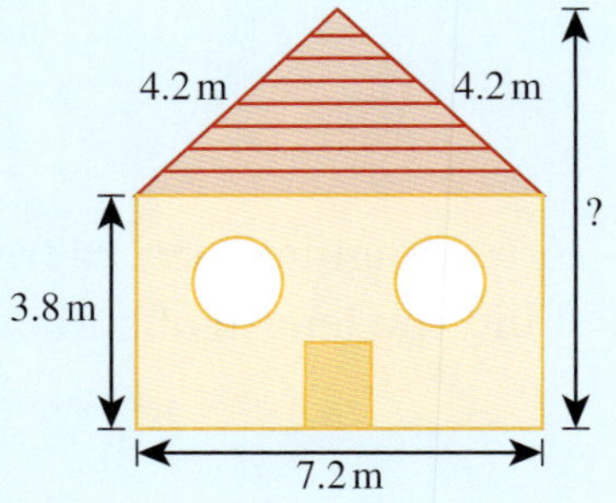

9. $ABCD$ is a rectangle and E is a point on AD. $AE = 4$ cm, $AB = 8$ cm and $BC = 20$ cm.

(a) Find the length of BE.

(b) Find the length of EC.

(c) Show that CEB is a right-angled triangle.

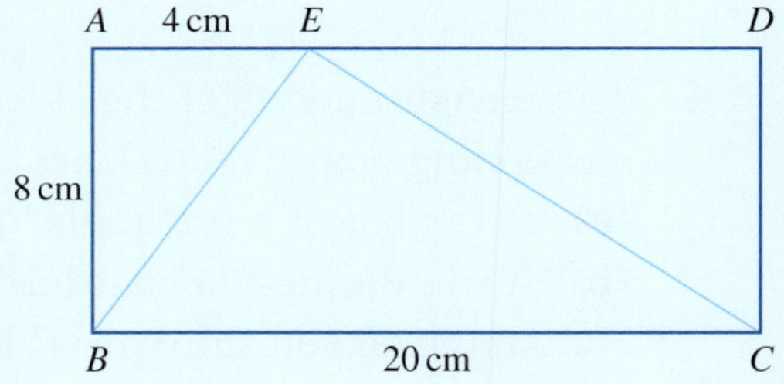

10. The diagonals of a rectangle are 10 cm. What could the length and width of the rectangle be?

OPEN QUESTION

REVIEW

Hypotenuse

In a right-angled triangle, the side opposite the right angle is called the hypotenuse. It is the longest side of the triangle.

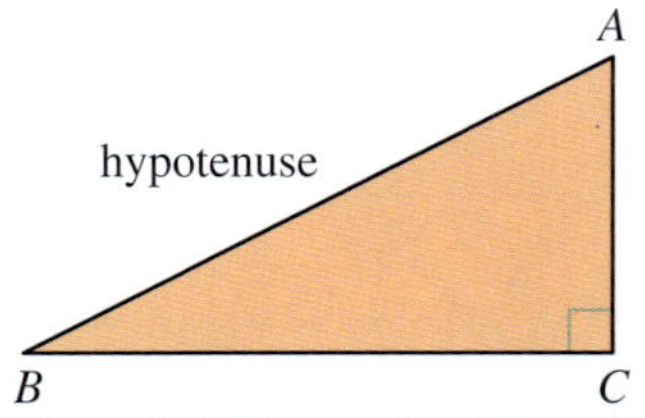

Pythagoras' Theorem

In ΔABC,
if $\angle ACB = 90°$, then
area of square on AB
= area of square on AC + area of square on BC
or $AB^2 = AC^2 + BC^2$
For example, given $AC = 28$ cm and $BC = 45$ cm,
find AB.

$$AB^2 = AC^2 + BC^2 \quad \text{(Pythagoras' Theorem)}$$
$$AB^2 = 28^2 + 45^2$$
$$= 784 + 2025$$
$$= 2809$$
$$AB = \sqrt{2809}$$
$$= 53\text{ cm}$$

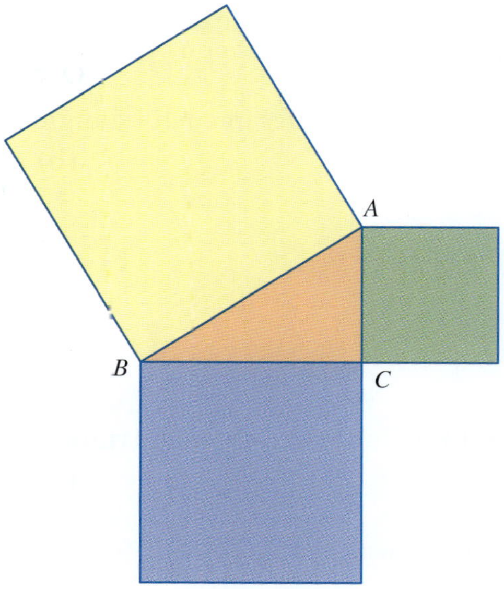

Converse of Pythagoras' Theorem

In ΔABC,
if area of square on AB
= area of square on AC + area of square on BC,
then $\angle ACB = 90°$.
or if $AB^2 = AC^2 + BC^2$, then $\angle ACB = 90°$.

CHALLENGE 10

ABCD is a lawn in the shape of trapezium. $AD = 40$ m, $BC = 54$ m and $CD = 50$ m. Find

(a) the length of AB,
(b) the area of the lawn.

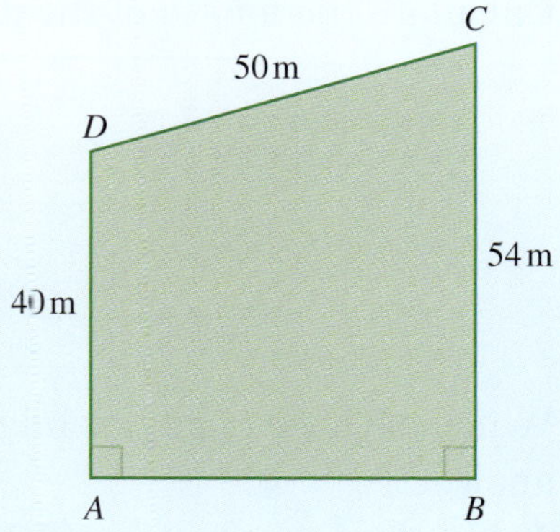

REVISION EXERCISE 10

In this exercise, give your answers to three significant figures if they are not integers.

1. Find the value of x in each triangle.

(a)

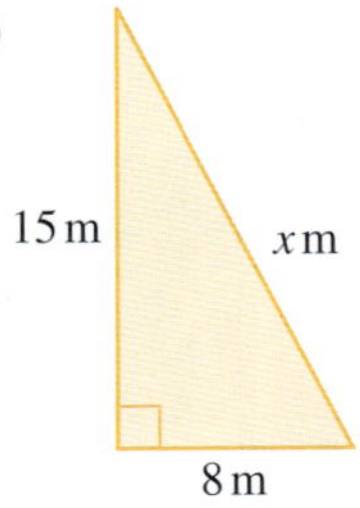

(b)

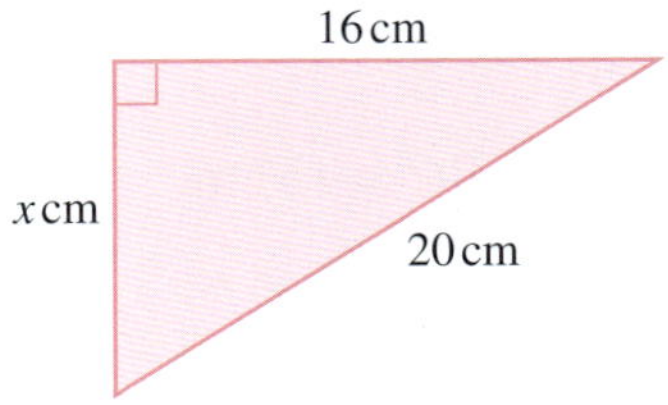

2. Find the value of a in each triangle.

(a)

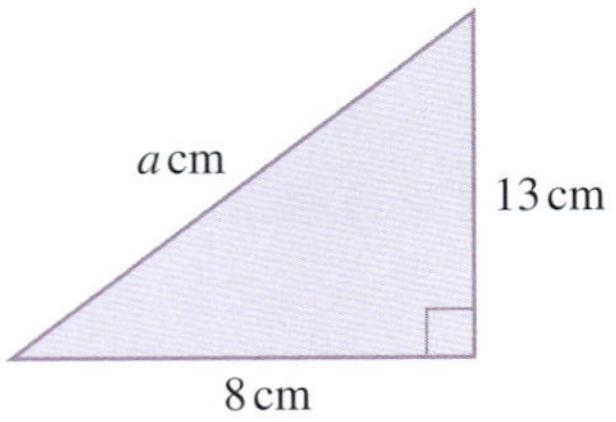

(b)

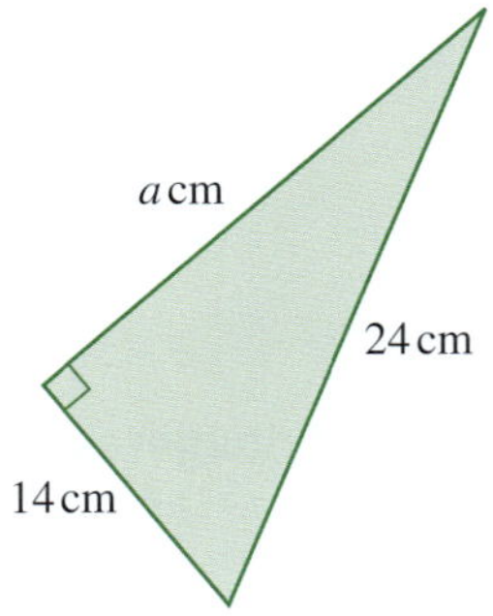

3. Could Pythagoras' Theorem be applied to each of these triangles? Explain your answers.

(a)

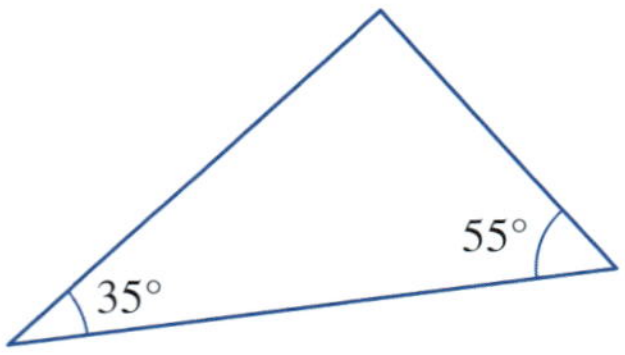

(b)

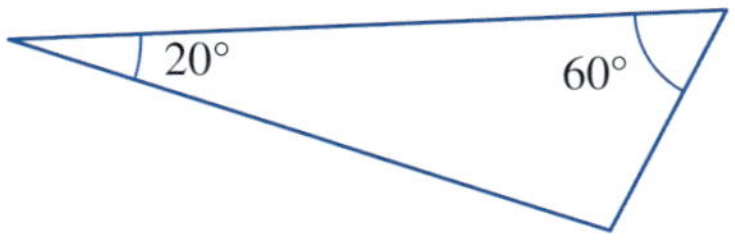

4. Which triangle with the given sides is a right-angled triangle? Explain your answer.

(a) 8 mm, 24 mm, 25 mm **(b)** 11 cm, 60 cm, 61 cm

5. Calculate the length of the diagonal of the rectangle shown.

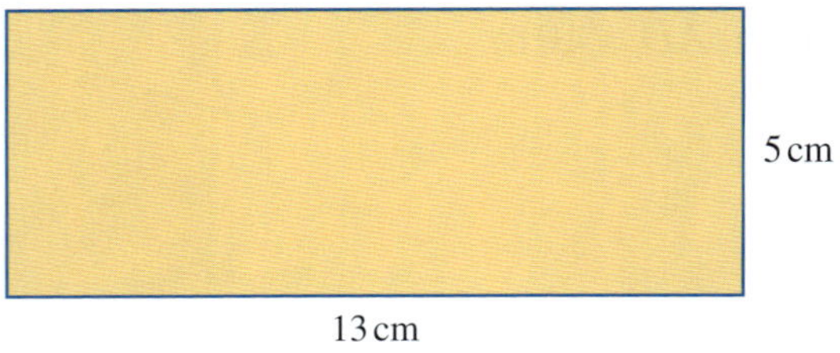

6. Which of these triangles might be the odd one out? Explain your answer.

Triangle A

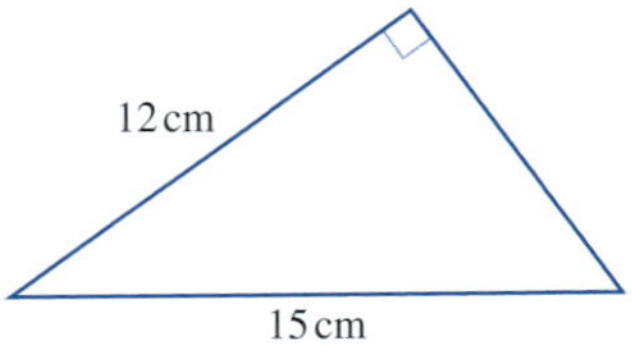

Triangle B

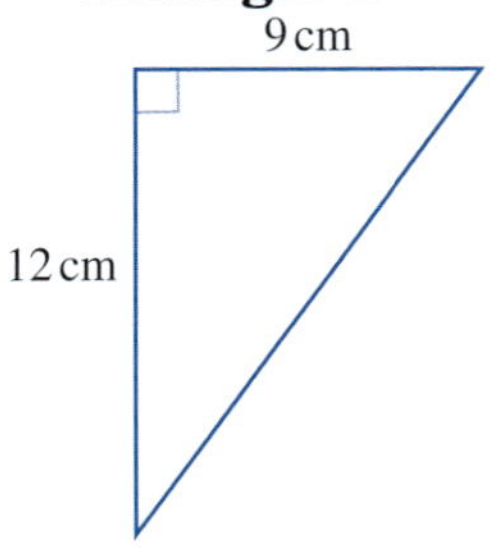

Triangle C

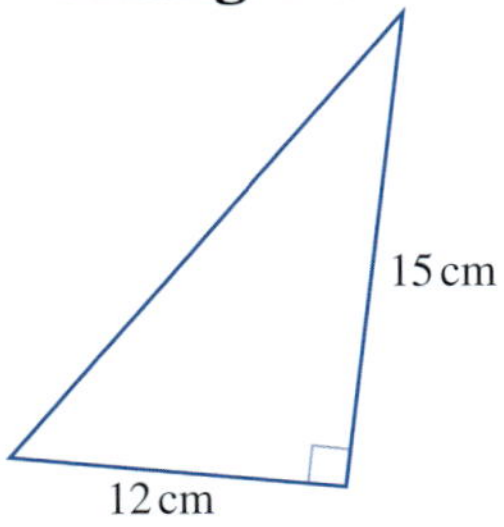

7. A ladder is propped up against a wall.
The ladder is 3 m long and the base of the ladder is 1 m from the base of the wall. Work out how far up the wall the ladder reaches.

8. Triangle *ABC* is an isosceles triangle. Find *CN*.

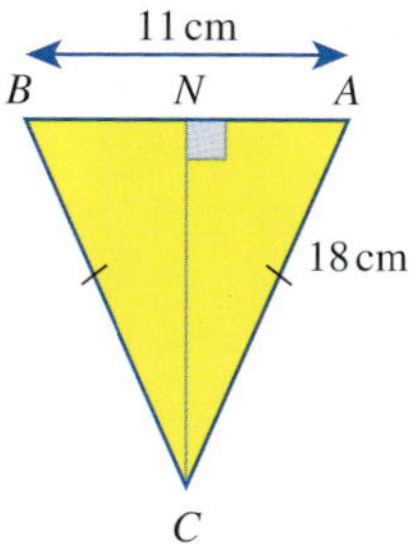

9. In the diagram shown, $AB = 10$ cm, $AC = 6$ cm, $CD = 15$ cm, $BD = 17$ cm and $\angle ACB = 90°$. Prove that points *A*, *C* and *D* lie on a straight line.

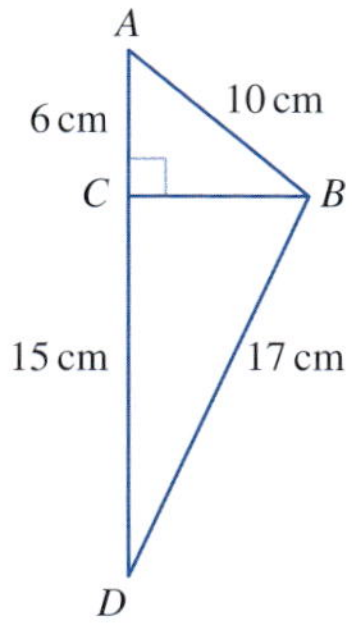

10. A tin for pencils has a rectangular base that is 14 cm long and 8 cm wide. A pencil is 16 cm long. Will the pencil fit in the bottom of the tin? Explain your answer.

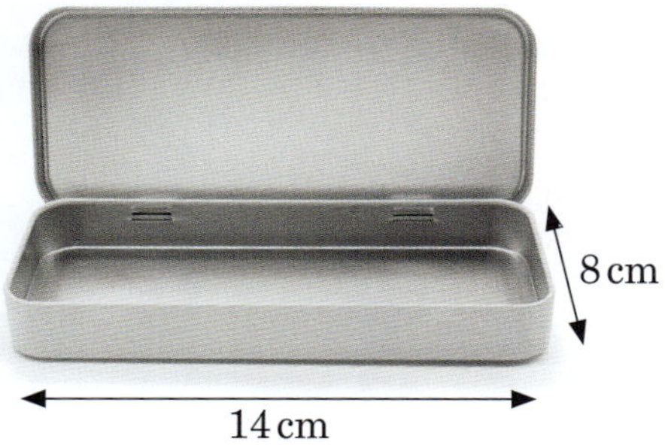

Write in Your Journal

1. Does an equilateral triangle have a hypotenuse?
2. Does an obtuse-angled triangle have a hypotenuse?
3. Can Pythagoras' Theorem be applied to
   (a) isosceles triangles, **(b)** scalene triangles?
4. Write down some examples of where people might use Pythagoras' Theorem in everyday life.

11 TRIGONOMETRY

WHAT IS IN THIS CHAPTER:

A surveyor uses a device called a theodolite for measuring angles. They can then use this to calculate heights, for example of buildings or bridges.

LET'S LEARN TO

- label the hypotenuse, opposite side and adjacent side of a right-angled triangle
- calculate trigonometric values
- find the unknown sides in right-angled triangles using trigonometry
- find the unknown angles in right-angled triangles using trigonometry

FLASHBACK

1. **Triangles**

   (a) A triangle has three sides and three angles.

   (b) $\angle a + \angle b + \angle c = 180°$

   (Angles in a triangle add up to 180°.)

   For example, if $\angle a = 90°$ and $\angle b = 38°$,

   then $90° + 38° + \angle c = 180°$

   $128° + \angle c = 180°$

   $128° - 128° + \angle c = 180° - 128°$

   $\angle c = 52°$

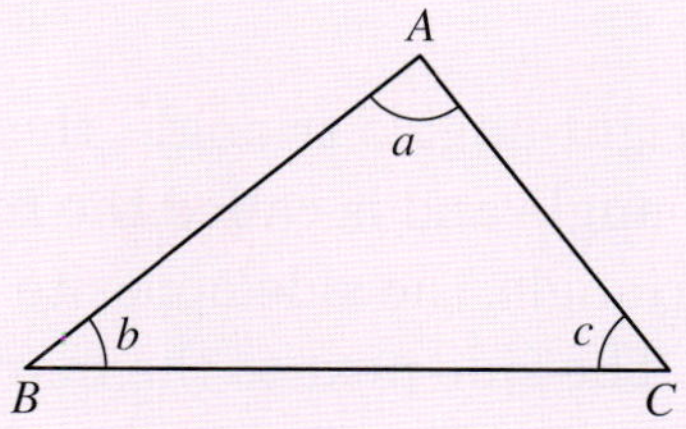

2. **Pythagoras' Theorem**

   In a right-angled triangle ABC, if $\angle ACB = 90°$, then area of square on AB
   = area of square on AC + area of square on BC
   (Pythagoras' Theorem)

   or $AB^2 = AC^2 + BC^2$

   The side AB facing the right angle is called the **hypotenuse** of the triangle.

   For example, given $BC = 15$ cm and $AC = 8$ cm,

   $AB^2 = AC^2 + BC^2$

   $AB^2 = 8^2 + 15^2$

   $= 64 + 225$

   $= 289$

   $AB = \sqrt{289}$

   $= 17$ cm (Since $AB > 0$.)

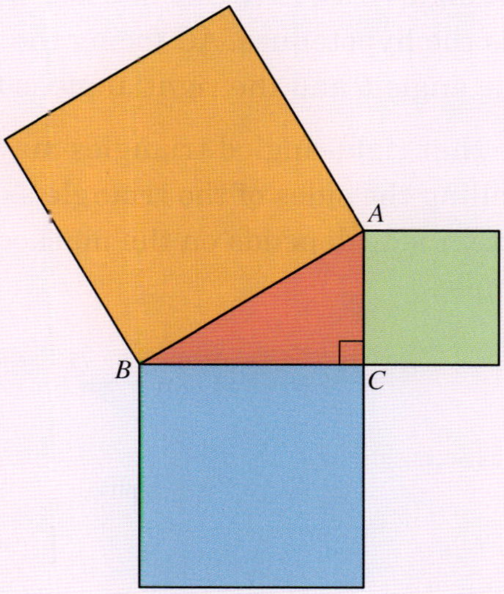

11.1 Introduction to Trigonometry

The triangle is an important shape in geometry. It has wide applications in architecture, engineering and construction. You will explore the relationship between the sides and angles of right-angled triangles in this chapter.

A Hypotenuse, Opposite Side and Adjacent Side

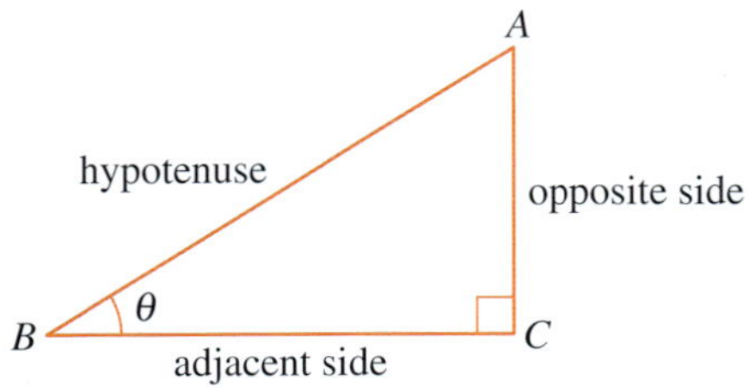

In a right-angled triangle, the longest side is always across from the right angle and is called the **hypotenuse**. For a marked acute angle in the triangle, the side opposite the marked angle is called the **opposite side**. The side next to the marked angle and the right angle is called the **adjacent side**.

In triangle ABC, $\angle ABC$ is marked with the Greek letter θ, read as theta. AB is the hypotenuse. AC facing the angle θ is the opposite side. BC next to the angle θ and the right angle is the adjacent side.

Note that right-angled triangles may have different orientations. Labelling the sides of the triangle as hypotenuse, opposite side and adjacent side depends on the marked angles. Here are two further examples.

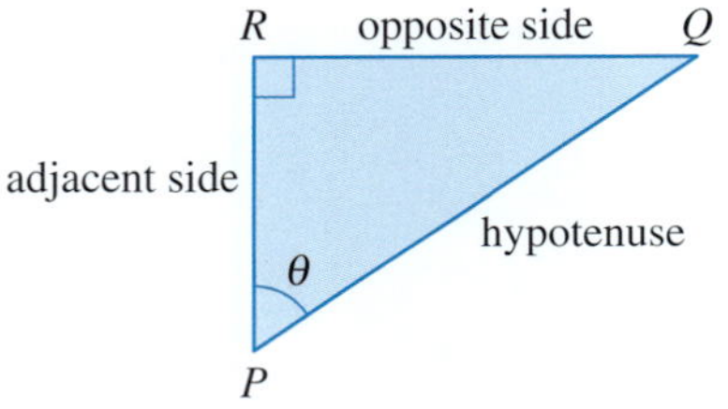

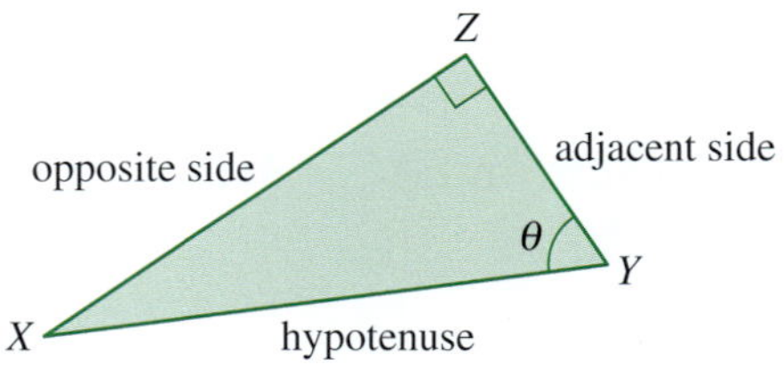

DISCUSS

What is the same and what is different about these triangles and the examples on the left of the page?

Can you label the sides of the triangle in each case?

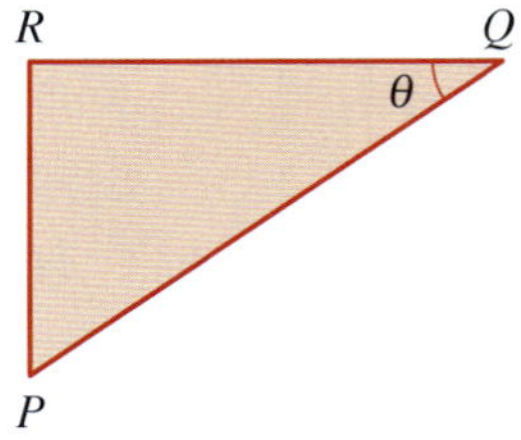

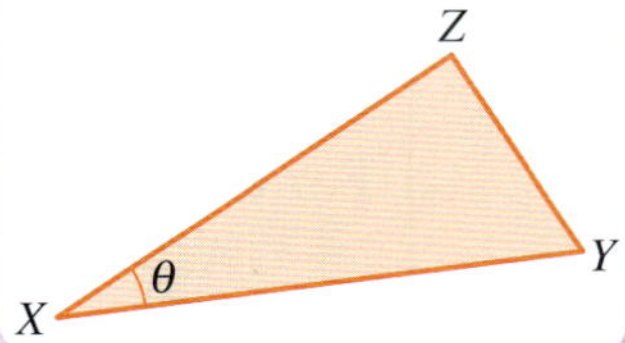

CLASS ACTIVITY 1

Objective: To label the sides of a right-angled triangle as hypotenuse, opposite side and adjacent side of a marked acute angle.

1. On a copy of the diagrams, label the hypotenuse, opposite side and adjacent side to the angle θ in each triangle.

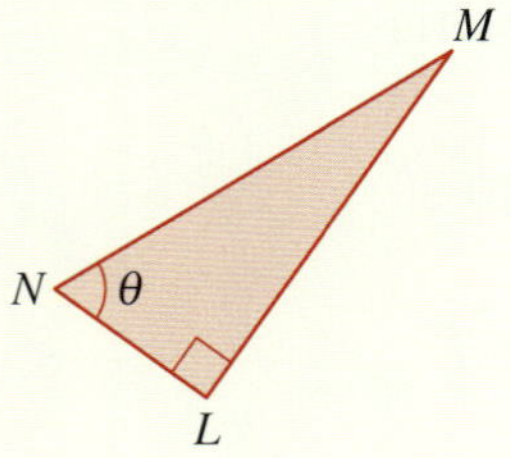

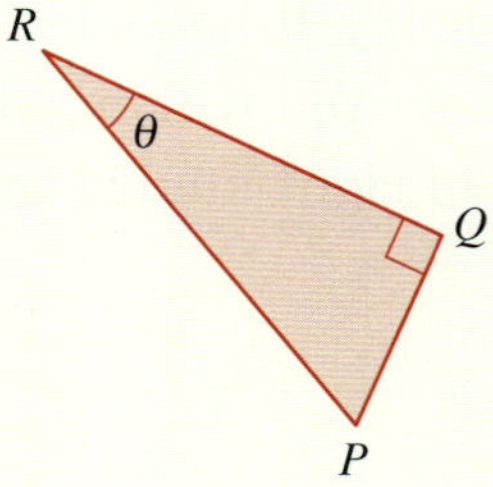

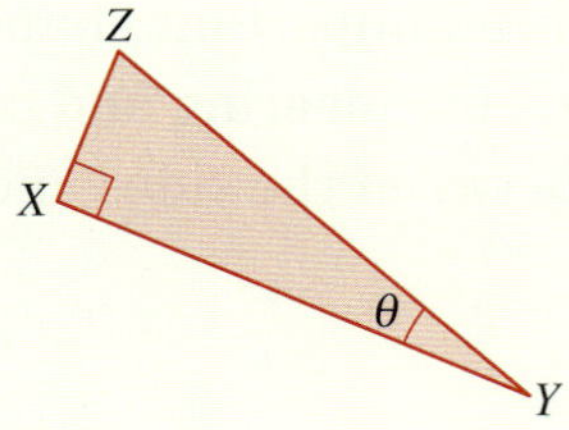

2. Draw your own right-angled triangle and label one of the acute angles θ.

3. Label the hypotenuse, opposite side and adjacent side to the angle θ in your triangle.

4. What is the same and what is different about these triangles?

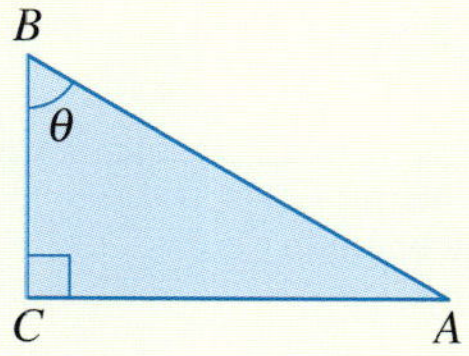

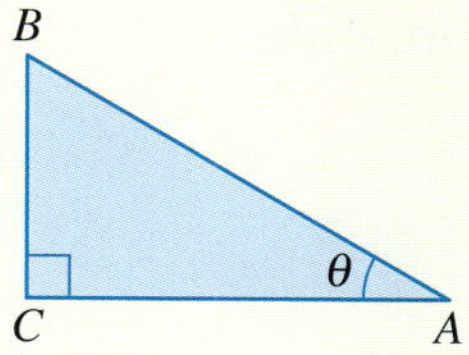

DISCUSS

Can you label the hypotenuse, opposite side and adjacent side to the angle θ in this triangle?

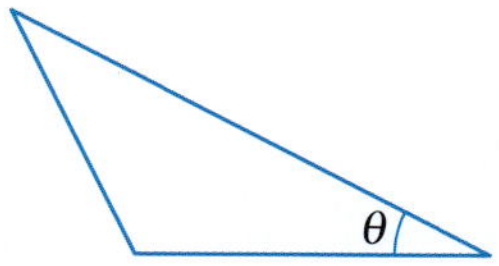

It is important that you can identify the hypotenuse, opposite side and adjacent side to an acute angle in a right-angled triangle. The working in this chapter is based on these terms.

B Trigonometric Values

Have a look at how the three sides of a right-angled triangle relate to each other in Class Activity 2.

CLASS ACTIVITY 2

Objective: To recognise the relationships between two sides and an acute angle of a right-angled triangle.

1. Use a ruler and protractor to draw any right-angled triangle with a 30° angle. Measure the lengths of the sides to the nearest millimetre.

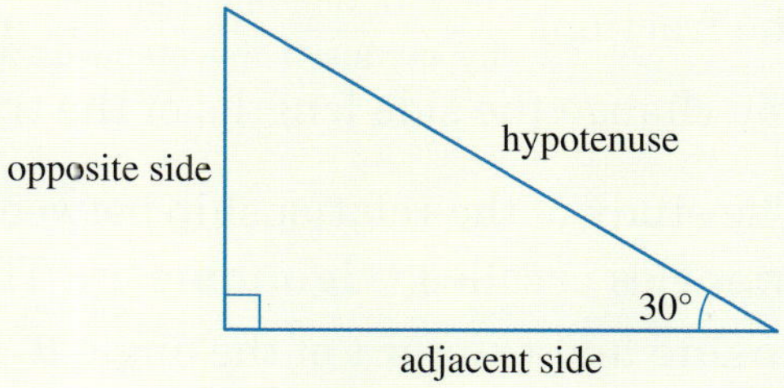

2. Use a calculator to work out the values of the fractions $\frac{\text{opposite side}}{\text{hypotenuse}}$, $\frac{\text{adjacent side}}{\text{hypotenuse}}$ and $\frac{\text{opposite side}}{\text{adjacent side}}$ using the correct side lengths of the triangle. Give your answers to one decimal place.

3. Repeat tasks **1** and **2** for a different right-angled triangle, still with a 30° angle.

   What do you notice about the value of the fractions $\frac{\text{opposite side}}{\text{hypotenuse}}$, $\frac{\text{adjacent side}}{\text{hypotenuse}}$ and $\frac{\text{opposite side}}{\text{adjacent side}}$?

4. Repeat tasks **1–3** for right-angled triangles with an acute angle of

   (a) 45°, **(b)** 70°.

   Repeat this task with two different triangles for each part.

In Class Activity 2, you saw that in the right-angled triangles you measured with an acute angle of 30°, the fraction $\frac{\text{opposite side}}{\text{adjacent side}}$ was approximately equal to 0.6 to one decimal place. This is always the case.

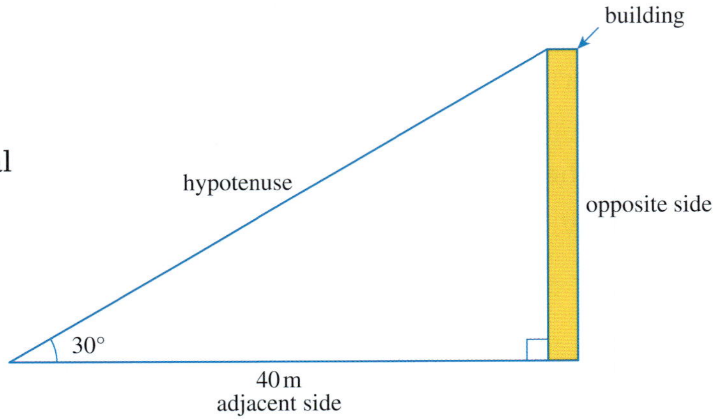

Recall the surveyor using a theodolite to work out the height of a building. Imagine they stand 40 m from the base of the building and uses the theodolite to measure the angle as 30°.

$$\frac{\text{opposite side}}{\text{adjacent side}} = 0.6$$

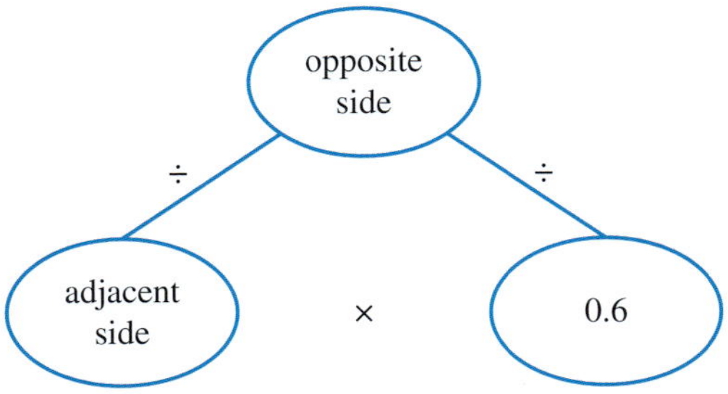

The factor tree shows you that

$$\begin{aligned}\text{opposite side} &= \text{adjacent side} \times 0.6\\ &= 40 \times 0.6\\ &= 24\end{aligned}$$

Thus, the height of the building is 24 m.

When an acute angle, θ, of a right-angled triangle is fixed, the values of the fractions $\frac{\text{opposite side}}{\text{hypotenuse}}$, $\frac{\text{adjacent side}}{\text{hypotenuse}}$ and $\frac{\text{opposite side}}{\text{adjacent side}}$ are also fixed, even if you change the side lengths of the triangle.

The study of the relationship between the side lengths and angles of triangles is called **trigonometry**. The fractions are called the **sine**, **cosine** and **tangent** of the angle θ. The sine of θ is given by $\frac{\text{opposite}}{\text{hypotenuse}}$ and is written $\sin\theta$. The cosine of θ is given by $\frac{\text{adjacent}}{\text{hypotenuse}}$ and is written $\cos\theta$. The tangent of θ is given by $\frac{\text{opposite}}{\text{adjacent}}$ and is written $\tan\theta$.

For a right-angled triangle as shown:

> the sine of angle θ is $\sin\theta = \frac{\text{opposite side}}{\text{hypotenuse}}$,
>
> the cosine of angle θ is $\cos\theta = \frac{\text{adjacent side}}{\text{hypotenuse}}$,
>
> and the tangent of angle θ is $\tan\theta = \frac{\text{opposite side}}{\text{adjacent side}}$.

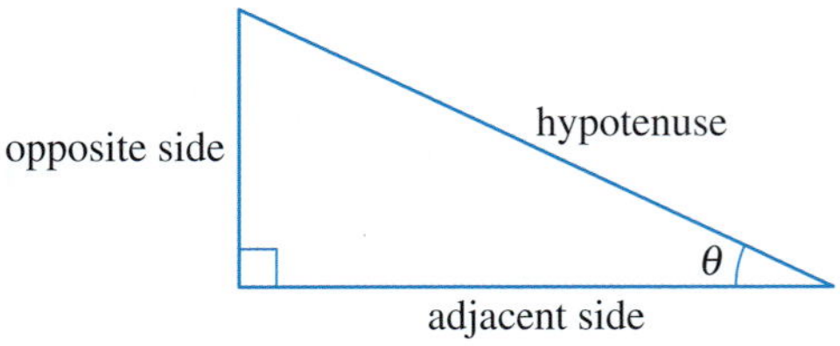

Example 1

Given the right-angled triangle ABC, find the values of $\sin A$, $\cos A$ and $\tan A$.

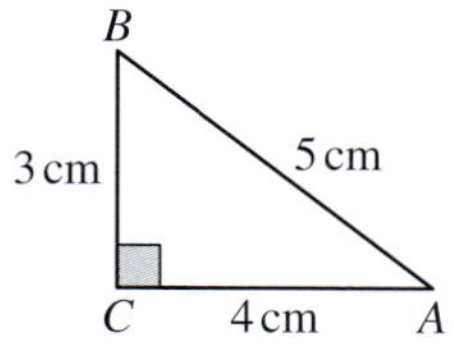

Solution

Hypotenuse $= AB = 5$ cm
For the angle A,
opposite side $= BC = 3$ cm
adjacent side $= AC = 4$ cm

$$\sin A = \frac{BC}{AB} = \frac{3}{5}$$

$\sin\theta = \frac{\text{oppsite side}}{\text{hypotenuse}}$

$$\cos A = \frac{AC}{AB} = \frac{4}{5}$$

$\cos\theta = \frac{\text{adjacent side}}{\text{hypotenuse}}$

$$\tan A = \frac{BC}{AC} = \frac{3}{4}$$

$\tan\theta = \frac{\text{oppsite side}}{\text{adjacent side}}$

Try It! 1

Given the right-angled triangle PQR, find the values of $\sin P$, $\cos P$ and $\tan P$.

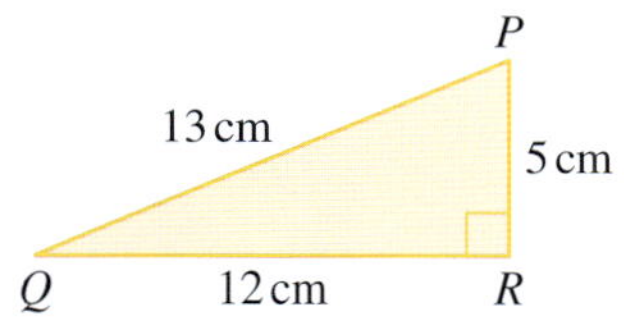

REMARK

$\sin A$ denotes the sine of angle BAC. It may be written as $\sin \angle A$ or $\sin \angle BAC$.

REMARK

For all trigonometry questions, start by identifying the hypotenuse, opposite and adjacent sides for the specified angle.

DISCUSS

What would you need to do differently if you were finding the values of $\sin B$, $\cos B$ and $\tan B$?

C Using a Calculator

You can use the keys [sin], [cos] and [tan] on a calculator to find the values of the sine, cosine and tangent of an angle. However, the calculator must be set to the DEGREE mode for angle measurement.

Example 2

Find these trigonometric values, giving your answers to three significant figures.

(a) $\sin 39°$ **(b)** $\cos 72°$ **(c)** $\tan 84°$

Solution

(a) Key sequence: [sin] 39 [=]
The display: 0.629320391
$\therefore \sin 39° = 0.629$ (to 3 sf)

REMARK

If your calculator is in the correct mode, then you will probably see a little 'D' or 'DEG' symbol at the top of the display. Different calculators may use different key sequences. You should be familiar with your own calculator.

REMARK

It is important to remember that $\sin 39°$ is a function, and does not mean $\sin \times 39°$.

(b) Key sequence: cos 72 =

The display: 0.3090169944

$\therefore$ cos 72° = 0.309 (to 3 sf)

(c) Key sequence: tan 84 =

The display: 9.514364454

$\therefore$ tan 84° = 9.51 (to 3 sf)

Try It! 2

Find these trigonometric values, giving your answers to three significant figures.

(a) sin 28° **(b)** cos 63° **(c)** tan 51°

DISCUSS

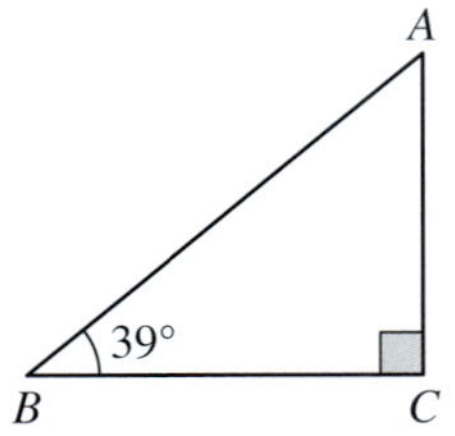

The result in part **(a)** means that

$\frac{AC}{AB} = \sin 39°$

$\approx 0.6293.$

How would you interpret the results in parts **(b)** and **(c)**?

PRACTICE 11.1

LEVEL 1

1. Name the hypotenuse, opposite side and adjacent side of the angle θ for each triangle. Give your answer as AC, FD and so on.

(a)

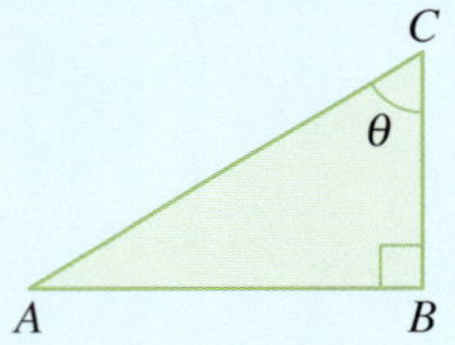

(b)

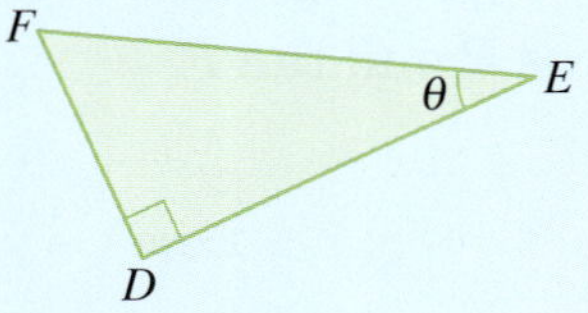

(c)

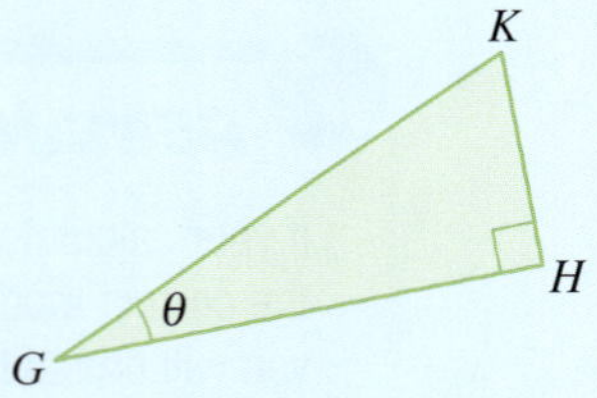

(d)

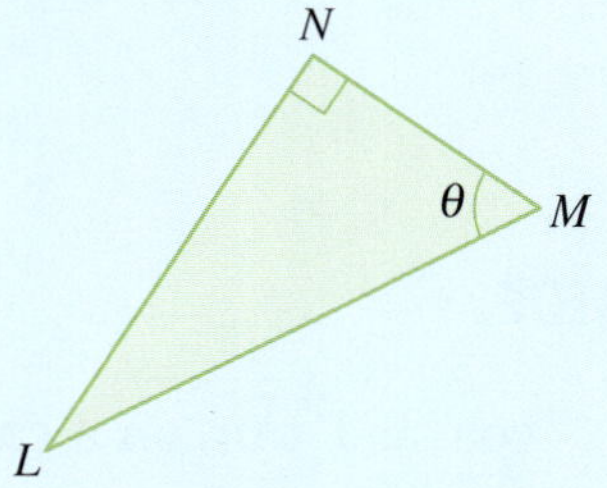

2. Copy and complete the following for the triangle LMN.

(a) $\sin\theta = \frac{\text{opposite side}}{\text{hypotenuse}} = \frac{}{}$

(b) $\cos\theta = \frac{\text{adjacent side}}{\text{hypotenuse}} = \frac{}{}$

(c) $\tan\theta = \frac{\text{opposite side}}{\text{adjacent side}} = \frac{}{}$

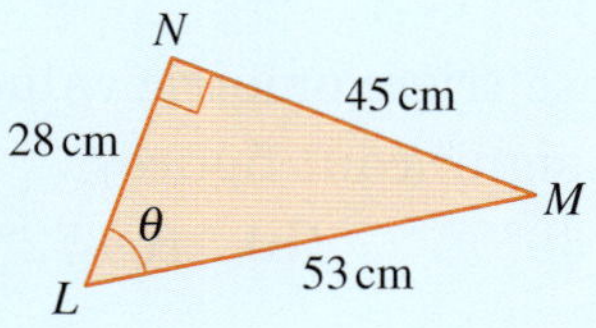

3. In ΔABC, find the value of $\sin A$, $\cos A$ and $\tan A$.

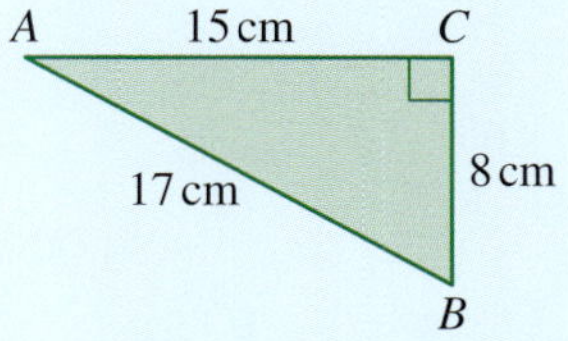

4. Which of these statements are incorrect? Explain your answer.

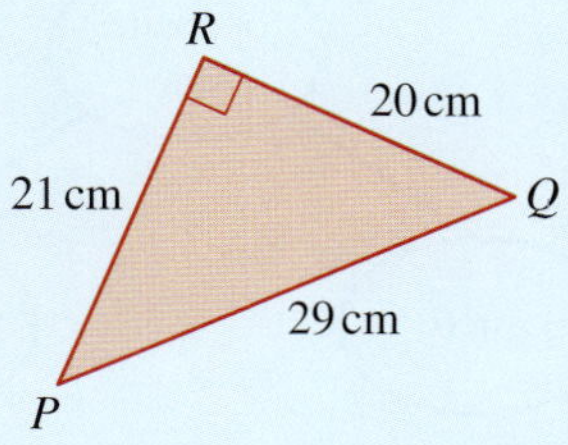

(a) $\sin P = \frac{20}{29}$

(b) $\tan P = \frac{21}{20}$

(c) $\cos Q = \frac{21}{29}$

(d) $\tan Q = \frac{21}{20}$

5. Find these trigonometric values using a calculator, giving your answers to three significant figures.

(a) $\sin 24°$ (b) $\cos 17°$ (c) $\tan 73°$

LEVEL 2

6. Express these in terms of a, b and c.

(a) $\sin\theta$ (b) $\cos\theta$ (c) $\tan\theta$

Hint: You can first write out each formula with the terms opposite, adjacent or hypotenuse before substituting a, b and c.

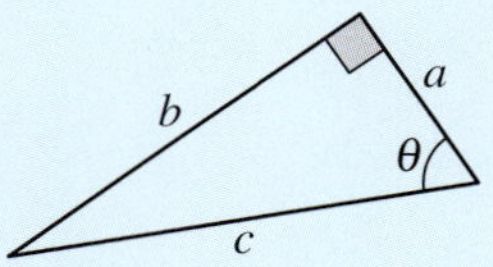

7. Refer to ΔABC.

PROBLEM SOLVING

(a) Express $\sin A$ in terms of a, b and/or c.

(b) Express $\cos B$ in terms of a, b and/or c.

(c) What is the relationship between $\sin A$ and $\cos B$?

Hint: Start by labelling the sides for parts **(a)** and **(b)** and writing out the relationships that you know.

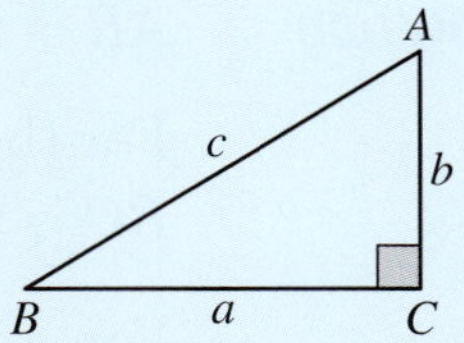

8. ABP and ACQ are straight lines.

PROBLEM SOLVING

(a) Express $\frac{CB}{AB}$ in terms of θ using trigonometry.

(b) Express $\frac{QP}{AP}$ in terms of θ using trigonometry.

(c) What is the relationship between $\frac{CB}{AB}$ and $\frac{QP}{AP}$?

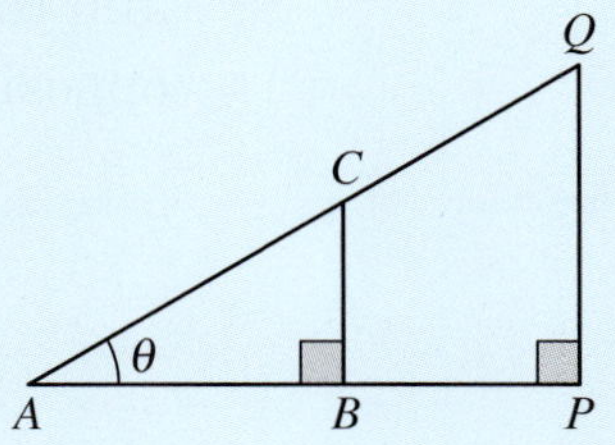

11.2 Finding Unknown Sides in Right-angled Triangles

When a side and an acute angle of a right-angled triangle are known, the other two sides can be calculated using trigonometry. Factor trees will help you to rearrange the formulae.

$\sin\,\theta = \dfrac{\text{opposite side}}{\text{hypotenuse}}$ $\quad\cos\,\theta = \dfrac{\text{adjacent side}}{\text{hypotenuse}}$ $\quad\tan\,\theta = \dfrac{\text{opposite side}}{\text{adjacent side}}$

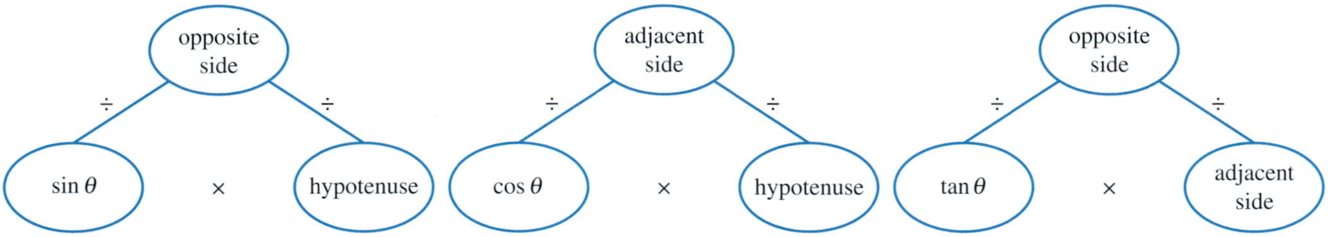

Now have a look at some examples.

Example 3

Use $\sin\,\theta = \dfrac{\text{opposite side}}{\text{hypotenuse}}$ to find the length of AC in the diagram.

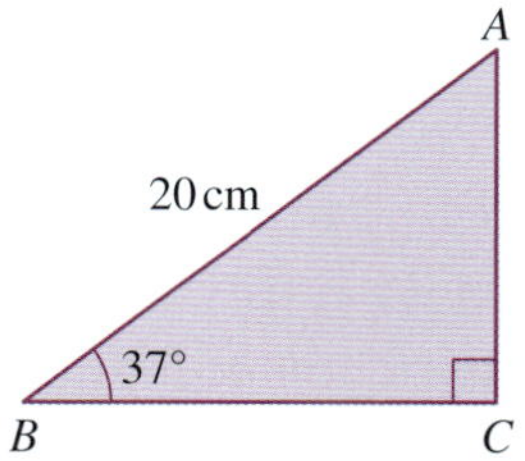

Solution

AB is the hypotenuse.

For the given angle 37°, AC is the opposite side and BC is the adjacent side.

You are told to use $\sin\,\theta = \dfrac{\text{opposite side}}{\text{hypotenuse}}$ since it involves a side you know the length of (the hypotenuse, AB) and the side you want to find the length of (the opposite, AC).

REMARK

For all trigonometry questions, start by identifying the hypotenuse, opposite and adjacent sides for the specified angle.

Using a factor tree for $\sin\theta = \dfrac{\text{opposite side}}{\text{hypotenuse}}$

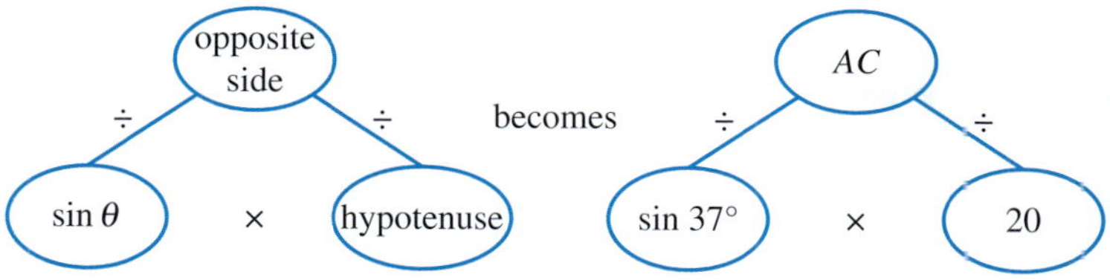

$\sin 37° = \dfrac{AC}{20}$ $\sin\theta = \dfrac{\text{oppsite side}}{\text{hypoter use}}$

$AC = 20 \times \sin 37°$

$= 12.0\,\text{cm}$ (to 3 sf)   Use a calculator.

Note: The calculator key sequence is:

20 [×] [sin] 37 [=]

Try It! 3

Use $\sin\theta = \dfrac{\text{opposite side}}{\text{hypotenuse}}$ to find the length of AC in the diagram, giving your answers to three significant figures.

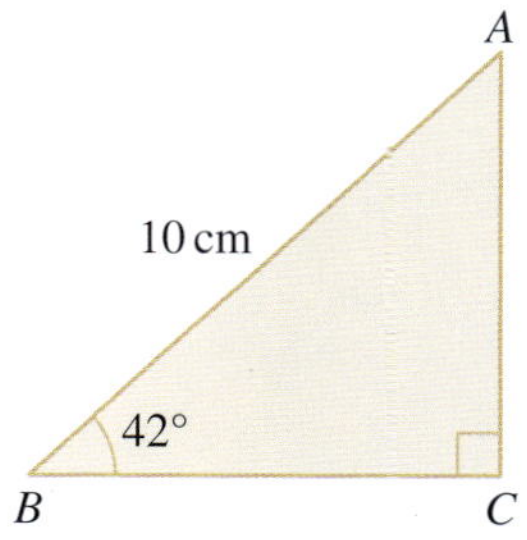

DISCUSS

What are the steps to make AC the subject of $\sin 39° = \dfrac{AC}{20}$ using algebra?

Example 4

Find the length of LM in the triangle LMN.

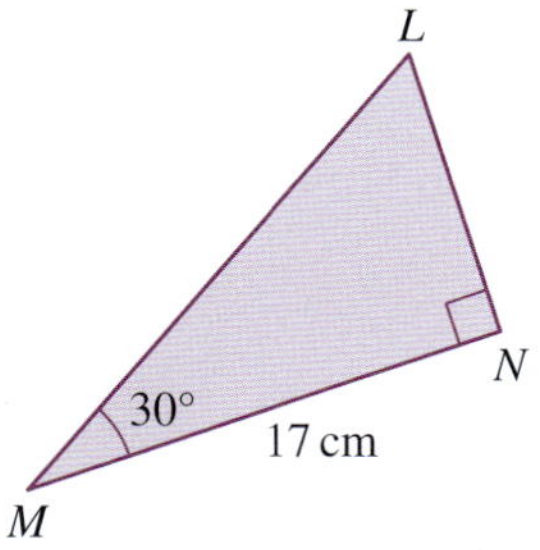

Solution

LM is the hypotenuse. For the given angle 30°, LN is the opposite side and MN is the adjacent side. You should use $\cos\theta = \dfrac{\text{adjacent side}}{\text{hypotenuse}}$ since it involves a side you know the length of (the adjacent side, MN) and the side you want to find the length of (the hypotenuse, LM).

REMARK

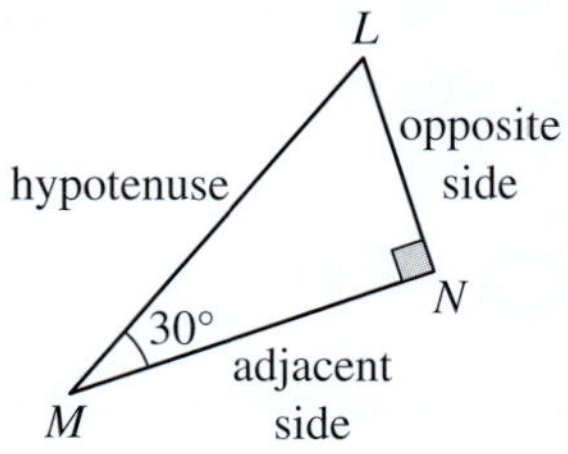

You should first identify the hypotenuse, opposite side and adjacent side to the angle 30°.

Using a factor tree for $\cos\theta = \frac{\text{adjacent side}}{\text{hypotenuse}}$

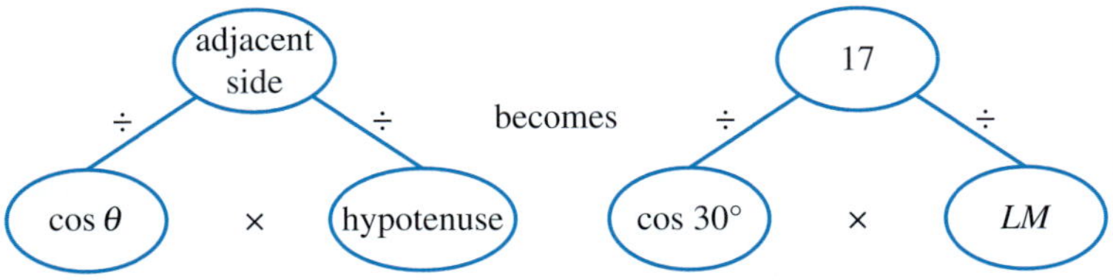

$\cos 30° = \frac{17}{LM}$ $\cos\theta = \frac{\text{adjacent side}}{\text{hypotenuse}}$

$LM = 17 \div \cos 30°$

$= 19.6\,\text{cm}$ (to 3 sf) Use a calculator.

Note: The calculator key sequence is:

17 [÷] [cos] 30 [=]

> **DISCUSS**
>
> What are the steps to make LM the subject of $\cos 30° = \frac{17}{LM}$ using algebra?

Try It! 4

Find the length of LM in the triangle LMN.

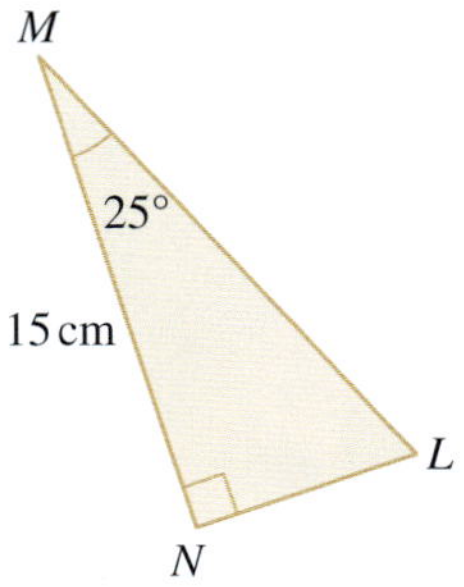

> **DISCUSS**
>
> How could you find the length LN in this triangle?
>
> Is there more than one possible method?

PRACTICE 11.2

In this exercise, give your answers for lengths to three significant figures.

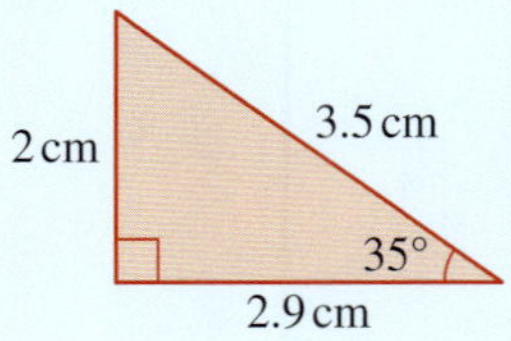

LEVEL 1

1. Copy and complete the factor trees for this triangle.

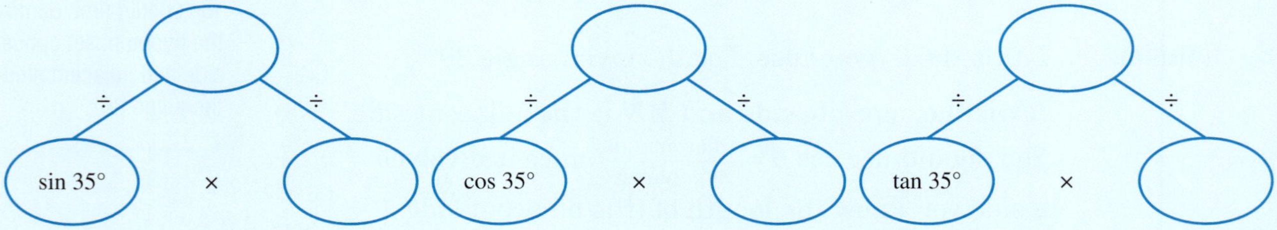

2. Use $\sin\theta = \frac{\text{opposite side}}{\text{hypotenuse}}$ to find the length of

(a) BC,

(b) YZ.

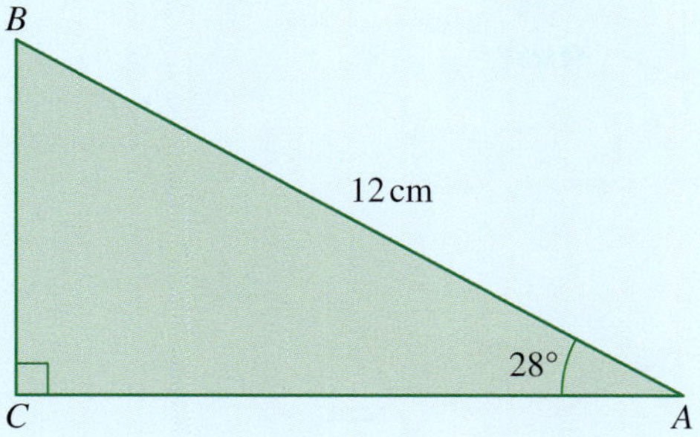

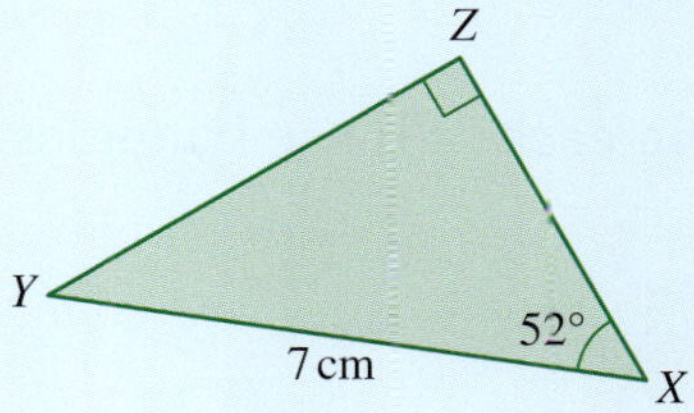

3. Use $\cos\theta = \frac{\text{adjacent side}}{\text{hypotenuse}}$ to find the length of

(a) AB,

(b) XZ.

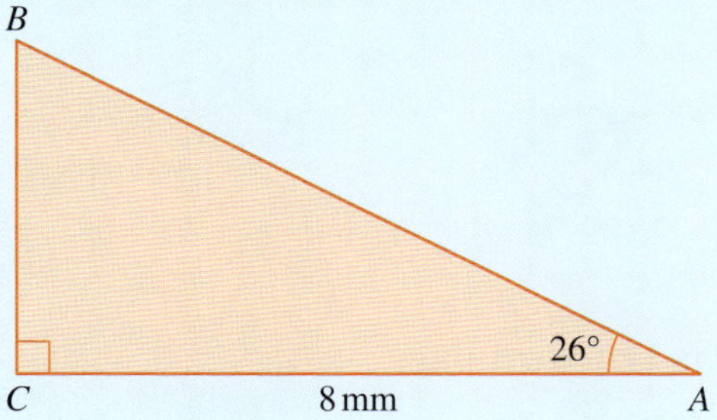

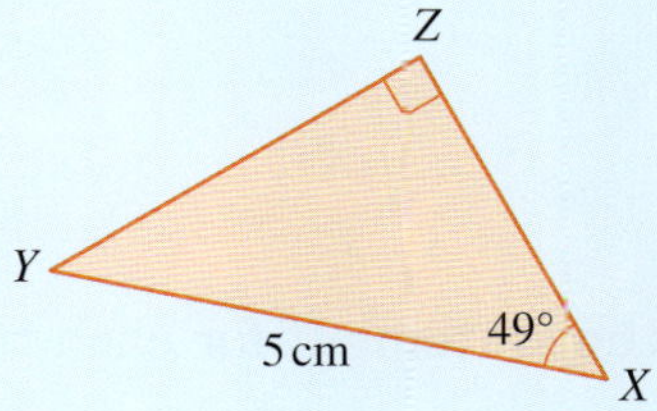

4. Use $\tan\theta = \frac{\text{opposite side}}{\text{adjacent side}}$ to find the length of

(a) BC,

(b) YZ.

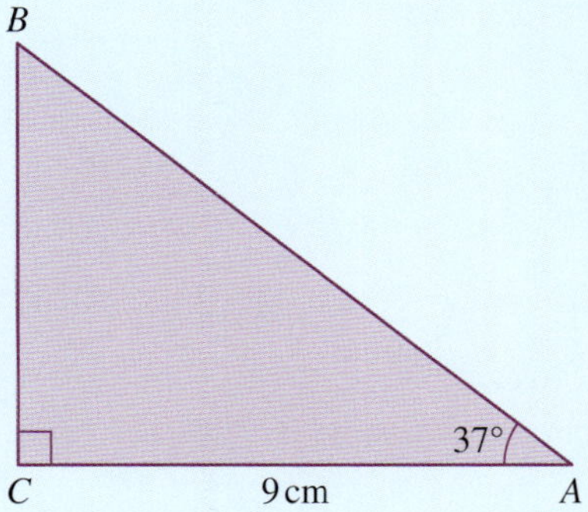

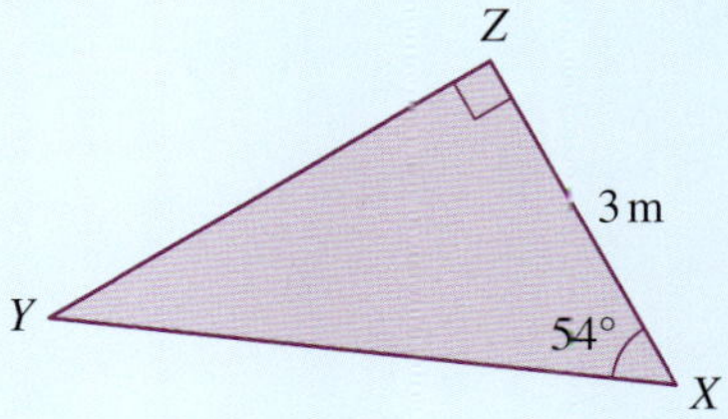

LEVEL 2

5. Find the value of x in each of these triangles.

(a)

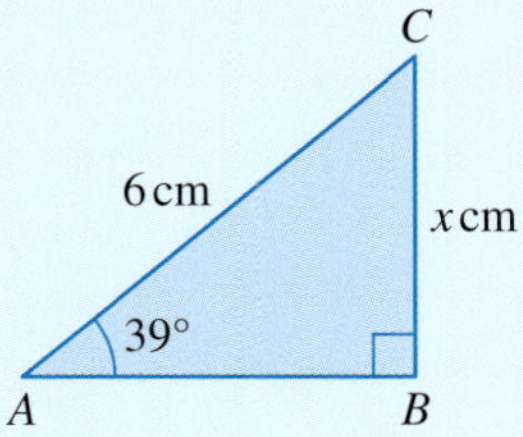

(b)

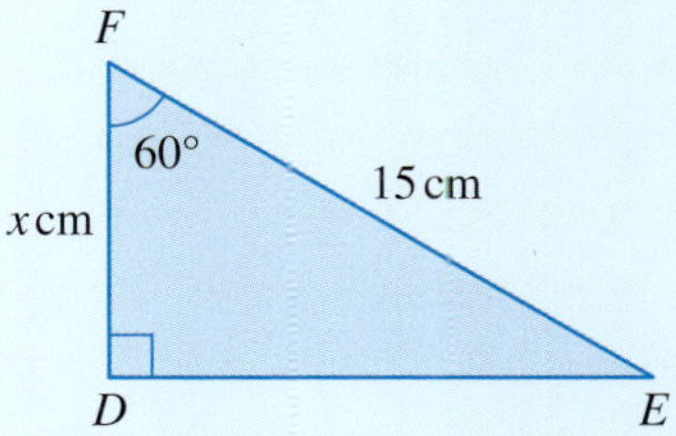

(c)

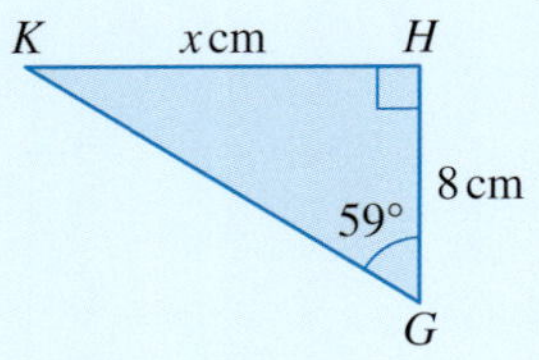

(d)

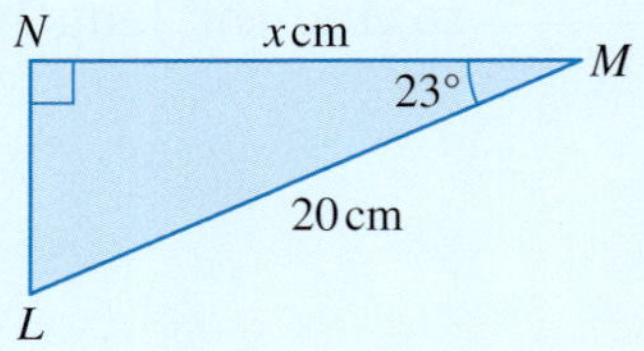

6. Find the value of z in each of these triangles.

(a)

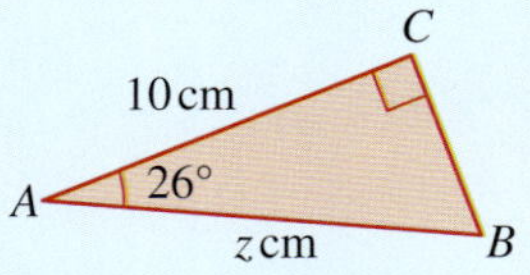

(b)

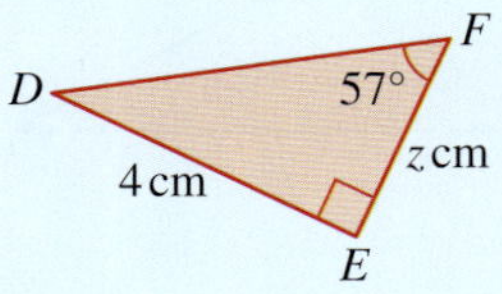

(c)

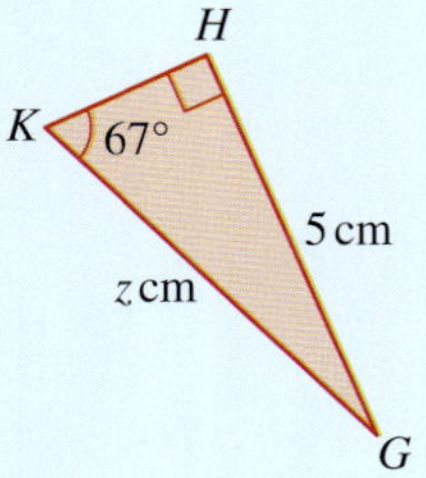

(d)

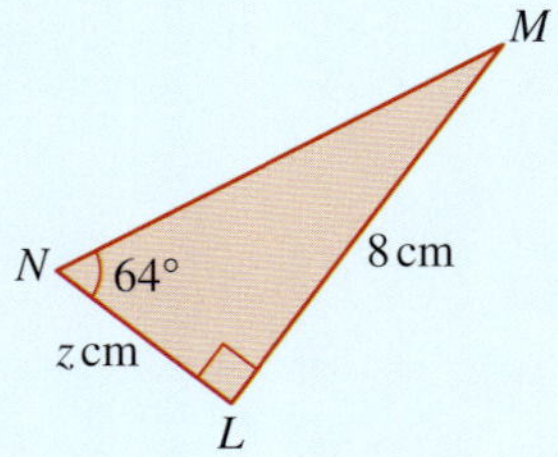

7. Determine whether the statement for each triangle is true or false.

(a) $x = 17 \times \sin 22°$

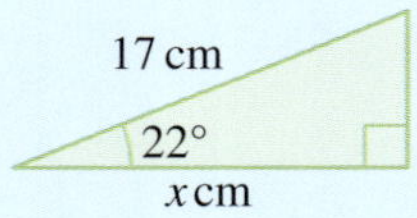

(b) $y = \dfrac{20}{\tan 63°}$

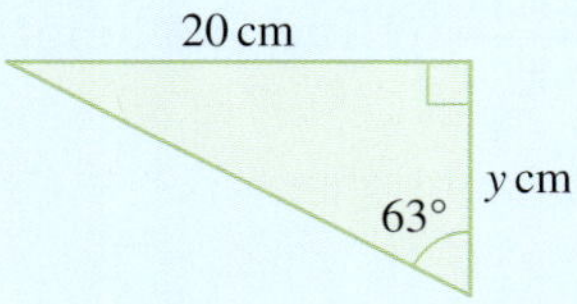

(c) $x = 35 \times \sin 53°$

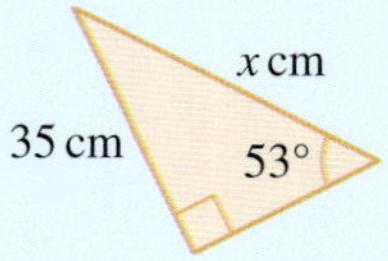

(d) $y = \dfrac{40}{\cos 58°}$

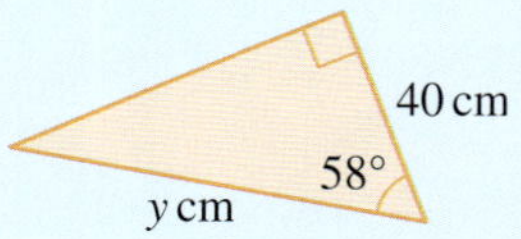

8. The diagram shows a triangular garden ABC.
Find the perimeter of the garden.

PROBLEM SOLVING

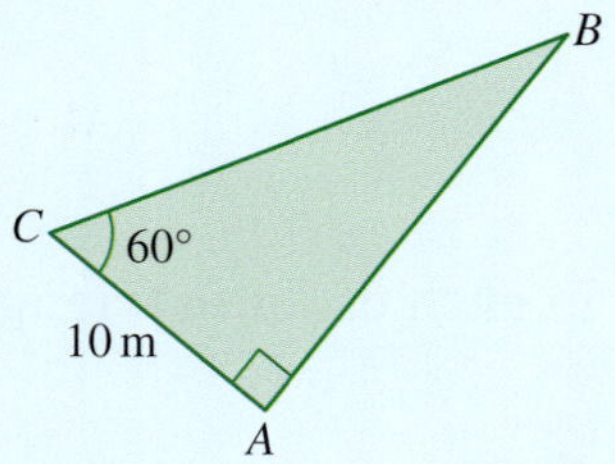

11.3 Finding Unknown Angles in Right-angled Triangles

A Finding θ for a Given Value of $\sin\theta$, $\cos\theta$ or $\tan\theta$ Using a Calculator

You already know what the inverse function of multiplication is, and you know the inverse function of addition. In the same way, trigonometric functions have inverses too. When a trigonometric value of the size of an acute angle θ is given, you can find θ by using the inverse function keys $\boxed{\sin^{-1}}$, $\boxed{\cos^{-1}}$ and $\boxed{\tan^{-1}}$ on a calculator. These keys are usually the second functions of the keys $\boxed{\sin}$, $\boxed{\cos}$ and $\boxed{\tan}$ respectively.

REMARK

To get the $\boxed{\sin^{-1}}$ key, you need to press $\boxed{\text{2nd F}}$ or $\boxed{\text{SHIFT}}$ and then press the $\boxed{\sin}$ key. You can get the $\boxed{\cos^{-1}}$ and $\boxed{\tan^{-1}}$ keys in a similar way.

Example 5

Find the size of the acute angle θ in each case, giving your answers to one decimal place.

(a) $\sin\theta = 0.48$ **(b)** $\tan\theta = \frac{7}{4}$

Solution

(a) For $\sin\theta = 0.48$,

$$\sin^{-1}(\sin\theta) = \sin^{-1}0.48$$
$$\theta = \sin^{-1}0.48$$

Take the inverse sine of both sides.

Key sequence: $\boxed{\sin^{-1}}$ 0.48 $\boxed{=}$

The display: 28.68540201

$\therefore\ \theta = 28.7°$ (to 1 dp)

(b) For $\tan\theta = \frac{7}{4}$,

$$\tan^{-1}(\tan\theta) = \tan^{-1}\frac{7}{4}$$
$$\theta = \tan^{-1}\frac{7}{4}$$

Key sequence: $\boxed{\tan^{-1}}$ 7 $\boxed{\div}$ 4 $\boxed{)}$ $\boxed{=}$

The display: 60.2551187

$\therefore\ \theta = 60.3°$ (to 1 dp)

Note: Angles are rounded to one decimal place in this chapter.

DISCUSS

Press this key sequence into your calculator:

$\boxed{\sin}$ 20 $\boxed{=}$

$\boxed{\sin^{-1}}$ $\boxed{\text{Ans}}$ $\boxed{=}$

What do you notice?

Try It! 5

Find the size of the acute angle θ in each case, giving your answers to one decimal place.

(a) $\tan\theta = 0.0328$ **(b)** $\cos\theta = \frac{2}{9}$

B Finding Unknown Angles in Right-angled Triangles

When two of the sides of a right-angled triangle are given, the two acute angles of the triangle can be found using trigonometry.

Example 6

Find the size of angle θ in each of these diagrams.

(a)

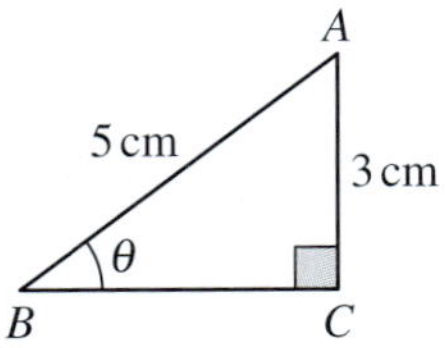

(b)

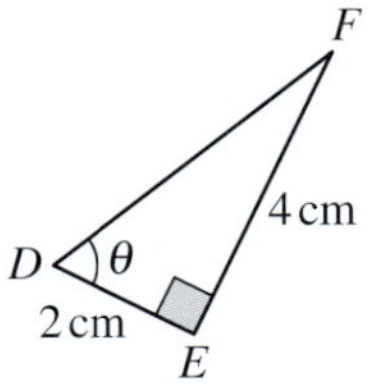

Solution

(a) In ΔABC,

$$\text{hypotenuse} = AB = 5\text{ cm}$$

opposite side to $\angle\theta$ is $AC = 3$ cm.

So, you need to use $\sin\theta$.

$$\sin\theta = \frac{3}{5} \qquad \sin\theta = \frac{\text{opposite side}}{\text{hypotenuse}}$$

$$\sin^{-1}(\sin\theta) = \sin^{-1}\left(\frac{3}{5}\right)$$

$$\therefore \quad \theta = \sin^{-1}\left(\frac{3}{5}\right) = 36.7° \quad \text{(to 1 dp)}$$

(b) In ΔDEF,

opposite side to $\angle\theta$ is $EF = 4$ cm

adjacent side to $\angle\theta$ is $DE = 2$ cm

So, you need to use $\tan\theta$.

$$\tan\theta = \frac{4}{2} = 2 \qquad \tan\theta = \frac{\text{opposite side}}{\text{adjacent side}}$$

$$\tan^{-1}(\tan\theta) = \tan^{-1}2$$

$$\therefore \quad \theta = \tan^{-1}2 = 63.4° \quad \text{(to 1 dp)}$$

Try It! 6

Find the size of angle θ in each of these diagrams.

(a)

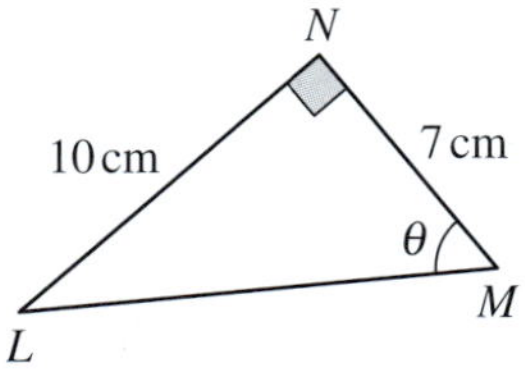

(b)

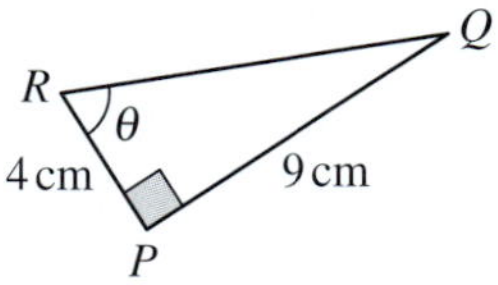

REMARK

You should label the given sides and the unknown angle to help you determine whether to use the sine, cosine or tangent of the angle.

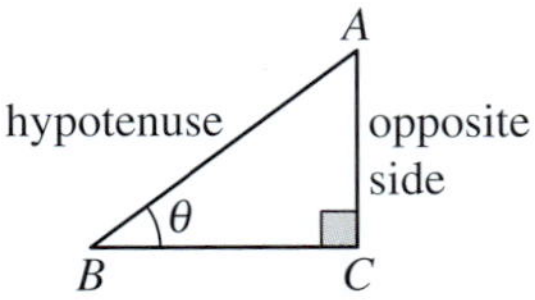

RECALL

$$\sin\theta = \frac{\text{opposite side}}{\text{hypotenuse}}$$

$$\cos\theta = \frac{\text{adjacent side}}{\text{hypotenuse}}$$

$$\tan\theta = \frac{\text{opposite side}}{\text{adjacent side}}$$

REMARK

You can continue to use factor trees to help you rearrange the formula.

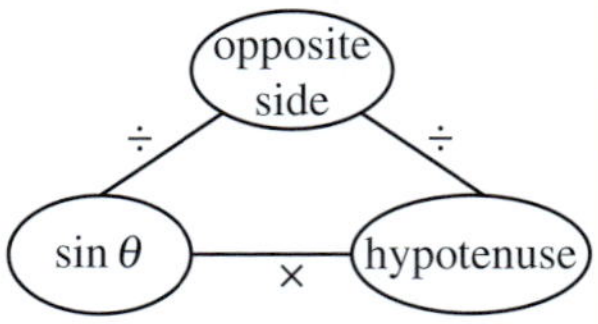

Can you draw the factor tree for tan θ?

PRACTICE 11.3

In this exercise, give your answers for angles in degrees to one decimal place.

LEVEL 1

1. Find the size of the acute angle θ in degrees.

(a) $\sin\theta = 0.3$ **(b)** $\cos\theta = 0.47$ **(c)** $\tan\theta = 1.5$

(d) $\sin\theta = \frac{2}{5}$ **(e)** $\cos\theta = \frac{3}{8}$ **(f)** $\tan\theta = \frac{9}{7}$

2. Use $\sin\theta = \frac{\text{opposite side}}{\text{hypotenuse}}$ to find the size of angle θ in these triangles.

(a)

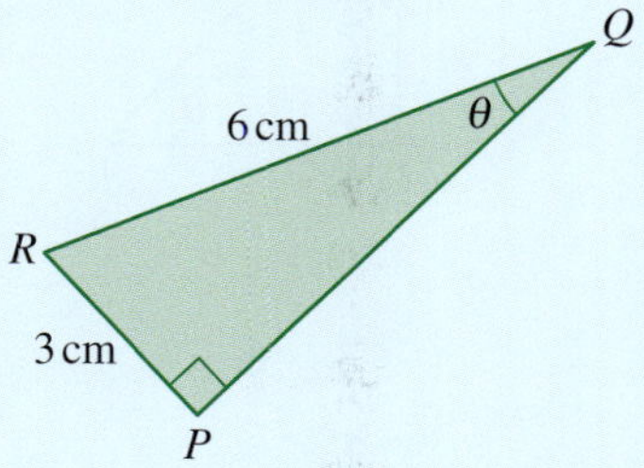

(b)

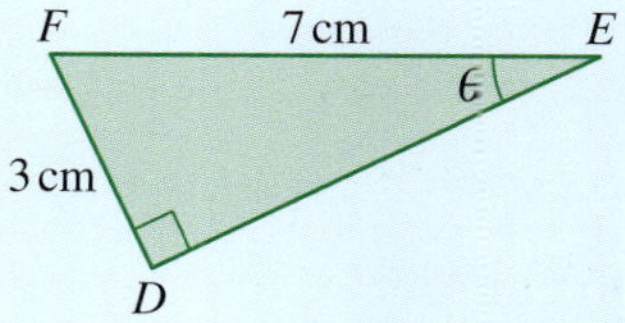

3. Use $\tan\theta = \frac{\text{opposite side}}{\text{adjacent side}}$ to find the size of angle θ in these triangles.

(a)

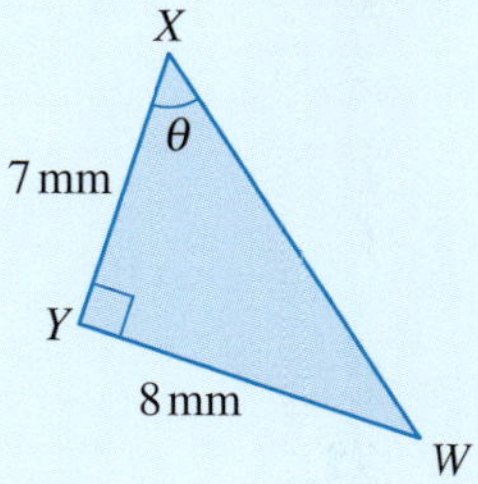

(b)

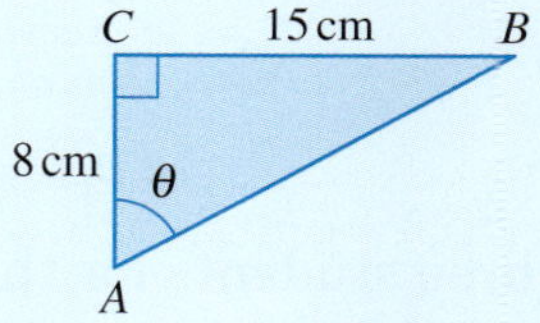

4. Use $\cos\theta = \frac{\text{adjacent side}}{\text{hypotenuse}}$ to find the size of angle θ in these triangles.

(a)

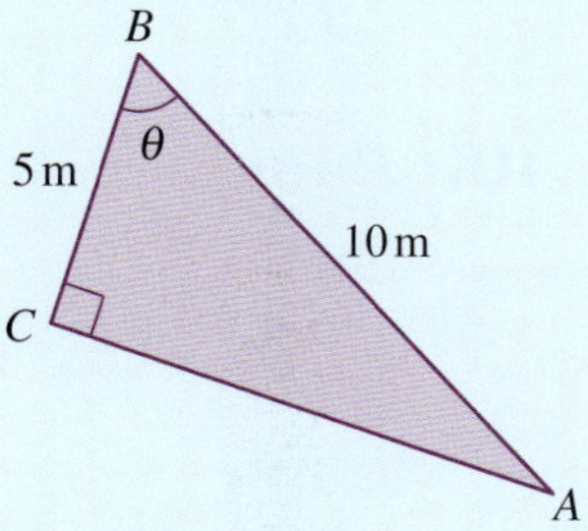

(b)

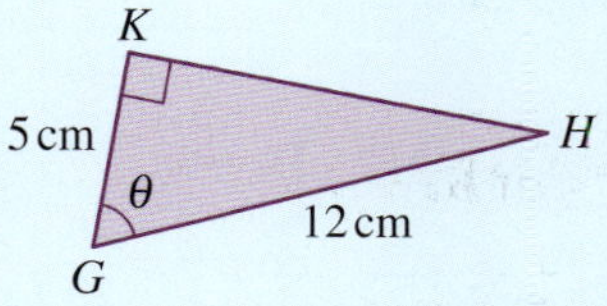

5. **(a)** Write down the values of $\sin a$, $\cos a$ and $\tan a$ for this triangle.

(b) Use your answers from part **(a)** to find the size of angle a.

(c) Can you answer part **(b)** in another way? Show your working.

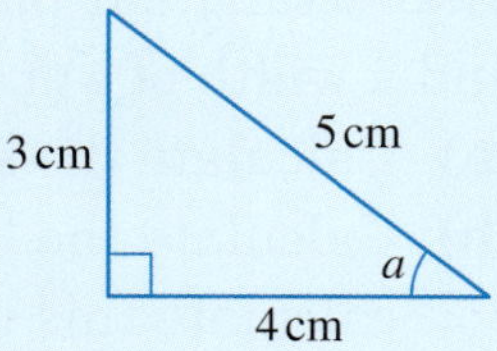

LEVEL 2

6. Find the size of angle θ in each triangle.

(a)

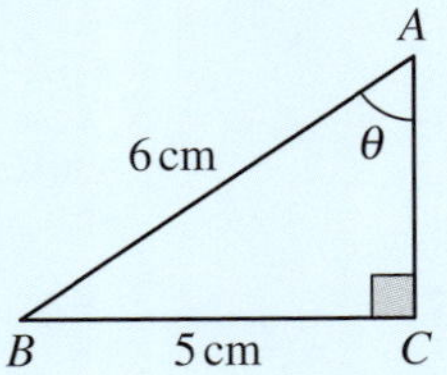

(b)

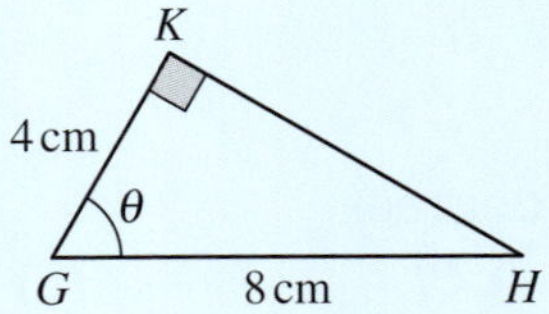

(c)

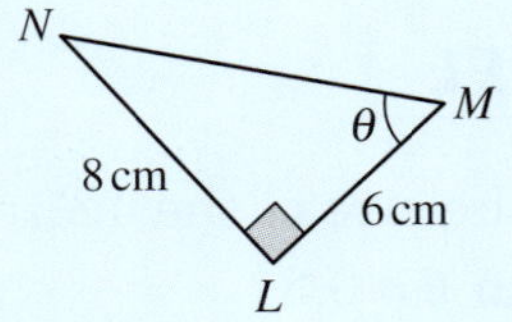

(d)

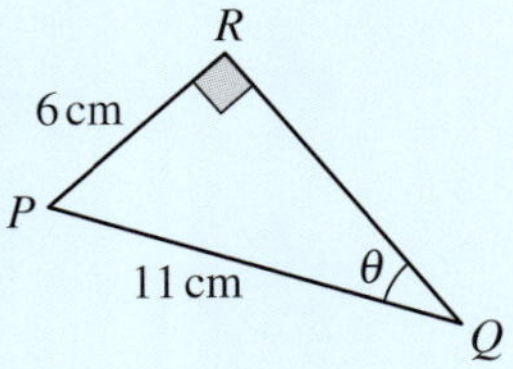

(e)

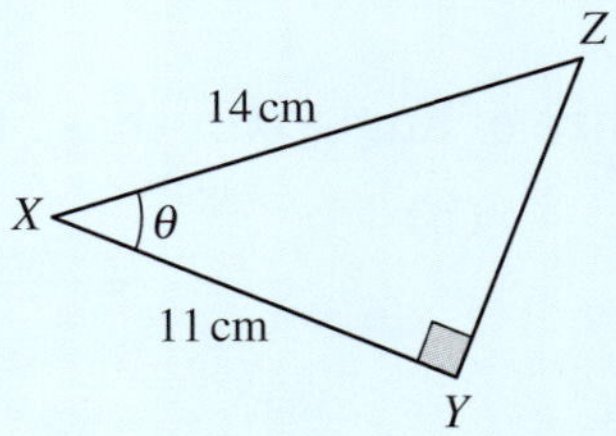

(f)

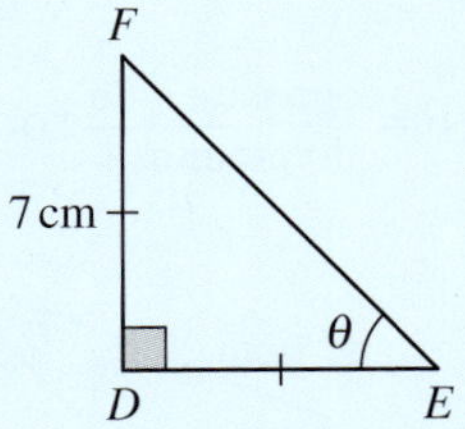

7. Which angle, x or y, is larger?

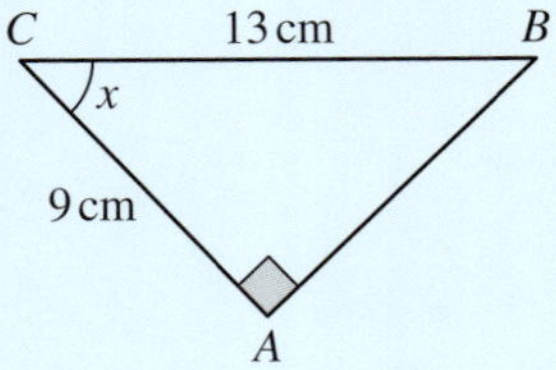

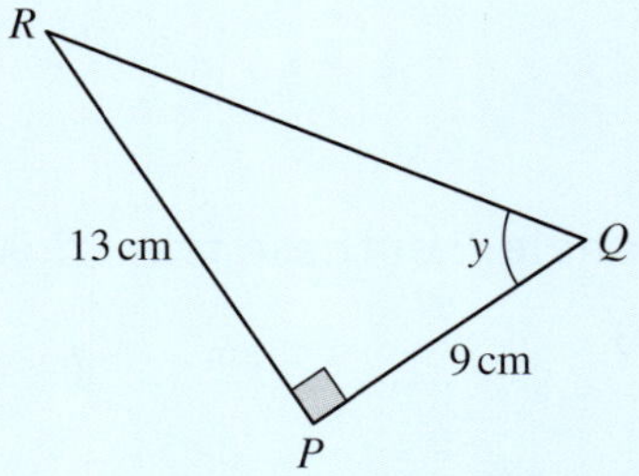

8. Here are the workings of three students for the size of angle θ.
Who is correct? Explain your answer.

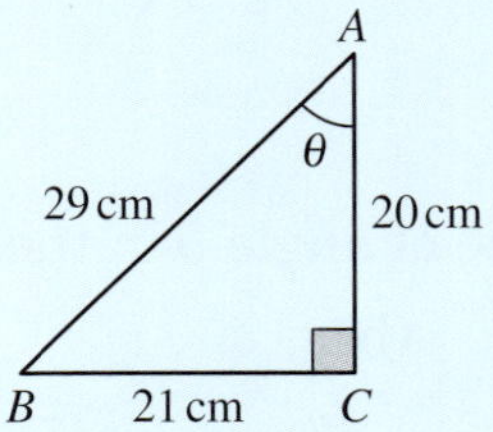

I. Alice

$\sin\theta = \frac{21}{29}$

$\theta = 0.8°$ (to 1 dp)

II. Betty

$\cos\theta = \frac{20}{29}$

$\theta = 46.4°$ (to 1 dp)

III. Clive

$\tan\theta = \frac{20}{21}$

$\theta = 43.6°$ (to 1 dp)

9. The rectangular playground shown has a length of 12 m and a width of 4 m. The diagonal is a path.

PROBLEM SOLVING

(a) Calculate the size of angle x.

(b) Calculate the length of the diagonal path. Can you calculate this length in more than one way?

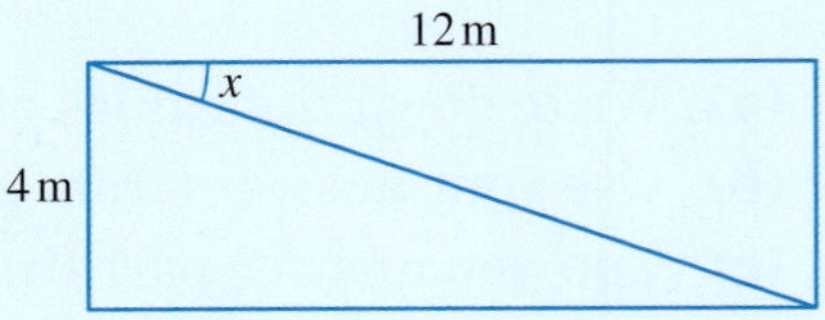

REVIEW

Trigonometry

$\sin\,\theta = \frac{\text{opposite side}}{\text{hypotenuse}}$

$\cos\,\theta = \frac{\text{adjacent side}}{\text{hypotenuse}}$

$\tan\,\theta = \frac{\text{opposite side}}{\text{adjacent side}}$

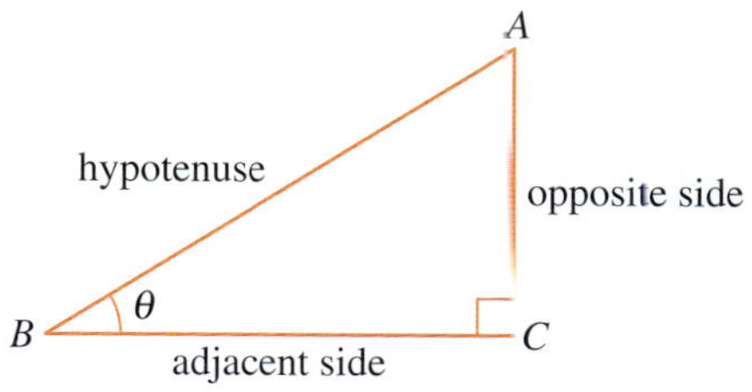

Finding Unknown Sides in a Right-angled Triangle

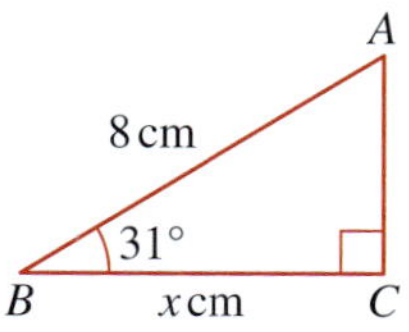

Using $\cos\,\theta = \frac{\text{adjacent side}}{\text{hypotenuse}}$,

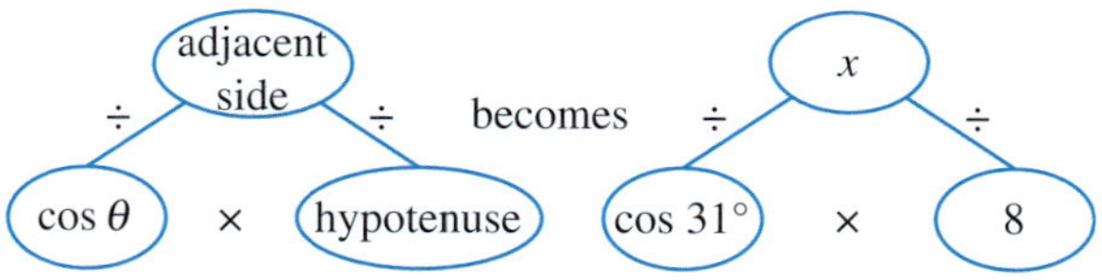

$\cos 31° = \frac{x}{8}$

$x = 8 \times \cos 31°$

$= 6.86\,\text{cm}$

Finding Unknown Angles in a Right-angled Triangle

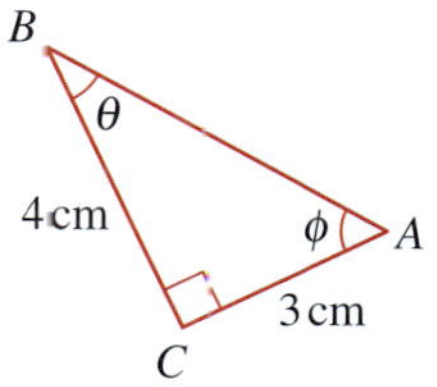

$\tan\,\theta = \frac{3}{4}$

$\tan\,\theta = \frac{\text{opposite side}}{\text{adjacent side}}$

$\tan^{-1}(\tan\,\theta) = \tan^{-1}\left(\frac{3}{4}\right)$

$\theta = \tan^{-1}\left(\frac{3}{4}\right)$

$= 36.9°$

Calculator key sequence:

tan⁻¹ 3 ÷ 4) =

CHALLENGE 11

ABC is an isosceles triangle. $AB = AC = 10\,\text{cm}$ and $\angle CBA = 31°$. Find the length of *BC*, giving your answer to three significant figures.

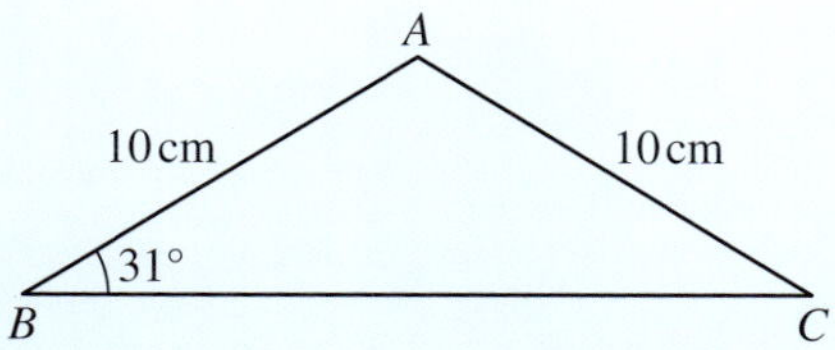

REMARK

First split the diagram into two right-angled triangles.

REVISION EXERCISE 11

In this exercise, give your answers for lengths to three significant figures and answers for angles to one decimal place.

1. State the hypotenuse, the opposite side and the adjacent side of the angle θ for each triangle.

(a)

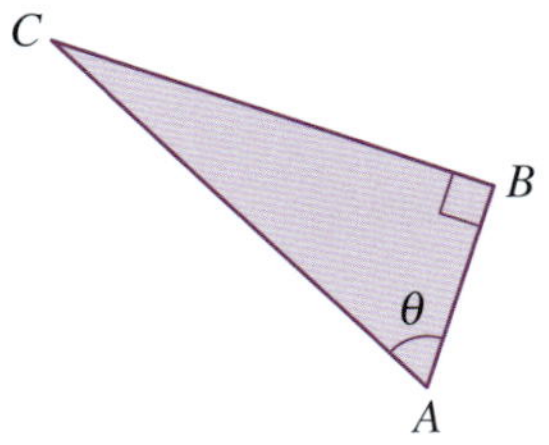

(b)

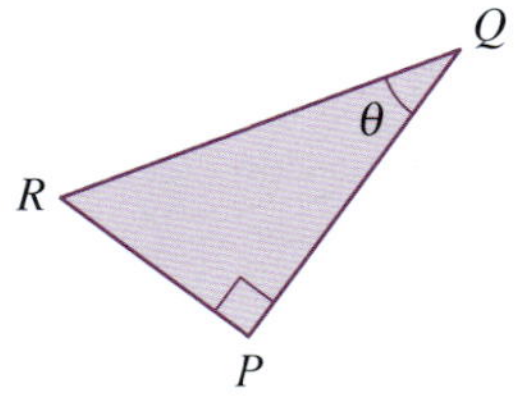

2. Express the values of $\sin\theta$, $\cos\theta$ and $\tan\theta$ as fractions for each triangle.

(a)

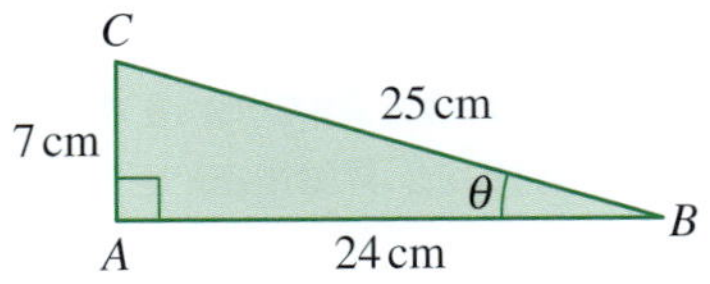

(b)

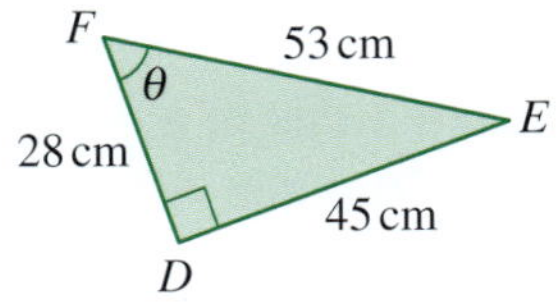

3. Which of these statements about ΔXYZ are incorrect?

(a) $\sin X = \frac{13}{12}$

(b) $\tan X = \frac{12}{5}$

(c) $\cos Y = \frac{12}{13}$

(d) $\tan Y = \frac{12}{5}$

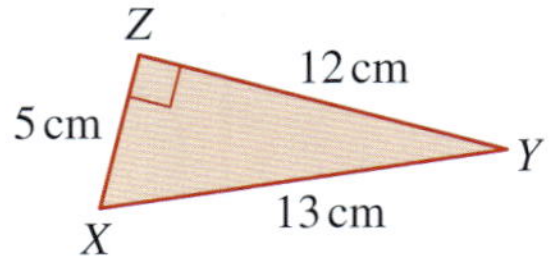

4. Find the unknown values x and y in each triangle.

(a)

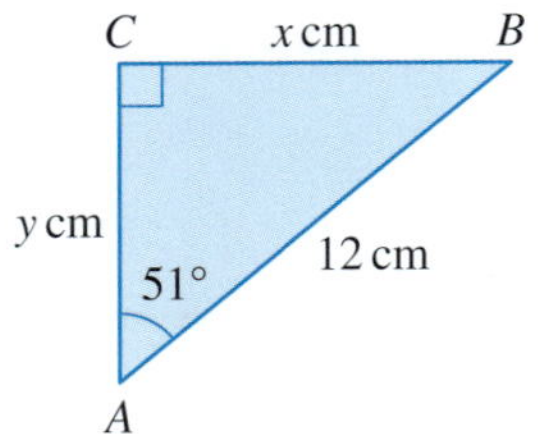

(b)

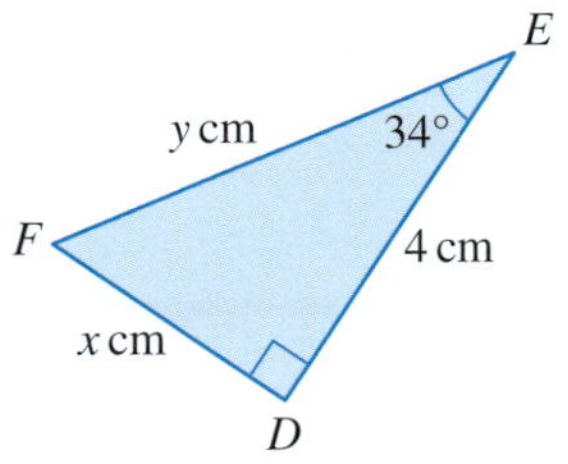

5. Find the size of angle θ in each case.

(a) $\sin\theta = 0.37$ **(b)** $\cos\theta = 0.926$ **(c)** $\tan\theta = \frac{2}{15}$

6. Find the size of angle θ in each triangle.

(a)

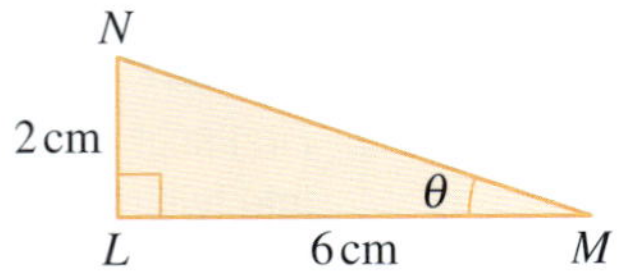

(b)

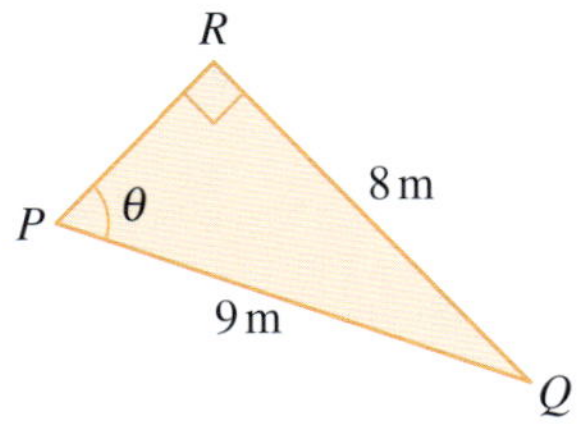

7. *LMN* is a triangular playground. Find

PROBLEM SOLVING

(a) the size of angle θ,

(b) the area of the playground.

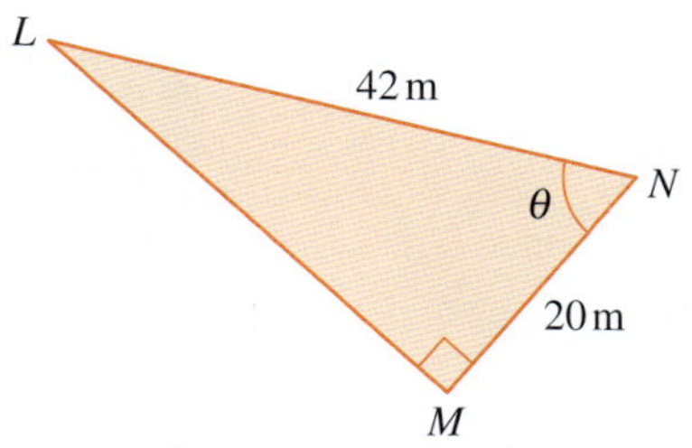

8. Boris makes two triangular boards *ABC* and *PQR*.

PROBLEM SOLVING

(a) Which angle, $\angle BAC$ or $\angle QPR$, is smaller?

(b) Which board has a longer perimeter?

(c) Which board has a larger area?

Write in Your Journal

How could you use trigonometry in your other subjects, or in a future career?

12 DATA ANALYSIS

WHAT IS IN THIS CHAPTER:

How would you compare the average incomes of employees in different industries? You would need to take samples of incomes from the different industries and then analyse them. One way to compare data is to use the average. There are different types of averages. You will learn about the mean, median and mode in this chapter.

LET'S LEARN TO

- understand the terms mean, median, mode and range of ungrouped data
- calculate the mean, median, mode and range of ungrouped data
- calculate the mean of grouped data
- make comparisons between sets of data

FLASHBACK

1. Collection of Data

(a) The purpose of collecting data is to get insight into certain situations. The data collected can be used for planning, and any decisions made can be justified and backed up by the data. Data collection is crucial in the fields of scientific research, business management and sociology.

(b) Depending on the objective of the data collection, data can be collected by

(i) taking measurements in experiments,

(ii) observing outcomes of events,

(iii) conducting surveys,

(iv) looking on the Internet, in newspapers or in statistical publications.

2. Organisation of Data

Raw data can be organised into a frequency table by tallying. For example, this frequency table shows the number of children in each family in a survey of 50 families.

Number of children	Tally	Frequency
0	~~IIII~~ III	8
1	~~IIII~~ ~~IIII~~ IIII	14
2	~~IIII~~ ~~IIII~~ ~~IIII~~ I	16
3	~~IIII~~ IIII	9
4	III	3

The table shows that there are 8 families with no children, 14 families with 1 child, and so on.

DISCUSS

What is the same and what is different about charts **(a)**, **(b)** and **(c)** in Question 3?

3. Presentation of Data

Data can be presented using a pictogram, bar chart, pie chart or line chart.

(a) Pictogram

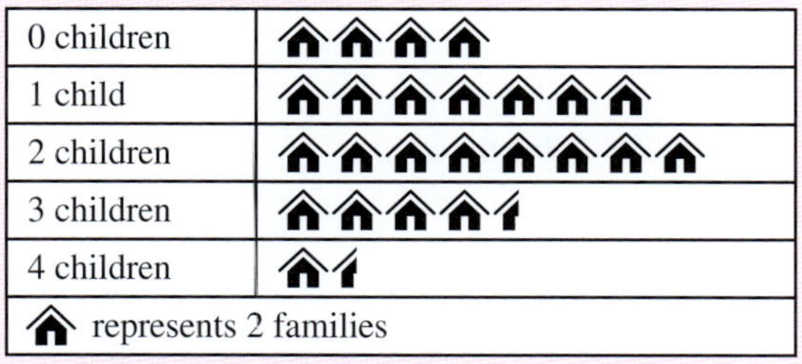

(b) Bar Chart

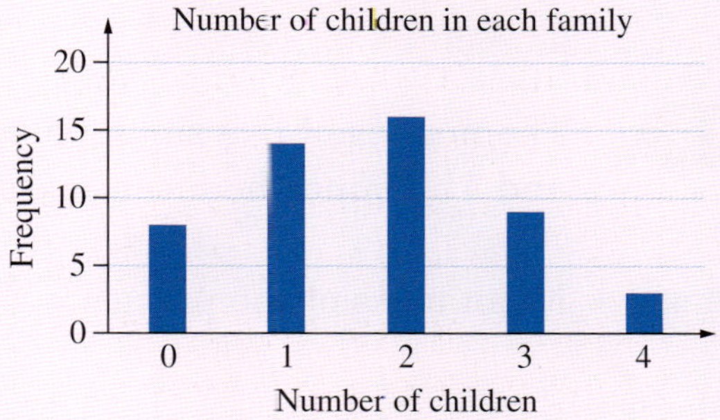

(c) Pie Chart

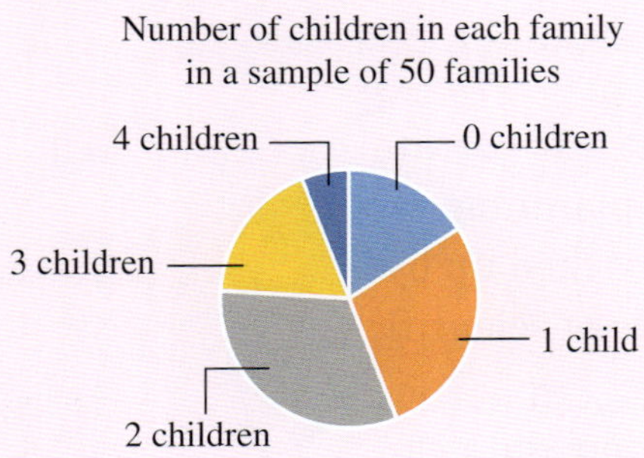

(d) Line Graph

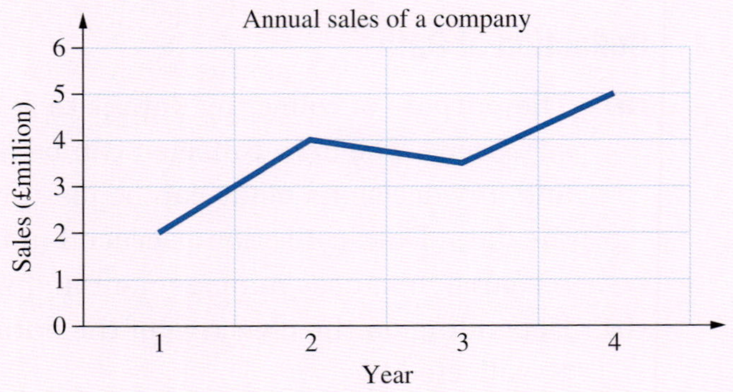

DISCUSS

Why should you not show the data on the number of children in a family on a line graph?

12.1 Mean

A school has two English classes. There are 10 students in each class. The marks of the students in the same end of topic test are shown.

Class A				
65	70	79	53	47
63	71	81	95	77

Class B				
55	72	93	82	54
68	75	51	42	80

How could the school assess which class performed better in the test?

You can compare the marks of the two groups by using an **average** of the individual marks. An average is a single value used to represent all the values in a data set. Three of the averages are **mean**, **median** and **mode**. This section will cover mean.

The mean is the sum of all data values divided by the total number of data items.

$$\text{Mean} = \frac{\text{total sum of all data values}}{\text{total number of data items}}$$

Example 1

The masses of five small parcels are 3 kg, 7 kg, 5 kg, 6 kg and 4 kg. Find the mean mass of the parcels.

Solution

$$\text{Mean mass of the parcels} = \frac{3 + 7 + 5 + 6 + 4}{5}$$

$$= \frac{25}{5}$$

$$= 5\,\text{kg}$$

You can represent the data with squares making five 'bars' of each showing the number as the height of a bar, and then rearrange the squares to make five bars of the **same** height. This new height is the mean, 5.

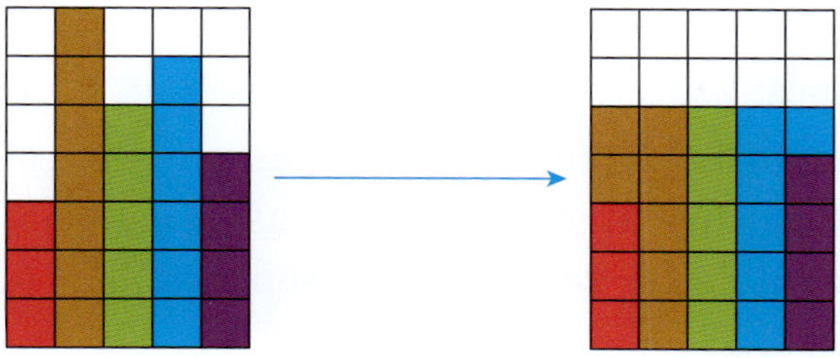

Try It! 1 The cost of four gifts are £3, £5, £2 and £6. Find the mean cost of the gifts.

DISCUSS

Represent the data with squares making four bars of different heights, and then rearrange the squares to make four bars of the same height. What does this height represent?

Example 2

The test marks of two classes of 10 students each are shown.

Class A				
65	70	79	53	47
63	71	81	95	77

Class B				
55	72	93	82	54
68	75	51	42	80

(a) Find the mean score of the students in Class A.

(b) Find the mean score of the students in Class B.

(c) Which class performed better in the test based on the mean scores?

Solution

(a) Total scores of students in Class A

$= 65 + 70 + 79 + 53 + 47 + 63 + 71 + 81 + 95 + 77$

$= 701$

Mean score of students in Class A $= \frac{701}{10}$

$= 70.1$

(b) Total scores of students in Class B

$= 55 + 72 + 93 + 82 + 54 + 68 + 75 + 51 + 42 + 80$

$= 672$

Mean score of students in Class B $= \frac{672}{10}$

$= 67.2$

(c) Since $70.1 > 67.2$,

the mean score of students in Class A is higher, so Class A performed better in the test.

RECALL

To divide by 10, move each digit one place to the right in the place value table.

DISCUSS

In what way might teachers use the mean scores for the two classes?

Try It! 2

The manager of a bus company wants to improve the service of two bus routes. They check the waiting time, in minutes, of passengers on the two routes. The results of ten passengers on each route are shown.

Route A waiting times: 3, 5, 8, 3, 6, 5, 8, 10, 4, 1

Route B waiting times: 2, 13, 7, 4, 9, 8, 7, 6, 1, 5

(a) Find the mean waiting time of route A passengers.
(b) Find the mean waiting time of route B passengers.
(c) Which route has a better service to passengers based on the results?

DISCUSS

What else might improve the service? Is there further data the manager could collect to check the service of each route?

Example 3

The frequency table shows the number of pets each student in a group owns.

Number of pets	0	1	2	3
Frequency	3	7	9	6

(a) How many students are in the group?
(b) Use a calculator to work out the mean number of pets owned.

DISCUSS

What do the numbers in the frequency row represent? How many students had 3 pets?

Solution

(a) Here, 3 students have 0 pets, 7 students have 1 pet each, and so on.

Number of students in the group $= 3 + 7 + 9 + 6$
$= 25$

(b) For 3 students with 0 pets,

the total number of pets $= 0 + 0 + 0$
$= 0 \times 3$

For 7 students with 1 pet each,

the total number of pets $= 1 + 1 + 1 + 1 + 1 + 1 + 1$
$= 1 \times 7$

For 9 students with 2 pets each,

the total number of pets $= 2 + 2 + 2 + 2 + 2 + 2 + 2 + 2 + 2$
$= 2 \times 9$

For 6 students with 3 pets each,

the total number of pets $= 3 + 3 + 3 + 3 + 3 + 3$
$= 3 \times 6$

Hence, the total number of pets in the group

$= (0 \times 3) + (1 \times 7) + (2 \times 9) + (3 \times 6)$
$= 0 + 7 + 18 + 18$
$= 43$

You could also add a row to the table to help work this out:

Number of pets	0	1	2	3	Total
Frequency	3	7	9	6	25
Number of pets × frequency	0	7	18	18	43

Mean number of pets the students own

$= \frac{43}{25}$ Mean $= \frac{\text{total sum of all data values}}{\text{total number of data items}}$

$= 1.72$

DISCUSS

Why do you not need the total for the 'Number of pets' row of the table?

Try It! 3

A coach wants to know the average age of students in a swimming squad for some promotional material. They recorded the ages of the students and summarised the results in this frequency table.

Age (years)	14	15	16	17
Frequency	4	9	6	11

(a) How many students are in the swimming squad?

(b) Use a calculator to work out the mean age of the students.

Example 4

A student is researching trends in the use of technology. They find this pictogram showing the number of mobile phones in a sample of households.

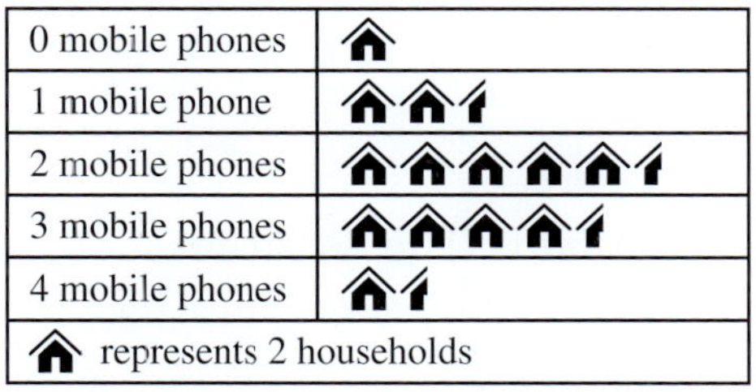

Use a calculator to work out the mean number of mobile phones in a household.

Solution

Start by transferring the information into a frequency table then fill in the row for 'Number of phones × frequency'.

Number of phones	0	1	2	3	4	Total
Frequency	2	5	11	9	3	30
Number of phones × frequency	0	5	22	27	12	66

Mean number of phones in the households

$= \frac{66}{30}$

$= 2.2$

Mean = $\frac{\text{total sum of all data values}}{\text{total number of data items}}$

Try It! 4

A student is researching the average age of part-time workers in a chain of cafés. They find a bar chart showing the ages of a sample of workers.

Use a calculator to work out the mean age of the workers.

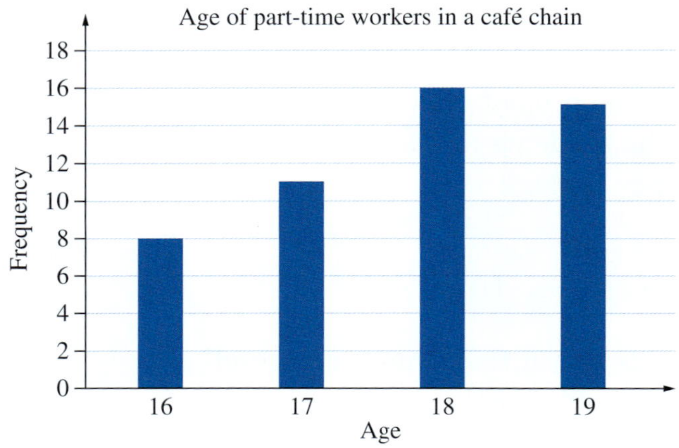

PRACTICE 12.1

You should use a calculator for this exercise.

LEVEL 1

1. A charity wants to know what the average donation is. The donations of four people are £10, £15, £25 and £30. Find the mean amount donated by these four people.
2. A basketball squad likes to advertise the average height of its team each week. One week, the heights of the players in the team are 193 cm, 186 cm, 192 cm, 205 cm and 189 cm. Find the mean height of these players.
3. A golfer has taken a mean average of 4 shots per hole for the first 17 holes of an 18-hole round of golf. They took 5 shots for the final hole. Will their mean average for the round be more than 4 or less than 4? Explain your answer.
4. By calculating the mean for each set, find which set of data is the odd one out.

   Set A: {4, 4, 4, 4, 4} Set B: {3, 4, 4, 5}

   Set C: {1, 2, 5, 7} Set D: {1, 2, 9}

5. Three siblings have a mean age of 8. The oldest is 12 and the youngest is 5. How old is the middle child?

Hint: Represent the middle child as x and write out your mean calculation.

LEVEL 2

6. A teacher is trying to improve how quickly their students can complete a times tables challenge. The first week they record the time taken by the class to complete the challenge. The data is shown in the frequency table.

Time taken (s)	11	12	13	14
Frequency	2	6	8	4

(a) How many students completed the challenge?

(b) Find the mean time taken by these students.

Before the second week's challenge, the teacher sets homework for them to practise their times tables. The teacher believes this will make them quicker. The numbers shown for the second week are in the table.

Time taken (s)	11	12	13	14
Frequency	9	5	4	2

(c) Is the teacher correct that the homework has improved the students' speed at the challenge? Explain your answer.

7. A workers' union records the hourly wages of some workers.

Hourly wage (£)	Frequency
12	8
14	9
16	6
18	12
20	5

(a) The union would agree to fight for a pay rise if the mean hourly wage of these workers is below £16. Should the union fight for a pay rise? Explain your answer.

(b) Without doing any further calculations, explain how the mean would change if

(i) one of the workers got a pay rise,

(ii) one of the workers earning £20 per hour left their job.

8. A building company is planning the amount of parking required for a new housing estate. They have this bar chart which shows the number of cars per household in a sample of 20 households.

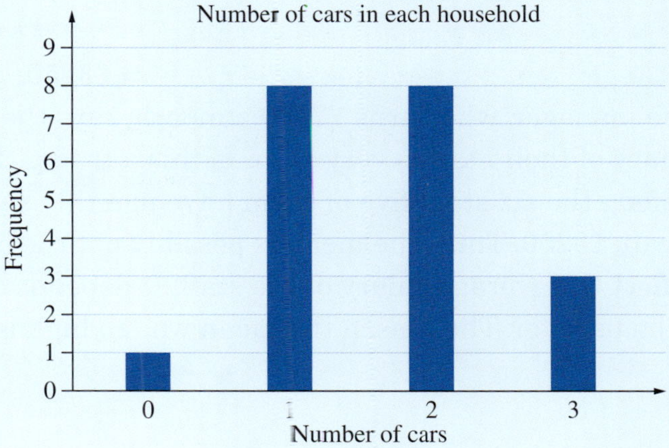

(a) Work out the mean number of cars for the households.

(b) Suggest how many parking spaces each house should have. Explain your answer.

9. A botanist uses different light levels to grow 10 plants from seeds. They measure the heights, in cm, of the plants after one month and record the results.

SCIENCE

Low light				
12	7	9	12	11
11	10	11	8	10

Bright light				
13	17	18	15	12
11	16	17	18	15

(a) Find the mean height of the plants grown with low light.
(b) Find the mean height of the plants grown with bright light.
(c) Which condition do you think is better for the growth of the plants? Explain your answer.

10. In a balance beam competition, the scores given by eight judges to two gymnasts are shown.

PROBLEM SOLVING

Scores of Rebecca			
8	10	8	9
9	8	7	7

Scores of Tania			
9	4	8	9
10	9	7	8

(a) Based on the mean scores of the eight judges, who has performed better?
(b) The competition uses a trimmed mean score system. The lowest score and the highest score for each gymnast are discarded. The trimmed mean score is the mean score of the remaining six judges. Based on the trimmed mean scores, who has performed better?
(c) What might be the advantage of using a trimmed score in this situation?

12.2 Median

A company has six staff, including the manager. The monthly salaries of the six staff are

£2100, £2300, £2500, £2600, £3000, £7000.

The mean monthly salary of these staff = £(2100 + 2300 + 2500 + 2600 + 3000 + 7000) ÷ 6
= £3250.

The manager, who earns £7000 a month, says that the average monthly salary of their staff is very high. Is this a true picture of the information? Among the six staff, five of them have monthly salaries lower than the mean, £3250. Thus, the mean is possibly not the best average to accurately reflect the average salary of the staff. It depends on what the average is to be used for. The reason the mean was so high is because £7000 is an extreme value or outlier from the rest of the data. In such a case, another average value, **median** could be used.

The **median** of a data set is the value in the middle position of the data when the data is arranged in ascending order.

Example 5

The midday temperatures, in °C, in a week were

22, 17, 23, 19, 8, 20, 16.

Find the median midday temperature in the week.

Solution

Arrange the temperatures in ascending order.

8 16 17 **19** 20 22 23

↑ middle position

Hence, the median midday temperature is the 4th item.

∴ median = 19 °C.

DISCUSS

Why might you want to use the median instead of the mean here?

Try It! 5

An office worker wants to know how much they spend on average buying lunch. The amounts they spent on their lunch every day for one week were

£3, £3, £4, £5, £20.

Find the median cost of their lunches.

DISCUSS

Would the mean be higher or lower than the median?

When there is an even number of values, there will not be a middle value. In this case, the median will be the mean of the middle two values.

Example 6

The masses of six apples are

230 g, 190 g, 200 g, 245 g, 178 g, 162 g.

Find the median mass of the apples.

Solution

Arrange the masses in ascending order.

162 g 178 g **190 g** ↑ **200 g** 230 g 245 g

middle position

The middle position is between the 3rd and the 4th items.
Median mass of the apples is the mean of the 3rd and 4th items.

$\therefore$ median $= \frac{190 + 200}{2}$

$= 195\,\text{g}$

Try It! 6

The age (in years) of a certain make of car in a car showroom are

3, 12, 5, 5, 4, 3.

The manager wants to advertise the average age of the cars of this make on the website.
Find the median age of the cars.

DISCUSS

What is the median monthly salary of the six staff in the opening paragraphs of this section?

Why might you want to use the median salary instead of the mean salary?

Example 7

The table shows the number of correct answers that some students obtained in a mental calculation test.

Number of correct answers	16	17	18	19	20
Frequency	1	2	3	6	2

(a) How many students took the test?
(b) Find the median of the number of correct answers of the students.

Solution

(a) Number of students who took the test
$= 1 + 2 + 3 + 6 + 2$
$= 14$

(b) When the values are listed in ascending order as:
16, 17, 17, 18, 18, 18, 19, 19, 19, 19, 19, 19, 20, 20,

you can see that both the 7th and 8th items are 19.

$\therefore$ median $= \frac{19 + 19}{2}$

$= 19$

DISCUSS

Max claims, 'The median is 18 because it is the value in the middle of the table.' Is this correct?

DISCUSS

Why do you list the data in ascending order first?

Try It! 7

The table shows the number of goals that a football team scored in some matches.

Number of goals	0	1	2	3	4
Frequency	7	4	2	2	1

(a) How many matches did the team play?
(b) Find the median of the number of goals scored by the team.

PRACTICE 12.2

You can use a calculator in this exercise where appropriate.

LEVEL 1

1. The working hours of a part-time worker on five days are 7 hours, 2 hours, 4 hours, 6 hours and 3 hours. What is the median number of working hours on these five days?

2. The prices of seven pairs of sports shoes are £45, £35, £30, £80, £60, £55 and £37. Sue chooses the pair with the median price to buy. What is the price of the pair of shoes that she buys?

3. The masses of six fish caught by Tom are 100 g, 400 g, 550 g, 300 g, 500 g and 450 g.
   (a) Find the median mass of these fish.
   (b) Why might Tom choose to use the median instead of the mean to describe the average mass of the fish he has caught?

4. A chemist tests the pH values of eight solutions. The results are
   4.7, 3.8, 8.5, 7.0, 6.9, 9.2, 3.1, 5.5.
   Find the median of these values.

SCIENCE

5. A farmer thinks that duck eggs are larger than chicken eggs. The farmer measures the masses of two samples of eggs.
   Chicken eggs: 60 g, 57 g, 62 g, 65 g, 59 g
   Duck eggs: 68 g, 70 g, 73 g, 62 g, 70 g, 71 g
   (a) Find the median mass of the chicken eggs.
   (b) Find the median mass of the duck eggs.
   (c) Do you think the farmer is correct? Explain your answer.

LEVEL 2

6. The throwing distances of two athletes in a javelin competition are as shown.

   Christina: 48 m, 50 m, 45 m, 51 m, 43 m, 49 m
   Sara: 51 m, 45 m, 50 m, 44 m, 47 m, 51 m
   (a) Find the mean and median throwing distance of Christina.
   (b) Find the mean and median throwing distance of Sara.
   (c) Whose overall performance is better? Explain your answer.

7. The ages of some racing drivers are given in the table.

Age (years)	18	19	20	21	22	26
Frequency	2	4	5	6	2	1

   (a) Find the median age of these racing drivers.
   (b) Give a reason why you might want to use the median to represent the average of these values.
   (c) What would be the effect on the median if the 26-year-old driver were to be replaced by a 30-year-old driver?

8. An observatory records the rainfall of a city on seven days of a week. The values are 11 mm, 0 mm, 13 mm, 8 mm, 120 mm, 6 mm and 10 mm.

SCIENCE

(a) Find the mean rainfall in these seven days.

(b) Find the median rainfall in these seven days.

(c) Give a reason why the observatory might want to use

(i) the median, **(ii)** the mean,

to represent the average of these values.

9. The times taken to swim 50 m freestyle by eight students are:

PROBLEM SOLVING

40 s, 35 s, 41 s, 32 s, 38 s, 29 s, 33 s, x s.

(a) Find the median time taken for the first seven students.

(b) If the median time taken for all the eight students is 36 s, find the value of x.

12.3 Mode

A shop sells jumpers. The sales manager records the sizes of a certain type of jumper sold in a week. Those sold are of sizes

12, 10, 14, 18, 10, 14, 12, 8, 14, 14, 8, 16.

The mean of these sizes $= (12 + 10 + 14 + 18 + 10 + 14 + 12 + 8 + 14 + 14 + 8 + 16) \div 12$

$= 12.5$

Arrange these sizes in ascending order.

8 8 10 10 12 12 14 14 14 14 16 18

The median of these sizes $= (12 + 14) \div 2$

$= 13$

The manager wants to order extra of the most popular size. However, the mean and the median cannot provide the information required. Neither the mean nor the median are jumper sizes. There is another measure of average which is useful for this sort of situation. It is called the **mode**.

> The mode of a data set is the data value that occurs most often.

In this case, the size 14 occurs four times. It has the highest frequency. Therefore, the mode (the modal size) = 14. The manager should order extra of this size.

The mode is also the only average that can be used when the data is non-numerical. For example, if the bar chart shows the favourite colours of some children, then the mode is blue since it has the highest frequency (7).

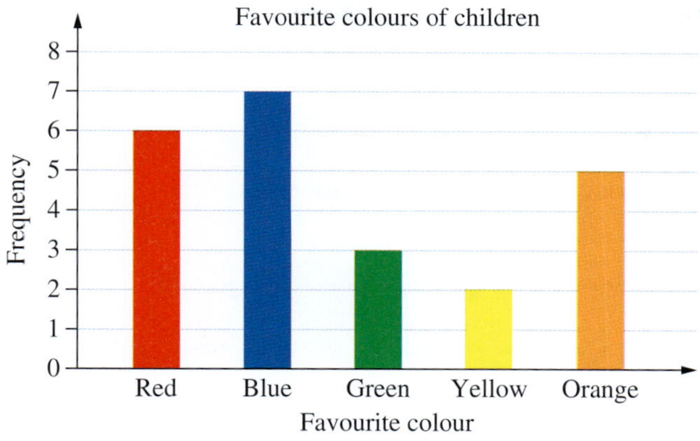

DISCUSS

Arya says, 'You cannot find the mean or median of this data.' Do you agree? Explain your answer.

Example 8

A company is considering where to set up a pizza takeaway restaurant. They conduct a survey of the current pizza takeaway restaurants in three different towns and record the cost of a plain, medium-sized pizza in each.

Town A:	£8, £10, £8, £8, £12, £11, £8, £6
Town B:	£7, £13, £7, £12, £6, £12, £12, £9, £7
Town C:	£6, £12, £8, £15, £9, £11, £14

Find the modal price of the pizza in each town.

Solution

For town A, £8 occurs four times. This is the highest frequency.

$\therefore$ the modal price in town A = £8.

For town B, both £7 and £12 occur three times, the other values only occur once each. Both are considered modes. The data set is said to be bimodal.

$\therefore$ the modal price in town B = £7 and £12.

For town C, the frequency of each price is 1. No price is higher than the others.

$\therefore$ there is no modal price in town C.

DISCUSS

Do you think the mode is the best average to use to decide in which town to set up the takeaway?

Try It! 8

A council needs to know the typical number of occupants of houses in some towns. A sample is taken from each town and the results are shown.

Town P: 2, 3, 3, 4, 1, 2, 1, 2, 2, 6, 2

Town Q: 1, 1, 3, 4, 2, 1, 3, 3, 1, 5, 3

Town R: 1, 5, 4, 2, 3, 1, 4, 5, 2, 3, 3

Find the modal number of occupants of the houses in each town.

Example 9

The table shows the number of correct answers that some students obtained in a test.

Number of correct answers	16	17	18	19	20
Frequency	2	3	3	5	1

A teacher wants to know what the most common number of correct answers was. Find the mode of the data.

Solution

The frequency for 19 correct answers is the highest frequency.

∴ the mode is 19.

DISCUSS

Why might you want to use the mode instead of the mean to represent the average number of correct answers?

Try It! 9

The table shows the number of goals that a football team scored in some matches.

Number of goals	0	1	2	3	4
Frequency	7	4	2	2	1

The coach wants to know the most common number of goals scored.

Find the mode of the data.

DISCUSS

Why might you want to use the mean instead of the mode to represent the average number of goals scored in a match?

CLASS ACTIVITY 1

Objective: To compare the mean, median and mode of some shoe sizes.

1. Survey the pupils in your class and record their shoe sizes.

2. Work out the mean, median and mode of the shoe sizes.

DISCUSS

How will you record and summarise the data?

3. Which value, mean, median or mode, involves all the data values in its calculation?

4. Which value, mean, median or mode, must be one of the data values?

5. Write why you might choose to use

   (a) the mean, **(b)** the median, **(c)** the mode,

   to summarise the data?

6. Ask your teacher for their shoe size. How will each of the averages be affected if you include your teacher's shoe size in the data?

PRACTICE 12.3

LEVEL 1

1. A human resource manager lists the ages, in years, of applicants for a job.

   24 24 25 26 24 28 40

   (a) Find the modal age of the applicants.
   (b) Find the median age of the applicants.
   (c) Find the mean age of the applicants.

2. A company is trying to decide on which colour sunglasses to manufacture. They survey 50 people and record the results in a table.

   (a) Write down the mode of the data.
   (b) Make a recommendation to the company.
   (c) Explain why you must use the mode to represent the average instead of the median or the mean.

Colour	Frequency
Blue	5
Brown	15
Black	25
Red	5

3. An estate agent is surveying the number of bedrooms in the properties listed on their website. The pie chart shows the number of bedrooms in 100 houses listed.

   (a) What is the most common number of bedrooms?
   (b) Which type of average is your answer to part **(a)**?

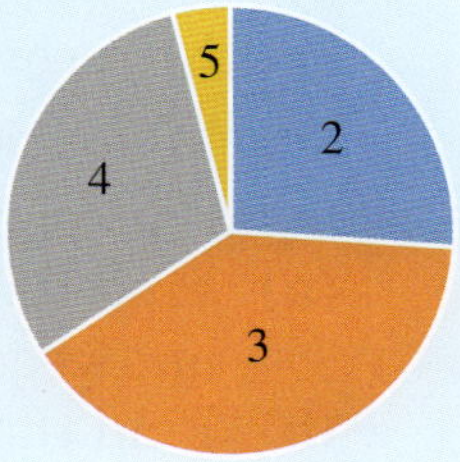

4. Elsie is planning a holiday. She searches the noon temperatures in three cities from 17 November to 23 November 2019 and presents the data in the table. She wants to visit the city with the coolest average noon temperature.

	17 Nov	18 Nov	19 Nov	20 Nov	21 Nov	22 Nov	23 Nov
Tokyo	19 °C	21 °C	20 °C	15 °C	15 °C	8 °C	15 °C
Singapore	34 °C	34 °C	34 °C	30 °C	30 °C	30 °C	31 °C
Perth	29 °C	33 °C	25 °C	21 °C	24 °C	27 °C	30 °C

(a) Find the modal noon temperature of this data for each city.
(b) Find the median noon temperature of this data for each city.
(c) Is mode or median more useful to Elsie when making her decision?
(d) Make a recommendation to Elsie.

LEVEL 2

5. An accountant records the amount of charity donations from some donors in a table.

£ FINANCE

Donation (£)	10	15	20	25	30
Frequency	8	9	3	13	7

(a) Find the mode of the donations.
(b) Find the median of the donations.
(c) Give a possible advantage of using the mode instead of the median to represent a typical donation.

6. A teacher records the time taken (to the nearest minute) for some students to complete a puzzle.
(a) Find the mode of the time taken.
(b) Find the median of the time taken.
(c) Find the mean of the time taken.

Time taken (min)	Frequency
8	4
9	7
10	9
11	5

7. At an after-school club there are five 13-year olds, seven 14-year olds and one 17-year old.
(a) What is the modal age?
(b) If the 17-year old left the club, how would this affect
(i) the mode, **(ii)** the mean?

8. A student is investigating whether most teenagers eat the recommended five portions of fruit and vegetables per day. They survey their classmates and represent the data in the pictogram.
(a) Find the modal number of portions of fruit and vegetables eaten.
(b) Find the median number of portions of fruit and vegetables eaten.
(c) What conclusion should the student make?

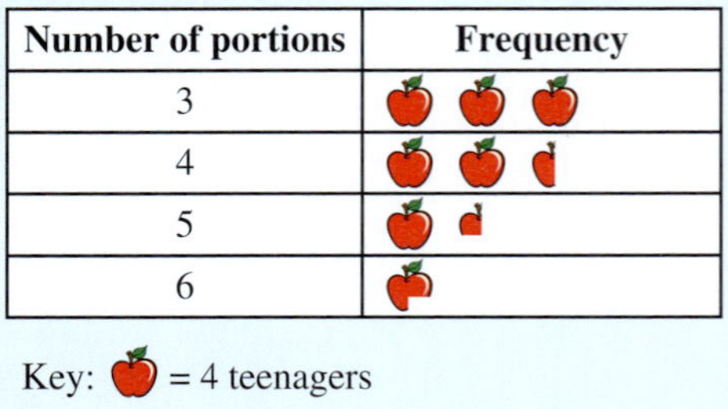

9. Create a data set with five values such that the mean, median and mode are all equal to 7.
OPEN QUESTION

10. Create a data set with six values such that the mean = 7, median = 6 and mode = 2.
OPEN QUESTION

12.4 Range

Consider the points scored by three basketball players in the five matches shown.

	James	Kevin	Robin
	20	16	10
	20	18	15
	20	20	20
	20	22	25
	20	24	30
Mean	20	20	20
Median	20	20	20

DISCUSS

What is different about the data for the three players? Which player would you rather have on your team?

The mean scores and median scores of these players are all equal to 20. However, you can see that there are some differences in each player's data. This is the **spread** or **variation** of the data. One of the measures of the spread of data is called the **range**.

Range = the largest value − the smallest value

Range of James' scores = 20 − 20
= 0
Range of Kevin's scores = 24 − 16
= 8
Range of Robin's scores = 30 − 10
= 20

A larger range indicates a larger spread of data.

DISCUSS

Which player is the most consistent? Which player has the largest fluctuation in performance?

Example 10

The long jump distances of Josh in six attempts are
5.8 m, 6.2 m, 5.9 m, 5.5 m, 6.1 m, 5.4 m.
Find the range of the data.

Solution

The largest value = 6.2 m
The smallest value = 5.4 m
$\therefore$ range of the data = 6.2 − 5.4   largest value − smallest value
= 0.8 m

Try It! 10

The heights of seven sunflowers are:
45 cm, 39 cm, 41 cm, 36 cm, 50 cm, 58 cm, 47 cm.
Find the range of the heights of the plants.

Example 11

A consumer council tests the lifetime, in hours, of some Brand A and Brand B dry batteries to check their quality. The results are listed.

Brand A: 13, 9, 8, 7, 17, 12, 8, 10

Brand B: 10, 13, 10, 9, 8, 11, 10, 12

(a) Find the mean and the range of the lifetimes of Brand A batteries.
(b) Find the mean and the range of the lifetimes of Brand B batteries.
(c) Based on the results in parts **(a)** and **(b)**, which brand would you prefer to buy? Explain your choice.

Solution

(a) For Brand A batteries,
mean = (13 + 9 + 8 + 7 + 17 + 12 + 8 + 10) ÷ 8 $\frac{\text{total sum of all data values}}{\text{total number of data items}}$
= 10.5 hours
range = 17 − 7   largest value − smallest value
= 10 hours

(b) For Brand B batteries,
mean = (10 + 13 + 10 + 9 + 8 + 11 + 10 + 12) ÷ 8 $\frac{\text{total sum of all data values}}{\text{total number of data items}}$
= 10.375 hours
range = 13 − 8   largest value − smallest value
= 5 hours

(c) The means of Brand A and Brand B are very close to each other.
However, the range of Brand A is much larger than that of Brand B.
This indicates that the lifetimes of Brand A batteries vary more than those of Brand B.
Hence, Brand B batteries are preferable.

Try It! 11

A coach checks the time it takes, in seconds, for two students to run 400 m in six trials. The results are

Kylie: 58, 63, 62, 57, 61, 61

Jenny: 62, 68, 56, 55, 59, 60

(a) Calculate the mean and the range of Kylie's times.

(b) Calculate the mean and the range of Jenny's times.

(c) Based on the results in parts **(a)** and **(b)**, should the coach choose Kylie or Jenny for the next competition? Explain your answer.

PRACTICE 12.4

LEVEL 1

1. A café manager checks the volumes of five cups of coffee prepared by her new staff member. The results are

210 ml, 205 ml, 192 ml, 200 ml, 198 ml.

Find the range of the data.

2. Five of the highest mountains in Britain and Ireland are

Ben Nevis 1345 m, Carn Eige 1183 m,
Snowdon (Yr Wyddfa) 1085 m, Carrauntoohil 1039 m,
Sgurr Alasdair 992 m.

Find the range of these heights.

Carrauntoohil, Ireland

3. A doctor checks the masses of six newborn babies. The results are

3.6 kg, 2.8 kg, 3.1 kg, 3.2 kg, 3.0 kg, 3.2 kg.

(a) Find the mean, median and mode of the data.

(b) Find the range of the data.

4. What is the same and what is different about these sets of data?

Set A: {15, 17, 18, 19} Set B: {1, 4, 4, 5, 5} Set C: {23, 25, 27}

5. The bar chart shows the number of siblings of a group of children.

(a) Find the mode of the data.

(b) Find the range of the data.

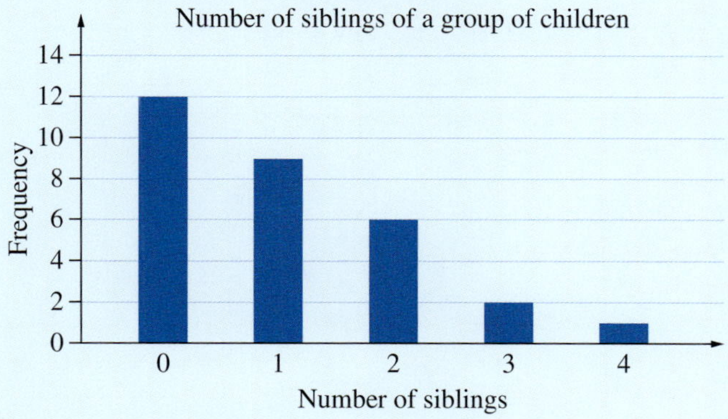

LEVEL 2

6. A teacher gives two mathematics tests to eight students. The scores of the students are shown.

Calculator test:	46	35	73	85	91	62	74	59
Non-calculator test:	63	78	51	90	66	58	75	62

(a) Find the mean and the range of the scores in the calculator test.
(b) Find the mean and the range of the scores in the non-calculator test.
(c) Which test did the students perform better in?
(d) Which test had a wider spread of scores?

7. SCIENCE Ava would like to compare the temperatures of London and Melbourne. She obtained the average highest temperature in each month from 2005 to 2015 from the Internet. The table shows the readings, where the unit is °C.

	Jan	Feb	Mar	Apr	May	Jun	Jul	Aug	Sep	Oct	Nov	Dec
London	8	9	12	16	18	21	24	22	20	16	12	9
Melbourne	28	27	25	21	18	15	15	16	19	22	24	26

(a) Find the mean and the range of the data for London.
(b) Find the mean and the range of the data for Melbourne.
(c) Which city is warmer on average?
(d) Which city has a greater variation in temperature?

8. The lengths of some leaves are

12 cm, 15 cm, x cm, 9 cm, 7 cm, 18 cm, 10 cm.

If the range of the lengths is 20 cm, find the possible values of x.

9. OPEN QUESTION Create two different sets of five numbers such that the mean for each set is 7 and the range for each set is 11.

REVIEW

Mean

$$\text{Mean} = \frac{\text{total sum of all data values}}{\text{total number of data items}}$$

For example, the expenses of a student in 5 days are £8, £5, £6, £10 and £6.

Mean expense
= £(8 + 5 + 6 + 10 + 6) ÷ 5
= £7

The table shows the masses of some dogs.

Mass (kg)	5	6	7	8
Frequency	3	10	13	4

Total mass = 5 × 3 + 6 × 10 + 7 × 13 + 8 × 4
= 198 kg

Total number of data items = 3 + 10 + 13 + 4
= 30

Mean mass = 198 ÷ 30
= 6.6 kg

The advantage of the mean is that its calculation involves all the data.

Median

When the data are arranged in ascending order, the median is the middle value of the data.

For example, if the data values are 7 s, 10 s, 13 s, 15 s and 18 s,

the median is the 3rd item, 13 s.

If there is an even number of data values, then you need to use the mean of the middle two values.

For example, if the values are 4 cm, 7 cm, 8 cm, 10 cm, 13 cm and 15 cm, the median is the mean of the 3rd and 4th values.

$\therefore$ median $= \frac{8 + 10}{2}$
= 9 cm

The advantage of the median is that it does not get affected by extreme values.

Mode

The mode of a data set is the data value which has the highest frequency.

For example, if the scores of some students are

(a) 63, 67, 72, 72, 72, 79, 85, mode = 72.

(b) 63, 67, 67, 72, 72, 79, 86, 72, 67, mode = 67 and 72.

(c) 63, 67, 70, 71, 72, 79, 85, there is no mode.

The advantage of the mode as an average is that it is always a value in the data. The mode can also be found from non-numerical data.

Range

The range of a data set
= the largest value – the smallest value.

It is a measure of the spread of the data.

For example, the masses of 5 cats are 3 kg, 2 kg, 6 kg, 4 kg and 5 kg,

range = 6 – 2
= 4 kg.

The smaller the range, the more consistent the data.

CHALLENGE 12

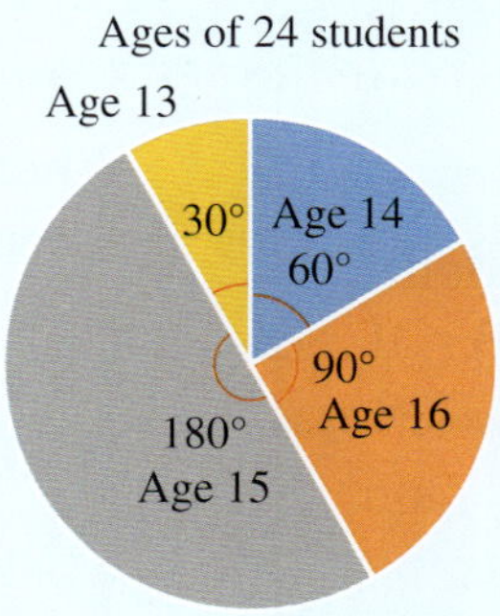

The pie chart shows the distribution of ages of 24 students. Find

(a) the number of students in each age group,

(b) the mean, median and mode of the ages of the students,

(c) the range of the ages of the students.

REVISION EXERCISE 12

Use a calculator in this exercise where needed.

1. A parent checks the prices of five workbooks. They are £6, £8, £7, £10 and £19.

(a) Find the mean price of these books.

(b) Find the median price of these books.

(c) Is the mode a good representation of the average price of these books? Explain your answer.

2. A restaurant manager records the amount spent by eight tables of customers. The amounts are

£ FINANCE

£30, £42, £58, £47, £36, £60, £42, £45.

The manager would like to know the average amount spent per table so they can work out how many tables they need to seat to make a profit.

(a) Find the mean of these amounts.

(b) Find the median of these amounts.

(c) Find the mode of these amounts.

(d) Which measure, mean, mode or median, would you advise they use? Explain your answer.

3. The amount spent by Tina on seven days of a week are £12, £5, £8, £17, £14, £40 and £9.

£ FINANCE

(a) Find the mean of these amounts.

(b) Find the median of these amounts.

(c) Why might Tina choose to use the median instead of the mean to represent the average amount she spent?

4. The heights of five rugby players are
190 cm, 198 cm, 179 cm, 180 cm, 183 cm.
The heights of six football players are
172 cm, 182 cm, 168 cm, 193 cm, 175 cm, 184 cm.
(a) Which group of players has the higher mean height?
(b) Which group of players has a greater range in height?

5. The lengths of six fish are
25 cm, 30 cm, 28 cm, 25 cm, x cm, 32 cm.
The mean length of these fish is 27 cm. Find
(a) the value of x,
(b) the median length of the fish.

6. **(a)** Write down a data set of five values with a median of 10 and a mean of 12.
OPEN QUESTION
(b) Write down a data set of six values with a median of 15 and a mode of 13.

7. The tables show the goals scored by Manchester City and Liverpool in the 2018/19 Premier League.

Manchester City

Number of goals	0	1	2	3	4	5	6
Number of matches	2	9	10	10	2	2	3

Liverpool

Number of goals	0	1	2	3	4	5
Number of matches	3	9	10	7	6	3

(a) Find the mean, median, mode and range for the number of goals of the matches of
(i) Manchester City,
(ii) Liverpool.

(b) Copy and complete these sentences to compare the number of goals scored by each team.

Use: less than/more than/the same as
(i) The mean number of goals scored by Manchester City was ________ the mean number of number of goals scored by Liverpool.
(ii) The median number of goals scored by Manchester City was ________ the median number of goals scored by Liverpool.
(iii) The range of the number of goals scored by Manchester City was ________ the range of the number of goals scored by Liverpool.

8. A tutor compares the weekly test scores of two students over six weeks.
Lucy: 17, 18, 10, 9, 23, 29
Syra: 18, 19, 21, 17, 20, 16
(a) Find the mean and the range of the scores of Lucy.
(b) Find the mean and the range of the scores of Syra.
(c) Who has performed better in the tests? Explain your answer.

9. The table shows the prices of a new toy in 20 different shops.
£ FINANCE
(a) Find the mean price of the toy.
(b) Find the median price of the toy.
(c) Find the modal price of the toy.
(d) Find the range of the prices of the toy.

Price (£)	Frequency
10	5
11	8
12	4
13	2
14	1

10. A farmer records the number of eggs laid by some hens in a week and presents the results in the bar chart.
(a) Find the modal number of eggs in a week.
(b) Find the mean number of eggs in a week.
(c) Find the range of the number of eggs in a week.
(d) The farmer claims that the median number of eggs in a week is 6 since this is the middle bar. Are they correct? Explain your answer.

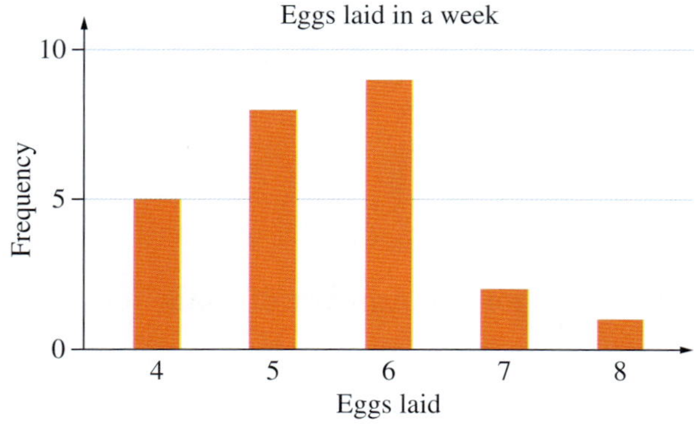

Write in Your Journal

'The weather in Singapore is better than the weather in Paris.'
Collect some data from the Internet that you could use to decide whether you agree with this claim.
Analyse the data using what you have learnt in this chapter and make your conclusions.

13 PROBABILITY AND SETS

WHAT IS IN THIS CHAPTER:

When you play a game at a fun fair, what do you think is your chance of winning a prize? The uncertainty about winning that you have when you play particular games can be modelled using a branch of mathematics called probability.

LET'S LEARN TO

- understand probability as a model of uncertainty
- define the terms sample space, outcome and event
- list the sample space for a simple chance situation
- find the probability of a single event
- draw Venn diagrams to represent sets
- use Venn diagrams to calculate probabilities

FLASHBACK

1. Number Types

(a) Whole numbers are 0, 1, 2, 3, 4, … .

(b) Even numbers are 0, 2, 4, 6, 8, … .

(c) Odd numbers are 1, 3, 5, 7, 9, … .

(d) Multiples of 3 are $1 \times 3, 2 \times 3, 3 \times 3, 4 \times 3, 5 \times 3, \ldots$ so 3, 6, 9, 12, 15, … .

(e) A prime number is a number that has exactly two factors: 1 and itself. The first 10 prime numbers are 2, 3, 5, 7, 11, 13, 17, 19, 23 and 29.

2. Fractions

(a) A fraction is a number of the form $\frac{a}{b}$, where a and b are integers and $b \neq 0$.

The number a is called the numerator and b is called the denominator of the fraction.

For example, $\frac{3}{7}$ is a fraction with numerator = 3 and denominator = 7.

(b) If the numerator and denominator of a fraction have a common factor, the fraction can be simplified by dividing both by the common factor.

For example, $\frac{12}{30} = \frac{12 \div 6}{30 \div 6}$

$= \frac{2}{5}$

13.1 Probability of an Event

A Introduction

Weather in Warrington

Today	Wed	Thurs	Fri	Sat	Sun
7°C	6°C	8°C	12°C	9°C	11°C
2°C	2°C	8°C	7°C	6°C	6°C
11%	15%	5%	88%	20%	74%

In everyday life you estimate the **likelihood** of events happening in the future. For example, you might estimate the result of an upcoming sports match or the weather later in the day. The weather forecast shows in percentages the chance that it will rain each day.

You can describe what you think is the **likelihood** of an event happening in the future with the terms **likely**, **unlikely**, **even**, **certain** and **impossible**. You can see how these words fit on a scale from impossible to certain in the diagram.

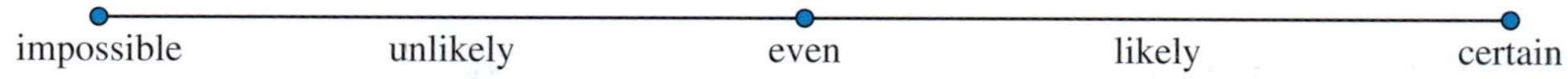

For example, most people, given their prior experience and understanding about how the world works, will agree with you if you say that you think that:

it is certain that the sun will rise from the east tomorrow,
it is impossible that you will turn 60 years old next year,
it is unlikely that the midday temperature tomorrow will be over 30 °C.

> **REMARK**
>
> The term 'even' here has nothing to do with even numbers. It just means the event is as likely to happen as it is to not happen.

CLASS ACTIVITY 1

Objective: To say what you think is the likelihood of some events happening.

1. Justify what you think is the likelihood of each of these events happening. Use the words likely, unlikely, even, certain and impossible.
   - **(a)** The sum of the angles of a triangle is 200°.
   - **(b)** The sum of two digits is greater than 3.
   - **(c)** There will be a new world record in the next Olympic Games.
   - **(d)** You will visit Singapore next year.
   - **(e)** A train will leave a terminal before the scheduled time.
   - **(f)** There will be a full moon in the next month.
   - **(g)** You will get a head when flipping a coin.
   - **(h)** The name of a month contains the letter J.
   - **(i)** A day in a week contains the letter d.
   - **(j)** You will see an ice cream van next week.
   - **(k)** You will hear your favourite song on the radio.
2. Copy the number line and write the letter of each event in the correct position above the line according to how likely you think it is. The first two have been done for you.

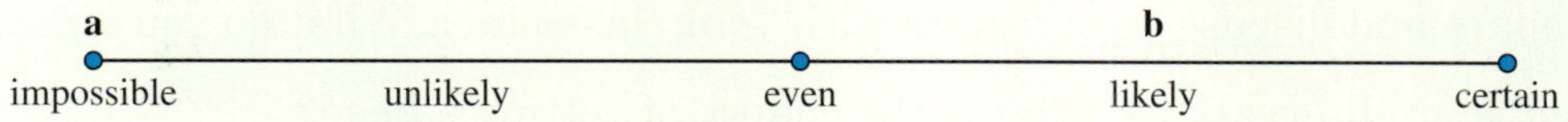

3. Make up four more sentences, **(l)** to **(o)**, like those in **Question 1**, with different likelihoods and ask a partner to add them to their number line.

B Terms and Definitions

In mathematics, when you decide what you think is the likelihood of an event happening, you call this the **probability** that the event occurs. The measure of probability is on a scale from 0 to 1.

What do you think the probability would be for

1. an impossible event,
2. a certain event,
3. an even event?

A process whose result cannot be predicted with certainty is called a **random experiment** or a **random trial**. A possible result of the experiment is called an **outcome**.

CLASS ACTIVITY 2

Objective: To observe long-term patterns when a coin is flipped.

Head

Tail

In the random experiment of flipping a coin, the two possible outcomes are getting a 'head' or getting a 'tail'.

Flip a coin into the air 20 times. Record the outcome of each trial in a copy of the table shown, up to the 20th trial. Use the notation 'H' for when the head lands face up and 'T' for when the tail lands face up.

Trial	1st	2nd	3rd	4th	5th	...	18th	19th	20th
Outcome									

1. Before a coin is flipped, are you able to predict correctly whether you will get a head or a tail?
2. In your results table, do you observe any pattern in the outcomes?
3. What percentage of your 20 trials resulted in getting a head?
4. Compare and discuss your results with your classmates. What do you notice?
5. From your observations, what is the chance of getting a head?
6. If you flipped the coin 100 times and got 40 heads, what might you think?
7. If you flipped the coin 1000 times and got 490 heads, what might you think? Would you think the same as for **Question 6**?

When a coin is flipped, you say that the result is random because it is not practical to measure the coin's movement precisely and quickly enough to predict the outcome accurately. You are not certain whether it is going to be a head or a tail. However, if you think the coin is **fair** or **unbiased**, then you have no reason to be more confident of getting a head or a tail. You say that the two outcomes, head and tail, are **equally likely**, and you say that the likelihood of getting a head is the same as getting a tail. You express this by saying that, 'The probability of getting a head $= \frac{1}{2}$' and also, 'The probability of getting a tail $= \frac{1}{2}$'.

REMARK

Jasper says, 'The probability of getting a head is $\frac{1}{3}$, because three outcomes are possible – heads, tails and standing on its edge.' Do you agree?

Example 1

A fair dice is thrown. Find the probability of getting

(a) a 3, **(b)** an even number,

(c) a number less than 3.

Solution

(a) The result of throwing a dice is the number on the upper face.

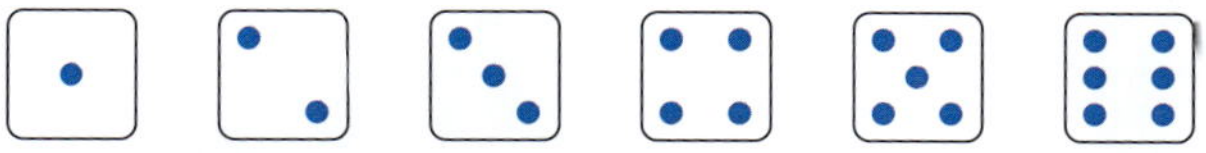

The possible outcomes are 1, 2, 3, 4, 5 and 6.

All the possible outcomes constitute the **sample space**.

Total number of possible outcomes is 6. There is no reason to be more confident of rolling a 3 than of any other outcome. Therefore,

Probability of getting a 3 $= \frac{1}{6}$.

(b) Outcomes which are even numbers are 2, 4, 6.

There is no reason to be more confident of rolling a 2, 4 or 6 than of any other outcome. Therefore,

Probability of getting an even number $= \frac{3}{6}$

$= \frac{1}{2}$.

(c) Outcomes which are less than 3 are 1 and 2.

There is no reason to be more confident of rolling a 1 or a 2 than of any other outcome. Therefore,

Probability of getting a number less than 3 $= \frac{2}{6}$

$= \frac{2 \div 2}{6 \div 2}$

$= \frac{1}{3}$.

DISCUSS

What is the sample space when a coin is flipped once? What is the sample space when a coin is flipped twice?

RECALL

Remember that to simplify $\frac{3}{6}$ you need to divide the top and bottom by a common factor. 3 is the highest common factor of 3 and 6, so divide both by 3.

Try It! 1

A fair dice is thrown. Find the probability of getting

(a) a 6, **(b)** an odd number,

(c) a number greater than 1, **(d)** a 7.

You call what happens an 'event'. An event can be one outcome (for example, rolling a 3) or more than one (for example, rolling an even number). If you think that all the outcomes of a random experiment are equally likely, you define the probability of an event happening, denoted by P(Event), as:

$$P(\text{Event}) = \frac{\text{number of equally likely outcomes which you want to happen}}{\text{total number of equally likely outcomes that could happen}}$$

DISCUSS

What is the sum of the probability of getting an even number and the probability of getting an odd number? Why?

Example 2

There are 3 brown rabbits and 4 grey rabbits in a pet shop. If a rabbit is to be chosen from the group at random, find the probability that the rabbit picked is

(a) brown, **(b)** grey.

REMARK

The sample space consists of the three brown rabbits and the four grey rabbits.

Solution

(a) The total number of possible outcomes $= 3 + 4$
$= 7$

The number of possible outcomes of picking a brown rabbit = 3.

Each rabbit is equally likely to be selected.

Hence, the probability of picking a brown rabbit,

$P(\text{brown rabbit}) = \frac{3}{7}$ $P(\text{brown rabbit}) = \frac{\text{number of brown rabbits}}{\text{total number of rabbits}}$

(b) The total number of possible outcomes = 7

The number of possible outcomes of picking a grey rabbit = 4.

Each rabbit is equally likely to be selected.

Hence, the probability of picking a grey rabbit,

$P(\text{grey rabbit}) = \frac{4}{7}$ $P(\text{grey rabbit}) = \frac{\text{number of grey rabbits}}{\text{total number of rabbits}}$

DISCUSS

What is P(grey rabbit) + P(brown rabbit) equal to? Why?

Try It! 2

There are 4 red balls and 5 blue balls in a bag. If a ball is picked at random from the bag, find the probability that the colour of the ball is

(a) red, **(b)** blue.

DISCUSS

What is the sample space of this experiment?

Example 3

A card is drawn at random from a pack of 52 playing cards. The pack consists of four suits and each suit has 13 cards. The suits are spades ♠, hearts ♥, diamonds ♦ and clubs ♣. Find the probability that the card drawn is

(a) red, **(b)** a diamond, **(c)** an ace.

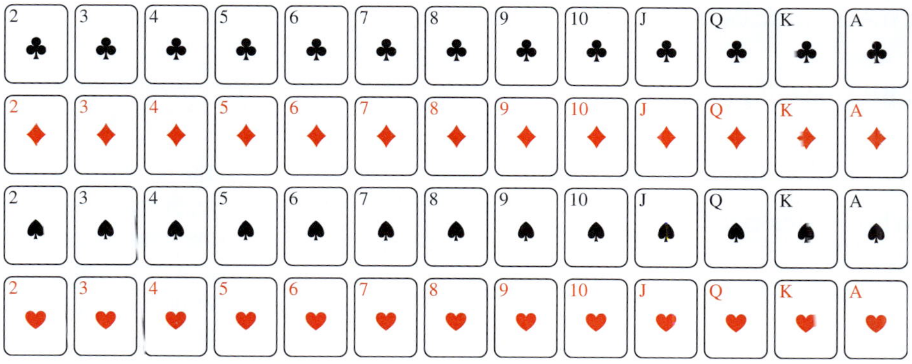

Solution

(a) There are 26 red cards (the hearts and the diamonds).

The sample space consists of all 52 playing cards. There is no reason to be more confident of drawing a red card than of any other outcome.

$$\text{P(getting a red card)} = \frac{26}{52} = \frac{1}{2}$$

(b) There are 13 diamonds. There is no reason to be more confident of drawing a diamond than of any other outcome.

$$\text{P(getting a diamond)} = \frac{13}{52} = \frac{1}{4}$$

(c) There are 4 aces. There is no reason to be more confident of drawing an ace than of any other outcome.

$$\text{P(getting an ace)} = \frac{4}{52} = \frac{1}{13}$$

REMARK

Divide the numerator and denominator by their common factor 26.

REMARK

P(getting a diamond) $= \frac{1}{4}$ also means that the probability of getting a diamond is 25%.

Try It! 3

A card is drawn randomly from a pack of 52 playing cards. Find the probability that the card is

(a) black, **(b)** a spade, **(c)** a red queen.

C Probability of an Event Not Happening

Example 4

There are 4 mathematics books and 8 science books on a shelf. A book is picked up at random from the shelf. Find the probability of getting

(a) a mathematics book,

(b) not a mathematics book.

Solution

(a) Total number of possible outcomes $= 4 + 8$
$= 12$

Number of mathematics books $= 4$

$$\text{P(mathematics book)} = \frac{4}{12} = \frac{1}{3}$$

(b) Number of books that are not on mathematics $= 8$

$$\text{P(not a mathematics book)} = \frac{8}{12} = \frac{2}{3}$$

DISCUSS

The number of non-mathematics books is the same as the number of science books. What would be the probability of getting a science book?

Try It! 4

A car park contains 3 black cars and 2 red cars. A car is selected at random. Find the probably the car is

(a) black, **(b)** not black.

DISCUSS

What do you notice about the answers to parts **(a)** and **(b)**?

In Example 4, you can see that

P(not a mathematics book) = 1 – P(mathematics book).

In general,

> P(not Event) = 1 – P(Event)

Example 5

There are 2 red pens, 3 blue pens and 5 black pens in a box. A pen is selected at random. Each pen is equally likely to be selected. Find the probability that the pen selected is

(a) red, **(b)** not red, **(c)** not blue,

(d) green, **(e)** not green.

Solution

(a) Total number of possible outcomes $= 2 + 3 + 5$
$= 10$

Number of red pens $= 2$

$$\text{P(pen is red)} = \frac{2}{10} = \frac{1}{5}$$

(b) P(pen is not red) = 1 – P(pen is red)

$= 1 - \frac{1}{5}$

$= \frac{5}{5} - \frac{1}{5}$ 1 whole = 5 fifths.

$= \frac{4}{5}$ 5 fifths – 1 fifth = 4 fifths.

DISCUSS

Is there another way to work out P(pen is not red)?

(c) P(pen is not blue) = 1 – P(pen is blue)

$= 1 - \frac{3}{10}$

$= \frac{10}{10} - \frac{3}{10}$ 1 whole = 10 tenths.

$= \frac{7}{10}$ 10 tenths – 3 tenths = 7 tenths.

(d) Since there are no green pens in the box, number of possible outcomes of getting a green pen = 0.

P(pen is green) $= \frac{0}{10}$

$= 0$

(e) P(pen is not green) = 1 – P(pen is green)

$= 1 - 0$

$= 1$

REMARK

It is **impossible** to select a green pen since there are no green pens in the box. Therefore, it is **certain** that the pen selected will not be green.

Try It! 5

There are 4 pink, 3 purple and 5 green colouring pencils in a box. One of the pencils is selected at random. Each pencil is equally likely to be selected. Find the probability that the pencil is

(a) pink, (b) not pink, (c) not purple,
(d) yellow, (e) not yellow.

Example 6

There are 8 marbles in a bag. Some of the marbles are blue and the remaining marbles are green. If a marble is picked from the bag at random, the probability of getting a blue marble is $\frac{1}{4}$. Find

(a) the number of blue marbles,
(b) the probability of getting a green marble.

Solution

(a) Draw a bar model. $\frac{1}{4}$ of the marbles are blue.

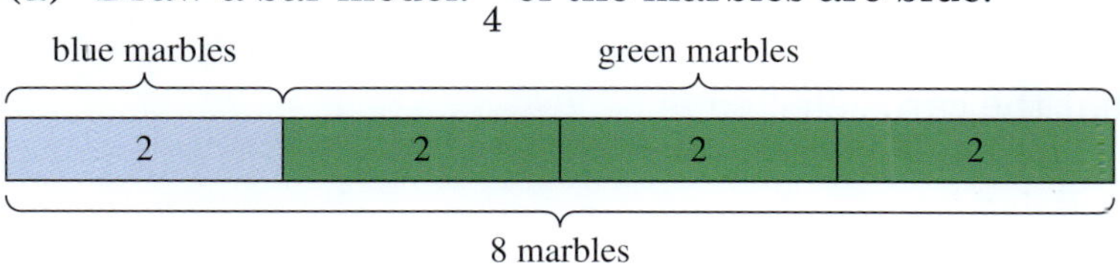

The total possible outcomes = 8

4 sections of the bar model represent 8 marbles.
1 section of the bar model represents $8 \div 4$
$= 2$ marbles.
Therefore, there are 2 blue marbles in the bag.

(b) The probability of getting a green marble,

$$\begin{aligned} \text{P(a green marble)} &= 1 - \text{P(a blue marble)} \\ &= 1 - \frac{1}{4} \\ &= \frac{4}{4} - \frac{1}{4} \quad \text{1 whole = 4 quarters.} \\ &= \frac{3}{4} \quad \text{4 quarters – 1 quarter = 3 quarters.} \end{aligned}$$

Try It! 6

There are 12 sweets in a bag. Some of the sweets are lemon flavoured and the remaining sweets are strawberry flavoured. If a sweet is picked from the bag at random, the probability of getting a lemon-flavoured sweet is $\frac{2}{3}$. Find

(a) the number of lemon-flavoured sweets in the bag,
(b) the probability of getting a strawberry-flavoured sweet.

PRACTICE 13.1

LEVEL 1

1. A fair dice is thrown. Find the probability of getting
(a) a 2, **(b)** a number greater than 4.

2. A set of 15 cards are numbered from 1 to 15. A card is selected at random from the set.
(a) Write down the sample space.
(b) Find the probability of getting a card with
(i) an odd number, **(ii)** a multiple of 5.

3. A letter is picked at random from the word 'BANANA'. Find the probability that the letter picked is
(a) the letter N, **(b)** not the letter N.

4. A card is selected at random from a deck of 52 playing cards. Which probability is the odd one out? The probability that the card selected is
(a) a black 7, **(b)** a 7, **(c)** a black 5, **(d)** a red 7.

5. There are five red, seven blue and nine green marbles in a bag. A marble is picked at random.
   (a) Find the probability that the marble picked is
      (i) green, (ii) not green, (iii) yellow.
   (b) Is the probability of picking a red marble less than the probability of picking a blue marble? Explain your answer.

LEVEL 2

6. There are 25 British and American tourists on a tour. If a tourist is selected at random, the probability of choosing a British tourist is $\frac{3}{5}$.
   (a) Find the number of British tourists on the tour.
   (b) Work out the probability of choosing an American tourist from this tour group.
   (c) What is the sum of the probability of choosing a British tourist and the probability of choosing an American tourist?

7. A wallet contains a total of 18 £10 notes and £20 notes. If a banknote is picked at random, the probability that it is a £10 note is $\frac{2}{9}$. Find
   (a) the probability of picking a £20 note,
   (b) the number of £10 notes in the wallet,
   (c) the probability of picking a banknote which is more than £5.

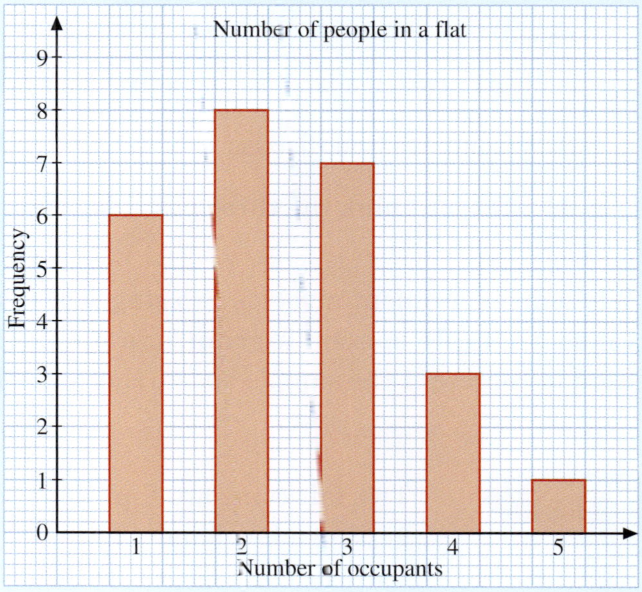

8. A survey is conducted in a block of 25 flats on the number of people per flat. The results are shown in the bar chart. A flat is selected at random and its occupants win a free meal at a new restaurant.
   Find the probability that the flat selected has
   (a) 2 occupants,
   (b) more than 3 occupants.

9. A survey was conducted among some students to find out their favourite colour. The pie chart shows the results of the survey.
   (a) Find the value of x.
   (b) A student is chosen at random.
      (i) What is the probability that their favourite colour is blue?
      (ii) What is the probability that their favourite colour is not green?

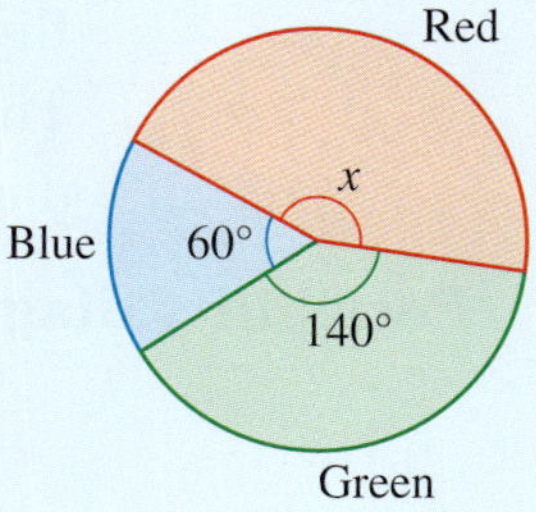

10. A letter is chosen at random from the word 'MATHEMATICS'. Define two events which have the same probability.
OPEN QUESTION

13.2 Using Sample Space Diagrams to Represent Events

CLASS ACTIVITY 3

Objective: To investigate the probabilities of different outcomes when two coins are flipped.

1. Flip two coins and record the outcome in a copy of the table shown. For example, if both coins show heads you would write HH. It is important to record the results in the correct order. HT and TH represent slightly different outcomes. Repeat this process until you have filled in the table.

Trial	1st	2nd	3rd	4th	5th	...	18th	19th	20th
Outcome									

2. What percentage of your 20 trials resulted in

   (a) two heads, **(b)** two tails, **(c)** one tail and one head?

3. Compare and discuss your results with your classmates. What do you notice?

4. Do you think the three possible outcomes given in **Question 2** are equally likely?

When an experiment involves two stages or two processes, a diagram called a **sample space diagram**, or a **possibility diagram**, can be used to represent the sample space. Have a look at some examples.

Example 7 Two fair coins are flipped. Find the probability of getting a head and a tail.

Solution There are two processes, flipping the first coin and flipping the second coin.
The sample space can be represented by a sample space diagram, either as a possibility diagram or as a table.

Possibility diagram

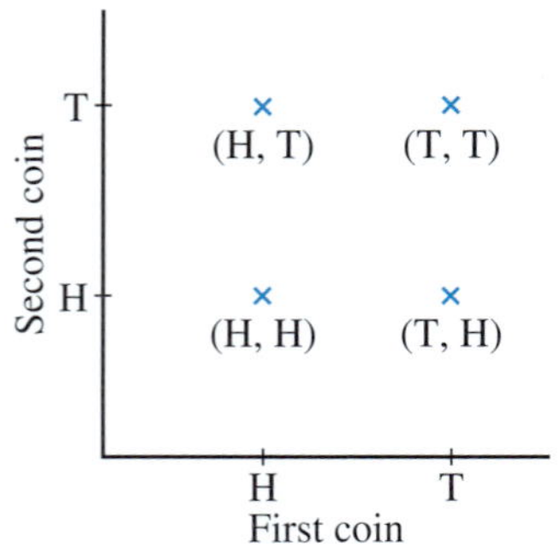

Table

		First coin	
		H	T
Second coin	H	HH	TH
	T	HT	TT

The sample space consists of the four outcomes (H, H), (H, T), (T, H) and (T, T), where there are two outcomes of a head and a tail: (H, T) and (T, H).

$\therefore$ P(getting a head and a tail) $= \frac{2}{4}$

$= \frac{1}{2}$

Try It! 7

A box contains one red ball and one green ball. Another box contains one red ball and one yellow ball. A ball is selected at random from each box.

(a) Draw a possibility diagram or table to show the sample space.

(b) Find the probability of getting

(i) two red balls,

(ii) one green ball and another ball,

(iii) two balls of different colours.

Example 8

In each spinner, the pointer is equally likely to land on each sector. When the pointers are spun, find the probability that the letters they land on are

(a) the same, **(b)** different.

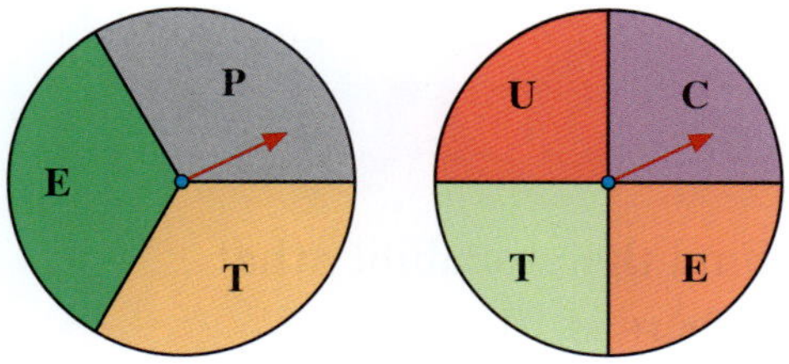

Solution

In the first spinner, the letters P, E and T are equally likely.

In the second spinner, the letters C, U, T and E are equally likely.

The sample space can be represented by a table as shown.

First spinner

Second spinner	P	E	T
C	PC	EC	TC
U	PU	EU	TU
T	PT	ET	TT
E	PE	EE	TE

There are 12 outcomes in the sample space.

(a) There are two outcomes where both letters are the same: EE and TT.

$\therefore$ P(both letters are the same) $= \frac{2}{12}$

$= \frac{1}{6}$

(b) P(both letters are different) = 1 – P(both letters are the same)

$= 1 - \frac{1}{6}$

$= \frac{6}{6} - \frac{1}{6}$

$= \frac{5}{6}$

Try It! 8

In each spinner, the pointer is equally likely to land on each sector. When the pointers are spun, find the probability that the letters they land on

(a) are both vowels,

(b) are one vowel and one consonant.

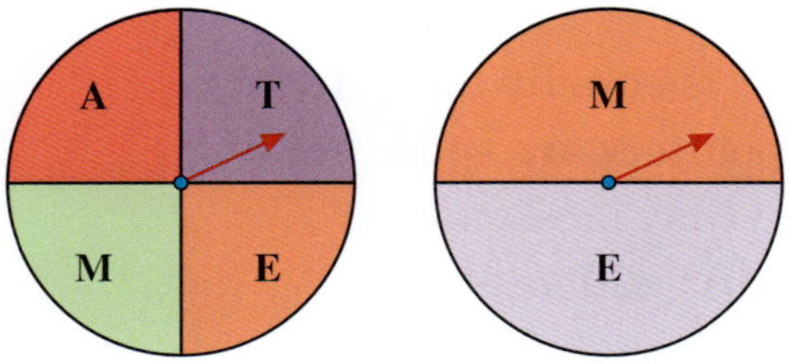

REMARK

Remember the vowels are: A, E, I, O and U. Every other letter is a consonant.

Example 9

Two fair dice are thrown. Find the probability that

(a) the sum of the two numbers is 10,

(b) at least one dice is a 3.

Solution

(a) The sample space can be represented by this sample space diagram.

1st dice

2nd dice	1	2	3	4	5	6
1	1, 1	2, 1	3, 1	4, 1	5, 1	6, 1
2	1, 2	2, 2	3, 2	4, 2	5, 2	6, 2
3	1, 3	2, 3	3, 3	4, 3	5, 3	6, 3
4	1, 4	2, 4	3, 4	4, 4	5, 4	6, 4
5	1, 5	2, 5	3, 5	4, 5	5, 5	6, 5
6	1, 6	2, 6	3, 6	4, 6	5, 6	6, 6

The sample space consists of 36 outcomes as you can see in the table.

REMARK

You can write the outcomes as ordered pairs, so (5, 6) means 5 on the 1st dice and 6 on the 2nd dice.

There are 3 outcomes with the sum of 10: (4, 6), (5, 5) and (6, 4).

$\therefore$ P(sum of the two numbers is 10) $= \frac{3}{36}$

$= \frac{1}{12}$

(b)

1st dice

2nd dice	1	2	3	4	5	6
1	1, 1	2, 1	3, 1	4, 1	5, 1	6, 1
2	1, 2	2, 2	3, 2	4, 2	5, 2	6, 2
3	1, 3	2, 3	3, 3	4, 3	5, 3	6, 3
4	1, 4	2, 4	3, 4	4, 4	5, 4	6, 4
5	1, 5	2, 5	3, 5	4, 5	5, 5	6, 5
6	1, 6	2, 6	3, 6	4, 6	5, 6	6, 6

There are 11 outcomes where at least one dice is a 3:
(3, 1), (3, 2), (3, 3), (3, 4), (3, 5), (3, 6),
(1, 3), (2, 3), (4, 3), (5, 3), (6, 3).

$\therefore$ P(at least one dice is a 3) $= \frac{11}{36}$

REMARK

The outcome (3, 3) means both dice are 3. It only counts once.

Try It! 9

Two fair dice are thrown. Find the probability that
(a) the sum of the two numbers is 7,
(b) both dice show the same number.

PRACTICE 13.2

LEVEL 1

1. There are two fair spinners, each with a green sector and an orange sector. When the pointers are spun, the colours where they land are recorded.

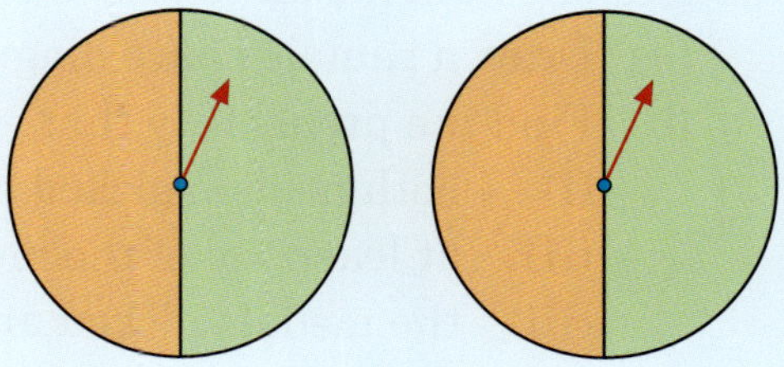

(a) Copy and complete the sample space diagram, where G stands for green and O stands for orange.

First spinner

Second spinner	G	O
G	GG	
O		

(b) Is the probability that both pointers land on the green sector equal to $\frac{1}{2}$? Explain your answer.

2. A letter is chosen at random from the word 'CAT'. Another letter is chosen at random from the word 'DOG'.
   (a) Copy and complete the sample space diagram.

	C	A	T
D			
O		AO	
G			

   (b) Find the probability that
      (i) one letter is C and the other letter is G,
      (ii) both letters are the same,
      (iii) both letters are different.

3. A fair dice is rolled, and a fair coin is flipped.
   (a) Represent the sample space using a possibility diagram.
   (b) Find the probability of getting
      (i) an even number and a head,
      (ii) a number greater than 4 and a tail.

4. Two fair dice are thrown.
   (a) Find the probability that the sum of the numbers is less than 5.
   (b) Is the probability of getting a sum of 5 less than the probability of getting a sum of 8? Explain your answer.

5. Two fair coins are flipped. Is the probability that at least one coin is a head greater than the probability that exactly one coin is a head? Explain your answer.

LEVEL 2

6. An athlete has one gold, one silver and one bronze medal for track events. They also have one gold, one silver and one bronze medal for field events. They pick at random one track medal and one field medal to take a photo.
   (a) Draw a sample space diagram.
   (b) Find the probability that
      (i) both medals picked are gold,
      (ii) at least one of the medals picked is gold,
      (iii) the medals picked are the same colour.

7. The first spinner has four equal sections labelled A, B, C and D. The second spinner has three equal sections labelled A, B and C. When the pointers are spun, find the probability that
   (a) the first pointer lands on A,
   (b) both pointers land on the same letter,
   (c) the pointers land on different letters.

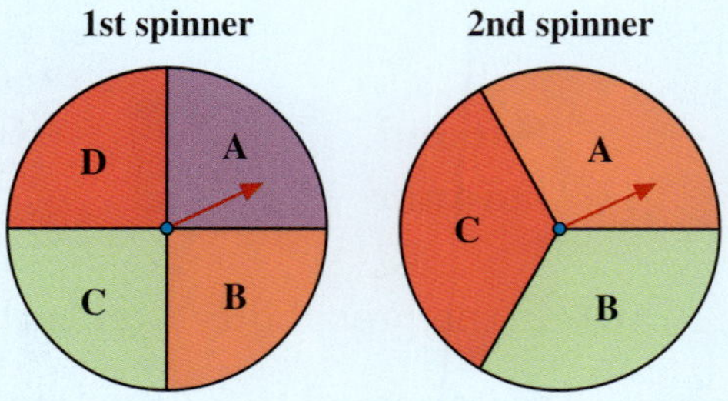

8. Which of these events is more likely:

'rolling a six with a fair dice' or

'rolling a six with a fair dice and at the same time getting a head when a coin is flipped'?

Explain your answer.

9. There are four mobile phones. One is black, two are white and one is pink. There are three mobile phone cases. One is yellow, one white and one pink. One phone and one case are picked at random.

(a) Find the probability that

(i) both of them are white,

(ii) they are both the same colour,

(iii) they are different colours.

(b) Write down two relationships between the answers in part **(a)**.

10. Every morning, both Maria and Peter will have a cup of coffee or tea. Can you say that the probability that both will have coffee is $\frac{1}{4}$? Explain your answer.

13.3 Sets and Venn Diagrams

A Sets and Elements

In daily life, a collective noun may refer to a group of animals or things. For example,

a **herd** of cows, a **flock** of seagulls,
a **school** of whales, a **pride** of lions.

In mathematics, the word **set** is used to refer to a collection of well-defined objects. The objects are called the **elements** of the set. A set may be denoted by a capital letter or enclosed in curly brackets.

For example, A = {positive even numbers less than 10}
= {2, 4, 6, 8}
and B = {polygons}
= {triangle, quadrilateral, pentagon, hexagon, …}

are two sets. The set A has a finite number of elements. It is called a **finite set**. The set B consists of an infinite number of elements, it is called an **infinite set**. The three dots (ellipsis) in the set indicate that the list continues indefinitely.

CLASS ACTIVITY 4

Objective: To understand the representation of sets and elements.

Copy and complete the table.

Name of set	Description	Listing	Finite or infinite
A	{positive odd numbers less than 10}	{1, 3, }	finite
B	{positive factors of 12}		
C	{negative integers}	{−1, −2, −3, ...}	infinite
D	{whole numbers}		
E	{first five square numbers}		
F		{2, 3, 5, 7, 11}	
G		{3, 6, 9, 12, ...}	
H		{2, 4, 8, 16, ...}	
I	{lower case letters before g}		
J		{x, y, z}	

Sets can be used to define collections of objects in many fields. Here are some further examples.

Example 10

Write down three elements in each set.

(a) {organs in a human body}

(b) {insects}

(c) {elements in the Periodic Table in chemistry}

Solution

(a) Heart, liver and kidney are three elements in {organs in a human body}.

(b) Bee, butterfly and dragonfly are three elements in {insects}.

(c) Carbon, oxygen and sodium are three elements in {elements in the Periodic Table in chemistry}.

Try It! 10

Write down three elements in each set.

(a) {gases in the Periodic Table in chemistry}

(b) {names of boys}

(c) {countries in Europe}

REMARK

If x is an element of a set A, it is denoted by $x \in A$.
If x is not an element of set A, it is denoted by $x \notin A$.
So in Example 10, bee $\in$ {insects}, but lion $\notin$ {insects}.

Example 11

Let the set C = {letters in the word 'eyes'}.

(a) Express the set by listing its elements.

(b) Is the letter z an element of C?

Solution

(a) C = {e, y, s}

(b) No, the letter z is not an element of C.

Try It! 11

Let the set D = {letters in the word 'dinner'}.

(a) Express the set by listing its elements.

(b) Is the letter r an element of D?

B Sets and Venn Diagrams

Sets can be represented by a **Venn diagram**. The rings in the Venn diagram can be used to sort elements according to some properties.

CLASS ACTIVITY 5

Objective: Use Venn diagrams to sort numbers.

1. **(a)** Copy the Venn diagram shown.

(b) What does each part of the Venn diagram represent?

(c) Sort the numbers from 1 to 12 into the correct part of the Venn diagram. Some have been done for you.

{numbers from 1 to 12}

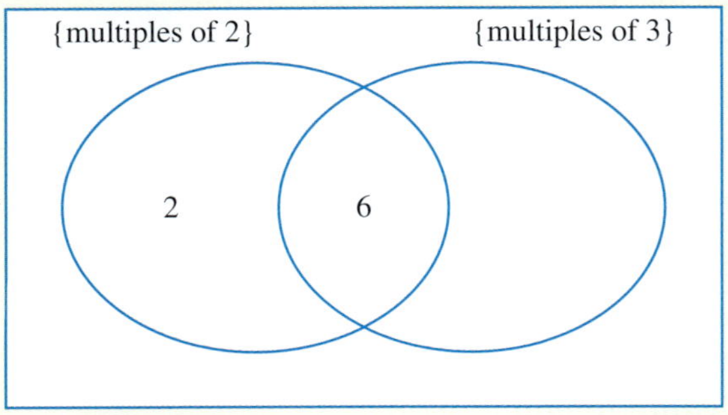

DISCUSS

Why are the numbers 2 and 6 in these positions in the Venn diagram?
Why do you need a rectangle around the rings? What set does the rectangle represent?

2. Draw your own Venn diagram to sort the numbers from 1 to 12 in a different way, for example you could use prime numbers, odd numbers or factors of 12. Ensure you label each of the sets in your Venn diagram.

Example 12

Draw a Venn diagram to sort the colours: red, orange, yellow, green, blue and purple using the sets, A = {primary colours} and B = {traffic light colours}.

Solution

The primary colours are red, blue and yellow, so A = {red, blue, yellow}.
The traffic light colours are red, orange and green, so B = {red, orange, green}.
Red is in both sets so will be in the middle section where the rings cross over.
Purple is not in either set A or set B, so will be outside of the rings.

The completed Venn diagram is shown.

{red, orange, yellow, green, blue, purple}

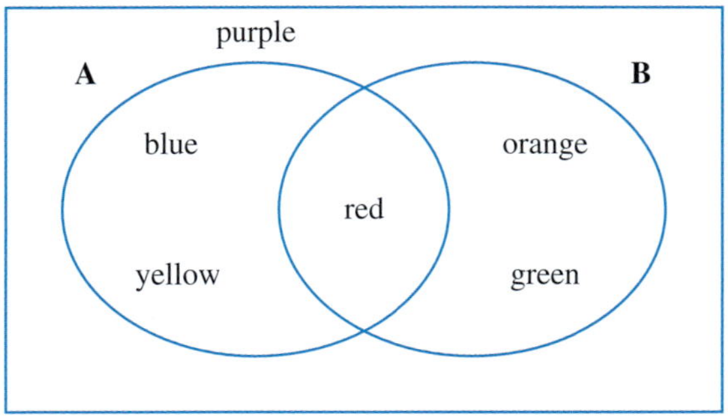

REMARK

The set of everything in the Venn diagram is called the universal set. The universal set is usually represented by the Greek letter ξ. In the example, ξ = {red, orange, yellow, green, blue, purple}.

Try It! 12

Draw a Venn diagram to sort the shapes: square, rectangle, rhombus, parallelogram and trapezium using the sets, A = {two pairs of parallel sides} and B = {all sides equal length}.

C Venn Diagrams and Probability

Probabilities can be calculated from Venn diagrams. Here is an example.

Example 13

The Venn diagram shows the residents of a care home. The residents are sorted according to the activities they enjoy.

{residents of a care home}

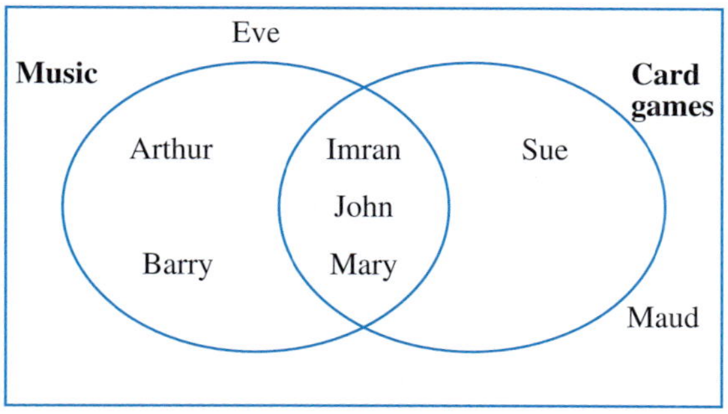

A resident is selected at random. Find the probability that they

(a) enjoy music,

(b) enjoy music and card games,

(c) do not enjoy either music or card games.

Solution

There are 8 residents in total.

(a) 5 of the residents enjoy music (Arthur, Barry, Imran, John and Mary).

$\therefore$ P(resident chosen enjoys music) $= \frac{5}{8}$

P(enjoy music) $= \frac{\text{number who enjoy music}}{\text{total number of residents}}$

(b) 3 of the residents enjoy both music and card games (Imran, John and Mary).

$\therefore$ P(resident chosen who enjoys music and card games) $= \frac{3}{8}$

(c) 2 of the residents do not enjoy either activity (Eve and Maud).

$\therefore$ P(resident chosen does not enjoy either card games or music) $= \frac{2}{8}$

$= \frac{1}{4}$

DISCUSS

On copies of the Venn diagram, can you shade in the section/s you need to look at for each part of the question? For example, for part **(a)**:

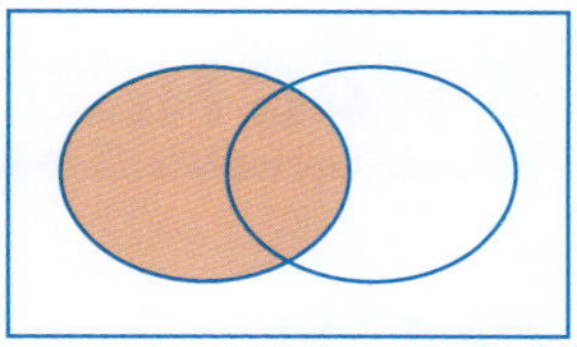

Try It! 13

The Venn diagram shows the employees of a pet shop. The members are sorted by what pets they have at home.

{pet shop employees}

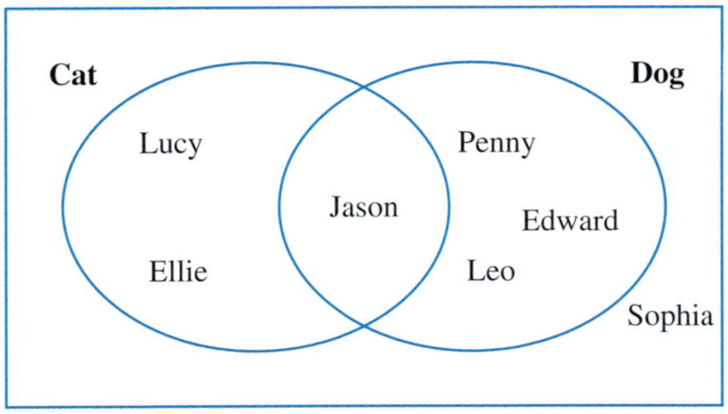

An employee is selected at random. Find the probability that they

(a) have a dog,

(b) have a dog and a cat,

(c) do not have a dog or a cat.

REMARK

If all the employees at the pet shop that had a cat also had a dog, the Venn diagram could be drawn like this:

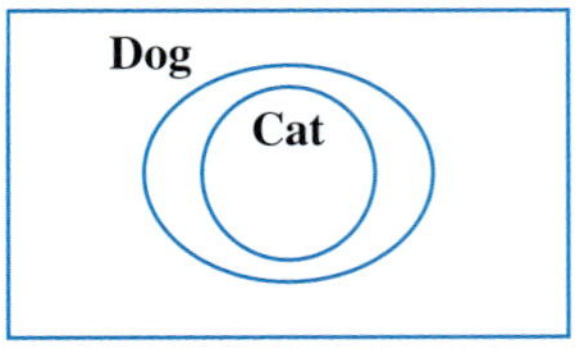

PRACTICE 13.3

LEVEL 1

1. List the elements in each set. State whether the set is finite or infinite.

(a) A = {integers from –3 to 3}

(b) B = {positive even numbers}

(c) C = {multiples of 3}

(d) D = {countries in the UK}

(e) E = {visible colours in a rainbow}

(f) F = {lower case letters in the alphabet}

2. Given that X = {quadrilaterals}, Y = {regular polygons} and Z = {shapes with rotational symmetry}. Which set(s) is each shape an element of?

(a) A square

(b) A rectangle

(c) An equilateral triangle

(d) An isosceles triangle

3. Copy and complete the Venn diagram to sort the integers from 1 to 12 using the sets {odd numbers} and {multiples of 3}.

{integers from 1 to 12}

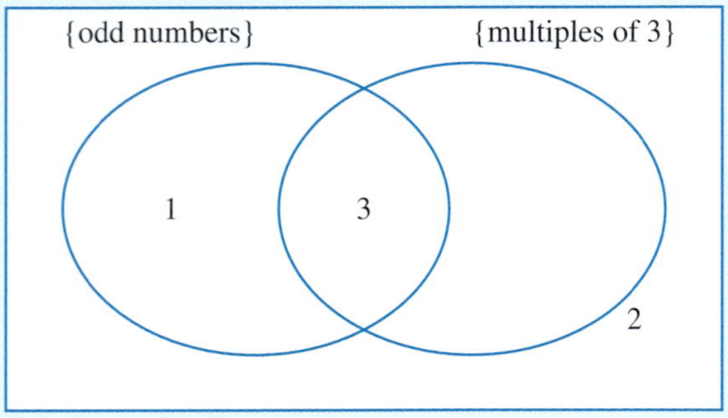

4. The Venn diagram shows the colours used in two paintings by some children.
{colours of paint available}

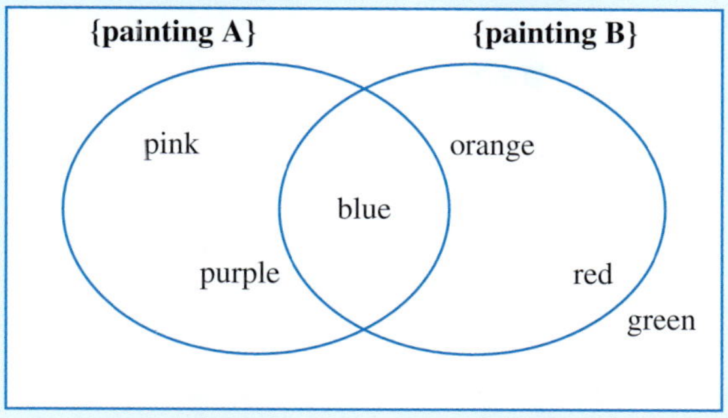

(a) Which colour was used in both paintings?
(b) Which colours were used in painting B?
(c) Which colour was available but was not used in either painting?

5. The Venn diagram shows the types of holiday a group of friends enjoy.
{group of friends}

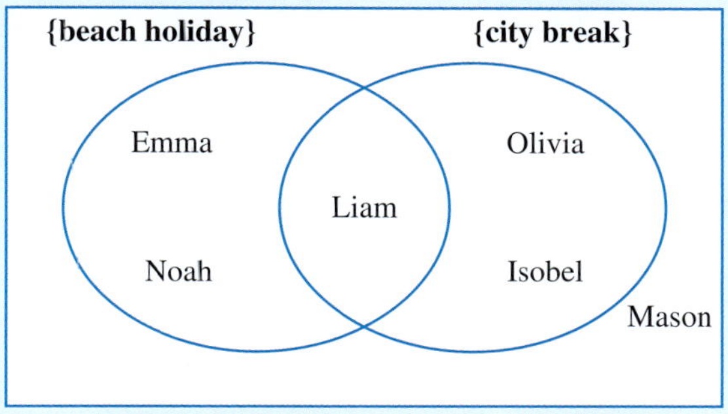

(a) How many people enjoy
  (i) beach holidays and city breaks, (ii) beach holidays?
(b) A person is chosen at random. Find the probability that they enjoy
  (i) beach holidays and city breaks, (ii) beach holidays.

LEVEL 2

6. Draw a Venn diagram to sort the integers from 10 to 20 using A = {odd numbers} and B = {multiples of 5}.

7. The Venn diagram shows the types of after-school club some students attend.
{Students}

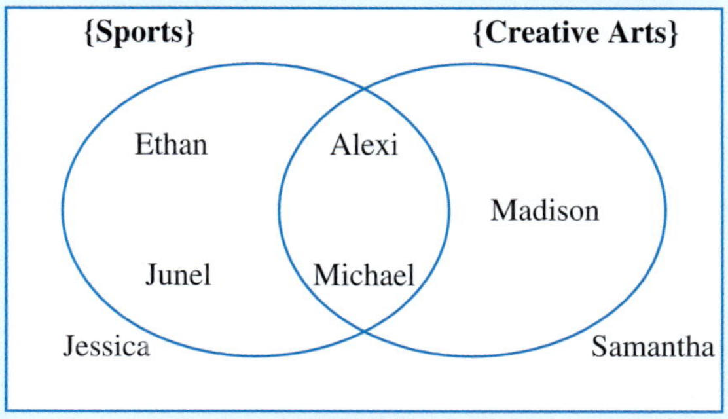

A student is to be selected at random from the group. Comment on the claim that the probability the student attends a Sports club is the same as the probability they attend both a Sports club and a Creative Arts club.

8. The Venn diagram represents a sample space of some letters.

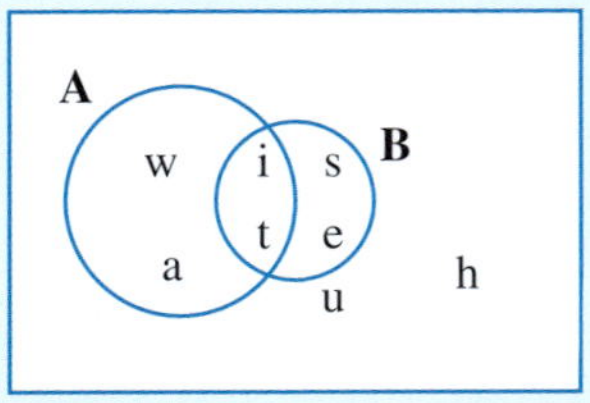

(a) List the elements in

(i) the sample space, **(ii)** the set A,

(iii) both set A and set B.

(b) If a letter is selected at random, find the probability that it is in set A.

9. Which of these Venn diagrams could be used to represent

(a) A = {odd numbers} B = {even numbers},

(b) A = {polygons} B = {quadrilaterals}.

(i)

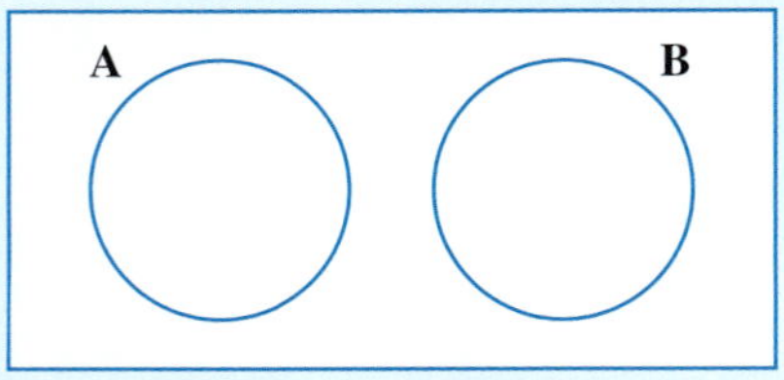

(ii)

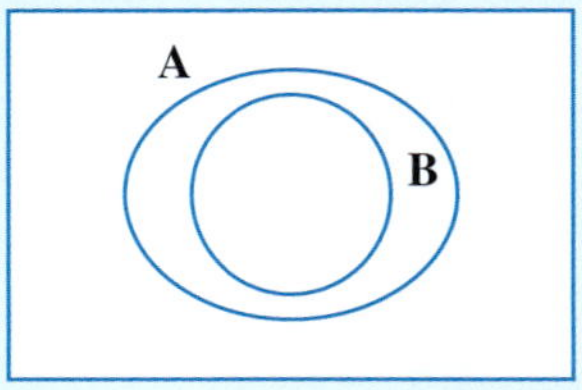

(iii)

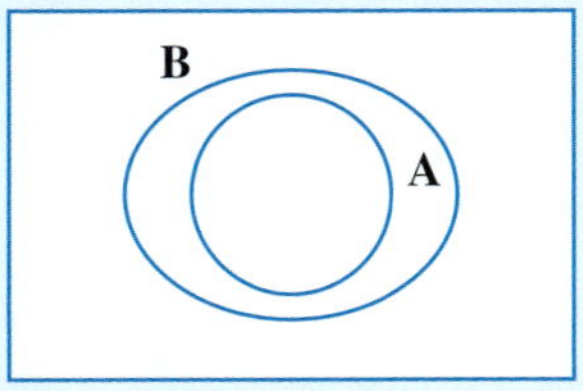

10. Let X = {factors of 18} and Y = {multiples of 3}.

PROBLEM SOLVING

A number is selected at random from set X. Find the probability it is also in set Y. Draw a Venn diagram to support your answer.

REVIEW

Definition of Probability

1. Probability is a measure of the likelihood of an event happening.
2. If all the outcomes of a random experiment are equally likely, the probability of an event, denoted by P(Event), is defined as:

$$P(\text{Event}) = \frac{\text{number of equally likely outcomes which you want to happen}}{\text{total number of equally likely outcomes that could happen}}$$

3. The sample space is all the possible outcomes.
4. The value of a probability is always between 0 and 1.
5. If E is an impossible event, then P(E) = 0.
6. If E is a certain event, then P(E) = 1.
7. P(not Event) = 1 – P(Event).

Sample Space Diagrams

The sample space of a two-stage process can be represented using a sample space diagram.

For example, in throwing two fair coins, the sample space can be represented as shown.

		First coin	
		H	T
Second coin	H	HH	TH
	T	HT	TT

There are 3 outcomes that have at least one tail: (H, T), (T, H) and (T, T).

Hence, the probability of at least one tail $= \frac{3}{4}$.

Sets and Venn Diagrams

1. A set is a collection of well-defined objects.

For example, A = {even numbers between 3 and 11}
= {4, 6, 8, 10}.

2. Sets can be represented on Venn diagrams.

For example, if A = {prime numbers} and B = {even numbers}, then the integers from 1 to 10 are sorted in the Venn diagram as shown.

2 is an element of both sets, so is placed in the part where the loops overlap.

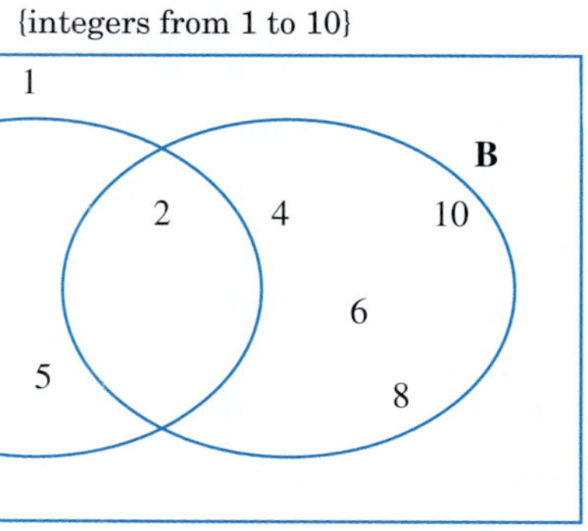

3. Probabilities can be found from Venn diagrams.

For example, if a number is selected at random from the Venn diagram,

probability of a prime number $= \frac{4}{10}$ — There are 4 prime numbers in the diagram: 2, 3, 5, 7.

$= \frac{2}{5}$

CHALLENGE 13

The performers in a band can all sing, and some can play one or more instruments as shown in the table.

Name	Instrument/s
Sarah	Guitar, drums
Miles	Keyboard, drums
Matt	Guitar, keyboard, drums
Jake	None
Michelle	Guitar, keyboard

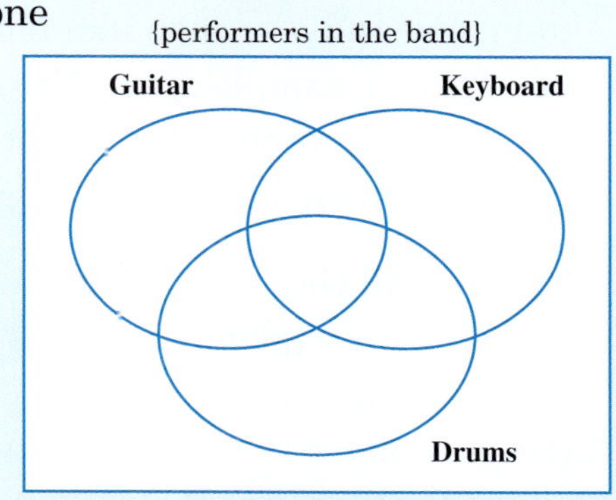

Copy and complete the Venn diagram to show all the band members.

REVISION EXERCISE 13

1. A fair dice is thrown. What is the probability that the number is

(a) a six, **(b)** greater than 4?

2. A letter is selected at random from the word 'PARALLEL'. Find the probability that the letter selected is

(a) the letter L, **(b)** the letter A.

3. There are 5 oranges, 7 apples and 3 pears in basket. If a fruit is picked at random from the basket, find the probability that the fruit is

(a) an orange, **(b)** a banana, **(c)** not an orange.

4. The probability of rain on a particular day is $\frac{1}{8}$. What is the probability of no rain?

5. A disc has eight equal parts with the numbers as shown. The pointer of the disc is spun once. Find the probability of getting

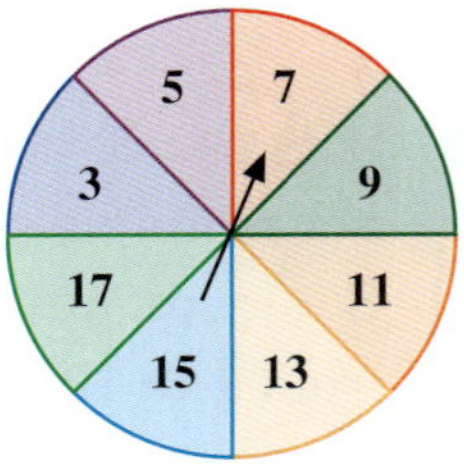

(a) a number more than 11, **(b)** an odd number,

(c) an even number, **(d)** a prime number,

(e) a factor of 99.

6. A bag contains one gold coin and one silver coin. A coin is drawn at random from the bag. A card is drawn at random from a deck of 52 playing cards.

(a) Copy and complete the sample space diagram for the type of coin and the suit of the card drawn.

Card suit

Coin

	♥	♦	♣	♠
Gold				
Silver				

(b) Find the probability of getting

(i) a gold coin and a spade (♠),

(ii) a silver coin and a red card.

7. John books a dentist appointment at random on a day from Monday to Friday and a session in a morning or an afternoon.

(a) Draw a sample space diagram for his choices.

(b) Find the probability that the session chosen is a morning session on a day beginning with the letter T.

8. **(a)** List all the elements of each set.

(i) A = {prime numbers less than 20}

(ii) B = {factors of 12}

(b) A number is selected at random from set A. Find the probability it is also in set B.

9. Sort the integers from 1 to 20 into a Venn diagram using
A = {multiples of 2} and B = {square numbers}.

10. The Venn diagram shows some GCSE choices of a group of students.

{group of students}

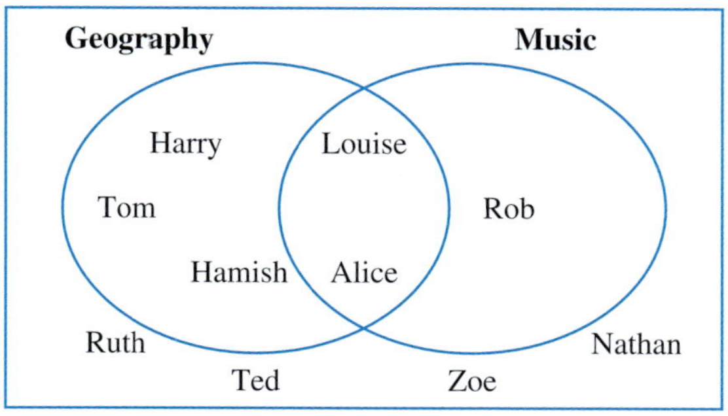

A student is be selected at random from the group.
Find the probability that they study

(a) geography,
(b) music but not geography,
(c) music and geography,
(d) neither music nor geography.

Write in Your Journal

A fair coin has been flipped 10 times. All the outcomes were heads. When the coin is flipped again, would you say it is more likely to land on a head or tail? Explain your answer.

INTEGRATED EXAMPLES AND REVIEW EXERCISE 3

Integrated Examples

Example 1

In ΔABC, $AB = 25$ cm, $BD = 24$ cm, $AD = 7$ cm, $\angle ACB = 60°$ and ADC is a straight line.

(a) Show that $\angle ADB = 90°$.

(b) Find the angle θ.

(c) Find the length of BC.

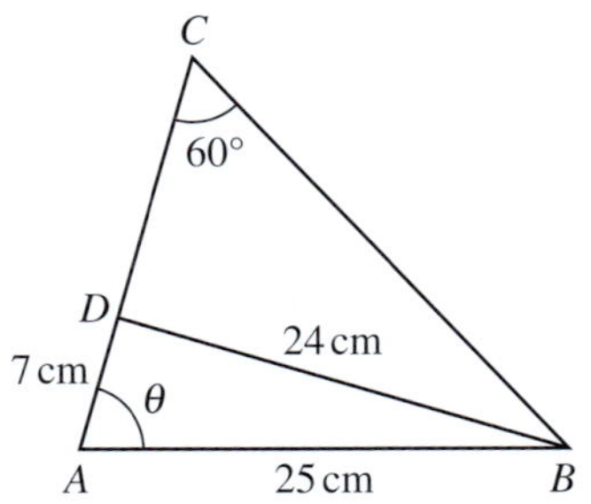

Solution

(a) $AB^2 = 25^2$

$= 625$

$AD^2 = 7^2$

$= 49$

$BD^2 = 24^2$

$= 576$

$AD^2 + BD^2 = 49 + 576$

$= 625$

$= AB^2$

$\therefore$ Hence, $\angle ADB = 90°$ (Converse of Pythagoras' Theorem.)

(b) In ΔABD,

adjacent side to angle $\theta = AD$

hypotenuse $= AB$

$\cos\theta = \frac{AD}{AB}$ $\quad$ $\cos\theta = \frac{\text{adjacent side}}{\text{hypotenuse}}$

$= \frac{7}{25}$

$\theta = \cos^{-1}\left(\frac{7}{25}\right)$

$= 73.7°$ (to 1 dp)

(c) In ΔBCD,

$\angle BDC = 180° - \angle ADB$ (Angles on a straight line add up to 180°.)

$= 180° - 90°$

$= 90°$

Hence, using the factor tree for

$\sin\theta = \frac{\text{opposite side}}{\text{hypotenuse}}$:

> **REMARK**
>
> If $\angle ADB = 90°$, then AB must be the hypotenuse because it is the longest side.

> **DISCUSS**
>
> Can you work part **(b)** out in another way using
>
> **(i)** sin,
>
> **(ii)** tan?

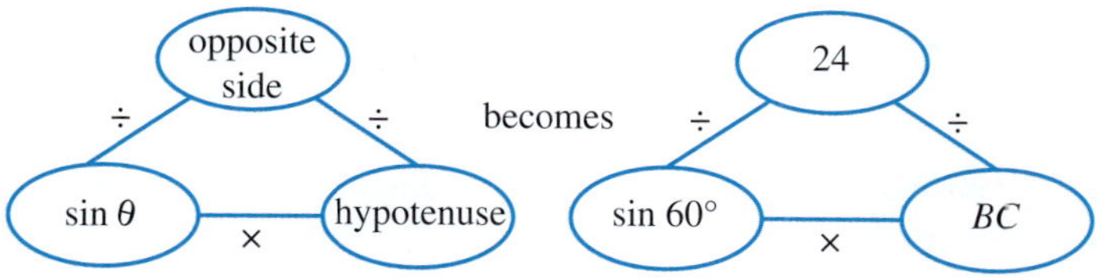

$$\sin 60° = \frac{BD}{BC}$$

$$= \frac{24}{BC}$$

$$BC = \frac{24}{\sin 60°}$$

$$= 27.7\,\text{cm} \qquad \text{(to 3 sf)}$$

$\sin\theta = \dfrac{\text{opposite side}}{\text{hypotenuse}}$

Try It! 1

In ΔPRS, $PS = 37\,\text{cm}$, $PQ = 12\,\text{cm}$, $QS = 35\,\text{cm}$, $\angle QSR = 40°$ and PQR is a straight line.

(a) Show that $\angle PQS = 90°$.

(b) Find the angle θ.

(c) Find the lengths of QR and RS.

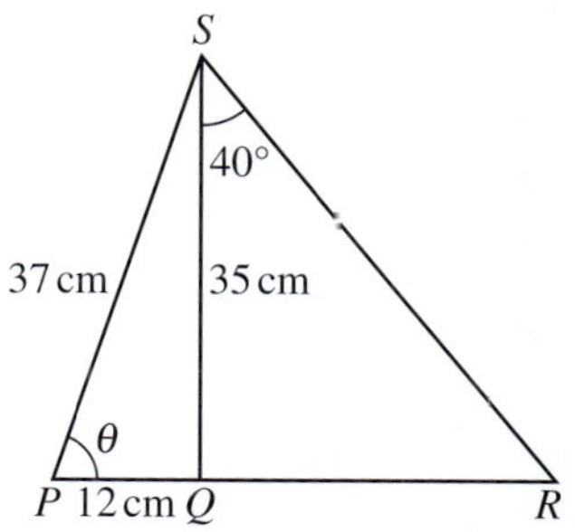

Example 2

Let P = {right-angled triangles} and Q = {isosceles triangles}.
ΔABC has sides $AB = 28\,\text{mm}$, $BC = 45\,\text{mm}$ and $CA = 53\,\text{mm}$.
ΔDEF has sides $DE = 7\,\text{mm}$, $EF = 4\,\text{mm}$ and $FD = 7\,\text{mm}$.
Copy the Venn diagram and place ΔABC and ΔDEF in it.

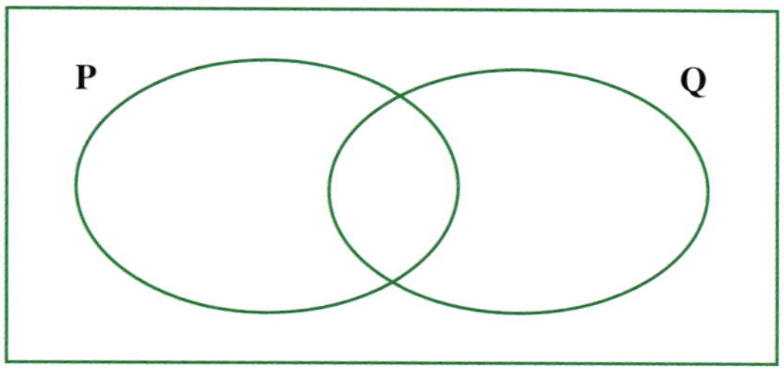

Solution

In ΔABC,

$$CA^2 = 53^2$$
$$= 2809$$
$$AB^2 = 28^2$$
$$= 784$$
$$BC^2 = 45^2$$
$$= 2025$$
$$AB^2 + BC^2 = 784 + 2025$$
$$= 2809$$
$$= CA^2$$

REMARK

You might find it helpful to sketch the triangles.

Hence, $\angle ABC = 90°$ (Converse of Pythagoras' Theorem.)

$\Rightarrow \Delta ABC$ is a right-angled triangle.

$\Rightarrow \Delta ABC$ is an element of P.

ΔABC is a scalene triangle, hence ΔABC is not an element of Q.

In ΔDEF, $DE = FD$ (given)

$\therefore$ ΔDEF is an isosceles triangle.

ΔDEF is an element of Q.

$FD^2 = 7^2$

$= 49$

$DE^2 = 7^2$

$= 49$

$EF^2 = 4^2$

$= 16$

$DE^2 + EF^2 = 49 + 16$

$= 65$

$\neq FD^2$

Hence, ΔDEF is not a right-angled triangle.

ΔDEF is not an element of P.

The required Venn diagram is:

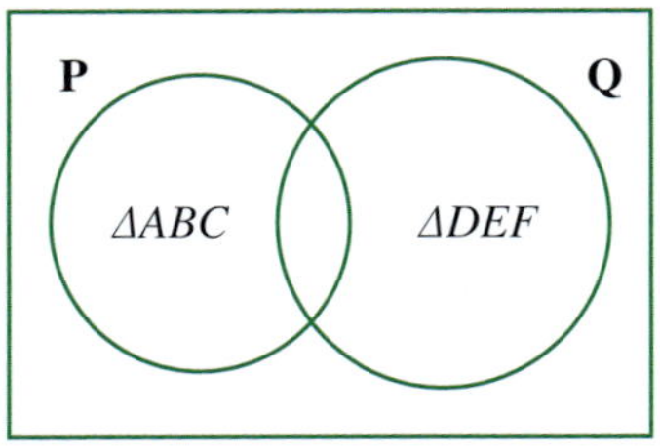

Try It! 2

Let P = {right-angled triangles} and Q = {scalene triangles}.

ΔABC has sides $AB = 11$ mm, BC = 5 mm and CA = 13 mm.

ΔDEF has sides $DE = 11$ mm, $EF = 60$ mm and $FD = 61$ mm.

Copy the Venn diagram and place ΔABC and ΔDEF on it.

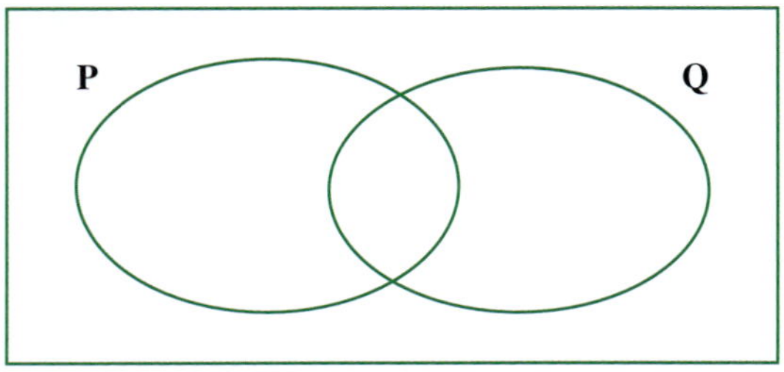

Example 3 A librarian studies the number of library books borrowed by students in a month. The table summarises the results of some students.

Number of books	2	4	6	8	10
Frequency	1	5	3	2	1

(a) Find the mean, median, mode and range of the number of books borrowed in this particular month.

(b) If one of these students is selected at random, find the probability that the number of books borrowed by the student is

(i) less than 7 books,

(ii) 7 books,

(iii) more than the mean.

Solution

(a) Total number of students surveyed = 1 + 5 + 3 + 2 + 1
= 12

Total number of books borrowed by these students
= (2 × 1) + (4 × 5) + (6 × 3) + (8 × 2) + (10 × 1)
= 66

Mean = 66 ÷ 12
= 5.5

Mean = $\frac{\text{total sum of all data values}}{\text{total number of data items}}$

> **DISCUSS**
> Looking at the data, do you think 5.5 is a sensible answer for the mean?

Write the data in ascending order:
2, 4, 4, 4, 4, 4, 6, 6, 6, 8, 8, 10

Median = mean of 6th and 7th values
$= \frac{4 + 6}{2}$
= 5

Median is the middle value of the data when arranged in ascending order.

Mode = the item with the highest frequency
= 4

Frequency = 5 is the highest.

Range = the largest value − the smallest value
= 10 − 2
= 8

(b) **(i)** Number of items in the sample space = 12

Number of students that borrowed less than 7 books = 1 + 5 + 3
= 9

P(borrowed less than 7 books) $= \frac{9}{12}$

$\frac{\text{number of equally likely outcomes that you want to happen}}{\text{total number of equally like outcomes that could happen}}$

$= \frac{3}{4}$

(ii) Number of students that borrowed 7 books = 0

P(borrowed 7 books) $= \frac{0}{12}$

$= 0$

(iii) Number of students that borrowed more than the mean

= number of students that borrowed more than 5.5 books

$= 3 + 2 + 1$

$= 6$

P(more than the mean) $= \frac{6}{12}$

$= \frac{1}{2}$

REMARK

If probability = 0, the event is impossible.

Try It! 3

The manager of a clothes shop records the number of items bought by customers. The table summarises the results of some customers.

Number of items	1	2	3	4	5
Frequency	6	4	5	3	2

(a) Find the mean, median, mode and range of the data.

(b) Give a reason why the mean could be a good average to represent the data.

(c) If one of these customers is selected at random, find the probability that the number of items bought by the customer is

(i) less than 6 items,

(ii) 3 items,

(iii) more than the mean.

REVIEW EXERCISE 3

1. Find the value of the unknown in each triangle.

(a)

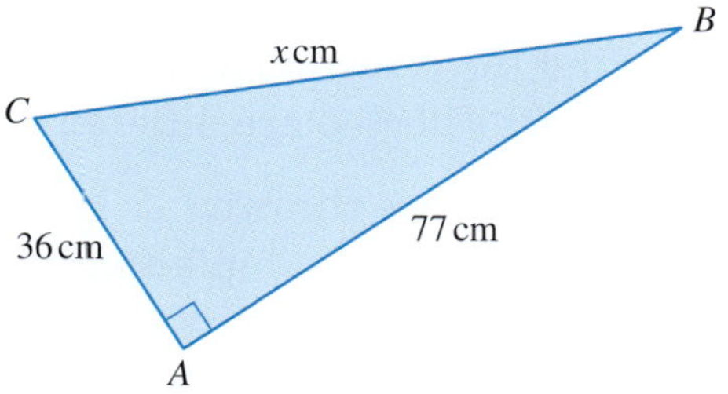

(b)

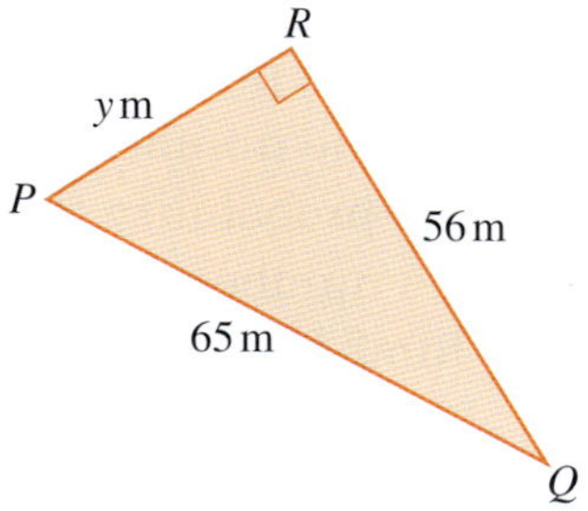

2. *ABCD* is a rectangular frame with a reinforcement beam *AC*.
Find the total length of the bars required to make the frame.

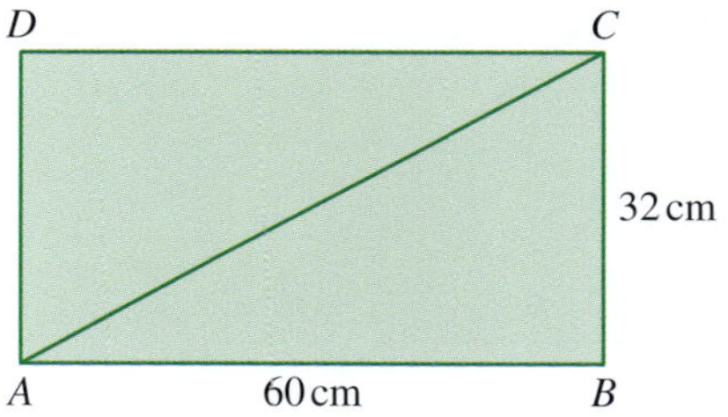

3. Which of these triangles is the odd one out? Explain your answer.

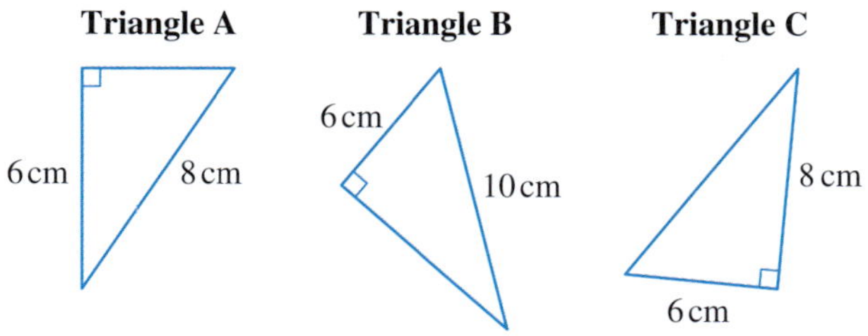

4. Which of these two triangles is a right-angled triangle? Explain your answer.
ΔABC with $AB = 40$ cm, $BC = 41$ cm and $CA = 10$ cm.
ΔDEF with $DE = 65$ cm, $EF = 97$ cm and $FD = 72$ cm.

5. Find the value of the unknown in each triangle.

(a)

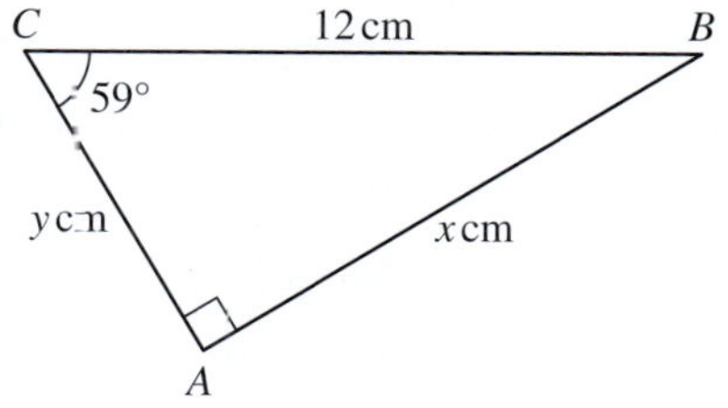

(b)

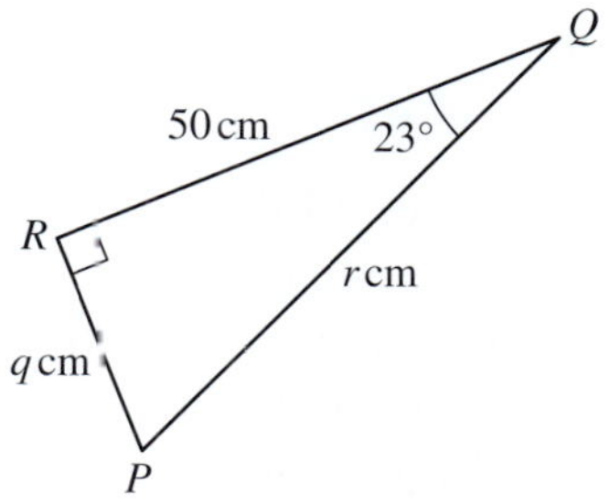

6. Find the size of the unknown angle in each of these triangles.

(a)

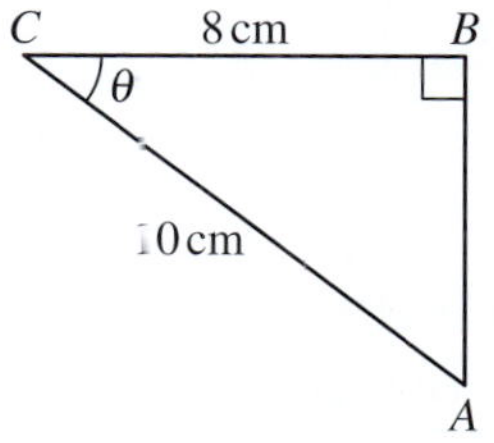

(b)

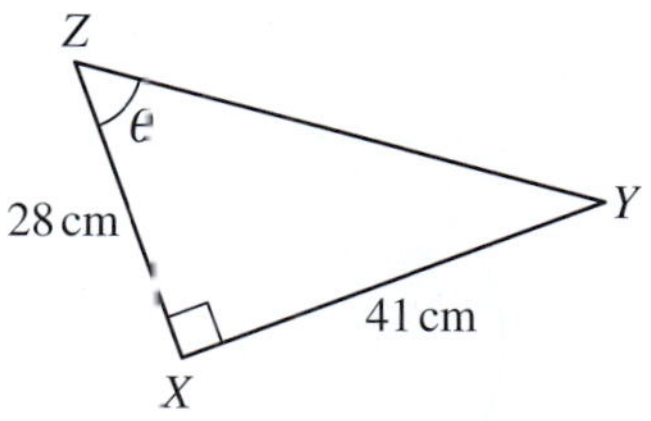

7. The volumes of hydrogen produced in five experiments are:
$25\,\text{cm}^3$, $30\,\text{cm}^3$, $29\,\text{cm}^3$, $30\,\text{cm}^3$ and $11\,\text{cm}^3$.

(a) Find the mean, median and mode of these volumes.

(b) Give a reason why you might

(i) use the mean as the average volume,

(ii) not use the mean as the average volume.

8. A consumer organisation checks the prices of a box of biscuits in 20 shops. The prices are summarised in the table.

Price (£)	2	3	4	5	6
Frequency	3	7	6	1	3

Find

(a) the mean price and the median price,

(b) the range of these prices.

9. Ten cards are numbered 21 to 30. If a card is selected at random, find the probability that the number on the card is

(a) a prime number,

(b) a multiple of 4.

10. Let A = {gold, silver, platinum, copper} and B = {zinc, iron, copper, gold}. Draw a Venn diagram to sort the metals gold, silver, platinum, copper, zinc, tin and iron using the sets A and B.

11. There are 2 red balls, 3 green balls and 5 blue balls in a bag. A ball is drawn at random from the bag. Find the probability that the ball drawn is

(a) blue, **(b)** not blue,

(c) yellow, **(d)** not yellow.

12. The Venn diagram shows the flower colours available to a gardener for roses and lilies.

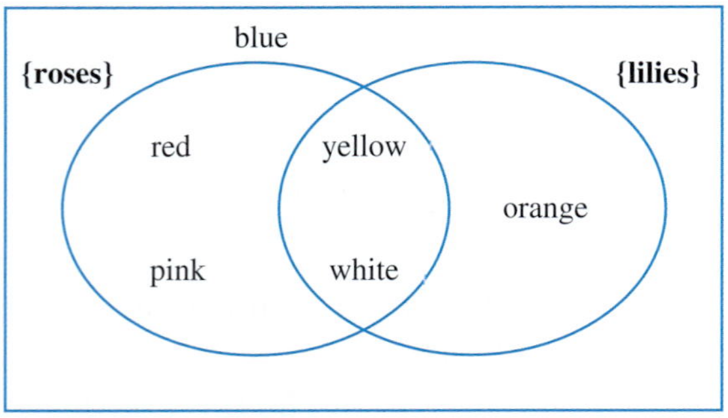

A colour is selected at random from the sample space. All colours are equally likely to be chosen. Find the probability that

(a) roses are available in the colour chosen,

(b) roses and lilies are available in the colour chosen,

(c) lilies are available in the colour chosen but roses are not.

13. A letter is selected at random from the word 'EAST'. Another letter is selected at random from the word 'WEST'.

(a) Represent the sample space using a possibility diagram or table.

(b) Find the probability that the letter E is selected from both words.

(c) Find the probability that the two letters selected are different.

14. Two fair dice are thrown.

(a) Represent the sample space using a possibility diagram or table.

(b) Find the probability that the sum of the numbers is 8.

(c) Tom says that the probability that the product of the numbers is even is equal to the probability that the product of the numbers is odd. Do you agree with him? Explain your answer.

15. PROBLEM SOLVING The diagram shows a triangular window. Work out the area of glass required to make the window.

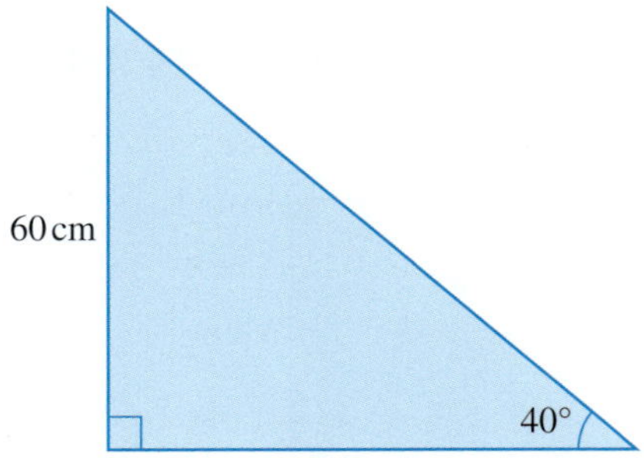

PROBLEMS IN REAL-WORLD CONTEXTS

A. Best Buy Restaurant Stock

Sam buys products in bulk for their restaurant. The prices of some of the products from three suppliers are given below.

Supplier A	Supplier B	Supplier C
Rice £1.50 per kg Onions 90p per kg	Rice £35 for 20 kg bag Onions £1.90 for 2 kg bag	Rice £24 for 15 kg bag Onions 72p for 6 onions (average mass 150 g each)
Takeaway containers 1p each	Takeaway containers £21 for 250 containers	Takeaway containers £9 for 100 containers
Delivery £8	Free delivery	Delivery £10

1. Which supplier offers the best value for rice?
2. Which supplier offers the best value for onions?
3. Sam needs to purchase 40 kg of rice and 400 takeaway containers. They want to buy everything from the same supplier. Which supplier should they use to get the best value?

B. Monthly Instalments

An appliance store offers a plan for its customers to pay for goods with monthly instalments:

- 20% of purchase price as an initial deposit payment,
- 6% interest rate on the remaining balance at the date of purchase,
- 12 equal monthly instalments for the balance and the interest.

The Smith family buys a television set for £1500.

1. Calculate the initial deposit payment they must make.
2. Work out the total interest on the remaining balance.
3. Find the price of the monthly instalment.
4. What is the difference between the retail price of the television set and the total amount that the Smith family will have paid using the monthly instalment plan?

DISCUSS

Do you think the Smith family will pay more in total if they pay in instalments or buy the TV outright initially?

C. Going on Holiday

Mr and Mrs Tan, who live in Singapore, would like to visit the UK for 7 days. They need to buy return flight tickets, book a hotel room and rent a car for 7 days. They check the prices online and find this information.

Flight ticket	SGD2900 per person, including tax
Hotel room and breakfast	£170 per day, excluding 20% VAT
Car rental	£700 for 7 days, including tax
Lunch	£15 per person per day, excluding 20% VAT
Dinner	£30 per person per day, excluding 20% VAT

REMARK

SGD means 'Singapore dollars'.

1. Find the total cost of the flight tickets in Singapore dollars (SGD).
2. Calculate the total cost of hotel room and car rental including VAT in pounds.
3. Calculate the total meal cost including VAT in pounds.
4. Assume the exchange rate is £1 = SGD1.79. Work out the total cost of the trip in Singapore dollars.

D. Staircase

The photo shows a staircase at the Tate Modern in London. The diagram shows the side view of a model of the staircase. Each step is 15 cm high and 30 cm wide. The platform GF is 150 cm wide. There are 10 steps in the lower part and 12 steps in the upper part.

1. Find the distances AD and DE.
2. Calculate the distance AE.
3. Calculate $\angle EAD$.

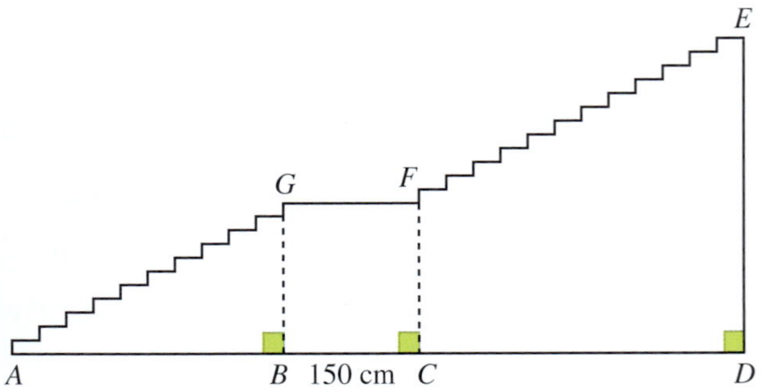

E. Premier League Statistics

Date	Venue	Result	GF	GA	Opponent
11/08/2018	Away	W	3	0	Huddersfield
18/08/2018	Home	W	3	2	Arsenal
26/08/2018	Away	W	2	1	Newcastle Utd
01/09/2018	Home	W	2	0	Bournemouth
15/09/2018	Home	W	4	1	Cardiff City
23/09/2018	Away	D	0	0	West Ham
29/09/2018	Home	D	1	1	Liverpool
07/10/2018	Away	W	3	0	Southampton
20/10/2018	Home	D	2	2	Manchester Utd
28/10/2018	Away	W	4	0	Burnley
04/11/2018	Home	W	3	1	Crystal Palace
11/11/2018	Home	D	0	0	Everton
24/11/2018	Away	L	1	3	Tottenham
02/12/2018	Home	W	2	0	Fulham
05/12/2018	Away	L	1	2	Wolves
08/12/2018	Home	W	2	0	Manchester City
16/12/2018	Away	W	2	1	Brighton
22/12/2018	Home	L	0	1	Leicester City
26/12/2018	Away	W	2	1	Watford
30/12/2018	Away	W	1	0	Crystal Palace
02/01/2019	Home	D	0	0	Southampton
12/01/2019	Home	W	2	1	Newcastle Utd
19/01/2019	Away	L	0	2	Arsenal
30/01/2019	Away	L	0	4	Bournemouth
02/02/2019	Home	W	5	0	Huddersfield
10/02/2019	Away	L	0	6	Manchester City
22/02/2019	Home	W	2	0	Tottenham
27/02/2019	Away	W	2	1	Fulham
03/03/2019	Home	D	1	1	Wolves
10/03/2019	Away	L	0	2	Everton
17/03/2019	Away	W	2	1	Cardiff City
31/03/2019	Home	W	3	0	Brighton
03/04/2019	Home	W	2	0	West Ham
08/04/2019	Away	L	0	2	Liverpool
14/04/2019	Home	D	2	2	Burnley
22/04/2019	Away	D	1	1	Manchester Utd
28/04/2019	Home	W	3	0	Watford
05/05/2019	Away	D	0	0	Leicester City
12/05/2019	Away	W	3	0	Huddersfield

REMARK

There is a lot of information in this table. You will not need all of it for the question.

The table shows the match results of Chelsea Football Club in the Premier League in the season 2018/19. The figures in the GF (Goals For) column are the goals scored by Chelsea in each match. The figures in the GA (Goals Against) column are the goals scored by the opposition team.

1. Draw a frequency table of the number of goals scored by Chelsea in the 39 matches.
2. Represent the data in the frequency table using an appropriate graph.
3. Find the mean, median, mode and range of the data.
4. Give a reason why a sports journalist might use the mode to summarise the results to the public.

ANSWERS

Chapter 1 Prime Factorisation, Indices and Standard Form

Try It!

1. $2 \times 2 \times 3 \times 5 \times 5$
2. 120
3. 12 cm
4. 660
5. 180
6. (a) 4^5 (b) 6^8 (c) $(-5)^6$ (d) p^7
7. (a) $25c^6$ (b) $16s^3$ (c) $-z^2$ (d) $27v^3$
8. (a) -64 (b) -17 (c) 1
9. $\text{HCF} = 2 \times 5^2 \times 7$, $\text{LCM} = 2^3 \times 5^4 \times 7^3$
10. (a) 1 (b) 1
11. (a) $\frac{1}{16}$ (b) $\frac{1}{49}$
12. (a) $\frac{7}{8}$ (b) $\frac{1}{64}$
13. (a) 5000 (b) 9 210 000
14. (a) 0.0009 (b) 0.000 002 45
15. (a) 7.3×10^3 (b) 3.25×10^5 (c) 4.652×10^7
16. (a) 4×10^{-2} (b) 4.7×10^{-4} (c) 4.78×10^{-6}
17. 4.95×10^6 litres
18. 5.2×10^{-5} m
19. (a) 1000, 1 000 000 000 000 (b) 1×10^9 kilobytes
20. 0.0003 m, 3×10^{-4} m

Practice 1.1

1. (a) $3 \times 3 \times 7$ (b) $2 \times 2 \times 2 \times 3 \times 3$
   (c) $3 \times 3 \times 3 \times 5$ (d) $2 \times 7 \times 11$
   (e) $2 \times 2 \times 5 \times 19$ (f) $2 \times 2 \times 2 \times 5 \times 11$
2. (a) 9 (b) 24 (c) 20 (d) 76
3. (a) 945 (b) 252 (c) 8360 (d) 462
4. (a) True (b) False (c) True
   (d) False (e) True
5. (a) False (b) False (c) False (d) True
   (e) True, but only for 1 times a prime number.
6. (a) 60 (b) 18
7. (a) True (b) False
8. 34 g
9. Ava = 5, Dan = 6
10. Student's answers, for example, 12 and 84

Practice 1.2

1. (a) 6^4 (b) -5^3 (c) 7^6 (d) -9^5
2. (a) 125 (b) -125 (c) 64 (d) 64
   (e) 1 (f) 1 (g) 1 (h) 1
3. (a) 6561 (b) 6561 (c) 16 807 (d) $-16\,807$
   (e) 1 (f) -1 (g) 64 (h) 0.015 625
4. (a) False, -2^3 (b) False, 3^2 (c) True
   (d) False, -1 (e) False, 3×10^{-1} (f) True
5. -2^3 and $(-2)^3$ are equal and the rest are different.
6. (a) $7r^3$ (b) $25t^4$ (c) $9x^5$ (d) $-8z^3$
7. (a) $\text{HCF} = 2^2 \times 3 \times 11$, $\text{LCM} = 2^3 \times 3^3 \times 11^2$
   (b) $\text{HCF} = 2^3 \times 5^2 \times 7$, $\text{LCM} = 2^4 \times 5^3 \times 7^2$
8. 117
9. (a) 14 (b) 5 (c) 100 (d) 8
   (e) 9 (f) $\frac{2}{5}$ (g) $\frac{3}{8}$ (h) $\frac{1}{9}$
10. 8^{-2}

Practice 1.3

1. 1×10^5, 2.9×10^{-4}, 3.08×10^{-2}
2. (a) 4000 (b) 4 200 000
   (c) 630 000 (d) 607 000 000
3. (a) 0.000 91 (b) 0.009
   (c) 0.000 0083 (d) 0.000 0803
4. (a) 6.3×10^3 (b) 6.3×10^5
   (c) 6.3×10^{-1} (d) 6.3×10^{-5}
   (e) 2.89×10^4 (f) 2.89×10^8
   (g) 2.89×10^{-4} (h) 2.89×10^{-7}
5. 1.27×10^4 km
6. 1.4×10^{-2} m
7. They all have the same digits and are all in standard form. They all have different powers of 10.
8. (a) 4.8×10^6 (b) 3.0×10^5
   (c) 3.6×10^{-2} (d) 3.6×10^{-4}
9. (a) 2×10^{-3} (b) 2.67×10^3 (c) 92 000
10. (a) Red blood cell = 7.8×10^{-6} m, white blood cell diameter = 1.2×10^{-5} m
    (b) The white blood cell

Practice 1.4

1. $4.38 \times 10^4\ \text{cm}^3$
2. $1.19 \times 10^6\ \text{m}^2$
3. 5.15×10^4 m
4. (a) 10 (b) 1.08×10^8 m
5. $7.6 \times 10^4\ \text{m}^2$
6. 0.0024 kg = 2.4×10^{-3} kg
7. 1.25×10^3
8. 100
9. (a) 2.63×10^7 bytes (b) No
10. Students' own answers.

Challenge 1

No, because it cannot carrier a mass greater than 7.5×10^{-5} kg

Revision Exercise 1

1. (a) 5^3 (b) 8^4 (c) -1 (d) 10^4
2. (a) 33 (b) 33 (c) 128 (d) -128
3. (a) $450 = 2 \times 3^2 \times 5^2$, $270 = 2 \times 3^3 \times 5$
   (b) 90 (c) 1350

4. (a) $150 = 2 \times 3 \times 5^2$, $105 = 3 \times 5 \times 7$ (b) 15 cm
5. For example, $2 \times 3^3 \times 5^2 \times 7 \times 13$ and $2^2 \times 3^3 \times 5^2 \times 7^2$
6. $2^3 \times 3^2 \times 7 \times 11^2$
7. (a) 1.0277... (b) 0.9876...
   (c) -5 (d) 1.75
8. (a) False (b) False (c) False (d) True
9. (a) $5^{-2}, 5^{-1}, 5^0, 5^3$ (b) $(-2)^5, -2^3, (-2)^0, (-2)^2$
10. $8.5 \times 10^6\,m^2$
11. (a) 3.9×10^{-4} kg (b) 1.5×10^{-4} kg
12. 10 times

Chapter 2 Algebraic Expressions and Manipulation

Try It!

1. (a) $8a$ (b) $3b$ (c) $-9c$
2. (a) $r + 7s$ (b) $-2u + v - 10$
3. (a) £$(2a + 3b)$
   (b) 5 burgers and 4 portions of chips (c) £$7(a + b)$
4. (a) £$(4t + s)$ (b) £90
5. (a) $9b - 4$ (b) $-q - 3$
6. (a) $-4x + 8y$ (b) $a - z - 15$
7. (a) £$5(x + y)$ (b) £$(x - 3y)$
8. (a) $24x + 30$ (b) $-24x + 30y$
9. $10x - 8y$
10. $x + 5$
11. 7
12. £$(50y + 30)$
13. (a) $2n^2 + n$ (b) $15p^2 - 40p$
14. (a) $xy + 5x$ (b) $2t^2 - 14tu$
15. (a) $3y^2 + 12y$ (b) $-3y^2 + 12y$
16. (a) $5(r + 4)$ (b) $4(4s - 3)$ (c) $-4(2s + 3)$
17. (a) $3(3x + y)$ (b) $7(2z - 3a)$

Practice 2.1

1. (a) $8x$ (b) $-2x$ (c) $2x$ (d) $-8x$
   (e) $-5y$ (f) $5y$ (g) $9y$ (h) $-9y$
   (d) is the negative of (a) and (c) is the negative of (b).
2. (a) $6x + 14$ (b) $3y - 2$ (c) $2x - 10y$
   (d) $-9x - 5y$ (e) $-x + 3 + 7y$ (f) $x - 3y$
3. (a) $-3a$ (b) $-3a - 5$
   (c) $-3a + 4$ (d) $-11a - 3$
4. All three expressions have the same four terms but in different orders, so they all simplify to the same expression: $-2x + 9y$.
5. $2x - 5x - 3x$ is the only one to simplify to $-6x$.
6. (a) $2a - 6$ (b) $2c - 3d + 4$ (c) $-p + 4q - 14$
   (d) $-2x - 3y - 6$ (e) $12s - t + 6u$ (f) $-11r - 2v + 10$
7. No, the coefficient of x is -8.
8. (a) £$(3p + 2n)$
   (b) How much more a pen costs than a notebook
   (c) Two pens and one notebook
   (d) £$(5p + 3n)$
9. (a) £$(2t + 3h)$ (b) £160
10. Student's own answers

Practice 2.2

1. (a) $5a + 5$ (b) $5a - 5$ (c) $6b + 4$
   (d) $-2b + 2$ (e) 0 (f) $-c - d$
2. (a) $-(2x + 4) \rightarrow -2x - 4$, $-(2x - 4) \rightarrow -2x + 4$, $-(-2x + 4) \rightarrow 2x - 4$, $-(-2x - 4) \rightarrow 2x + 4$
   (b) $-(3y + 2x - 5) \rightarrow -3y - 2x + 5$, $-(3y - 2x - 5) \rightarrow -3y + 2x + 5$, $-(3y + 2x + 5) \rightarrow -3y - 2x - 5$, $-(-3y - 2x - 5) \rightarrow 3y + 2x + 5$, $-(-3y - 2x + 5) \rightarrow 3y + 2x - 5$, $-(-3y + 2x - 5) \rightarrow 3y - 2x + 5$
3. (a) $3t - 3$ (b) $3t + 3$ (c) $u + 7$
   (d) $7u - 7$ (e) $-7v + 7w$ (f) $-5v$
4. $(6x - 4y) - (2x + 3y)$. This simplifies to an expression with a $-7y$ term. The others simplify to an expression with a $+7y$ term.
5. (a) $5a - 2b + 2$ (b) $-a + 8b - 10$
   (c) $-g - 10h - 4$ (d) $-4k + 12$
6. $(7a + 2b) - (7a - 2b)$. This expression simplifies to a multiple of b. The other expressions simplify to a multiple of a.
7. There is a mistake in the first line when expanding the brackets: $-(-4x) = +4x$ and there is a mistake in the last line with the final term: $-5 + 6 = 1$. $6x - 4y + 1$
8. (a) $(2r + 2b)$ cm or $2(r + b)$ cm
   (b) $(8r + 2b)$ cm or $2(4r + b)$ cm
   (c) $6r$ cm
9. (a) £$(2m + 8n)$ or £$2(m + 4n)$ (b) £$2n$
10. (a) $(4x + 2y)$ cm (b) $(2y - 12)$ cm

Practice 2.3

1. (a) $15x + 24$ (b) $-15x - 24$ (c) $6y - 2$
   (d) $-6y + 2$ (e) $-8x + 24$ (f) $-8x + 24$
2. (a) $20a + 14$ (b) $22b - 12$ (c) $6c - 5$
   (d) $11c + 19$ (e) $28h - 11k$ (f) $-5m + 10n$
3. (a) $2 - 12p$ (b) $-6p + 3$ (c) $7q$
   (d) $22q - 4$ (e) $24r - 27s$ (f) $-36r - 15s$
4. $3(4x - 5) - 2(6x + 1)$
5. The expressions have the same variables but different signs.
6. $2(8x + 3)$ cm
7. (a) £$(90x + 120)$ (b) £$(80x + 100)$
   (c) £$(170x + 220)$
8. (a) $3 + n$ (b) $30 + 11n$
9. Student's own answers, for example:
   (a) $2(6x + 5)$ and $2(3x + 1)$
   (b) $4(x - 4y)$ and $2(2x - 2y)$
10. Student's own answers, for example:
   (a) $2(6x + 5)$ and $9x + 4$ (b) $4(2x - y)$ and $4x + 3y$

Practice 2.4

1. (a) $2a^2 + 7a$ (b) $2a^2 - 7a$ (c) $6a^2 + 21a$
   (d) $6a^2 - 21a$ (e) $4b^2 + 20b$ (f) $4b^2 - 20b$
   (g) $20b + 24b^2$ (h) $20b - 24b^2$
2. (a) $xy + 2x$ (b) $xy - 2x$ (c) $3xy + 6x$
   (d) $3xy - 6x$ (e) $3xy + 3x^2$ (f) $3xy - 3x^2$
   (g) $xy + 3x^2$ (h) $2xy - 3x^2$

3. Only (c) is correct: $5y(3y-7) = 15y^2 - 35y$
4. No, he has added 2 and 3 to work out the coefficient instead of multiplying them.
5. $a(6b - 9a)$: this simplifies to the negative of the results of the other expressions.
6. (a) $5a + 2a^2$ (b) $6a^2 + 3a + 3$ (c) $20b^2 + 9b - 1$ (d) $20b^2 + 34b - 6$
7. $2x(10x - 6)$: this simplifies to the negative of the results of the other expressions.
8. $(6x^2 + 10x)\,\text{cm}^2$
9. $(2x^2 + 4x)\,\text{cm}^2$
10. Students' own answers, for example, $2x$ and $3 + 4x$; x and $8x + 6$.

Practice 2.5

1. (a) $2(2x+3)$ (b) $6(x-2)$ (c) $3(3x+1)$ (d) $4(5x-2)$ (e) $5(x+2)$ (f) $5(x-2)$ (g) $-5(x-2)$ (h) $-5(x+2)$
2. (a) $2(2a+3)$ (b) $2(2a-3)$ (c) $4(a+2)$ (d) $7(3f-4)$ (e) $-7(3f+4)$ (f) $7(4-3f)$ (g) $5(5x+3)$ (h) $5(5+3x)$ (i) $5(5-3x)$
3. (a) $2(3h+2k)$ (b) $2(3h-2k)$ (c) $4(4h-k)$ (d) $6(3t+5u)$ (e) $6(-3t+5u)$ (f) $18(t-2u)$ (g) $14(a-2b)$ (h) $14(b-2a)$ (i) $-14(b+2a)$
4. Correct answer $= 10(x+3)$: neither Amy nor Ben has removed the highest common factor of the two terms.
5. $30a + 45b = 15(2a + 3b)$
6. (a) $8(b-3) = 2(4b-12) = 4(2b-6)$ (b) $8(b-3)$
7. $5(2-a)$
8. $£(x+4)$
9. 2 cm and $(2x + 6y)$ cm or 4 cm and $(x + 3y)$ cm.
10. Students' own answers, for example, $2y(4x-7) = 8xy - 14y$, $3x(4x-7) = 12x^2 - 21x$

Challenge 2

(a) $(10x^2 - 8x)\,\text{cm}^2$ (b) $2x(5x-4)$

Revision Exercise 2

1. (a) $7a + 4$ (b) $-b + 4c$ (c) $-2p + 4q - 6$ (d) $-8x - 5y - 7$
2. (a) $7m - 7$ (b) $-6n + 11$ (c) $-5p + 6$ (d) $9q - 8$ (e) $9r - 3s$ (f) $-2x - 14$
3. (a) $8x + 28$ (b) $6x - 15y$ (c) $11p - 25$ (d) $-10q + 39$ (e) $9u + 31v$ (f) $34y - 9x$
4. $(2x+y) + (x-5y)$ and $2(2x+y) - x - 6y$
5. $2x - 15y$
6. (a) $3a^2 + 5a$ (b) $9b - 4b^2$ (c) $3c^2 + 3cd$ (d) $2de - d^2$ (e) $11x + 6x^2$ (f) $2y^2 + 4y$
7. (a) $(2x+4)$ cm (b) $(3x^2 + 19x)\,\text{cm}^2$
8. (a) $5(3a+5)$ (b) $2(4b-3)$ (c) $4(5+7n)$ (d) $15(2p-3)$ (e) $6(4s+3t)$ (f) $7(2x-3y)$
9. $4(5x-4)$: Daniel's terms in the brackets still have a common factor of 2.
10. (a) Nathan buys 2 sandwiches and 4 cans of drink. Max buys 5 sandwiches and 1 can of drink. (b) $£(7s + 5d)$ (c) $£(3s - 3d)$
11. (a) $£(19x + 7)$ (b) $£(2x + 1)$
12. Student's answer: any two expressions which multiply together to give $24x + 12$
13. (a) $(4x+6)$ cm (b) $(x^2 + 3x)\,\text{cm}^2$ (c) $(x+2)$ cm
14. $£(20 + x)$

Chapter 3 Linear Equations

Try It!

1. (a) $x = 8$ (b) $y = 3$
2. (a) $x = 4$ (b) $y = 5$
3. 23
4. (a) $x = 3$ (b) $x = 11.5$ (c) $x = 3$
5. (a) $t = 2$ (b) $q = -1$
6. (a) Student's diagram (b) (i) $m = 11 - p$ (ii) $p = 11 - m$
7. (a) $p = \frac{9}{8}$ (b) $R = 4V$ (c) $b = \frac{10}{A}$
8. (a) Student's diagram (b) $\frac{d}{s}$ (c) 3 hours
9. (a) $r = \frac{s-3}{5}$ (b) $z = 4(y+1)$
10. (a) $r = \frac{C}{2\pi}$ (b) 4 cm

Practice 3.1

1. (a) $x = 4$ (b) $x = 5$ (c) $x = 5$ (d) $x = 4$
2. (a) $p = 6$ (b) $p = 16$ (c) $p = 8$ (d) $p = 4$
3. (a) $a = 2$ (b) $a = -2$ (c) $a = 2.75$ or $\frac{11}{4}$ (d) $a = 4$ (e) $a = 9$ (f) $a = 8.5$ or $\frac{17}{2}$
4. Yes
5. (a) Student's proof (b) $y = 6$
6. (a) $x = -1$ (b) $x = -4$ (c) $x = -2$ (d) $x = 5$
7. (a) $m = 1$ (b) $m = 2.5$ or $\frac{5}{2}$ (c) $m = 4$ (d) $m = -2$ (e) $m = 5$ (f) 6.5 or $\frac{13}{2}$
8. $2(3x-1) = 16$, $3(2x-1) = 15$ and $3(1-2x) = -15$
9. 12
10. £24

Practice 3.2

1. (a) Student's answers, for example $y = 15 - x$, $x + y = 15$, $x = y - 15$ (b) Student's answers, for example $a = \frac{13-b}{2}$, $b = 13 - 2a$, $b + 2a = 13$
2. (a) Student's answers, for example $P = QR$, $Q = \frac{P}{R}$, $Q = \frac{P}{Q}$ (b) Student's answers, for example $w = \frac{xy}{3}$, $x = \frac{3w}{y}$, $y = \frac{3w}{x}$
3. (a) M (b) b (c) V (d) I
4. (a) $x = y - 3$ (b) $x = y + 3$ (c) $x = y - k$ (d) $x = \frac{y}{7}$ (e) $x = 7y$ (f) $x = \frac{k}{y}$
5. (a) 10 (b) 10
6. (a) $x = \frac{z-1}{2}$ (b) $x = 2(z+1)$ (c) $x = \frac{1-t}{3}$ (d) $x = \frac{2t-k}{3}$

7. (a) $m = \frac{y}{2x}$ (b) $m = \frac{4r}{5s}$
(c) $m = \frac{24v}{b}$ (d) $m = \frac{2}{a}$
8. (a) 0 (b) 18
9. (a) Student's diagram (b) No, $V = \frac{M}{D}$.
(c) 30 grams
10. Student's diagram (b) $a = \frac{v-u}{t}$ (c) $3\,m/s^2$

Challenge 3

$k = \frac{y-L}{Lt}$

Revision Exercise 3

1. (a) $x = 6$ (b) $x = 16$ (c) $x = 2$ (d) $x = -2$
2. (a) $y = 12$ (b) $y = 4$ (c) $y = -6$ (d) $y = 3$
3. (a) $p = 2$ (b) $q = -2$ (c) $a = 2$ (d) $b = -2$
4. $4x - 1 = 6x + 5$
5. $x = 3y \rightarrow, y = \frac{x}{3}, x = y + 3 \rightarrow y = x - 3, x = y - 3 \rightarrow y = x + 3, x = 3 - y \rightarrow y = 3 - x, x = \frac{y}{3} \rightarrow y = 3x; x = \frac{3}{y} \rightarrow$ missing formula $y = \frac{3}{x}$
6. (a) $x = 50 - y$ (b) $x = \frac{z-5}{3}$ (c) $x = \frac{1-u}{2}$
(d) $x = 2(v+4)$ (e) $x = \frac{p}{F}$ (f) $x = \frac{2r}{t}$
7. (a) 33 (b) 3 (c) −2
8. (a) 55 (b) 2 (c) 0
9. 3 kg
10. 18 years old
11. (a) Student's diagram (b) $t = \frac{C-30}{25}$
(c) 2 hours
12. (a) Student's diagram (b) $a = \frac{F}{m}$

Chapter 4 Functions and Graphs

Try It!

1. (a) $P = (3, 1), Q = (-2, -1)$
(b) P = first quadrant, Q = third quadrant
(c) Student's diagram
2. (2, −2)
3. (a) (3, −3)
(b) Area = 25 square units, perimeter = 20 units
4. (a) $y = x + 3$ (b) $x = 13, y = 4, 7, 11$
5. (a) $y = 10x$ (b) 10, 20, 30, 40, 50
6. Student's graph
7. Student's graph
8. (a) Student's graph
(b) They lie on a straight line.
9. (a) Student's graph (b) $y = 7 - t$
10. (a) Student's graph (b) 35
11. Student's graph
12. Student's graph
13. 3
14. $\frac{-2}{3}$
15. $y = -2$ is a horizontal line so the gradient of the line is 0. $x = 2$ is a vertical line, so the gradient of the line is undefined.
16. (a) Gradient = 2, y-intercept = 5
(b) Gradient = −6, y-intercept = −4
(c) Gradient = 0, y-intercept = 5
(d) Gradient = −1, y-intercept = 5
17. (a) $y = 3x - 5$
(b) Student's answer, for example, $y = 3x$
18. $y = x + 2$
19. (a) Student's graph
(b) The h-intercept of the graph
(c) The gradient; the increase in height is 2 cm per day.
20. (a) Student's graph
(b) The y-intercept; the amount of cement when time x is zero
(c) The gradient; the decrease in cement is 15 kg per hour.
21. (a) 5, 4, 8 (b) Student's graph
22. (a) 8, 0, 2 (b) Student's graph
23. (a) 2, 0, 6 (b) Student's graph
24. (a) 0, 4, 3 (b) Student's graph
25. (a) 30 m (b) 35 m
(c) The initial height of the ball
26. (a) $y = -1$ (b) $x = 0.5$

Practice 4.1

1. (a) $A(1, 4), B(-4, 3), C(-2, -3), D(1, -2), E(3, -4), F(0, 2), G(-3, 0)$
(b) (i) A (ii) C (iii) G (iv) F
2. (a) Student's graph
(b) (i) Second quadrant (ii) Fourth quadrant
3. (a) (i) 0 (ii) −7
(b) y-axis
4. (a) Same x-coordinate = 5, different y-coordinates
(b) Same y-coordinate = −4, different x-coordinates
5. (−3, −4), all others are in the second quadrant
6. (a) (i) (1, 5) (ii) (1, −5)
(b) (i) Northern Cliffs (ii) East Haven
(c) 5 (d) (−4, 2), (−4, 0), (−5, 1) and (−3, 1)
7. (a) (2, −2)
(b) Student's answer, for example (4, 0)
8. D is at (1, −1), perimeter 20 units, area = 25 square units
9. (3, 6) and (−3, 6) or (3, −6) and (−3, −6)

Practice 4.2

1. 'y is 5 less than x' $\rightarrow y = x - 5$, 'y is 5 times x' $\rightarrow y = 5x$, 'y is x less than 5' $\rightarrow y = 5 - x$, the missing equation is $y = x + 5$.
2. (a) (i) −3, −2, −1, 0, 1, 2, 3 (ii) Student's graph
(b) (i) −6, −4, −2, 0, 2, 4, 6 (ii) Student's graph
(c) (i) −5, −4, −3, −2, −1, 0, 1 (ii) Student's graph
(d) (i) −1, 0, 1, 2, 3, 4, 5 (ii) Student's graph
3. (a) Student's graph
(b) (i) $y = 3$ or $y = -3$ (ii) $x = 3$ or $x = -3$
(iii) $y = 3$ and $y = -3$ or $x = 3$ and $x = -3$
4. (a) Student's graph
(b) The graphs are parallel lines.
5. (a) 7, 15 (b) (0, 3), (2, 7), (4, 11), (6, 15)
(c) Student's graph
6. (a)–(d) Student's graphs

7. (a) $y = 3x + 2$ (b) Student's graph
(c) No, when $x = 3$, $y = 11$
8. (a) $y = 4x$ (b) Student's graph
9. (a) Student's graph (b) No
10. (a) Student's graph (b) 3.5 seconds

Practice 4.3

1. (a) The slopes are the same but one slope is longer than the other.
(b) Both slopes have a vertical change of 2 and a horizontal change of 4. However, the LHS gradient is negative the RHS gradient is positive.
2. (a) Negative (b) Zero (c) Undefined
(d) Undefined (e) Undefined (f) Positive
3. (a) Gradient = 1, y-intercept = 1
(b) Gradient = $-\frac{1}{3}$, y-intercept = 2
(c) Gradient = $-\frac{1}{2}$, y-intercept = 0
(d) Gradient = $\frac{2}{3}$, y-intercept = −1
4. (a) Gradient = 3, y-intercept = −7
(b) Gradient = 3, y-intercept = 1
(c) Gradient = 4, y-intercept = 0
(d) Gradient = −2, y-intercept = −5
(e) Gradient = 0, y-intercept = −5
(f) Gradient = −2, y-intercept = 4
5. (a) (3) and (6) (b) (1), (2) and (4)
(c) (1), (4) and (5) (d) (5)
6. (a) $y = -2x - 2$
(b) Gradient = −2, y-intercept = −2
7. (a) Student's graphs (b) 3
(c) Same gradient, but intersect the y-axis at different points
8. Any three of these four pairs of lines: $y = 6x + 3$ and $y = 6x + 2$; $y = -6x + 2$ and $y = 3 - 6x$; $y = 3x + 1$ and $y = 3x$; $y = -3x + 6$ and $y = 1 - 3x$
9. (a) Student's graph
(b) Gradient = 3, y-intercept = 5
(c) Laura's initial distance in metres
(d) Laura's speed in m/s
10. (a) Student's graph (b) 4
(c) The initial amount owed for the sofa
(d) The amount paid per month

Practice 4.4

1. (a) 4, −5, −1, student's graph
(b) 3, 0, 12, student's graph
(c) 2, 0, 6, student's graph
(d) −5, −1, −2, student's graph
2. (a) 3 (b) $y = x^2 + 2x$
3. (a) $y = \frac{6}{x}, x \neq 0$ since the graph is a reciprocal, undefined at 0.
(b) $y = x^2 - 6$ since the graph is a parabola which is open upwards.
(c) $y = -x^2 + 6$ since the graph is a parabola which is open downwards.
4. (a) 6 (b) −12
5. (a) Student's graph
(b) Both are parabolas, open upwards and symmetric about the y-axis, with a y-intercept of −1. $y = 2x^2 - 1$ is steeper than $y = x^2 - 1$ for all values of x (except on the y-axis).
6. (a) Student's graph
(b) Both are parabolas, open downwards and symmetric about the y-axis, with the same gradient. They have different y-intercepts.
7. (a) Student's graph (b) $x = 1$ and 3
(c) (i) (2, 0) (ii) (0, 4) (d) (2, 0)
8. (a) Student's graph (b) 2 seconds
(c) The initial height of the ball in m
9. (a) 12, 4 (b) Student's graph (c) 48
(d) The distance in km from Northampton to Manchester

Challenge 4

(a) (i) £30 (ii) £40
(b) Gradient = 10 (£ per hour), y-intercept = 20

Revision Exercise 4

1. (a) $A(1, 0)$, $B(0, -3)$, $C(-2, -3)$, $D(-3, 3)$, $E(3, 4)$
(b) C (c) B (d) (−1, 0)
2. (a) −1, 5, 13 (b) Student's graph (c) No
3. (a) (i) $\frac{1}{3}$ (ii) Undefined
(iii) Zero (iv) −3
(b) $y = -3x + 2$
4. (a) (i) Gradient = 2, y-intercept = −5
(ii) Gradient = −3, y-intercept = 1
(iii) Gradient = 3, y-intercept = 0
(iv) Gradient = −4, y-intercept = −5
(v) Gradient = 0, y-intercept = −4
(vi) Gradient = −2, y-intercept = 6
(b) None
5. (a) Student's graphs
(b) They all have a y-intercept of 1 but gradients are different.
6. (a) Student's graph
(b) Gradient = 3, y-intercept = 4
(c) 3 is the price in £ per mango, 4 is the price in £ of a watermelon.
7. (a) 0, −4, 12, student's graph
(b) −8, 0, −2, student's graph
(c) 0, −2, 0, student's graph
(d) −11, −3, −6, student's graph
8. (a) Student's graph
(b) (i) (−1, 0) and (3, 0)
(ii) (0, −3)
(c) (1, −4)
9. (a) 4 seconds (b) 20 m (c) 15 m
10. (a) 24, 15, 12 (b) Student's graph (c) 10
(d) The total cost in £ of hiring the minibus

Integrated Examples and Review Exercise 1

Try It!

1. (a) $2^2 \times 5^2$ (b) 25, 20, 10, 5, 4
   (c) Student's graph
   (d) $X = \frac{100}{y}$ (e) 5×10^{-3}
2. (a) $10x + 5y$ (b) $5(2x + y)$ (c) $y = -1$
   (d) $y = 3 - 2x$ (e) Gradient = −2, y-intercept = 3
3. (a) Student's proof (b) Student's graph
   (c) $16\,\text{cm}^2$

Review Exercise 1

1. (a) $125 = 5^3$ (b) $250 = 2 \times 5^3$
   (c) HCF = 125, LCM = 250
2. (a) $\frac{8}{9}$ (b) Yes, both = 1 (c) No
3. (a) 3.6×10^4
   (b) (i) Influenza virus: 8.5×10^{-8} dust particle: 2.5×10^{-7}
   (ii) Influenza
4. (a) $17x + 32$ (b) $-2x + 13y$
   (c) $x^2 - x$ (d) $6x^2 + 10x$
5. (a) $3(3a + 2)$ (b) $5(p - 3q)$
   (c) $12(x + 2y)$ (d) $6(-p + 3r)$
6. (a) $p = -11$ (b) $q = 4$
   (c) $r = 6$ (d) $s = -2$
7. (a) $x = y - 7$ (b) $x = \frac{y}{7}$
   (c) $x = \frac{k}{3y}$ (d) $x = 3(2y - k)$
8. (a) $v = \frac{I + 10}{2}$ (b) 15
9. (a) Student's diagram (b) 25 square units
10. (a) Gradient = 5, y-intercept = −4
    (b) Gradient = −2, y-intercept = −3
    (c) Gradient = 0, y-intercept = 3
    (d) Gradient = −3, y-intercept = 9
11. (a) Student's graph, −9, −6, −3, 0, 3
    (b) Student's graph, 8, 5, 2, −1, −4
    (c) Student's graph, 7, 0, −9, 0, 7
    (d) Student's graph, −8, 0, 0, −8, −24
12. 30 cm
13. (a) Student's graph
    (b) Both graphs have a y-intercept of 6 and the same level of slope but one is negative.
    (c) $x = \frac{6 - y}{2}$
14. (a) Student's graph
    (b) The total volume in ml to be divided into equal parts
    (c) $x = \frac{80}{y}$
15. (a) Student's graph (b) 5 m (c) No

Chapter 5 Proportion

Try It!

1. (a) 10, 15, 20, 25 (b) Student's diagram
   (c) Yes (d) Student's graph
2. (a) No (b) Student's graph
3. (a) 8 (b) Student's diagram
   (c) 9 (d) $y = 2c$
4. £21
5. The small pack
6. (a) 10, 5, 2 (b) Yes (c) Student's graph
7. (a) 10, 5, 0 (b) No
8. (a) 3 hours (b) 2 km/h
9. 45 ml
10. (a) $t = \frac{12}{s}$ (b) (i) 4 (ii) 3

Practice 5.1

1. (a) Shop B (b) (i) £20 (ii) £14 (iii) 5
2. (a) Cyclist A (b) Student's diagram
3. (a) Student's diagram (b) $p = 40$, $q = 14$
   (c) Student's graph (d) $T = 4x$
4. No
5. (a) (i) £12 (ii) £18 (b) (i) £4 (ii) £5
6. 1440 m
7. (a) Student's diagram (b) 65 minutes
   (c) $y = 13x$
8. (a) 375 ml (b) 38
   (c) 600 g (d) $m = 10e$
9. Student's proofs
10. Brand X

Practice 5.2

1. (a) (i) £5 (ii) £20 (b) 10
2. (a) 12, 8, 4 (b) Yes
3. (a) Project B (b) Student's graph
   (c) 2 hours 24 minutes or 2.4 hours
4. Graph A
5. (a) £10 (b) 40 (c) $C = \frac{600}{p}$
6. Yes
7. No
8. 6 hours
9. This is unlikely: 60 workers might be too many to work in the same space at the same time, and certain processes might take a fixed length of time regardless of the number of workers.
10. No

Challenge 5

£10

Revision Exercise 5

1. (a) (i) £6 (ii) £9
   (b) (i) 4 hours (ii) 6 hours
2. (a) Yes (b) Student's diagram (c) £21
3. (a) Student's table (b) £24 (c) £10
4. (a) Yes (b) 88 Euros (c) $y = 1.1x$
5. (a) Inversely proportional (b) Neither
   (c) Neither (d) Directly proportional
6. (a) £9 (b) $14\,\text{m}^2$ (c) Student's graph
7. (a) Student's proof (b) Student's graph
   (c) $V = \frac{900}{n}$ (d) 100 ml
8. (a) 322 g (b) 264 g
9. Budget
10. 8 hours 24 minutes or 8.4 hours

Chapter 6 Rate and Speed

Try It!

1. (a) 4 boxes per minute (b) £2 per can
2. (a) 5 litres per minute (b) 60 litres
   (c) 13 minutes
3. (a) £12 per day (b) Student's graph
   (c) 12, spending rate per day
4. (a) Copper is £3 per metre (m) more expensive than iron.
5. (a) 28 EUR (b) 17.86 GBP (to 2 dp)
6. (a) 360 RUB (b) 2.20 GBP approximately
7. £140
8. £180
9. £6600
10. 90 km/h
11. 22 km
12. 1 hour 30 minutes
13. (a) 20 m/s (b) 30 m/s (c) 22.5 m/s
14. (a) $26\frac{2}{3}$ m/s (b) 18 km/h

Practice 6.1

1. (a) 4 (b) 40 (c) 5
2. (a) Student's diagram (b) 3
   (c) 42 (d) 3 minutes
3. (a) 2 chairs per hour (b) £25 per hour
   (c) £12.50 per chair
4. (a) 6 tyres per hour (b) Student's diagram
   (c) 18
5. Rate of serving = $\frac{1}{2}$ customer per minute, time to serve 100 customers = 200 minutes
6. (a) £25 per m^2 (b) £600
7. (a) £2.50 per kg (b) £7.50
   (c) 4.8 kg (d) Student's graph (e) Price per kg
8. (a) Student's diagram (b) 9 g/cm^3
   (c) 72 g
9. (a) Yes (b) Yes
   (c) John's rate is measured in km per litre and Nazia's rate is measured in litres per km.
10. Supermarket B

Practice 6.2

1. (a) Student's diagram (b) 13.56 EUR
2. (a) Yes (b) 66.67 USD (to 2 dp)
3. No, Terry should have divided by 8.41.
4. (a) 160 THB (b) 5 GBP
5. (a) Shop A (b) 507 SGD
6. 730.69 GBP (to 2 dp)
7. The US website
8. (a) 3.6 CHF (b) 1 GBP = 1.2 CHF
9. £857.14 (to 2 dp)
10. No, you only get back £988.20.

Practice 6.3

1. (a) £15 (b) £92 (c) £180 (d) £200
2. 3% of £1000
3. (a) (i) £20 (ii) £40 (b) Bank B
4. (a) (i) £560 (ii) £2240 (b) Bank A
5. (a) £1728 (b) £8128
6. Peter has multiplied by 8 rather than 8%, £120
7. 5% simple interest for 6 years
8. 4% simple interest for 11 years
9. £120
10. (a) They receive the same amount of interest each year.
    (b) £400

Practice 6.4

1. (a) 80 (b) 1.25
2. (a) 64 km (b) 3 hours
3. The speed is given in km/h, so convert the time in minutes to a time in hours first; 20 km
4. (a) 80 km/h (b) $\frac{1}{4}$ hour
   (c) The speed is constant.
5. (a) (i) 15 m/s (ii) 25 m/s
   (b) (i) 90 km/h (ii) 72 km/h
6. 7.92 m/s (to 2 dp)
7. 55 km/h; all the others equal 72 km/h
8. 2 hours 35 minutes
9. 52.5 mph
10. No, the average speed is not the same as taking the average of the two speed figures. You need to work out total distance travelled divided by the total time.

Challenge 6

(a) 80 km/h (b) 70.6 km/h (to 1 dp)

Revision Exercise 6

1. (a) £6 per box (b) £20 per hour
   (c) 3 vases per minute (d) 7 cm per hour
2. (a) Student's diagram
   (b) 36 revolutions per minute
   (c) 324 (d) 3 minutes
3. The 8 pack
4. 635 USD
5. 1900.83 GBP (to 2 dp)
6. (a) 7.80 GBP (b) 1.8
   (c) The exchange rate of Singapore dollars to a British pound
7. (a) £280 (b) £3780
8. Deal A
9. (a) (i) 6 km/h (ii) $1\frac{2}{3}$ m/s (b) 2.5 hours
10. 6.1 m/s (to 1 dp)

Chapter 7 Triangles, Quadrilaterals and Polygons

Try It!

1. (a) Acute-angled, $\angle z = 57°$
   (b) Right-angled, $\angle x = 57°$
2. $\angle y = 53°$
3. (a) Equilateral, $\angle t = 60°$ (b) Isosceles, $\angle x = 65°$
4. $\angle u = 63°$, $\angle v = 54°$
5. $\angle q = 110°$
6. (a) $PS = 8$ m (b) $QT = 6$ m
7. $\angle u = 49°$, $\angle v = 96°$

8. $\angle a = 70°$, $\angle b = 40°$
9. Irregular pentagon, $\angle x = 40°$
10. 60°
11. 10 sides
12. $\angle y = 110°$
13. 8 sides

Practice 7.1

1. (a) (i) Scalene (ii) Right-angled
   (b) (i) Scalene (ii) Acute-angled
   (c) (i) Isosceles (ii) Obtuse-angled
   (d) (i) Isosceles (ii) Right-angled
2. (a) 65° (b) 52° (c) 64° (d) 133°
3. (a) 60° (b) 70° (c) 130°
4. (a) Equilateral (b) 60°
5. 124°
6. (a) Both equilateral triangles, but their side lengths are different.
   (b) Both isosceles triangles, but ΔPQR has two angles of 30° and ΔXYZ has one angle of 30°.
7. (a) $\angle BCA$ could be either 70° or 55°, depending on which two sides are equal.
   (b) 40° is the only possible value for $\angle QRP$.
8. (a) 35° (b) 20°
9. (a) $\angle x = 40°$, $\angle y = 100°$ (b) $\angle x = 70°$, $\angle y = 110°$
10. (a) Yes (b) Yes

Practice 7.2

1. (a) $\angle x = 150°$ (b) $\angle y = 100°$
2. 12 cm
3. $XY = 13$ cm, $TY = 20$ cm
4. (a) Both have two pairs of parallel sides and diagonals that bisect each other, but a rectangle has two opposite pairs of equal sides and four right angles while a rhombus has four equal sides, two opposite pairs of equal angles and perpendicular diagonals that bisect the interior angles.
   (b) Both have a pair of parallel sides, but a parallelogram has two parallel pairs of equal opposite sides whereas the sides of a trapezium could all be different lengths.
5. Yes
6. $\angle x = 125°$, $\angle y = 55°$
7. $\angle x = 65°$, $\angle y = 115°$
8. $\angle x = 60°$, $\angle y = 60°$
9. Yes, diagonals intersect at right angles
10. (a) Parallelogram (b) Trapezium
    (c) Irregular quadrilateral

Practice 7.3

1. (a) 1080° (b) 1260° (c) 2340°
2. (a) $\angle x = 90°$ (b) $\angle x = 50°$
3. (a) $\angle x = 85°$ (b) $\angle x = 120°$
4. No, interior angles do not add to 360°.
5. (a) Exterior angle = 72°, interior angle = 108°
   (b) Exterior angle = 45°, interior angle = 135°
   (c) Exterior angle = 40°, interior angle = 140°
6. (a) 9 (b) 18 (c) 5 (d) 15
7. No
8. $\angle x = 108°$, $\angle y = 72°$, $\angle z = 36°$
9. $\angle x = 150°$, $\angle y = 75°$, $\angle z = 30°$
10. (a) Student's proof (b) $\angle HGF = 150°$
    (c) $\angle FHG = 15°$

Challenge 7

$\angle x = 36°$, $\angle y = 108°$

Revision Exercise 7

1. (a) $\angle x = 90°$, right-angled triangle
   (b) $\angle x = 40°$, isosceles triangle
2. Triangle (c) might be the odd one out.
3. $\angle x = 40°$, $\angle y = 160°$
4. (a) 12 cm (b) 8 cm
5. (a) No (b) Yes
6. (a) 16 cm (b) $\angle x = 60°$, $\angle y = 120°$
7. $\angle x = 134°$, $\angle y = 46°$
8. No
9. $\angle x = 60°$, $\angle y = 60°$, $\angle z = 120°$
10. 10 sides
11. No

Chapter 8 Geometric Constructions

Try It!

1. Student's drawing, $\angle BAC = 35°$
2. Student's drawing, $\angle ACB = 35°$
3. Student's drawing
4. Student's drawings
5. Student's drawing
6. Student's drawing
7. (a) Student's drawing (b) Student's answer
8. Student's drawing

Practice 8.1

1. (a)–(b) Student's drawings
2. (a) (i)–(ii) Student's drawings
   (b) (i) $\angle BAC = 119°$ (ii) $\angle BAC = 51°$
3. Student's drawing
4. (a)–(b) Student's drawings
5. (a) Yes (b) Yes
   (c) No; this can be constructed in two ways.
6. Student's drawing
7. Student's drawing
8. Student's drawing
9. Student's drawing
10. (a) The sum of the two shortest sides needs to be longer than the longest side.
    (b) Angles in a triangle should add up to 180°; the two angles given add up to 190°.
    (c) The longest side is opposite the largest angle in a triangle. 90° must be the largest angle (since in total the angles will add up to 180°) but 7 cm is not the longest side.

Practice 8.2

1. Student's drawing
2. Student's drawing
3. Student's drawing
4. Student's drawing
5. **(a)–(b)** Student's drawing
6. Student's drawing
7. **(a)–(c)** Student's drawing
   (d) $MN = \frac{XZ}{2}$
8. **(a)–(b)** Student's drawing
   (c) They all intersect at a point the same distance from each vertex.
9. **(a)–(b)** Student's drawing
   (c) They all intersect at a point the same distance from each side of the triangle.
10. **(a)–(c)** Student's drawing **(d)** $\angle AED = 90°$

Practice 8.3

1. Student's drawing
2. Student's drawing
3. Student's drawing
4. Student's drawing
5. **(a)–(b)** Student's drawing **(c)** 5.2 cm
6. **(a)–(b)** Student's drawing **(c)** 4 cm
7. **(a)–(c)** Student's drawing **(d)** $BN = PD$
8. **(a)–(c)** Student's drawing
   (d) They all intersect at a common point.

Challenge 8

(a)–(b) Student's drawing

Revision Exercise 8

1. 28°
2. Student's drawing
3. 7.4 cm
4. **(a)** No, the sum of the two shortest sides is less than the length of the longest side.
   (b) No, two of the angles added together equal 185°.
   (c) No, an arc of length 3 cm from C does not intersect the angle line for B.
5. Student's drawing
6. Student's drawing
7. **(a)** Student's drawing **(b)** 12 cm
   (c) Student's drawing
   (d) The two bisectors are perpendicular to each other and the point of intersection is on the hypotenuse of the triangle.
8. **(a)–(b)** Student's drawing **(c)** $\angle PIQ = 105°$
9. **(a)–(b)** Student's drawing
10. **(a)–(c)** Student's drawing
    (d) AD, BE and CF intersect at a common point.

Chapter 9 Congruence, Similarity and Enlargement

Try It!

1. Student's drawing
2. Student's drawing
3. Student's drawing
4. B and G; C, K and N; E, H and M
5. $PQ = 6.7$ cm, $QR = 7$ cm, $RS = 3$ cm, $SP = 7.9$ cm, $\angle PQR = 90°$, $\angle QRS = 90°$, $\angle RSP = 118°$, $\angle SPQ = 62°$
6. **(a)** Yes, 2 **(b)** No
7. Student's drawing
8. Student's drawing
9. Student's drawing
10. Student's drawing
11. 12 cm
12. $\angle x = 36°$, $y = 10$ cm
13. $x = 4$ cm, $\angle y = 135°$
14. $x = 36$ cm

Practice 9.1

1. **(a)–(c)** Student's drawings
2. **(a)–(c)** Student's drawings
3. **(a)–(c)** Student's drawings
4. **(a)–(b)** Student's drawings
5. **(a)** Rotation: the size and shape of the triangle has not changed but the orientation of the shape has changed.
   (b) Reflection: the size and shape of the triangle has not changed but the orientation of the shape has changed. It has been reflected across a vertical line of reflection.
6. **(a)** 3 units left and 2 units down
   (b) 4 units right and 2 units up
7. **(a)** 90° anticlockwise **(b)** 180°
8. **(a)** Rotation, 180°, (6, 4) **(b)** Student's diagram

Practice 9.2

1. A, C, G and I; B and F; D and H
2. **(a)** $AB = DE$, $BC = EF$, $CA = FD$
   (b) $AB = PQ$, $BC = QR$, $CD = RS$, $DA = SP$
3. **(a)** No **(b)** Yes
4. $\Delta ABC \equiv \Delta PQR$
5. **(a)** No **(b)** $ABCD \equiv PQRS$
6. **(a)** $x = 1$ cm, $y = 3$ cm **(b)** No, different lengths
7. **(a)** $\angle x = 36°$, $\angle y = 72°$ **(b)** $\angle x = 63°$, $\angle y = 117°$
8. **(a)** $\angle x = 55°$, $\angle y$ 35° **(b)** $\angle x = 18°$, $\angle y = 115°$
9. **(a)** $x = 7.8$ cm, $\angle y = 110°$ **(b)** $x = 12$ cm, $\angle y = 110°$
10. Student's diagram

Practice 9.3

1. **(a)** **(i)–(ii)** Student's diagrams
   (b) Same shape and orientation, different sizes
2. **(a)** **(i)–(ii)** Student's diagrams
   (b) Same shape and size, different positions
3. ΔPQR, enlargement scale factor = 2
4. $EFGH$, enlargement scale factor = $\frac{3}{2}$
5. No, different shapes
6. **(a)–(b)** Student's diagrams
7. **(a)** Student's diagram
   (b) Yes, angles do not change under an enlargement.
8. **(a)** **(i)–(ii)** Student's diagrams
   (b) Same shape and size but in different positions
9. **(a)** $\frac{1}{2}$ **(b)** Z
10. **(a)** 2 **(b)** Student's diagram

Practice 9.4

1. A and G, B and I, C and L, D and J, E and H, F and K
2. *PQRS*
3. **(a)** 15 m **(b)** 16 mm
4. $x = 2$ cm, $\angle y = 75°$
5. $\angle x = 52°$, $y = 3$ cm
6. No, different angles
7. $\angle x = 24°$, $y = 6$ cm
8. $x = 4$ cm, $\angle y = 95°$
9. 4 m
10. **(a)** 108° **(b)** Student's diagram **(c)** Yes

Challenge 9

(a) A rotation **(b)** 124°
(c) $DE = 6$ m, $EF = 10$ m, $FA = 8$ m

Revision Exercise 9

1. **(a)–(b)** Student's diagrams
2. **(a)–(c)** Student's diagrams
3. $\angle x = 56°$, $y = 10$ cm
4. $x = 8$ cm, $\angle y = 100°$
5. Student's diagram
6. **(a)–(c)** Student's diagrams
7. **(a)–(b)** Student's diagrams
8. **(a)** 30 cm **(b)** 0.375 m
9. **(a)** Student's diagram **(b)** Yes
   (c) Student's diagram
10. **(a)** Student's diagram **(b)** 2.7 cm **(c)** 64°

Integrated Examples and Review Exercise 2

Try It!

1. **(a)** Student's proof **(b)** 4 hours
   (c) EUR 37.44
2. **(a)** 720, 1440 **(b)** No **(c)** 75°
3. **(a)** Student's diagram
   (b) It is at the centre of the rectangle and midpoint of *AC*.
   (c) Yes **(d)** Student's diagram

Review Exercise 2

1. 225 cm
2. 4 oranges
3. **(a)** 5 m/s **(b)** 50 m
4. Bright is better value because the price per kg is lower.
5. £300
6. **(a)** 60° **(b)** Acute-angled scalene triangle
7. **(a)** 14 cm **(b)** 110°
8. **(a)** 9 cm **(b)** 90° **(c)** 25°
9. **(a)** 200 km/h **(b)** 93.60 EUR
   (c) 1008 passengers
10. No
11. 18 sides
12. **(a)–(d)** Student's diagrams
13. 28 cm
14. **(a)** 15 m **(b)** 4 m/s **(c)** 20 seconds
15. **(a)–(b)** Student's diagram **(c)** 126°

Chapter 10 Pythagoras' Theorem

Try It!

1. **(a)** *FE*, $d = 5$ cm **(b)** *YZ*, $y = 8$ cm
2. **(a)** $b = 7.75$ cm (to 3 sf) **(b)** $z = 9.66$ cm (to 3 sf)
3. *ABC* is right-angled, *XYZ* is not right-angled
4. 7.07 m (to 3 sf)
5. 4.31 cm (to 3 sf)
6. **(a)** 20 cm **(b)** 15 cm **(c)** Student's proof

Practice 10.1

1. **(a)** No **(b)** Yes
2. **(a)** 81 cm² **(b)** 144 cm²
   (c) 225 cm² **(d)** 15 cm
3. **(a)** $a = 10$ cm **(b)** $b = 26$ cm
4. **(a)** $x = 20$ cm **(b)** $y = 5$ cm
5. They are all right-angled with one side measuring 4 cm and one measuring 5 cm, but have different orientations. The first two triangles are congruent and the 5 cm side is the hypotenuse, whereas in the third triangle one of the sides next to the right angle measures 5 cm.
6. $x = 8$ cm
7. **(a)** $a = 4.47$ cm **(b)** $b = 31.3$ cm
   (c) $c = 4.24$ cm
8. **(a)** $x = 5.20$ cm **(b)** $y = 14.7$ cm
9. **(a)** $a = 6.26$ mm **(b)** $b = 8.09$ m
10. **(a)** 15 cm **(b)** 40 cm **(c)** 60 cm²

Practice 10.2

1. **(a)** No **(b)** Yes, $\angle EDF$
   (c) Yes, $\angle GKH$ **(d)** No
2. 14.1 cm (to 3 sf)
3. 54.1 cm (to 3 sf)
4. **(a)** No **(b)** A parallelogram
5. **(a)** *PQRS* **(b)** Student's proof
6. **(a)** 12 cm **(b)** 9.17 cm (to 3 sf)
7. 30 m²
8. 6 m (to the nearest metre)
9. **(a)** 8.94 cm (to 3 sf) **(b)** 17.9 cm (to 3 sf)
   (c) Student's proof
10. Student's answers, for example, $x = 6$ cm and $y = 8$ cm; or $x = 5$ cm and $y = 8.66$ cm (to 3 sf)

Challenge 10

(a) 48 m **(b)** 2256 m²

Revision Exercise 10

1. **(a)** 17 m **(b)** 12 cm
2. **(a)** 15.3 cm (to 3 sf) **(b)** 19.5 cm (to 3 sf)
3. **(a)** Yes **(b)** No
4. **(a)** No **(b)** Yes
5. 13.9 cm (to 3 sf)
6. Triangle C
7. 2.83 m (to 3 sf)
8. 17.1 cm (to 3 sf)
9. Student's proof
10. Yes, the diagonal is 16.1 cm

Chapter 11 Trigonometry

Try It!

1. Sin $P = \frac{12}{13}$, Cos $P = \frac{5}{13}$, tan $P = \frac{12}{5} = 2.4$
2. **(a)** 0.469 **(b)** 0.454 **(c)** 1.23
3. 6.69 cm
4. 16.6 cm (to 3 sf)
5. **(a)** 1.9° **(b)** 77.2°
6. **(a)** 55° **(b)** 66°

Practice 11.1

1. **(a)** Hypotenuse = AC, opposite side = AB, adjacent side = BC
   (b) Hypotenuse = EF, opposite side = DF, adjacent side = DE
   (c) Hypotenuse = GK, opposite side = HK, adjacent side = GH
   (d) Hypotenuse = LM, opposite side = LN, adjacent side = MN
2. **(a)** $\frac{45}{53}$ **(b)** $\frac{25}{53}$ **(c)** $\frac{45}{48}$
3. Sin $A = \frac{8}{17}$, Cos $A = \frac{15}{17}$, tan $A = \frac{8}{15}$
4. **(b)** and **(c)** are incorrect.
5. **(a)** 0.407 **(b)** 0.956 **(c)** 3.27
6. **(a)** $\frac{b}{c}$ **(b)** $\frac{a}{c}$ **(c)** $\frac{b}{a}$
7. **(a)** $\frac{a}{c}$ **(b)** $\frac{a}{c}$ **(c)** $\sin A = \cos B$
8. **(a)** $\tan\theta$ **(b)** $\tan\theta$ **(c)** $\frac{CB}{AB} = \frac{QP}{AP}$

Practice 11.2

1. top row: 2, 2.9, 2; bottom row: 3.5, 3.5, 2.9
2. **(a)** 5.63 cm (to 3 sf) **(b)** 5.52 cm (to 3 sf)
3. **(a)** 8.90 mm (to 3 sf) **(b)** 3.28 cm (to 3 sf)
4. **(a)** 6.78 cm (to 3 sf) **(b)** 4.13 m (to 3 sf)
5. **(a)** 3.78 cm (to 3 sf) **(b)** 7.5 cm
   (c) 13.3 cm (to 3 sf) **(d)** 18.4 cm (to 3 sf)
6. **(a)** 11.1 cm (to 3 sf) **(b)** 2.60 cm (to 3 sf)
   (c) 5.43 cm **(d)** 3.90 mm
7. **(a)** False **(b)** True **(c)** False **(d)** True
8. 47.3 m (to 3 sf)

Practice 11.3

1. **(a)** 17.5° **(b)** 62° **(c)** 56.3°
   (d) 23.6° **(e)** 68.0° **(f)** 52.1°
2. **(a)** 30° **(b)** 25.4°
3. **(a)** 48.8° **(b)** 61.9°
4. **(a)** 60° **(b)** 65.4°
5. **(a)** Sin $a = \frac{3}{5}$, Cos $a = \frac{4}{5}$, tan $a = \frac{3}{4}$
   (b) 36.9° **(c)** Yes
6. **(a)** 56.4° **(b)** 60° **(c)** 53.1°
   (d) 33.1° **(e)** 38.2° **(f)** 45°
7. $\angle y$
8. Betty
9. **(a)** 18.4° **(b)** 12.6 m (to 3 sf), yes

Challenge 11

17.1 cm

Revision Exercise 11

1. **(a)** Hypotenuse = AC, opposite side = BC, adjacent side = AB
   (b) Hypotenuse = QR, opposite side = PR, adjacent side = PQ
2. **(a)** Sin $\theta = \frac{7}{25}$, Cos $\theta = \frac{24}{25}$, tan $\theta = \frac{7}{24}$
   (b) Sin $\theta = \frac{45}{53}$, Cos $\theta = \frac{28}{53}$, tan $\theta = \frac{45}{28}$
3. **(a)** and **(d)** are incorrect.
4. **(a)** $x = 9.33$ cm, $y = 7.55$ cm
   (b) $x = 2.70$ m, $y = 4.82$ m
5. **(a)** 21.7° **(b)** 22.2° **(c)** 7.6°
6. **(a)** 18.4 **(b)** 62.7°
7. **(a)** 61.6° **(b)** 369 m^2
8. **(a)** $\angle QPR$ **(b)** Board ABC
   (c) Board ABC

Chapter 12 Data Analysis

Try It!

1. £4
2. **(a)** 5.3 minutes **(b)** 6.2 minutes **(c)** Route A
3. **(a)** 30 **(b)** 15.8 years
4. 17.76 years
5. £4
6. 4.5 years
7. **(a)** 16 **(b)** 1
8. 2 in town P, 1 and 3 in town Q and 3 in town R
9. 0
10. 22 cm
11. **(a)** Mean = 60.3 seconds (to 3 sf), range = 6 seconds
    (b) Mean = 60 seconds, range = 13 seconds
    (c) Kylie; higher mean and smaller range so more consistent

Practice 12.1

1. £20
2. 193 cm
3. More than 4
4. Set C
5. 7 years old
6. **(a)** 20 **(b)** 12.7 seconds
   (c) Correct; mean time has decreased
7. **(a)** Yes, mean = £15.85
   (b) **(i)** Increase. **(ii)** Decrease
8. **(a)** 1.65 **(b)** Student's answer
9. **(a)** 10.1 cm **(b)** 15.2 cm **(c)** Bright light
10. **(a)** Rebecca **(b)** Tania
    (c) It removes extreme values/outliers.

Practice 12.2

1. 4 hours
2. £45
3. **(a)** 425 g
   (b) The 100 g value is much lower than the other values, and lowers the mean but not the median.
4. 6.2
5. **(a)** 60 g **(b)** 70 g **(c)** Yes

6. (a) Mean = 47.7 m (to 1 dp), median = 48.5 m
(b) Mean = 48 m, median = 48.5 m
(c) Sara, as her mean throwing distance is greater.
7. (a) 20 years old
(b) One driver is much older than the others
(c) No change
8. (a) 24 mm (b) 10 mm
(c) (i) The median is not affected by the extreme value of 120 mm.
(ii) The mean uses all of the data values collected.
9. (a) 35 s (b) 37 s

Practice 12.3

1. (a) 24 years old (b) 25 years old
(c) 27.3 years old (to 3 sf)
2. (a) Black (b) Manufacture black sunglasses
(c) The data is not numerical so you cannot calculate the mean or median.
3. (a) 3 (b) Mode
4. (a) Tokyo: 15 °C, Singapore: 30 °C and 34 °C, Perth: no modal temperature
(b) Tokyo: 15 °C; Singapore: 31 °C; Perth: 27 °C
(c) Median (d) Visit Tokyo
5. (a) £25 (b) £22.50
(c) The mode is always one of the actual values donated.
6. (a) 10 minutes (b) 9 minutes (c) 9.6 minutes
7. (a) 14 years old
(b) (i) No effect (ii) It would be lower.
8. (a) 3 (b) 4
(c) Most do not eat the recommended five portions.
9. Student's answer
10. Student's answer

Practice 12.4

1. 18 ml
2. 353 m
3. (a) Mean = 3.15 kg, median = 3.15 kg, mode = 3.2 kg
(b) 0.8 kg
4. Same range, do not have a single mode (but set B is bimodal); different numbers of values, different means and different medians
5. (a) 0 siblings (b) 4 siblings
6. (a) Mean = 65.625, range = 56
(b) Mean = 67.875, range = 39
(c) The non-calculator test
(d) The calculator test
7. (a) Mean = 15.6 °C (to 3 sf), range = 16 °C
(b) Mean = 21.3 °C (to 3 sf), range = 13 °C
(c) Melbourne (d) London
8. $x = 27$ cm
9. Student's answers, for example, set A= {1, 12, 3, 10, 9}, set B = {4, 15, 6, 5, 5}

Challenge 12

(a) Number aged 13 = 2, number aged 14 = 4, number aged 15 = 12, number aged 16 = 6
(b) Mean = 14.9 years (to 3 sf), median = 15.5 years, mode = 15 years
(c) 3 years

Revision Exercise 12

1. (a) £10 (b) £8 (c) No mode
2. (a) £45 (b) £43.50 (c) £42 (d) Mean
3. (a) £15 (b) £12
(c) Median is not affected by the outlier
4. (a) The rugby players (b) The football players
5. (a) 22 cm (b) 26.5 cm
6. (a) Student's answer, for example, 8, 9, 10, 11, 22
(b) Student's answer, for example, 13, 13, 13, 17, 64, 64
7. (a) (i) Mean = 2.5, median = 2, mode is 2 and 3, range = 6
(ii) Mean = 2.3 (to 1 dp), median = 2, mode = 2, range = 5
(b) (i) More than (ii) The same as
(iii) More than
8. (a) Mean = 17.7 (to 1 dp), range = 20
(b) Mean score = 18.5, range = 5
(c) Syra
9. (a) £11.30 (b) £11 (c) £11 (d) £4
10. (a) 6 eggs (b) 5.44 eggs (c) 4 eggs (d) No

Chapter 13 Probability and Sets

Try It!

1. (a) $\frac{1}{6}$ (b) $\frac{1}{2}$ (c) $\frac{5}{6}$ (d) 0
2. (a) $\frac{4}{9}$ (b) $\frac{5}{9}$
3. (a) $\frac{1}{2}$ (b) $\frac{1}{4}$ (c) $\frac{1}{26}$
4. (a) $\frac{3}{5}$ (b) $\frac{2}{5}$
5. (a) $\frac{1}{3}$ (b) $\frac{2}{3}$ (c) $\frac{3}{4}$
(d) 0 (e) 1
6. (a) 8 (b) $\frac{1}{3}$
7. (a) Student's diagram
(b) (i) $\frac{1}{4}$ (ii) $\frac{1}{2}$ (iii) $\frac{3}{4}$
8. (a) $\frac{1}{4}$ (b) $\frac{1}{2}$
9. (a) $\frac{1}{6}$ (b) $\frac{1}{6}$
10. (a) Student's answer, for example, helium, neon and argon
(b) Student's answer, for example, Ross, Joey and Gunther
(c) Student's answer, for example, Greece, Spain and Germany
11. (a) D = {d, i, n, e, r} (b) Yes
12. Student's diagram: A = {square, rectangle, rhombus, parallelogram}, B = {square, rhombus}
13. (a) $\frac{4}{7}$ (b) $\frac{1}{7}$ (c) $\frac{1}{7}$

Practice 13.1

1. **(a)** $\frac{1}{6}$ **(b)** $\frac{1}{3}$
2. **(a)** {1, 2, 3, 4, 5, 6, 7, 8, 9, 10, 11, 12, 13, 14, 15}
   (b) (i) $\frac{8}{15}$ **(ii)** $\frac{1}{5}$
3. **(a)** $\frac{1}{3}$ **(b)** $\frac{2}{3}$
4. **(b)** is the odd one out
5. **(a) (i)** $\frac{3}{7}$ **(ii)** $\frac{4}{7}$ **(iii)** 0
   (b) Yes
6. **(a)** 15 **(b)** $\frac{2}{5}$ **(c)** 1
7. **(a)** $\frac{7}{9}$ **(b)** 4 **(c)** 1
8. **(a)** $\frac{8}{25}$ **(b)** $\frac{4}{25}$
9. **(a)** 160° **(b) (i)** $\frac{1}{6}$ **(ii)** $\frac{11}{18}$
10. Student's answer, for example, P(choose M) = P(choose T)

Practice 13.2

1. **(a)** Student's table **(b)** No, P(both green) = $\frac{1}{4}$.
2. **(a)** Student's table
   (b) (i) $\frac{1}{9}$ **(ii)** 0 **(iii)** 1
3. **(a)** Student's table **(b) (i)** $\frac{1}{4}$ **(ii)** $\frac{1}{6}$
4. **(a)** $\frac{1}{6}$ **(b)** No
5. Yes
6. **(a)** Student's table
   (b) (i) $\frac{1}{9}$ **(ii)** $\frac{5}{9}$ **(iii)** $\frac{1}{3}$
7. **(a)** $\frac{1}{4}$ **(b)** $\frac{1}{4}$ **(c)** $\frac{3}{4}$
8. 'Rolling a six with a fair dice'
9. **(a) (i)** $\frac{1}{6}$ **(ii)** $\frac{1}{4}$ **(iii)** $\frac{3}{4}$
   (b) P(both white) < P(same colour); P(same colour) + P(different colours) = 1
10. No, we cannot assume each makes an independent random choice.

Practice 13.3

1. **(a)** A = {−3, −2, −1, 0, 1, 2, 3}, finite
   (b) B = {2, 4, 6, ...}, infinite
   (c) C = {3, 6, 9, ...}, infinite
   (d) D = {England, Northern Ireland, Scotland, Wales}, finite
   (e) E = {red, orange, yellow, green, blue, indigo, violet}, finite
   (f) F = {a, b, c, ..., x, y, z}, finite
2. **(a)** A square ε sets X, Y and Z.
   (b) A rectangle ε sets X and Z.
   (c) An equilateral triangle ε sets Y and Z.
   (d) None
3. Student's diagram
4. **(a)** Blue **(b)** Blue, orange and red
   (c) Green
5. **(a) (i)** One **(ii)** Three
   (b) (i) $\frac{1}{6}$ **(ii)** $\frac{1}{2}$
6. Student's diagram
7. P(attends a Sports club) is double P(attend both a Sports and a Creative Arts club).
8. **(a) (i)** {a, w, i, t, s, e, u, h}
   (ii) {w, i, t, a} **(iii)** {i, t} **(b)** $\frac{1}{2}$
9. **(a)** (i) **(b)** (ii)
10. $\frac{2}{3}$, Student's diagram

Challenge 13

Student's diagram

Revision Exercise 13

1. **(a)** $\frac{1}{6}$ **(b)** $\frac{1}{3}$
2. **(a)** $\frac{3}{8}$ **(b)** $\frac{1}{4}$
3. **(a)** $\frac{1}{3}$ **(b)** 0 **(c)** $\frac{2}{3}$
4. $\frac{7}{8}$
5. **(a)** $\frac{3}{8}$ **(b)** 1 **(c)** 0
   (d) $\frac{3}{4}$ **(e)** $\frac{3}{8}$
6. **(a)** Student's table **(b) (i)** $\frac{1}{8}$ **(ii)** $\frac{1}{4}$
7. **(a)** Student's table **(b)** $\frac{1}{5}$
8. **(a) (i)** A = {2, 3, 5, 7, 11, 13, 17, 19}
   (ii) B = {1, 2, 3, 4, 6, 12} **(b)** $\frac{1}{4}$
9. Student's diagram
10. **(a)** $\frac{1}{2}$ **(b)** $\frac{1}{10}$ **(c)** $\frac{1}{5}$ **(d)** $\frac{2}{5}$

Integrated Examples and Review Exercise 3

Try It!

1. **(a)** Student's proof **(b)** 71.1° (to 1 dp)
   (c) QR = 29.4 cm, RS = 45.7 cm (to 3 sf)
2. Student's diagram
3. **(a)** Mean = 2.55, median = 2.5, mode = 1, range = 4
   (b) The mean uses all of the data.
   (c) (i) 1 **(ii)** $\frac{1}{4}$ **(iii)** $\frac{1}{2}$

Review Exercise 3

1. **(a)** x = 85 cm **(b)** y = 33 m
2. 252 cm
3. Triangle A
4. ΔDEF
5. **(a)** x = 10.3 cm (to 3 sf), y = 6.18 cm (to 3 sf)
   (b) r = 54.3 cm (to 3 sf), q = 21.2 cm (to 3 sf)
6. **(a)** θ = 36.9° (to 1 dp) **(b)** θ = 55.7° (to 1 dp)
7. **(a)** Mean = 25 cm^3, median = 29 cm^3, mode = 30 cm^3
   (b) (i) It uses all the data values.
   (ii) It is affected by the outlier value.
8. **(a)** Mean = £3.70, median = £3.50 **(b)** Range = £4
9. **(a)** $\frac{1}{5}$ **(b)** $\frac{1}{5}$
10. Student's diagram
11. **(a)** $\frac{1}{2}$ **(b)** $\frac{1}{2}$ **(c)** 0 **(d)** 1

12. **(a)** $\frac{2}{3}$ **(b)** $\frac{1}{3}$ **(c)** $\frac{1}{6}$

13. **(a)** Student's diagram **(b)** $\frac{1}{16}$ **(c)** $\frac{13}{16}$

14. **(a)** Student's diagram **(b)** $\frac{5}{36}$ **(c)** No

15. 2150 cm^2 (to 3 sf)

Problems in Real-world Contexts

A. **1.** Supplier A
2. Supplier C
3. Supplier A

B. **1.** £300
2. £72
3. £106
4. £72

C. **1.** SGD5800
2. £2128
3. £756
4. SGD10 962.36

D. **1.** $AD = 8.1$ m, $DE = 3.45$ m
2. $AE = 8.80$ m (to 2 dp)
3. 23° (to 2 sf)

E. **1.** Student's table
2. Student's graph
3. Mean = 1.69 (to 2 dp), median = 2, mode = 2, range = 5
4. The mode is not affected by extreme values and it is one of the data values.